SpringerWienNewYork

Eric Dieth

Integration by Cooperation

A Constructivist Social Theory
and a Theory of the State and the Law

SpringerWienNewYork

Dr. Eric Dieth
Bonaduz, Switzerland

This work is subject to copyright.
All rights are reserved, whether the whole or part of the material is concerned, specifically those of translation, reprinting, re-use of illustrations, broadcasting, reproduction by photocopying machines or similar means, and storage in data banks.

Product Liability: The publisher can give no guarantee for all the information contained in this book. The use of registered names, trademarks, etc. in this publication does not imply, even in the absence of a specific statement, that such names are exempt from the relevant protective laws and regulations and therefore free for general use.

© 2011 Springer-Verlag/Wien
Printed in Germany

SpringerWienNewYork is part of
Springer Science+Business Media
springer.at

Typesetting: Camera ready by the author
Printing: Strauss GmbH, 69509 Mörlenbach, Germany

Printed on acid-free and chlorine-free bleached paper
SPIN: 12717156

With 26 Figures

Library of Congress Control Number: 2011936878

ISBN 978-3-211-99415-3 SpringerWienNewYork

Contents

A. Introduction   1

B. Social construction of "reality"   7

1. Different worlds   9
   a) Reciprocity and/or selfish individuality?   9
   b) Social construction of poverty   13
2. Value-based "reality"   17
   a) Fighting with reality   17
   b) Consensus-based constructivism   20
   c) Decision instead of cognition   24

C. Concept of humankind and community   27

1. Neo homo oeconomicus – selfish individualism   28
   a) Selfish monads imprisoned   29
   b) Market-integration as divine harmony   31
   c) Religious hope or cynical disinterest instead of justice   38
   d) Core value – freedom to consume   40
2. Homo interactivus – interdependent individuals   41
   a) "I" as me and the other   42
   b) Constitutive recognition by and of others   45
   c) Others   46

		d) Community – society	48
		f) The visible and responsible hands	52

D. Integration process — 55

1. Consensus — 57
- a) Constitutive consensus and value consensus — 57
- b) Routine consensus — 58
- c) Institutional consensus — 60
- d) Legitimation consensus — 61

2. Construction phases and integration modes — 64
- a) New construction phase — 64
- b) Reproduction — 65
- c) Deconstruction — 66
- d) Deviant behavior – dissent — 71

3. Integration quality — 76
- a) Direct violence, structural violence, cultural violence — 77
- b) Authoritarian, competitive, or cooperative integration — 80
- c) Integration work — 87
- d) Winner/loser arrangement — 89

4. Fragile stability — 92
- a) Contingency – need for stability — 92
- b) Scapegoat politics — 94
- c) Stable change — 106

5. Collective identity — 107

6. Value-based constructivism — 111
- a) Pleading for values — 111
- b) Social construction of values — 113

	c)	Value-based or procedural? Partisanship or neutrality?	115
	d)	Happiness	119
	e)	Everything is about values	121

E. Integration elements — 124

1. Basic values — 124
- a) Life as hope — 126
- b) Freedom as work in progress — 136
- c) Responsibility — 150
- d) Justice — 159
- e) Solidarity — 172

2. Recognition — 180
- a) Economic absolutism – negated personhood — 180
- b) Constitutive and universal recognition, recognition of potential — 202
- c) Recognition denial – fight for recognition — 208

3. Respect — 211
- a) Listen to others — 211
- b) Homogeneity v. plurality — 212
- c) Manichaeism and collectivism — 221

4. Reciprocity — 226
- a) Morality first — 227
- b) Greed alone is not enough — 239

5. Trust — 245
- a) Functions of trust — 245
- b) With trust to democracy — 249

6.	**Decision-making process**	266
	a) Monopoly of violence by consensus	266
	b) Interactive construction of the state – consented state power	291
	c) Integration by law	301
	d) Law and identity	332
7.	**People – Space**	343
	a) Racist market	345
	b) Imposed and chosen ghettos	371
8.	**Symbolic link – Time concept**	387
	a) Symbolic link	387
	b) Time concept – past, present, future	407
9.	**Elementary consensus**	421
	a) Approval of the core elements	421
	b) Integration is more than democracy or politics	426
	c) Greatness thanks to cooperation	428
	d) Cooperation instead of confrontation	431
Acknowledgments		435
References		437
Index		487
About the author		497

A. Introduction

The last thirty years were lost years. People didn't manage to build up a just and free community. They didn't establish respectful and supportive relationships. A small strata of the society manipulated and forced people to compete with each other, to be greedy selfish individuals, subjected to a totalitarian market: Every realm of life had to obey the exigencies of the market, understood as a godlike force, nobody was and is responsible for.

This book proposes an alternative to the economic absolutism neoliberal ideology established successfully. According to this ideology, only the market has to decide, only the market knows what is best, only the market is able to harmonize the actions of individuals not capable and not willing to take the interests of others into account. Instead of the market system, which ruled by miraculous means, I want *responsible individuals*: Individuals interested in others, supporting the members of a community, supported in turn by the community when there is need. Individuals interacting with each others create the reality we live in. Our major goal should be a community that provides its members equal opportunities to freedom. This freedom is not understood as freedom against others, but as an option given by others, built up together and effective only, if the participants are willing to contribute their necessary support. Furthermore we should give up the belief, that to compete with each other makes people creative and is much more effective. Cooperation yields trust, why costs of control in form of people, time, and police or even army can be reduced. In addition, the individuals as much as the community can be more creative, can take more risks, because the others are positively interested in our results, and do not look for any weakness to push the competitor out of the market. Giving up the winner-takes-it-all logic frees people for risky creative inventions. Quality of life is enhanced, because others aren't a competitive threat anymore, but make things possible one alone couldn't achieve.

Neoliberal market-absolutism and the heydays of individualism and competition were fundamentally questioned by the financial market crisis of 2008. The religious belief in the market force was irritated and led us forlorn. Indoctrinated over decades by the mantra, that selfishness and aggressive competition is best for all, many had to note, that the neoliberal years were best for a vanishingly small group of people. Unfortunately, we are not used anymore to think in alternatives. Many have drawn the conclusion, that the end of soviet totalitarianism was necessarily the end of justice, solidarity or responsibility. The "end of history" had arrived and the competitive market system won forever. Paradoxically, the joyous loss of the oppressive system that prevailed in the Eastern bloc brought political freedom to some parts, but it also made us dependent on the neoliberal monopoly of thinking. We lost a critical position to ourselves, the ability to think in alternatives. The end of the absolutist concept of the collective was perceived as legitimization of the absolutism of the individual.

An alternative to this celebration of the competitive war of all against all has to rethink many different aspects. First, our concept of humankind, our worldview. What is a human being? Which are the possibilities to build up a community? Is greed and selfishness a natural element of human nature nobody can question? Is the homo oeconomicus *the* reality we have to adapt to? To liberate our thinking and our future opportunities and to propose a debate that doesn't exclude others by using so called realistic arguments that can't be questioned, the explanations brought forward in this book are based on a *constructivist approach*. There is thus not one exclusive reality. Based on my constructivist conviction, there are the "realities" people construct according to their interests and needs. The term "reality" put in quotation marks stands for the "reality" we construct, we are responsible for. Without quotation marks it denotes *the* objective reality independent of ourselves, the unique one, the one used in Realism. Realism is an effective tool to exclude other ways of thinking, to disqualify as "unrealistic" proposals we don't like. Being qualified as "unrealistic" means not to have the right to participate in the debate. This competitive approach to the conviction of other people is replaced here by a cooperative understanding, based on the idea, that *every position has the same right to exist and be heard*. Cooperation doesn't mean absence of conflict. It is important to debate intensely positions we do not like. However, the debate should not be based on the ontological quality of arguments, but rather on the grounds of their advantages versus their

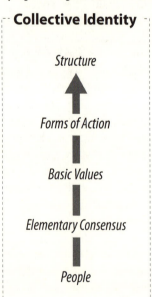

costs. The ideas discussed here will thus have an impact, if readers are sufficiently convinced to live according to them. *What is, is, because we decide it to be, in the way we want it to be.*

The alternative proposed in this book is a model of integration that is based on a set of elements that constitute the collective identity of a community. At the center of every "reality" proposal stands the basic values, that characterize the relationship of individuals and community. Contrary to the values dominating today's neoliberal "reality", which are selfish freedom and material wealth, I try to make plausible an interactive concept of freedom, justice, solidarity, and responsibility. Individuals are perceived as part of a community – made by others and making others – and not as lonesome cowboys who look only for themselves. The main premise of this construction is the avoidance of direct, structural, and cultural violence. "Reality" proposals are measured against this criteria: How are they able to avoid violence, recognize people and communities as equal and respect their originalities and differences, and to support them enough to ensure that members' hopes are realized.

From a structural point of view, people are integrated, when their actions are coordinated, so that they don't hinder each other. There are many forms of integration – our own creativity sets the limit. People can adapt to overwhelming direct violence, such as torture and killings, and are by this integrated. They can adapt to economic structures that dramatically restrict their job opportunities, not having the power to change the employer's dominance over workers (structural violence). Or they conceive the "reality" they live in as the only possible, even though it confines them to a low social status, because the educational and ideological system explains inequality as natural or inevitable (cultural violence). According to the basic values relevant in this book, is a *high quality integration* a form of coordination that increases justice, solidarity, and freedom. All the members are able to improve their situation, and any economic or social burden is carried by the community as a whole. A presumed trickle down effect has been the justification for the accumulation of wealth over the past few decades by a very few at the top. While some money may trickle down to the disadvantaged, this fatalistic acceptance of injustice is in my view low quality integration. The same holds true for political structures that exclude people from power. Not to recognize the equal dignity of others, not to respect their creative originality, not to support the ones in need is in my mind a short-term concept of life, which likely will lead to fewer opportunities, increased suffering, and reactive violence.

Against the constructivist backdrop, nothing is given, everything has to be built up by the interactors. "Integration" means to develop a collective identity. It is a quite complex, never ending process, depending on the engagement of the people. Beside committing to the basic values, the actors have to decide, who is part of "we the people", how they want to interact (forms of action), who are the decision-makers, and how decisions will be implemented (decision mechanism, part of the community's structure). The time concept as structural element also plays an important role: What story do the people want to tell about their origin, past, and their aspired future? Additionally, a symbolic link helps to focus people's engagement and to highlight over time, why people act together. Finally, all the elements relevant in the shared "reality" only exist, if the interactors support them day in and day out (elementary consensus). This applies to institutions too, like the family unit or the state, if we decide to construct one. The state is one of many tools a community uses to stabilize itself, to secure the integration reached. As an institution acting on behalf of the community, the state fulfills specific tasks as long as the constitutive support prevails.

Collective identities are concretized worldviews, are applied concepts of mankind. What is the role of the community, which the one of individuals? How, if ever, do individuals depend on each other? Do communities need political institutions and if yes, what should they look like? Is freedom possible or are human beings determined by God or by their gene pool? Does solidarity, justice, and responsibility make humans humane? From a constructivist point of view, the right worldview is not a truth to be recognized. It is a chosen experience. What has to take place is accordingly a debate about the pro's and con's of political, social, cultural, and economic arrangements, and not a fight over the truth of exclusively defended absolutisms.

This book is at the same time a social theory as it is a theory of political institutions, the state, and the law. Convinced that institutions originate within a specific community and depend on the engagement of its members, talking about integration needs a holistic approach. Just another useless big theory? Farber and Sherry recommend that scholars "focus less on [...] grand theories and more on solving particular constitutional conundrums."[1] In their appeal for "a pragmatic alternative to grand theory" they criticize mainly two aspects: The "foundationalism and a penchant for novelty."[2] For them, "foundationalism" stands for theories that try to establish a justification system within which "answers could be derived from a small number of

---

[1] Farber, Daniel A./Sherry, Suzanna (2002), p. 6
[2] Id.

abstract principles."³ According to Farber and Sherry this sort of theory isn't needed, because "so far, judicial review has served well enough" and "has been emulated by most other democracies."⁴ "Democratic governments around the world have adopted judicially enforceable written constitutions featuring various protections for individual rights against majority action. What calls out for justification and legitimization today is not so much judicial review as its absence in some legal systems."⁵ I'm not sure if the recourse to the wide diffusion of an organizational principle is justification enough. Big numbers in my opinion do not automatically stand for quality. Populist movements use this argument with sometimes very unpleasant effects on freedom of the others or on justice. Simple "pragmatism" or the argument that for example the methodology of the common law "has served the rule of law reasonably well"⁶ is in my mind a conservative and unreflected approach to conflict resolutions. For whom was it good enough, under which circumstances and what does "reasonably well" mean? Is it sensible to state that something was "well enough" without specifying the values on which this judgment is based?

I think it is not a waste of time or reflection to step back and try to think of alternatives to the way things are currently done, and to question our own fundamentals, our own beliefs. Farber and Sherry recommend the following solution: "[…] we think the most fruitful lines of scholarly inquiry lie elsewhere: in doctrinal critique, empirical studies, comparative law, and historical research."⁷ However, the results produced by this research won't be uncontested. We will dispose of different doctrinal, empirical, or historical answers to our problems and still have to decide which one to favor. And this decision, so the proposal made in this book, will be based on a specific set of values. Farber and Sherry's inductive methodology and majoritarian empiricism are useful, when minor disagreements occur, when a smoothly running routine is slightly disturbed. But when central elements of the collective identity are questioned, a discussion about our worldview and our concept of humankind is needed. Grand theories, theories trying to explain the origins and the impact of conflicts on a larger scale, have at least four benefits:

---

3   *Id.*
4   *Id.*, p. 141
5   *Id.*, p. 145
6   *Id.*, p. 141
7   *Id.*, pp. 141 f.

- Possible *advantages and costs of a statement are better evaluable* if the model we are working with tells the story of many interconnected elements.

- *Statements are made against a specific background, based on assumptions* about the amount of freedom individuals have, the relevance of God or other transcendental forces, or the importance of the community for ones own existence. Highlighting these assumptions *helps to understand the opponent and to hold an open discourse* about integration problems.

- A theory should be without contradiction. Not because it makes her look nice, but because it subjects its developer to a *higher justification requirement* and makes it more difficult to act arbitrarily.

- Novelty is in my opinion an important quality criteria of theories: By *establishing alternative ways of thinking* our convictions can be relativized and freedom becomes possible. Without choice, no freedom.

Against the reductionist understanding of human beings relevant in neoliberalism, a comprehensive view of the individual's complex existence is proposed. The selfish isolated monad shall not be the ideal anymore, but rather the supportive individual as a responsible constructor of her or his own "reality", cooperatively engaged with others in realizing dreams that are about more than just material wealth.

B. Social construction of "reality"

The world we live in could be so simple. We could commission people to find out what the truth is (so-called "scientists"). We would listen to their objective results and would behave according to the facts, the reality the experts discovered. We would have experts for every single problem, be it medical, psychological, technical, economic, legal, cultural, or political. Being reasonable individuals, we wouldn't discuss the cognition of the experts. Because we would want to survive, we would follow the unequivocal expertise produced by the knowledge-elite: You cannot live against the reality, otherwise you die. In the enlightened society, the scientists have taken the place of the priests, who were the ones giving advice in earlier societies. In my point of view, however, the guidance by scientists fails, because there are as many "realities" as there are scientists. If reality was such a helpful orientation point, why are there always such intense disputes between the scientists about this very reality? Why are there so many different factions within the sciences, competing each other over the real knowledge?

Benjamin Barber criticizes the current political situation in the United States because of its lack of scientific approach. "[…] it is the epistemological deficit that is putting democracy at risk. Epistemology signifies the 'science of knowing' and expresses a civilizational conviction that truth, objectivity, science, fact, and reason are fundamentally different from opinion, subjectivity, prejudice, feeling, and irrationality. The science of knowing insists on the fundamental distinction made by the Greeks between episteme (true knowledge) and doxa (opinion or prejudice, a root of our word 'orthodoxy'). […] This doesn't mean there is perfect truth, but it does mean there are good and bad arguments – claims that can be verified by empirical facts or rooted in logically demonstrable arguments and those that cannot be. […] None of this means science is 'absolutely true' or that belief is false. But what is true is that science is falsifiable and belief is not. When as an evolutionist I claim man is descended from apes and their historical/biological predecessors, I am claiming something that can be corroborated or falsified by reference to fossil records, genetic affinities, geology and other kinds of empirical data and testable hypotheses. When I claim God created man and then woman from a rib of man, there is no way to confirm or falsify the claim, no 'evidence' that can counter what is a subjective belief."[1] Barber's belief in the scientific method to qualify knowledge as "real" or "unreal", as "true" or "prejudice", doesn't take into account the multitude of contradicting positions that science produces. He supposes that the question of the human's descent from apes can be answered definitely by recourse to empirical research. In my opinion, however, the stories told in this respect vary according to the world we prefer to live in. Supposed, we opt for the descent-from-apes theory, which one of these creatures shall be our ancestor? Which is the one that mirrors our behavior best? Most often scientists refer to the chimpanzees, a male-dominated society with a high level of aggression. This social structure best suits the interests of a patriarch who wants to justify his hierarchical and competitive claims. On the other hand one who is interested in a much more peaceful form of conflict settlement, will opt for the Bonobos as our biological role model. The Bonobos, another great ape (also called Pygmy Chimpanzee), is genetically as near to the humans as the common Chimpanzee, but it doesn't fit the traditional explanation of reality. This species is dominated by females (matriarchal structure) and their conflicts are solved by sexual intercourse.[2] "Puritan patriarchs" weren't attracted to this model so the common Chimpanzee became the animal standard for our predecessors.

What endangers democracy is the claim to absoluteness. In my point of view it is not the scientific method that will solve the problems Barber describes. Rather it is a lack of respect for the equally legitimate position of opponents. As Barber holds, is "our polarized antidemocratic politics of personal prejudice [...] all about the certainty that we are right paired with the conviction that nothing can change our mind."[3] We do not need *the* reality or *the* truth, be it scientific or religious, to avoid this problem. We need *modesty and the willingness to cooperate*. The way people debate and try to find a common ground counts, not the type of knowledge used. The agora has to be organized universally so that everybody has the right to talk and has the guarantee to be listen to. There is *no prevailing argument because of its origin*, no prerogative of a form of knowledge, be it scientific, religious, financial, social, political, racial, or ethnical. A monopoly of knowledge should be avoided to ensure the individual's autonomy. "Those who manipulate [...] our lives are the agents, publicists, marketing departments,

---

[1] Barber, Benjamin R. (2010)
[2] About the Bonobos see de Waal, Frans (1991), pp. 173-228, de Waal, Frans (1989), de Waal, Frans/Lanting, Frans (1997), or National Geographic Society (1993), pp. 42 f., 105.
[3] Barber, Benjamin R. (2010)

promoters, script writers, television and movie producers, advertisers, video technicians, photographers, [...] wardrobe consultants, fitness trainers, pollsters, public announcers, and television news personalities who create the vast stage for illusion. They are the puppet masters. [...] Commodities and celebrity culture define what it means to belong, how we recognize our place in society, and how we conduct our lives."[4] According to Hedges, this form of information control is dangerous because it is illusionary, free from truth[5]. From a constructivist point of view, however, it is not a problem that people create their own stories. This is part of their creative autonomy. Stories become a threat for equal freedom when they are decreed as the only valuable ones and when segments of the population are forbidden to contribute or even worse: are not talked about. "[...] the working classes, comprising tens of millions of struggling Americans, are shut out of television's gated community. They have become largely invisible."[6] Furthermore, focusing on entertainment and "fast-food" information, we lose a reservoir of rich alternatives, as well as the ability to construct complexity. Not a problem of truth, but of choice.

1. Different worlds

There are as many "realities" as there are people. Different "realities" occur, because people have different needs and try to fulfill different interests, to build up divergent worldviews and concepts of humankind.

a) Reciprocity and/or selfish individuality?

Poverty questions the ability of a community to integrate its members. "To see poor people leads – especially in an affluent society – to irritation, disgust, or fear: This sight confronts everyone with the fragility of their own status, but also with the discrepancy between poor and rich, and with difference in general."[7] There is no objective, unique-compulsory answer to be given to this irritation. Every community finds the answer that fits its basic idea of the world. The definition of poverty, for example, in the Middle Ages had to fit the biblical "reality with its orientation to God and its fatalistic ac-

---

[4] Hedges, Chris (2009), pp. 15 f.
[5] Id., pp. 44 f., 51
[6] Id., p. 26
[7] Renz, Ursula/Bleisch, Barbara (ed.) (2007), p. 9

ceptance of the actual situation. Poverty thus had to be explained in a way that gave it a sensible place in the divine order. That's why they declared it to be an imitation of the life of Christ."[8] Most of the time this justificatory explanation worked, though it didn't totally avoid protests or violent conflicts rooted in blatant inequality. A community needs, besides the symbolic narrative (see pp. 387 ff.), a reciprocity arrangement (see p. 225 ff.) to become integrated. Therefore, a social fabric based on "give and take" was built up: The wealthy gave money to the poor while the latter prayed to God for the sake of the donors.[9] Two problems could be solved at once this way. The poor could, at least for the moment, overcome their dire straits. The rich, on the other hand, feared being barred from salvation because of their wealth.[10] Thanks to their generosity they hoped to gain access to the kingdom of God. At the time, because material and spiritual needs were equivalent such an arrangement between the classes was possible. "[…] the poor were rather less concerned with inverting the social order than in ensuring that those who stood at its apex fulfilled their traditional obligations. Although modern observers might be appalled by the complacency of a world-view in which all would be well so long as the rich were kind and the poor were patient, the idiom in which social relations were negotiated was one of social justice rather than one of economic quality. […] rich and poor alike shared a strong sense of the paternalistic obligations of the rich."[11]

Modern society forced materialism and individualism and lessened moral obligations. In combination with the industrialization process, the social fabric of pre-modern times got destroyed. Former mechanisms of self-reliance based on a subsistence economy and family business weren't available anymore so society was confronted with the "social question". Poverty became an important integration challenge to which two answers were mainly given. One answer understood poverty as failure of the individual and the other insisted on the responsibility of the community. Convinced, that anyone could get rich if one tried hard enough, Reverend Russell Conwell[12] gave a lecture around the United States entitled "Acres of Diamonds" to preach his morality to success:

---

[8] Tanner, Jakob (2007), p. 88
[9] See hereto Simon-Muscheid, Katharina (2002), pp. 153 f.
[10] Mark 10:25: "It is easier for a camel to squeeze through the eye of a needle than for a rich person to get into the kingdom of God."
[11] Hindle, Steve (2001), p. 117
[12] Conwell (1843-1925) was American Baptist minister, lawyer, and writer and is the founder of Temple University in Philadelphia (Penn.).

"I say that you ought to get rich, and it is your duty to get rich. [...] Because to make money honestly is to preach the gospel. [...] The men who get rich may be the most honest men you find in the community. 'Oh,' but says some young man here to-night, 'I have been told all my life that if a person has money he is very dishonest and dishonorable and mean and contemptible.' My friend, that is the reason why you have none, because you have that idea of people. The foundation of your faith is altogether false. Let me say here clearly [...], ninety-eight out of one hundred of the rich men of America are honest. That is why they are rich. That is why they are trusted with money. That is why they carry on great enterprises and find plenty of people to work with them. It is because they are honest men. [...] A man is not really a true man until he owns his own home, and they that own their homes are made more honorable and honest and pure, true and economic and careful, by owning the home. [...] I sympathize with the poor, but the number of poor who are to be sympathized with is very small. To sympathize with a man whom God has punished for his sins [...] is to do wrong [...]. [...] let us remember there is not a poor person in the United States who was not made poor by his own shortcomings. [...] It is all wrong to be poor anyhow."[13]

In Reverend Conwell's worldview rich people owe their wealth just to themselves, to their high morality, which is why moral incapacity creates poverty. The bourgeois materialistic entrepreneur is his role model, and there is no claim for solidary behavior or for social responsibility. Poor people were no longer perceived as an imitation of the life of Christ, but more as vagabonds, beggars, or benefit fraudsters.[14] Against this background the idea arose to educate the poor in order to eliminate their moral incapacity. "Pauperism appeared to them as a pathological condition. Hence, in part, the need to isolate paupers as if they were the victims of cholera or smallpox."[15] Victorian society used workhouses to force the poor to learn to work, to deter them from asking for relief,[16] to separate them from the better off and to control them to avoid riots, as "the nation seemed on the brink of revolution."[17] "Only by this means could the independent labourer be protected from 'pauperism,' the potential 'pauper,' particularly the child, be trained and educated to independence and the real 'pauper' be subjected to a disciplined regime which would encourage or frighten him into self

---

[13] Zinn, Howard (1999), p. 262
[14] Simon-Muscheid, Katharina (2002), p. 162
[15] Rose, Michael E. (1988), p. 57
[16] Brundage (2002), p. 66
[17] *Id.*, p. 59

reliance."[18] However, all the Poor Laws didn't suffice to make sure that the workers, the poor lower class, would renounce violence. Against the background of chronic unemployment, the lack of reciprocity mechanisms, and the absence of a form of a convincing justification for the inequality, the excluded used any means at their disposal. On the other hand, these excluded established a support structure within the under class to moderate the worst effects of the new economic regime. As a form of social insurance, these associations were tolerated by the upper class. As soon as they became a political power though, they were repressed.[19] Modern capitalism promised progress and general wealth, which is why, for a certain time, people were willing to follow this promise. But many were forced to realize that the promise would become true just for a segment of the society.

Contrary to Conwell's individualistic description of poverty, George Henry[20] was convinced, that destitution is the result of social and economic structures and nothing the individual can be blamed for.

> "Go into one of the new communities where Anglo-Saxon vigour is just beginning the race of progress; where the machinery of production and exchange is yet rude and inefficient; where the increment of wealth is not yet great enough to enable any class to live in ease and luxury; where the best house is but a cabin of logs or a cloth and paper shanty, and the richest man is forced to daily work – and though you will find an absence of wealth and all its concomitants, you will find no beggars. There is not luxury, but there is not destitution. No one makes an easy living, nor a very good living; but every one *can* make a living."[21] "It is true that wealth has been greatly increased, and that the average of comfort, leisure, and refinement has been raised; but these gains are not general."[22] "This association of poverty with progress is the great enigma of our times. It is the central fact from which spring industrial, social and political difficulties that perplex the world, and with which statesmanship and philanthropy and education grapple in vain. [...] So long as all the increased wealth which modern progress brings goes to build up great fortunes, to increase luxury and make sharper the contrast between the House of Have and the House of Want, progress is not real and cannot be permanent. The reaction must come. The tower leans from its foundations, and every new story but hastens the final catastro-

---

[18] Rose, Michael E. (1988), p. 67
[19] Langford, Paul (2001), pp. 431 ff.
[20] Henry George (1839-1897) was social philosopher and journalist, published in 1879 "Progress and Poverty", a book proposing remedies to the problem of inequality. It was a huge success, having been sold more than three million times.
[21] George, Henry (2005), p. 10
[22] *Id.*, p. 11

phe. To educate men who must be condemned to poverty, is but to make them restive; to base on a state of most glaring social inequality political institutions under which men are theoretically equal, is to stand a pyramid on its apex."[23]

Whereas Conwell defends the interests of the ones at the top of wealth, Henry writes in favor of an inclusive community based on justice.

To overcome the disintegrative effects capitalism had generated because of industrialization and the disbandment of moral obligations support entitlements were established. Before, the relationship between the rich and the poor was mainly based on the contract-principle,[24] which led to charity at the discretion of the rich. There was no guarantee for the needy to get support. A form of non-contractual reciprocity had to be developed on a national level, alike the one that had been part of traditional communities and had characterized families. The welfare state provided an answer in the form of a deficiency guarantee. The former exclusive focus on individualization got balanced by common responsibility. And the individuals were entitled to get relief when they conformed to the requirements. The world of Conwell, which was based on freedom and material greed and dominated the beginning of the capitalist bonanza, got replaced by a solidary and responsible concept of community. Neoliberalism, though, tried everything to prove Conwell right.

b) Social construction of poverty

Intensive fights between the haves and the have-nots took place over "poverty." Not only has the origin of and the reaction to poverty been disputed, but also its definition. To solve this problem an empirical or scientific approach would recommend analyzing the true suffering of the people and its origins in order to define objectively who is "poor" and if they are entitled to our compassion or financial support. However, there seems to be no Archimedian point from which the true "reality" could be recognized. What sort of poverty are we talking about? Is poverty in the modern society still relevant or has the welfare state found the final answer to this question? Is poverty a situation that affects individuals existentially or can somebody be poor and still have enough to eat? Is there a so-called "new poverty" or a "two-thirds society" in which one-third is locked in poverty? The answer to these questions is in my opinion more than a description of reality. It is

---

[23] *Id.*, p. 12
[24] Fraser and Gordon speak of the "ideology of contract-versus-charity" (Fraser, Nancy/Gordon, Linda [1994]).

more than an objective approach to facts. It is a social construction of "reality" based on specific goals that the builder of the "reality" intends to reach.

The definition of poverty is a controversial one. As early as the 18th century, Grosses vollständiges Universal-Lexikon states that it is impossible to assess who is poor.[25] And, according to Klocke, poverty as a sociological category is not clearly determined because an exact scientific fixing of the threshold between poor and rich is impossible.[26] Lipsmeier, in turn, stipulates, that every definition of the threshold demands normative decisions.[27] For Simmel, poverty is not an objective state, but a social construction, the result of a social reaction within a specific community.[28] In western states, we find today mainly two definitions of poverty: Absolute and relative poverty. Absolute poverty is based on a universal concept of minimal needs of human beings and relates to an existential food, health, housing, and education minima. However, there remains a wide range of interpretation because the term poverty can't be regarded as an absolute and unquestioned need. Even the physiological criterion is not easily measurable or evident, but leaves an important margin to judge and decide. The relative understanding of poverty was already used by Seneca, who didn't define it as a specific amount of wealth, but as a deficit relative to the rest of the community: "Poverty doesn't mean to have little, but not to have a lot: so it isn't named after the amount of possession, but after the missing."[29] Adam Smith used them same relative concept, putting the needs into their social context:

> "By necessaries I understand not only the commodities which are indispensably necessary for the support of life, but whatever the custom of the country renders it indecent for creditable people, even of the lowest order, to be without. [...] Custom [...] has rendered leather shoes a necessary of life in England. The poorest creditable person of either sex would be ashamed to appear in public without them. [...] All other things I call luxuries [...]. Beer and ale, for example [...] I call luxuries. A man of any rank may, without any reproach, abstain totally from tasting such liquors. Nature does not render them necessary for the support of life; and custom nowhere renders it indecent to live without them."[30]

---

[25] Zedler, Johann Heinrich (1732-1754)
[26] Klocke, Andreas (2000), p. 313
[27] Lipsmeier, Gero (1999), p. 281
[28] Simmel, Georg (1992), pp. 548, 551
[29] Seneca, Lucius Annaeus: Ad Lucilium Epistulae Morales LXX-CXXIV, 11. Book, Letter 87, Sect. 39: "Paupertas enim est non quae pauca possidet, sed quae multa non possidet: Ita non ab eo dicitur, quod habet, sed ab eo, quo ei deest."
[30] Smith, Adam (1994 [1776]), pp. 938 f. [Book V, Chapter II, Part II, Article IV]

In my view, being poor is more than a material question – it also has an important moral impact. Beside material hardship, there is, on the one hand, the feeling of personal failure to be dealt with. On the other hand, there may be a profound feeling of injustice. Poor people are marginalized, which is why they try to improve their economic situation and fight for recognition (see pp. 208 ff.).

Defining poverty is a *value-based decision*.[31] Amartya Sen for example basis his definition on equal opportunity as element of justice. "Poverty" is therefore a deficit in regard to someone's capacities to reach her or his own goals. This "deprivation of basic capabilities"[32] is due to "deprivations that are intrinsically important," like well-being, freedom, health, or longevity.[33] Sen, however, is convinced that low income is just one of many different origins of poverty. The capability of individuals is as much influenced by age, gender,[34] social role, location, an unhealthy environment,[35] violence, or warfare.[36] To make sure that the people's personal experiences are respected, he highlights the necessity to avoid standardizations. And, like Henry, Sen is convinced that poverty has mainly social origins. Against this background, a respectful idea about poverty becomes possible, adapted to the personal situation of the concerned people, and stressing the responsibility of the community to find solutions. Poverty then is a form of structural and even cultural violence (see p. 77 ff.) only avoidable if people are willing to share wealth and to support each other. Also based on a structural approach, Paugam distinguishes three degrees of poverty:[37] "Integrated poverty" describes lower classes still able to fulfill their basic targets as they are integrated in social, mainly familial networks and can refer to an informal economy. "Marginal poverty" stands for a fundamental form of exclusion, as the concerned people lack the capacity to participate in the wealth of the community and the community doesn't take note of this disability. We can say, that they do not exist in the "reality" of the majority, they're not recognized as such. Paugam's "disabling poverty" stands for a social structure that makes it almost impossible to realize one's own capacities such as in a community with high unemployment rate and a pronounced individualism that destroyed the traditional social networks and extensively controls the

---

[31] In this sense see Sen, Amartya (1999), p. 110.
[32] *Id.*, p. 87
[33] *Id.*, p. 93
[34] *Id.*, pp. 104 ff.
[35] *Id.*, p. 88
[36] *Id.*, p. 103, 96
[37] Paugam, Serge (1998), pp. 49-52

informal economy. According to Paugam, disabling poverty is to be found especially in the most advanced capitalistic societies. Muhammad Yunus confirms this idea when he writes that the actual economic structure doesn't help to solve problems, but rather worsens the situation of the poor: "Unfettered markets in their current form are not meant to solve social problems and instead may actually exacerbate poverty, disease, pollution, corruption, crime, and inequality."[38] He is convinced, that every human being has its own potential and almost everybody can be an entrepreneur.[39] That's why he criticizes the benevolent but haughty behavior of the actual development aid.[40] As poverty means a loss of control over ones own destiny, – "the ultimate denial of human rights"[41] –, concrete projects within a respectful, cooperative relationship have to be established.[42] He posits that "the poor aren't lazy. They work often harder and longer than the ones better off."[43]

Thus, "poverty" is a social construction devised according to the interests of the people in power. A neoliberal understanding individualizes the origins of and the solutions to poverty. In this way, responsibility can be negated and selfish material greed pursued without any qualms. In this worldview, individuals have to fight for their own interests in a worldwide competition. The ones who fail are not strong enough, are lazy or they chose the wrong field to make money. As solidarity doesn't play a role, it's up to the individual to find a way out of her or his misery. A community-based concept, however, stresses not only everybody's responsibility for the quality of life of all members of the community, it also makes it possible to discuss the effects poverty has on individuals and the community itself. The stability of the social arrangement or the quality of democracy may suffer.[44] To construct poverty as a community's problem has many ramifications, it is not an innocuous act. As soon as the lack of opportunities is recognized as an injustice, poverty becomes a plea,[45] a call for action and help, an invocation for change. This change has to overcome structural exclusion mechanisms, necessitating a fundamental overhaul of the community. Some dollars spent once a year won't be enough. A long-term engagement is needed.

---

[38] Yunus, Muhammad (2007), p. 5
[39] Id., p. 54
[40] Id., pp. 11 ff., 56
[41] Id., p. 104
[42] Id., p. 112
[43] Stiglitz, Joseph (2002), p. 103
[44] Kronauer, Martin (2002), p. 17
[45] Linke calls "poverty" a "plea-word" (Linke, Angelika [2007], p. 39).

2. Value-based "reality"

a) Fighting with reality

A realist can't negotiate reality, because to be a realist means to admit the limitations that reality imposes on us. Not to accept these limits leads inevitably to failure or to death because of our hubris. With Galbraith: "In the end of course reality is decisive."[46] For Kirchgässner the "homo oeconomicus" is a realistic concept because it matches reality: "Modern economic theory [...] is based on a realistic concept of humans and admits that individuals with their value judgment (preferences) are givens. It doesn't try to 'improve' them; it doesn't pretend that under different circumstances the individuals would be 'better.' Other economic situations don't make egoistical (bad) human beings become altruistic (good)."[47] Realism is finally an easy concept: We just have to accept the world as it is and stop hoping for a change. People are as they are, period. Beinhocker, an economist like Kirchgässner, unfortunately makes this simple truth complex by qualifying the "homo oeconomicus" as unrealistic: "Of all the assumptions in traditional economics, perhaps the strongest and most obviously unrealistic is its model of human behavior."[48] "Human beings are neither inherently altruistic nor selfish; instead they are what researchers call conditional cooperators and altruistic punishers. [...] The universality of strong reciprocity behavior is staggering. [...] The evolutionary logic for strong reciprocity is simple: In a world of non-zero-sum games, conditional cooperators perform better than agents following either purely selfish or purely altruistic strategies."[49] Beinhocker further criticizes the use of physics and mathematics in traditional economics: "When Walras imported the concept of equilibrium from physics into economics, he gained mathematical precision and scientific predictability. But he paid a high price for that gain – realism. The mathematics of equilibrium required Walras and later economists to make a set of highly restrictive assumptions that have increasingly detached theoretical economics from the real world."[50] According to Beinhocker, a realistic economic theory has not to relate on physics or mathematics, but on evolution, network, and system theory: "[...] modern science, in particular evolution-

---

[46] Galbraith, John Kenneth (2005), p. 11
[47] Kirchgässner, Gebhard (1991), p. 27
[48] Beinhocker, Eric D. (2006), p. 5
[49] Id., p. 419; see also p. 121
[50] Id., p. 48

ary theory and the theory of complex adaptive systems, provides us with a radically new perspective on these long-standing economic questions."[51] Thanks to these tools it will be possible to recognize economic laws and to predict the future: "Saying that there are laws of economics does not imply that we will ever be able to make perfect predictions about the economy, but it does imply that we might someday have a far deeper understanding of economic phenomena than we do today. It also means that economics in the future may be able to make prescriptive recommendations about business and public policy with a level of scientific authority that it has not had before."[52] In both cases, Kirchgässner as well as Beinhocker, use the argument of "realism" not to add some important information to their theory, but to *discredit contradicting opinions*. To be "real" or "realistic" means, therefore, simply to have the right to silence opponents characterized as "unrealistic." Realism is a *competitive fight over the power to decide* what currently has to be accepted. This "epistemologically veiled fist fight"[53] gives the opportunity to quiet the opposite side, to *end and refuse discussion* because truth can't be discussed.

However, both Kirchgässner and Beinhocker, economists, well respected in their profession, seem to talk about totally different "realities." Realism would be more convincing if the invoked reality were to give clear indications about how we human beings have to act. This, according to the realist[54] Popper, won't be the case. Popper states that science attempts to describe and explain reality.[55] The target of science has to be to propose "theories which come a little nearer to the truth than those of our predecessors."[56] "Truth is correspondence with the facts"[57] and "the idea of truth is absolutist, but no claim can be made for absolute certainty: we are seekers for truth but we are not its possessors."[58] "[…] while we cannot ever have sufficiently good arguments in the empirical sciences for claiming that we have actually reached the truth, we can have strong and reasonably good arguments for claiming that we may have made progress toward the truth."[59] Hence, sure cognition isn't possible. We are able to discover the reality without ever

---

[51] *Id.*, p. 5
[52] *Id.*, p. 14
[53] Mitterer, Josef (1992), p. 110
[54] Popper, Karl R. (1992), p. 22
[55] Popper, Karl R. (1979), p. 40
[56] *Id.*, p. 44
[57] *Id.*
[58] *Id.*, pp. 46 f.
[59] *Id.*, pp. 57 f.

being sure of having caught it.[60] There's no possibility, according to Popper, to prove our knowledge as being true.[61] The only thing we can do, so his proposition goes, is to test our conceptions of reality in a discursive way, as our knowledge increases thanks to critical discussion. "[…] I look upon criticism […] as our main instrument in promoting the growth of our knowledge about the world of facts."[62] Popper's argument demonstrates the contradictory character and uselessness of realism. First, he states that, on the one hand, people can't acquire sure cognition. On the other hand, however, they can approach or even find reality. Doesn't that suppose, that at minimum Popper knows what the reality looks like? Otherwise he couldn't measure the rapprochement. Second, his solution for the lack of certainty, the critical discourse, doesn't need reality, because the relevant criteria is the consensus of the debaters. Realism only works if sure cognition is possible and if contradicting positions can be excluded. However, it then becomes *totalitarian*, what Popper for example wants to avoid. If we take the freedom of others seriously, if we respect other positions ontologically as equal, realism isn't justifiable,[63] isn't needed, and is even dangerous.

Beside its totalitarian claim, realism contains another risk for freedom – its *tendency toward elitism and standardization*. An important part of realistic worldviews is the selection of the people who are responsible to find the truth. Before the Enlightenment God was the orientation point, which gave the religious experts the right to know what was best for the people. In modern society, it is science that claims this privileged position. Scientists, therefore, decide what we have to believe and how we have to act. Within the scientific community, though, there is fierce competition to gain the power to decide. Because of the competitive setup, the search for the one and only truth has a reductionistic effect: If the knowledge-producing community comes to the conclusion that my knowledge is "false," I risk being excluded. All the work I invested to reach the summit of scientific recognition may have been done in vain. That's why many decide not to take any risk and to reproduce the point of view of the ones in charge.

This uniformization is also supported by the members of the scientific powerhouse. To demonstrate objective truth to the non-scientific outside world and to immunize the caste of pundits against criticism, unity has to

---

[60] Popper, Karl R. (1994b), pp. 49 f.
[61] *Id.*, p. 234
[62] Popper, Karl R. (1979), p. 318. See also p. 121, or Popper, Karl R. (1994b), pp. 39 f., 232; Popper, Karl R./Eccles, John C. (1996), p. 188, 190
[63] A position, Popper also defends, but on epistemological grounds: "[…] realism is neither demonstrable nor refutable" (Popper, Karl R. [1979], p. 38).

be feigned. Quarreling scientists do not suit the idea of a community on its way to *the* reality. Another problem for alternative thinking is the standardization of knowledge creation. What in French is called "la pensée unique" stands for a monoculture attracted by uniformity. Everything has to fit the same criteria. Knowledge becomes in combination with economic interests a commodity to be consumed effortlessly. One pays for knowledge to climb some steps on the career ladder and not to be questioned by unexpected, different ways of thinking. Liessmann talks of the "industrialization and economization of knowledge"[64] and warns of the "control-society" we are rapidly heading to.[65]

b) Consensus-based constructivism

Truth is, in my opinion a concept without any helpful information. Its function is solely to prioritize a statement over another by pretending, that it is of higher quality. The problem, though, is that the criteria used to demonstrate its prerogative are also man-made. We, therefore only move the discussion about the truth of statements to another level. This shift can take place infinitely, and in the end it is still up to us to decide, what *we* think is worth being called "truth". To avoid this infinite regress and to highlight our responsibility for the "reality" we live in, I propose the *consensus-based constructivism* as an alternative. It is a form of community-construction that states a *conflicting, ambivalent relationship between indeterminism and interdependence* within the human existence. Ensuring that the freedom of the ones can be realized as much as it respects the freedom of others, responsibility and solidarity are part of this construction theory, too. As I intend a comprehensive form of liberty, "reality"[66] is understood as the result of our actions. As much as we are constitutive for each other's liberty we bring "reality" into existence by acting. Out of this construction power follows our responsibility for what is, as there is nothing without us acting: "Real" is what we want to be.

The "reality" we live in is the child of our *hopes* and our hopes are revealed in our *actions*. Our actions, in turn, are *proposals* to the others which we hope they will accept. Proposals intend to realize a specific form of com-

---

[64] Liessmann, Konrad Paul (2006), p. 8
[65] *Id.*, p. 173
[66] Contrary to the reality of realism, which stands for an existence independent of ourselves, given and to be recognized, "reality" in quotation marks is what interacting individuals originate.

munity. If our counterpart *approves* the proposed form of social relation, we have *interactively constructed "reality"* based on the *consensus* of its members.

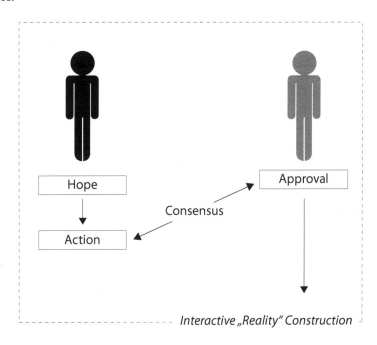

Interactive "Reality" Construction

Against this background every "reality" element is the *result of a negotiation process*, of debates though not necessarily an elaborated or very nuanced or detailed one. Already the possibility to say "no," but answering "yes" stands for a reflection, a choice that could be different. The approval or denial can be explicit or non-verbal. As long as there is no opposition, the proposed action will have its way and decide, at least for the moment, what is "real." The "reality" we construct is existent as long as we and others are ready to behave in the manner that leads to the intended result. Without us acting there is no "reality."

Following this exclusive focus on action, there aren't any superhuman forces or institutions relevant in this consensus-based constructivism. There also isn't any objective truth, no absolute reality that has to be taken into account. We are the originators and the ones who set the limits of our "reality." As discussed earlier (see p. 9 ff.), there is a multitude of "reality" proposals that concretize different basic values. This consensus-based constructivism is founded on and characterized by the following values:

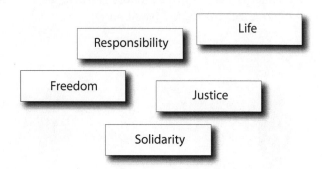

This set of interconnected values is supposed to make sure that every individual has the equal opportunity to realize her or his hopes (see in detail pp. 124 ff.). Underlying this is a concept of humankind that sees individuals as part of a social arrangement, constituting community and, at the same time, made by it. Being responsible for what we do and are is the basis for being creatively free. Responsibility also generates trust, which, in turn, is central for enhancing the room to maneuver.

There is no objective justification for consensus-based constructivism, no compelling argument to be made. If freedom is a basic value, it is up to the readers to approve the proposal made here. Perhaps it will convince by itself, by the experience of a "reality" that is qualified as positive. The opportunity to get rid of rules proscribed by nature or to decide on our own if limits decreed by pundits will be abided by, could make this proposal attractive. On the other hand, this freedom is a burden because it implies our responsibility for the "reality" we build. Consensus-based constructivism is justified by a (usually proscribed) circular argument: A "reality" is proposed that realizes basic values. Why?: Because the actor cherishes this way of living. Why does he cherish this way of living? It is a satisfying experience incorporating the values important for him. To change the values will change the construction which will make possible new experiences. These will be satisfying because they are what we are looking for just now: A combination of advantages and disadvantages currently attractive enough to be supported. These pros and cons, in turn, are qualified against the background of the relevant basic values ...

Circular arguments are in my view unproblematic when they are made explicit because they do not hide a lack of justification. They are necessary because of the abandonment of justification strategies referring to externalities. There is nothing left to justify our decisions except ourselves.

Value-based "reality"

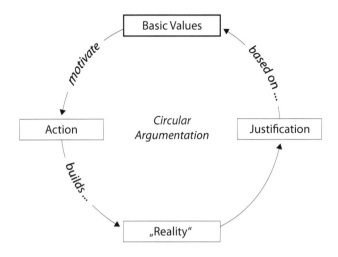

Circular arguments end infinite regresses by declaring what is at the origin of the "reality" proposal, by declaring the motives of the constructor and the expected pros and cons. Based on the principle of *equal construction opportunities*, there is no claim for universal truth or an objective duty to comply with the proposal. What is left is a discussion over the values that motivate our "reality" construction and the decision about which "reality" we want to live in, which form of community we favor and which ones we disapprove of.

What do we lose be giving up *the* reality?

- The possibility to avoid or end discussions because truth has been found.
- The excuse not to do something because it is unrealistic.
- The ability to counter claims for a change by qualifying them as "naive".
- A mechanism to reduce complexity as we become responsible for the events in our world.
- We also loose a very effective justification for establishing privileged knowledge, the prerogative of an elite of people who think they know better than others.

What do we gain?

- The possibility to meet each other on fundamentally equal grounds.

- Comprehensive freedom: The possibility to build the world we want to live in, if we are able to convince others to join in.
- And the possibility to be thoroughly responsible for the world we chose.

Eternal truths like "the market demands ...", "human beings can't ...", "black people are ...", or "men and women can't understand each other ..." lose their status as truth and become "reality" proposals. As a result, our "reality" elements are contingent, meaning, they can change in every interaction: There is no guaranteed future.

Interaction is the fundamental form of "reality" construction. It shouldn't be confused with "discourse." Whereas "interaction" stands for *every form of action related to others*, it denotes "discourse" interactions that comply with specific quality criteria, such as equality, openness, or respect (see p. 171). To interact means to act and react to others. Interactions can take the form of dictatorships or the form of a coercion-free discourse.

c) Decision instead of cognition

Realism looks for an orientation point, for an instance that decides what is the truth and where we go wrong. Faced with the multitude of "reality" proposals to be found about every topic, one wonders where this judgment should come from. "There are many eyes. […] that is why there are many 'truths' and hence no truth."[67] "It is evident that every existence different from us senses other qualities and thus lives in a different world than we do."[68] Invoking a meta-position doesn't solve the problem as there will again be several meta-positions, needing a meta-meta-position able to decide. This infinite regress makes *the* reality a lure everybody runs after and nobody will ever find. We, therefore, at least as proposed in this book, are confronted with the task *not to recognize what is true, but to decide what we want*. It is a choice based on values, on a favored form of relationship, a worldview that seems for the chooser attractive enough with which to agree. It is a specific arrangement of freedom and obligation, of autonomy or interdependence, of responsibility for our own deeds and solidarity toward others that we opt for. The question then isn't: "What is?" or "What has to be?", but "*Who do you want to be?*"

---

[67] Nietzsche, Friedrich (1996), p. 369
[68] *Id.*, p. 385

What is the role of science in a "reality" without reality? *Scientific action* – like any action – *creates "reality,"* and the question is, for what and for whom is this useful? In my opinion, there are two tasks that science should be up to. First, it should construct solutions that satisfy the needs of the people, of the community. How can conflicts be solved? How can people be healed, fed, and sheltered. How can stable and energy-efficient houses be built? How the mobility wish of people be addressed in a sustainable way, or how can business be made in a just way? Second, its role could also be to develop as crazy as possible alternatives to the dominant way of thinking. It seems that this second role of court jester is not serious enough for modern scientists. They would risk being thought of as "unrealistic," losing the respect of the scientific community, the status, and by this the power science provides.

The Enlightenment criticized the claim of the priests that they knew the truth and were, therefore, entitled to lead the people as a father figure. Enlightened people were supposed to decide autonomously by using their critical and sceptical mind.[69] In my opinion, however, modern science replaced "the father" by *the* reality. To abandon the concept of realistic truth would make us seriously autonomous, would set us free to construct the unknown other, the surprising alternative, or the unexpected creation.[70] Scientific court jesters would criticize the rulers and their active or passive supporters and keep the community dynamic by embracing difference. Creativity and courage should be favored over obedience. This would also mean to distance oneself from method-fetishism. Just to follow the existing rule is not a justification by itself. What counts is the readiness to discuss and defend the proposals. The quality of knowledge shouldn't depend on its origin but on its ability to launch discussions, to make people think of alternatives, or to bring solutions. I share the position of Poppy, the fundamentally optimistic freethinker and main character in the movie "Happy-go-lucky," who doesn't want to be realistic, because it's too dull and restrictive a philosophy.[71]

To renounce *the* reality is a decision in favor of liberty and equality. The "reality" of others is then not recognizable anymore from an objective external standpoint, which has consequences for the way we approach them. Getting to know somebody means in the consensus-based constructivism to share "reality" with this person, to listen, to ask, and finally to talk.

---

[69] Abosch, Heinz (1993), pp. 193 f.; Popper, Karl R. (1994a), p. 162
[70] Popper highlights the importance of taking risks and being creative (Popper, Karl R. [1979], pp. 54 ff.).
[71] Mike Leigh (2007), Min. 4' 22"

Bronislaw Malinowski, the founder of the method of participant observation, describes the task of the ethnographer "to grasp the native's point of view, his relation to life, to realize *his* vision of *his* world."[72] In his viewpoint, ethnographers become a part of the world of the people they observe as scientists and are themselves changed by this contact: "In field research the ethnographer traverses a sort of second socialization. Through personal experience he appropriates the foreign culture in all its aspects."[73] This "observation" is in my point of view not a one-to-one portrayal of the others' "reality". It is a construction based on one's own principles, even though it is enriched by the "disturbances" that the interaction provides. The people described quite probably see themselves differently, as the report of Father Baldwin shows, who met the Trobrianders after Malinowski. He submitted them Malinowski's text to them and noted the following reaction: "[…] Malinowski would be regarded in some ways naïve by the people he was studying. That the people he describes would still seem somewhat foreign to the Trobrianders themselves. They did not quarrel with facts or explanation, only with the coloring, as it were. The sense expressed was not the sense they had of themselves."[74] Insofar as writing *about* others is as much writing about oneself and reveals as much about the writer as about the subject.[75] In this construction process we delineate ourselves from others, defining at the same time who we are.[76] The free and equal solution out of this self-referencing description is a *cooperative construction of the identity others want to have*. Interactively, we work on a "reality" that the others decide to be their own. In a constructivist "reality" there is no difference between recognizing the subject and object anymore and we have to give up the idea of seizing comprehensively the object of our interest.[77] Constructivists aren't passive observers of the present, but active constructors of the future. They respectfully build with others, if justice counts for them.

---

[72] Malinowski, Bronislaw (1922), p. 25
[73] Kohl, Karl-Heinz (2000), p. 112
[74] Quoted in Därmann, Iris (2002), p. 22
[75] Därmann, Iris (2002), p. 23
[76] Kohl, Karl-Heinz (2000), p. 26
[77] About the difficulties to differentiate between subject and object see Jamme, Christoph (2002), p. 191. For relative recognition abilities see for example Wierlacher, Alois (1993), p. 48, Waldenfels, Bernhard (1999), p. 113, Zingerle, Arnold (1993), p. 431, and Cappai, Gabriele (2000), p. 272.

C. Concept of humankind and community

Every action is a "reality" proposal and poses the question of integration: "Integration" is *an interactive process leading to a specific form of humankind and community*. To talk about "integration" means to talk about our concept of human beings, means to talk about the role of the individual within the community, and the amount of freedom and obligation, solidarity and responsibility. What is the world we want to live in? What is the concept of humankind and community do we intend to establish? The answer is a political project based on an arrangement of values. Reflecting on what we are doing needs us therefore to discuss the concept of humankind and community that underlies our decisions. And we are able to understand each other when we are able to grasp what is important in the "reality" of the other, what is her or his worldview.

For Dahrendorf there is a permanent conflict between the scientific concepts of humankind like the homo oeconomicus, the homo sociologicus, the psychological man, and the homo politicus[1] and the everyday experience: "What is the relation between the human being of our everyday experience and the transparent concept of the social sciences? Do we have to and is it possible to defend our constructed, abstract human being against the real one?"[2] "The whole human being can't be described by one discipline on its own and has perhaps to rest as an undefined figure in the background."[3] This impossibility is according to Dahrendorf accountable to the scientific necessity to simplify and standardize its object to make possible a systematic reconstruction and testability. Realistically speaking, we are interested in the real human being. If science can't provide a description of the reality, why then not renounce to the scientific method? We do not need it, as Dahrendorf seemingly knows; otherwise he wouldn't be able to state the deficits of the scientific approach. And why hold on to scientific standardization if it doesn't tell the whole story? The answer of consensus-based constructivism is: Let's renounce the search for scientific truth and

---

[1] Dahrendorf, Ralf (2006), pp. 19 f.
[2] Id.
[3] Id., p. 21

build up the concept of humankind and community that satisfies us most, that makes as good a life as possible.

In this chapter, I will discuss two forms of humankind. The *neo homo oeconomicus*, exclusively oriented toward freedom and the dominating model since the 1980s, and the *homo interactivus* as a relationship based on freedom, responsibility, justice, and solidarity. The latter is conceived as an alternative to the selfish monad which has not made the majority of people happy, but has been *imposed by a few as the standard of a good life*.

1. Neo homo oeconomicus – selfish individualism

The neo homo oeconomicus is grounded on the methodological individualism. "The ultimate constituents of the social world are individual people [...]. Every complex social situation, institution, or event is the result of a particular configuration of individuals, their dispositions, situations, beliefs, and physical resources and environment."[4] Hayek, often referred to as the father of neoliberalism, defends a "true individualism," as "a theory of society" that tries to explain "the formation of spontaneous social products"[5] recurring to individual action.[6] Stating that the actors aren't totally rational,[7] he defines rationality as the result of "an interpersonal process in which anyone's contribution is tested and corrected by others."[8] Individualism isn't identical with anti-social behavior, because in the point of view of Hayek "selfish interest" doesn't mean "egotism in the narrow sense of concern with only the immediate needs of one's proper person."[9] The "self" can include family and friends and "anything for which people in fact did care". In this *classic* liberal sense "selfishness" stands for the freedom from compulsory prescriptions, stands for the freedom "to strive for whatever [one] think[s] desirable"[10] and against "central control of all social processes"[11] or centralization, nationalism and socialism.[12] Hayek perceives the individual as part of a social arrangement. But this arrangement has to be organized freely,

---

[4] Watkins, John W.N. (1959), p. 505
[5] Hayek, Friedrich A. (1949), p. 10
[6] Id., pp. 3 ff. Hayek speaks of "the true individualism" as "primarily a theory of society [...] and only in the second instance a set of political maxims" (p. 6).
[7] Id., pp. 10 f.
[8] Id., p. 15
[9] Id., p. 13; see also p. 23
[10] Id., p. 15
[11] Id., p. 27
[12] Id., p. 28

shall it find the approval of Hayek: "What individualism teaches us is that society is greater than the individual only in so far as it is free."[13]

a) Selfish monads imprisoned

The *neo*-liberal concept of the individual clearly goes beyond this classic understanding and *isolates egoistic men and women in a materialistic world*, basically referring to themselves. Within a competitive arrangement selfish individuals only seeking their own interests are integrated by the market. At the core is a concept of negative freedom, understanding others as a potential threat to a pre-given liberty.

The homo oeconomicus underlies the neoliberal concept of humankind and states that individuals always act rationally: They balance costs against benefits before acting. On the grounds of scarcity the reasonable decision is taken, trying to maximize utility.[14] Individuals choose the opportunity that provides the greatest benefit. Giving in to critics from psychology, economists relativized this absolute rationality. This weighing process, therefore, isn't necessarily "objective" or "deliberate" anymore because human beings aren't computers.[15] Kirchgässner talks of "restricted rationality,"[16] embedding rationality in its social context. And in the point of view of Becker, the actors aren't expected to have complete information for their decisions, neither do they have to be aware of their optimization attempts.[17] But still: The whole system is based on rationality because irrationality is sanctioned by *the* reality: "Irrational deciders are also obliged to recognize the reality and can't act beyond their possibilities."[18] Thus, their possibilities are determined by external restrictions and the actors try to realize their main preferences within this restrictions. "Preferences" are values of the individuals that help them to decide which of the opportunities they should choose.

Why does the economic theory insist so much on the aforementioned "rationality?" Scientific concepts of humankind are established on the grounds of practicality. The leading model for economists, the homo oeconomicus, has to be simple enough to be operationalizable[19] and to make formalization possible. In this way, the economy hopes to come close to the

---

[13] *Id.*, p. 32
[14] Kirchgässner, Gebhard (1991), p. 91
[15] *Id.*, p. 28
[16] *Id.*, pp. 31 f.
[17] Becker, Gary S. (1993), pp. 5 f.
[18] *Id.*, p. 184
[19] Wiese, Harald (1994), p. 67

credibility that natural sciences have acquired. The behavior of individuals is best measurable if scientists can focus on externalities and do not have to bother about the individual's motives, about the imponderabilities of psychological processes.[20] Because the interior life of people isn't objectively verifiable[21] and measurability counts most, economic theory simply declares preferences as stable, unchangeable.[22] Only the external restrictions are left to be analyzed so that the economic research can concentrate on income, GDP, or education level. Behind the statistics, then, the individual disappears.

The homo oeconomicus is used to pursue egotistic interests – it is a *selfish utility-maximizer*. Economic theory is based on a concept of human beings modelled not on the cooperative, solidary mother or father, but on the prisoner in solitary confinement. The prisoner's dilemma[23] is used to explain, why people act in a specific way and has the advantage to be easily applicable. Furthermore, it suits the idea that economists seem to have of human beings. Within the prisoner's dilemma nobody knows anything of each other, and every individual tries to obtain as much as possible, independent of the demeanor of others, because the self-interest axiom is universal.[24] Love or solidarity can't develop because these competencies are founded on direct contact. Cooperation or the protection of collective interests only occur in this worldview, if legal coercion is used.[25]

Economic "reality" is based on a concept of humankind that, out of a profound desire to predict the actions of human beings, renounces to psychological reflections and strips them of any social competence. To predict one's behavior means to try to reduce the other to a standardized object that doesn't use its liberty to act in a creatively new way. Paradoxically, the ones who base their whole theory on individualistic freedom (freedom detached from any social dependencies) try to get rid of contingency by attempting to control the future. But contingency, or the possibility to change our way to act in any moment, is in my viewpoint a constitutive prerequisite of freedom (see p. 136 ff.). To facilitate the work of scientists, people have to renounce to their unpredictability. According to Taleb, "there is a strong link between rationality, predictability, and mathematical tractability. […] Rational actors must be coherent: they cannot prefer apples to oranges, or-

---

[20] Kirchgässner, Gebhard (1991), p. 26
[21] Id., p. 39; Becker, Gary S. (1993), pp. 4, 15
[22] Kirchgässner, Gebhard (1991), p. 38
[23] Id., pp. 53 f.
[24] Id., p. 16; see also p. 45
[25] Id., p. 55

anges to pears, then pears to apples. If they did, then it would be difficult to generalize their behavior. It would also be difficult to project their behavior in time. In orthodox economics, rationality became a straitjacket."[26] Furthermore, the concept of immutable preferences is contradictory, as, for example, Kirchgässner pretends that preferences are the result of socialization processes.[27] How comes, that something built up interactively, suddenly becomes something that can't be changed anymore? Are people social beings or determined existences whose freedom is a lure? Shouldn't it be the laudable task of science, not to predict or focus on standardized similarities, but rather to create alternatives nobody until now thought of? The standardized utility maximizer looses individuality and freedom.

b) Market-integration as divine harmony

It is not probable that an isolated selfish monad could be able to play an important role in the integration process. Because everyone just looks after her- or himself and tries to fulfill their own egoistic interests, respectful cooperation is all but expectable. Furthermore, the integration work is according to the economic proposal, too complex to be done by human beings. Thus, besides the lack of motivation there is also a cognitive deficit to be taken into account. Individuals or institutions do not have the necessary knowledge to integrate the society by central governance.[28] And still, people seem able to live together. How come? The economists' answer is that the market integrates individuals like an invisible hand. The "market" is, in this understanding, a place where demanders and providers meet. Pursuing their own materialistic interests the market principle helps the individuals to make choices that are, on the one hand, ideal for themselves and, on the other hand, lead to an increase of the common wealth.[29] Markets are understood as self-regulating systems[30] with an impressive integration-power that brings forth a spontaneous order.[31] President Reagan called this "the magic of the marketplace,"[32] which only works, if its integrative power isn't disturbed by non-market forces, like, for example, the state because "[…] gov-

---

[26] Taleb, Nassim Nicholas (2008), p. 184
[27] Kirchgässner, Gebhard (1991), p. 13
[28] Giddens, Anthony (1997), p. 102; Baecker, Dirk (2006), p. 97
[29] Heilbroner, Robert (1994), p. 90
[30] Polanyi, Karl (1978), p. 71
[31] Kirchgässner, Gebhard (1991), p. 22
[32] Reagan, Ronald (1982)

ernment is not the solution to our problem; government is the problem."³³ Following this philosophy, Reagan's policies "called for reductions across the board in the size and scope of government and for shrinking the government's revenue base. This reduction of the federal role was the unifying element of Reaganomics."³⁴

By focussing on the selfish actor pursuing his own best material interests, social values like solidarity, responsibility, or justice aren't of any importance. That's why Friedman gives priority to economic freedom. He is convinced, that "economic freedom [...] is a necessary condition for political freedom."³⁵ For Friedman, the most important social problem is the coordination of the economic activities of large numbers of people.³⁶ Because the state isn't able to replace the multitude and diversity of individual actions,³⁷ the market is that for the best technique.³⁸ What's left for the state is, according to Friedman, the preservation of law and order, the protection of the individual's liberty against private violence,³⁹ the guarantee of private propriety, the responsibility for the monetary system, the prevention of monopolies,⁴⁰ and the protection of lunatics and children who can't subsist on the market.⁴¹ Whatever results the markets yield, they have to be accepted as the best solutions for the individuals and the common wealth. That counts also for inequality, which is a "result of arrangements designed to satisfy men's tastes,"⁴² and is, therefore, "required."⁴³ Inequality is simply the result of individual choices, due to "initial differences in endowment, both of human capacities and of property."⁴⁴ Even if that poses some ethical questions, according to Friedman, we just have to trust that the market will distribute payment in accordance with performance ("product").⁴⁵ Furthermore does inequality in his point of view fulfill a useful function, because

---

33   Reagan, Ronald (1981)
34   Cannon, Lou (1991), pp. 198 f.
35   Friedman, Milton (2002), p. 4. According to Stöger all other liberties do follow out of the economic one (Stöger, Roman [1997], p. 65).
36   Friedman, Milton (2002), p. 12
37   Id., p. 4
38   Id., p. 14
39   Id.
40   Id., pp. 26 ff.
41   Id., p. 33
42   Id., p. 163
43   Id., p. 162
44   Id., pp. 163 f.
45   Id., pp. 166 f.

"it enables distribution to occur impersonally without the need for 'authority'" and gives the better-off the possibility to invest in unpopular or novel ideas.⁴⁶ And even if one would be concerned about inequality, it is non of his business because it's the market that is responsible for ethical questions, not the economic actors: "There is one and only one social responsibility of business – to use its resources and engage in activities designed to increase its profits so long as it stays within the rules of the game, which is to say, engages in open and free competition without deception or fraud."⁴⁷

Why this blind trust in the market forces? Because there is *market equilibrium*, the most efficient form of integration: "At every moment, some people are buying while others are selling [...]. Yet in the midst of all this turmoil, markets are constantly solving the what, how, and for whom. As they balance all the forces operating on the economy, markets are finding a market equilibrium of supply and demand. A market equilibrium represents a balance among all the different buyers and sellers."⁴⁸ This interest accommodation is according to Varian/Buchegger, inevitable. There sometimes can be a disturbance of this equilibrium, but they are convinced, that it is just the exception and not the rule.⁴⁹ In the end, so the conviction of the economists go, the price mechanism will lead to common wealth (not identical with equality).⁵⁰ That's why "neoliberalism considers the growth of poverty to be a pathology, not a consequence of the economic system. Hence, it isolates poverty from the process of capital accumulation and economic development, and reduces the solution to designing specific social policies."⁵¹ This belief in the transcendental benign power of the market goes back to Adam Smith, who in the "Theory of Moral Sentiments" and in "The Wealth of Nations" talks of an "invisible hand" that leads the people.⁵² For him, a religious-transcendental First Cause was behind all existence, a cause he called God,⁵³ the divine Being, the Author, or Jupiter. In the worldview of the still mainly deistic eighteenth century, God is the origin of a

---

⁴⁶ *Id.*, p. 168
⁴⁷ Friedman, Milton (1970), p. 236
⁴⁸ Samuelson, Paul A./Nordhaus, William D. (2001), p. 27
⁴⁹ Vairan, Hal R./Buchegger, Reiner (2007), pp. 3 f.
⁵⁰ Mankiw, Gregory/Taylor, Mark (2008), p. 13 and 14
⁵¹ Vilas, Carlos (1996), p. 16
⁵² For example in Smith, Adam (1994 [1776]), Book IV, Chapter II, p. 485
⁵³ Smith, Adam (1980 [1795]), p. 113: "The idea of an universal mind, of a God of all, who originally formed the whole, and who governs the whole by general laws, directed to the conservation and prosperity of the whole, without regard to that of any private individual [...]."

preordained and basically harmonious world. "It was common for seventeenth- and eighteenth-century deists to perceive God as a creative demiurge who desisted from direct intervention in human affairs via miracles, visions and so on. On this view, God is the First Cause, a 'general' rather than special 'providence' pre-existing the world, creating it perfect and equipping it with uniform laws of Nature in order to keep it in motion."[54] The moral structure and the language of "The Theory of Moral Sentiments" is dominated by religious elements combined with the enlightened self-responsible individual with the transcendental force making sure to rein in the immense amount of freedom given.

> "In every part of the universe we observe means adjusted with the nicest artifice to the ends which they are intended to produce; and in the mechanism of a plant, or animal body, admire how every thing is contrived for advancing the two great purposes of nature, the support of the individual, and the propagation of the species. [...] When by natural principles we are led to advance those ends, which a refined and enlightened reason would recommend to us, we are very apt to impute to that reason, as to their efficient cause, the sentiments and actions by which we advance those ends, and to imagine that to be the wisdom of man, which in reality is the wisdom of God."[55]
>
> "The administration of the great system of the universe, [...] the care of the universal happiness of all rational and sensible beings, is the business of God, and not of man."[56]

These two "realities", the "reality" of the individuals and the superhuman one have to be respected for their irreducible differences, and nobody has to interfere in the sphere reserved for God, "that divine Being, whose benevolence and wisdom have from all eternity contrived and conducted the immense machine of the universe so as at all times to produce the greatest possible quantity of happiness."[57] Against this background, Smith asks for modesty of human beings, not trying to exercise influence on a large scale. Not up to the task they only should pursue their immediate desires and leave the ruling of the game to the designing power.[58]

"Wealth of the Nation," which was published seventeen years latter, indicates a move toward a more secular language. However, still looking for an ordering, superhuman authority, "nature" replaces God and becomes

---

[54] Hill, Lisa (2001), p. 5
[55] Smith, Adam (2006 [1759]), Part II, Section II, Chapter III, p. 87
[56] Smith, Adam (2006 [1759]), Part VI, Section I, Chapter III, p. 238
[57] Id., pp. 237 f.
[58] Hill, Lisa (2001), p. 14

the 'invisible hand' of Providence.⁵⁹ "The non-human authority/standard that Smith does retain is nature, as manifested in his pitch for the 'natural system of perfect liberty and justice'⁶⁰ that would support the 'natural progress of opulence', the 'natural course of things,' the 'natural progress of things toward improvement,' the 'natural law of succession,' the 'natural progress of law and government,' the 'natural effort of every individual to better his own condition,' the 'natural employments' of industry and capital, the 'natural division and distribution of labour' [...]."⁶¹ Even though he describes the importance of individual acts, he is not ready to give up the superhuman ordering authority, thus accepting fundamental restrictions on freedom. *The common good is still at the fore.*

The belief in a concept of a transcendental steering mechanism is to be found in many areas. Nozick describes them as "invisible-hand explanations," as explanations of "what looks to be the product of someone's intentional design, as not being brought about by anyone's intentions."⁶² Evolutionary theory (random mutation, natural selection, genetic drift, etc.), the ecological regulation of animal populations, or the equilibration of markets are examples of the effect of an invisible-hand. Nozick prefers this sort of explanation to the straightforward ones because "they don't explain complicated patterns by including the full-blown pattern-notions as objects of people's desires or beliefs."⁶³ According to him, the invisible hand is, realistically spoken, a better explanation than the straightforward one.

Neoliberalism uses the same religious belief in transcendental integration forces, but, contrary to Smith, gives up the notion of social obligation, of responsibility. For Smith, there is a need for reciprocity, for cooperation, not organized by the anonymous regulator, but by interdependent individuals. And he expects people to be humane, helping the ones in need: "[...] public spirit [...] is founded upon the love of humanity, upon a real fellow-feeling with the inconveniencies and distresses to which some of our fellow-citizens may be exposed."⁶⁴ Smith defended the idea of a just society

---

[59] *Id.*, pp. 12 f. "The deistic theology of the Moral Sentiments is carried through to the Wealth of Nations with the effect that Smith's economic views are informed by the moral and theological assumptions set out in the Moral Sentiments" (p. 4).
[60] Smith, Adam (1994 [1776]), Book IV, Chapter VII, Part III p. 655
[61] Minowitz, Peter (2004), pp. 407 f.
[62] Nozick, Robert (1974), p. 19
[63] *Id.*
[64] Smith, Adam (2006 [1759]), Part VI, Section II, Chapter II, p. 233

and was convinced of the necessity of betterment for the underclass.⁶⁵ He further criticized people who were critical of high wages.⁶⁶ He "was a consistent advocate of the labouring class, believing that the powers inherent in those who employed labour were often wielded in a collusive fashion against the best interests of society. Few of his immediate successors were to exhibit the same concerns. Using Smith's mode of analyses but jettisoning his concern that it should be used to improve the lot of the poor, these successors were responsible for making economics into what came to be called the 'dismal science.'"⁶⁷ Smith was convinced that social change had to be made to forward humanity and benevolence. To make these changes possible, reason and persuasion, not force or violence, had to be used.⁶⁸ That's why cooperation between the state and the human society would be needed, to avoid "the highest degree of disorder."⁶⁹ Adam Smith defended the idea that selfishness had to take place within a competition regulated by the state because not every market would have benign effects. "The interest of the dealers, however, in any particular branch of trade or manufacture is always in some respects different from, and even opposite to, that of the public. [...] It comes from an order of men whose interest is never exactly the same with that of the public, who have generally an interest to deceive and even to oppress the public, and who accordingly have, upon many occasions, both deceived and oppressed it."⁷⁰ Smith argues here to the advantage of the bourgeois and against colonial monopolies favoring

---

65 Smith, Adam (1994 [1776]), Book I, Chapter VIII, p. 90: "Is this improvement in the circumstances of the lower ranks of the people to be regarded as an advantage or as an inconveniency to the society? The answer seems at first sight abundantly plain. Servants, labourers, and workmen of different kinds, make up the far greater part of every great political society. But what improves the circumstances of the greater part can never be regarded as an inconveniency to the whole. No society can surely be flourishing and happy, of which the far greater part of the members are poor and miserable. It is but equity, besides, that they who feed, clothe, and lodge the whole body of the people, should have such a share of the produce of their own labour as to be themselves tolerably well fed, clothed, and lodged."

66 Id., p. 93: "The liberal reward of labour, therefore, as it is the effect of increasing wealth, so it is the cause of increasing population. To complain of it is to lament over the necessary effect and cause of the greatest public prosperity."

67 Brundage (2002), p. 30

68 Smith, Adam (2006 [1759]), Part VI, Section II, Chapter II, p. 234

69 Id., p. 235

70 Smith, Adam (1994 [1776]), Book I, Chapter XI, Conclusion of the Chapter, pp. 287 f.

only a small part of the community. "Book IV of 'Wealth of Nations' is a withering criticism of the trade distortions caused by monopolizing colonial trade and fighting wars to protect that trade, at significant cost to the British economy and to the development of home prosperity."[71] Friedman also defends measures to avoid monopolies[72] and expects the state to organize the "infrastructure" the market depends on. This argument seems to me paradoxical. The state and individuals are, according to Smith, responsible and able to construct the market. They, however, aren't capable taking over the functions that the market fulfills? I suppose that it is only the neoliberal market that is constructed by Friedman that is able to deliver the divine integration-function. All other forms of integration that communities have built up are in this regard deficient, the multitude of market-orientated models[73] is of no importance, and only the neoliberal dichotomy of the good market and the bad state can be justified. Where the neoliberal market-model wants to realize selfish freedom, the mixed economy (also called the "social-democratic model"[74] or "great compression,"[75] to be found in Europe or the United States from the Second World War to the end of the seventies) tries to establish freedom and justice in the sense of equal opportunity and solidarity. Therefore, it allocates an important role to rules concerning the quality of life defined by the community. Another example is the Japanese model, which can be described as "bureaucratic centralism" and is characterized by a tight cooperation between administration, politics and big companies.[76] The main target here is the collective welfare by solidary sacrifice.

The idea of market harmony got criticized in the aftermath of the financial market crisis of 2007/2008. Soros, for example, is convinced, that "market prices do not deviate from a theoretical equilibrium in a random manner" and that "markets never reach the equilibrium postulated by economic theory."[77] He further criticizes the exclusion of reflexivity because there is an "imperfect understanding of the situation."[78] The attempt of economic theory to imitate natural sciences to establish "timelessly valid

---

[71] Kennedy, Gavin (2009), p. 251
[72] Friedman, Milton (2002), pp. 26 ff.
[73] Stiglitz, Joseph (2002), p. 249
[74] Dahrendorf, Ralf (1999), p. 9
[75] Krugman, Paul (2009), pp. 37 ff.
[76] Yergin, Daniel/Stanislaw, Joseph (1998), pp. 145 ff., van Wolferen, Karel (1989)
[77] Soros, George (2008), p. X
[78] *Id.*, p. 6

generalizations"[79] results, to Soros, in the wrong believe, that the future is predictable. For him, "financial markets follow [a course that] is indeterminate and unique."[80] "The inability to predict the course of history"[81] is also strongly vindicated by Taleb. Both Soros and Taleb base their statements on the their better knowledge of *the* reality. For Taleb we have to adapt to Black Swans and overcome our natural tendency to naïve empiricism if we want to be realistic.[82] And for Soros, the rational expectation theory is "so far removed from reality,"[83] that he didn't bother to study it. For me, the difference lies in the concept of humankind that is used.

c) Religious hope or cynical disinterest instead of justice

Freedom and egoism are the main values characterizing the neoliberal concept of humankind. Social obligations aren't needed because integration is done by the divine market. Also, the economic theory is not interested in an ethical discussion of needs.[84] These have to be accepted as givens, as a social facts.[85] Others are perceived as competitors, as co-prisoners unable to cooperate in favor of something that exceeds the single existence. The required mutual disinterest excludes highly praised forms of behavior and leads to a fairly simple-minded, poor existence of the self-centered monad. People who are ready to donate anonymously big amounts of money for helping others, or who renounce to their many advantages in favour of their children, who donate blood, or who commit to military service, or mutual help at the workplace or in the neighborhood – all of these people act irrationally because their selfish interests do not prevail. By declaring cooperation and altruism as "deviant," "abnormal," unnatural, unrealistic,[86] the range of possible action is reduced and people are incited to be anti-social.

In my view, there are mainly two factors motivating the unshakable belief in the market. First, there is a religious need to trust in a superhuman force that can arrange all for the best. "Markets in our culture are a totem; to them can be ascribed no inherent aberrant tendency or fault."[87] This is

---

[79] *Id.*, p. 52
[80] *Id.*, pp. 17 f.
[81] Taleb, Nassim Nicholas (2008), p. XX
[82] *Id.*, pp. 56 ff.
[83] Soros, George (2008), p. 57
[84] Woll, Artur (2000), pp. 48 f.
[85] *Id.*, p. 50
[86] Kirchgässner, Gebhard (1991), pp. 47 f.
[87] Galbraith, John Kenneth (1994), p. 24; see also pp. 22 and 106 f.

why "to question the ideology of the free market became, even among the liberal elite, a form of heresy."[88] Against this background we do not have to care about the quality of our life. We just do what pleases us without thinking of others or the future condition of our world. The magic of the market will do what's needed and we are relieved of the sometimes heavy burden of "reality" construction and responsibility. This economic fundamentalism establishes a frightening amount of fatalism. Human or ecological effects of short-term egoism do not have to be addressed. If there will be a market for the protection of human beings or the protection of the environment, these disintegrative conflicts will be solved. We, therefore, do not have to care about this. The same applies to market equilibrium. Whatever it is, it is what it has to be. Besides this religious hope and fatalistic acceptance, there is *cynical disinterest*, using other people as a tool to fulfill one's own goals, without respect to others' hopes, passions, and sufferings. Contrary to the "classic" liberalism which insists on the combination of economic freedom and moral duty, neoliberalism denies any moral duty, negates comprehensive obligations toward others, negates the social aspects of the human existence.[89] Even though the selfish and competitive monad active on the decisive market is today understood as a universal and realistic concept of humankind, it is a political postulation[90] that got established over the centuries. The same accounts for the principle of profit maximization and dominating self-interest, which originated in the 16th century and unfolded in the middle of the 18th century in England and was politically intended and propagated.[91] With this change the community became the servant of the selfish entrepreneur and human relationships mutated to market be-

---

[88] Hedges, Chris (2009), p. 148
[89] Nollert, Michael (2005), pp. 44 ff.
[90] According to Vacarie et al. homo oeconomicus is a "moral and political representation of human beings" (Vacarie, Isabelle/Allouache, Anissa/Ginon, Anne-Sophie/Ferkane, Ylias/Leroy, Sonia [2008], p. 1107). "Homo oeconomicus is a standard in the form of a model of behavior. That means that it understands itself as normativity" (*Id.*, p. 1108). For them, this model is a reduction of plurality: "The economic human being reduces the multitude of qualities and of the actual social relationships by focusing on only one situation, the one between consumer [...] and supplier" (*Id.*, p. 1107). They disapprove of the uncritical acceptance and application of the concept of homo oeconomicus, with the effect, that this anthropology is now understood as the only possible description of humankind.
[91] Wiebe describes the intense process of conviction that had to be done to win over people who believed in the former religiously justified order as "revolution in values" (Wiebe, Robert H. [1967], pp. 133-163, 134 f.). It took decades to establish the competitive individualism as the new value-standard.

havior free of moral demands.

The last steps to get rid of moral qualms about economic activities, of limits given by reflections about justice or responsibility, were taken scientifically from the 1930s on in the form of neoliberal theories and politically in 1979 by Margaret Thatcher. She declared about collective responsibility and the existence of society: "There is no such thing! There are individual men and women and there are families and no government can do anything except through people and people look to themselves first."[92] Egoism was decreed as natural, and collective actions as nonexistent. Claims for social justice became a problem that one had to solve him- or herself by beating competitors on the market basis. Political power was no longer available for the social or economic interests of the majority, but was reduced to a security policy that protects the interests of a small group of people.[93] Politics is, from now on, perceived to be under the supremacy of economics over the state, whereby the basically bad state has to justify its existence. And the market is the good force in this Manichaean battle.

d) Core value – freedom to consume

The freedom to consume is the only thing left in the materialistic world of neoliberalism once all aspects of justice, solidarity, and responsibility were eliminated. With economic freedom being the most important one that dominates everything, materialism now penetrates all aspects of life. There is not one element that isn't subject to the principle of permanent competition, of buying and selling, of testing one's own market-value. Only what is demanded, only what is consumable exists.

But consumption is also a very shallow value because it is self-eliminating. Every time consumption takes place, it loses its satisfying potential. To consume a product means to end the necessity to have it. You can't buy the same car again and again. So you have to find new products. This is why fashions have to be changed as fast as possible and new needs have to be created permanently. As a result, consumption and change appear to be the only important values in a thoroughly materialistic world. This superficial materialism contains a considerable risk of identity crises because people begin to define themselves as made by what they have and consume. The cult of the isolated self replaced the interest in deciding over the form of the

---

[92] Thatcher, Margaret (1987)
[93] Hirsch, Joachim (1998)

community and, for example, the role of the economy.[94] "Human beings [have] become a commodity" and lasting values an obstacle for the economy. Random change is needed to make the system run so people have to alter themselves continuously. Change the job, the clothes, the relationships, start a new formation, change the electronic devices, or the social network – then you're sure not to miss what you currently have to be. There is no discussion about the future because only short-term satisfaction counts. Lacking a common political project, the evanescence of consumption disorients people. This void is filled with intensified and permanent distraction. "This cult of distraction [...] conceals the meaninglessness and emptiness of our own lives. It seduces us to engage in imitative consumption. It deflects the moral questions arising from mounting social injustice, growing inequalities, costly imperial wars, economic collapse, and political corruption."[95]

This dogmatic materialism is, according to Wesel, not a universal element of the human nature. Collector and hunter communities aren't dominated by the pure amount of wealth. That's why they have to work less than the so-called civilized people to satisfy their needs.[96] Accordingly, it seems doubtful that the chase for material wealth is a gain in liberty because markets and the law of the economy decide how we have to live.[97] Alternatives besides the religious neoliberal ideology of the market do not exist so it has become very difficult to criticize, to think differently. Hence, we are just free to act according to economic principles, to selfishly amass as many things as possible. The rest is decided on our behalf.

2. Homo interactivus – interdependent individuals

The homo oeconomicus and especially the neo homo oeconomicus was *built to serve a capitalist economy*. Therefore, people had to be isolated socially and to be reduced to competing individuals, focused primarily on the use of their economic freedom. The concept of humankind I wish to propose, follows fundamentally different goals. It intends to avoid

---

[94] Hedges, Chris (2009), p. 33
[95] *Id.*, p. 38
[96] Wesel, Uwe (1985), p. 75
[97] According to Schnepf the concept of freedom is used twofold: First there is no freedom because of the laws of the economy, determining our existence. Second, *talking* about rights and democracy, a strong concept of freedom is defended, portraying ourselves as "higher beings" (Schnepf, Robert [2007], pp. 127 f.).

- relationships based on power-abuse,
- social injustices that thwart the creative potential of individuals and therefore their freedom,
- community-structures that exclude specific categories of people, or
- create permanent losers.

My concept attempts to realize

- relationships which are supportive of the individuals, so that everyone is recognized as equal, respected as unique, and
- gets the opportunity to fulfill her or his hopes.

For the homo interactivus, human behavior is much more than self-reference and selfish competition. And against a systemic or essentialist point of view, interacting individuals have the full power over their "reality". Hence, "structures," "systems," or "societies" are not "durable, coherent entities,"[98] but an ever precarious arrangement, dependent on the goodwill of the community-members.

a) "I" as me and the other

We are what the others say we are. Or we are, what we explicitly uphold against the judgment of others. If we don't like what others say we are, we can try to change their mind. Doing this, we tell others what we think they are and how they are supposed to perceive ourselves. "Identity" occurs when the behavior of an individual is attested by ourselves or by others over a certain regularity of time.[99] To recognize somebody, to identify an individual, means to associate a set of behaviors with this person. His or her the physiognomy plays a role, but isn't decisive when we talk about an particular individual. That's why we sometimes don't recognize a person anymore because he totally changed, he became so gentle, so respectful, so supportive. When, on the other hand, the particular individual is of no interest because stereotypes are looked for, then the person's origin, skin color, ethnicity, or religion become the decisive criteria.

---

[98] Emirbayer, Mustafa (1997), pp. 282-291, 285
[99] Erikson, Erik H. (1999), p. 36: "Ego-Identity [as] ability to experience one's self as a continuity that stays the same".

We try to realize our interests in a specific geographical, temporal, and social context. But to be the man or the woman we intend to be needs the approval of others. To become a doctor means to learn all the techniques the community has defined as essential, to pass the tests, and to convince the patients of our quality. A President is the one who mobilizes the majority of people to vote in her or his favor. Even the hermit defines himself in relation to the others because solitude stands for the absence of a community, for the decision to leave community. Only the opportunity to go back into the community makes hermitism a willful and original act. Even people forced to leave are, as outsiders, still defined by their relationship to others.

The reactions of others to our "reality" proposals are as much helpful as they are a nuisance. We are enriched by their offered alternatives, by their criticism. But they may be unwelcome because they may stop us, may hinder us from going further on the path we hoped to pursue. Whatever the result of these interactions, the feedback of others is an information about ourselves, and our identity "emerges within the societal realm of experience and activity."[100] To be a human being means to be in relation to others. "[…] everything that exists for us results out of communication and is orientated toward communication. […] To be alone would be a non-existence."[101]

> No man is an island entire of itself; every man
> is a piece of the continent, a part of the main;
> if a clod be washed away by the sea, Europe
> is the less, as well as if a promontory were, as
> well as any manner of thy friends or of thine
> own were; any man's death diminishes me,
> because I am involved in mankind.
> And therefore never send to know for whom
> the bell tolls; it tolls for thee.[102]

Developing an identity means to choose the actions we think are important. From the richness of actions stored in the cultural heritage of a community we select the ones we are currently in favor of.[103] Or we develop against this

---

[100] Mead, George Herbert (1993), p. 177
[101] Jaspers, Karl (1984), p. 374. And for Hannah Arendt, "a life without speaking and acting […] wouldn't be a life anymore, but a lifelong dying" (Arendt, Hannah [1987], p. 165).
[102] Donne, John (1839 [1572-1631]), p. 575
[103] According to Bréchon et al. "cultures and individual identity are connected concepts. Everybody's identity is built by active learning of a culture" (Bréchon, Pierre/Laurent, Anne/Perrineau, Pascal [2000], p. 12).

background alternatives and by this enhance the pool of possibilities. In both ways, "identity has to be chosen consciously by the individual."[104] As long as I take over the "reality" proposals of others, I imitate them by developing an identity that is as near as possible to the mainstream. "It is tragic how few people ever 'possess their souls' before they die. [...] Most people are other people. Their thoughts are someone else's opinions, their lives a mimicry, their passions a quotation."[105] The envy being part of the world of others, being the same is understandable because it guarantees to a certain degree stability and foreseeability. Being different requires the courage to answer creatively to proposals, to propose one's own "reality" elements that can be accepted by the others, or to stand up to their criticism. Difference or uniqueness will exist if the others are ready to support it: "This human being is different, intrinsically different than I am, and it is this difference I mean, I conform when I want him as he is."[106] Our actions aren't determined by others, but strongly influenced. If the counterparts turn out to be friendly cooperators, the intended "reality" will be realized because we were approved as a valuable and influencing member. If there is some opposition to our suggestion, we have to decide how important the intended "reality" element is and which obstacles we are ready to overcome. The higher we estimate this specific form of action and relationship, the more we are ready to fight for it. That's why "value" is a relative concept, initiated and proposed by the actors and influenced by the reaction of the others.

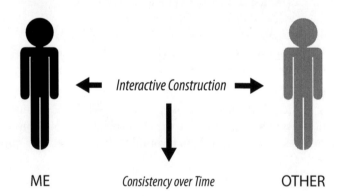

---

[104] Heckhausen, Heinz (1987), p. 177
[105] Wilde, Oscar (2005), p. 176
[106] Buber, Martin (1992), p. 233

What is built up as "identity," the recognized set of behaviors, isn't guaranteed to last. As the homo interactivus is grounded on consensus-based constructivism (see p. 20 ff.), "identity" is the result of a *permanent debating process*. It's not an inborn or, once built up, a fixed character of the individual.[107] Established forms can change in every forthcoming interaction. Whether we decide to head for a different future, we are induced by others to do so, or others qualify what we are doing differently. As a consequence of freedom, the contingency of human acting includes the possibility to build any time a new "reality."

b) Constitutive recognition by and of others

Human beings are in my view highly dependent existences. Before being able to go our own way, we need *substantial support* from others to our existence. To come to life, to be nurtured, fed, and clothed, to be supported making our first steps, to be educated and guided toward "realities" are not thinkable without the help of parents, friends, and the wider community; it is a network of supportive cooperation that makes things possible. Besides this, there is a *dialogic constitution of identity*. Everything I am doing in the presence of others has an impact on them. Acting isn't neutral or innocuous because it's always creating a specific "reality" with certain consequences. We are a constitutive part of a debating context, within which "reality" proposals are introduced and accepted or denied. This interplay of claim and answer[108] is a *quest for recognition*. We want our "reality" proposals to be accepted by the others; we try to convince them that it's worth recognizing our proposal as meaningful. As much as we depend on the others' recognition, they need our approval to fulfill their purposes. For all the "reality" elements we try to build within a community, the responsiveness of our counterparts is needed. As a consequence of this constitutive interdependence the *responsibility of the participants for each other* is pointed out.

This interdependence becomes especially visible in the context of what is often referred to as "humane." For example for "love," "respect," "empathy," "trust," "support," "solidarity," "generosity," or "humor" – all of these characteristics are per definition realizable only in social relationships. Süs-

---

[107] According to Mouffe, "there aren't any 'natural' and 'native' identities, as every identity is the result of a constitutive process. Identity is practically the result of a multitude of interactions" (Mouffe, Chantal [1998], p. 843). Identity is a "basically instable discursive structure" (*Id.*, p. 845).

[108] Waldenfels, Bernhard (1998), p. 77

kind describes in his novel, "Perfume," Jean-Baptiste Grenouille, a young man, born in the most abominable place on earth, grown up on the streets, mistreated by everybody, but trying to survive by looking for perfection, for the absolute, for the most wonderful perfume that has ever been made. He could withdraw himself from the society that abused him, that until now has been a source of the worst experiences. And, yet, he keeps up the hope of finding something valuable, something that will make life worth living. Killing many wonderful women and taking their scent, he develops a perfume nobody can resist. However, he has to realize that to be loved is something you can't enforce. It is a gift "that other people become because their born and that was refused to him alone."[109] He can't enjoy his triumph, he can't be satisfied by the adoration of all these people because they don't adore him because of himself, but only because of "trick". He never learned to cooperate with others, never experienced love. Having been the victim of violence and disrespect, he used the same tools to realize his goal and was unable to step out of his "reality." Using other people and denying their dignity made it impossible for him to develop the empathetic respect that love necessitates. The way we behave toward others always has an impact on ourselves.

c) Others

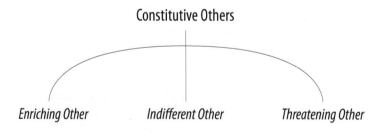

Every individual and every community constructs the selves and others they think will realize their interests. Crudely stated, the role the others can play within the interactive construction process can be threefold:

---

[109] Süskind, Patrick (1985), p. 304

The

- enriching, the
- indifferent, and the
- threatening other.

Whatever form the other takes, it always plays a constitutive part of the identity of the community's members.

The *enriching other* is perceived as a positive counterpart, as part of a relationship that opens new horizons, that spurs by challenging, that frees because of the alternatives proposed, and that gives the opportunity to be original because of its difference. Others are not only enriching because of their difference, but also because they function as a role-model. People who don't know who to be are happy to copy as much as possible the successful and/or beloved others. The most creative form of an enriching other is to be found within a critical discourse, where challenging another's views is as important as listening to their statements, trying to understand the world they live in and which are the assets and drawbacks they're confronted with. *Indifferent others* are part of our collective "reality" without personally influencing us in a decisive way. On a train, in the mall, or at the concert, they constitute for example the mass society based on individualistic consumption, and we follow this flow of people to the places they declare as "hip." Though we're rarely interested in the personality of the indifferent others, they confirm the rightness of our decision to be part of the norm – that many people can't be wrong. Not only mass consumption, but also mass political protests or mass entertainment are experiences of indefinite others and are part of our identity. The particular individual is of no importance, but the number of people going in the same direction is. A third possibility to construct others is the Manichaean one of good and evil. *Threatening others* function as a projection screen for all negative things. For example in racist "realities" with their dichotomous literally black and white elements. Other examples are the terrorist Islam, the flood of immigrants, and asylum seekers, or the Jewish conspiracy theory of world domination. The advantage of this form of "reality" construction is its simplicity and its potential to unify the "good" people against "axes of evil." However, the price to pay is freedom because the community has to fight the evil that has been constructed. It has to mobilize all possible means to control everybody and everything. For the ones forced to be the bad guys, an important loss of equal possibilities has to be deplored. The good guys, on the other hand, force themselves into an authoritarian identity that dramatically reduces the realm of opportunities.

d)   Community – society

To live as a human being means, for most of us, to live in a community, to live with others. Our concept of what a community is, how it comes into existence, and what role the individual plays in it depends on the basic values relevant to each of us. The neo homo oeconomicus isn't interested in community because everything is based on the competitive selfish individual. The integration-task is delegated to the market. The homo interactivus, though, originates in community and, at the same time, makes community possible. A *community* is a *field of expectations of a certain intensity* between at least two people, lasting longer than just an accidental encounter and developing an idea of itself.

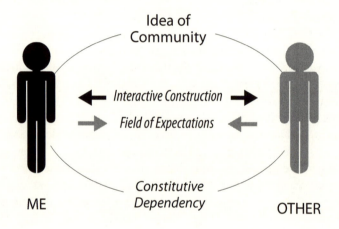

A hazardous aggregation of people can be the core of a future community, but does not inevitably lead to one. People in the subway do not build a community even though they have the expectation that everybody behaves decently. If a technical breakdown occurs, people start to interact more intensely and then they may develop a common goal (idea of community). To perceive others as fellow sufferers unites them and makes them expect some minimal respect and support. The longer their relationship lasts, the more they expect solidary behavior. Expectations characterizing a community are projections of the current relationship into the future. Hopefully the others will act next time according to the identity the community developed. These expectations build a social net between the community members, between me and others – a field of expectations.

According to Tönnies "community is the permanent and real living together."[110] It is a "living organism,"[111] based on the "community of the blood"[112] and the biological bond created by birth.[113] Society, on the other hand, is an aggregation of people that lives beside each other, "essentially unconnected."[114] In societies "everyone is alone and in tension against all others. [...] there is in reality no common good. Such a thing only can be created in a fictional form by the subjects."[115] In his understanding, the distinction between community and society equals the distinction between nature and culture. Community, therefore, develops naturally, society is the result of a cultural performance. For Dahrendorf, society is a fact and this fact exists independently of individuals even though it would be a senseless fiction to think of it without particular individuals.[116] Society isn't an acting subject,[117] it is a fact that is more and something different than the sum of the individuals.[118] In the point of view of Dahrendorf, society is a "nuisance for the individual"[119] "because we can't avoid it."[120]

It seems to me that Dahrendorf constructs a conflict between a basically free pre-societal individual and a society that exists independent of individual actions. If the individual fulfills what society wants him or her to do, the goodwill of the society will be granted.[121] Social roles are, according to Dahrendorf, compulsory institutionalized expectations that have to be learned by the individual[122] – the so-called "socialization process." At the same time, he describes individuals as social beings only free in society.[123] Paradoxically, "society" that exists independent of its members can be changed by individuals.[124] What do we "society" as an independent existence need for, when acting individuals can change this "objective fact"?

---

[110] Tönnies, Ferdinand (1991), p. 4
[111] Id.
[112] Id., p. 12
[113] Id., p. 7
[114] Id., p. 34
[115] Id.
[116] Dahrendorf, Ralf (2006), p. 21
[117] Id., p. 47
[118] Id., p. 48. For a logical argumentation in favor of the existence of societal elements independently of the human action, see Lukes, Steven (1977), pp. 179 ff.
[119] Dahrendorf, Ralf (2006), p. 21
[120] Id., p. 31
[121] Id., p. 31
[122] Id., p. 52, 61
[123] Id., p. 13
[124] Id., p. 65

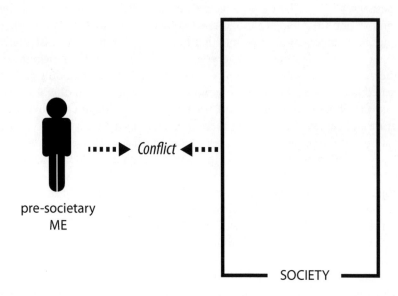

Wouldn't it be easier to construct the social "reality" on the basis of interacting individuals with their own interests, which sometimes are identical, sometimes complementary, and sometimes conflicting/excluding? It seems to me, that the society as an objectified fact is a helpful construction for the sociology as a science, because it's more efficient to talk about society than about the myriad of actions that influence each other and can't be localized and reduced to simple elements that fit a mathematical or statistical formulae. In this sense, Dahrendorf's homo sociologicus is a concept that relates society and the individual as "the incorporation of socially preformed roles."[125] Homo sociologicus isn't however a real woman or man, it is a scientific construction.[126] "It is a tool that helps to rationalize, explain, and control a part of the reality we live in."[127] "In an important sense the atom or the social roles are, though invented, not just invented. They are categories, that impose themselves in a manner difficult to explain […] on the people who try to seize the object nature or the human being in society over time and space. And as soon as they are invented, they aren't just useful but also

---

[125] *Id.*, p. 24
[126] *Id.*, p. 25
[127] *Id.*, p. 76

evident categories."[128] That's why sociology has to recognize the structures of social roles.[129] Even though there is social construction, it is a construction that is imposed by *the* reality. And as scientific cognition it is objective, neutral, and free of morality: "As long as sociology understands its duty as a moral problem, it has to renounce to the rationalization and analysis of the social reality; because when it comes to scientific cognition, the moral request of the individual and his or her liberty have to step back."[130]

In his quest for truth and scientific efficiency Dahrendorf builds up a dichotomy between society and the individual that, according to him, doesn't reflect the freedom-experience people make in their life.[131] Being himself an engaged liberal on the one hand and sociologist on the other, he didn't manage to combine both aspirations. Renouncing to the conflict between politics and science, between community building and reality-recognition, the consensus-based constructivism proposes "reality" elements as the result of engaged individuals. If they need a society, they will build it. If they prefer community, they will act according to their wishes. In the "reality" of homo interactivus both community and society are an interactively constructed field of expectations. They differentiate according to their underlying values. Whereas *society* is a relationship focusing on individual interests, on loose bonds, and a low level of expectations, *community* points out the interdependence of individuals. Society can be characterized by individualized competition, community by solidary cooperation between responsible actors. Contrary to Tönnies, both of these are social constructions and no one has a natural advantage over the other. They differentiate over the way of life, not over their origins.

Considering the contingency of individual actions (see p. 136 ff.), the existence of communities is fragile. To perpetuate a community, a story is needed that is told by its members. This story is about the past, the origins of the relationship, and the future. Furthermore, it is about the importance of basic values, about rights and duties, and about the way problems may be solved. The bigger the community the more rare it is to meet many of its members and the more symbols representing the story are used. The field of expectations is nothing physical, but becomes visible only in the actions of its members, and is existent as long as people act on behalf of it. Even if the community builds up libraries, museums, banks, trains, streets, or electric and water infrastructures, these objects are only a part of the community if

---

[128] *Id.*, p. 25
[129] *Id.*, p. 24
[130] *Id.*, p. 89
[131] *Id.*, p. 90

the individuals decide to refer to them, to talk about them, to understand them as an element of their "reality." The same is to be said for institutions like the government, the judiciary, the army and the police, or other parts of the "state."

f) The visible and responsible hands

Instead of the invisible hand of a system nobody can hold responsible for its effects, I favor the visible hand of "reality" constructing individuals. Chandler differentiates a capitalism based on small traditional family firms and managerial capitalism. According to him, "the activities of one of these small, personally owned and managed enterprises were coordinated and monitored by market and price mechanisms."[132] This family capitalism lasted from 1790 to 1840. Chandler is of the opinion that this traditional market mechanisms doesn't work anymore in the managerial capitalism because big modern companies bring much more economic activities under their control. It took about sixty years to develop a system that made it possible to control competition.[133] "[…] modern multiunit business enterprise replaced small traditional enterprise when administrative coordination permitted greater productivity, lower costs, and higher profits than coordination by market mechanisms."[134] The reason for this change is to be found in an increase of economic activities that are to be ascribed to new technology and expanding markets.[135] Against this background, to Chandler, administrative coordination was more efficient and profitable than market coordination.[136] "What the new enterprises did do was take over from the market the coordination and integration of the flow of goods and services from the production of the raw materials through the several processes of production to the sale to the ultimate consumer. Where they did so, production and distribution came to be concentrated in the hands of a few large enterprises."[137] In the "reality" of Chandler, the "market" finally doesn't stand for an impersonal system acting on its own like a superhuman black box or godly power. It is much more about the freedom the individuals are able to develop. The more freedom people accord to each other, the

---

[132] Chandler, Alfred D. (1977), p. 3
[133] *Id.*, p. 186
[134] *Id.*, p. 6
[135] *Id.*, p. 8
[136] *Id.*, p. 8; see also p. 208
[137] *Id.*, p. 11; p. 285

more Chandler would talk of market processes that help to integrate quite powerless entities into a bigger whole. He seems to suppose that the economic actors were too powerless to control the business interactions, so he uses the metaphor of the market to explain its working. The more the big companies took the economy under their control, the less the market-explanation is helpful. In my view, Chandler wouldn't need the objectified market[138] to describe family capitalism. In every detail he convincingly pictures all the decisions people have to make, the relationships they have to develop, and the people they have to convince to make the intended economic arrangement work. It is their personal engagement, their passion, and their readiness to invest their time, knowledge, and money, as well as the time, knowledge and money of others, that brings this "reality" into being. The same intense work of individuals trying to build up a "reality" that satisfies the interests of its members is described in detail by Adam Smith.[139] The reference to the "invisible hand" or "Providence" is, in my view, not needed. There are *so many visible hands building up a collection of economic and social actions*[140] that we don't have to trouble transcendental superhuman forces.[141] In a variation of Thatcher's dictum: In the consensus-based constructivism, *there is no such thing as the market*.

Putting forward *visible and* by this I mean *responsible hands*, instead of anonymous market processes, gives us the opportunity to decide where to go. We then are finally responsible for our "reality" and it is up to us to seize and use this power in an ethical way. Questions of justice, freedom, and solidarity can then be asked. Economic actions become a "moral" activity, a political decision to be justified. Offenders and victims can be identified and the argument that the market forces people to do something doesn't work anymore. Furthermore, if there is a harmonious equilibrium, it isn't a miraculous phenomenon, but the achievement of hundreds and thousands of people ready to trust each other and cooperate widely. To choose the "reality" of the neo homo oeconomicus is a political decision in favor of the

---

[138] Ganssmann talks of market platonism and is convinced, that markets aren't any actors (Ganssmann, Heiner [2003], pp. 478 ff.).

[139] Smith, Adam (2006 [1759]), Part IV, Chapter I, pp. 181 f. See also Smith, Adam (1994 [1776]), Book IV, Chapter II, pp. 483 ff.

[140] Kennedy, Gavin (2009), p. 241: "Complex systems like language and markets do not emerge suddenly or spontaneously and most certainly do not emerge by design; a long maturation period is required to bring them to term and great and persistent effort."

[141] For Kennedy, Smith anyway used "the invisible" hand as a metaphor, and not as description of an existing object (Kennedy, Gavin [2009], p. 240).

freedom of the powerful who realize their selfish interests which they hide behind invisible hands. That's not an objective mistake or an unreal way of living.[142] It is a freedom-based "reality" construction that helps the oligarchy win at the expense of justice, solidarity, and democracy.[143]

It is up to us to visualize all the hands that make available the richness of our heritage. The answer to the end of God doesn't have to be an overwhelming and mysterious system. It simply should be – if freedom is intended – the creativity of interacting individuals.

---

[142] Against Braudel (Braudel, Fernand [1997], p. 45) I don't think that the concept of the invisible hand is a self-deception.

[143] Joffrin, Laurent (2001), p. 137

D. Integration process

"Forget your past, your customs, your ideals. Select a goal and pursue it with all your might. No matter what happens to you, hold on. You will experience a bad time but sooner or later you will achieve your goal [...] A bit of advice for you: Do not take a moment's rest. Run, do, work and keep your own good in mind. A final virtue is needed in America – called cheek [...] Do not say. 'I cannot; I do not know.'"[1]

New York at the end of the 19th century was looking for workers and the immigrants were looking for work. Price recommends two forms of behavior for successful integration in the USA: The willingness to work and the belief in the American philosophy "everything is possible." A core element of the community building was work. The loosely knit community in New York at this time was characterized by economic freedom alone. This economic absolutism didn't foresee any support structures for immigrants. There wasn't any collective project based on solidarity, which is why these costs had to be borne by the small communities of immigrants, families, or isolated individuals: "The cunning and unscrupulousness that were often incidental to material rise, the anxiety that accompanied the blistering pace of frontier industries, and the fear of poverty and unemployment took a heavy toll on physical and psychological well-being. [...] The contrasts between the successful and those less fortunate produced chasms which law, the state, and society were slow to bridge. As the apparel trades grew to be without a peer in the industrial life of the city, the voice of protest would sound with ever-mounting resonance. The community of responsibility that had been shattered by the combined pressures of immigration, industrialization, and urbanization would be rewoven upon new looms."[2]

Integration is an accommodation of actions of people. Being integrated means being able to fulfill ones own interests within a social arrangement. Integration requirements dependence on the goals people want to fulfill.

---

[1] Recommendation of G.M. Price to immigrants from 1892, cited in Finkelstein, Norman H. (2007), p. 91
[2] Rischin, Moses (1977), p. 75

The more their intentions are based on the contribution of others, the longer the community is supposed to last, the higher the prerequisites to be respected. Accommodation is a process, a form of deliberation, within which the interactors negotiate the amount of freedom and obligation relevant for the community to be established. This deliberation is mainly characterized by the repartition of power and the relevant basic values. It can be equally marked by a severe power imbalance. Against the backdrop of consensus-based constructivism, the consensus of the interactors is a constitutive precondition, a consensus, that can be bought, enforced, or that occurs because of convincing arguments. Even though the term "integration" is almost exclusively used in relation to immigration, I understand integration as a prerequisite for community building. Every community is permanently challenged by integration-problems, be it an existing community trying to uphold what they achieved, a community that is challenged by immigrating people with different needs and claims, or a community about to be established. In any case, acting means proposing a specific relationship and we can never be sure if our opponents are willing to support our proposals. *Being approved is being integrated.* As soon as two people meet and no conflict occurs we can say that they're integrated. There is no need for a comprehensive approval of all the elements characterizing the community. "Very often a more or less conscious fiction of total consenting is enough and even the mutual acceptance of possibly very heterogeneous norms or norm justifications suffice, as long as a plausible and reliable coordination of the relevant actions is possible."[3] Minorities who are submitted to harsh treatment can be integrated, as long as they don't rebel against inequality, lack of freedom and respect and the use of arbitrary power. Not protesting, they "support" the existing arrangement, and uphold the governing "reality." Given the unjust form of integration, though, it is quite probable that fundamental resistance will bring down this community and replace it with a new arrangement. Integration is long lasting if it is cooperative, if the members are respected and treated equally. However, as soon as conflicts occur it is necessary to address the differences, to highlight which elements of the collective identity (see p. 110) are problematic, and to debate possible solutions.

On February 13, 2009, Representative DeFazio (D-OR) introduced a bill (H.R. 1068) called: "Let Wall Street Pay for the Restoration of Main Street Act." The proposal intended to raise $150 billion per year through a securities transaction tax. The tax revenues would have been used to create jobs

---

[3] Weiss, Johannes (1993), p. 227

and reduce the federal deficit. The conflict between "Main Street" and "Wall Street" and, in the aftermath, between "Washington" and "the people" is contrary to the question of immigration, an integration problem that affects core institutions of the American society. The combination of the limitless bonus-culture, the enormous financial state support for the banks, and the difficulties "ordinary" people have in paying their bills or to find a job – all this nourishes the idea of an oligarchy responsible for the crisis which is making a profit once again. A fundamental cleavage becomes a major integrative challenge. The proposal didn't become law.

1. Consensus

The consensus needed to integrate two or more people is at the outset nothing more than the renouncement to oppose. To consent means to re-enact submitted "reality" proposals and can comprise every form of action. Depending on the relevant values, the degree of reflexivity, and the readiness to fight for ones convictions, different forms of consensus can be differentiated.

a) Constitutive consensus and value consensus

To debate with somebody about something presupposes the readiness of the interactors to recognize the others existence and relevance. Without this *constitutive consensus* there is on the one hand no interaction taking place or, on the other hand, a specific topic not debatable. Illegal immigrants, those hired by companies looking for cheap manpower, who live in the underground so as not to be caught by the police and expelled from the country, do not exist – for most of the people living legally in the country. Perhaps they appear as an abstract number or a collective threat in the headlines, but not as individuals with their own histories, sufferings, and hopes. In the small country of Switzerland they amount to about 150'000 - 300'000[4] and are called "sans-papiers" – paperless people (undocumented immigrants). The more face-to-face relations are rare, the more evident becomes the need to recognize the others and their problems to make them existent.

Supposed the existence of sans-papiers is consented. To accept them as equal partners in the debate over their future is part of a *value consensus*

---
[4] Spescha, Marc (2002), p. 134

– equality would be admitted as relevant. Whereas the constitutive consensus concerns the opening of a deliberation, the entrance ticket into the debate, is the value consensus focussed on the conflicting relationship between freedom and obligation, between rights and duties, between solitary autonomy and interdependence. Constitutive consensus makes the development of a relationship possible, while value consensus is about the power-arrangement characterizing this relationship. Which amount of liberty corresponds to whom? What is the sort of liberty people want to establish? Is mutual support a part of the human condition? Does freedom originate within relationships or is it a given, just to be used? Neo homo oeconomicus or homo interactivus are concretizations of a set of values to be consented to, if a community were to be integrated on these grounds.

b) Routine consensus

To build and keep up a community is a process based on everyday actions of its members. This construction can take place consciously or outer consciously. *Conscious construction* stands for a reflected pursuit of interests that takes note of the similar or conflicting interests of others and is ready to debate the pros and cons of the involved proposals. To be permanently in a conscious construction mode is very demanding and may lead to overload and a lack of efficiency. As long as there is no serious conflict about "reality" elements, as long as the interacting members are satisfied with the power arrangement and are able to realize their interests, there is no need for profound debate. At this point an *outer conscious reproduction* can take place. What until now worked, will also work in the future, why it isn't necessary to rethink it. The former ways of interaction are reproduced quasi "automatically."

The longer relationships are routinely reproduced, the more community members develop trust into coming interactions. Routinized and standardized expectations stabilize the social existence and lead to a more efficient management of resources.[5] As a result of the routine consensus, members begin feeling "at home" and take their collective identity for granted. "Routinization is vital to the psychological mechanisms whereby a sense of trust or ontological security is sustained in the daily activities of social life. Carried primarily in practical consciousness, routine drives a wedge between the potentially explosive content of the unconscious and the reflexive moni-

---

[5] Heckhausen, Heinz (1987), p. 151

toring of action which agents display."[6] Contrary to Giddens, I understand "outer consciousness" not as the subconsciousness made famous by Freud. Outer consciousness isn't a force on its own, based on a physiological heritage that determines our being beyond our knowledge, but an interactively built up social "reality," whose *origins get lost over time*. To admit the existence and relevance of a subconscious force is a choice people have to make. The concept of humankind can foresee an uncontrollable element that breaks through now and then, only recognizable by specialists called psychoanalysts or by the concerned individuals after year-long therapy. Defending freedom and autonomy, the homo interactivus qualifies violence or the so-called "evil," not as a break-through of an animal energy, but a social construction people use for specific reasons.

Routine isn't formed easily. According to Braudel, thousands of gestures are needed, gestures that are accumulated over time and not controlled by a central power.[7] We reproduce these actions because they're here, proposed by others, by our parents and friends, schoolmates, or the coworkers. They are to be found in books, movies, songs, or paintings, and they incorporate our heritage of positively selected actions. Tradition building, normalization, and learning procedures are developed[8] and expectations are transmitted to the next generation by education or inculcation. Most of the expectations are taken over outer-consciously. As soon as these procedures become ingrained they fulfill their stabilizing function.

From the point of view of freedom has routinization an ambivalent effect, helps to stabilize a social arrangement that, for example, in the form of the constitutional state protects freedom. On the other hand it contains the risk to standardize people, to avoid dissent and difference and to reduce by this the possible richness of human existence. Furthermore, it can petrify current relationships. Especially so when the community's origins are hidden and attributed to transcendental forces, natural laws, or timeless tradition to avoid criticism. What has been created by God, follows the prerogative of the dominant race, or has succeeded for centuries and proven by this to be right, can't be questioned anymore. This sort of conservative stability eternalizes the present, excludes social development, and denies responsibility of the former or current generations.

---

[6] Giddens, Anthony (1984), p. xxiii
[7] Braudel, Fernand (1997), p. 16
[8] Waldenfels, Bernhard (1998), p. 198

c) Institutional consensus

The institutional consensus is a specialized form of the routine consensus. "Institutions" are a social arrangement built to stabilize interactions and to *reduce the construction costs by delegation* (p. 295 ff.). To "institutionalize" certain functions means to hand over construction competencies to a (defined or personally open) group of people. Thus, the majority recognizes and builds up the power of an institution, which is supposed to decide on their behalf. The state, government, universities, libraries, churches, or hospitals are required to use the power they were entrusted with, according to the principles contained in the institutional consensus.

The privileged ones have to prove that they deserve their prerogatives. Acting convincingly every day, a *concrete institutional consensus* develops, strengthening their reputation and, by this, their power. After a while the trust gets generalized, isn't bound to particular people anymore and starts to be identified with the now impersonal institution: A *general institutional consensus* has been acquired. In this way, institutions can outlast the lives and engagement of people and stabilize the community. Different measures can be taken to intensify this development. The life tenure of the appointed judges of the US Supreme Court or the robes they are expected to wear are among other things supposed to render impersonal the actors and to focus on the function they are fulfilling for the community. Since the seventeenth century British judges wore wigs in all court proceedings to stress their function and hide the person behind the role[9]. And the Queen is supposed to behave not as Elizabeth but as part of the symbolic institutions of the country. One day, her mortal body will pass but her mystical body will endure, embodied by her son.[10]

Even though the general institutional consensus makes the dissociation from the individual's action possible, its status is ever fragile. The current members of the institution who profit from the work of heir forbearers, can destroy the reputation built up over generations in no time. Trust and stability is a relationship needing permanent persuasion to work by convincing results (see p. 248 ff.). Consensus is always provisional.

---

[9] Since 2007, however, judges sitting in the civil and family courts no longer wear wigs. But in criminal courts the tradition is uphold to give the judges a certain amount of anonymity and authority.

[10] About the two bodies of the king or queen see Kantorowicz, Ernst H. (1994).

d) Legitimation consensus

"To consent" is not per se identical with moral approbation. Different reasons motivate people to endorse "reality" proposals. Depending on the power, that interacting others can build up, people are more or less free to approve. The more we live under the rule of law and under democratic circumstances, the more we can be assured that the absence of opposition reflects approbation based on conviction. However, there's no guarantee that the consenting majority is consenting as a result of a reflected, intense and critical discussion and that the political decision suits best their values (*consensus by conviction*). Possibly, they are just uninterested in politics because their interests are only material, and a highly developed, affluent society serves this need best. As long as the community fulfills its material desires or doesn't prevent them from consumption, people adapt to whatever are the political or moral ramifications (*consensus based on satisfaction*). Or people are intellectually overwhelmed by the claims democracy asserts and, thus, prefer to stay private and quiet and lose their interest (*consensus because of incapacity*).

In a dictatorship we can find many different forms of consensus. A dictatorship works, first, when an engaged minority fights for its convictions (*consensus by conviction*) or benefits from the gifts and bribery of the dictator (*consensus by satisfaction*). Second, a powerless majority is willing to live in the dictatorship because they are mainly interested in their everyday life, so politics is not of great importance (*consensus based on convenience*). Third, the opposition is limited to some convinced people who are ready to risk even their life (*dissent by conviction*). As long as the deeply motivated opposition is small and isolated, the ruler is able to control them by inflicting very strong punishments in the form of imprisonment, torture, or media-hyped executions. Fourth, even fierce critics adapt then to the overwhelming power (*consensus for lack of alternatives*). Referring to the former GDR (Deutsche Demokratische Republik), Glaessner and Neckel describe two forms of existences: A political public and an everyday private sphere. On the one hand there was an official political culture in the form of the communist party and the state leaders. On the other hand, more and more a social culture came into being, based on a finely woven network of families, friends, and associations.[11] These private communities were characterized by reciprocity and trust.[12] Creating an informal and

---

[11] Glaessner, Gert-Joachim (1992), p. 40, 44. See also Lemke, Christiane (1991), p. 14, 48.
[12] Neckel, Sighard (1992), p. 262

apolitical living space, that people could retreat to, the majority renounced to declare publicly their discontent with institutions and ideas that had lost their attraction quite a time ago. Thus, they supported to a certain degree the authoritarian system, because "[…] the [social] security the authoritarian system made possible was quite nice."[13] In this sense writes civil rights activist Bärbel Bohley (who was imprisoned in 1982 because of her pacifist engagement and forced to leave the country for six months), "this system was based on the consensus of the individual. As soon as I don't accept it, it gets weak very fast."[14]

Dictatorships work best when a majority of people is convinced, that an authoritarian government is needed. If that isn't the case, at least a majority should be satisfied or they are not courageous enough to fight against dictator. People who are overwhelmed by what is happening shouldn't be a problem. Democracy, on the other hand, is much more complex to realize, because its quality depends on the engagement of its members. Democratic decisions have to be reflected (based on conviction) and are based on alternatives, without which a critical debate isn't possible. The control of all forms of power, be it economic, state, or social, needs attentive citizens, not satisfied only by the newest consumer goods, but by heading to a future based on justice and solidarity. It's the silent majority that helps demagogues and authoritarian rulers to come to power: "The silent majority has spoken with a resounding roar."[15]

Totalitarian systems build up a power that excludes any alternative. A moral condemnation of the people adapting to the system isn't therefore justified. But thoroughly totalitarian systems seem to be rare. According to Götz[16] and Browning,[17] even the national socialist state accepted autonomous decisions. There was for Germans the possibility to decide differently. The authors hold the view that the Holocaust wasn't the result of a tightly organized Fuehrer state, but a political project that was also supported by people not forced to act. Not to do a job within this totalitarian system didn't necessarily mean it was sanctioned. For example soldiers who were unable to execute people in a firing squad (*specific dissent*) were assigned another job. Only *fundamental dissent* with the system was consequently and thoroughly sanctioned. For Sofsky, the participation in this systematized killing was, for not a few, a temptation to experience absolute power,

---

[13] Bohley, Bärbel (1992), p. 13
[14] Id., p. 11
[15] Sally Heep, in: Boston Legal, Season 1, Episode 12
[16] Aly, Götz (1995), pp. 333, 374, 385
[17] Browning, Christopher R. (1993), pp. 99, 109, 172

excessive killing power.[18] "The perpetrator wasn't a will-less subject, he did more than he had to. He did what he was allowed and he was allowed to do everything. [...] Modern system terror isn't characterized by the all-powerful, invulnerable master, but by the immoderate acting of the servants of the power."[19] According to Hilberg, there was a form of approval even by the Jews because they didn't oppose or flee.[20] However, in this case a moral condemnation is not possible, as the whole system was built in a way that made an escape highly difficult and very often impossible. And any opposition was exterminated without hesitation.

	Function	Forms
Constitutive Consensus	Enter in contact and debate the construction of a community.	Accepting the existence of others and of "reality" elements.
Value Consensus	Construct a specific community based on a set of values.	Interactive adjustment of each others behavior according to the conflicting relationship between freedom and obligation. Power arrangement.
Routine Consensus	Stabilization by perpetrated reproduction of successful social arrangements.	Habits, Rituals, Institutions
Institutional Consensus	Functionally motivated power delegation to enhance effectiveness.	First, concrete institutional consensus (connected to specific actors) Second, general institutional consensus (abstract approval)
Legitimation Consensus (Motivation based)	Justifying "reality" proposals by reproducing them.	1. Consensus by conviction 2. Consensus for lack of alternatives 3. Consensus based on satisfaction 4. Consensus based on convenience 5. Consensus because of incapacity
Dissent	Question "reality" elements and claim for a more or less radical change.	1. Specific dissent 2. Fundamental dissent

---

[18] Sofsky, Wolfgang (1993), pp. 317 f.
[19] *Id.*, p. 318
[20] Hilberg, Raul (1999), pp. 11, 28, 195 f., 228, 328 ff., 518 f., 1100

2. Construction phases and integration modes

Communities are an integration success, otherwise they wouldn't exist. The integration challenge that people are confronted with varies according to the construction phase the community is in. Building up a community needs different work on consensus processes than keeping up what has been existing for quite some time. A reached consensus, though, isn't a guarantee, it is provisional and comes daily under pressure because of the creative freedom human beings are able to. Questioning certain aspects or even the fundamentals of the community's "reality," the interactors have to decide whether they intend to uphold or to break up what until now had been their home. Communities are built in the *new construction phase*, kept alive and stabilized during *reproduction* and destabilized, or even disintegrated, in the *deconstruction phase*.

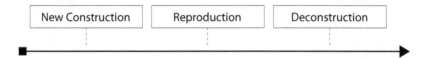

New construction and reproduction contain integration measures that have to be taken to build up and stabilize the community. During deconstruction signs of destabilization or disintegration will necessitate some reconstructive action.

Construction phases	Integration modes	
New Construction	*Basic Integration*	Goal setting, definition of basic values and membership, power arrangement, conflict settlement
Reproduction	*Stabilization*	Institutionalization, harmonization
Deconstruction	*Criticism (Destabilization)*	Questioning parts or the fundamentals of the community, producing alternatives, protesting, destabilization, disintegration

a) New construction phase

People interested in community construction launch deliberations over the structure of their future social arrangement. A *basic integration* process takes place that is quite a challenge for those involved. Dependent on the degree of novelty, the actors can rely on pre-existing forms of action or creatively develop new ones. If a totally unknown "reality" is intended and the interactors do not know each other well, they have to act with a high degree of uncertainty and risk, making decisions based on premature trust. The more they can relate to a common cultural heritage, the easier the communication and the faster consent can be reached. In both cases, the actors have to be open-minded and as inclusive as possible to appreciate the richness of the proposals. During the new construction phase, the future members have to clarify their goals and to define their relevant basic values. They have to decide who is allowed to be part of the deliberation process and how membership can be acquired at a later time. Immigrating in the Chesapeake, the newcomers had different handicaps that made successful community construction quite improbable. First, they weren't interested in community building. What they wanted most was to make money as fast as possible. Their basic values didn't include solidarity or long-term cooperation. And they lacked the experience and the knowledge to overcome the dire conditions they had to confront in the New World. The Puritans, to the contrary, arrived as a community and could rely on the experiences of former immigrants, and they were interested in a lasting settlement. Not just wealth, but quality of life was important to them.

To "construct" means to use power to create "reality" and to build up new power with cooperation. One of the main questions during the new construction phase is, therefore, to decide over the repartition of power (*power arrangement*). Another essential is the *conflict settlement*. Long term integration only works if conflicts can be solved effectively, respectfully, and in an early stage.

b) Reproduction

A community becomes stable if it manages to reproduce the benefits of the arrangement and to tackle its negative side effects. The reproduction phase doesn't take place automatically. On a lower level, community structures are reproduced if people re-enact former interactions in a widely routinized way. Getting used to certain forms of interaction, they become "normal," aren't discussed anymore and are only sometimes questioned, usually by individuals or a minority (*stabilization*). The longer reproduction lasts, the more the routinized interactions become institutions, becoming uncoupled from particular individuals (*institutionalization*).

It is at this point that "law" and what is called "the state" develop their stabilizing function. "Law" refers to the actions people want to uphold against all odds. The majority is willing to use different sanctions against a minority not ready to accept the behavioral standards. Actors taking over the governing function are assigned to make sure that unlawful behavior is sanctioned and to apply the conflict settlement established during new construction. Furthermore, to stabilize dear-won social arrangements, all possible cultural, political, scientific, or economic tools are used. Buildings are built, ceremonies held, stories about the origins rooted in the mists of times are developed, the future is outlined, and retirement plans are established. Making sense of the community's life and projecting a current being into the future establishes a place people can call "home".

If the community succeeds to establish reproduction, members are relieved from caring permanently about what's next. Everyday activities steadily reproduce elements of the collective identity. The longer this reproduction phase lasts, the more people take their "reality" for granted. The intense construction process gets lost with time. All the original conflicts, all the conviction work that had to be done to build the community, is no longer present. During reproduction, the conflicts that occur are minor ones, limited because slight adjustments within a defined realm of possibilities will suffice (*harmonization*). As long as there aren't any loud or silent protests, as long as there aren't any deep-seated frustrations about the current state of affairs making people withdraw from the public sphere and giving up their interest in the community, the reproduction phase can be qualified as best integrated. The longer stabilization processes apply, the more the community is apt to develop different strategies to perpetuate its social arrangement.

c) Deconstruction

Contingency, the possibility to act differently, always looms in the background. Reproduction is effective as long as the consensus of the actors is given. But this can change in every forthcoming interaction. Conflicts, deviant behavior, or social change point out the inherent fragility of "reality" constructions.

To *criticize* "reality" elements ends smooth reproduction and opens the debate over the work or even the existence of institutions, over the goals the community has set up, or over the power arrangement that now is perceived as being unjust. There is a lot of criticism in the reproduction phase. But it concerns details, that are not significant for the functioning of the community. These conflicts can be fixed by minor adjustments (specific dissent). The criticism relevant in the deconstruction phase, however, concerns the basics of the community, core elements that were until now cherished as supporting parts of the collective identity (*fundamental dissent*[21]). We are confronted with *destabilization* when the community's institutions are questioned and their output is no longer easily accepted. The more important the "reality" elements are that are being criticized, the higher the risk of total deconstruction. And if there's no possibility anymore to come back to the former consensus because, for example, of revolutionary protests and changes, *disintegration* takes place: The community ceases to exist.

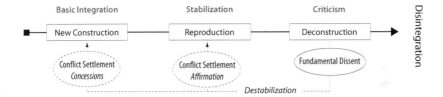

Criticism leads to destabilization, relativizing former certainties. It depends on the reaction of the members, if this destabilization ends as disintegration or becomes an affirmation of the preceding "reality." Opponents of the currently relevant consensus have to be aware that a lost debate or fight can strengthen the loathed "reality." A failing political protest, therefore, confirms the norm opponents wanted to change or abolish. On the other hand, from the point of view of the winners conflicts even destabilizing ones can help clear and enhance convictions which had started to fade and become self-evident. If the deliberators make many concessions to uphold the community, a new collective identity will be built up with more or less the same members.

After twenty-three years of dictatorship, Tunisian president Ben Ali had to flee the country: The Jasmin Revolution abruptly ended the reproduction phase everybody expected to endure. A tightly-knit police state with an important army, reckless police, and ubiquitous informers was overthrown by simple protests in the streets of Tunisia. Ignited by the highly symbolic act that Mohammed Bouazizi committed, setting himself ablaze, the youth of the country wiped out the firmly established power within twenty-three

---

[21] Hirschman, Albert O. (1994), p. 301 talks of dividable conflicts (specific dissent) and categorical conflicts (fundamental dissent). But his categorical conflict is understood in an absolutist way. According to Hirschman they are unsolvable, because the "reality" concepts involved aren't negotiable. Fundamental dissent, as I understand it, can be absolutist, but doesn't have to be. It is still possible to compromise, if the interactors are ready to change their positions.

days. Even though more than sixty people died in clashes with the security forces, the young who represent half of the population weren't willing to back off. The former regime based its legitimization on different grounds. On the one hand, the very small elite and clans that profited from the dictator (consensus based on satisfaction) and/or was convinced that an elite has to rule over a majority not capable of ruling itself (consensus by conviction). The majority of the Tunisian population had never experienced another ruler than Ben Ali because half of the population is under 25 years old and 60 % are under the age of 30. For them this seemed to be the natural order of things (routine consensus) and, therefore, couldn't be questioned (consensus by conviction based on inculcation and tradition). Growing up and, one, discovering alternatives thanks to globalized information, and two, realizing that the government's promises wouldn't be fulfilled (high unemployment rate [around 30 % for the under 30 years old], dire future prospects, increased food prizes), fundamental dissent occurred. Against the backdrop of a highly unequal and corrupt society governed by a "kleptomaniac autocracy"[22] the renouncement to freedom could no longer be justified. Good jobs were only available to the ones who knew a relative of Ben Ali. "Trabelsi" not only stood for the name of Ben Ali's wife and her clan, but also for a mafia-like economy that extorted payments from companies. Those not willing to submit were dispossessed.[23] The dictator and the ruling families accepted at his court controlled all economic sectors.

The well-educated youth felt they were a lost generation without a future. The case of Mohammed Bouazizi was symbolic of their situation: Not having the money to go on with his studies, not finding a job with his Bachelor degree, he tried to make a living for himself and his family by selling vegetables and fruits in the streets. Lacking the authorizations needed, the police confiscated his goods and a policewoman slapped his face. This lack of respect and perspective, the abuse of authority made him protest with one of the most powerful symbolic means an individual has: self-immolation. Claiming economic integration and social justice, many young people were ready to fight a system that reacted in a way never seen since the "bred insurgencies" of 1984 under president Bourguiba. Tunisian society had moved from decades-long reproduction to deconstruction as the dictatorship got destabilized. Neither knew if they would succeed. Would the regime be overthrown or would it be the winner, keeping up the oppression for some more years? But the state's excessive violence heated

---

[22] Le Monde of January 16, 2011, p. 1
[23] Suplement du Monde of January 20, 2011, p. V

up the protests and led to further delegitimization. Ben Ali tried to keep the discontent within reproduction by treating it as a specific dissent. He promised to create 300'000 jobs through 2012, said he would dismiss the Secretary of the Interior, and would liberate protesters. But this second reshuffling of the government nor the announcement that he would install an investigative commission to verify the allegations of corruption did attenuate the protests and bring back routinized reproduction. Also the dictator's declaration that the instigators of the protests were foreign terrorists, didn't have the unifying effect he hoped for. His last proposal that he would resign in 2014 changed nothing, which is why on January 14, 2011 he escaped to Saudi Arabia. On this day it became clear that a conflict settlement in the form of affirmation wouldn't take place.

Prime Minister Ghannouchi stated on TV that he would take over the same day and would create a government of national unity which would organize new elections. The opposition, was allowed to come back to Tunisia. The protesters, believing that there were still too many people of the old inner circle in power, kept on protesting, which is why three ministers of the transition government stepped down and interim president Fouad Mebazaa and Prime Minister Ghannouchi left the RCD, Ben Ali's party. Still, the old followers tried to stay in power, keeping the most important ministries for themselves, not understanding how much the country already had changed. Fundamental concessions had to be made if a new construction would be possible to overcome the current disintegration. In subsequent protests of now older generations, the police seemed to have learned because they reacted without using violence, but just trying to maintain order. On January 27, 2011, transition Prime Minister Ghannouchi declared after intense negotiations with all political parties and members of the civil society who accepted participating that the most important former ministers of Ben Ali were dismissed – twelve in total. The street had been heard.

In contrast to the Jasmine Revolution is the Tea Party "revolution" a movement of specific dissent that doesn't challenge the fundamentals of the American collective identity. The very heterogeneous[24] movement didn't question the institutional arrangement built up over 200 years ago. They were ready to participate in democratic elections and to use their power within the legal framework, in reproductive ways. The references used are

---

[24] Zernike, Kate (2010), p. 143: "To some Tea Partiers it was a vessel for grievance, inchoate or specific. To others it was a means to electoral victory against the Democrats. Libertarians hoped it would force the Republican Party to fight more for fiscal discipline, while constitutional purists hoped it would cleanse the country of its New-Deal-Great Society sins."

part of the cultural heritage – the Boston Tea Party, the American Revolution, the Declaration of Independence, and foremost, the Constitution. The part of the movement able to make itself heard does not propose to change the Constitution, but claims a conservative interpretation of the text. It reproduces the "classic" schism between liberals and conservatives that has been defining American politics since the Great Depression. In the same tradition is Barry Goldwater's pledge for small-government in 1964, Reaganomics from 1981 onward (with a soaring deficit and debt during his tenure), and the Republican's Contract with America of 1994. In the version of Dick Armey, the Tea Party philosophy is a neoliberal program because he just wants to be free, is convinced that individual freedom and economic liberty are interdependent, wants to limit government by referring back to Anti-Federalist arguments, asks for fiscal responsibility,[25] and urges everybody to trust the market and its self-healing power.[26]

Specific dissent can lead to harsh debates. Reproduction doesn't have to mean smooth routine. Conflicts can be very intense, the criticism sometimes unfair and often disrespectful. But the collective's identity fundamentals aren't questioned, the basics characterizing the community are reproduced while battles are fought about single aspects. To avoid destabilization or disintegration especially in violent forms, community members have to be very sensitive to every form of disapproval. As soon as protest movements reach a critical mass, it is very difficult to contain them with convincing reform offers. Integration means to listen and to adapt to claims in a cooperative way. Give and take and the avoidance of absolutist positions are at the centre of a free debate between people critically enriching each other.

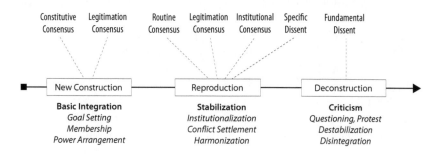

---

[25] Armey, Dick (2010), pp. 65 ff., 123
[26] Id., p. 44 and p. 52

d) Deviant behavior – dissent

aa) Social construction of abnormality and criminality

To "dissent" means to behave differently, to manifest identity not by copying, following, or consenting, but by marking a difference. To be different means to propose another "reality," to question what others do, to be convinced that another path has to be taken. It is a demonstration of autonomy and of critical thinking. It is also a sign of courage, as the deviant doesn't know if his or her "reality" proposal will be appreciated or dismissed.

There are two different aspects to be distinguished when it comes to deviant behavior. First, a specific action has to be qualified as "deviant." Second, the community has to decide how to react to their construction of "deviance." What sort of reaction shall take place, which sanction shall be applied, who has to act? The construction of "deviance" is nothing innocuous, as it may include and exclude, it may appreciate or punish people. There is, according to consensus-based constructivism, no given norms people have to apply, no set of actions human beings can't elude. Deviance is a social construction that is based on more or less clear knowledge of "normal" or "standard" behavior. As routinized behavior very often develops without us noticing, we become aware of it when others act in a way that irritates us. Irritation doesn't mean something by itself. It stands for an expectation-deception, a so-called cognitive dissonance. We are confronted with a form of action that doesn't fit our expectations. The meaning and relevance of this deception is up to us. Is there a majority that judges the problematized act as "deviant?" And is this conflict just an accident or is it a wilful act that contradicts the majority's consensus? How should we react to this irritation?

Deviance-construction is the result of a debate, of more or less explicit negotiations. If the community established explicit norms – be they legal, moral, or ethical – it, at the same time, established deviance. Even though these norms may be intended as unequivocal, their actual content is open to interpretation, can even change over time and go against the explicit wording. In spite of their professionalism and their long-standing tradition and technicality, legal rules aren't evident. There is a scope of interpretation that can be used in many different ways. They're interactively constructed (see p. 320 ff.) so the opposing parties have to find a consensus about their meaning. Or the more powerful try to impose their interpretation by using violence. Moral or ethical expectations are usually less concrete and do not have the same degree of formality. It is also less evident who is officially responsible for the interpretation work. Whatever the norm, whatever the expectation, the final result, the final arrangement about norm and deviance, is interactively built, influenced by many more people than the professionals of norm-interpretation. Besides the priests and the ethics commission, the representatives, the senators, the administration, or the judges, there are all the people who are trying to realize their own interests. A debate takes place about what is, for now and for the near future, "normal" and what has to be qualified as "abnormal." Within this political fight the parties try to win over as many people as possible to support their understanding of normality and to establish this understanding as "standard behavior."

"Criminality" is therefore a social construction that serves the interests of its constructors. It doesn't reflect universal, natural, imperatively to fight behavior. "Killing people in times of war or in our name by the hands of the public executioner is legitimate. [...] What we describe as infanticide was absolutely legitimate for the Spartans, testing the survivability of the newborn by putting them on a cold roof for one night."[27] "Legal" is what a powerful group of people is able to define as such and impose on others.[28] Thus criminality is used to control a minority or relatively powerless people.[29] It helps to build up the collective identity of the rulers,[30] and the "criminals" are the ones not powerful enough to counter this construction. No objective, neutral criteria like, for example, the damage potential or the effective harm produced determines which acts are qualified as "criminal". Hundreds of billions in losses were generated by those so-called 'responsible' players on the financial market. But no prosecutions of top figures have taken place, as Morgenson and Story in bewilderment point out.[31] The enormous damage resulting from the consumption of legal drogues like alcohol or cigarettes are not qualified as "criminality." And not long ago, it wasn't criminal for a husband to beat his wife. Damaging activities of states/societies against individuals or minorities, so-called macro criminality are most often justified.[32] It is only in the last years that a new construction takes place, trying to hold responsible the ones who until now could hide behind diplomatic immunity. The debate over the creation and power of the International Criminal Court in Den Haag and the role of ius cogens shows that it is a question of power, of decision, and not of recognition of the true values and forms of actions.

---

[27] Phillipson, Michael (1974), p. 127
[28] Turk, cited in: Michalowski, Raymond (1988), pp. 39 f.
[29] Peters, Helge (1989), p. 20
[30] Frehsee, Detlev (1991), p. 38
[31] Morgenson, Gretchen/Story, Louise (2011), p. 1
[32] See Jäger, Herbert (1989), p. 65

Deviance-construction has to be done in a responsible manner because it can affect considerably the ones who have to live with this attribution. To be qualified as "different" means for the individual to be treated differently. Not necessarily in a negative way, but there is a risk that the quality we assign to people leads to their devalorization. To produce or avoid stigmatization is in the responsibility of the currently dominant group. According to Laing, psychological illness isn't a given. It is the result of the joint action of family, doctor, health care officer, psychiatrist, nurses, social worker, and often other patients.[33] Laing qualifies the practice of the sixties concerning people who were labeled "schizophrenic" as a degradation ceremony, robbing them of their personal liberty. Laing supposes that these stigmatizations are made to stabilize the civic order.[34] For Goffman, mental illness is a social breach of standard rules. The one labeled as mentally ill doesn't behave according to the means of social control and doesn't try to hide or neutralize his or her breach.[35] Understanding this person means, to Goffman, to understand the "reality" she or he is living in.

bb) Dissent between disintegration and confirmation

Deviance is the result of a political process, of interactive negotiations over "normality." It is at the same time the construction of the collective identity of the successful majority. People who want to be part of this community have to be normal. A community is integrated when a clear notion of what is part of the collective and what is too different to be accepted is established. Dissenting from the concept of normality is, therefore, an integration challenge, it is a *validity test for the rules of a community*. How seriously the existence of the community is questioned depends, on the one hand, on the criticism itself, on the seriousness and intensity of the dissenting action, and, on the other hand, on the openness of the community, the readiness to discuss central elements. What is qualified as a "nuisance" doesn't need to be answered with intense protection measures. It's okay not to do anything. To enjoy this curiosity is even possible because the discussed behavior has no impact on the community's reproduction mechanisms. However, if the community has opted for an authoritarian concept of homogenization, if it is an absolutist "reality" and the least criticism is perceived as existential threat, then, of course, every irritation has to be eradicated. Thus, authori-

---

[33] Laing, Ronald D. (1969), p. 110
[34] *Id.*, p. 111
[35] Goffman, Erving (1982), p. 460

tarian communities have to react to almost everything with a lot of resources, which risks overextension. Everything that is different is combated by all means, avoiding whatever relativization of the absolutely true foundation of the collective.

	Dissent-construction based on respectful multitude	Dissent-construction based on authoritarian homogenization
Irritation (cognitive dissonance)	Enrichment, nuisance, or fun	Offence
Criticism (challenge)	Discursive prerequisite for improvement	Forbidden questioning of the authority
Alternative (freedom)	Precondition to freedom	Dangerous heterogeneity that will destruct the chosen and singular truth
Threat (absolutist and irrevocable acts)	Existential protection of basic values in exceptional cases	Existential protection of basic values in a almost every case

"Realities" that accept different forms of life will be able to qualify criticism as a chance for improvement. Critical statements help to clarify our own position, to reason out what we are doing and if it's worth it. Or to think about the alternative proposed by others. To have the possibility of choice makes freedom available. Against this background different people, including crazy ones, can have an important function within the construction of a personal and collective identity. For Schopenhauer, geniuses are people outside of the standard way of thinking, nearer to madness than to science.[36]

Every actor and every community has to decide how intense the reaction has to be, what the price is that everyone has to pay, and if it's worth focusing that much on what is constructed as different. Building up a threatening bogeyman helps to mobilize people, money, and time and can justify wide-ranging measures. What neither the authoritarian nor the pluralistic approach to dissent know is whether the criticism will lead to a confirmation of the currently relevant "reality", or if it is the precursor of the new "reality."[37]

---

[36] Schopenhauer, Arthur (1987), pp. 269 ff., 272
[37] Waldenfels, Bernhard (1998), p. 255: "Contingency which appears out of the ordinary doesn't only slip through the meshes of order. It becomes a possible core of new orders."

cc) The minority we make

As the construction of deviant behavior creates majorities and minorities and integrates and segregates, we have to reflect on our conception of normality and the possible victims it produces. There is no metaphysical or natural justification for the inclusion and exclusion processes we generate. If a community thinks to need minorities to build up its identity, from a standpoint of justice, freedom, and solidarity, we should ask ourselves the following questions:

- What is the integration goal? Which form of collective identity is the community aiming at?
- How far is the construction of a collective self producing minorities and what is the status of these minorities?
- Are these minorities supported in their integration work or just used to integrate the majority?
- Does the community have the resources to stabilize the intended relationship?
- Are the advantages the community gains important enough to justify the possible negative effects on the minority?
- Which are the gains for the minority in the intended arrangement?

The more minorities are constructed and the more the majority imposes its own values on them, the more the aspired to "reality" has to be important and indispensable. If deviance becomes an integration problem, it will depend on the

- motives to construct deviance, the
- way deviance is built (how exclusionary it is), the
- reasons that lead to the deviant behavior, the
- reaction of the majority, and the
- resources the majority has either to impose its concept or to propose a new form of living that attracts the dissenting person and leads to a new community.

Moral or legal expectations are not an end in themselves, but should be at the service of human beings.[38] Fundamental opposition highlights an important consensus-problem that has to be taken seriously. To act in an integrative way means to take up this manifestation of dissent as an offer for discourse. "The riots in East Anglia in 1815–16 or the more widespread 'Swing' riots of 1830–31 persuaded the ruling classes of the appalling consequences of creating a pauper class, dependent or semi-dependent upon public funds."[39] Civil disobedience is a sign of quality as long as the debate over the shared "reality" is respectful. Deviance often helps communities to change, to find solutions that integrate better and on a larger scale.[40] Whatever we do, we have to leave room for the different, if we agree with the idea, that there is no absolute truth and everything we think today may no longer convince us tomorrow. *Dissent prevents us from absolutism*, from an exclusionary concept of truth, from the limitation of our own fantasy. Thus the normative legal and moral securitization of expected behavior should be reduced to the core elements of our "reality." And even in this, an open-minded reaction to criticism helps us to rethink what we once thought is the best for our community. Deviant behavior is basically healthy because it is a manifestation of the autonomy of the people. It is to be fought if it acts in an irrevocable way and destroys opportunities.

3. Integration quality

People are integrated as soon as their actions reach a minimal form of co-ordination, as soon as they are able to act within a social field without to much distortion. This minimal definition of integration, however, is not really useful for a critical debate about the quality of social arrangements. Integration is not a goal per se, as some communities have deleterious effects on their members. If life, integrity, freedom, and justice matter, a form of integration has to be found that guarantees equal opportunities as much as equal protection against power abuse. The central question is, therefore: *How much power do people have in relative and absolute terms to influence the "reality" they live in?*

---

[38] See also Galtung, Johan (1994), pp. 67 ff.
[39] Rose, Michael (1988), p. 58
[40] Spescha discussed different examples of illegality leading to social change, Spescha, Marc (1988).

a) Direct violence, structural violence, cultural violence

Violence is not just a fact simply evident. *Violence is a social construction* as much in relation to its origins as to its qualifications. Violence is an act within a network of possibilities provided by the community of which one is member. Accordingly, every violent act has its history and doesn't occur out of nowhere. Violence can be qualified as virtue, as strength, as an essential political measure to break the resistance of enemies. It can be seen as an unavoidable remedy to secure people against illegitimate violence. And it can be qualified as violation of the potential of people to construct a "reality" according to their wishes.

Galtung's differentiation of direct, structural, and cultural violence convincingly reflects the social embeddedness of violent acts. He describes violence as an "avoidable insult to basic human needs [...], lowering the real level of needs satisfaction below what is potentially possible."[41] He sets out four classes of basic needs: Survival needs (negation: death, mortality), well-being needs (negation: misery, morbidity), identity – meaning needs (negation: alienation), and freedom needs (negation: repression).

> "We shall refer to the type of violence where there is an actor that commits the violence as personal or direct, and to violence where there is no such actor as structural or indirect. In both cases individuals may be killed or mutilated, hit or hurt in both senses of these words, and manipulated by means of stick or carrot strategies. But whereas in the first case these consequences can be traced back to concrete persons as actors, in the second case this is no longer meaningful. There may not be any person who directly harms another person in the structure. The violence is built into the structure and shows up as unequal power and consequently as unequal life chances. Resources are unevenly distributed, as when income distributions are heavily skewed, literacy/education unevenly distributed, medical services existent in some districts and for some groups only, and so on. Above all the power to decide over the distribution of resources is unevenly distributed."[42] "The important point here is that if people are starving when this is objectively avoidable, then violence is committed, regardless of whether there is a clear subject-action-object relation, as during a siege yesterday or no such clear relation, as in the way world economic relations are organized today."[43]

---

[41] Galtung, Johan (1990), p. 292; Galtung, Johan (1969), p. 168: "[...] violence is present when human beings are being influenced so that their actual somatic and mental realizations are below their potential realizations."

[42] Galtung, Johan (1969), pp. 170 f.

[43] *Id.*, p. 171

Different techniques are used to secure inequality that best serves best the top-dog minority: *Penetration* of the mind and the spirit of the victims restricts their protest potential by *segmentation*, giving them only a partial view of the origins of their misery. Controlling their living area is described as *marginalization* and through *fragmentation* (divide et impera) the organization of resistance is avoided.[44] Cultural violence "preaches, teaches, admonishes, eggs on, and dulls us into seeing exploitation and/or repression as normal and natural, or into not seeing them (particularly not exploitation) at all."[45]

The concept of "direct violence" finds the approval of many a people because it reflects the protection of the "classical" values to be found in a liberal worldview, such as life, physical integrity, or freedom. However, to qualify social structures and ideologies as "violent" questions order and the identity of communities at their basis. In this way, the morality of worldviews and social arrangements are put on the spot and our responsibility in the social construction of violent structures and justifications is pointed out. Even though we are not directly making people starve or excluding them from access to education or work, we have to ponder our role in supporting lifestyles, economic, or political concepts that have this impact on others. Furthermore, it points out injustice in the form of equal chances, repartition of wealth, and questions the meritocratic principle that seldom honors justly people's performance. It also highlights the constitutive necessity of mutual support for the individual's success. In this way, the core elements of capitalism are made responsible for violence and the suffering of many people. "The archetypal violent structure […] has exploitation as a center-piece. This means that some, the top-dogs, get much more […] out of the interaction in the structure than others, the underdogs."[46] To criticize structural violence and its cultural legitimization mechanisms is only possible within a non-deterministic setting of human beings. Only if we can change our relationships, only if freedom of construction is given, only if we are not condemned to aggression, exclusionary competition, inequality, or authoritarianism can we try freedom, solidarity, or justice. That's why the constructivist approach is helpful: It gives us the opportunity to be responsible for the present and the ability to change the future. "The human potential for direct and structural violence is certainly there – as is the potential for direct and structural peace."[47] Following cultural concepts can,

---

[44] Galtung, Johan (1990), p. 294
[45] *Id.*, p. 295
[46] *Id.*, p. 293
[47] *Id.*, pp. 295 f.

according to Galtung, be "violent" because they give reasons for structural or direct violence. "The Chosen People" having religiously justified prerogatives over others; the modern state used for nationalist goals; linguistic exclusionary mechanisms;[48] the doctrine of comparative advantages in the economy, serve as justification for a rough division of the world.

Contrary to the scientific claim for objective neutrality, science is used as much as a tool to liberate people by creating alternatives, as it is to control them very effectively by limiting their construction-power. Cultural violence appears, in my view, not only as justification of the two other forms of violence, but also as regulation and limitation of the resources of people. Personal and collective identities are forced on others thanks to the control of the knowledge creation of the community. Feminist critics of patriarchal science highlight these mechanisms. In this sense, writes Honegger, of a scientific cover used to establish the psycho-physiological difference between the genders.[49] For Modelmog "rationality" is a patriarchal attempt to conceal male affects as "objective" and "factual."[50] In a patriarchal "reality" men dispose of the symbolic means that women have limited possibilities to build up their own identity.[51] And scientific norms like "objectivity," "universality," or "neutrality" are, according to Betzler, used to pursue the interests of men.[52] The same accounts for racist constructions, for nationalist-historical stories developed in science, or for the scientific explanation of injustice claimed as inevitable in an effective capitalistic system.

In other words, these three types of violence are about *physical, material, political, and ideological control over others*. What therefore is needed is, on the one hand, the protection of life and integrity of people. On the other hand, political and social justice are required to guarantee "egalitarian distribution of power and resources."[53] However, changing structures and culture that favor violence takes time and has to be carried out by fundamental alterations, by a non-violent "revolution."

---

[48] See e.g. Trömel-Plötz, Senta (ed.) (1984), Hellinger, Marlis (1990), or Pusch, Luise F. (1984).
[49] Honegger, Claudia (1991), p. 192
[50] Modelmog, Ilse (1989), p. 11, 20, 99
[51] Lerner, Gerda (1991), p. 248, 285
[52] Betzler, Monika (1998), p. 783
[53] Galtung, Johan (1969), p. 183

b) Authoritarian, competitive, or cooperative integration

Depending on the underlying values, we can schematically differentiate three forms of integration:

	Authoritarian	Competitive	Cooperative
Life	X	X	X
Integrity	X	X	X
Freedom		X	X
Responsibility	(X)	(X)	X
Justice		(X)	X
Solidarity	(X)		X

They mainly differ according to the amount of freedom and of support.

aa) Authoritarian integration

Authoritarian integration is a top-down concept. The charismatic or dictatorial leader decrees the relevant "reality" that everybody has to adapt to. This form of integration works only, if the authority is able to build up such big a power, that possible opposition can instantly be controlled or destroyed. Because of the contingency of human actions, a multitude of measures have to be used to uphold this one-sided form of integration. The religious function the leader incorporates, promising redemption, can be one of these. Another one is bribery, thanks to economic advantages given to the fervent and loyal supporters. Political offices also help convince people of the greatness of the leader. As a last resort, terror, torture, and killings can be used to rein in people who don't accept that the leader knows best what the people need. The main problem of the authoritarian integration is its disdain for human dignity and equality. This morally unbound use of power often leads to instability, because disrespected individuals fight for recognition. It is difficult for the leader to trust people, since he never knows if they support him just for the material or political advantages they receive, or because they are convinced that work is done for the society. Sole oppression without anything in return will sooner or later lead either to violent protests or to withdrawal. In any case, the society disintegrates. First, the counterpower using violence against the totalitarian system will cost more lives and injuries than before, and the leader isn't able to present a convincing justification for this civil war. Second, the society looses the potential of people who withdraw from the public realm and don't want to engage anymore in favor of the collective. This reduction of opportunities also takes place because nobody wants to take risks or to be creative. Everyone who crosses "normality" endangers her or his own life. The result is a highly reduced monoculture that limits the possibilities the society has to react to conflicts. Any change, therefore, challenges the core elements of the imposed collective identity because conflicts most of the time end violently. Totalitarian systems exclude the possibility to let ideas die rather than people.

Authoritarian Integration

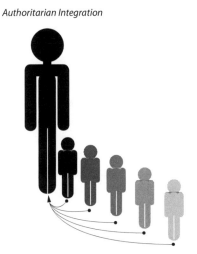

However, an authoritarian government in the form of a caring parent will last, if it takes responsibility for the people's happiness and well-being. The price to pay is freedom. But people in different places on earth seem willing to accept this restriction, as long as support, material security, ideological justification, affiliation to a sort of "home," and fairness in the sense of equal treatment and opportunities prevail.

bb)   Competitive integration

The core idea of competition is to coordinate actions of at least two people in a *mutually exclusive way*. Their goal is the same, but it is not possible for both of them to reach it. *The success of the one diminishes or excludes the reward of others.*

Mutually exclusive future Success

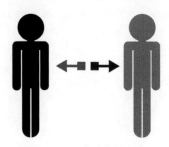

Competitive Integration

Competition is, according to von Cube, a morally just and effective way to attribute to individuals their adequate status.[54] In a just competition, where everybody knows and respects the rules and all participants have equal chances, this procedure will select the best members of society. Human beings, so the conviction of Cube goes, are genetically determined to competition, it is their natural form of behavior.[55] To be the most efficient, competitive systems shouldn't be restricted by ethical, moral, or esthetical expectations.[56] Competitions are neutral forums to judge performances because the results can't be criticized. It is, therefore, comparable to market integration as a transcendental, unquestionable, and infallible decision-making process. Consistently the economic worldview has postulated competition as a unique form of action, characterizing true human nature.

Another understanding is proposed by biologist Markl. For him, competition is a possible, but not an ineluctable form of action.[57] Maturana goes even so far as to write that nature doesn't know competition.[58] Interested in an *undetermined* concept of humankind, I am convinced that competition is a social construction that creates scarcity,[59] injustice and exclusion.[60] It furthermore individualizes failure and restricts the people's opportunities.

---

[54] von Cube, Felix (2001), p. 313
[55] *Id.*, p. 131
[56] Rosa, Hartmut (2006), p. 89
[57] Markl, Hubert (1982), p. 38, 28
[58] Maturana, Humberto R. (1994), p. 235
[59] Kohn, Alfie (1986), p. 4
[60] Longino, Helen E. (1990), p. 189; Ackelsberg, Martha A./Addelson, Kathryn Pyne (1990), p. 158; Traoré, Aminata (2002), p. 183

"Our collective creativity seems to be tied up in devising new ways to produce winners and losers."[61] Competition is fundamentally aggressive: "Every competition, be it in sports, games, or in business, implies the conscious and willful damage of another."[62] This aggression, though, isn't perceived as such because competition is part of everyday[63] behavior, justified by an educational system that pushes competition and declares it an unavoidable universal part of the war of all against all.[64] During the reign of neoliberalism, we saw two developments. First, competition became a unique form of action. Based on their negative concept of (ethically or morally widely unrestricted) freedom, everybody needed to compete with everybody everywhere. Against the background of serious inequality of opportunities, this arrangement benefitted most the ones who were already winning. Not surprisingly, the level of inequality dramatically increased during this time and reached the extent of the twenties of the last century.[65] Second, the competition culture established a justification system for inequality. Individuals were now solely responsible for their failure and not entitled to claim any corrective measures from the society. The wealthy minority had, thus, established a game only they could win.

This perfidious arrangement takes from isolated and unsupported individuals every chance to meet others on a level playing field. To protect themselves and to affirm their self-respect, some turn to violence in order to achieve the goals set by the society. Juvenile delinquency is, therefore, a rational reaction,[66] an attempt to get the status symbols that materialism requires. Insofar a form of counter violence[67] against the structural violence that excludes them from participation. Another reaction may be the exclusion or violence against people weaker than ourselves. Xenophobic constructions are such examples. Enhanced stress, burn-out, or drug consumption highlight a self-destructive attempt to cope with the enormous pressure an isolating competition generates.

Competition arguably enhances the liberty of some. In general, though, in my view, there is a reduction to be noted. Because only winning counts,

---

[61] Kohn, Alfie (1986), p. 2
[62] Brandt, Lewis Wolfgang (1982), p. 171
[63] *Id.*, p. 171
[64] Kohn, Alfie (1986), p. 25
[65] Krugman, Paul (2009), pp. 4 f.
[66] Engel, Uwe/Hurrelmann, Klaus (1993), pp. 238 ff.; see also Eisenberg, Götz/Gronemeyer, Reimer (1993), pp. 28 ff.
[67] Burgherr, Simone/Chambr, Siegfried/Iranbomy, Shahram (1993), p. 86

most of the participants in the competitive setup fear becoming a modernity-loser.[68] They, therefore, avoid any risks by copying the majority. To stand out makes one vulnerable, which is how the norm becomes the way to be. Because just a few can win, it is better not to be seen as a loser, to disappear in the mass of all those who do what everyone else does. Hence, instead of furthering a risk-culture that supports those who fall, *competition pushes mediocrity because of fear*. This serious reduction of alternatives reduces the choices available in the society as well as the freedom of all.

A modern economy asks for flexible individuals who are ready to adapt all the time and to be used wherever and for whatever (economic absolutism). Whereas before modernity the "religion of the stability"[69] was the dominant philosophy, today it is the "religion of change." To change has become a dogma, an obligation, a value by itself; not to change seems to be the end of one's capacity to compete. This glorification of change in all realms of our existence puts enormous pressure on the individual who never knows if he or she will meet the requirements. As a result, we are permanently and everywhere subjected to competition; we react instead of act by ourselves. Subsequently, we lose control of our life, our self-assurance, our "sense of character."[70] "The other is missing"[71] and there is no shared narrative and no shared destiny anymore that would create a meaning of life. This exclusive focus on economic growth and total flexibility has put strain on the social fabric: "[…] such growth comes at a high price: ever greater economic inequality as well as social instability. […] Only a certain kind of human being can prosper in unstable, fragmentary social conditions."[72] Usually it's the ones who make great profit thanks to this system and who route it to their advantage.

cc) Cooperative integration

Hunter-gatherers would perceive competition as barbaric and cruel because succeeding thanks to the failure of others was qualified as a form of torture.[73] Traditional communities (often described as "primitive") are based on cooperative non-individualistic behavior. "Possession of material

---

[68] Rosa, Hartmut (2006), p. 101
[69] Dupront, Alphonse (1978), p. 190
[70] Sennett, Richard (1998), p. 110
[71] *Id.*, pp. 146 f.
[72] Sennett, Richard (2006), p. 3
[73] Laing, Ronald D. (1969), p. 62

goods is not seen as desirable; wealth circulates freely, and there is therefore no competition in the economic sphere."[74] *Cooperation means to be successful if others are.* Self-interest and interest-in-the-others are both served best. "Competition" is, in my understanding, based on a one-dimensional idea of human beings, requiring nothing else then him- or herself and the victory over others. On the other hand, to cooperate means to

- *recognize* the existence of others as constitutive for one's own "reality" and identity (constitutive interdependence), to
- *respect* others' differences, to
- *support* each other
- on the way toward a shared future, and to
- allocate equally losses and advantages.

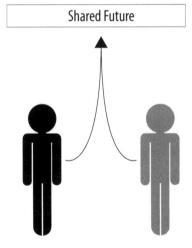

Cooperative Integration

Furthermore, it means to

- challenge one another in a way that
- enhances the respective potential.

---

[74] Kohn, Alfie (1986), p. 35

Others aren't a nuisance or an obstacle on our way to fame and glory per se. They sometimes can be, but the potential that lies in cooperation overcomes the capacities of an individual alone. Thanks to alternative proposals, to criticism, and to moral, political, and financial support, success is an inclusive team performance, surpassing the zero-sum-game-logic of competition.

Cooperation is historically at the origin of human beings because it holds people together and makes possible a higher quality of life for the biggest part of the community. Following the idea that basic needs have to be organized and distributed by the community, the goods that had been gathered and hunted were shared independent of the individual's success.[75] This "ethos of sharing" was a key concept in these communities and only people able to unconditionally share were respected and accorded authority to.[76] It is this traditional form of integration that motivated the policy of Roosevelt. For him, cooperation was part of "the American grain, from Puritan town democracy to the frontier." Accordingly, he understood relationships as "interdependency [...] of individuals, of businesses, of industries, of towns, of villages, of cities, of states, of nations."[77] In the following decades, the underclass improved their situation considerably.

Cooperation doesn't exclude self-interest, autonomy, or difference. It only moderates possible negative effects of egoism by the relevance of others. Total altruism is not intended, but rather a mix of self-interest and altruism. The integrative effect of cooperation lays mainly in the recognition, respect, and reciprocity that it generates. These three forms of actions (see p. 179 ff., p. 211 ff., pp. 225 ff.) are the core elements of an enduring relationship because they bring humanity to the fore.

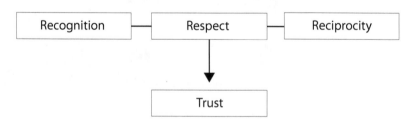

To be recognized as an equal element of the construction process, to be respected in one's own uniqueness and difference, and to be supported when

---

[75] Mayer-Tasch, Peter Cornelius (1991), p. 114
[76] Luig, Ute (1990), p. 86
[77] Lawson, Alan (2006), p. 39

and where needed, motivates people to take responsibility. Experiencing each other as part of an arrangement that tries to find solutions for a shared future, leads to trust.[78]

Trust is a central part of the integration process. Without trust people have to control each other permanently, they have to build up an important apparatus of army, police, secret services, and to use bribery to make sure that the others, perceived as threatening competitors, won't overthrow the rulers. An autonomous conduct of life is much more difficult when trust is missing and fear dominates. Cooperation is the best way to develop this important resource[79] and has, therefore, a decisive effect on the stability of the present and the future.

c) Integration work

When one reads the newspapers and watches the news, one could think that the world we are living in may fall apart at any moment. In my view, though, our "reality" is most often not determined by single events, but rather by the work engaged in that and courageous people fulfill every day. Individuals are the *active and decisive constructors who make and are made by others*. To be "integrated" isn't a static state but a relationship, the future of which is unknown. Even though an arrangement has been found that is currently reproduced and justified by its pros and cons, deconstruction can occur at any moment. Learning how to behave successfully in this community, in family, school, and in the workplace doesn't end with maturity. We constantly have to be aware of changes in the behavior of others. Indeed, routinized interactions reduce the necessity to debate everything all the time. And thanks to our experience of positive interactions in the past, we may sensibly trust the future. But to expect a specific future will be guaranteed would abolish freedom. Thus, integration is not only an intense work, it is also a permanent, never ending story written by each of us.

The amount of work to be done for a successful integration varies widely, depending on the situation, the social environment, ones own resources and history, and the pursued objectives. The ruling elite or majority has a relatively easy integration task, because they managed to construct a "real-

---

[78] According to Sztompka, the "most complex systems of trust appear in the situation of cooperation" (Sztompka, Piotr [1999], p. 62).

[79] Misztal, Barbara A. (1996), p. 199: "The greater the level of trust within a society, the greater the likelihood of cooperation, which in turn contributes to the establishment of trust relationships."

ity" that others have to adapt to. It is up to the powerless to take over the values and convictions of the rulers. This ease ends when opponents try to change the course of events. However, to be heard isn't easy. An equal social, cultural and economic capital is needed to have one's say in the "reality" construction. Lack of money or relationships can be countered to a certain degree by intense personal engagement. But to reach the same social status is under such circumstances much more difficult. That's why I distinguish

- *simple* and
- *multiple integration work.*

Upper class children need to learn a lot of things and to do their integration work in order to function within the community. But, compared to immigrants or to the under class, the necessary investment for children is clearly lower. The upper class has fewer obstacles to overcome to be a successful part of the community because they are quite "automatically" "standard" or "normal" as expected. And success is – as is everything in the consensus-based constructivism – a social construction. Talking about experiences in Germany, Neckel states: "[…] even similar education levels or material assets don't guarantee equal status, because social ranks not only depend on objectively available resources, but also on their qualification."[80] "The bigger the distance between the weaker groups and the strong milieus, the smaller their social chances."[81] For immigrants, there may even be language and administrative barriers to overcome. They further may have to learn how to organize their everyday life in the new "reality." And last but not least they have to endure different forms of exclusion mechanisms. The "racial" construction form is especially problematic for the person concerned because it is impossible to change this attribution imposed by others. "Ethnicity" or "race" are based on biological and by this unchangeable grounds: You are what you are – your genetic heritage determines your existence. There are mainly two forms of ethnical construction. First, it is a result of domination or oppression and exclusive stigmatization. Second, it is a result of autonomous self-assurance, as counter definition of a minority.[82] Imposed, ethnicity or race may be used to fix a group of people on a specific social status, to force them to certain tasks that nobody else wants to carry out. By constructing insurmountable obstacles, social advancement is excluded. Whatever the engagement, equal integration won't be possible.

---

[80] Neckel, Sighard (2003), p. 160
[81] *Id.*, p. 161
[82] See about this distinction Wieviorka, Michel (2001), p. 80

d) Winner/loser arrangement

One of the central questions of the integration process is whether or not the construction of the collective identity tends to include or to exclude. Who gains by this construction and who has to pay the price and what price is it? "Due to which expulsion-system, due to whose eradication, due to the drawing of which line of demarcation, due to which game of negation and exclusion can a society begin to work?"[83]

aa) Delimitations

People integrating each other have to know where to go. They have to decide which community they want to construct. An important part of this process is the determination of the community's members: Who shall participate in the construction process, who shall be a part of ourselves? By delimitation an in- and an outside is built, some relationships are declared as "ours," and others belong, at least for the moment, to different individual or collective identities.

This selection doesn't mean that other forms of life are worthless and have to be fought. Delimitation isn't identical with exclusion. Delimitation is not avoidable, exclusion is. Basically, it is a process of mutual construction, as our and the others' identities are made at the same time within a shared relationship.[84] This interaction is itself a form of community and can be cooperative, confrontational, authoritarian, or even exclusionary-destructive (about the cooperative plurality-structure, see p. 141 ff.). To cooperate between communities requires the mutual readiness to interact on equal grounds. Cooperation expects us to be curious about the other, to be eager to get to know the "reality" the others live in. *Asking* questions in a respectful way is the first step for working cooperation. Second, we have to *listen* to the answers the other is willing to give. And only in the third place comes our self-portrayal, comes *talking*. Asking and listening can be interchanged, talking should come last. Against a cooperative background delimitation is not exclusionary, but keeps the others within the negotiation. The others are an opportunity, the pre-condition for new and different things, for a critical debate on ourselves, others, and possible alternatives.

---

[83] Foucault, Michel (1976), p. 57. See also Schroer, Markus (2001).
[84] Waldenfels, Bernhard (1998), p. 77

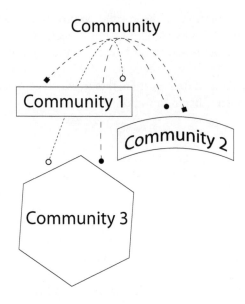

If there is no common ground on which cooperation can take place, delimitation can be used to protect one community against the now threatening others. In the world of neoliberalism everything different is basically a competitor. Under these circumstances delimitation is used to beat the other individual, other teams, or communities, even countries. Globalization is consequently an economic war of all states against all, may the best win. After years of international deregulation favoring the gains of big multinational companies, a more cooperative approach should be tried, in order to avoid exclusion and disintegrative effects. For Krugman international trade is not a sort of war[85] and no zero-sum-game.[86] He is also convinced that states do not compete with each other.[87] Thus, globalization can be understood as community-building on the principles of cooperation, bringing together the outstanding capacities of peoples and communities. The delimitation left is then the earth.

---

[85] Krugman, Paul (1996), pp. 69 f.
[86] *Id.*, p. 10
[87] *Id.*, p. 8

bb) Equal construction power

Quality of life depends fundamentally on the possibility of each individual to construct her or his "reality" (freedom) and on the amount of support he or she finds for this purpose (solidarity). Furthermore, justice is of great importance because generalized social or economic problems are most often accepted. But when a crisis concerns only a small, and always the same part of the community, protests are highly probable, as the examples of Tunisia, Egypt, and others demonstrate.

A long lasting and seemingly unchangeable inequality of construction power humiliates those who can't make an impact on their life. They have to react and adapt to the ruler's orders. As *permanent losers* they have basically two choices: Give up their hopes and dreams and accept the place assigned to them. Or they can try to preserve their dignity and start to fight with the means needed to get the recognition and respect they long for. If their will hasn't been systematically destroyed or the development of an autonomous personality hasn't been made impossible by the use of educational or indoctrinatory techniques, people will fight their loser-status and will develop a counterpower. The more thorough the exclusion is, the more insignificant the resources the excluded have, and the more they will use extreme measures to be heard, be it by violence alone or in combination with religious or ethnical fundamentalist[88] ideology,[89] and the fight will be rude and heavy in victims. The world that rejected their attempts to build up their life may become an object of hatred. As a result, inequality of power originates counterpower, costly conflicts, and freedom restrictions.

Cooperation is based on equal construction power or at least on the equal right to talk and be heard. Human dignity is generalized (recognition) and difference is respected. Measures to protect the minorities and structures guaranteeing equal access to power are essential for a long-term integration. The step from monarchy to a republic and then to democracy is an example of increased equality of construction power. Enlarged integration into the core political process is just one part of the story. In combination with the constitutional state and welfare elements a set of mechanisms was established to avoid disintegrative permanent losers.

---

[88] Meyer, Thomas (1997), p. 330. According to Meyer it is regularly the experience of denied recognition or denied material solidarity that renders the political offer of fundamentalist organizations attractive and effective.

[89] Heitmeyer, Wilhelm/Anhut, Reimund (2000), p. 14

4. Fragile stability

Human existence is fragile. Against the background of homo interactivus, nothing is given, everything has to be built up. And everything lasts only as long as people are willing to support it. This enduring existential challenge is answered in different forms. One, often seen, is scapegoat politics: A group of people builds its collective identity by excluding and oppressing others and holding them responsible for whatever. A much more constructive way to moderate the provisionality of our existence is cooperation, an inclusive search for a common project based on give and take. Instead of producing enemies, partnership is built up. Cooperation can be quite complex because the others are taken seriously in their difference and uniqueness, and because the common future isn't fixed, but will be debated on equal footing.

a) Contingency – need for stability

What is "contingent" happens by chance. There is no determination, no given, no necessary action taking place. Predicting the future is impossible because every actor may act differently next time. Being free means having the opportunity to change. Insofar is contingency the *conditio sine qua non of liberty* and consequently of responsibility and solidarity. Neither would exist; individuals would be determined to be and to behave in one way and no other. On the other hand, contingency is the source of insecurity or even fear. Not to know what is coming, being obliged to develop one's own meaning of life, and having to decide what is valuable – all this is a *permanent burden*.

> "That is our true state. That is what makes us incapable of certain knowledge or absolute ignorance. We are wandering in a vast atmosphere, uncertain and directionless, pushed hither and thither. Whenever we think we can cling firmly to a fixed point, it alters and leaves us behind, and if we follow it, it slips from our grasp, slides away in eternal escape. Nothing remains static for us, it is our natural state yet it is the one most in conflict with our inclinations. We burn with desire to find a firm foundation, an unchanging, solid base on which to build a tower rising to infinity, but the foundation splits and the earth opens up to its depths. So let us not look for certainty and stability. Our reason is always disappointed by the inconstant nature of appearances."[90]

---

[90] Pascal, Blaise (1995), p. 70. In French: Pascal, Blaise (1977), Fragment 185, pp. 157 f.

To ease the burden of contingency, people look for worldviews that will reduce or end our responsibility for the "reality" we live in. The following theories are attempts to get rid of contingency. Theories about genetic determination or disposal, about a core barbarian character of human beings (the man will always be a hunter, the woman always the care taking element), about human "aggressive instinct," natural and dominating selfishness, the "war of all against all," or the ones about the godly origins and destination, about a unidirectional civilization process (and progress), or a given sense in history. The search for truth or *the* reality is another attempt to find what is unquestionable, what has to be accepted, which sets limits to our realm of possibilities. Contrary to Freud, who established a concept of humankind with an important physiological determinism, Fromm bases his construction on the contingency of human actions. "The most beautiful as well as the most ugly inclinations of man are not part of a fixed and biologically given human nature, but result from the social process which creates man."[91] The *quest for freedom and the quest for stability* are central motives of human beings. Human existence is ambivalent: To be free frightens as much as it pleases. Courageous and creative individuals will understand contingency as an opportunity. Many however try to build "realities" that offer a clearly structured and predictable home: Not too complex, not too much change or regularities, but a certain predictability that people can count on. Especially if the society we live in is competitive, aggressive, and exclusionary, its members will look for stable grounds and for certainty in order to reduce the risk of failing or to be failed. A lack of mutual support and fragile individual identities amplify the need for stability. Collectivist or authoritarian proposals will, under these circumstances, seem to be a solution: "[…] in our effort to escape from aloneness and powerlessness, we are ready to get rid of our individual self either by submission to new forms of authority or by a compulsive conforming to accepted patterns."[92] From cooperation to totalitarian solutions, everything can occur any time, it just depends on us – that's contingency. "It's possible that tomorrow people decide to establish fascism, and the rest is possibly coward enough and perplex, not to do anything against. At this moment, fascism will be humanity's truth – tough luck. It will be like people decide it has to be. Does that mean giving me up and to adopt quietism? No. First I have to engage."[93]

The importance of a cooperative arrangement becomes evident when we think of the necessity of develop meaning of life. To live is not enough,

---

[91] Fromm, Erich (2001), p. 9
[92] *Id.*, p. 116
[93] Sartre, Jean-Paul (1996), p. 50

one has to know what for he or she lives.[94] Senselessness is a nightmare for human beings because contingency gains its full impact. Being without sense, not knowing what we want to achieve, makes unpredictability self-destructive. Cooperation is a highly integrative answer to the question of meaning, because it recognizes individuals as equal and unique, accepting them as part of the collective. Thanks to reciprocity (see pp. 225 ff.), a structure based on mutual obligation, and a long-term focus is established that exceeds the individual. And trust reduces considerably the fear of what's next.

b)   Scapegoat politics

Establishing scapegoats is an often used and very effective way to reduce complexity, to make life simple, to delegate responsibility, and to give sense to an existence burdened by contingency. "Reality" is constructed along good and bad, whereas the bad is responsible for everything rejected and motivates the good to live and act passionately.

aa)   Witches against disorientation

In 1692 Massachusetts was a world where God and the Devil were omnipresent. Witches were understood as a form of devilish appearance, embodying maleficium, the magic used to harm people. When two little girls who were living in the household of Reverend Parris had fits, witchcraft was suspected. They screamed, uttered strange sounds, or complained of being pricked with needles. This could have been a reaction to the fanciful tales told them by the slave, Tituba, who had shown them voodoo magic and experiments in fortune-telling. The Puritan children knew that these sorts of stories were strictly forbidden, that they had conjured up evil spirits, and felt pangs of remorse. Living within a "reality" that was religiously very strict and moralized, betraying God was too heavy a burden for young girls. Shortly after, other girls or young women between the ages of 12 and 20 years, who had been part of the same group of children that had infringed the community's moral principles, began to show the similar intense and frightening symptoms. Several physicians were consulted, but no one could explain the events. Dr. William Griggs first thought it could be epilepsy, but finally diagnosed witchcraft.[95] This event in Salem Village trig-

---

[94]   Dostojewski, Fjodor M. (1966), p. 23
[95]   Wilson, Lory Lee (1997), p. 23

gered many other stories of victims of maleficium. Over more than a year different proceedings took place, trying about 185 people (141 women, 44 men) who were charged with witchcraft. The Massachusetts body of Liberties of 1641 ruled in Article 94 no. 2 that any male or female witch shall be put to death. This criminal offence was still in force in 1692. Many of the accused were in jail for a long time, 20 were executed, and three women and a man died in custody. What made the Salem Trials[96] unusual was not the criminal prosecution of witchcraft, because this happened quite often at the time. What was unique was the number of the accused, the geographical scale, the credulous belief in the witnesses and accusers, and the speed with which the accused were judged.[97] Sir William Phips became governor of the Province of Massachusetts Bay in May 1692. At his arrival the jails were overcrowded with suspected witches, so he created the Court of Oyer and Terminer to speed up the trials. The judges he selected were upper class merchants, church members, landowners, and magistrates.

The trials took place during a fundamentally unruly time with existential instabilities and threats from inside and outside the community. The Massachusetts colony was confronted with powers that seemed big enough to wipe it off the map the settlements. In New England's northeast and in Canada French and English troops were fighting with the support of Natives over the control of the area (the so-called King William's War, one of the French and Indian Wars). Settlements in Main were wiped out and families had to leave their home for the South. On the other hand, the Massachusetts government was unauthorized, the relationship to England, mother country was tense, and the treasury empty.[98] In 1684 the charter of 1629 was revoked by King James II, who appointed Governor Andros to exercise tighter control of the colony. There no longer was a legislative authority representing the people. Puritan judges were replaced with Andros' people, the courts were centralized in Boston, taxations were increased, land titles challenged, and Anglicans had to be accepted. After more than fifty years of autonomous government, rights taken for granted were abolished in one blow. With King William III a more moderate regime took place. But the charter of 1691 made Massachusetts a royal colony and introduced liberty of conscience. Hitherto disenfranchised religious groups had to be integrated, questioning the core criteria of the religious identity of the Puritans (see pp. 227 ff.). Based on homogeneity (see p. 213 ff.), their worldview

---

[96] The trials took place in many different villages. It is only the beginning of the conflict that was located in Salem.
[97] Norton, Mary Beth (2002), p. 8
[98] Roach, Marilynne K. (2004), p. XXV

was shaken to the core. "Thus the death blow was given to New England theocracy, for political privilege was henceforth to depend on wealth and not on church membership."[99] Modernization also became a threat to the tightly knit and very close Puritan community. The more trade and materialism became important, the more the traditionally thinking Puritans were frightened about losing their moral economy.

Against the background of general instability and threat, the accused people were chosen because of their connection to these abstract menaces. It was an arbitrary selection of people who somehow were linked to Natives or had connections to Maine,[100] who were opponent parties of a legal procedure, or had been related to witchcraft before. Further, the girls or adults surrounding the accused people held a grudge because of personal conflicts[101] or of the social humiliation they had experienced.[102] Rivalries between political factions also played an important role. One of these schisms occurred between people who wanted to live the godly, modest life of farmers who were focused on morality, and not dominated by the interest in money or in commercial development like the wealthy farmers and merchants.[103] In 1689 Salem Village engaged Reverend Samuel Parris as minister and established an independent church to strengthen morality. Thomas Putnam led the religiously motivated faction and had intense quarrels with parts of his family, the wealthy Porters. He was also one of the most active in the witch trials and successfully launched many proceedings against accused.[104] This conflict was, in my view, not just an economic one, as Goss[105] suggests, it was about basic values, forms of action, and the future of the community: The collective identity was at stake.[106]

At the beginning, most of the accused were poor, old, widows, people "from the fringes of the community,"[107] not highly integrated. These victims were powerless, without support, somehow symbolizing the generalized threat of the outside world. Preliminary examinations that formerly were kept private, were now exposed in public to meet the curiosity and power-need of the people. Contrary to the recommendations of Reverend Rich-

---

[99] Osgood, Herbert L. (1907), p. 441
[100] Norton, Mary Beth (2002), p. 12
[101] Dickinson, Alice (1974), p. 59, 62; Wilson, Lory Lee (1997), p. 71
[102] Goss, David K. (2008), p. 64
[103] Boyer, Paul/Nissenbaum, Stephen (1974), p. 60, 106
[104] Rosenthal, Bernard (ed.) (2009), p. 30
[105] Goss, David K. (2008), p. 56
[106] Boyer, Paul/Nissenbaum, Stephen (1974), p. 103, 180
[107] Weisman, Richard (1984), p. 76

ard Bernard's *Guide to Grand-Jury Men*, published in England in 1627, principles of due process weren't respected anymore. "[...] the examining magistrates ignored one crucial piece of advice offered by Richard Bernard. The afflicted, the individual witnesses, and the suspects, he directed, should be questioned 'apart, & not in the hearing one of another'. Only after they had been carefully examined 'alone' should they be brought together and the suspects be confronted in person by their accusers."[108] The trials were a demonstration of power, a tool to assure that the chosen people would control the appearances of the Devil. Legal rules weren't of any protection to the ones selected to be the scapegoats.

To be able to use further these trials as a battle against the forces of evil, against the social, economic, and political changes, an increasing number of perpetrators were needed: A "seemingly endless cycle of suspicion, gossip, and complaints, leading to more suspicion, more gossip, and additional complaints."[109] The more it was used as a political tool, the more direct opponents of the upper class were targeted.[110] This social elite who until now willingly used the trials to integrate the people, became uncomfortable with the new development because they risked losing control over the conflict. Suddenly "many powerful people openly questioned the reliability of the evidence accepted by the court, [...] the court's methods of determining guilt."[111] Up to this point, the magistrates had played the decisive role in the trials, had influenced the discovery of the devil's appearances and the selection of the accused. "The afflicted were free to define the shape of the conspiracy only insofar as their formulations did not conflict with those of their official sponsors. [...] it was the magistrates who decided upon the identity of the afflicted as well as upon the validity of their testimony. Not until the accusers began to cry out against civil and ecclesiastical authorities and their near relations did these judicial prerogatives become explicit."[112] The court cases were ended by the powerful as fast as they had begun.

Motivated by a general destabilization because of important existential changes, different political goals were intended by the Salem Witch Trials:

- The construction of scapegoats was supposed to *strengthen the collective identity*. During the trials, the central elements of the community's "reality" were reproduced in a highly emotional way.

---

[108] Norton, Mary Beth (2002), p. 42
[109] *Id.*, p. 113
[110] Weisman, Richard (1984), p. 146
[111] LaPlante, Eve (2007), pp. 175 f.
[112] Weisman, Richard (1984), p. 147, 165

- Refocusing on problems the community perceived as solvable (witchcraft), the feeling of general powerlessness could be overcome.
- The reciprocity structure was reinforced, as the political institutions listened to the people and recognized their fears.

Scapegoat politics has its own dynamic, it can fall back on the originators, so the rulers have to use it carefully. As soon as the mechanism of exclusion and oppression is introduced, it is legitimized and then must be at the disposal of everybody. To construct scapegoats also demonstrates the limited validity of human dignity. This universally understood value, though, doesn't bear relativization without losing its normative content. Hence, the dignity of all suffers, be it as perpetrators, current or potential victims.

bb) Exclusion for inclusion

"Scapegoats" are characterized by three elements. First, they are held responsible for everything negative. Second, this group of people solely exists as a collective, described by a few criteria. Individuals in this group do not count. Third, scapegoats are excluded from the construction process, having to suffer what others decide. Manichaean scapegoat constructions are highly effective because they meet the goal of *simplification by polarization*. In this way, the rulers can, on the one hand, demonstrate their capacity to govern and, on the other hand, confirm the identity of the ones now described as "good."

Increased immigration to the USA at the end of the nineteenth and the beginning of the twentieth century brought many conflicts, mainly rooted in gross inequality. The lack of solidarity and justice led to a highly stratified society. To avoid class conflicts, to make sure that the majority of workers wouldn't organize against the ones making profit out of this individualized and competitive situation, the rulers built up a foe based on skin-color, against which the Whites (independent of their wealth) could unite. What economically and socially didn't make any sense – the common interests of antagonistic classes – was made possible by racist stereotypes. Problems weren't rooted anymore in changeable social relations, but in natural differences, which were impossible to overcome. "While European ethnics displayed tremendous hostility toward each other – which explains the peculiarly segregated labor market of New York at the beginning of the twentieth century, with its stereotyped Irish cops, Jewish garment workers, and Italian laborers – exclusion was most effective when African Americans were its victims."[113] "Most white Brooklynites – immigrant or native, Catholic or Protestant, wealthy or poor – were in conflict on all but a single local issue: the subjection of free black people, a cornerstone of proslavery politics."[114]

After having relentlessly played the nationalist card and having insisted on the "identité nationale" to win over Front National voters, French president Sarkozy had to face the loss of the regional elections, growing opposition concerning his retirement plans, the Woerth affair (his minister of labor, solidarity and public service was accused of corruption and illegal party financing), and increasing problems of inner security, highlighted by riots in different cities, prominently Grenoble. Over the years he had tried to build up a reputation as top minister tough on crime and highly effective. But the events of the last month were tarnishing his reputation. To exemplify his determination and strength, he constructed the supposedly dangerous minority of the Roma and Sinti. On July 21, 2010, president Sarkozy announced in the council of ministers a "war against criminality."[115] By declaring it a "war," the president made illegal residence and petty crimes a national existential threat. He blinded out all the other challenges, like the relation between state and economy, the future of capitalism, the necessity of an ecological conversion of the economy and the society, the relevance of the nation-state, the effect of globalization, or social inequality. Symbol politics or mini-politics,[116] was chosen instead of tackling integration challenges that are fundamental and based on a problematic structure of society. To make sure that the targeted won't fire back, it has to be unorganized, not beloved, and supposedly without support. The Roma and Sinti were a good fit. According to Brice Hortefeux, minister of the interior at the time, "in all three cases – Roma, vagrant peoples sedentary or not – the consequences are the same: an increase of delinquency."[117] French Gendarmerie had also contributed to the construction by establishing *illegal* files based on ethnic criteria like "Roma" or "vagrant peoples," linking them to different forms of criminality.[118] Instead of defending the fundamental basis of the universalistic republic as described in Article 1 of the French Consti-

---

[113] Wilder, Craig Steven (2000), p. 143; as well p. 137
[114] Id., p. 67
[115] Le Monde of July 22, 2010 (http://abonnes.lemonde.fr/politique/article/2010/07/21/nicolas-sarkozy-huit-ans-de-declarations-de-guerre_1390764_823448.html), retrieved on July 27, 2011
[116] Alain Touraine : " Nous sommes à l'heure de la 'mini-politique'", in: Le Monde of September 5, 2010, p. 7
[117] Le Monde of July 29, 2010, p. 8
[118] Le Monde of October 8, 2010, p. 1

tution – "[France] shall ensure the equality of all citizens before the law, without distinction of origin, race or religion," the president used his power for electoral purposes only. Thus, he didn't fulfill his role as protector of the Constitution, as an arbitrator securing the proper functioning of the state (Article 5 Constitution). Evacuating the Roma and Sinti from their illegal encampments[119] is a strong form of symbol politics. But it doesn't solve the problems of the poor in Europe to find a place to live in dignity. On the contrary, it made them into a problem without a voice. "If we are allowed to stay or have to go, if we have to hibernate jammed together on resting places or to live in ghetto-tenements, if our children are educated in special kindergarten, special classes, special schools and by whom, if we ever will get work or the permission to carry on a trade, if we were allowed to enter a pub, if you gaze at us like circus animals or despise us as strangers, if once we were perceived as individual human beings or again and again thrown all together in one pot: all this depends on you. On your decisions about us and without us."[120]

The history of vagrant peoples in Europe is the history of governments constructing minorities as they please. Only recently organized, these individuals, families, and groups are forced by political decision to be part of a community that didn't exist before. The notion of "gypsy" is the attribute the majority forced on a multitude of different groups it wanted to collectivize. In 14th century Greece the name "atsinganoi" was given to nomads who probably moved from Northwestern India through Persia and Armenia over Southern Europe and North Africa to Europe. In their own perception they do not see themselves as a closely knit entity. "One of the most salient characteristics of the Roma […] is their diversity."[121] A multitude of languages, religions, professions, and different forms of adaptation to the cultures they encountered, stand for a large variety of existences. There are as much commonalities as there are differences between the people constructed by the ones in power as "gypsies."[122] What makes all these people "Roma" is the same negative experience with the rulers, the "Gadsche", as the majority is called by the reacting minority. Themselves, these Middle Europeans want to be called "Rom" (human being, Romania), "Manush" (true human being, Transilvania), or based on their professions "Kalderash" (boiler maker), "Lovari" (horse dealer), or "Baiesi" (basket maker). Realizing that they had to organize themselves to protect the interests they

---

[119] Le Monde of August 14, 2010, p. 7
[120] Leidgeb, Ellen/Horn, Nicole – Roma-Union Ffm. (Hrsg.) (1994), p. 9
[121] Matter, Max (2005), p. 15
[122] Leidgeb, Ellen/Horn, Nicole – Roma-Union Ffm. (Hrsg.) (1994), p. 42

had in common, they began in the 1980s to use the designation of "Roma and Sinti". To gain at least some counterpower, they had to build up a collective identity. Hence, minorities often come into being as a reaction to the oppression of current rulers.

Most of the Roma and Sinti live under very poor conditions in so-called "gypsy-settlements" on the border of great cities in Eastern Europe. There are only estimates about their numbers because they preferred to lie about their affiliation, knowing from experience that these data could be used against them at any time.[123] The French Gendarmerie's practice showed, once again, that they're were right. Grass estimates their number at twenty million, making them the biggest minority in Europe.[124] Their marginalization results from historical conditions like slavery, for example, in Romania, the industrialization that annihilated their traditional economy, the consequences of the Holocaust that destroyed family structures, the absence of reparation, the nationalist politics of the states they were living in, and the scapegoat-politics based on old and easily available prejudices.[125] The biggest number of Roma and Sinti live in Romania, where they had to suffer the systematic and arbitrary abuse of power by former dictator Ceausescu. The revolutionary change in 1989 didn't bring any improvement, but even more violence[126] and poverty[127] than before, though their legal situation progressed. The intense social change made nationalistic concepts attractive at their expense and they became the first victims in the different civil wars in Eastern Europe. The second largest group lives on the territory of former Yugoslavia, where their already very difficult position worsened after the death of Tito. They weren't recognized as a national minority and, therefore, couldn't invoke the protection of the Constitution. "The Kosovo-Roma became in the 'Serbian-Albanian war the greatest victim."[128] They paid with their lives and many of them lost the little they had accumulated over years.

Already in the sixteenth century many of the Sinti began to settle and ended their nomadic life. Others were forced by the states to sedentariness. But this "normalization" didn't protect them against xenophobic harassment, violence, or persecution. Assimilationist politics (p. 213 ff.) of many governments forced them to give up their culture, their smaller and

---

[123] Matter, Max (2005), p. 13; Leidgeb, Ellen/Horn, Nicole – Roma-Union Ffm. (Hrsg.) (1994), p. 60.
[124] Grass, Günter (2000), pp. 34 f.
[125] Leidgeb, Ellen/Horn, Nicole – Roma-Union Ffm. (Hrsg.) (1994), pp. 43 f., 6
[126] Id., p. 68
[127] Bercus, Costel (2005), p. 29
[128] Jakšić, Božidar (2005), p. 47

bigger differences to become "civilized". There was an ideological-cultural motive, too, that interested in the enforcement of the perfect citizen. And there was an economic interest in the industrial workforce. Both goals were only reachable if the social structure and collective identity of the Roma and Sinti were destroyed. Vagrancy, their languages, and the professions they exercised were forbidden. As the Roma and Sinti resisted and sought to preserve their family structure as fundamental to their heritage and their different identities, the states began to take their children away by force. To end cultural reproduction, the children were brought into foster homes, or even psychiatric hospitals or prisons, if there weren't enough homes. Parents defending their rights and the rights of their children were often placed under disability. In Switzerland for example, the authorities tried to register all Roma and Sinti and to prevent biological and cultural procreation,[129] making sure that the society would be freed of this evil source of reproducing neglect.[130] Dr. Siegfried, responsible staff member of the aid organization "Kinder der Landstrasse" (created in 1926 as a project of the foundation "Pro Juventute") was convinced that the Roma and Sinti had an inferior genetic makeup, so a change of their anti-moral, anti-social behavior was not possible. To exterminate the evil of the vagrancy[131] the children had to be saved from their parents and entourage.[132] The aid organization forcibly took away around 630 children. These re-modelled children would be integrated into the industrial production process and become an ethnically unidentifiable workforce.[133] "Kinder der Landstrasse" based their decision on Article 369 ZGB,[134] which gave (and gives) the guardianship authority the right to place under disability "imbeciles" or "insane", and on Article 370 ZGB, describing "vicious moral conduct" as reason for administrative actions. According to Article 284 ZGB (today Article 311 ZGB), the guardianship authority had the duty to withdraw the children if the parents weren't able to act sufficiently in favor of the child's well being. These terms, highly open to interpretation, gave the authority all possible means to pursue their discriminatory intentions. The stigmatization of the vagrant peoples as criminals, lazy, neglected, and genetically afflicted was a consequence of this registration policy.[135] Besides the guardianship authority was

---

[129] Egli, Andina (1998), pp. 90 f.
[130] Leimgruber, Walter/Meier, Thomas/Sablonier, Roger (1998), p. 33
[131] Egli, Andina (1998), p. 96
[132] Galle, Sara/Meier, Thomas (2009), p. 18, 35
[133] Egli, Andina (1998), p. 93
[134] Zivilgesetzbuch, Swiss Civil Code.
[135] Leimgruber, Walter/Meier, Thomas/Sablonier, Roger (1998), p. 34

the psychiatry a very active part, providing expertise to justify the official politic of racial hygiene.[136]

The Swiss State had subsidized this program until 1967. More than twenty years after the Holocaust governments still acted on the basis of racist criteria. Many civil organizations supported anti-vagrant politics.[137] It is only in 1973 that the aid organization was abolished. The parents whose children were stolen became reparation from the Swiss Confederation: Between CHF 2'000.- and 7'000.- per person, limited to the maximum of CHF 20'000.-. Once again, the supposedly neutral and objective bureaucracy had struck. The properly collected and stored information about the Roma and Sinti were often highly pejorative and reproduced the bogeyman criteria used over centuries.[138] The examination of their personal files shocked many of the Roma and Sinti, because they had to learn the atrocities those responsible had written about them. Some, in the aftermath, committed suicide.[139]

In the aftermath, there was no criminal prosecution against none of the responsible people. Did they commit genocide against the Roma and Sinti? The Convention on the Prevention and Punishment of the Crime of Genocide of 1948 qualifies in Article II lit. e "genocide" as the forcible transfer of children of one group of people to another group with the intention to destroy, in whole or in part, a national, ethnical, racial or religious group. The intention to annihilate is a necessary condition for punishment.[140] Not decisive, however, is the number of victims or if individuals or groups are concerned.[141] According to Gschwend, there are many indications to be found that a conviction for genocide of active individuals in Pro Juventute as well as in the guardianship authorities could be possible, not based on Swiss penal law, because the relevant Article 264 StGB[142] wasn't in force at the time the acts were perpetrated, but based on customary international law.[143] It is possibly a "crime against humanity" in accordance with Article 7 of the Rome Statute. The International Criminal Tribunal of Rwanda has ruled

---

[136] *Id.*, pp. 59 ff.
[137] *Id.*, pp. 67 ff.
[138] Galle, Sara/Meier, Thomas (2009), pp. 129 ff.
[139] *Id.*, p. 98
[140] See Article 6 of the Rome Statute.
[141] Botschaft betreffend das Übereinkommen über die Verhütung und Bestrafung des Völkermordes sowie die entsprechende Revision des Strafrechts vom 31. März 1999, Bundesblatt Nr. 28, 20. Juli 1999, pp. 5327-5353, 5338.
[142] Strafgesetzbuch, Swiss Penal Code
[143] Gschwend, Lukas (2002), pp. 384 ff.

that genocide and crimes against humanity are of equal gravity even though genocide includes a morally specially abject intention, because genocide, according to the tribunal, constitutes the "crime of crimes."[144] Barth states in regard to the "stolen generation" in Australia that an established democracy like the Australian one can't commit genocide.[145] In my opinion it is not the form of government that counts, but the intended and realized result. Democracies can be as destructive as totalitarian or authoritarian systems. It is not because a majority decides that this majority is objectively right and wouldn't under any circumstances commit violent acts. According to Tatz, Aborigines were killed in the first decades of the nineteenth century, "because they were Aborigines."[146] Later a mix of a politic of protection-segregation and an era of wardship[147] took place, resembling the one applied in Switzerland. "By 1886 forced assimilation was in full swing," based on racial criteria, including "the forcible removal of children from parents and family."[148] Pure Aborigines were lost, the ones with white blood could be saved, but had to be controlled to "avoid the dangers of blood call."[149] Administrative persecution was not direct violence, it was not physical killing, "but it was assuredly a practice directed at child removal, 'breeding them white', and 'transforming to white' everyone who was regarded as less than 'full-blooded.'"[150] The responsible people "certainly intended the disappearance of the 'part-Aboriginal' population by 'eugenicising' many of them."[151] That it didn't totally succeed doesn't exclude genocide because the Genocide Convention punishes in Article III lit. d) the attempt to commit genocide. What makes these acts so atrocious is their hidden violence, their rational way of proceeding, and the pretext of helping people. It is the normality, the rationality, the calmness, the unagitated way the worst things are committed, that makes this violence so dreadful and difficult to fight. Structural violence is as much if not even more effective than direct violence, but disappears behind its complexity and behind small little steps within a bureaucracy. The same accounts for responsibility.

---

[144] Prosecutor v. Serushago (Case No. ICTR-98-39-S), Trial Chamber I, February 5, 1999, para. 13 ff.
[145] Barth, Boris (2006), pp. 21 f.
[146] Tatz, Colin (2003), pp. 78 f.
[147] Id., p. 86
[148] Id., p. 88. The victims of this politic are called the "stolen generations".
[149] Id., p. 90
[150] Id., pp. 91 f.
[151] Id., p. 92

Minorities used as scapegoats have under certain circumstances the chance to become "victims," to change the status as "personification of the evil" into an "oppressed people." "Victim" is a social construction, a form of recognition. "Victims" can be recognized because of truthful remorse, as a political measure against the former rulers, or because of a revolutionary change in the distribution of power. If a formerly oppressed minority manages to take over government, it is in their hands to punish the perpetrators and to enforce compensation. If their minority-status prevails, they are dependent on the readiness of the new rulers to accept their status as victims. The better the minority is organized and the more powerful the states or organizations that support its claim, the more it can influence this decision. The heterogeneity of the Roma and Sinti, the lack of organization, and their tendency to be unobtrusive due to historical experiences made it difficult for these victims to be heard. There is a debate over the exact number of Roma and Sinti killed by the National Socialists and whether they suffered as much as the Jews.[152] Whatever the legal assessment of the acts perpetrated against Roma and Sinti, the debate over their status as victims is humiliating. "Establishing a hierarchy of the victims is for the victims of the genocide and the survivors of the minority of the Sinti and Roma hurting and offending."[153] "Even dead the Roma are excluded."[154]

Wanting to become members of the European Union, Eastern European countries were ready to improve the situation of the Roma and Sinti in the field of education, (construction of kindergartens, development of teaching aids in Romanes, lessons in Romanes, formation and support of teachers in general and Romanes teachers in particular, a sort of affirmative action for the access to university), housing, cultural institutions, community centers, and professional integration (Roma became, for example, members of the police force).[155] Besides the EU the OSCE or the Council of Europe were important institutions that helped to build up the necessary international pressure for change. One major problem persists: Extreme poverty because of economic and social exclusion: structural violence. For Romania, for example, the de iure segregation can be said to have ended, but the de facto

---

[152] For Lewy for example the deportations of Roma and Sinti to the east lacked the intention to exterminate them as a group as such (Lewy, Guenter [2001], p. 366, 370). Acts of forced sterilization based on the Auschwitz-Erlass he however qualifies as "genocidal" (Lewy, Guenter [2001], p. 371).
[153] Romani, Rose (1989)
[154] Grass, Günter (2000), p. 73
[155] Matter, Max (2005), pp. 24 f.

segregation prevails.[156] "The circuit of poverty, within which the Roma are imprisoned, becomes evermore a dead end."[157] It's not for nothing that the neoliberal theory focusses on individuals and sets aside the question of social inequality. To remedy this injustice is costly and needs much more of a change than "just" the important but easier to achieve legal equality. The elite especially has to share the wealth it accumulated.

Scapegoat-politics violates justice as much as freedom, solidarity, and responsibility. And this bogeyman politics reduces the freedom of the ruling majority too. What's often a welcomed effect because it eases the burden of indetermination. Patriotic rhetoric is an effective example of this sort. "The tragedy of our day is the climate of fear in which we live, and fear breeds repression. Too often sinister threats to the bill of rights, to freedom of the mind, are concealed under the patriotic cloak, of anti-communism."[158]

c) Stable change

"Stability" is as little as "change" a value per se. Both, however, are essential preconditions for freedom and justice. Too fast a change makes it difficult to build up construction power and to preserve identity. No change at all excludes the opportunity to act differently. Change is problematic, if it isn't inclusive, if it profits some at the expense of the others. Forced exclusion of change, on the other hand, will lead to violent attempts to modifications, especially if the social structure is perceived as unjust. *Stable change* is, therefore, a mixture of stability and development, made possible by a cooperative arrangement. *Respectful cooperation* gives the community members the possibility to realize their own interests. Their originality and difference is respected and their meaning of life is the result of negotiations of a shared future. This just integration leads to trust and to readiness for joint change. People know, that the gains and the costs the development yields will be shared and that the ones in need will be supported.

Reached stability is not identical with immutability. By establishing procedures that make change possible without producing permanent losers, modifications become an integrative part of the community. Rearrangements of the existing relationships on the other hand can keep the community alive, can bring new members in and persuade old ones to stay. Thanks to its flexibility, the changes individuals want to make can be integrated,

---

[156] Bercus, Costel (2005), pp. 31 ff., 41
[157] Jakšić, Božidar (2005), p. 66
[158] Stevenson, Adlai (1952)

which is why the community goes on. New forms of actions are developed, the relationships evolve, but the people involved are still convinced that the "reality" constructed interactively is worth it. Thus, "stability" refers to the actors, not necessarily to the character of their relationship. A stable community tries to keep its members on board by *discussing and implementing change in a cooperative way*.

5. Collective identity

A community's identity is *the story its people tell about themselves*. It is the *sum of integrative acts* that people want to *reproduce* in the future and are *ready to uphold against criticism*. Storytelling is more than just entertainment. Telling a story is *giving a sense to people's existence by building interrelations* and by *locating them within time*. To whom are we important? Who made us? Who did we influence and how? What is our present state, how does it differ from the past, and what should our future look like?[159] What is the past we want to have and how does it determine the present? By telling stories, "realities" are constructed. Insofar are modern written societies not different from communities based on orality.[160] It is within our stories that our heroes accomplish what is necessary for the establishment of an important nation. It is within our stories that people go on living though they are physically dead, often having a deeper impact than alive. As soon as we stop talking about people who have died or people to come (as in many religious "realities"), they no longer exist and our collective identity changes: "The only certainty [...] was to be found in uninterrupted telling, in the continuous retelling over thousands of years. [...] It's this telling that stood for the world, more real than reality, because all this existed just as long as it was told. What wasn't told anymore, was forgotten, didn't exist. [...] It lived as long as one existed to tell and another to hear."[161] "Stories so rich and dreadful, so cruel and absurd, that they linked over death and oblivion the lives on generations, as all family members knew them."[162]

It doesn't matter, which sort of narrative people create to integrate each other. Local, regional, national, religious, cultural, economic, legal, or other criteria are used to construct a form of belonging. If the community man-

---

[159] About the importance of a big story, see Postman, Neil (1999), p. 16.
[160] For the characterization of oral and written cultures see Ong, Walter J. (1982).
[161] Forte, Dieter (1995), pp. 109 f.
[162] Forte, Dieter (1998), p. 215

ages to generate a feeling of trust, reliability, and predictability going along with the story, people will call it "home." "Home" stands for a feeling of security, a feeling, "being in the bosom of a shared room,"[163] "a non-arbitrary, intimate feeling."[164] Rites like religious and/or traditional festivities, annual celebrations of memorable events, or elections help to create and intensify the feeling of eternity people are looking for – against their background of existential contingency. "Home" in form of "tradition" has to be built up and cherished again and again as, for example, through the work of priests, politicians, savants/scientists, patriarchs, artists, or others.[165] And a "tradition" fulfills its stabilizing function only if the community manages to establish its reproduction automatically, so that these rites are perceived as coming from time immemorial.[166] This is why communities – as long they are in reproduction phase – don't like to talk about the creation of their collective identity: "Few individuals spend much of their time consciously worrying over their own or their community's 'identity,' while many spend none whatever. Social (including national) collective consciousness is none the less constantly transmitted onwards. In fact it may be powerfully transmitted, over surprising periods of time, and against great apparent odds – for centuries, rather than just generations. 'National identity' has […] a non-genetic but long-range sociocultural inheritance. While of course it must pass through consciousness, its residence within any social fabric is largely 'unconscious' in the familiar sense of being 'taken for granted.'"[167] One of the tools to "eternalize" collective identity is to reify some or all of its elements. Thus, a community's identity shall be perceived as "natural" and by this unquestionable.[168] The "uniqueness of a folk," the "natural dominance of the colonizers over the colonized," or the national socialist "Aryan race" are examples of natural origins not allowed to be criticized.

Collective identity is, according to the consensus-based constructivism, the result of intense and permanent integration work, requiring people ready to engage for their idea of community.[169] Developing a collective identity means to reach a *consensus over elements* perceived as *essential*. In the following I propose elements that interactors have to find an answer to

---

[163] Gauchet, Marcel (1996), p. 228
[164] Bronfen, Elisabeth/Marius, Benjamin/Steffen, Therese (ed.) (1997), p. 1
[165] Giddens, Anthony (1997), pp. 77 f.
[166] De Saint Martin, Monique (2003), p. 115
[167] Nairn, Tom (1997), p. 246
[168] Douglas, Mary (1991), p. 84
[169] See also Habermas, Jürgen (1996), p. 330; Kirsch, Jan-Holger (1999), p. 316; Hondrich, Karl Otto (1992), p. 47; Rosanvallon, Pierre (1998), p. 356

if they are interested in *human dignity lasting over time*. Interactors have to

- recognize the existence of the people they want to be members of their community and treat them as equal; they have to
- respect the uniqueness of every individual and to
- develop a form of exchange and compensation, of solidarity; they have to
- make sure, that its members trust each other and are willing to
- determine who is allowed to decide and how the decisions have to be made in situations of conflicts.

The basic values a society or a community wants to realize and to live by, are the core elements of integration is about. *Economy, science, or law are functional means used to fulfill these values.*[170] Economic action is needed, people have to eat, to drink, to have a shelter etc. Also important is not the economy per se, but what is produced, how it is produced, and how the output is distributed. The same accounts for science: Who has access to this powerful construction tool? What are the worldviews, the concepts of humankind? Are its results bearable? Law, also, is not a value per se. It is a formalized decision-making process that serves specific goals. What, therefore, counts, are the goals and the meaning of life a community aspires to.

---

[170] Peters distinguishes three forms of social integration and describes "functional coordination" as instrumental (Peters, Bernhard [1993], p. 116).

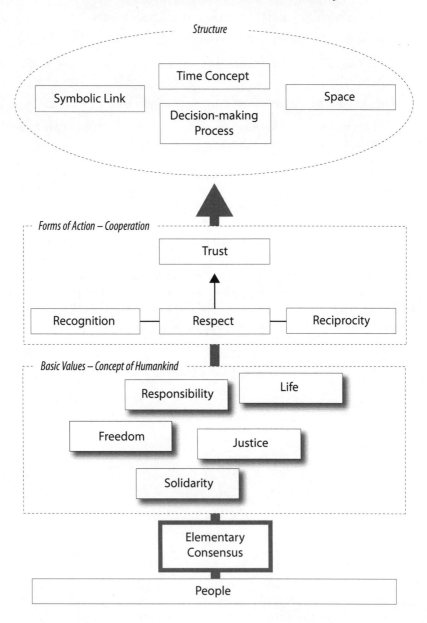

6. Value-based constructivism

Modern society is proud of being a value-free zone that's based only on rationality and efficiency. Instead of ethical or moral reflections of our future actions, of our goals, our concepts of humankind, and our worldview, pure functionalism is what counts.[171] "Values" are perceived as outdated concepts of traditional or religious communities. This loss of points of reference[172] helps the powerful to pursue their interests as they please and to use other people therefore. To protect the equal dignity of people, we need reasoned limitations of power. Not in the sense of absolute norms, but as debatable grounds for decision-making.

To act means to opt for something that we value more than something else. Decisions are therefore concretizations of values, which brings them into the world, visible and relevant to others. In the consensus-based constructivism there aren't any actions without preferences. The "reality" we live in can be understood as the embodiment of what is important for the constructors. Everything that is is of value because it either is or was defended by somebody, or by another wants to change it because it hinders her or his interests.

a) Pleading for values

Values are expectations. Values stand for the hope that others as much as ourselves will behave in a specific way. They are nurtured by former experiences qualified as positive. Values come into existence because we take others seriously enough to look for their sensible contribution. Forced social isolation is a very effective punishment because the person concerned loses the ability to preserve expectations, to keep and build up hope. "What does 'nihilism' stand for?: Our highest values are devaluated. There's no goal, no answer to the question 'why'?"[173] For Nietzsche, in my interpretation, nihilism isn't the final goal, it isn't a value by itself. It is a way to overcome the limitations current society imposes on its members. To be free to develop your own point of view, your own deep convictions, means, for Nietzsche, first to attack common morality, the expectations of the ruling majority, inculcated as absolute.[174] He argues against a metaphysical concept of truth used to propagate specific interests – concealed human dominion[175] – as

---

[171] Luhmann, Niklas (1997), pp. 406 f.
[172] Arendt, Hannah (1993), p. 22
[173] Nietzsche, Friedrich (1996), p. 10
[174] *Id.*, pp. 11 f., 23
[175] *Id.*, p. 16

values.[176] The modern world's exclusive focus on the dichotomy of suffering v. hedonistic pleasure is, in the opinion of Nietzsche, problematic,[177] because it isn't an autonomous way to determine one's own will, the meaning of life.[178] Nietzsche's passionate fight for autonomy strongly criticizes social expectations and defends an ideal of the powerful individual fighting without any regard to others.[179] Concepts like "justice" or "equity" are to him a simple nuisance hindering the strong to realize their vocation. That's why "socialism is the thought-through tyranny of the least, the most stupid and shallow."[180] I like Nietzsche's passion for autonomy and his concept of self-responsible "reality" construction. But I do not embrace his rage against every social expectation. I am convinced that all of our values are the result of an interactive "reality" construction and to be free means to be free within a social arrangement that supports and hinders at the same time. Nietzsche's passion and his values gain their intensity thanks to the others he perceives as obstacles. It is out of these interactions that he develops the importance and concrete configuration of, for example, "freedom."

Discussing the values incorporated by a proposal helps clarify their advantages and their negative effects, and it helps to clarify who the winners are of the arrangement. Values are points of reference to judge. Everything can be brought back to our values and, thus, to our responsible freedom. That's why discussions about personal and collective identities are sensibly referring to the values involved, to the expectations people hope to realize. Neoliberalism defends economic freedom as the most important value, eclipsing all others. In combination with the transcendental and comprehensively responsible market, this position seems to me nihilistic, as there is no expectation left toward others. Freedom identified with selfishness is the renouncement of the richness of human relationships, of the possibilities only interacting people can originate. And the supremacy of the economy finally destroys its own founding: "Wealth isn't enough to protect the system that makes it possible. [...] Many start to realize, that societies not exclusively motivated by economy are showing considerable strength and even predominance because of their regulated, belief-based restriction of need. [...] Conflicts arise, which won't be pacified only on economic grounds."[181]

---

[176] *Id.*, pp. 14 f.
[177] *Id.*, p. 27, 54
[178] *Id.*, p. 28
[179] *Id.*, pp. 84 ff.
[180] *Id.*, p. 90
[181] Strauss, Botho (1999), pp. 58 f.

b) Social construction of values

"We hold these truths to be self-evident [...] that all men are created equal, that they are endowed by their Creator with certain unalienable Rights [...]." The preamble of the United States Declaration of Independence from 1776 holds one of the main arguments justifying the separation of the American colonies from the British state: People are by nature universally equal and free to determine how to live. Nobody from whatever origin is entitled to decide on behalf of others without their consensus. There is no prerogative of descent or wealth, every community has to find its own organization. Even though the idea of the universal equality of human beings wasn't new and had been thought of by several English, Scottish, and French thinkers during the preceding two hundred years – the emancipation from the British world power was an incredibly courageous revolutionary step. Monarchies had been the essence of political and social organization over centuries had become because of their widely unquestioned reproduction an everlasting principle. How to justify the new government against a political organization that had religious support and seemed to be the natural order of things? The American revolutionaries used a traditional form of argument, but changed its inherent meaning: First, the declaration refers to the same origin – God ("Nature's God," "Creator," "Supreme Judge," "Devine Providence"). Second, the invoked God isn't exclusively the one of the Bible, it isn't the Christian one, but rather, according to my interpretation, it is a universal principle that's relevant for everybody, independent of her or his religious beliefs. By withdrawing these enlightened principles from the sphere of influence of human beings, the founders of the declaration tried to make absolute the values of freedom and justice, which would be concretized later in a democratic organization of government. The overwhelming presence of God, standard in medieval worldviews, wasn't questioned, but didn't anymore legitimize a specific group of people with prerogatives because of their privileged access to the Creator.

Against the backdrop of consensus-based constructivism, values "do not have any reality-character"[182] in an ontological sense. That includes their origins as much as their scope. Values indicate *the wishes of particular people at a specific time and in a particular place*. This wish is orientated toward other people or toward objects; it is not given, but is created interactively. That people in 1636 would pay some 3'000 florins (in today's value: $25'000 to $50'000) for a tulip bulb called Semper Augustus, isn't due to

---

[182] Geiger, Thomas (1987), p. 274

the bulb itself, but to a social construction called "speculation." "Nobles, citizens, farmers, mechanics, seamen, footmen, maid-servants, even chimney-sweeps and old clotheswomen, dabbled in tulips. People of all grades converted their property into cash, and invested it in flowers. [...] money poured into Holland from all directions."[183] The same value-construction applies to gold, which isn't valuable per se. It's the people who look for a symbol for economic or social reasons that give it its value. Values are of relative importance and are weighed against each other. European traders imported beaver furs that were hunted and treated by Natives in the American colonies for making hats and trimming fine clothes. This commodity had become scarce in Europe because of over-hunting. For practical reasons, Natives exchanged the furs for knives and kettles. But most valued were beads – a product, that seemed to Europeans childish. Within the animistic "reality" of Natives, however, all living and material objects possessed spiritual power, which the Algonquian called "manitou". They were convinced that "manitou" was concentrated in especially bright and shiny objects like copper ornaments, polished seashells, or the colorful glass beads Europeans offered. "Displayed on the body or carried to the grave, the new trade goods demonstrated high status and access to manitou."[184] Peter Minuit, representative of the Dutch West India Company, "purchased" Manhattan in 1626. He paid the natives 60 guilders (in today's money something around $670).[185] Thinking of the prices paid today for a square meter in New York, this sum in retrospect seems to be ridiculously low. The Lenapes were probably paid in axes, hoes, needles, awls, scissors, knives, and kettles, an enormously useful "high-end technology transfer."[186] Furthermore, the Natives and Dutch didn't have the same concept of possession and of the use of land. For Natives, there was no exclusive right to use the land, a land all had to live from. They lacked the concept of permanent transfer of ownership. It had much more to do with a mixture of rental and an alliance between two communities.[187] For the Dutch, possession was an investment possibility, for the Natives it was a value to be used to create social bonds within a cooperative context.

Constructively speaking, are values not a given, not something to be recognized. They are expectations *orientated to the future, nourished by the past* by our foregoing experiences and *concretized and changed in the pres-*

---

[183] Galbraith, John Kenneth (1994), pp. 31 f.
[184] Taylor, Alan (2001), p. 94
[185] Burrows, Edwin G./Wallace, Mike (1999), p. XV
[186] Id.
[187] Shorto, Russell (2007), pp. 69 f.

ent. These expectations can be securitized by ethical, moral or legal forms of reaction. An ethical support is given if an individual is personally convinced of an expectation. Some want this to be because they think that good people behave this way. Not to meet these expectations toward themselves yields shame and self-criticism. Moral expectations are directed toward others and an infringement could lead to social exclusion. The legal reaction is formalized and has to be paid with money or freedom. Combined with moral and ethical expectations they have the greatest impact on the preservation of values. Actors then defend expectations because they're convinced of their importance and because life with others will be difficult otherwise.

c) Value-based or procedural? Partisanship or neutrality?

Modern society is often described as "over-complex," "pluralistic," and "individualistic,"[188] and because of this *no longer* integrated on the basis of values. The multitude of individual moralities questions the ability of a community to find an answer to integration challenges. If the thesis of plurality and over-complexity is right, then every modern community is threatening to disintegrate. Isolated individuals without common moral grounds can't build a community because philosophical and ethical arbitrariness becomes the dominating form of living. To avoid disintegration institutions have to be established that follow typical procedures and use coercive power.[189] Döbert qualifies modern societies as procedure societies par excellence.[190] And Luhmann states as a prominent exponent of this thesis that social systems are the answer to the high complexity of modern society.[191] These systems have to be widely autonomous not to be disturbed by the environment (see also pp. 153 ff.). They reduce complexity by determining what can happen within the system.[192] Applied to the judicial system, Luhmann highlights the following points for an effective integra-

---

[188] For example Durkheim, Emile (1990), p. 395: "The more societies grow, the more they get complex, division of labour occurs, the differences between the individuals multiply, and at a certain point, there is nothing common anymore for the members of this group beside the fact, that they are human beings." Fuchs, Peter (1992), p. 61: "[Society] is hypercomplex, polycontextural, and because of this (and causing this) heterarchically structured." Fuchs talks of "radical plurality" (p. 81).
[189] Geiger, Thomas (1987), p. 265
[190] Döbert, Rainer (1996), p. 328
[191] Luhmann, Niklas (1989), p. 41
[192] *Id.*, p. 69

tion based on procedures. First, the concrete result of the procedure is of no importance. It has to be accepted, whatever its content, independent of its accuracy.[193] Second, most important is the openness of the procedure. The result of the procedure should not be determined,[194] can be influenced by the defendant. Third, there is a chance to win a further procedure[195] – the loser can hope to be more effective in the next judicial battle. According to Luhmann, procedures include social roles that proscribe possible forms of behavior of the participants.[196] People have to be educated to become part of the procedure, to fulfill the foreseen functions, independent of their personal convictions.[197] According to Luhmann, what matters is a conclusive acceptance of the procedure and the norms applied in a court as an authoritarian institution.[198] Procedural integration is, in my view, nothing more than a power game. It is a form of society building, using coercion to *force the relevant values onto the deviant or opponent*. Refractory losers of a procedure have to be isolated and if necessary excluded, writes Luhmann.[199] In this regard, there is no difference between traditional and modern society.

The differentiation between a *procedural* concept of liberalism that's orientated toward justice, on the one hand, and a *material* (content orientated) concept, based on convictions of the good life, is in my opinion not really helpful.[200] Both need the consensus of the participants to be realized. There's not a difference of quality, but of quantity, of degree. Liberal concepts based on justice accept plurality from the beginning and try to avoid homogenous community concepts, whereas, on the other hand, the convictions of the good tend to monopolize a specific form of living and to exclude everything abnormal. The criticized intolerance of conceptions of the good life comes to the fore in procedural concepts, too, as soon as their basic values are questioned. To suppose that cultural plurality within a liberal society leads automatically to the cultural neutrality of the liberal state and, by this, to its objective rightness, is problematic. As much as the homogenous ver-

---

[193] *Id.*, pp. 4, 29 f.

[194] *Id.*, p. 40, 51, 107; 116. See also Luhmann, Niklas (1993), p. 209

[195] Luhmann, Niklas (1989), p. 77

[196] *Id.*, pp. 82 ff.

[197] *Id.*, p. 111

[198] *Id.*, p. 114

[199] *Id.*, pp. 3 f., 35, 49, 117 ff.

[200] See for this discussion for example: Honneth, Axel (ed.) (1993), pp. 8, 60 f., 78 f., 109 and 122 f., 133 f.. Dreier distinguishes a material and a procedural theory of justice (Dreier, Ralf [1991], p. 19). For Sandel, there is a difference between the national and the procedural republic (Sandel, Michael [1984]).

sion, the liberal one universalizes a form of living at the expense of others. "Liberalism is not a possible meeting ground for all cultures, but is the political expression of one range of cultures, and quite incompatible with other ranges. [...] liberalism can't and shouldn't claim complete cultural neutrality. Liberalism is also a fighting creed."[201] And to realize freedom in an equitable way, there is more needed than just disinterested neutrality. We have to engage in a responsible and solidary way: "You realize good life by preserving liberality every day, by respecting all citizens, by being open minded, tolerant and sensitive to the problems and fights of others, by protecting basic human rights, and by resolving problems using your mind in a violence-free atmosphere, characterized by cooperation."[202]

The procedural concept works, in my opinion, in the reproduction phase. Basic decisions have been taken during the new construction and a part of the integration work has been delegated to a group of people who is responsible to act against offenders (stabilization). Only individual cases of deviant behavior have to be solved (harmonization). Institutionalized procedures provide a certain degree of predictability, without being predetermined. As long as their results are consented to by the ruling majority, as long as they are "acceptable results, making possible further actions,"[203] they fulfill an important integrative role. Ruling the world, self-assured majorities do not have to reflect the values underlying their "reality." It is because of the consensus of the biggest part of the society, the majority's behavior is perceived as "normal," as "standard," and by this as "neutral." "Liberal state," "secular state," "laïcité" stand for political institutions that are independent of any religious movement. There is no religious group dominating the institutions of the state, which makes a plurality of values possible. However, that doesn't mean that these concepts are value-free, or neutral. On the contrary, they incorporate freedom, plurality, and respect – values even defended militarily if threatened. The discussion of the role of Islam in Europe or the USA shows, that freedom isn't simply permission to do whatever one pleases. Time and again the restrictions the majority wants to uphold, have to be discussed. As soon as the conflict reaches the level of deconstruction, the involved values become visible. To secure integration, the former elementary consensus has to be affirmed, or, if necessary, a new one has to be established during new construction. If both are not possible, disintegration will take place.

---

[201] Taylor, Charles (1992), p. 62. Jullien on the contrary defends "universality" in the form of plurality and respect as neutral (Jullien, François [2010], p. 14, 56).
[202] Rockefeller, Steven C. (1992), pp. 99 f.
[203] Döbert, Rainer (1996), p. 331

After the unification of the BRD and the former GDR the new community needed time and several different procedures to find an acceptable solution for abortion. The former GDR had known a quite liberal regulation (abortion was allowed within the first months of pregnancy)[204] and people in the new Bundesländer wanted to preserve this liberty after unification. When the former generous GDR state support for families and single mothers wasn't available anymore,[205] an increasing number of women recurred to abortion, not to lose their university place or their job.[206] These different understandings of life, beginning of life, and the autonomy of women to decide their own future had to be brought to an integrative solution for a united Germany. First, it took parliament a long time to draft a law regulating abortion in a quite liberal way. Then the Bundesverfassungsgericht (the German Supreme Court) declared in 1993 some parts of the law unconstitutional, stating the basic interdiction of abortions, and the duty to deliver the child.[207] In the same decision the court expressed an obligation of the state to do everything necessary to protect women against social or economic emergency situations and disadvantages in education and profession.[208] The unconstitutional parts had to be debated again in parliament and came into effect in 1995. A compromise was found between embryos as "legal persons" and on the other hand the possibility to abort within the first three months. Before medical intervention a woman would have to go to an official information center. Liberals strongly criticized the important influence the German Supreme Court had played during this debate and were especially bothered by its non-democratic, elitist character and its decision against the autonomy of women.[209] Others, however, were convinced that the Court had protected the Constitution against a parliament incapable of deciding within the realm of constitutionality. Even though in-

---

[204] About the history of abortion laws in the GDR see Lippold, Michael W. (2000), pp. 49 ff.

[205] According to Lippold it's not so much the legal rule that shows an impact on the amount of abortions, but the social conditions, women live in (Lippold, Michael W. [2000], pp. 225 f.). Insofar is the will to have children an interactive construction, within which the community plays an important role. The number of births depends not so much on contraceptive methods than on the will to have children (Roloff, Juliane [1997], p. 37), a will, that is heavily influenced by social and economic conditions (*Id.*, pp. 39, 112).

[206] Der Spiegel 20/1990, p. 79

[207] BVerfGE 88, 203, D.I.2 of August 4, 1992. Cf. Eser, Albin (1994), pp. 53, 57

[208] BVerfGE 88, 203, D.I.3

[209] Berghahn, Sabine (1998), pp. 401, 415

stitutionalized procedures were applied, the debate was about values, about the right way to live. And as this conflict has preoccupied western societies since the end of the 1960s, it presumably will rise again. However rational an institution is, however detailed the procedure to be applied is described, it is still a form of conflict resolution that takes part in a power play over the future "reality" and creates values by deciding in favor of some and against others, hence bringing forward a specific value arrangement.

d) Happiness

What makes people happy? According to the idea of consensus-based constructivism, there is no universal answer to this question, if we want to respect the individual's right to be different. The orthodox economic answer would be: The more income and assets one has, the happier he or she is, which suits the ideology of the consumer society. But according to Graham, "focusing purely on income can miss key elements of welfare. People have different preferences for material and non-material goods."[210] "Income surely matters to happiness among individuals within countries, but other key variables, such as age, marital and employment status, and health, matter as much (if not more in some instances)."[211] Interestingly, people adapt quickly to income gains, which means that its positive effect on happiness gets lost soon, whereas the effect of status gains lasts much longer.[212] According to this, it's not material wealth that matters most, but the recognition we get from others. Consumer societies are characterized by a happiness-paradox: On the one hand, material progress is the major motive of the individualistic consumer. The growth-based economy, on the other hand, *only works if the consumer is never satisfied*. Like the hamster on his wheel the consumer is continually running after a happiness that should never be reached, otherwise the wheel comes to a halt. It is, therefore, the unhappiness of the individual that makes the economy happy.

In consensus-based constructivism is *happiness an interactive construction*. Satisfaction with the developed arrangements leads to high approval rates. If freedom and justice count, we first have to make sure that individuals experience *equal construction opportunities*. Thus, we have to avoid direct, structural, and/or cultural violence. These forms of violence reduce the ability of people to live or act, to make independent decisions, or to

---

[210] Graham, Carol (2009), p. 7
[211] *Id.*, p. 48
[212] *Id.*, p. 154

think in alternatives (p. 77 ff.). Second, *political as much as social or economic insecurity should be avoided*, because insecurity leads to fear and fear to paralysis. A highly problematic future makes people risk-averse and hinders them from establishing trust. "Insecurity is associated with lower happiness levels. [...] As is the case of being able to insure against future income shocks by saving, the ability to insure against future health shocks seems to have positive effects on happiness above and beyond those of wealth and education levels."[213] It is constant uncertainty and by this: anxiety that has an important influence on the quality of life.[214] I approve these statements not because they're the objective truth, but because they suit my concept of humankind. They especially reflect the idea that contingency is a burden for the individual's life (see p. 92 ff.). Unpredictability puts our construction-power under permanent threat. To enhance this uncertainty and unpredictability by a competitive social arrangements doesn't further quality of life.

Feeling unhappy is bearable if it is a transient state, because it will probably change in the future. If alternatives are available and are within reach, hope prevails. That people are happy even though they are poor economically has a lot to do with the expectations and the possibilities one has to reach one's goals. Rulers who want to keep the underclass in their inferior status have to work on their expectations. Using cultural violence, poverty and inequality can be constructed as "natural," "divine," or "eternally given." If the construction works, the underclass will fatalistically resign to its destiny. They will be happy to reach the goals assigned to them. "Individuals are remarkably adaptable [...] and in the end can get used to most things."[215] Against this background, it is "typically not the poorest people who are most frustrated or unhappy with their conditions or the services that they have access to."[216] As soon as people perceive inequality as man-made, it becomes a source of unhappiness, if it is "high and persistent."[217] Lacking the power to alter the injustice, "[...] concerns for relative income differences arise at surprisingly low levels of income."[218] Even if people improve their material situation, inequality outweighs it.[219] An effective upper-class answer is the American dream, which individualizes poverty and

---

[213] *Id.*, pp. 129 f.
[214] *Id.*, pp. 139 f., 142
[215] *Id.*, p. 15
[216] *Id.*, p. 151
[217] *Id.*, p. 132. See also 154.
[218] *Id.*, p. 158
[219] *Id.*, p. 165

makes everybody self-responsible for whatever he or she achieves. By relentless hard work everybody can succeed. This lure generates high hopes, nurtured by Hollywood stories about the proverbial dishwasher's success and some statistical outliers corroborating this ideology. Out of this hope follows happiness,[220] because the current state is only a transitional vale of tears. The ones not succeeding despite trying have to come to grips with this personal defeat. In my view, a network of support and a lot of luck is needed to become successful. We, therefore, have to take care that everybody gets the chance to *shape her or his own life*. Happiness is greatest when a mixture of freedom and support are available … in cooperation.

e) Everything is about values

Basic values can be used to *characterize communities*. Neoliberal capitalism is an individualistic concept of "reality," which doesn't expect any solidary behavior of the people because the market will integrate the isolated monads. The only task of individuals is to selfishly follow their interests. Actually this is not even a task because it is their nature to be egoistic, so they do not have a choice. An individualistic concept of freedom is at the core of the neoliberal value system, solidarity doesn't exist, and everybody is just responsible for her- or himself. And if they don't want to be responsible, that's all right, too. The endangered lives of people fare away who are working for multinational companies are nothing we have to care about. Justice plays a role only with regard to the market structure, which shouldn't be monopolistic or oligopolistic. "Classic liberalism" wasn't interested in solidarity, but it did insist on the responsibility, for example, of the "patrons" for their employees or the well-being of the nation. Justice has to be respected, but freedom stays dominant. The entrepreneur with morality is the representative of classical liberalism and the short-sighted bonus orientated manager represents the neoliberal "reality". Two experiences motivate communitarianism: First, the accelerated individualization has a destructive effect on communities. Second, freedom is a philistine concept originating out of nothing. A substantial communitarianism propagates the prerogative of the community over the individual (for example Alasdair MacIntyre or Michael Sandel) and by this the prerogative of solidarity over freedom. The more liberal communitarianism refers to an enlarged idea of values, which originate in community (for example Charles Taylor's dialogue based self). Accordingly, liberal freedom conceptions have

---

[220] Bok, Derek (2010), p. 79. Bok therefore concludes that inequality isn't the problem.

to be moderated by equity and solidarity. Authoritarian Socialism in the form of the Soviet Union or the Chinese party dictatorship isn't interested in freedom or responsibility. The only behavior that counts is obedience toward the collective, represented by the party. Obedience in these cases means overall solidarity, limited personal interests and justice in the sense of equal opportunity (even though party members may be a bit more equal than others). If individuals act against the clear will of the nation, their life doesn't count. There is no limit to the power of the authority. According to Article 37 § 1[221] and 41 § 1[222] of the Chinese constitution personal liberty and freedom of speech are guaranteed. But these civil rights have to step back as soon as national interests are concerned:

> **Article 51 Constitution**
>
> The exercise by citizens of the People's Republic of China of their freedoms and rights may not infringe upon the interests of the state, of society and of the collective, or upon the lawful freedoms and rights of other citizens.

Since Deng Xioaping, however, economic freedom has gained in importance. For minorities, the Chinese constitution guarantees their equality and protects them from discrimination and against oppression. "The people of all nationalities have the freedom to use and develop their own spoken and written languages, and to preserve or reform their own ways and customs."[223] At the same time the prerogative of the "unity of the nationalities", the interdiction of secession,[224] and in general the "unity of the country"[225] prevail. National Socialists used the same value-order. Justice, however, was reserved only for blue-eyed blond-haired Aryans, and the right to life of Jews didn't exist from 1941 on.

---

[221] Article 37 § 1 Constitution: The personal freedom of citizens of the People's Republic of China is inviolable.
[222] Article 41 §1 Constitution: Citizens of the People's Republic of China have the right to criticize and make suggestions to any state organ or functionary. Citizens have the right to make to relevant state organs complaints and charges against, or exposures of, any state organ or functionary for violation of the law or dereliction of duty.
[223] Article 4 Constitution
[224] Article 4 Constitution
[225] Article 52 Constitution

L = (⇑); J = ⇓, F ⇑ S = 0, R ⇓	L = (⇑); J < F, R ⇑, S ⇓	L = (⇑); J ⇑, F = 0, R = 0, S ⇑
Neoliberalism	Liberalism	Sowjet or Chinese Socialism
L = 0, J ⇓ , F = 0, R = 0, S ⇑	L = ⇑; J > F, R ⇓, S ⇑	L = ⇑; J < F, R ⇑, S ⇓
National Socialist Totalitarianism	Communitarianism	Constitutional welfare democracy

L = Life; I = Integrity; J = Justice; F = Freedom; S = Solidarity; R = Responsibility

⇑ = big; ⇓ = small; 0 = inexistent

E. Integration elements

Market-based integration is simple: Do whatever you want, the rest is up to the market. This model of the individual and its relation to others best suits the logic of the consumer society ... self-orientation and short-termism. Sustainability and long-term planning includes the respect of others, the environment, and the next generations and is not simply motivated by economic reflections, but looks for a just repartition of construction power over time. In this chapter I describe the elements we should be aware of if we want to take equal freedom seriously and avoid exclusionary mechanisms that will lead to violent clashes. These elements reflect the afore-presented idea of mutual dependence and support and highlight a cooperative form of interaction.

1. Basic values

Basic values are *general expectations*, a orienting of our actions in a broad direction without determining exactly how to behave. They are permanently concretized and enriched by problems to be solved, by successful solutions found, by failures, and by the hopes people don't want to give up. Nurtured by experiences with others they change their content as well as their importance, their encouraging character, and their identificatory attraction. Thus, the general expectations incorporated in values are "interacting" with everyday experiences in politics, economics, culture, and the personal or wider social realm. "Democracy" contains an important promise of self-ruling autonomy and freedom. This promise has to prove its validity day in and day out, not just in official speeches. If its members aren't recognized and respected, they do not know what happens in government, and can't be sure that criticism has an impact on politics, then people will prefer a monarchy with an identifiable leader and a convincing staging, rooted in the past and giving the impression it will last forever. The freedom that democracy promises isn't interesting if it doesn't go along with construction power. Frustrated freedom-expectations often motivate an opting for an authoritarian regime.

There is a form of discourse between general values, concretizing forms of action, and the structure that the political community builds up. Basic values help to make decisions. These decisions in turn highlight what it means to be free within this community and which form of solidarity can be expected. In the neoliberal "reality" the meaning of freedom became clear in the deregulation process beginning in the 80's and with the enhanced individualization and competition (concretization). Leading to the financial market crisis, this experience will hopefully have an impact on the prevailing basic values and on the understanding of freedom, which should be more than just the absence of obligation (critical reflection). It also highlighted the necessity to find new structures that incorporate companies into a cooperative setup that is focused on the common good.

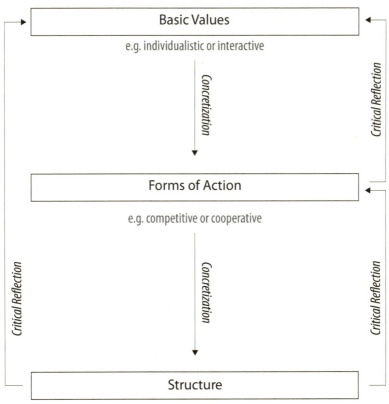

a) Life as hope

Human beings are fragile and existentially interdependent. A person needs considerable support and recognition to develop the desire to live and to have the courage to be free. Reciprocity structures help to overcome ones own limits. And people taking their responsibilities for their "reality" aren't restricted by boundaries imposed by others. Equal access to the construction process and respect for differences guarantee dignity. These complex appearances of human relationships are, in my opinion, made possible by the following five basic values:

There is no prerogative of any of these values. All of them are needed, all of them are constitutive for each other. That also accounts for life, which is conceived here as much as of a constitutive as a dependent value. In the consensus-based constructivism human nature is undetermined. To make freedom out of this indeterminacy needs the support of parents and others. Equally shared resources are needed and alternatives have to be reachable or at least imaginable to establish construction power. Because of this interdependence between members of the community, irresponsible and unjust use of freedom will lead to counterpower or even exclusion and then to the loss of freedom itself. Freedom without solidarity doesn't exist and freedom without responsibility and justice destroys its bases.

aa) Social construction of life

On May 31, 2009, George Tiller's life was taken by a pro-life activist who defended life as an absolute value. The assassin was convinced that Tiller, director of a clinic providing late-term abortions, was a "mass-murderer" and, therefore, had to be killed to protect the unborn life. Life, perceived as an absolute value, is taken to protect life – a paradoxical answer to a problem that has complex ramifications. On a constructivist base, life is *not* a given, it is *not* something that simply exists and has to be respected because of its sole existence. Arguing this way would be a naturalistic fallacy,[1] helpful for the ones who want to delegate their responsibility to decide to nature and restrict or even end freedom. In my opinion, life is procreated, is given birth, nourished, protected, clothed, healed, supported psychologically, motivated, educated, and so forth. Its existence as much as its quality depend on the engagement of people. An absolutist position that doesn't take into account the comprehensive social origins of life, becomes, in my view, destructive. What is needed are not unquestionable principles enforced against all critical reflection. Moral, social, economic, or medical support is needed for people who do not feel able to be responsible for the life of a child. Won't the life both of the child and the parents be miserable if they're not helped morally and financially, or if the parents aren't motivated at all to take care of the vulnerable toddler? The life we want to protect is seriously endangered if we do not take into account the future conditions the person will live in. Undesired children run the high risk of dying during their first year[2] or of being abused.[3] Forcing people to have a child is at the origin of many traumas and diseases.[4] Good parents aren't created by force, but by personal conviction and a network of cooperative support.

According to the Federal Court of Switzerland, the life of a human being is worth CHF 100'000.- a year.[5] The judges had to determine whether health insurers are obliged to pay the treatment of a woman suffering from Morbus Pomp. For reasons of justice (equality of human beings) and against the background of limited financial resources, the funds have to be rationed, entitling everybody to limited benefits. The CHF 750'000 to 900'000.- that patient would have needed was, therefore, denied. Would all sick people in the same situation get the support the plaintiff claimed for, costs of about CHF 90 Billion would have resulted – according to the court 1.6 times the yearly amount of the health care costs in Switzerland, and therefore not bearable. To decide, who is entitled to get medical treatment, the so called "senior death discount" takes into account years of life expectancy. Persad et al. defend this "complete lives system" which prioritizes younger people who have not yet lived a complete life, because it satisfies

---

[1] Lippold, Michael W. (2000), pp. 336 ff.
[2] Amendt, Gerhard/Schwarz, Michael (1990), p. 69
[3] Id., p. 123
[4] Id., p. 163
[5] BGE 9C_334/2010, decided on November 23, 2010.

all ethical requirements for just allocation.[6] The following five principles are therefore relevant: 1. Youngest-first (the ones with the least life years), 2. prognosis for saved life-years, 3. number of lives saved, 4. lottery (random selection, treating everybody as equal), and 5. instrumental (future usefulness). If this system is implemented, individuals aged between 15 and 40 years will profit most. It is, in my view, a political question, how much a community is willing to spend for saving a life. Considering the increases in health care costs, decisions like reducing defense expenditure or increasing taxes have an impact on the lives that could be saved.

The support structure needed to help people manage their lives as satisfyingly as possible has also to be established in the terminal phase of life. Terry Schiavo's case can be understood as a conflict between an absolute concept of life and the claim for an autonomous decision about the moment when life isn't worth being lived. Terri Schiavo suffered a cardiac arrest on February 25, 1990, which injured her brain due to a lack of oxygen. There was no living will and the County Court decided her husband, Michael Schiavo, was her legal guardian, a decision at this point not disputed by her parents. Up until 1994, different forms of therapy were applied to try to reanimate her brain activity. However, it was in vain. "Her neurologic examinations were indicative of a persistent vegetative state, which included periods of wakefulness alternating with sleep, some reflexive responses to light and noise, and some basic gag and swallowing responses, but no signs of emotion, willful activity, or cognition. There is no evidence that Ms. Schiavo was suffering, since the usual definition of this term requires conscious awareness that is impossible in the absence of cortical activity."[7] According to Judge Greer, Michael Schiavo had been "very motivated in pursuing the best medical care for his wife."[8] In May 1998 Michael Schiavo filed a petition to remove the feeding tube. Judge Greer approved because five witnesses confirmed that Terry had expressed the wish that, in such a case, she would want life support to be removed.[9] According to the medical experts, she had "no hope of ever regaining consciousness and, therefore, capacity, and that without the feeding tube she will die in seven to fourteen days."[10] The Schindler family didn't want to accept the diagnosis of persistent vegetative state and was convinced that her condition could improve

---

[6] Persad, Govind/Wertheimer, Alan/Emanuel, Ezekiel J. (2009), p. 428
[7] Quill, Timothy E. (2005), p. 1630
[8] Greer, George W., Circuit Judge (2000-02-11). "In re: the guardianship of Theresa Marie Schiavo, Incapacitated," File No. 90-2908GD-003, p. 3
[9] Id., p. 9
[10] Id., p. 6

with additional treatment. They took different legal steps, but the Florida Second District Court of Appeal upheld the decision to end artificial hydration and nutrition. Their appeals to the Florida and the U.S. Supreme Court were denied a hearing. There were possibly other motives at stake than only altruistic ones. The very good relationship Michael Schiavo had with Terry's parents broke down in 1993. He had received compensation for malpractice leading to her cardiac arrest: $300'000 for loss of consortium. Further, $700'000 for the Guardianship of Terri Schiavo was to be used for medical treatment. The severance of this "amicable relationship [...] was predicated upon money and the fact that Mr. Schiavo was unwilling to equally divide his loss of consortium award with Mr. and Mrs. Schindler. The parties have literally not spoken since that date. Regrettably, money overshadows this entire case and creates potential of conflict of interest for both sides."[11] There was also debate about who would inherit the estate of Terry.

This part of the conflict could be called "semi-private." "In tens of thousands of cases each year, patients and families handle catastrophic illness or injury without going to court. They do so with unsung courage, in the face of fear, anguish, and sometimes bitterness. [...] end-of-life questions are almost always resolved in the private sphere, by patients, their physicians, and their family members, working with nurses, social workers, and members of the clergy."[12] To be just, the *individual* case has to be judged on the grounds of the concrete circumstances, trying to defend the interests of the patient according to her or his personality. The law and by this those not directly concerned should only set the basic rules without intervening too much by regulating details. Life is too complex and manifold to be controlled. As long as the interests of the patient are respected as well as possible, families in cooperation with the medical staff seem to be the appropriate forum in these existential situations. "[...] caregivers should encourage conversation about end-of-life questions among patients, family members, and others who are closely involved. And when the clinical picture takes a catastrophic turn and a patient can no longer formulate preferences, caregivers should give high priority to detecting hints of discord. At the first sign of tension, physicians, nurses, and social workers should become active listeners in search of smoldering feelings that might give rise to conflict."[13] Also makes the absence of external interventions mourning easier. We are *responsible to support and protect life, but not to force one to live*.

---

[11] *Id.*, p. 2
[12] Bloche, Gregg M. (2005), p. 2371
[13] *Id.*, pp. 2372 f.

In the case of Terri Schiavo, private conflict resolution wasn't possible, which is why court decisions were needed and helpful. Besides the protection of the patient and possible material interests that had to be taken into account, decisions about ending the life of a person are incredibly difficult, sometimes exceeding the capacities of family and friends. There is, however, a second act in this drama, when the originally private conflict was exploited by right-wing Republicans for their battle for the absolute. They tried to push through their exclusive truth, regardless the dignity and autonomy of the concerned people. On October 20 and 21, 2003, the Florida Legislature hastily passed "Terri's Law," giving Governor Jeb Bush, brother of President George W. Bush, the right to intervene in the case. Using his new power he ordered the feeding tube to be reinserted. This law is a one-case law, as the Governor's authority lasted only for 15 days. On May 5, 2004, the Florida Circuit Court held: Terri's Law "is unconstitutional on its face because it is an unconstitutional delegation of legislative power to the Governor and because it unjustifiably authorizes the Governor to summarily deprive Florida citizens of their constitutional right to privacy."[14] Finally, on September 23, 2004, the Florida Supreme Court judges over the appeal of Jeb Bush and confirms the violation of the constitutional principle of separation of powers. Jeb Bush's appeal to the U.S. Supreme Court was denied a hearing (January 24, 2005). On March 8, 2005, the fight over the life of Terri Schiavo became a federal affair, as Republican Representative David Weldon introduced legislation to force review of cases of incapacitated persons by the federal courts.[15] US media tycoon, Robert Herring, offered Michael Schiavo one million dollars for passing the Guardianship on to Terri's parents, which he declined to do. To avoid the removal of the feeding tube after another decision of Judge Greer on March 18, 2005, the House Government Reform Committee subpoenaed Michael and Terri (!) Schiavo to appear at a hearing in Washington concerning an inquiry into the long-term care of incapacitated adults. Another draft[16] was introduced in the Senate and approved by the three present Senators (Palm Sunday Compromise, March 25, 2005). As no one opposed the absence of the other Senators, a quorum was reached. Contrary to the draft in the House of Representatives, this one focused only on the Schiavo case, as it granted the

---

[14] Baird, W. Douglas, Circuit Judge. (2005-05-05). "Michael Schiavo, as Guardian of the person of Theresa Marie Schiavo, Petitioner, v. Jeb Bush, Governor of the State of Florida, and Charlie Crist, Attorney General of the State of Florida, Respondents, Case No. 03-008212-CI-20"
[15] H.R. 1151
[16] S. 686: Terri Schiavo Incapacitated Protection bill

jurisdiction of the US District Court for the Middle District of Florida for alleged violations of the rights of Terri Schiavo without regard to prior state court decisions. Only her parents were entitled to file a suit and the validity of the law was limited to thirty days after its enactment. On March 21, 2005, the law was approved by the House of Representatives, 41 % of its members being absent. President Bush came to Washington, suspending his holiday, to sign the law half an hour immediately afterwards.[17] Ten days later Terri Schiavo died.

Defending their absolute conviction, in my view, Republicans were ready crossing elementary constitutional limits that protect the individual and the states against abuse of power. First, laws should be prospective and not retrospective and ruling a previously unknown amount of cases and people (general and impersonal quality). Second, parliament acted like a court, not respecting the separation of power. Third, the right of patients to refuse extraordinary life-saving treatment, established in Cruzan v. Missouri Dep't of Health, wasn't respected. Fourth, all the personal and legal debates that took place during the foregoing seven years weren't taken into account. A lot of people tried in an almost uncountable number and a variety of proceedings to find a suitable solution. Many different aspects were discussed, indicating that the involved people took the problem seriously. On the federal level, though, there are serious indications, that not only ethical convictions and compassion played an important role, but also "political point-scoring, [...] symbolic, politicized legislating,"[18] satisfying political ambition.[19] As this case shows, legal provisions do not guarantee a specific conflict resolution. What law finally is and which form of legal protection individuals get, depends on the people acting on behalf of the law (see p. 320 ff.).

The improvement of reanimation techniques forces the medical staff to rethink if and when an intervention has to take place. In Switzerland, for example, the responsibility to decide whether people are alive or dead has been delegated to the medical science. In 1972 decided the Federal Court of Switzerland that "a person is dead [...] as soon as vital body functions totally and irrevocably end working. Medical science has to decide about the

---

[17] Paradoxically, in 2005, six-month-old infant Sun Hudson dies after his life-sustaining treatment was discontinued. The first time in the USA artificial nutrition was stopped against the will of a guardian, in the case his mother. The decision was taken in application of the Texas Advance Directives Act, a bill, Governor George W. Bush had signed into law in 1999.

[18] Lazarus, Edward (2005)

[19] Cassel, Elaine (2005)

relevant criteria. Because of [...] new scientific knowledge the former death diagnose based on cardiac arrest respectively circulation arrest has been questioned fundamentally. [...] While the failure of the respiratory and cardiac activity can be compensated, it is recognized that a total failure of brain activity can't be remedied."[20] Presently relevant are the "Richtlinien der Schweizerischen Akademie der Medizinischen Wissenschaft" from 2005 concerning, for example, the decision about reanimation or the relevant point in time for organ transplantations. The end of our life lies, therefore, to a considerable degree in the hands of a few people called "doctors."

bb)   Hope from support

Values understood in an absolute sense are norms independent of time, geography, culture, or people. Certain forms of behavior are proscribed independent of the conflict they apply to. To rein in human contingency, eternal and universal validity is claimed as an unquestionable given. Against an interactive backdrop, though, values aren't given, they are made. Whatever we want to be valuable gets this quality, because we are able to convince ourselves and others to engage in this future. It is within a network of cooperative or competitive people, of supportive, indifferent, or abusive people that a person builds up hope. Without hope, there is no expectation, fatalism reigns and the necessary passion for life doesn't occur, it fades away.

In 1995 Jean-Dominique Bauby, journalist and editor of the French magazine ELLE suffered a stroke that totally paralyzed him – except the control of his left eyelid. His mind intact, he was a prisoner in his body. His speech therapist, Henriette Durand, realized that he could communicate. She was willing to "listen," to try to enter into communication with Bauby. She realized that by moving his eyelid he was able to interact. She developed a communication system that gave him the opportunity to triumph over his useless body's limits. According to the frequency of the letters in French, she recited the alphabet and Bauby winked to choose the one he needed. Publisher Robert Laffont commissioned former ghostwriter, Claude Mendibil, to work with him over two months, seven days a week, three hours a day, to write down the manuscript of the a 130-page book[21] Bauby dictated, using over 200'000 blinks. Three days after the book was published, he died.

What, if there is no reaction to bedside stimuli? These people awake from the acute comatose state without any sign of consciousness. Monti et al. try to determine with the MRI whether somebody is in a vegetative state

---

[20]   BGE 98 Ia 508, 515 f.
[21]   Bauby, Jean-Dominique (1998)

or whether the patient retains the capacity for a purposeful response to stimulation. If there is communication, subsequent care and rehabilitation can be implemented because there is hope for improvement. "[…] a small proportion of patients in a vegetative or minimally conscious state have brain activation reflecting some awareness and cognition. Careful clinical examination will result in reclassification of the state of consciousness in some of these patients. This technique may be useful in establishing basic communication with patients who appear to be unresponsive."[22]

The passion to live and for life has to be brought up by others within ourselves, and to be preserved and nurtured by our own decisions day in and day out. It is hope, the hope for betterment, that keeps people alive even in dire straits. "[…] people need no medicine more than hope."[23] Having made the experience that life is valuable, it grows in importance, which is why it's not easily given up anymore. Then, "the belief in the meaning of life is incorporated in every fibre of human beings, it's an essence of human nature."[24] Without hope though, life is meaningless, which is why some people hope to find relief in ending life: "People get vulnerable to death when they have to take the lesson that their actions are in vain and hopeless."[25] Suicide is, therefore, the decision of a person, opting for the least negative choice. There aren't any alternatives left attractive enough to balance the difficulties people are in.[26]

Hope is increased if reciprocal structures are established and every individual life is protected in its complexity. Solidarity, the contact with supportive others, is accordingly essential to stay alive and to enjoy life. It's not for nothing that incommunicado detention is used in various countries as a technique either to break the resistance of people or to torture them in hidden places. According to the Commission on Human Rights, "prolonged incommunicado detention may facilitate the perpetration of torture and can in itself constitute a form of cruel, inhuman or degrading treatment.[27] This fragile arrangement is put at risk when some are abused or excluded.

---

[22] Monti, Martin M. et al. (2010), p. 1
[23] Becker, Jurek (1976), p. 193
[24] Levi, Primo (1998), p. 84. Primo Levi was a Jewish Italian chemist and writer, deported to Auschwitz in 1944.
[25] Seligman, Martin E.P. (1999), p. 160
[26] Lindner-Braun, Christa (1990), p. 35, 59
[27] Commission on Human Rights resolution 1997/38, para. 20

cc) Bringing people to kill

Mass-killing is nothing natural; it is not ingrained in human nature. There is, in the consensus-based constructivism, no aggressive instinct that sometimes suddenly breaks through the crust of civilization established by education. Violence and especially mass killing is a socially constructed tool used for specific purposes. It is not an easy thing to create killers (see also p. 157 ff.). When people had positive experiences with others, when they had had the opportunity to be respected, loved, or supported, life will be of great value. Because hurting or killing others is hurting or killing a little bit of oneself, there are deep seated reticencies to be overcome.

Absolute denial of life took place in the Rwanda Genocide in 1994. Hundreds of thousands (at least 500'000, some estimations go as high as 1'000'000) of Tutsi and moderate Hutu were killed within about hundred days. Contrary to he systematic mass killing of the Holocaust, the Rwanda Genocide was more "hand-made" and seemed to be a spontaneous outbreak of hate. Typically the murderers (militia, neighbors, or fellow villagers) hacked their victims with machetes, the militia also used rifles. This genocide wasn't due to a barbaric state of civilization or a genetically inevitable ethnic conflict. It was organized, planned, and willfully constructed by extremist Hutus. "[...] mass violence [...] must be organized; it does not occur aimlessly. Even mobs and riots have a design, and great and sustained destruction requires great ambition. It must be conceived as the means toward achieving a new order [...], compellingly simple and at the same time absolute."[28] As ideology "Hutu Power" was used. This absolutist concept, published in the form of the "Hutu Ten Commandments" in 1990, propagated a separation between Hutu and Tutsi or a clear domination of the Hutu over the Tutsi: No intermarriage, the Rwandan Armed Forces should only be Hutu, all strategic positions in politics, administration, or the economy had to be entrusted to Hutu, the education sector should be dominated by Hutu, and Hutus should never trust the always dishonest Tutsi. The government used different means to build up the hatred needed for this slaughter: Systematic propaganda, supported by the very effective Radio Télévision Libre des Milles Collines, demagogic speeches and songs of Hutu popstars, recurring massacres in the nineties also understood as exercises in killing, and a form of apartheid. The collective identities used in this conflict weren't traditional ones that had existed over centuries. In their competitive and finally deadly exclusivity they were the result of a "dual

---

[28] Gourevitch, Philip (1999), p. 17

colonialism"[29] fostered by the colonizing Germans at the end of the nineteenth century. According to Chrétien, being Tutsi or Hutu didn't mean the same in 1594, when the communities began to build in 1794, when the kingdoms were at their pinnacle in 1894, or when the Europeans arrived, or in 1994, during the genocide.[30] Originally "Tutsi" or "Hutu" were clans, structuring-criteria that helped to integrate people. These delimitations weren't used as exclusionary tools (see p. 89 ff.). Interconnections transcending the clans over a wide geographical area were common and stood for the identities' openness.[31] According to Shyaka, neither "race", nor "cast" nor "class" nor "ethnic group" applies to this loose network of interrelated people.[32] "During the pre-colonial era, the Hutus, Tutsis, and the Twas of Rwanda [were groups that] swore allegiance to the same monarch, 'Umwami', had the same culture, the same language 'Ikinyarwanda' – and lived together on the same territory from time immemorial. That set of links was also an important element of social cohesion. Everybody recognized one another as being Banyarwanda [people of Rwanda]."[33] It is only as a European import that the identities were constructed as absolute and that ethnicity became a manipulative element in politics,[34] overshadowing the multitude of former relationships. Protected and supported by the Germans, the Tutsi built up their hegemony over the Hutu. The Belgians, taking over Rwanda after the First World War, used the polarization of the now clearly defined two ethnic groups for their colonial interests, reproducing and strengthening these identities. The unity in language, religion, and law got lost and ethnicity became taken for granted.

Genocides are used by the ruling majority to constitute and stabilize its identity. It is an "exercise in community building."[35] Scapegoat politic helps to legitimize coming atrocities: "[…] the ideology […] of genocide was promoted as a way not to create suffering but to alleviate it. The spectre of an absolute menace that requires absolute eradication binds leader and people in a hermetic utopian embrace."[36] People have to be conditioned to be able to kill others. The same can be said about love.

---

[29] *Id.*, p. 54
[30] Chrétien, Jean-Pierre (2000), p. 68
[31] *Id.*, pp. 73 ff.
[32] Shyaka, Anastase (2005), pp. 3 f.
[33] *Id.*, p. 5
[34] *Id.*, p. 12
[35] Gourevitch, Philip (1999), p. 95
[36] *Id.*, p. 95

b) Freedom as work in progress

The be free means to have the *power to construct the "reality" that suits our interests*. Construction power is a *grant, asked for by us and given by others*. That's why the amount of power we have depends on the readiness of others not to oppose our "reality" proposals and even to support them. This is especially the case when the intended construction goes beyond our individual capacities, which is most of the time.

aa) Contingency – freedom

People are not born free, they are born undetermined. Indetermination stands for genetical openness … everything is possible. Whatever people want to accomplish, they will be able to. With the necessary support of others, every thinkable "reality" can be constructed. Indetermination also means, that the *future isn't foreseeable, it is contingent*. It might be different of what we already know. Contingency doesn't mean that change has to come. But change can take place at any time in any form. Many a people like stability so they try to establish social arrangements which make the future predictable. Social conventions and technical measures can reduce the probability of unforeseen events. In a casino, for example, many different measures are taken to control the improbable. Staff and clients have to adhere to strict rules. Big money is invested in security and in machines running precisely and reliably. Insofar is "[…] gambling sterilized and domesticated uncertainty. In the casino you know the rules, you can calculate the odds, and the type of uncertainty we encounter there."[37] The financial markets, however, in the form developed over the last thirty years, had much more to do with Russian roulette than with the risk-controlled games of hazard. The goal wasn't to stabilize society, but to make as much money as fast as possible, whoever would have to pay the price. Successful thanks to the financial-market-Russian-roulette, they didn't care about the future and they opposed regulations. Clearly defending the homo oeconomicus concept of "*freedom from*" (obligations), responsibility for the future was and is not the problem of economically active individuals. This irresponsible freedom is justified by the wondrous and perfect functioning of the market, which shouldn't be disturbed by regulations. Trying to rein in the worst effects the homines economici produced, the US Congress enacted the Financial Reform Bill. Promoting a responsible freedom (*freedom for*),

---

[37] Taleb, Nassim Nicholas (2008), p. 127

president Obama said: "[…] our market is only free, when there are clear rules and basic safeguards, that prevent abuse, that check access, that ensure that it is more profitable to play by the rules than to game the system."[38] Legal rules alone won't be enough. As long as the main actors are passionately willing and supported by many others to go on as before, creative new ways will be found. The law has to be supported by a moral and ethical self-restraint, an economic and managerial culture that contains elements of responsibility, solidarity, and modesty. The so-called "elite" has to become aware that their freedom is given and made possible by the people. Without them, they wouldn't be.

We are born *undetermined but not free* because freedom is a *resource-intensive social construction*. Indetermination opens to infinite possibilities without guaranteeing any specific relationship. Indetermination is the precondition of freedom, but doesn't automatically lead to it: Freedom is possible, but not a sure thing. On the other hand, freedom is a form of contingency reduction because it is a social arrangement that's usually developed over time and anchored in the culture and history of a community. Out of the limitless possibilities undetermined human beings can realize, the freedom that is built up interactively by individuals restricts on just a few forms of action. It nevertheless gives people the opportunity to act according to their wishes within the scope the community thinks is currently possible and admissible.

bb) Interactively constructed

The 1776 United States Declaration of Independence, the Massachusetts Constitution of 1780, and the French Declaration of the Rights of Men and of the Citizen of 1789 are proclamations of a universal and natural freedom. As proposals they have to be heard, taken seriously and supported by as many people as possible to become a shared "reality." It is an intense construction process that can take any direction. "We now take these principles to be 'self-evident.' But what did they mean in 1776, when an […] observer might […] conclude that all men were created unequal, and when the impartial historian would report that no government had ever been instituted on the basis of popular consensus? And what about those 'unalienable' rights that all men were supposed to enjoy but had been denied to virtually every people through history?"[39] The political aspect of freedom,

---

[38] President Obama, July 21, 2010, signing into law the Financial Reform Bill.
[39] Onuf, Peter S. (2008), p. IX

its social foundation becomes evident when we have a look at the "universality" of the aforementioned declarations. Universality wasn't intended. It was an effective argument to fight the elite of the time and to help the upcoming bourgeoisie to take over power. These biased universal claims were *not* aimed at liberating *everybody* and accepting them *all* as equal, as can be seen in the twenty-seventh grievance concretizing the preamble of the Declaration of Independence. Who are the people who have to dissolve the political bands? Who holds these truths to be self-evident? It's not every man and woman, and it's especially not the "king nor his helpers, the 'merciless savages' and 'domestic insurrectionists.'"[40] With the "merciless savages" Congress excluded African Americans and Native Americans from the community to be built. Exposing the king's tyranny, the grievances helped to unite a multifarious group of people. Combined with long-held prejudices against Blacks and Natives that had grown throughout the colonial period, an elementary consensus began to be established. For political needs of independence, Congress played upon these racist fears "in the name, and by authority of the good people of the colonies."[41] Thomas Jefferson, however, with the approval of John Adams and Benjamin Franklin, intended true universalism when he criticized in his original draft the slave trade waged by King George III as a "cruel war against human nature itself, violating it's most sacred rights of life & liberty in the persons of a distant people who never offended him, captivating & carrying them into slavery in another hemisphere, or to incur miserable death in their transportation thither." He, therefore wasn't surprised that the King "is now exciting those very people to rise in arms among us."[42] In complaisance to South Carolina and Georgia, Congress struck out the clause criticizing the slave trade. The second part, though, was withheld, stating the "exciting domestic insurrections amongst us." Congress was well aware of the pains slaves had to endure, which made insurrections against the colonists and conspiracies with the British quite probable and even understandable.[43] They nevertheless used populist and xenophobic statements to mobilize white colonists and to create by this the "American people." This doesn't totally delegitimize the proposal of liberty and equality and the impressive courage of the few people sitting in Philadelphia. But it highlights the *political aspects of the construction and of the use of freedom.*

---

[40] Parkinson, Robert G. (2008), p. 17
[41] *Id.*, pp. 17 f.
[42] Cited in Kaplan, Sidney (1976), p. 244
[43] Kaplan, Sidney (1976), pp. 249 ff.; 253 f.; 255. See also Armitage, David (2007), pp. 59 f.

Likewise the French Revolution served mainly the male wealthy white bourgeoisie. The universalistic statements in the French Declaration of the Rights of Men and of the Citizen only meant men, not women and not slaves. And the Constitution of 1791 distinguished between the propertied active citizens and the poorer passive citizens. Only active citizens were given the right to vote.[44] And to be a propertied active citizen one had to pay at least a tax amount of three days of salary,[45] what counted for about 15 % of the population. According to Olympe de Gouges, the universally understood declaration didn't really help women in their life and was exclusively oriented to the interests of men.[46] De Gouges, born 1748 in Montauban, Languedoc, was interested in writing, even though he wasn't allowed to go to school. She wrote plays and engaged herself in political publications from 1788 on – considered an unseemly activity for women at the time. Her Declaration of the Rights of Woman and the Female Citizen of 1791 was a criticism and an answer to the questions raised by the Declaration of 1789. The seventeen articles contained concrete recommendations about how to change society, so that in the end universal equality would be reached. Amongst other things, she stated freedom of speech of men and women, specifying the right of women to denounce the father of their illegitimate child.[47] She justified the right to speak in public by referring to the right of women to ascend the scaffold:[48] If women are given the right to suffer capital punishment, it is, according to de Gouges, a simple question of logic to recognize them the other rights, too. On November 3, 1793, she was put to death in Paris. Grounds for the judgment: "She wanted to be a statesman, and it seems as had the law punished this conspiratress, because she forgot the virtues behooving her sex."[49] The postulated universality of the Declaration of 1789 also didn't apply to slaves, even though a comprehensive universality was claimed for by, for example, La Société des Amis des Noirs led by Jacques-Pierre Brissot (motivated by the abolitionist movement in Great Britain) or the Club Massiac (a group of colonial planters). The "Code Noir," decreed in 1685 by Louis XIV, established the main lines for policing slavery in French colonies, was abolished in 1794, it's abolishment though was never implemented. Napoleon revoked in 1802 the repeal of the decree and declared its validity in 1805.

---

[44] Chapitre premier Section II Article 1 Constitution de 1791
[45] Id.
[46] Hassauer, Friederike (1990), p. 328
[47] Article 11
[48] Article 10
[49] Hassauer, Friederike (1990), p. 333

From a constructivist point of view freedom is not a recognition of universal principles, but the result of decisions, the result of a form of cooperation. I respect the claims for freedom of others, I behave in a way that their wishes to be free become possible. To be free we have to convince our counterparts, that

- the freedom we are hoping for won't restrict them unduly, that
- the intended goal justifies their support, and/or that
- they even could benefit from this arrangement.

Liberal or neoliberal concepts of freedom do not conceive others as constitutive. After having been fed, loved, cherished, and financed by our parents, after having been educated by patient and engaged teachers, after having been trained on a job in the different companies at the beginning of our professional career, it seems pretentious to me to perceive individuals as "born free." This "negative freedom"[50] qualifies others as competitors, as the ones who hinder ourselves living our natural, given freedom. A constructive concept, on the other hand, focuses on the interaction of people, an interaction that can make freedom impossible. It is as much our merit as the merit of others which makes us free. To fight the others to get freedom will lead to counter power and, therefore, tie forces not available anymore for our ventures. If we renounce to compete with others, but recognize, respect and support them, they will be much more willing to support our liberty-claims.

Freedom as a "social construct" is mainly helpful because of two reasons. First, it highlights the necessity of a thorough and permanent engagement of everybody to make freedom happen. Second, it points out all the restrictions individuals can encounter when trying to realize their dreams. Not only direct violence can make freedom unattainable. Structural violence hinders access to the resources needed to develop our plans, as well. And cultural violence can make freedom even unthinkable. Structural and cultural violence are much more effective in controlling other people, because they are more complex and more difficult to attribute to individual actors. As part of the cultural heritage, of the stories people tell about their origins, are sensed as "natural," "given," and everlasting. To overcome this obstacle the victims need to step out of the current "reality" and develop an alternative, a culture of their own. "Even semantics have conspired to make that which is black seem ugly and degrading. In Roget's Thesaurus there

---

[50] Taylor, Charles (1988), pp. 118 ff.

are 120 synonyms for blackness and at least sixty of them are offensive, as for example, blot, soot, grim, devil and foul. And there are some 134 synonyms for whiteness and all are favorable, expressed in such words as purity, cleanliness, chastity and innocence. A white lie is better than a black lie. The most degenerate member of a family is a black sheep. Ossie Davis has suggested that maybe the English language should be reconstructed so that teachers will not be forced to teach the Negro child sixty ways to despise himself, and thereby perpetuate his false sense of inferiority, and the white child 134 ways to adore himself, and thereby perpetuate his false sense of superiority."[51] Language matters, language builds up identities and determines the way we can think and act. With Wittgenstein: "The limits of my language are the limits of my world."[52] Language is for Heidegger "the home of existence."[53] But this home can become instead of a place of empowerment a place of imprisonment: "Words interpret the world; the one who's able to enforce his interpretation is the master of the souls."[54] That's why we have to take care of a fair language[55] and reflect the distribution of power, the exclusion-inclusion-mechanism our language contains. We have to be aware that the exclusion of people out of language-production, out of the circle defining admissible words and concepts, may engender violent reactions.[56] Being at the mercy of a language others shape, can motivate the recourse to communication forms that are louder and more explosive.

The system built up by language is never perfectly knit. There are always contradictions, different interpretations. Thanks to this, change is possible.[57] If the creation and use of language were totally controlled, alternatives would be unthinkable.

cc) A need for alternatives – pluralism

To dispose of alternatives is the structural precondition of freedom. Feyerabend pleads for a creative, brave and somewhat "crazy" variation to the common, well known reality. With regard to scientific theories he hopes for audacious, sketchy, and risked theories: "Theoretical pluralism is assumed to be an essential feature of all knowledge that claims to be objective.

---

[51] Martin Luther King, Jr., SCLC Presidential Address, 1967
[52] Wittgenstein, Ludwig (1995), p. 67
[53] Heidegger, Martin (1979), p. 90
[54] Schneider, Wolf (1989), p. 149
[55] Trömel-Plötz, Senta (1992), p. 128; Pusch, Luise F. (1984), p. 65
[56] Rorty, Richard (1989), p. 127
[57] Hellinger, Marlis (1990), p. 53

Alternatives must [...] be developed in such detail that problems already 'solved' by the accepted theory can again be treated in a new and perhaps also more detailed manner. [...] it would be very unwise to bring the process to a standstill in the very beginning by the remark that some suggested new ideas are undeveloped, general, metaphysical. It takes time to build a good theory. The function of such concrete alternatives is, however, this: they provide means of criticizing the accepted theory in a manner which goes beyond the criticism provided by a comparison of that theory with the facts. [...] such a plurality allows for a much sharper criticism of accepted ideas than does the comparison with a domain of 'facts' which are supposed to sit there independently of theoretical considerations."[58] Being able to choose is the precondition of freedom. Accordingly we should support fantasy instead of certitude and develop risky alternatives to the current convictions.[59] What makes power bearable is the possibility to change it. And it becomes changeable if options are available. Wild constructions of another world[60] help us qualify what we have, to have an outside look at the current "reality" and, possibly, to step into another future. It is not for nothing that dictatorships fight against an open, critical discourse, and against minorities, against difference in general – because it is the precondition of freedom.

There are basically two ways of plurality-construction: First, the ones who want to be different leave the actual community and build a new one in a different place. Assumed there is enough space, this side-by-side-plurality based on mutual disinterest provides every community the possibility to live in accordance to their wishes. To avoid conflicts, these communities will tend to confine themselves and reduce contacts to an absolute minimum. As the world gets smaller and the probability of encounters increases, an evasive community construction is less and less an opportunity. Furthermore, politics of separation misses the opportunity of mutual enrichment, of challenges that may be the core of new social arrangements and, hence, emanations of freedom. Therefore, communities should *build within themselves a plurality structure* so that alternatives are available and a permanent debate about the quality of life becomes possible. Constructing plurality is a challenge because different forms of collective identities have to be integrated within an overarching community. Thus, integration work has to take place on different levels in different communities at the same time.

---

[58] Feyerabend, Paul K. (1999), p. 80
[59] Rorty, Richard (1994), pp. 24 f.
[60] See also Foucault, Michel (1978), p. 113, 117, 185, 195

Basic values 143

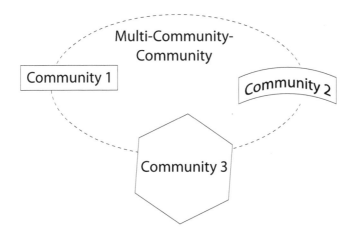

This multi-community community is a social structure that arises out of the continuous interactions the different communities and individuals perform. Like every other community it originates in communication and exists as long as individuals refer to it. The multi-community community is the result of arrangements that help the member-communities to live their life, to find the support needed from other member-communities or the multi-community community, and to solve conflicts the member-communities can't solve themselves. It also provides a collective identity concretized in its specific arrangement between the different communities. Difference has to be recognized and supported by material and immaterial means. Plurality, hence, is the result of engagement, not of passive disinterest.

Article 1 Sec. 7.5. of the Declaration of Rights of the California Constitution states that "only marriage between a man and a woman is valid or recognized in California." This declaration in favor of an exclusively heterosexual understanding of marriage is the result of a year-long fight between different concepts of love, partnership, parenthood, and sexuality. In 2000, the voters of California adopted a clarification of the state's Family Code, which provided marriage only between man and woman. In a clear breach of the law, San Francisco Mayor Gavin Newsom ordered in 2004 the city clerk to issue marriage licenses to same-sex couples. Within nine days nearly 3'200 same-sex marriage licenses were issued. Newsom explained that denying gay men and lesbians the right to marry "is wrong and inconsistent with the values this country holds dear. […] And if that means my political career ends, so be it."⁶¹ This act of civil disobedience wasn't confirmed by the courts because the California Supreme Court judged the decision of Newsom as illegal, ordered San Francisco to stop its practice, and nullified the marriage licenses that same-sex couples had received.⁶² Subsequently, San Francisco and other parties filed state court actions challenging the constitutionality of § 308.5 Cal Family Code. In 2008, the California Supreme Court declared prohibition of same-sex marriages unconstitutional⁶³ because of its violation of the state's equal protection doctrine. However, the fight over the legal status of homosexual partnerships didn't end. Within four-and-a-half months after the ruling of the California Supreme Court, San Francisco and other California counties issued approximately 18'000 marriage licenses to same-sex couples. Conservatives who couldn't accept the Court's decision in favor of plurality launched an initiative forbidding same-sex marriages on the level of the state constitution. During the campaign over Proposition 8 both sides spent together more than $70 million.⁶⁴ The conservatives won with 52% of the votes and the following lawsuits filed by the proponents of plurality weren't approved. In 2009, the "pluralists" filed a complaint in the U.S. District Court for Northern District of California and Justice Walker approved the arguments of the plaintiffs because "Proposition 8 fails to advance any rational basis in singling out gay men and lesbians for denial of a marriage license. Indeed, the evidence shows Proposition 8 does nothing more than enshrine in the California Constitution the notion that opposite-sex couples are superior to same-sex couples. Because California has no interest in discriminating against gay men and lesbians, and because Proposition 8 prevents California from fulfilling its constitutional obligation to provide marriages on an equal basis, the court concludes that Proposition 8 is unconstitutional."⁶⁵ It probably will be up to the U.S. Supreme Court to decide whether or not the U.S. Constitution's 14th Amendment was violated by Proposition 8 because the defeated "monistics" will go on fighting for their exclusive family model.

It's not the first time that a fight over plurality took place in Californian society. In the 1960s, gay and lesbian organizations worked for equal recog-

---

61   articles.cnn.com of February 22, 2004 (http://articles.cnn.com/2004-02-22/justice/same.sex_1_marriage-licenses-couples-political-career?_s=PM:LAW), retrieved on July 27, 2011
62   Lockyer v City & County of San Francisco, 95 P3d 459 (Cal 2004)
63   In re Marriage Cases, 183 P.3d 384 (2008)
64   The Wallstreet Journal of November 6, 2008 (http://online.wsj.com/article/SB122594011478104085.html), retrieved on July 27, 2011
65   Perry v. Schwarzenegger, 09-02292 (2010), p. 135

nition and against discrimination and police persecution. Harvey Milk was part of the counterculture of the 1960s, a movement that strongly criticized the absolutist claim for a monistic understanding of family life. He became city supervisor in 1977 – a revolution in favor of equality and freedom because he was elected on the basis of a campaign he openly conducted as a gay man. More than hundred years before was California was a highly pluralistic society. It is only over the past few decades that it has become increasingly monistic.

When Gold was found in California in 1848 the small group of inhabitants was overwhelmed by an endless number of immigrating fortune seekers (by 1845 Yerba Buena – later San Francisco – counted about 150 inhabitants; in 1850 it has risen to 35'000). At the time the dominating Spanish missionaries were too small a community to uphold their social structure against the incoming flood of people. The culture of the Natives wasn't perceived as valuable, which is why it didn't serve as a core of the new community. On the other hand, the immigrants came from so many places and origins that no specific group could impose its identity. People coming together didn't know each other and the numerical dominance of men in the first years (at some places eleven men to one woman; in the Southern Mines it was 97 percent men) made classical family building impossible. Social distinctions relevant in other parts of the country couldn't be upheld. "Worries surfaced about how eating, sleeping, or even sitting in close proximity to one's social inferiors might subvert class distinctions and lead to a radical and disturbing kind of leveling."[66] This social aggregation – loosely interacting people without institutionalized structures – had to quickly solve many daily problems. Lacking housing, servants, and women, and searching daily for gold, men lived in hotels and boardinghouses, ate in restaurants, and brought their clothes to the laundry. Even though the service industry mushroomed, it couldn't match the explosive increase in the numbers of people flocking to the new bonanza. Houses were built fast and everywhere, so that sumptuous residences came to stand next to run down shanties. A "climate of promiscuous social mixture in the city's eateries and hostelries"[67] reigned, which made different forms of living possible. Cabins and tents were populated by people from all different corners of the world and often groups of two to five men lived together, alternating the household tasks like washing, cooking, sewing, or taking care of the sick and sharing, if they existed, the profits.[68] Cross-gendering was often found

---

[66] Berglund, Barbara (2007), p. 18
[67] Id., p. 23
[68] Lee Johnson, Susan (2001), p. 106. See also pp. 122, 127

during dancing-evenings when some of the men wore a sign distinguishing them as a woman for the night.[69] It is against this backdrop that, for example, homosexual identities could be developed and assumed – not publicly, but at least in private –, that a "heritage of tolerance" originated, thanks to the absence of the patriarchal heterosexual social norms.[70] In general, tolerance toward other forms of sexual behavior was much larger in the late 19th and early 20th centuries than in the following decades.[71] And California was known for a more liberal structure of prostitution in the early years, particularly outside San Francisco.[72] The same was true for Los Angeles, which in the 1850s was "a town of 'free-and-easy customs,' in which people could 'do practically as they pleased.' There were no city ordinances against gambling, nor against drunkenness, drugs, prostitution, or high-noon showdowns in the middle of the street."[73] Because of the loose social organization the moral code known in the East of the U.S. wasn't established, which is why "homosexual ties flourished in California."[74] "San Francisco's overlap of cultures and communities, foreign and native born, contributed to a live-and-let-live sensibility. […] Despite periodic anti-vice crusades, a wide range of adventure-seekers, homosexuals among them, made their way through the Golden Gate."[75] Also "sex between men [was] an accepted fact of life in mining, logging and railroad camps on the western frontier in the United States and Canada during the 19th century,"[76] homosexuality could be lived without too much contradiction against the background of a widely accepted culture of plurality. Homosexuality was at this time perceived as a sin like drunkenness or gambling, but not as an identity trait,[77] which is why an active politic in favor of homosexuals didn't exist.[78]

The more the European-American identity began to take over, the more this pluralistic society became a monistic one, based on the "moral spaces of the urban and even rural communities of mid-nineteenth-century America."[79] Within fifty years the former indistinct aggregate of people

---

[69] *Id.*, p. 173
[70] Richards, Rand (2007), p. 234
[71] Kissack, Terence (2008), p. 1
[72] Lee Johnson, Susan (2001), p. 78
[73] Faderman, Lillian/Timmons, Stuart (2006), p. 14
[74] Lee Johnson, Susan (2001), p. 163
[75] Boyd, Nan Alamilla (2003), pp. 4 f.
[76] Beemyn, Brett Genny (2006), p. 159
[77] Lee Johnson, Susan (2001), p. 173
[78] Kissack, Terence (2008), p. 3
[79] Wright, Les (1999), p. 164

became an American place in the sense of specific race, class, and gender relations, or white dominance in a patriarchal community, structured along capitalistic principles.[80] Homosexual sodomy, this "infamous crime against nature," became liable to prosecution for the first time in California in 1872.[81] Cultural frontiers between the races and classes were built up in restaurants, hotels, boardinghouses, as well as in the living areas. An "increasingly powerful, conservative middle class desired to rid their fair city of the low-class and debauched Barbary Coast. [...] a Red Light Abatement Act was passed in 1914 and was upheld by the California Supreme Court in 1917, dealing the Barbary Coast its final death blow. The passage of the Prohibition in 1919 shut down completely legal drinking establishments. 'Vice,' – alcohol, gambling, prostitution – came under the control of the newly organized criminal class, old social habits became 'dirty,' 'immoral,' 'outrageous' – and illegal, and a new criminal class was born, the 'sexual deviant.'"[82] Besides legal means different cultural forms of identity-construction were developed to make the advent of an "orderly society" possible, meaning that the advent of a society clearly structured on European-American criteria of "normality" according to class-distinctions,[83] traditional family ideas (female and male roles), and appropriate sexual behavior. So, for example, the Jordans museums that displayed certain forms of sexual practices as diseased or deviant and helped by this to establish the heterosexual marital sexuality as the "dominant normative arrangement."[84] The importance of cultural work to construct a community's identity becomes visible. It also demonstrates the deep impact that cultural violence can have on the life of people and how much people are in- and excluded culturally. It's not just economy or politics that makes us and our world, it is also through the control of key cultural sites and institutions that hierarchies are erected and societies shaped.[85]

Prohibition repealed many queer entertainment facilities that had emerged in San Francisco. But it is only later that a political consciousness, or a collective identity, developed, which could be used in political contexts: "Through the 1930s, 1940s, and 1950s, tourist-based queer cultures mutated and exploded, shooting off in multiple directions. [...] With little more than same-sex attraction and/or gender-transgressive behavior to bind

---

[80] Berglund, Barbara (2007), p. 9
[81] Faderman, Lillian/Timmons, Stuart (2006), p. 28
[82] Wright, Les (1999), p. 169
[83] Berglund, Barbara (2007), pp. 157 ff.
[84] Id., p. 83
[85] Id., p. 225

them together, the queer communities that existed in San Francisco during these years did not form a cohesive whole."[86] In a hostile environment it is quite difficult to develop a different "reality." It is mainly in the course of World War II that the homosexuals started to realize their numbers and to establish a sense of a "quasi-ethnic minority."[87] During the war, the armed services had become aware of the large numbers of homosexual enlistees and draftees and discharged thousands of them. This overt discrimination and labeling by state institutions helped homosexuals establish themselves as a group or even a community with common interests and experience.[88]

The multifarious beginnings of the European community in California helped to develop a culture of open-mindedness and tolerance. This culture of respect and recognition is still visible when it comes to the status that homeless people have. Contrary to Paris or New York, for example, the homeless feel at home in San Francisco. So in the streets and parks or in public buildings like libraries, where they are tolerated. The homeless also aren't afraid to address people they don't know and who are obviously not living the same experience. San Francisco can be qualified as a widely democratic town according to its architecture as well as to its usage of the city space. There aren't, for example, too many areas of rich gated communities. The mixture of social strata is quite high. And ghettos, as a result of a segregationist policy, are hard to find. "As San Francisco grew into a modern American metropolis it did so organically, such that hetero and homo spaces, public and private spaces, upper- and lower-class spaces intermingled, invisible to the tourist's eye but assuredly known by the habitués."[89]

The monistic and the pluralistic concepts differ in the importance of freedom of others, respect for their differences, and equality of life choices. Monistic approaches are dichotomously simple and exclusionary and reductionistic. To make alternatives unthinkable in the context described here, they recur to biological justifications of the twofold gender-"reality:" The reproductive function binds men and women, who have to fulfill their duty for the sake of the community's existence. Or it is stated that the bipolar gender-reality is given by God who prohibits transgression of this divine order. That's why the Vatican perceives homosexuality as a "deviation" and an "irregularity" and the act of homosexual sex as a sin.[90] "As in every moral disorder, homosexual activity prevents one's own fulfillment and happiness

---

[86] Boyd, Nan Alamilla (2003), p. 5
[87] Wright, Les (1999), p. 173
[88] Licata, Salvatore (1981), p. 166
[89] Wright, Les (1999), p. 170
[90] Pope Benedict XVI on a visit in Portugal, Telegraph of May 13, 2010

by acting contrary to the creative wisdom of God."[91] The monistic concept of human beings adheres to assimilatory integration (see pp. 213 ff.). On the contrary, if we intend to establish freedom and equality, *multiple* identities become thinkable and communities with a pluralistic sex-model[92] acceptable. Native Americans like the Yurok, for example, recognized biological men who dressed and lived as women and often made them shamans because they were more spiritual. Transvestite men married men of Juaneñ, who found them especially attractive because of their physical strength. Biological men or women Mohaves could choose in puberty which gender they wanted to assume.[93] Besides these cases that are biologically undisputed but socially open, there are intersexuals, where the genital type doesn't suit the chromosomal or gonodal type.[94] Intersexuals often are made "man" or "woman" by surgery because the state and medical establishment are convinced that this abnormality has to be normalized.[95]

Because of the freedom of individuals, because of their creativity, every society and every community has to repeatedly answer new challenges to their collective identity. As people change, they want to live in a different way, try out new things, and question routinized behavior and institutions, that were taken for granted. The answer to this innovation can be pluralistic or monistic. The pluralistic answer favors freedom, equity, and life. The monistic answer is absolutist and forces other people to assimilate, emigrate, or die. To avoid destructive effects on individuals and communities, we should favor difference over homogeneity, create alternatives to become free to choose, integrate change as an ordinary pattern, and look at others not as members of a rigid and inescapable collective, but as individuals interacting with others on fragile common ground: "Where two or three Quakers are gathered together, one is liberal, one is conservative, and a third keeps asking the others to define their terms."[96]

---

[91] Congregation for the Doctrine of the Faith: Some Considerations concerning the response to legislative Proposals on the non-discrimination of homosexual Persons, Vatican 1992, I. 3.
[92] Gildemeister, Regine/Wetterer, Angelika (1992), p. 211; Hagemann-White, Carol (1984), pp. 34 f.
[93] See Faderman, Lillian/Timmons, Stuart (2006), pp. 10 ff.
[94] Lorber, Judith/Farrell, Susan A. (1991), p. 7. Sax defends the position of the normality of two genders (Sax, Leonard [2002]).
[95] For Switzerland see Büchler, Andrea/Cottier, Michelle (2002).
[96] Thomas Mullen, quoted in: Hamm, Thomas D. (2003), p. 142

c) Responsibility

"Destiny is not a matter of fate, it's a matter of choice."[97] If life and the "reality" within which we live is the result of a choice, the ones who choose are responsible for their selection. The reactions to the financial market crisis, however, didn't bring forward people ready to take responsibility. Defenders of the free market idea were convinced not having been a decisive contributing factor. Does that mean that responsibility doesn't have anything to do with freedom? Or does it mean that individuals were forced by the financial market to act the way they did?

aa) Delegation

Lloyd Blankfein, CEO of Goldman Sachs, describes himself as "a blue collar guy," just a banker helping "companies to grow by helping them to raise capital. Companies that grow create wealth." He's, therefore, "doing God's work."[98] That this blue-collar guy made in 2007 $68m is, according to him, a reward for the success he made possible. The standards, the market practice, and the competitive situation justify this salary.[99] During the Senate Hearings in April 2010 neither Blankfein nor Swenson, Sparks, or Tourre admitted any mistake or responsibility for the financial market crisis. Sorking, columnist for The New York Times, perplexedly noted: "I must say that one of the frustrating parts of researching my book came when I finally got to ask the question of Wall Street chief executives and board members [...]: Do you have any remorse? Are you sorry? The answer, almost unequivocally, was no. (Or they just didn't answer.) They see themselves as just one part of a larger problem, with many constituencies to blame."[100] Honegger et al. describe this delegation-strategy as "structured irresponsibility". Different arguments are used to explain the crises and to get rid of one's own responsibility:

- Everybody is responsible (and by this nobody) as the greed of human beings made it happen. This greed is understood as an anthropologi-

---

[97] Mario Gonzalez, Sioux, in: 500 Nations, part 8, 41'
[98] The Times-Online of November 8, 2009 (http://www.timesonline.co.uk/tol/news/world/us_and_americas/article6907681.ece), retrieved on July 27, 2011
[99] Interview with Lloyd Blankfein on CNN, May 2, 2010 (http://transcripts.cnn.com/TRANSCRIPTS/1005/02/fzgps.01.html), retrieved on July 27, 2011
[100] Sorkin, Andrew Ross, Author of "Too big to fail", on: The New York Times of October 19, 2009 (http://www.nytimes.com/2009/10/19/business/media/19askthetimes.html?pagewanted=all), retrieved on July 27, 2011

cal constant and thus unavoidable. Bankers did, what everybody else would have done.
- Others are responsible: Investment bankers, financial engineers, rating agencies, the clients, politics, the state and so on.[101]
- "The most powerful exculpation machinery is 'the market', determining one's own actions supposedly like a natural force, declared by the neoliberal believers [...] as the absolute authority."[102]

Paradoxically, the support of the banks with taxpayer's money – a clear violation of the neoliberal credo – didn't lead to modesty, but to the feeling of being indispensable. They think that the community self-evidently had to bear the consequences of the crises and they feel even more powerful than before. Accordingly, they deny the need for a fundamental change in the banking business.[103]

Again, the lopsided upper class[104] cleverness of the neoliberal economy becomes visible: First, everybody is free to act according to his or her own interests. Second, individuals are not responsible for the community, this task is taken over by the market which integrates all individuals into a functioning whole. Third, all the gains belong to the individual taking the highest risks. Fourth, if there is failure, the individual can rely on the community, which has to act and support the ones who took such big risks that the existence of the community is at stake. It is in my view that not only Wall Street that is to blame, but also the lending practices of the subprime-companies, and the deregulation-decisions of the Republican and Democrat governments alike that led to the crisis. But all actors were convinced of the inimitable wisdom of the market and the usefulness of the selfish homo oeconomicus. "What Francis Fukuyama prematurely called 'the end of history' was [...] the apparent end of intellectual opposition to the dogmas of economic liberalism."[105] "All it takes for evil to succeed is for good people to say 'it's a business.'"[106]

---

[101] Oswald Grübel, former CEO of Credit Suisse and today CEO of UBS declared the market and the rating agencies being responsible, on: Tages-Anzeiger of December 31, 2008 (http://www.tagesanzeiger.ch/wirtschaft/unternehmen-und-konjunktur/ berbezahlt-Ich-habe-kein-schlechtes-Gewissen/story/25271295), retrieved on July 27, 2011.
[102] Honegger, Claudia/Neckel, Sighard/Magning, Chantal (2010), pp. 305 f.
[103] Id., pp. 310 f.
[104] People making $68m a year are in my point of view part of the upper class, even when they perceive themselves as part of the blue collar community.
[105] Strange, Susan (1998), p. 8
[106] Alan Shore, Boston Legal, Season 2, Episode 11, adapting the well-known saying.

bb)   Acting and responding

I distinguish two forms of responsibility:

- The *individual and collective opportunity* and burden *to decide* about the "reality" one wants to live in.
- The *ability to listen* to others and to *respond* respectfully.

The first form is described, for example, by the existentialist Sartre, who perceives human beings as damned to be free: They are responsible for the world and for themselves. Being responsible means being consciously the originator of an event or an object,[107] which is why no regrets or excuses in transcendental form can be used.[108] Being responsible, though, not only is a burden, it is as much a chance. "Reality" originates in our actions, it is what we do, what we manage to convince others to support. We, therefore, have the chance to construct our individual and collective identity according to our wishes. Neither God nor the party nor the market are responsible for what we are. Responsibility delegation is, in my opinion, used, because we do not want to carry the burden or because we want to hide our decisive contribution to injustice. People can *choose between adaptation or creation*. You can prefer to be like everybody else, act by the rules, reproducing the accepted standards, and adapt to all changes the ruling majority claims. Or you may decide to be creative, different, to look for alternatives and, if there aren't any, to develop them yourself, to be the master of your "reality." In the second case we are responsible for the "reality" we construct. In the first, we negate responsibility because we just follow orders made by more powerful people than we are. But according to the consensus-based constructivism, to reproduce "reality" proposals of others doesn't abolish our responsibility. The reproduced "reality" wouldn't prevail without our support. It is, in my view, important to point out the responsibility of mass-movements or trends that are followed by many people without thinking about the origin or the consequences. The worst things in history happened because of uncritical followers who brought führers, for instance, into existence.

The *ability to listen and to respond* focuses on others and their needs. Being responsible, therefore, also means being attentive, interested, fascinated by difference, and solidary with the ones in need. As soon as we recognize the existence of others, they become a part of our "reality" and our way of behaving influences their existence. If there are people claiming their existence and crying for recognition, but aren't heard by us, they won't be part

---

[107]   Sartre, Jean-Paul (1943), p. 598
[108]   *Id.*, p. 601

of our "reality." We, therefore, have to be ready to answer when we are taken to task.[109] Thus, it is our duty to be attentive and to be willing to listen to people. As soon as we hear them (recognition), we have to listen carefully (respect) to try to understand the world they live in. Possibly, we have to relativize or change our "reality" to increase opportunities and to bring others into the construction-process on an equal basis. Within this cooperative debate the involved parties should fight for their ideas and try to convince others, without stopping listening to others and reflecting their own belief.

cc) Systemic "reality" – politics without individuals

The methodological individualism that grounds the homo oeconomicus doesn't use societal elements like "roles," "statuses," "class," "institutions," or "society." In the "reality" of sociological theories, however, they play a central role and are the result of macro-laws sui generis, not explicable by reference to the behavior of individuals. Social "reality" is in this sense a superhuman world, as the societal concepts are irreducible to something else – they aren't explainable by referring to psychological, physical, economic, or philosophical ideas. In sociology, a society does not exist without individuals, but has, nevertheless, an existence independent of the individual action (see also p. 49 f.).[110] Luhmann's system theory is a consequent application of this very idea and is exemplary for the modern society that's understood as an aggregate of isolated individuals, organized by something that happens beside their realm of influence or knowledge.

At the heart of Luhmann's system theory is the functional differentiation of modern society.[111] This differentiation process led, according to Luhmann, to an overly complex social structure. To come to grips with this

---

[109] Buber, Martin (1992), p. 206; Coelho, Paulo (2001), p. 82

[110] See for this discussion for example Berger, Peter L./Luckmann, Thomas (1980), p. 20. They differentiate between the objective facticity of society and its subjective meaning. And for them society is a reality sui generis. See also Amann, Anton (1991), p. 140; Mandelbaum, Maurice (1959), pp. 476 ff.; Castoriadis, Cornelius (1997), pp. 246 ff.; Weber, Max (1973), p. 121. Simmel is convinced, that the individual stands toward society like toward nature (Simmel, Georg [1992], p. 236). Durkheim talks of social facts as a reality "in the outer world" (Durkheim, Emile [1990], p. 361, 365. For Giddens, societies "'stand out' in bas-relief from a background of a range of other systemic relationships in which they are embedded. They stand out because definite structural principles serve to produce a specifiable overall 'clustering of institutions' across time and space" (Giddens, Anthony [1984], p. 164).

[111] Luhmann, Niklas (1997), p. 743

complexity, the different functional systems build simplifications,[112] meaning that processes operate in an *autopoietic* way. Autopoietic systems are closed and reproduce themselves self-referentially on the grounds of an identity building criterion, the so-called "codes."[113] The survival of a system depends essentially on its capacity to neutralize external disturbances. Modern society is, thus, based (psychologically speaking – something Luhmann wouldn't do) on "autistic" systems that are able to answer in an autonomous way the disturbances (called by Luhmann "interferences"). In this context, "autonomous" means the communication of the system that decides if there is a disturbance and how the system has to react to it.[114] These self-referential systems "filter" all information in application of the identity-building code. The political system uses the code "power/powerlessness," the economic system the code "to pay/not to pay," the scientific system uses "truth/falsity," and the legal system uses the difference "legal/illegal." With these criteria the systems define what is part of themselves and what belongs to the environment. According to Luhmann, the constitutive difference between system and environment can't be overcome without risking the survival of the system. By demarcating itself from the overly complex environment the system comes with its own function into being.[115]

The acute functional differentiation and the system-specific code make communication between systems impossible, according to Luhmann. The legal system, for example, just works on its own, regardless of the output the political system produces. A *target-orientated cooperation can't be realized* because the autistic character of the systems prevents them from mutual understanding or compassion. Other systems only exist in the unknown and unknowable environment. If there is cooperation between the systems, then only by chance, unintentionally. Systems irritated by interference try to avoid this disturbance of their reproduction process and, hence, without knowing anything about the other system, may possibly adapt to them. To overcome the system's isolation, Luhmann proposed the concept of "interpenetration:" One system makes available its own complexity to the construction of another system and vice-versa.[116] Mutual penetration is supposed to be an answer to the question of how autopoietic systems can

---

[112] *Id.*, pp. 437 f. and Luhmann, Niklas (1989), p. 41. To ground a concept of society on the action of individuals is according to him under complex (*Id.*, pp. 153 f.).
[113] Luhmann, Niklas (1997), p. 223
[114] Luhmann, Niklas (1991a), p. 146. About the notion of "autonomy" see Luhmann, Niklas (1989), p. 69.
[115] Luhmann, Niklas (1991a), pp. 242 ff., 602
[116] *Id.*, p. 290

integrate into society. But it questions strongly the central element of his theory ... the autopoiesis.

Münch, who wants to construct a political system that controls societal processes[117] and who is interested in an intense cooperation of politics and non-politics,[118] attenuates the closeness of the involved systems and defends the idea of relative autonomy and openness.[119] Through the interconnection of politics and non-politics the political system gains the possibility to decide society-wide and, hence, to perform the central integration function.[120] From the point of view of the legal system Teubner and Willke also propose a modification to Luhmann's autopoiesis. Teubner defends a gradual concept of autopoiesis to reach a form of interactive relation between the political and legal system.[121] And Willke wants a legal system that's able to structure inter-system-relations,[122] which is why he develops the idea of collective communication in a functionally differentiated society.[123]

The concept of the autopoietic system is from the point of view of freedom and responsibility helpful as much as it is dangerous. It is helpful to construct inclusion- and exclusion-processes and to highlight power-abuse. That a group of people obliges new members to learn a specific language, to take over the basic principles, and to adapt to the rules can be well described in systemic terms when a sort of an absolute frontier is built up. There is only one code, one way to live and people have to assimilate or can't be part of the system. Another relationship that can well be described in systemic terms is the world Franz Kafka created in his novels: Acute powerlessness of individuals at the mercy of not clearly identifiable forces that take place behind their back. "Structural violence" can also be thematized with system theory. On the other hand, the systemic perception is a risk for the relevance of individuals and their autonomy. Indeed, system theory knows a "psychic system" that stands for the individual and its autopoietic identity construction. But the psychic system isn't constitutive for the social system "society." Both exist independently of each other. The power and the responsibility of individuals to create and alter the society they live in, isn't an element of the systemic "reality."

---

[117] Münch, Richard (1976), p. 85
[118] Münch, Richard (1994), pp. 394, 404
[119] Id., pp. 393 f.
[120] Id., p. 400
[121] Teubner, Gunther (1989), pp. 81 f.
[122] Willke, Helmut (1992), p. 206
[123] Id., p. 207

For realists like Luhmann, Münch, Teubner, or Willke the functional differentiation as much as the autopoietic reproduction are irrefutable facts about modern society. So Luhmann writes, for example, that "all recognizing systems are real systems in a real environment and that because of this they exist."[124] Furthermore, the necessity of an autopoieticly structured systems is given because the reality Luhmann wants to describe is so complex that only a systemic answer can be given (a non-declared circular argumentation).[125] For Teubner, only autopoieticly structured systems are able to stabilize the complex self-reproduction of autopoieticly structured systems (also a circular argumentation).[126] According to these authors, the functional differentiation has to be accepted as a given fact, it can't be discussed. For other scientists, though, this fact is a "functionalist fallacy" and its ontological pretension is at least debatable.[127]

Used as an objective and, thus, an exclusive description of the reality, the system theory is a loss of individual construction power and responsibility. It is a world within which nobody is responsible for the origination of society or of all the processes that are bigger than the individual. It is not for nothing that the market concept that the neo homo oeconomicus uses has a systemic character: This impenetrable solution to every problem does what has to be done without anybody understanding exactly how this wonder is achieved. Even though contradicting one of its core elements (the methodological individualism), it helps to realize a world, within which responsibility is evinced. The market system takes over the place God had before.

dd) Standardization, bureaucratization

Standardization and bureaucratization are central elements of a modernity focused on efficiency and simplicity. Difference, originality, and the unexpected are obliterated to make sure that everything runs smoothly. An engineered and industrialized monoculture is built up, adapted to the capitalistic production system. According to Fasching, this development is dangerous because of its oppressing and exclusionary effect on opponents. Reinforced within a globalized context this monoculture spreads every-

---

[124] Luhmann, Niklas (1988), p. 13
[125] Luhmann, Niklas (2000), p. 17
[126] Teubner, Gunther (1989), p. 24
[127] Critics of the concept of functional differentiation are for example Joas, Hans (1992), p. 336; Wagner, Gerhard (1996), pp. 89 ff.; Mayntz, Renate (1997), p. 39; Greven, Michael Th. (1999), p. 94. Schwinn calls it a "functionalist fallacy" (Schwinn, Thomas [1997], p. 391).

where without any control.¹²⁸ Modernity is a centralistic project that treats difference or strangeness as a "problem."¹²⁹ Critical self-reflection is only possible if we have at our disposal a multitude of "realities" without any priority rank.¹³⁰ Therefore a dialectic of diversity and homogeneity,¹³¹ of interactive individualism instead of dominating collectivism, is needed.¹³² According to George Bernard Shaw: "The reasonable man adapts himself to the world; the unreasonable one persists in trying to adapt the world to himself. Therefore, all progress depends on the unreasonable man."¹³³ To choose abnormality means to be master of one's own destiny and to look for a fundamental change. It is this sort of courageous act that improves communities, that controls power, that shakes routine, and proves that freedom exists. This barbaric uncontrolled politic¹³⁴ is a declaration of autonomy because one wants to be responsible for his or her present and future.

The danger of the technical and bureaucratic character of modern society is convincingly pointed out by Zygmunt Bauman. Even the National Socialists' propaganda machine wasn't able to eradicate the value of "life". After years of indoctrination, after intense construction of the inhuman and worthless Jew threatening the good German, the policemen and soldiers responsible to kill the men, women, and children had many qualms in fulfilling their job. Browning describes the working of the Reserve-Polizeibataillon 101 (reserve battalion consisting of policemen). On July 11, 1942, it got the assignment to bring the 1'800 Jews of Józefów (Poland) to one of the camps of Lublin. The men were supposed to be used as "Arbeitsjuden" (working Jews) and the order was to kill women, children, and old people. Lieutenant Heinz Buchmann was expected to be one of the killing officers but refused to do the job and was therefore allocated the escort the 300 male Jews selected to work. The others were brought to a forest nearby. The shooting started after the first company was informed how to target their victims. The executions lasted hours and alcohol was brought by to "ease" the duty of the soldiers. The second company had some problems killing effectively the Jews. Not instructed in the right technique, men, women, and children often weren't instantly dead or were hit in a way, that parts of the bodies of

---

[128] Fasching, Gerhard (1996), pp. 3 ff., 94 f.
[129] Baykan, Aisegul (1999), p. 158
[130] Fasching, Gerhard (1996), p. 92
[131] Baykan, Aisegul (1999), p. 160
[132] Id., p. 158
[133] George Bernard Shaw, "Man and Superman", 1903
[134] Bertho, Alain (1999), p. 95

the victims and blood "spattered around and soiled the shooters."[135] Many policemen couldn't bear the executions and were replaced; back to the quarters, others got drunk. The ones who didn't participate didn't want to hear about details, and the killers didn't want to talk about ever again.[136] "To destroy human beings is almost as difficult as to create them."[137] As this killing technique wasn't successful (too stressful for the policemen and soldiers and not effective enough), the Nazis invented the bureaucratized and industrialized systematic killing, later called "Holocaust."[138] The "advantage" of this technique was that the perpetrators were not directly confronted with the men, women, and children they were gassing. By splitting responsibility into small parts, every individual was much better able to function smoothly within this modern type of systematic killing. The Holocaust was, according to this, a rational, bureaucratic form of problem-solving and very horribly effective because of its modern character. "The Holocaust was born and executed in our modern rational society, at the high stage of our civilization and at the peak of human cultural achievement, and for this reason it is a problem of that society, civilization and culture."[139] "Without [civilization], the Holocaust would be unthinkable. It was the rational world of modern civilization that made the Holocaust thinkable."[140] "The more rational is the organization of action, the easier it is to cause suffering – and remain at peace with oneself."[141] To make sure that killing isn't questioned, it has to be reproduced relentlessly.[142] What becomes a normal routine can't be wrong anymore. The Holocaust was barbaric in its result, but modern in its technique.

Rationality and efficiency are some of the dogmas of modern society. Thanks to the highly developed division of work, responsibility becomes free-floating,[143] not attributable to somebody in particular anymore. The overwhelming trust into processes deviates the attention from the effects produced. And the celebrated individualism helps to deny social obligations. Empathy and solidarity are perceived as outdated concepts of communities of a much smaller scale and with an incomparably modest output.

---

[135] Browning, Christopher R. (1993), p. 97
[136] *Id.*, pp. 101 ff.
[137] Levi, Primo (1998), p. 179
[138] Browning, Christopher R. (1993), p. 79
[139] Bauman, Zygmunt (1989), p. x
[140] *Id.*, p. 13
[141] *Id.*, p. 155
[142] *Id.*, p. 158
[143] *Id.*, p. 163

This inbuilt tendency to the volatilization of guilt and responsibility eases the commission of exclusion and violence. As part of the big machinery called "modern society," we are just insignificant details in a story that takes anyway place regardless of what we intend to do. An interactive, constructivist understanding of the individual and her or his community brings the individual back into the game – both as actor and as a responsible person.

d) Justice

"Freedom" is about the possibility to be myself, to act according to my wishes, to have a say in the construction-process. "Justice" is about the organization of the construction-process, about access to the negotiation determines "reality." A just debate gives the participants the same right to question, to talk, and to be listened to and, thus, to influence the shared "reality."

aa) Human dignity – protection

Our physical existence and our identity are built up interactively. We are what we are out of the interactive process that restricts contingency and opens a particular set of opportunities. Against this constructivist background there aren't any objective criteria to define human dignity. Like every "reality" element human dignity is the result of debates, of an "always renewable process of reflection and communication."[144] A consensus has to be established whether racism, slavery, inequality, harsh working conditions, and sexual or physical abuse are violations of human dignity. At the age of 38, physician Kurt Heissmeyer wanted to become a professor, which is why he had to present a habilitation thesis. For his research on the ways to fight tuberculoses, he ideally wanted to make tests on living bodies, on human beings, to observe the effects one-to-one. Heissmeyer began his test-series on adults in the concentration camp Neuengamme in 1944. He therefore injected tuberculosis viruses directly into the lungs of his laboratory humans. Hitler had already decided in 1942 that human experiments for the benefit of the state were allowed. It would have been a glaring injustice to have, on the hand, German soldiers suffering, whereas, on the other hand, inmates would be spared from making any contribution to the Thousand-Year Reich.[145] Heissmeyer's test subjects were better fed than other inmates to ensure that their health problems would have a viral

---

[144] Müller, Jörg Paul (1999), p. 151
[145] Schwarberg, Günther (1997), p. 12

cause: Inmates volunteered. As the tests didn't produce the results he had hoped for, he began tests on children. Twenty Jewish children were ordered to Auschwitz and transported to Neuengamme. For Heissmeyer, there was no difference between laboratory animals and Jewish children[146] because the latter weren't real human beings.[147] "The scientific value of a physician was and is measured by the amount and quality of his publications. Besides two papers [...], Heissmeyer had nothing to put forward. To become recognized he had to do what 'everybody' did ... human experiments."[148] Contrary to Frankenberg, I do not think that human dignity becomes evident when we see people abused, tortured, or killed or that the content of human dignity can only be recognized out of its violation, "ex negativo."[149] I think that our hopes, our plans for the future, the ideals of life we develop give human dignity the contours that are relevant for us. Constructively spoken, there is no objective, a-historic, abstract, universal description of the human being and of its dignity.[150] For Heissmeyer, nothing was universally evident. The only dignity he knew was the German dignity and the dignity of his social and professional status. What counts, in my view, is the idea of dignity, the projection of relationships we think are most important. These projections are concretized by negative experiences, as well by positive ones. Without alternatives, without an idea of how life should and could be, we miss a touchstone. Human dignity means to me to be

- recognized as existent, to be
- heard as interactor, to be
- respected as a unique individual, and to be
- supported if needed.

It is thus by cooperation that human dignity is established and preserved.[151] Self-assurance originates in the experience of human dignity. People who are treated with dignity are able to act freely, to conceive alternatives, to weigh their pros and cons, and to engage in the chosen "reality." To be able to develop a personality, one needs to be heard. Individuals listened to will realize that they exist, that they are different, and that their actions matter.

---

[146] *Id.*, p. 42
[147] *Id.*, p. 98
[148] *Id.*, p. 100
[149] Frankenberg, Günter (2003), p. 276
[150] Greven, Michael Th. (1999), p. 196
[151] Luhmann, Niklas (1999), p. 68

The German Bundesverfassungsgericht decided on February 9, 2010, that, according to Article 1 § 1 and Article 20 § 1 of the Constitution, a humane subsistence level has to guarantee one's physical existence and a minimum of societal, cultural, and political participation.[152] That means that the decent survival of people and their involvement in interactions has to be secured by the community. So it is not the solitary individual that grounds this decision, but the homo interactivus, a human being becoming human, who takes initiative, is engaged, powerful, and creative thanks to respectful and equal interactions. Without cooperative social contacts, people become, in the worst case, sole physical bodies: They lose "the social, the vita activa, and the vita mentalis."[153]

In capitalist logic, making money is what counts. Greed is a venerated motivation because it enhances selfish competition and by this the output the market can produce. The American health care industry demonstrates that in capitalism human dignity often comes second behind material reflections. Wendell Potter worked four years at Humana and 15 years at CIGNA, two global health service companies. At CICNA he was the head of corporate communications. He quit the job in 2008 and began to speak out about the practices in the health care industry he could no longer support. More and more insurance companies had changed their business concept from cooperation to competition: Originally a form of collective solidarity and responsibility between insurance companies, employers, and individuals, the new politic individualized the risks by overburdening the health care costs onto the backs of individuals.[154] When Potter for the first time met the victims of the economic practices he had helped to establish, it was an attitude changing epiphany. He was confronted with the needs and sufferings of people using the free medical services of a health care expedition he learned about in a newspaper.

> "[…] what I saw were doctors who were set up to provide care in animal stalls. Or they'd erected tents, to care for people. I mean, there was no privacy. In some cases – and I've got some pictures of people being treated on gurneys, on rain-soaked pavement. And I saw people lined up, standing in

---

[152] BVerfG, 1 BvL 1/09 vom 9.2.2010, Absatz-Nr. 1: "Das Grundrecht auf Gewährleistung eines menschenwürdigen Existenzminimums aus Article 1 Section 1 GG in Verbindung mit dem Sozialstaatsprinzip des Article 20 Section 1 GG sichert jedem Hilfebedürftigen diejenigen materiellen Voraussetzungen zu, die für seine physische Existenz und für ein Mindestmaß an Teilhabe am gesellschaftlichen, kulturellen und politischen Leben unerlässlich sind."
[153] Sofsky, Wolfgang (1993), p. 230
[154] Potter, Wendell (2009a)

line or sitting in these long, long lines, waiting to get care. People drove from South Carolina and Georgia and Kentucky, Tennessee – all over the region, because they knew that this was being done. A lot of them heard about it from word of mouth. There could have been people and probably were people that I had grown up with. They could have been people who grew up at the house down the road, in the house down the road from me. And that made it real to me. […] It was absolutely stunning. It was like being hit by lightning. It was almost – what country am I in? It just didn't seem to be a possibility that I was in the United States. It was like a lightning bolt had hit me."[155]

How can it be that a well-educated man never reflected the effects his acts had on others?

"I had been in the industry and I'd risen up in the ranks. And I had a great job. And I had a terrific office in a high-rise building in Philadelphia. I was insulated. I didn't really see what was going on. I saw the data. I knew that 47 million people were uninsured, but I didn't put faces with that number. […] when you're in the executive offices, when you're getting prepared for a call with an analyst, in the financial medium, what you think about are the numbers. You don't think about individual people. You think about the numbers, and whether or not you're going to meet Wall Street's expectations.[…] And it helps to think that way. […] That enables you to stay there, if you don't really think that you're talking about and dealing with real human beings."[156]

These companies are short-term and are self-interested well-oiled machines, running standardized procedures that are focused on efficiency and high profits and are not, therefore, interested in the needs of human beings. Within this competitive environment, they are convinced that defense of the interests of individuals is naïve and unrealistic. The shareholder logic can't be overstated because these companies do not work for their insured, their clients, but for the value of their stocks. Analysts will only favor insurers if "they made more money during the previous quarter than a year earlier and that the portion of the premium going to medical costs is falling."[157] A company, therefore, has to get rid of less profitable policyholders or of the ones who get sick, if it wants to meet the interests of potential investors. Protecting their financial interests, the health care industry was ready to invest heavily in lobbying:

---

[155] Potter, Wendell (2009b)
[156] Id.
[157] Potter, Wendell (2009c), pp. 3 f.

"The industry has always tried to make Americans think that government-run systems are the worst thing that could possibly happen to them, that if you even consider that, you're heading down on the slippery slope toward socialism. So they have used scare tactics for years and years and years, to keep that from happening. If there were a broader program like our Medicare program, it could potentially reduce the profits of these big companies. So that is their biggest concern. [...] That means that part of the effort to discredit [the film "Sicko" of Michael Moore] was to use lobbyists and their own staff to go onto Capitol Hill and say, 'Look, you don't want to believe this movie. You don't want to talk about it. You don't want to endorse it. And if you do, we can make things tough for you.' [...] By running ads, commercials in your home district when you're running for reelection, not contributing to your campaigns again, or contributing to your competitor."[158]

Human dignity isn't taken seriously if the possibility to make money is rated higher than life, health, or freedom of people. This is what Simmel called "Mammonismus" – money that becomes and end in itself, money that is adored, independent of its practical use[159] – blinds out social aspects of human beings. Our existence is hence reduced to material criteria and we are happy, when our bank account tops that of others.

bb) Equal construction power

To recognize and to respect the other as a human being necessitates equal construction-power. Every person has to have *the same opportunity to influence the construction of the community*. Without an impact on one's own surrounding, it is hard to develop self-esteem. This impact has to be at least optionally equal and, up to a basic level, egalitarian. The goal is not to become identical, but to have equal opportunities to realize one's own hopes. The integration quality of a community depends, accordingly, not least on its capacity to enhance its members' life prospects.[160] It is justice and solidarity that makes freedom possible, because "to be free means to overcome all obstacles hindering human development."[161]

The "glass ceiling" that stops women from climbing the career ladder is an example of *structural inequality* that counters the promise of meritocracy. Even though men and women are legally equal in western societies and

---

[158] Potter, Wendell (2009b)
[159] Rammstedt, Otthein (ed.) (2003), pp. 312 f.
[160] Dahrendorf, Ralf (1979), p. 27
[161] *Id.*, p. 36

are perceived as having the same abilities, there are structural (as well as cultural and mental) obstacles not easily overcome. To remove these barriers means to change the society on many different levels and in a variety of ways. Contrary to this interactive understanding of the origins of inequality and its possible solutions, a "reality" based on the methodological individualism won't, first, see any structural problems at all and will, second, deny the necessity of a common approach. Convinced that everyone forges her or his own destiny and that the meritocratic principles – that everybody gets what one deserves – have to be respected, then the community bears no responsibility for inequality. Dishwashers who do not become millionaires have to attribute this failure to themselves. "Les hommes naissent libres et égaux en droit. Après ils se démerdent."[162] There is equality at birth and if we abolish legal inequalities, the road to success is open for all. This *formal concept of equal opportunities* (based only on rights, not on individual construction power) doesn't seem to be enough to establish justice.[163] Social or economic advantages are usually not based on personal capabilities. The main factors for inequality are, in my view, pre-existing wealth, social and political favoritism, and cultural bias. Thus, a *substantial concept of justice* is needed that takes the resources of people into account.

In the solitary competitive capitalism one of the main factors to become and to stay rich is *heritage, not performance*.[164] High salaries have an impact on the important rise in inequality over the last thirty years: The incomes of the highest 10 % of all wage earners increased since the 1970s by 70 % or more.[165] But more important than income are the assets. One percent of the worldwide richest people possess 40 % of the world's fortune. And the richest 10 % own 85 %.[166] The relation between the biggest and the average fortune in the U.S. was in 1790 of 4000:1, in 1890 it was 370'000:1, and in 1999 1'416'000:1.[167] And it is not only out of big fortunes that one can obtain high incomes. Big fortunes are bequeathed to the next generation, which often didn't contribute. These forms of income have nothing to do with the favorite justification system of capitalism: meritocracy. Rather it has more in common with a feudal social fabric.[168] According to Kissling,

---

[162] Jean Yanne (French humorist, actor, and director): People are born free and equal in rights. Than they have to fend for themselves.
[163] Rössler, Beate (ed.) (1993), p. 8
[164] Mäder et al. (2010), p. 11, 393
[165] Id., p. 37
[166] Id., p. 56
[167] Id., p. 62
[168] Kissling, Hans (2008), p. 16

is for example Switzerland a "principality" because big fortunes and by this privileges are inherited, they are built up through descent.[169] Interactively speaking, individual performance on the so-called "market" depends on a multitude of sociocultural factors and isn't solely influenced by the one remunerated.[170] The success and the failure of individuals is not based on an anonymous decision of the "market" or on the individuals' merit alone, but is attributable to others, too. Because success is a collective performance, it is also *a societal and a political decision whether inequality is created and increased.*[171]

Accepting the market-logic means to accept unjustified increases in inequality and serving mostly the interests of the fortunate hereditary oligarchy. In this way, social classes with their different construction opportunities are reproduced over time, leading to a "dynastic capitalism."[172] Since the market was declared sole responsible integration factor (in Great Britain starting in 1979, in the USA in 1981), social inequality has significantly increased. Even though the worst economic downturn since the Great Depression happened in 2007/2008, Wall Street is already back in 2009 with the highest earnings ever. Main Street, on the other hand, struggles for a living and has problems finding and keeping its jobs to satisfy basic needs. Giving up the model of mixed economies in favor of the neoliberal market-absolutism, the U.S. economy developed into "a capitalist oligarch[y] like Brazil, Mexico, and Russia. [...] America's runaway rewards for the affluent have not unleashed an economic miracle whose rewards have generously filtered down to the poor and middle class."[173] The trickle-down promise, made to *make people wait and accept*, has not been fulfilled. According to Hacker and Pierson, this drift toward economic oligarchy is "the story of a thirty-year war."[174] Central elements of a policy that favors the top and neglects the middle and the bottom are according to them: A reduction of taxes for the very top; a reduction of benefits for the vast majority of Americans (reduced redistribution); a lack of adaptation of the laws of a shifting economy because political leaders do not want to adapt out of ideological reasons or by giving in to the pressure of powerful lobbyists; a weakening of unions (the main political players addressing middle-class economic concerns), keeping down the minimum wage, supporting corporate gov-

---

[169] *Id.*, p. 61
[170] Albert, Hans (1978), p. 148
[171] Kreckel, Reinhard (1992), p. 13
[172] Joffrin, Laurent (2001), p. 153
[173] Hacker, Jacob S./Pierson, Paul (2010), p. 4
[174] *Id.*, p. 6

ernance in favor of the management, and comprehensive deregulation of the financial markets without adapting existing rules. Hacker and Pierson criticize the idea of the "market as some pre-political state of nature […]. Politicians are there at the creation, shaping that 'natural' order and what the market rewards. Beginning in the late 1970s, they helped shape it so more and more of the rewards would to got the top."[175] "The winner-take all economy threatens to undo the critical social progress of the last hundred years and returns us to a quasi-Robber Baron economy, where the rich control an increasing portion of society's wealth and resources, while those who do the lion's share of labor in America increasingly fail to share in the benefits of economic growth."[176]

The inequality at the beginning of the 20th century could be overcome and a more just society could be established if there was cooperation between the main political forces. Within a few years after World War II a middle-class-society was established. "The golden age of economic equality roughly corresponded to the golden age of political bipartisanship."[177] Up to the end of the 1970s inequality was low and workers could live a dignified life. However, from 1979 on neoliberal forces, not interested in equal opportunity, quit the cooperative agreement and began to implement the dominance of competition and economy in every realm of life. This "erosion of the social norms and institutions that used to promote equality ultimately driven by the rightward shift of American politics, played a crucial role in the surging inequality."[178] That the cooperative arrangement was terminated became evident in the politics against unions: "Business interests, which seemed to have reached an accommodation with the labor movement in the 1960s, went on the offensive against unions beginning in the 1970s. And we're not talking about gentle persuasion, we're talking about hardball tactics, often including the illegal firing of workers who tried to organize or supported union activity. During the late seventies and early eighties at least one in every twenty workers who voted for a union was illegally fired; some estimates put the number as high as one in eight."[179] This important weakening of the unions' counterweight made place for a sort of management autocracy, considerably increasing the inequality of construc-

---

[175] *Id.*, p. 56
[176] Garfinkle, Norton (2005), p. 39
[177] Krugman, Paul (2009), pp. 5 f.
[178] *Id.*, pp. 8 f.
[179] *Id.*, p. 150. See also Hacker, Jacob S./Pierson, Paul (2010), p. 59: "Reported violations of the NLRA (National Labor Relations Act] skyrocketed in the late 1970s and early 1980s."

tion-power.[180] The conflict in Wisconsin between governor Scott Walker, public employees, and their unions highlights the ongoing battle over influence.[181] Since the Republicans won the mid-term elections in November 2010 and were in control of many more state legislatures and governorships, they launched a series of attempts to restrict the unions' bargaining rights. Besides Wisconsin, Indiana, and New Jersey, Ohio,[182] too, used the pretext of financial problems to deal a blow to democracy. To avoid "a third-world-style oligarchy"[183] it is essential to equalize construction-power.

Inequality is a political decision. The powerful establish it willfully or at least hazard the consequences. Important integration problems like fear, distrust, stress, poverty, illness, death, xenophobia, scapegoat politics, or violence against minorities[184] may result. All the more if the situation of the people becomes more fragile, if their perspectives are gloomy, if the near future is unknown, if there aren't any support structures, or if inequality is perceived as illegitimate. Exclusionary minority-constructions are, there-

---

[180] Flanagan, Robert J. (2005), pp. 60 and 44 ff.
[181] Nichols states that "the governor has made his budget decisions not with an eye toward fiscal responsibility, but with an eye toward rewarding his political benefactors" (Nichols, John [2011]). Do the $140 million tax breaks for multinational corporations engineered by Walker have to be compensated by the workers and the rights of unions to defend their interests? There seems to be a broad GOP attack against unions. The majority of House Republicans voted in February 2011 to slash the funding of the NLRB (National Labor Relations Board) by one-third. According to Meyersohn, they go in a generalized way against the unions because they "remain the most effective part of the Democratic coalition in turning out minority voters come election time and in getting working-class Whites to vote Democratic. As such, they are the linchpin of progressive change in America. Taking them off the political map isn't about budgets. It's about removing a check on right-wing and business power in America" (Meyersohn, Harald ([2011]). Walker's bill intends to eliminate most collective bargaining for public employees and would strip the unions of their financial means. They would no longer be entitled to deduct dues from the payroll and would lose their right to require members to pay dues (See Legislative Reference Bureau [2011], pp. 1 f.).
[182] Ohio passed the Anti-Union Bill on March 30, 2011. The bill bars public employees from striking and prohibits binding arbitration for police officers and firefighters. Public-employee unions are only allowed to bargain if the public employers opt for it. Does the negotiation not come to terms, it is the legislative body that has the right to take the final decision.
[183] Krugman, Paul (2011), p. A17
[184] Hahn, Alois (1994), p. 153; Anhut, Reimund/Heitmeyer, Wilhelm (2000), p. 53; Rüssmann, Kirsten et. al (2010), pp. 281-301; Vester, Michael (1997), p. 165

fore, a sensible crises-indicator.[185] Inequality has also a negative impact on the economy because "countries with high inequality grow more slowly, on the average, than countries with low inequality."[186] To avoid these developments, to avoid structural violence, *political, social, and economic equity* is needed, incorporated by a large middle class. The middle class may be defined as people who are able to fulfill their hopes without too many problems.[187] Moderate hopes, rather long-term orientated and within the reach of ones own possibilities, therefore often satisfied and satisfying. One could say that the middle class represents a decent average, the so-called common sense. Engaged, responsible for family and friends, trustworthy, conscientious workers[188], they are essential for the stabilization of the community, the core integration-factor. Not revolutionary and moderately critical, the middle class stands for the reproduction-phase, for keeping up the interactions that proved successful. The larger the middle class, the more the extremes are "neutralized" in a community and the easier it is to establish solidarity-mechanisms. The relative balance between the rich, middle class, and underclass can be seen as a compromise, which has the most integrative effect when the middle class makes around 60 % or more of the society.[189] Besides their political stability, middle classes are also essential for economic development because "the middle-class consumer is the engine driving the modern economy."[190] Competitive neoliberal politics has mainly three negative effects on this stabilizing element:

- It put the middle class under economic and social pressure by increased competition throughout all realms of life (economic absolutism) and by reducing the benefits and grants.
- It motivated people to give up their long-term orientation and instigated a debt culture. A development strongly supported by structural changes.

The last point is symptomatic of a selfish devil-may-care attitude. Long-term planning and reflecting on our actions according to their effects on

---

[185] Imhof, Kurt/Romano, Gaetano (1996), p. 263
[186] Frank, Robert H. (2007), p. 116
[187] The way I use "middle class" here is not a description of *the* reality. I just want to point out the problems a community has, when to many people have problems to make ends meet. See Bosc, Serge (2008), pp. 29, 109 f., about the heterogeneity of what is called "middle class".
[188] Lamont, Michèle (1992), pp. 61, 85
[189] Vester, Michael (1997), p. 163
[190] Garfinkle, Norton (2005), p. 39

the community and the next generation is not perceived as "hip."

Middle-class communities "have to be created through political action"[191] based on reciprocity, that is mutual support over time. In the USA, it was built up very fast thanks to the "New Deal legislation, union activity, and wage controls during World War II."[192] The strong position of the unions also reined in the salaries of management as well as the incomes of the stockholders. "Top executives knew that if they paid themselves huge salaries, they would be inviting trouble with their workers; similarly corporations that made high profits while failing to raise wages were putting labor relations at risk."[193] "A labor movement that withers will likely trigger only greater disparities in the nation's distribution of wealth."[194] At the time, the large consensus was that there had to be equal construction power in all areas of life, otherwise inequality and the feeling of powerlessness would put important strain on the integration process. In the words of Republican Dwight D. Eisenhower: "Today in America, unions have a secure place in our industrial life. Only a handful of reactionaries harbor the ugly thought of breaking unions and depriving working men and women of the right to join the union of their choice. I have no use for those – regardless of their political party – who hold some vain and foolish dream of spinning the clock back to days when organized labor was huddled, almost as a hapless mass. [...] Only a fool would try to deprive working men and women of the right to join the union of their choice."[195]

The neoliberal era, however, enormously favored the rich and richest[196] and may thus be qualified as "trickle-up economics:" "The rich are getting fabulously richer while the rest of Americans are basically holding steady or worse."[197] To keep the economic level they had, the American household had to work many more hours than in the late 1970s.[198] According to Warren & Warren Tyagi, parents with children have the highest risk of going bankrupt. "[...] married couples with children are more than twice as likely to file for bankruptcy as their childless counterparts. [...] Most are [...] ordinary middle-class people united by their determination to provide a

---

[191] Krugman, Paul (2009), p. 18
[192] Id., p. 137
[193] Id., p. 138
[194] Francia, Peter L. (2006), p. 154
[195] Quoted in American Labor Studies Center (2010)
[196] At the expense of the middle class and the poor, so Bosc, Serge (2008), pp. 92, 98.
[197] Hacker, Jacob S./Pierson, Paul (2010), p. 20
[198] Id., pp. 22, 26

decent life for their children."[199] Most of the time both parents work, try to keep their money together, and still do not have enough to make ends meet. The two-income families earn far more than did the traditional family some years ago, but in the end, have less at their disposal. It is not because of over-consumption[200] that they are in dire straits, but because of the social environment where the family lives. In order to have access to the right schools that give their children a start good enough to succeed professionally, families have to choose the right school district.[201] The run for a district that guarantees safety and good education launched a bidding war.[202] Increasing house prices weren't exclusively attributable to the competition of the middle class for promising locations. The house prizes also increased, because the rich upper class was willing and had the possibilities to spend rising amounts for their living space.[203] As every child needs preschool support and the costs of colleges and universities rose over time, the earnings are spent quite fast. Without any reserve, jobs are lost, families break up, and medical problems drive them into bankruptcy.[204] The promise, that inequality is not too bad, as everybody has the opportunity to rise in status and income, lost its credibility as this opportunity "may well have declined over the last generation, even as inequality has risen."[205]

Equal construction-power is central for individual well-being. It is also a decisive element of democracies and vital for long-term oriented integration. A powerful labor movement is needed to defend the interests of workers in the economic realm and to mobilize them to take part in the political debate[206]. The neoliberal focus solely on the power of the state that has to be controlled, is a diversion. Private power is as important and as much a danger for the individual's quality of life as is the one of the state – if not even more because it lacks the state's transparency and its obligation to justify its acts. In the political realm, democracy is political cooperation: First, the pure form of democracy guarantees one man one vote and no one is disre-

---

[199] Warren, Elizabeth/Warren Tyagi, Amelia (2003), pp. 6 f.
[200] Id., p. 15, call it the "over-consumption myth".
[201] Frank, Robert H. (2007), p. 45: "[Parents] can either send their children to a school of average quality by purchasing a house that is larger and more expensive than they can comfortably afford, or they can buy a smaller house that is within their budget and send their children to a below-average school."
[202] Warren, Elizabeth/Warren Tyagi, Amelia (2003), p. 23, 28
[203] Frank, Robert H. (2007), pp. 5, 43 f.
[204] Warren, Elizabeth/Warren Tyagi, Amelia (2003), p. 81
[205] Hacker, Jacob S./Pierson, Paul (2010), p. 28
[206] Francia, Peter L. (2006), pp. 15 f., 155

spected. The unanimity rule makes sure that everybody has to be considered and convinced. Concessions toward efficiency made the majority rule attractive, giving way though to power abuse. The different provisions of the constitutional state, especially human rights and mechanisms of checks and balances are used as safeguards for individuals. Minority rights make sure that there are many points within the political debate where the weaker can step in. But formal democratic processes do not guarantee equal construction power. Politicians, parties, and governmental institutions can be hijacked by lobbying groups, and the "reality" construction by mass media leads to a mediacracy, with a tendency to mediocracy. Out of this power-arrangement follows the difficulty for a large part of the people to make their voices heard. Political protest and unorthodox forms of resistance are possible ways to attract, at least for a short time, the attention of the media. The Tea Party is an example of a movement that has had an effective impact. In the economic realm, though, workers are less and less represented and have only a few opportunities to defend their interests. Individuals are, therefore, confronted with the power of the state, which is for an important part public and is widely checked and balanced. And there is, second, the power of companies, fast changing, with a little degree of formalization, sometimes internationally active, potentially diffuse and difficult to seize, and taking decisions that have often existential effects on the ones with few power.

To make sure that the "reality" construction is organized in a just way, a coercion-free discourse is needed, a discourse organized on the basis of freedom, responsibility, and justice (equality, respect). Alexy defined it as follows: 1. Every subject with the competence to speak and act is allowed to take part in a discourse; 2a. Everyone is allowed to question any assertion whatever; 2b. Everyone is allowed to introduce any assertion whatever into the discourse; 2c. Everyone is allowed to express his attitudes, desires, and needs; 3. No speaker may be prevented, by internal or external coercion, from exercising his rights as laid down in (1) and (2)[207]. To make sure that integration is general, we should add the necessary support to bring into the discourse everybody or at least to make the access equally available. Furthermore, we have to think about the necessity of being able to speak: Is it sensible to exclude the mentally ill or people suffering from senile dementia, nature, animals, and so on? Or could somebody represent their interests? However, a substantial understanding of equal opportunities is needed[208] so that all members have the same probability of being successful

---

[207] Alexy, Robert (1995), p. 130
[208] O'Neill, Onora (1993), pp. 148 ff.

and realizing their interests. It is not relevant if I am a blue-collar worker, black, a white woman, or rich, whoever I am, my ability to influence my "reality" has to be as important as that of the others. Formal equality and universal rights are shallow when the society is very unequal and many a people do not have the resources to express, defend, and fulfill their interests: "The law, in its majestic equality, forbids the rich as well as the poor to sleep under bridges, to beg in the streets, and to steal bread."[209]

A just community is orientated toward equal construction-power and is ready to share the resources needed to develop ideally the potential of its members. Without cooperation, justice isn't possible: "Danny Crane: Do you have any idea what would happen if all the little people stop paying their taxes? Alan Shore: Rich people would have to start paying theirs ..."[210]

e) Solidarity

"Solidarity" is about weakness, failure, fear, and powerlessness. It is also about identity, resources, enrichment, and support. Solidarity reflects the social character of human beings, it reflects their dependence on each other as well as their mutual enhancement. The homo oeconomicus doesn't know solidarity or social interdependence.[211] This rational, self-referential individual makes himself and isn't made by others. For the homo interactivus, however, solidarity is a central form of relationship, it is the *interaction that shapes the character of the individuals and the community*. Solidarity is also *unconditional support to make life for others possible and to protect their dignity*. And it stands for a long term engagement, for the *responsibility for others* and, thus, for the community. Solidarity sets the conditions needed for a just community made out of free individuals.

---

[209] France, Anatole (1894), Chap. 7, § 118, p. 81: "Cela consiste pour les pauvres à soutenir et à conserver les riches dans leur puissance et leur oisiveté. Ils y doivent travailler devant la majestueuse égalité des lois, qui interdit au riche comme au pauvre de coucher sous les ponts, de mendier dans les rues et de voler du pain. C'est un des bienfaits de la Révolution. Comme cette révolution a été faite par des fous et des imbéciles au profit des acquéreurs de biens nationaux et qu'elle n'aboutit en somme qu'à l'enrichissement des paysans madrés et des bourgeois usuriers, elle éleva, sous le nom d'égalité, l'empire de la richesse."
[210] Boston Legal, Season 2, Episode 19, 21'
[211] Vacarie, Isabelle/Allouache, Anissa/Ginon, Anne-Sophie/Ferkane, Ylias/Leroy, Sonia (2008), p. 1108

aa) Constitutive effect

I am what we are, even though I am more than what we are and the we is more than I am. Interactively I become myself thanks to the demarcation from others. The others, therefore, are constitutive to my identity, on the one hand, because of their difference and, on the other hand, because of their support for myself as a child or as grown up. Between the interactors stretches the "we," the community, which is dependent on the actions of the individuals (see before, p. 42 ff.). This "we" has its own quality, it is something an individual alone couldn't establish and it has an enriching impact on the identity of the interactors. The "I" is at once myself and me as a member of "we." Over the years one develops many different personal and collective identities, whereby the new experiences add to the foregoing ones. Deciding to interact with somebody is, thus, a decision for a "we," for a community. It is a decision *for* a specific social arrangement and it stands for the readiness to *act in favor of commonality*. Solidarity is, therefore, the *willingness to take responsibility for a particular set of freedoms and obligations*. This responsibility can vary in intensity and range. The more the interactors are ready to engage for the "we," the more it is stable and the longer it will last. A "we" isn't simply given by the consumption of cheap products. It's neither identical with sport events or big concerts. The "we" transcending the individual existence incorporates rights and obligations and includes a common perspective. *Every community is based on a minimal form of cooperation.*

To be able to realize the potential that communities provide, which is a potential that overcomes the limits of individuals, the existence of others has to be recognized. The more their difference and uniqueness is respected, the richer the reservoir the actors have at their disposal. And if there are reciprocal forms of support, it is only the lack of engagement of the creators that restricts their possibilities. A community, however, based on oppression, abuse, or competition will heavily underperform. Individuals then are confronted with obstacles that others put have built up, using lots of creative energy just to limit the possibilities of the competitors. Insofar is "a life in form of the first person singular [...] a mutilated life.[212] [...] we need to be [...] part of a social succession overtopping and magnifying us."[213] Waldo Emerson wrote about friendship as "a friend may well be reckoned the masterpiece of Nature,"[214] which stands for the uniqueness of supportive

---

[212] Debray, Régis (2009), p. 14
[213] *Id.*, p. 17
[214] Emerson, Ralph Waldo (1993), p. 108

communities. What makes us rich are the friends we have and cherish,[215] not the shallow materialism that currently dominates. That is the case of the meaning of life, which originates in relationships, in literature, scientific work, music, architecture and other symbolizations that tell a story about the past and the future of the interactors. "Sense" is about "connecting [...] the ephemeral with the durable [...]; the prolongation of the self by affiliation with a 'we' that precedes and survives me."[216]

Because of the interdependence of individuals, a *mirroring-effect* takes place: What happens to others, happens to ourselves. Treating people as "inhumane" or as "animals" lowers the level of expectations toward everyone. Central values like justice or human dignity are strongly relativized and become evidently arbitrary and at the mercy of the rulers. This arbitrariness makes all the community members insecure, not just the victims. Nobody can trust that the cherished values will be upheld in the future, the abused people might come to power and act on the same deep level of morality. Or the rulers may decide to change their mind and construct a new enemy.

bb) Support

Cooperation comprises rights and obligations and basically involves all members. There are, however, people who are not able to fulfill obligations. A lack of resources makes them unequal contributors.

> "The streets are very dirty
> Me shoes are very thin
> I have a little pocket
> To put a penny in
>
> I have a little pocket to put a penny in.
> If you haven't got a penny, a ha' penny will do.
> If you haven't got a ha' penny then God bless you."[217]

They try to survive. Their only hope is the support of God if they're religious and/or the support by others. To treat them in a just way means to take into account their individual capacities. Human beings are equal according to

---

[215] Calogero: C'est Dit, on the album "L'embellie" 2009
[216] Debray, Régis (2009), p. 34
[217] Sting: Soul Cake, on the album "If on a Winter's Night" 2009

their dignity, as well as to their potential or their right to be recognized and respected. But they are often not equal with regard to their current opportunities which are mainly determined by direct, structural, and cultural violence. To make sure, that equal construction power becomes possible, *unconditional support* has to be offered.

The dignity of men and women is best preserved if the support takes the form of help to self-help. Yunus is convinced that very poor people also know how to survive, otherwise they wouldn't be alive anymore.[218] It is, therefore, not a problem of knowledge, but a problem of resources and obstacles. Structures are needed that have a lasting impact on inequality. Charity may be helpful in individual cases or when unexpectedly immediate support is required. In the long run, though, structures at the origin of inequality have to be changed, because support within an excluding social structure is ambivalent. If it doesn't lead to change it reproduces and confirms the exclusion, and is, hence, an ambivalent measure of relief and reproductive oppression at the same time. Support within an unequal community also may lead to dependency be it of private or state help. To break the social, economic, political, and cultural barriers that hold people back, the barriers that incapacitate people to develop equal freedom,[219] is a challenge that has to be answered at the community level. It can't be executed by individuals alone. It doesn't need too much to liberate people and to make opportunities available for them.[220] The readiness to cooperate, though, is essential.

Neoliberal ideas of modern life mainly focus on the anti-social individual. To give up the notion of the common good makes it much more difficult to create the "reality" we would like to live in. Most of the individuals become re-actors instead of actors because the changes are too important to be assumed by one alone: The present and future slip through our fingers. Italy's chief anti-mafia prosecutor, Piero Grasso, holds that the Mafia can't be beaten by repression, but by a cultural revolution. People have to give up their indifference for others and for the community. State power is limited and can only be effective if individuals in their everyday life are ready to cooperate and support the state actors. To get rid of the Mafia with its deep roots within society "a culture is needed that is the contrary of consumerism and egocentricity. Today we put the individual first, not the community. We only react, if our personal interests are at stake […]. This indifference toward the community has to be overcome."[221]

---

[218] Yunus, Muhammad (2007), p. 113
[219] Moore, Barrington (1982), p. 148
[220] *Id.*, p. 167
[221] Grasso, Piero (2010)

cc) Exchange – reciprocity

For many tourists, the Palio of Siena is a horse race. For the Sienesi, it is the core of their identity, dating back to medieval times. Siena, a city in Tuscany, Italy, is the venue of two horse races that take place every year in July and August. The city is split into seventeen city wards called "Contrade," the borders of which were determined in 1729. From the 14th century on races took place in the city, but it is in 1633 that the form seen today got established. In 1721, a catalogue of rules was set up and which is still applied. Every Contrade has its own name (Tortoise, Wave, She-Wolf, Goose, Shell, Porcupine, Dragon, Owl, Snail, Panther, Eagle, Caterpillar, Unicorn, Ram, Giraffe, Forest, and Tower), constitution, and political institution, a hymn, an emblem, a patron saint, its church where its people get married, a baptismal font, a museum within which the victory banners are kept, and some historical palaces. People become burghers of the Contrada where they are born. Members in need are supported by their community without having to ask.[222] Every Contrade passionately nurtures its allies and enemies. A very fragile equilibrium of love and hate characterizes their relationships. In songs and poems the others are venerated or mocked and people do not get married with members of an enemy Contrade.

Communities use symbolic links (see p. 387 ff.) to represent, reproduce, and stabilize their collective identity. The more this link is dynamic, the more it helps bring people together and to motive their engagement. On the other hand, too much dynamism can have disintegrative effects. Social inequality and permanent losers have to be avoided if a community wants to last. That's why Siena's horse race uses the drive that a non-destructive and non-exclusionary competition can yield, but moderates it with many equalizing rules. Because of the size of the Piazza del Campo, the number of race participants had to be reduced to ten in 1721. The ones not participating will automatically take part the following year and the other three are drawn by lot. Every Contrada brings its horse to the trial runs where the most equal horses are selected. The horses are chosen and trained by the individual Contrada. For the race, though, since 1676 they are assigned by lottery to make sure that all the Contrade have the same chance to win. Otherwise, the rich and/or aristocratic Contrade harboring for example one of the oldest banks of the world, the Monte dei Paschi di Siena (Contrada Lupa) would probably win most of the time. The jockeys are "mercenaries" and with the horse are decisive for the victory. Even though they're well paid, nobody really trusts them. They are controlled day in and day

---

[222] Dundes, Alan/Falassi, Alessandro (1994), p. 29

out to make sure that no other Contrada bribes them. If a jockey is caught working for another, he will probably be beaten up. Negotiations and pacts between the Contrade, however, are allowed and are perceived as a complex barter system that enhances the thrill of the event. The winner gets enormous reputation, its enemies, however, will be laughed out during the year. What the winner gains in reputation is equalled with money, which is why it has to "compensate" all the participants, except, of course, its enemy.[223]

The Palio keeps the people of Siena busy during the whole year and, therefore, becomes an important element of the people's meaning of life. All the preparations, the trials, trainings, and festivities reproduce time and again the basic elements of the collective identity and strengthen the bonds between the interactors. The race further integrates two identities: The Contrada identity, with its clear demarcations and its self-perception as the state, on the one hand, and the city identity uniting the wards, on the other hand.[224] A complex *net of rights and obligations and important forms of repartition* secure equal opportunities for the interactors and effectively avoid exclusion and permanent losers.

Solidarity is a form of reciprocal exchange (see p. 225 ff.) and stands for a give and take over time. Some *renounce something for somebody*, expecting a direct or indirect *payback* in the long run. "Brother, can you spare a Dime?" was a number one hit during the Great Depression and perfectly describes the mutual obligation solidarity represents.

Brother, Can You Spare A Dime?
E.Y. Harburg (lyrics) – Jay Gorney (music) – 1931

They used to tell me
I was building a dream.
And so I followed the mob
When there was earth to plow
Or guns to bear
I was always there
Right on the job.

They used to tell me
I was building a dream
With peace and glory ahead.
Why should I be standing in line
Just waiting for bread?

---

[223] *Id.*, pp. 78 f.
[224] Civai, Mauro/Toti, Enrico (1997), p. 55

Once I built a railroad
I made it run
Made it race against time.
Once I built a railroad
Now it's done
Brother, can you spare a dime?

Once in khaki suits
Gee we looked swell
Full of that yankee doodle dee dum.
Half a million boots went sloggin'
through hell

Once I built a tower up to the sun
Brick and rivet and lime.
Once I built a tower,
Now it's done.
Brother, can you spare a dime?

And I was the kid with the drum!
Say don't you remember?
They called me Al.
It was Al all the time.
Why don't you remember?
I'm your pal.
Say buddy, can you spare a dime?

Effective and lasting power originates in acts of reciprocity. One could say that the bigger the power somebody claims and the longer it is supposed to last, the more the people have to be taken seriously and have to find advantages in this arrangement.

dd) Freedom, thanks to solidarity

Enhanced individualization propagated by neoliberalism imposes the market-logic on every relationship and has, therefore, a destructive impact on social bonds[225] – the solidary soil on which freedom and justice grow. Twenge and Foster who interviewed college students, state a considerable increase in narcissistic traits over the generations.[226] This heyday of the self, this narcissism is self-limiting as much as it limits the community the narcissists live in. It is the choice of a conflict-avoiding life that looks for simple need-satisfaction. However, to become a distinguished character is only possible if one is courageous enough to step apart from the masses and confront others with one's own "reality" proposals. It is thanks to conflicts with others that we get to be ourselves.[227] Uniqueness results from interactive

---

[225] Green, E.H.H. (2002), p. 290: "[…] the emphasis on market relations which had informed much of the political, economic, and social agenda of the 1980s and 1990s appeared to have brought about the possibility of […] a fracturing of social cohesion."
[226] Twenge, Jean M./Foster, Joshua D. (2010), p. 103
[227] Nassehi, Armin (2004), p. 31

identity-work[228] which uses and nurtures the solidarity that relationships offer. I would qualify as free only unique, self-assured people, those who are able, if necessary, to decide against the majority. Furthermore, selfish materialism doesn't seem to make us happy. According to Headey et al., "people who consistently prioritize non–zero-sum altruistic goals or family goals are more satisfied with life than people who prioritize goals relating to their own careers and material success. Giving priority to altruistic goals is strongly associated with higher life satisfaction, whereas family goals are also satisfaction enhancing."[229]

To force individualization is politically of interest for right-wing goals because counterpower based on solidarity becomes highly difficult to develop. Isolated people have many more problems to mobilize and be mobilized because solidarity is the central resource for effective political action.[230] Democracy on greater levels becomes possible if people organize in social movements, parties, or interest groups to make themselves heard.[231] The ruling oligarchy is in a better position because of the small number of people and the existing networks they can rely on. In any case, solidarity is the "technique" which makes the cooperation of free individuals possible, without forcing them to give up their own interests. It is a flexible relationship, able to answer the challenges people are confronted with[232] and preserves freedom best.[233] Complexity, plurality, and freedom result from interacting individuals supporting the creativity of others.[234]

To be solidary in a just and responsible way means to be surrounded by human beings, to develop empathy, to be able to imagine the "reality" others live in, to respect others' suffering, and to support their hopes.

---

[228] Keupp, Heiner (1992), p. 109
[229] Headey, Bruce/Muffels, Ruud/Wagner, Gert G. (2010), p. 3
[230] Meyer, Thomas (1994), p. 67
[231] Frankenberg, Günter (1994), pp. 222 f.
[232] Hondrich, Karl Otto/Koch-Arzberger, Claudia (1992), pp. 119 f.
[233] Bauman, Zygmunt (1995), p. 21
[234] Morin, Edgar (2008), p. 48

2. Recognition

Basic values are quite abstract principles. Forms of action concretize what people mean when they talk about freedom or justice. Often a consensus is found about basic values, about the general direction of the society's development, without, however, sharing the concrete steps to realize these ideas. In this book cooperation is the form of action that is meant to realize best the basic values and to have therefore longest lasting integrative effect. Cooperation conflates recognition, respect, and reciprocity, all of which yield trust. Democracy and the constitutional state developed in Europe and in the USA are political applications of recognition, respect, and reciprocity. Nevertheless, European and American history is full of violations of the equal dignity of people. People were used for political and economical goals and, therefore, they were neither recognized nor respected. Plumelle-Uribe highlights three main genocidal experiences: The massacre of Natives in the Americas, the annihilation of the Blacks, and the exterminations effected by the Nazis.[1] In her opinion the last of these atrocities is based on the preceding abuses of power. Their master- and slave-race totalitarian politic was built up upon the experiences and justifications made during colonization and slavery.[2] As the "result of an over four centuries lasting process,"[3] they used the same philosophical concepts and based their "reality" on the same values. "Hitler made visible a racist insanity established long before the twentieth century [...], a system of annihilation of human beings, that until then only colonized people had had to experience."[4]

a) Economic absolutism – negated personhood

"Slavery" is the archetype of economic absolutism, of a politic that sets economic interests higher than any other consideration. The elite of first the European nations and then the United States created from the 16th to the 19th century a way to make money in a more efficient way than ever. Slavery existed in many different forms and long before it became a thriving business that played a central role in the economic development of the West. But the Europeans perfected the system by introducing industrial produc-

---

[1] Plumelle-Uribe, Rosa Amelia (2001), p. 23
[2] *Id.*, p. 29
[3] *Id.*, p. 137
[4] *Id.*, p. 30

tion forms. There is nothing natural[5] or inevitable about slavery. It is the decision of an economic and political upper class to make materialism the sole guideline of life.

aa) Looking for workforce

Throughout history slaves served their masters in many different roles: As agricultural laborers, as builders, in the armed forces, as household servants, as concubines or wives, or as the proverbial sacrificial lamb. They were captured during warfare and enslaved, regardless of their ethnical, religious or national origins. Slave markets existed in ancient and medieval times and the masters had the right to hold them like chattels: Slaves could be bought and sold, punished and even killed at the will of their owners. From the 6th to the 9th century Christians used and supported slavery regardless of the religious identity of the enslaved.[6] In medieval society it became increasingly important to delimit Christians from other denominations, which is why slaves then had to be, for example, Jews, Muslims, heretics, or pagans. Christendom took over from Islam a rule already known in the Old Testament but never applied until then: It was no allowed to enslave co-religionists.[7] In Europe slaves had never been the dominant workforce and were from the 11th century on increasingly replaced by serfdom. Even though serfdom was deeply unequal, it was a more equitable arrangement because within the feudal system the lord had certain duties to fulfill toward the vassal:[8] He had to protect him, guarantee general security, and to be solidary. Even the serfs in Russia, who had one of the lowest status levels, enjoyed certain rights like holding land, getting married, or forming communal organizations around shared interests. The total arbitrariness characterizing slavery was exceptional and, contrary to slave-owners, the lords were forbidden to take the lives of the serfs. In the 15th century, serfdom began to lose its importance and got replaced by paid free landless labourers. When, in the 16th century, the concept of individual liberty gained ground, the emerging nation states wanted to be free of slavery. Nevertheless, European states didn't stop buying and selling slaves and justifying it theologi-

---

[5] Elkins, Stanley M. (1959), p. 37
[6] Blackburn, Robin (1998), p. 38
[7] *Id.*, p. 42: "Islamic law went [even] further and prohibited the enslavement of Christians and Jews so long as they were living peaceably under Islamic rule, and paying a special tribute."
[8] Schulze, Hans K. (1998), p. 58

cally.⁹ From the 12th to the 15th century the universal concept of humankind dear to Christians restricted the use of slaves. Even though important religious leaders like Thomas Aquinas justified slavery because of its utility and factual necessity,¹⁰ political leaders were reluctant to make use of it.¹¹ Economic interests were still dominated by moral reflections, which is why the number of slaves was limited. It is only in capitalism, in this economic totalitarianism that these limits were abolished. Nevertheless, these religious qualms didn't improve the slaves' conditions. The promised redemption wasn't supposed to take place here and now but in the kingdom to come.¹² And there were no differences between the religions because Catholics as well as Protestants treated their human propriety awfully.¹³

Prosperity in feudal Europe increased the demand for sugar. The technique to extract this luxury commodity from cane was invented in India and brought to Europe by Arabs and then Italian merchants, who used it in Crete, Cyprus, and Sicily. Cane had to be ground and the obtained juice to be boiled, which was a hard and labor-intensive work. The colonization of the Canary Islands by the Spanish and the Portuguese led to another labor-shortage, as there was too small a workforce in the Isles. Especially on the Azores, Madeira, and the Cape Verde Islands, which were previously uninhabited, slave trade labourers were needed.¹⁴ Colonization as well as the slave trade were supported by the Pope, who understood them as promotion of Christianity. According to the Papal Bull "Romanus Pontifex" of 1455, the captivation and trade of slaves was allowed, as long as the Portuguese tried to "win them for Christ."¹⁵ The economy established by the Portuguese – agricultural production, employment of slaves, and international trade – became the core economic model for the coming three centuries.

---

[9] Blackburn, Robin (1998), p. 62-76

[10] Aquinas: Summa Theologica – Justice – Question § 57, Article 3, Objection 2: "[…] slavery among men is natural, for some are naturally slaves". Reply to Objection 2: "[…] the fact that this particular man should be a slave rather than another man, is based, not on natural reason, but on some resultant utility, in that it is useful to this man to be ruled by a wiser man." Article 4: "[…] a son belongs to his father, since he is part of him somewhat, […] and a slave belongs to his master, because he is his instrument."

[11] Blackburn, Robin (1998), p. 83

[12] Sala-Molins, Louis (2005), p. 66

[13] Id., p. 69

[14] According to Fogel, Robert William/Engerman, Stanley L. (1974), p. 17, about 117'000 Blacks were imported from 1451 to 1550.

[15] Blackburn, Robin (1998), p. 103

Contrary to the Portuguese orientation toward trade, the Spanish pursued a political and religious project. They intended to establish an empire[16] organized along absolutist feudal principles. Huge tracts of land would have to be colonized, souls saved from paganism, and the natural resources of the Americas exploited, especially the gold and silver mines. Emperor Charles V of Spain legalized in 1521 the slave trade to his colonies by establishing the asiento system (an exclusive right on slave trade granted to privates). About 190'000 legal slaves and thousands of smuggled slaves were brought to Spanish America from 1551 to 1650. The Spanish built up a royal central administration and imposed a tribute system to secure the important investments that had to be made in order to conquer these lands and people. Spanish America had by 1630 five archdioceses, 29 dioceses, 10 universities, 334 monasteries, and 74 convents.[17] Political-religious integration was dominant because "Spanish authorities [...] did not trust independent merchants and their aggressive pursuit of self-interest."[18] Slaves were needed to replace the Native labour force that had been decimated by overwork, diseases, and punishment inflicted by rapacious conquistadores. To avoid revolt, the Crown forbad Native slavery in the second half of the 16th century. African slaves were easier to control, because they were isolated from their original communities and forced to live far away from home. Notwithstanding, morality put a limit to this business, which is why the King of Spain tried to rein in the worst excesses. Same moderation is to be found in the Portuguese colonies. Royal preacher Father Vieira, assigned with the task of missionary work in Brazil, criticized the enslavement of Natives,[19] wherefore it was outlawed at his behest in 1655.

English colonizers hoped to "get-rich-quick" by finding gold mines and by pirating Spanish ships at sea. But these endeavours were too expensive and highly risky so long-term engagements began to be favored. Contrary

---

[16] Taylor, Alan (2001), p. 51, 59
[17] Blackburn, Robin (1998), p. 132
[18] Taylor, Alan (2001), p. 476
[19] He also criticized the cruelties of slavery in general: "Are these people the children of Adam and Eve? Were not these souls redeemed by the blood of Christ? Are not these bodies born and do they not die as ours do? Do they not breath the same air? Are they not covered by the same sky? Are they not warmed by the same sun?" Addressing the masters, he asks: "[...] your slaves, why must you sell them too, putting your lust for gold ... ahead of their salvation?" Vieira invokes even a right to resist: "If the master orders the slave to do something, or wants from a slave anything that gravely harms his soul and conscience, the slave is not obliged to obey". (Cited in Blackburn, Robin [1998], p. 209).

to the Spanish, however, English interests were purely economic. Virginia, for example, was at the beginning of the 16th century, little more than a speculative object of the Virginia Company of London, which tried to sell shares to the highest bidder. Whatever the motivation, all colonial projects needed lots of workers, because agricultural production was labour-intensive and the land that was supposed to make them rich was sparsely populated. The Dutch had just a few domestic workers willing to emigrate, because the conditions at home were satisfying enough.

In England, however, an important mass of people had lost their economic existence because of the privatization of the common land.[20] Thanks to this agricultural reform rationalization was made possible, yielding higher profits for the aristocrat's estates.[21] On the other hand, the "lower sort" was excluded and lost their economical basis and autonomy. To escape their dire straits and to find hopefully a decent life abroad, many people were willing to take the risk. Most of this poor went to the Chesapeake, Virginia, and the West Indies. The majority was engaged as indentured servants – a fixed-term contract, during which they had almost the status of slaves. Their engagement was time-limited, based on their consensus, and included different rights. Unable to pay for the passage to the new lands, they mortgaged four to seven years of their lives to a ship captain or a merchant who sold them on the other side of the Atlantic to a planter. During their engagement, they weren't allowed to marry and their freedom was restricted. When their contract expired, they were entitled to a piece of land (in Virginia, for example, fifty acres[22]), clothes, tools, and food – the so-called "freedom dues." Compared to the desolate situation in Britain all in all this was an interesting offer. They didn't expect to die of overwork or disease in such large numbers. Also, they weren't told that planters readily resorted to the whip, convinced that the serfs were "loose, vagrant people, vicious and destitute of a means to live at home."[23] Event though their rights were guaranteed by contract, to gain redress was difficult. The judges, themselves wealthy planters, often defended the interests of their equals. The convicts were a second group of people used as manpower in the colonies. In England they were perceived as the detritus of society and potentially dangerous, which is why the government supported their shipment to America. Instead of having to pay for prisoners at home, they would be used in the colonies as unskilled workers. It was an easy way to get rid of the commu-

---

[20] Finzsch, Norbert/Horton, James O./Horton Lois E. (1999), pp. 56 f.
[21] Taylor, Alan (2001), p. 120
[22] Id., p. 133
[23] Id., p. 143

nity's responsibility for its members, for the social conditions and lack of opportunity that had motivated criminal acts.

Financed by the state and by licensed private companies these investments were of high risk. Mainly at the beginning, the lack of experience, the different climatic conditions, and unknown forms of diseases led to significant losses. To assure the investment, supplies for the workforce had to be organized – not an easy task because the investors had to rely on free laborers. The solution was African slaves. Having been experimented before in Spanish and Portuguese America, African slaves had four big advantages: First, the slaves were commodities the buyer could own indefinitely and treat and sell according to his own discretion. Second, there seemed to exist an indefinite supply of slaves, which was very helpful in satisfying the ever increasing demand for sugar, tobacco, coffee, cotton, or indigo. Third, the color of their skin made escaping much more difficult. Fourth, thanks to the legal status of slaves, mothers passed their chattel status on to their children, which meant a self-perpetuating labor force.

In 17th century Northern Europe mass demand developed considerably. Smoking tobacco and serving tea or coffee with sugar became status symbols for an increasingly waged and salaried working class. In particular, the sugar production gained momentum and replaced gold and silver as the most valued commodity. During the 17th century, the former sugar monopoly of the Spanish and Portuguese ended as the British (on Barbados, Jamaica for example), French (on Haiti), and the Dutch (in Guayana and Surinam) became sugar-trade powers. It is only in the 19th century that Spain again played an important role in the sugar trade, when it started producing on extensive plantations in Cuba and Puerto Rico.

Labor-intensive cash crops like rice but above all cotton or sugar, and an ever-growing worldwide demand motivated the rationalization of agricultural production forms. Heavy investments were needed, especially in the sugar production, for refining machinery, land, and workers. This hard calculating form of managed large-scale economic activity[24] developed integrated plantations, where the slaves worked in gangs, planting in incessant cycles, weeding and harvesting, and grinding during the night. Furthermore, the selling and the transportation of the commodities had to be organized. On a plantation in the Caribbean fifty to three hundred slaves were working up to eighteen hours a day. Under these harsh conditions, planters estimated an average life expectancy of young Africans to be little more then seven years.[25] Within these seven years, the investment had to pay off.

---

[24] Fogel, Robert William/Engerman, Stanley L. (1974), pp. 67 ff., 129, 199
[25] Blackburn, Robin (1998), p. 339

In summary: The labor-intensive industrialized agriculture necessitated a limitless number of workers. Free workers were difficult to find, not enough convicts were available, and the working conditions were so harsh, that too many workers died and women were much less able to bear and nurse children. And the ratio of about 65 males to 35 females in the Atlantic slave trade didn't help procreation. Because of all these reasons the planters needed a permanent influx of slaves, a never ending supply of very cheap and easy to handle workers. A service the African-American trade system was apt to provide.

bb) Slaves – a profitable commodity

The slave trade was big business for the state, the families, and the companies involved. The purchase of slaves was a highly profitable investment, yielding rates of return comparable with the most outstanding investments in manufacturing,[26] which is why investors were ready to take the high risks inherent in every voyage. *Modern wealth of the European and North American[27] states is fundamentally based on the trade with and the work of slaves.* Slave traffic and the plantation-related trades played a decisive part in the economic development of Europe because they fueled its capitalist accumulation.[28] Colonies based on the plantation and by this the slave-system were much wealthier than others,[29] which is why for decades the most important economic assets were land and slaves. Slavery didn't just profit the slave-traders and owners, but also other economic areas. For example, the colonial trade needed a growing volume of shipping which contributed to the importance of shipbuilding, another major industry. "By the middle of the eighteenth century, half of all Britain's overseas trade consisted of shipments of sugar or tobacco; sugar and coffee comprised more than half of all French overseas commerce."[30] On the other hand, the colonies required equipment for the plantations, which was produced in Britain or in the northern colonies. In this way, Britain had developed an international economic system that yielded a surplus going far beyond the subsistence economy.

---

[26] Fogel, Robert William/Engerman, Stanley L. (1974), p. 4
[27] Farrow, Anne/Lang, Joel/Frank, Jenifer (2006), p. XXIX: "The nation's wealth, from the very beginning, depended upon the exploitation of black people on three continents."
[28] Blackburn, Robin (1998), p. 376
[29] Morgan, Kenneth (2007), p. 36
[30] Blackburn, Robin (1998), p. 396

The plantation economy and the triangular trade yielded the profits necessary for the investments that boosted industrialization in Great Britain. In 1770, the triangular trade is estimated to have furnished from 21 to 55 per cent of the British gross fixed capital formation. Combined with the profits of the plantations they constituted the largest single source of imperial gains.[31] Furthermore, they provided the crucial industrial input – row cotton – at a cheap price, which helped British manufacturers compete decisively successfully with Indian textile producers and to establish a global hegemony. "By the eve of the Civil War, Great Britain was largely clothing the Western world, using Southern-grown, slave-picked cotton."[32] On the other hand, the success of the capitalist industrialization boosted the slave economy because of the ever-rising world demand for cotton, the U.S. production rose from 3'000 bales in 1790 to over 178'000 bales in 1810 to 732'000 in 1830 and to 4'500'000 in 1860,[33] creating great wealth in North America. To the total exports of the United States, cotton contributed 30 percent in 1820, 50 percent in 1840, and 60 percent in 1860.[34]

Within this capitalist economy, the slave trade was a business like any other trade of commodities. Slaves weren't people, they were a workforce and only valuable for that. Like animals, the men and women were caught in Africa, branded with a hot iron, and forced onto the ships waiting offshore. Europeans didn't catch Africans by themselves, but were sold them by leading merchants and chiefs of the coastal kingdoms. "Although they did not directly seize slaves, the European traders indirectly promoted the wars and kidnapping gangs by offering premium prices for captives."[35] Future slaves were not only captured from the coastal areas but also from the interior of Africa. In the latter case the slaves had to walk hundreds of miles to the coast in coffles and shackled in a line.[36] Since the early 17th century European nations had established warehouses called "castles" on the west coast of Africa to stock the kidnapped merchandise before embarking on the overseas voyage. In total, the slave *raids* led to the death of a least two million Africans.[37]

The following transatlantic voyage, the so-called "Middle Passage," had to be organized to ensure that the shipping companies would make highest

---

[31] Blackburn, Robin (1998), pp. 542 f.
[32] Farrow, Anne/Lang, Joel/Frank, Jenifer (2006), p. 10
[33] Fogel, Robert William/Engerman, Stanley L. (1974), p. 44
[34] Finzsch, Norbert/Horton, James O./Horton Lois E. (1999), p. 163
[35] Taylor, Alan (2001), p. 325
[36] Morgan, Kenneth (2007), p. 71
[37] Taylor, Alan (2001), pp. 323 f.

profits. Basically, transporting kidnapped people in such densely crowded ships over such long a distance was a huge risk, but could generate ten times the profit of an ordinary trade voyage.[38] The more men and women that could be transported and the more of them survived the passage in a not too bad a shape, the higher were the gains. The "loose packers" defended more room and food for the captured, hoping to deliver their cargo alive to the Americas. The "tight packers," on the other hand, preferred shipping as many people as possible and risking the life of some of the victims. To avoid uprisings on the boats, slaves were shackled to the rack and to each other. Furthermore, the traders assembled cargos of diverse ethnic groups and languages to hinder mutual support. The slavers blamed the slaves for this harsh treatment because they weren't willing to accept their fate. "The many acts of violence they have committed by murdering whole crews and destroying ships when they had it in their power to do so have made these rigors wholly chargeable on their own bloody and malicious disposition, which calls for the same confinement as if they were wolves or wild boars."[39] During the 17th century, about 20 percent of the slaves were killed on the Middle Passage. Later it "improved" to about 10 percent mainly thanks to a more varied diet. Compared to these numbers, English convicts were lucky, as "only" about 4 percent of them died during their passage. Arriving abroad, the customers checked the merchandise thoroughly according to the contracts signed at public auctions.

cc) Capitalism – deadly materialism

In Latin America, an estimated 80 million Natives in 1500 was diminished to 10 million in 1650[40] due to, on the one hand, a willful decimation of the population and, on the other hand, the appalling effects of a political, religious, and economic absolutism. The Natives were killed because they resisted. They died of overwork in the mines or because of contagion for unknown viruses. The search for fast money had genocidal effects on communities which had successfully lived here for about 15'000 years.[41] Hunting potential slaves in Africa killed about two million people. Ten to 12 million living slaves were transported over the Atlantic within about three hundred years.[42] Until 1830, forced migration significantly exceeded vol-

---

[38] Farrow, Anne/Lang, Joel/Frank, Jenifer (2006), p. 98
[39] Quoted in Taylor, Alan (2001), p. 327
[40] Plumelle-Uribe, Rosa Amelia (2001), p. 36
[41] Taylor, Alan (2001), pp. 38 f., 43, 52 ff., 63 ff.
[42] Morgan, Kenneth (2007), p. 12

untary immigration. Arriving didn't mean surviving: during the 18th century, for example, in the Chesapeake about one quarter died within the first year. "Brazil and the Caribbean were graveyards for Africans and their descendants."[43]

The origin of this abominable suffering and loss of human lives was capitalism, the *absolutized materialism, a totalitarian economy*. "The overriding motive of merchants and planters in their involvement with slavery and the slave trade was economic."[44] Profit-orientation before anything else and the desire for cheap products made this mass-killing possible. Using direct violence for establishing structural violence justified by cultural violence: Life, justice, freedom, and solidarity were flouted because *material wealth dominated everything*. What made this economy "capitalistic" was its *unrestricted pursuit of material goals*, whatever it may cost even in human lives. It is, in my opinion, not the right to property or economic freedom that makes a society capitalistic. These are the elements characterizing a partly liberal society. In the center of a capitalistic society is an *important inequality of power, resources, and rights used for personal material gain*. The bigger part of the society is used by the ruling majority to increase the elite's wealth. Elkins called this an "unmitigated capitalism" that led to "unmitigated slavery" because nobody stopped the sacrifice of black people. "The planter was now engaged in capitalistic agriculture with a labor force entirely under his control."[45] As in every community, there were restrictions, there were rules that the Whites had to observe. But when it came to their power over slaves, the slave society "was based on devolution of authority to the masters on the plantations. Moreover, the relationship between masters and slaves was a total relationship that covered virtually everything that made up human contact."[46] This blatant inequality is enhanced by the fundamental irresponsibility of the rulers for the "side effects" this absolutist materialism inevitably produces. Based on pure commercial calculations the homo oeconomicus sacrificed the lives of millions of people to such banal needs as sweet tea and chocolate, smoking, and dressing elegantly. Just for fun and well-being, lives were destroyed and the human dignity of millions was violated. The consumer society was made possible thanks to the extermination of people.

---

[43] Kolchin, Peter (2003), p. 22
[44] Morgan, Kenneth (2007), p. 34
[45] Elkins, Stanley M. (1959), p. 49
[46] Morris, Thomas D. (1996), p. 13

dd) Slave society – philosophically justified violence

English law didn't foresee the possibility of possessing slaves, which is why Barbados passed a slave code in 1661[47] to ensure a labour force for the plantations. Based on the concept of Blacks as heathenish, brutish, and dangerous people, the laws, on the one hand, securitized the masters' possession, and, on the other hand, intended to control the slaves to avoid rebellion. Barbados became the precursor of many English colonies. Copying the Barbadian model, Virginia declared slaves as "real estate" that could be bequeathed.[48] To make the slave trade easier, it latter changed the legal status of slaves into chattels. In any case the slaves were *things* owned by somebody else.[49] Perpetuating the social order of "master-slave" and securing the master's investment in the long run, the slave codes stipulated slavery as a natural quality: "Born to a slave inheritance,"[50] the slaves' children automatically became the master's property. The legal basis of slavery was partly found in statutes. But most of the legal justification of the master's power over African-Americans was included in court judgments applying common law and protecting class interests among Whites, racist interests of the Whites against colored people, economic interests, and religious convictions.[51]

The relationship between master and slave was basically a violent one because the "Negro had to be broke."[52] From physical over verbal (as part of direct violence) to structural and cultural violence, all forms of oppression were used to break the will of the imported commodity. Supported by the state and justified by the law, masters were entitled to use their property at their own discretion. In 1669, the Virginian Assembly decreed: "Be it enacted by this grand assembly, if any slave resist his master (or other by his master's correcting him) and by extremity of correction should chance to die, that his death should not be accompted felony … since it cannot be presumed that prepensed malice (which alone makes murther felony) should induce any man to destroy his own estate."[53] Whipping, branding, nose slitting, amputation of ears, toes, and fingers, castration, or burning at the stake, owners and courts alike used these punishments. Even though

---

[47] Hening, William Waller (1819), 3:252
[48] Morris, Thomas D. (1996), pp. 66 f., 71
[49] *Id.*, p. 80
[50] *Id.*, p. 81
[51] *Id.*, pp. 2 f.
[52] Taylor, Alan (2001), p. 330
[53] Blackburn, Robin (1998), p. 251; Morris, Thomas D. (1996), pp. 163 f.

these were quite common punishments in the seventeenth century, they were much more easily applied to slaves, who, contrary to Whites, didn't have the possibility defending their interests. And as these coercion means fell into desuetude for Whites, they prevailed for slaves and were executed in much harsher forms. Being entitled to use force against slaves was the basic advantage of slave work compared to the employment of free people. Nobody free would do the same work under these dire conditions without being forced. Such a low wage, such hard work, so humiliating the circumstances: even paying considerably more after the abolition of slavery didn't make the now free people accept this totalitarian oppression.

The more slaves were imported, the more the Whites were outnumbered, the more they developed means of repression to secure their dominance as ruling minority. The Whites were well aware that their treatment of the Africans destroyed the need of people to be recognized and respected – one of the main sources of resistance and rebellions. For deterrence, different punishments for insubordinates were enacted: "Placing defiant slaves in an iron cage hung from a tree, there to die slowly of hunger and thirst […]. In 1694, for the crime of stealing a pig, judges had a black man sliced into quarters for public display."[54] Protests or rebellions were qualified as a violation of the natural order, justifying harsh reactions. Irish physician and philanthropist Hans Sloane wrote in 1706: "The Punishments for Crimes of Slaves, are usually for Rebellions burning them, by nailing them down on the ground with crooked sticks on every Limb, and then applying the Fire by degrees from the Feet and Hands, burning them gradually up to the Head. […] These punishments are sometimes merited by the slaves, who are a very Perverse Generation of People."[55] The death penalty was inflicted to deter other Blacks from resisting, but had the disadvantage of destroying the possession of a master. In 1690, on Santo Domingo alone in the quarters of Rochelois, Nippes, Petit-Goave, and Grand-Goave 1'136 Blacks were executed. That's why Article 40 of the Code Noir introduced an insurance fund, ruling that the masters have to pay a contribution into the "caisse des nègres justiciés". Out of this fund the master's losses were compensated.[56]

On Santo-Domingo in the 1780s planter Marylis invited friends to play boule (French ball game). Some slaves were buried up to their neck, so that their head was still visible. The friends shot balls against the heads of the slaves, until an hour later, all of them were dead. "This sort of scene is inevitable everywhere where […] the humane quality of a group of people

---

[54] Taylor, Alan (2001), p. 213
[55] Sloane, Hans (1706), p. LVII
[56] Sala-Molins, Louis (2005), pp. 170 f.

is negated."⁵⁷ Establishing such an oppressive totalitarian economic system against the background of the enlightenment, the American and the upcoming French Revolution had to find a convincing justification. A natural, deterministic argument had to be found to legitimate the violation of the idea of universal freedom and equality of human beings. Color-based racism was the solution. It's major advantage was that people can't change the color of their skin, which is why they are trapped. The black person had to resign her- or himself to the given natural order. Blackness was identified with the Devil and the Blacks' suffering was explained by Noah's curse on the son of Ham.⁵⁸ Blacks were different because of their lusty and savage nature, they were less rational, "relying more on the putatively lower sense of smell, sound, and touch."⁵⁹ For slaveholders, the black skin was best suited to plantation labor. "While nimble enough to pick cotton, black hands were coarse, clumsy, and awkward, and a good, light hoe was wasted on them. [...] And, of course, tough skin had to be punished especially hard, just to ensure that pain was felt."⁶⁰ Connecting slavery with racism was historically new, as most of the societies as, for example, the Romans, didn't make this differentiation.⁶¹ Even though there existed many negative feelings toward Jews, Irish Catholics, or Scottish Highlanders among the English, these groups weren't enslaved.⁶² It was easier to create disdain against people who at first glance seemed to be different than against people who too much resembled the rulers. This racist justification continued to be used to justify existing prerogatives and advantages. Ernest Renan, for example, wrote in 1871: "Nature made a race of workers, that's the Chinese race, with an exceptional manual skill and without almost any sense of honour; [...] a race of peasant laborers, the Negroes; [...] a race of masters and soldiers, the Europeans. [...] Each of them shall do what they are made for, and everything will be fine."⁶³

The universalist philosophy of the enlightenment most of the time wasn't meant to be "universal." It was a powerful argument to criticize the monarchy and to defend the interests of the upcoming bourgeoisie. The English philosopher John Locke for example admittedly wrote very pas-

---

[57] Plumelle-Uribe, Rosa Amelia (2001), p. 63
[58] See about this religious argument used to justify slavery Sala-Molins, Louis (2005), pp. 21 ff., 35 ff.
[59] Smith, Mark E. (2006), p. 12; see also p. 43.
[60] Id., p. 23; see also p. 46.
[61] Morris, Thomas D. (1996), p. 18
[62] Morgan, Kenneth (2007), p. 22
[63] Renan, Ernest (1871), pp. 93 f.

sionately against slavery. Freedom for him was a chief value and slavery "so vile and miserable an estate of Man," that Englishmen have to reject any concept trying to subordinate them as slaves of the royal power.[64] Contrary to, for example, Aristotle, Locke didn't defend the natural origins of slave-master-relations because "all men are naturally in [...] a state of perfect freedom to order their actions and dispose of their possessions and persons [...]. A state also of equality, wherein all the power and jurisdiction is reciprocal, no one having more than another."[65] Under extraordinary circumstances, Locke accepts slavery. When innocent people defend their right and property against an unjust aggressor they are waging a "just war." "[...] captives taken in a just war, are by the right of nature subjected to the absolute dominion and arbitrary power of their masters."[66] Beside this right-based origin of slavery, there are factual situations where protection justifies subordination: "[...] to turn loose to an unrestrain'd Liberty, before he has Reason to guide him, is not the allowing him the privilege of his nature, to be free."[67] Locke's argument, however, wasn't intended to free slaves, but to criticize the absolute monarchy; no universal social and legal revolution was intended but rather a breakthrough of an upcoming new social class. Looking at the draft of the Constitution of Carolina Locke wrote in 1699, his relative concept of freedom and equality becomes evident. In his function as secretary to the Lords Proprietors of Carolina, he stated in Article 110 of the "Fundamental Constitutions of Carolina": "Every freeman of Carolina shall have absolute power and authority over his negro slaves, of what opinion or religion soever." Proclaiming religious freedom (Article 109), slaves are entitled to choose their religion and to be "as fully members as any freeman" of the church (Article 107). "But yet no slave shall hereby be exempted from that civil dominion his master hath over him, but be in all things in the same state and condition he was before." Just above the slaves Locke situates the serfs (called "leet-men"). Their legal position was identical in many other countries. Locke though secured the existing social order by adding the rule, that the social position of the serfs is bequeathed to all following generations (Article 23). Only interested in the freedom and protection of property[68] of the upper class, he visibly didn't want to challenge the social order, to question the inequality characterizing

---

[64] Locke, John (1824), Book I, Chapter 1, § 1, p. 4
[65] Id., Book II, Chapter 2, § 4, pp. 131 f.
[66] Id., Book II, Chapter 7, § 85, p. 179; see also Book II, Chapter 16, § 179.
[67] Id., Book II, Chapter 6, § 63, p. 165
[68] According to Lock, the chief end of civil society is the "preservation of property" (Locke, John [1824], Book II, Chapter 7, § 85, p. 179).

the society he lived in. The "Royal African Company" had been granted monopoly over the English slave trade in 1660. Locke was one of its investors, which is why he probably had important financial interests in slavery. He further was secretary of the Council of Trade and Foreign Plantations from 1672-1674. As commissioner of the Board of Trade, he was from 1696 responsible for colonial matters. Instructions drafted in 1698 required Governor Nicholson of Virginia to fight the illegal slave trade and assure the monopoly of the Royal African Company, to encourage the Conversion of Negroes and Natives to the Christian Religion, and to pass laws restraining inhumane severities.[69] Locke "was mobilizing his political theory for practical purposes"[70] and Africans or the poor, forced to live under dire circumstances, weren't part of his engagement. This ambiguity between universalism, on the one hand, and the unwillingness to change society according to these principles, on the other hand, is also to be found in the person of Thomas Jefferson. Drafting the fundamentals of the Declaration of Independence, he defended passionately a truly universal concept of freedom. He, therefore, intended to abolish slavery. At the same time, he was the owner of at one time about 250 slaves and doubted the aptitude of Blacks to be equal. In 1784, he wrote that "Blacks, whether originally a distinct race, or made distinct by time and circumstances, are inferior to the Whites in the endowments both of body and mind."[71]

The different European states didn't accept slavery on their home ground. First, because the family ties and the community's support that people had in Europe would have helped them resist. Second, religious convictions forbid the enslavement of Christians and, third, the respect between the monarchs made the enslavement of captives of the others' subjects unacceptable.[72] Fourth, to negate the human quality of some individuals within a state contains a risk to generalization. The debasement of others debases ourselves, and this total degradation can at any time be used against the current rulers. As long as the criteria can't be applied to the masters and are exclusively implemented in a foreign land, this potentially explosive practice can be contained outside the realm of bourgeois coziness. Hitler transgressed both limitations because he exerted it at home and he blurred the distinction between Whites and others. Some Whites were supreme to other withes, the Aryan master race was superior to other European races.[73]

---

[69] Farr, James (1986), pp. 268 f.
[70] Id., p. 282
[71] Jefferson, Thomas (1853), Query 14, p. 155
[72] Blackburn, Robin (1998), p. 359
[73] Plumelle-Uribe, Rosa Amelia (2001), p. 163

ee) Slavery – a question of identity

In the Southern United States, slavery became over time part of the collective identity, a point on and around which the society was built up. Slavery was no longer only a form of production, but also it became a way of life. This change from a purely economic to a community orientation led to slight improvements of the situation of the slaves. Compared to, for example, the Caribbean colonies slaves weren't solely commodities anymore. They became part of the wider "family" of the master. An owner feeling more responsible for his possession tried to protect them and keep them alive as long as possible. For example the Alabama slave code of 1852 stipulated that "the master must treat his slave with humanity, and must not inflict upon him any cruel punishment." But the power-relation was so much one-sided that the enforcement of such rights was almost impossible. The legal rule that slaves weren't allowed to testify against Whites didn't help.

Northern America was predominantly agrarian and needed an increasing number of workforce for the production of tobacco and rice, some sugar, and, later, cotton. Overall, just a small number of natives was enslaved. They were too familiar with the areas, which made escaping easy. And contrary to the captured and by this socially isolated Africans, the Natives were able to rely on their community's solidarity, which helped to develop counterpower. "Because it has historically been difficult to enslave people on their home turf, the English found it convenient to export Indians captured in battle rather than hold them locally."[74] The number of English immigrants decreased at the end of the 17th century because of the improvement of the political and economic situation at home. Also, the English government tried to prevent people from emigration in order to improve agriculture and manufacturing and to strengthen its national economy. To remedy this shortage of workforce the American colonies began to rely increasingly on imported African slaves. The biggest part of the 10 to 12 million Africans were brought to Brazil and the Caribbean colonies. North America imported around 650'000 men and women. This comparatively a small number would finally develop into the largest slave population in the Western World. This was due to a much higher survival rate in the U.S. thanks to better living conditions: A healthier diet, the absence of most of the tropical diseases, and the lesser harsh working conditions, as the harsh production of sugar was the exception. As a consequence the reproductive rate was higher and Creoles (American-born slaves) outnumbered Africans from the middle of the 18th century on. Planters who provided medical care

---

[74] Kolchin, Peter (2003), p. 8

for their slaves or supported family building didn't do it because of a philanthropic conviction, but rather to protect and augment their workforce.

In Brazil and the Caribbean, the planters were most of the time absentees, not living on their estates or living totally separated from their slaves because integration in a community was neither intended nor thinkable because of its size, its inequality, and its disproportion between the few Whites and the great number of black workers. In North America estates holding slaves were smaller[75] and the master and the slaves lived together (resident masters, semi-domestic slavery[76]) in a more integrated, but not equal or just way. This forced integration developed, contrary to the industrialized agriculture of the big plantations, a more personal form of relationship. The private and working sphere were often intermingled because slaves worked in the house of the masters, cooked, mended clothes, or fostered the master's children. The slaves' and the master's children often also played together. Nevertheless, the Whites were keen to uphold racial borders to ensure their superiority. As a result there were two segregated communities, with the black community forced to behave like the Whites wanted them to.

In spite of the enormous violence, the slaves managed to preserve their own "reality," to protect their world. Many obstacles had to be overcome: First, the newly imported slaves often didn't talk the same language and shared only certain cultural elements. Their relationships destroyed by the kidnapping, they had to begin anew, developing a common ground, trusting each other enough to resist the external pressures. Second, privacy was difficult to uphold because the totalitarian arbitrary power of the owner could strike at any moment and everywhere. Family bonds were fragile because of the perpetual threat that one of them could be sold. The runaway ads published in newspapers offering rewards for those taking up and securing the fugitives provide evidence of the slaves' recurring attempts to flee. Many of the runaways were looking for family members who had been sold to other farms. The third obstacle to overcome was their economic dependency, which considerably reduced available alternatives. Developing their own culture and tradition, with the time the slaves built up a sphere of autonomy beyond the long arm of the white supremacists. The construction of their own identity was also a form of resistance and self-affirmation. In this way, they were able to recognize, respect, and support each other and, therefore, build up dignity. Religion, food, or music were, for example,

---

[75] Sugar plantations on Jamaica for example had an average size of about 180 slaves at the end of the 18th century, whereas in Virginia and Maryland less than 13 slaves were usual.

[76] Blackburn, Robin (1998), p. 468

the domains within which they created themselves, mixing different African and European-American elements.

The more slavery became a core element of Southern identity, the more it was difficult to abolish it. But slavery was contested. In 1758 the Quakers in Philadelphia condemned it in general and threatened to exclude any member of their society who was involved in the slave trade. In 1772 the Slave James Somersett won a trial against his proprietor Charles Stuert from Boston before the Court of King's Bench. Somersett's lawyers argued that neither common law nor any statute ever stipulated slavery or allowed the enslavement by oneself. Stuert's lawyers on their side put forward the predominant value of property. Lord Chief Justice Mansfield judged that British law never knew any legal ground for "so odious as the conditions of slaves." Somersett was freed and with him about 15'000 slaves. The work of the abolitionists gained momentum thanks to the American Revolution. The highly venerated and self-evident truth, that all men are created equal and free put much pressure on the economic and social institution of slavery: It now had to be justified. To avoid a scission between the thirteen colonies, neither the revolution nor the constitution of 1787 did abolish bondage. But still, a new tone was set: In the aftermath, slavery was legally abolished in the North and in 1808 the slave trade was prohibited. Furthermore, moral pressures on the South increased over time and made the justification of this blatant inequality the more difficult. In the antebellum era, the natural master-slave-order became fundamentally questioned and people willing to keep up with this economic practice had to develop unquestionable arguments. As discussed earlier (see p. 190 ff.), "race" became the main criterion: "[…] the only logical answer […] was to assert that those held as slaves were somehow so different from free Americans that they were not entitled to the same rights and privileges. Because race was the most easily identifiable difference, it became an increasingly important justification for slavery."[77]

This amplified racism had besides its defense of slavery, also an integrative effect. Three social groups were constructed in the slave society of the South: White slave-owners, non-slaveholding Whites, and black slaves. Even though there very often were jealousy conflicts between the most of the time richer slave-owners and the rest of the Whites, racism dominating everything helped to unite the Whites. This community building mechanism already worked in the 17th century when the economic differences between groups of Whites became too big and integration became a problem. It's the change from indentured servants to black slaves that helped the

---

[77] Kolchin, Peter (2003), pp. 90 f.

Whites to understand themselves as superior, even though their financial situation wasn't what they had hoped for.[78] The "scapegoat-technique" helps the morally weak become politically strong at the expense of the ones excluded from the community-construction. The image of dangerous Blacks capable of any atrocity created racial fear which further helped to unite the Whites.[79]

The Southern states underwent an important change *from a slave-holding society to a slave society* when the relation master-slave crystallized as the core element of the collective identity. Not just an economic organization principle anymore, slavery was constructed by political, legal, cultural, economic, and scientific means. Every criticism of slavery was forbidden, mail from the North censured people who didn't respect the "sanctity of slavery" and were dislodged from their function and position.[80] "To most masters, slavery represented a civilization or way of life that ordered their very existence. [...] Masters saw their slaves not just as their laborers but also as their 'people,' inferior members of their extended households from whom they expected work and obedience, but to whom they owed guidance and protection."[81] The increasing importance of slavery was also reflected in the number of slaves present in the South. From about 700'000 slaves in 1790 their numbers increased to almost 4 millions in 1860. All these workers were needed for cultivating and harvesting cotton, the cash crop that became predominant in the late 18th century and was sold to the insatiable British textile industry. The interest of the masters in the well-being and stable family life of their property was also economic reflections because captive breeding was the cheapest way to increase workforce – especially since the slave trade was prohibited. The structure and quality of family life depended on the will of the master, and marriages of slaves weren't protected legally. Their children were in any case automatically property of the mother's owner.

As in every totalitarian system, the antebellum South developed into a community that not only affected the slaves, but also had a deep impact on the masters themselves. Slavery made the white slave-holders, in general, very rich, but the material wealth had to be paid for with a lack of freedom and the omnipresence of violence. The fear of revolts required a permanent control over the oppressed. A community based on horrible injustice needs equal horrible means to preserve the direct, structural, and cultural

---

[78] Taylor, Alan (2001), p. 140, 157
[79] Blackburn, Robin (1998), p. 323
[80] Finzsch, Norbert/Horton, James O./Horton Lois E. (1999), pp. 270 f.
[81] Kolchin, Peter (2003), p. 111

violence that's applied. Violence becomes a normal element of everyday life: "The more the requested obedience is intense, the more the sanctions against disobedience have to be merciless."[82] A police state was developed within which Whites, regardless if they were slave-owners or not, had to be members of the slave patrols controlling routes of transportation and preventing the grouping of Blacks or their leaving from the estate without permission. An aggressive culture of honorable white men developed, which made violence an omnipresent element of Southern identity.[83] Their fear of fights for freedom was fueled by events like the Stono Rebellion in South Carolina in 1739, during which 20 Whites and 44 slaves were killed. Securing the totalitarian prerogative of Whites, securing the masters' way of life, a multitude of legal regulations were established to control the slaves' behavior, their movement, and their potential to resist. Several states enacted the principle that manumission needed the consensus of the legislature and that freed people had to leave the state or were forbidden entry. As in 1850 only 0.45 per thousand slaves were freed,[84] the Whites' massive fear of a black revenge becomes visible.

Slavery wasn't only a Southern problem, it "[…] was a national phenomenon. The North shared in the wealth it created, and in the oppression it required."[85] Because of their economic interdependence, Northern States participated at least indirectly in the slave-economy in the South. By selling comestible goods to the South, by financing investments, by building and insuring ships used to transport slaves[86] and cotton, by distilling Southern molasses into rum, by buying Southern cotton to be processed in the hundreds of textile mills in the North (in 1860, 472 in New England), by being a hub in the triangular trade (the South provided more than half of New York's exports) – out of all these economic connections the more or less slave-free states in the North sustained and profited from slavery. "For the half century before the Civil War, cotton was the backbone of the American economy. It was king, and the North ruled the kingdom. From seed to cloth, Northern merchants, shippers, and financial institutions, many based in New York, controlled nearly every aspect of cotton production

---

[82] Schoelcher, Victor (1998 [1842]), p. 86
[83] Finzsch, Norbert/Horton, James O./Horton Lois E. (1999), pp. 194 f. Plumelle-Uribe, Rosa Amelia (2001), p. 57: "[…] barbary leads inevitably to a culture of destruction."
[84] Fogel, Robert William/Engerman, Stanley L. (1974), p. 150
[85] Farrow, Anne/Lang, Joel/Frank, Jenifer (2006), p. XXV
[86] Some of them with built-in crates and supersize water tanks adapted to the human cargo to be transported.

and trade."[87] "Cotton thread holds the union together; unites John C. Calhoun and Abbott Lawrence. Patriotism for holidays and summer evenings, with music and rockets, but cotton thread is the Union."[88] In the middle of the 18th century, about 80 percent of New England's overseas exports went to the British West Indies which depended so heavily upon the supply from the North, that it's stop during the American Revolution led to famine on the sugar islands. "Plantation slavery created tremendous wealth in the New World and the Old. It was the engine of the colonial Atlantic economy."[89] Compared to the South and the West Indies, the New England and the Middle Colonies had fewer slaves. But in 1760, at least 41'000 Africans were enslaved under the same legal conditions: They were property of the master and could be punished at his own will and even killed. More visibly than others, Rhode Island participated intensely in the slave trade and transported, in the 18th century until its ban, over 106'000 slaves to the Americas. Eighteen ships a year brought rum to Africa and slaves back, controlling by this between 60 and 90 percent of the American slave trade.[90] New York also played an active part in this business: in the first half of the 18th century about 10'000 Blacks were brought to America and after 1747 they increased their import capacity from 17 to 103 ships.[91] Besides the economic interdependence, the importance of the Southern states is visible in the so-called "Virginia Dynasty," meaning that four of the five first American presidents came from Virginia: In the 72 years since the creation of the USA there were during fifty years of slave-owners as presidents. The USA was for quite a time a slave republic.

ff) From slavery to class-based injustice

Ending slavery in 1865 had the effect that former slaves were now legally the owners of their own human capital. And even more important, there was nobody entitled anymore to sell or mistreat them. But besides this formal liberation, the economic, social, and political inequality persisted.[92] The *slave system changed into a class-system*, whereas Blacks weren't called slaves

---

[87] Farrow, Anne/Lang, Joel/Frank, Jenifer (2006), p. 13
[88] Emerson, Ralph Waldo (1971), p. 420
[89] Farrow, Anne/Lang, Joel/Frank, Jenifer (2006), p. 55
[90] Greene, Lorenzo Johnston (1942), p. 30
[91] Finzsch, Norbert/Horton, James O./Horton Lois E. (1999), p. 59
[92] Writing about the antebellum situation, Fogel et al. write: "For Blacks, the alternative to slavery was not freedom, but […] 'quasi-freedom'" (Fogel, Robert William/Engerman, Stanley L. [1974], p. 150).

anymore, but free workers. Freed Blacks tried to start over, but lacking resources, it was almost impossible to quit former economic dependencies. They were now legally entitled to negotiate their working conditions and their wages. But, even though there was labor shortage and a national political climate in favor of Blacks, their bargaining power wasn't strong enough to have a decisive impact. An exceptionally small group of white people managed to acquire real estate because congress had renounced to confiscate and redistribute the land. Blacks hadn't access to land and couldn't, therefore, built up economic autonomy. The prevailing dependency made the promise of legal freedom mostly a lure. "[…] with the overthrow of slavery Southern social relations underwent a fundamental transformation. The market, with liberal assistance from the law, replaced the lash as the arbiter of labor relations."[93] In summary, the same social strata as before prevailed, made up of rich Whites, poor Whites, and poor Blacks. But now, as the African Americans were legally free, they could be blamed for their lack of success. After the Civil War "the life expectations of Blacks declined by 10 percent between the last quarter century of the antebellum era and the last two decades of the nineteenth century. The diet of Blacks deteriorated. […] The health of Blacks deteriorated. […] The skill composition of the black labor force deteriorated. […] The gap between wage payments to Blacks and Whites in comparable occupations increased steadily from the immediate post-Civil War decades down to the eve of World War II."[94] They were freer than before and got certain rights, but as racism prevailed and black codes went on segregating the community, they found themselves again in the least attractive place, confronted with insurmountable obstacles. As soon as the Reconstruction governments were replaced by the former rulers in the South ("home rule", "redemption"), they repealed the civil rights of Blacks and gave up financial support of education. Politics was made by Whites for Whites and massive electoral fraud took place to secure specific results in states with a majority of Blacks. Violence against Blacks – fueled by the humiliation of a lost war and the fear of loosing Southern identity – terrorized freed people all over the South. Racism became much more virulent and was no longer controlled by the master's interest in the well-being of his property. "In certain respects the surviving caste system shows even more resistance to change than did slavery. The main economic significance of slavery was that the employer really owned his labor. Because of that he also had a vested interest in its most profitable utilization. […] It is true that

---

[93] Kolchin, Peter (2003), p. 236
[94] Fogel, Robert William/Engerman, Stanley L. (1974), p. 261

the slaves were robbed of their freedom to move on their own initiative. But as factors of production, they were moved by the economic interest of their owners to their 'most advantageous uses'. [...] After Emancipation no such proprietary interest protected Negro laborers from the desire of white workers to squeeze them out of skilled employment."[95]

b) Constitutive and universal recognition, recognition of potential

To recognize somebody means to

- treat him or her as *existent*, to
- treat them as *equal*, and to
- make sure they have the same construction power, the same potential to influence "reality".

An individual exists socially only if its actions are taken into account by others. This *constitutive recognition* is needed to exist at all. The fight of individuals or minorities to be heard is a profound necessity of human beings to exist in the eyes of others. To be fastened by the eyes of others gives our existence sense, without it, the void of contingency and an undetermined future threatens. That somebody is constitutively recognized doesn't determine the form of actions of the people involved. It only means that we take note of the existence of the other. Contrary to slaves, who were constitutively recognized but treated like chattels, justice needs us to treat everybody equally. To be a human being entitles us to equal treatment. This *universal recognition* abstracts from particular individuality and bases our judgment and decisions of formal equality.[96] Taking this recognition seriously means to make sure that equality isn't just a permanently unkept promise, but an effective potential to shape the "reality" we live in. Our interactions have, therefore, to be organized in a way that gives the participants their say within the construction process. It is this *recognition of potential* that makes freedom available. The debate over the common "reality" has, therefore, to be widely open, the "res publica" to be taken seriously, so that "everything that concerns and moves the citizens [...] gets the dignity of public articulation and controversy."[97] There is no prerogative per se of any knowledge or statement. Every position counts and has to be recognized as valuable by

---

[95] Myrdal, Gunnar (1996), p. 222
[96] Benhabib, Seyla (1989), p. 468
[97] Rödel, Ulrich/Frankenberg, Günter/Dubiel, Helmut (1989), p. 177

consensus or by criticism. Not a monologue, but a serious dialog is needed within which a "no" of the counterpart is respected.[98] We have to appreciate the resistance and stubbornness of the interactors who are demonstrating their dignity. Politics, as much as the economy, culture as much as the private sphere should be understood and organized as a debate of equally speaking, heard, and responsible actors. Universal recognition means to recognize "the inherent dignity and [...] the equal and inalienable rights of all members of the human family."[99] Constructively spoken, these rights are not "inherent," but have to be recognized by establishing social and political structures giving equal access to debate-forums, an equal right to speak and to be heard, and the resources needed to build up an existence as valuable as that of others. There is no natural or social limit to the recognition we can give and get. I, therefore, agree with Sennett[100] that a scarcity of recognition is man-made. Recognition as well as exclusion are interactive processes "launched in the center of society."[101] But contrary to Sennett, I do think that recognition is costly.[102] Personal engagement in time as much as in attention and the willingness to change is needed. If personal behavior, structures, or cultural exclusion mechanisms aren't transformed according to the wants of the people involved, recognition won't be made.

Universalism isn't interested in the uniqueness of the people, in their particular history, their current power, hopes and sufferings, their social or economic support. Universalism treats people as the same in rights, as if they were acting behind Rawls' veil of ignorance. In this way, every individual gets at least the guarantee not to be discriminated against or killed because of some arbitrary criterion. This formal approach is important, but not sufficient. It is too disinterested in the concrete resources people have to fulfill their hopes. Human existence is highly dependent and, therefore, highly fragile. Hence, many preconditions have to be met to avoid direct, structural, and cultural violence. Slavery denied Africans recognition in all forms. Africans were not recognized as human beings, they didn't have any possibility of influencing the "reality" they were the victims of. Reduced to an "animal" workforce, they were forced to renounce to their opportunities. The abolishment of the legal discrimination made them equal in regard to certain rights, but didn't change their living situation. Thus, their hopes remained only hopes.

---

[98] Bauman, Zygmunt (1995), pp. 113 ff., 116
[99] Preamble of the Universal Declaration of Human Rights
[100] Sennett talks of "respect", a term used differently in this book.
[101] Kronauer, Martin (2002), p. 210
[102] Sennett, Richard (2003), p. 3; see also p. 46.

Using people for economic objectives didn't end with the legal abolishment of slavery. Most of the time immigrants are not perceived as human beings, but as a workforce. It is not the man or woman who attract attention, but the economic potential they incorporate for others. "What [the United States'] more highly developed economy lacked [in the nineteenth century] was an industrial working class. The Second Immigration coincided with the industrialization of the United States and furnished the bulk of the manpower for it. [...] To make adequate use of the enormous supply of illiterate European peasants who became available around the end of the 19th century, it was necessary to simplify and routinize factory work. Accordingly, a dependence on unskilled immigrant labor encouraged the introduction of automatic machines and processes. [...] Only in America did the immigrants constitute a mass proletariat engaged in manufacturing; and because they did, America was able to develop to the full a system of mass production."[103] As long as the workers were needed, as long as their workforce fitted the economy and didn't represent a direct competition or contained a risk to joblessness, they were welcomed, even recruited. From the 1870s on, the United States began to perceive immigration also as a threat, which is why it restricted it. Integration based solely on economic terms treats workers as a "commodity" to be used as long as necessary. However, if human dignity counts, individuals coming to live and work within a community have to get the opportunity to build up equal construction power. Max Frisch noted in the 1960s about Switzerland: "A small master people sees itself in danger: Work force has been called, but human beings came."[104] These human beings most of the time are left to themselves. Thus, they have to organize a support structure, a community that's able to attenuate the risks an isolated existence would have to endure in form of illness, joblessness, illiteracy, or age. Widely neglected by the ruling majority, immigrants establish communities to give each other a helping hand: "One common response to the disadvantages imposed on a minority group by the larger society is group solidarity among the members of that minority."[105] The better this cooperative support-structure works, the more likely the problems connected with immigration can be solved: "[...] Vietnamese refugees dispersed in isolated neighborhoods recovered more slowly from the trauma of war and defeat and were more likely to feel homeless, displaced, and unwelcome than those who were resettled as groups."[106]

---

[103] Higham, John (1984), p. 23
[104] Frisch, Max (1965), p. 7
[105] Zhou, Min/Bankston, Carl L. III (1998), p. 10, 74
[106] *Id.*, p. 72

"There are more slaves today than at any point in human history"[107] writes Skinner. Even though slavery is forbidden worldwide and the people can't legally be owned anymore, there are more than ever people who are "forced to work, through fraud or threat of violence, for no pay beyond subsistence."[108] The International Labour Organization estimates, that at least 12.3 million people around the world are enslaved.[109] Slavery today is less visible than in its historic form, but it is to be found everywhere. One of the most effective means of controlling the victims is to confiscate their passports. In this undocumented status, the slaves risk being deported at any moment, which makes them accept any harsh conditions and treatments. States pursuing a legalistic and deterrent politic to keep away migrants support this tactic by expelling asylum seekers without checking if they are slaves who have to be protected. "In a typical case, traffickers forced a seventeen-year-old Congolese boy into sexual slavery in a gay club in London. When a patron rescued him, facing threats from the traffickers, the boy claimed asylum. British authorities denied his claim and deported him to Spain, where earlier he had been held in brutal bondage."[110]

Besides this forced labor, there is a labor market that abuses of people who don't have any economic or social perspectives in their home country. Emigrating to Europe they hope to make use of their potential. In Italy or Spain they work as harvesters 15 hours a day for €15 to 20. Housed in barracks or under plastic awnings without light or electricity, sometimes one toilet for 200 workers, they have to pay rent to their employers. Being *illegal* immigrants, they accept almost any working conditions. All of Europe knows similar destinies – situations widely accepted because they are at the basis of cheap food, the main criterion in the consumer society. According to Emmanuel Terray, illegal workers is exactly what neoliberals hoped for: "They claim for as possible docile and flexible workers, without social security. [...] They are the mass of perfectly flexible workers, as they can be hired and fired whenever the situation needs it."[111] Contrary to the slave owners of past centuries, who had to take care of their possession, the masters of today do not need to posses the workers, because there are enough poor people who need to work and can't rely on alternatives. According to international conventions, these people aren't qualified as "slaves" because

---

[107] Skinner, Benjamin E. (2008), p. 17
[108] *Id.*, p. 329
[109] ILO (2009), p. 1
[110] Skinner, Benjamin E. (2008), p. 328
[111] Terray, Emmanuel (2004), p. 121

they're not physically forced to work.[112] "Forced labour cannot be equated simply with low wages or poor working conditions. Nor does it cover situations of pure economic necessity, as when a worker feels unable to leave a job because of the real or perceived absence of employment alternatives. Forced labour represents a severe violation of human rights and restriction of human freedom, as defined in the ILO Conventions on the subject and in other related international instruments on slavery, practices similar to slavery, debt bondage or serfdom."[113] The problem with this definition is that only direct violence qualifies as "slavery," not structural violence. Structural violence, though, can have the same effect. The supposed freedom of people *not* to take whatever job, to negotiate the conditions, and if not pleased to look for another job – these people do not have this alternative. This is the violence the so-called "market" exerts. This "market", though, is not a anonymous force. It is the relationship of, on the one hand, the consumers, eager to buy cheap cloths and food, and, on the other hand, the employers, only interested in the biggest profits to be made thanks to exploitation. To change this structural violence means to change the behavior of many people, to make responsible all of those with considerable construction power, and to establish relationships based on interactive freedom, justice, and solidarity. The measures against slavery proposed by Anti-Slavery International would on all accounts also help to solve the problem of the aforementioned immigrant workers or poor workers in general: 1. Labor organizations should be able to represent these people; 2. Businesses and the civil society have to take their responsibilities; 3. Social development is needed, having an impact on the vulnerability and material poverty of the workers; 4. Government action has to be increased.[114] In this way, all previously discussed forms of recognition could be realized.

Universal recognition is denied children or young women who are killed because of their gender. This so-called gendercide is a form of direct, structural, and cultural violence. Based on the prerogative of men over women, India has a considerable number of so-called "Dowry deaths." According to Newman, about 72'000 young brides have been burned to death in India over 45 years. Furthermore, almost all cases of abortion after amniocentesis were female fetuses. This deadly preference of males is due to "the devastat-

---

[112] See also Article 2 no. 1 of the Forced Labour Convention, 1930 (No. 29): "For the purposes of this Convention the term forced or compulsory labour shall mean all work or service which is exacted from any person under the menace of any penalty and for which the said person has not offered himself voluntarily."

[113] ILO (2009), p. 5

[114] McQuade, Aidan (2008), p. 10

ing financial impact of the dowry typically required of a woman's family in order to arrange a proper marriage. This dowry can cost a family up to five years' income as it is generally computed to be commensurate to the estimated earning potential of the groom. The only compensation for the bride's family is the prestige that results from their daughter marrying into a good family."[115] In China the combination of the one-child-politic and the preference of boys over girls leads to a higher rate of abortions of female fetuses and to the neglect and killing of the undesired children.[116] "In China the imbalance between the sexes was 108 boys to 100 girls for the generation born in the late 1980s; for the generation of the early 2000s, it was 124 to 100. In some Chinese provinces the ratio is an unprecedented 130 to 100. This discriminatory violence is worst in China, but has spread far beyond. Other East Asian countries, including Taiwan and Singapore, former communist states in the western Balkans and the Caucasus, and even sections of America's population (Chinese- and Japanese-Americans, for example), all have distorted sex ratios. Gendercide exists on almost every continent. It affects rich and poor; educated and illiterate; Hindu, Muslim, Confucian and Christian alike. Wealth does not stop it. Taiwan and Singapore have open, rich economies. In China and India, the areas with the worst sex ratios are the richest, best-educated ones. And China's one-child policy can only be part of the problem, given that so many other countries are affected."[117]

All three forms of recognition are, in my view, needed to generate human dignity. Combined with "respect" (see p. 211 ff.) and reciprocity (see p. 225 ff.), the individuals are comprehensively taken into account. In consensus-based constructivism interdependent people are more than abstract rights, why a dignified life is based on a whole range of obliging as much as liberating relationships. The dignity of one is respected if treated in a generalized way as human being and in a concrete way as the individual existing here and now. Discrimination is avoided by abstracting from the particular men and women, focussing solely on their equal quality as human beings. At the same time they will get construction power only if the relationships are organized in a way that best suits their concrete needs.

---

[115] Newman, Alizabeth (1992), p. 114
[116] French, Marilyn (1992), p. 51
[117] Gendercide, on: The Economist, March 4, 2010 (http://www.economist.com/node/15606229), retrieved on July 27, 2011

c) Recognition denial – fight for recognition

Human beings are permanently looking for sense: *There is no innate sense, the meaning of life has to be made.* Sense is developed interactively, it gives the individual a sensible place within the community, it recognizes her or him as valuable. Honneth differentiates three forms of recognition: Love, law, and morality.[118] "Love" stands for personal relationships, for the interactions with friends and family. "Law" represents the political and legal recognition, and "morality" describes the social status one is able to acquire on the basis of shared values.[119] According to Honneth, to experience disregard motivates people to fight for recognition.[120] In my view, this fight for recognition is a fight for existence, for sense, for a meaning of life found by myself while interacting with others. A deep sense of injustice, the feeling to be less valuable than others results from the denial of recognition. Humiliated and disparaged, the disintegrative effects are important. People choose mainly two different reactions to protect their dignity:

- Violent, criminal acts against others, political protest, and

- addiction or suicide as acts against oneself.

Violence becomes a tool to claim recognition, to develop power in a form that forces the community to recognize at least ones existence and to overcome the feeling of being at the mercy of others.[121] "[…] the recognition I didn't get freely, I provide myself using violence."[122] Exclusion based on structural violence has the effect that people are deprived of their recognition, are treated like simple bodies,[123] which is why these superfluous existences fight to be noticed. The more disintegrated a community is, the more violence it experiences.[124] Some sort of terrorism can be explained as an attempt to affirm identity.[125] Experiencing power by killing or frightening others leads to an existence at minimum, even though it is based on hate and most probably yields violent counter attacks. Violence therefore can be

---

[118] Honneth, Axel (1992), p. 148, 111
[119] Honneth, Axel (1994), p. 90; Honneth, Axel (1992), p. 152
[120] Honneth, Axel (1992), p. 219
[121] Neckel, Sighard (1999), p. 161
[122] Todorov, Tzvetan (1996), p. 111
[123] Schroer, Markus (2000), pp. 446 f.
[124] Babka von Gostomski, Christian (2003), p. 255
[125] Scheerer, Sebastian (2002), p. 138

seen as an *indicator of a community in deconstruction phase*. Political protest and civil disobedience may be the first signs of a disintegration conflict, if there is no serious reconstruction effort made.[126]

Suicide is, on the one hand, resignation because a person is convinced not to find the recognition he hoped for. At the same time it is a form of protest and revolt,[127] a criticism of the current situation that one lives in. Not able to make sense out of his existence other than crying out loud for help (attempted suicide) or by quitting a world that didn't provide the recognition he was looking for.[128] It is a willful act demonstrating one's autonomy and dignity, even though possibly for the last time.[129] Suicide is an act of desperation, on the one hand, but also as an act of proud resistance.[130] The more somebody is integrated, the more he or she finds recognition, the more they count for others, the less they will fall back on suicide or other forms of self-destruction like drogue abuse. As much as the social arrangement can take the form of competition, exclusion, or violence, it can be a support-structure[131] that integrates people by cooperatively creating meaning of life.

In a society within which work is the central integration measure, within which work is the path to status and security, joblessness is at the origin of dishonor and the feeling of unworthiness.[132] Young people who have difficulties finding a job have to grapple with self doubts and the inability to develop confidence.[133] Being excluded from the labor market can isolate people and make material, political, and cultural participation impossible.[134] If one is not needed, one is not necessary for others and, thus, isn't recognized, apathy can result.[135]

Competition is basically exclusionary and yields unrecognized losers. It is also a arrangement that profits the elitist small minority at the expense of the majority. To make sure that the majority stays calm and accepts this inequality, a minority is created against which everybody is entitled to talk or to act. Immigrants often have to take this role because citizenship is used

---

[126] Kleger, Heinz (1993), pp. 395 ff.
[127] Rufer, Marc (1988), p. 99
[128] Amendt, Gerhard/Schwarz, Michael (1990), p. 143
[129] Sartre, Jean-Paul (1943), p. 584
[130] Pamuk, Orhan (2005), p. 476
[131] Heitmeyer, Wilhelm (1997), p. 30
[132] Forrester, Viviane (1997), p. 14
[133] *Id.*, p. 81
[134] Kronauer, Martin (2002), pp. 151 f.
[135] Sennett, Richard (1998), p. 146

to decide in- and exclusion.¹³⁶ The "real" citizens are protected thanks to measures focused against foreigners.¹³⁷

---

[136] Sackmann, Rosemarie (2004), p. 95
[137] *Id.*, p. 117

3. Respect

Human dignity originates in interactions that recognize individuals as *universally equal*, respect their uniqueness, their *particular difference*, and build up a *reciprocal structure* (supportive, opportunity orientated). Contrary to the universal claim of recognition, which focuses on an abstract human being stripped of its history and geographical and temporal concreteness, to respect somebody means to look for difference, for uniqueness. Constructively speaking "difference" is not given, but made: A community has to debate which sort and how much of difference it is willing to accept and support. It is a conflict between "normality" and "originality," a tension every community resolves according to its characteristic basic values.

a) Listen to others

Respect is an interaction based on *tolerance*, on *interested disinterest*, on active passivity. To respect somebody means to act in a way that the difference she wants is made possible. We do not bother about her difference, we decide not to react to her difference, or, best, we are interested in her difference, try to understand this difference, and perhaps learn from her. Plurality, thus, is not a disinterested tolerance, but an *active acceptance of the way of life somebody has opted for*. If people want to be different, their interactors have to be willing to listen to their claim, ask to make sure that they understood the request, and decide whether the difference will be supported by acceptance or fought. The ones claiming for difference have to engage for the "reality" they propose, they have to justify their claim, and listen to the arguments the counterpart proffers. Cooperatively organized, this debate will yield a rich set of alternatives around which to organize life and exclude the ones which violate the majority's cherished basic values. What Taylor calls the "politics of difference" can be understood as counterweight to universalism. To respect somebody means to respect the particular person in its history and its complexity. Its "individualized identity"[1] shall be part of the community's interactions. Universalism is a chance for justice and freedom, if it claims equality. It can be dangerously understood as a "pensée unique," a formalistic and exclusive way of thinking and living. Under these circumstances it becomes a collectivism, which is why universalism needs a counterweight, giving individuals and communities the possibility to be unique.

---

[1] Taylor, Charles (1992), p. 28

To be part of a community, to have a collective identity is essential for human beings. Our interdependence as well as our need for a meaning of life, make us build up memberships. Affiliations, however, become problematic, when they are imposed on others and go along with a negative, pejorative, exclusionary qualification. This sort of generalization based, for example, on national, cultural, or ethnic criteria, forces individuals to become part of a story they didn't choose. They have to live in compliance with cliches others would like to become "reality." Most often these generalizing judgments are used to build up inequality and exclude others from access to power. Or, they are used to justify violence against the "barbarian others." "[…] the main hope of harmony in our troubled world lies in the plurality of our identities, which cut across each other and work against sharp divisions around one single hardened line of vehement division that allegedly cannot be resisted."[2] As "race" for the moment isn't politically correct anymore, collectives are based on culture, religion, or ethnicity with the same intention, to make sure that a specific position of a group of people, that their social status can't be changed by themselves. Contrary to this deterministic and eternalized construction of collective identities, consensus-based constructivism opts for a permanent interactive construction of options. Individuals are, in my view, a patchwork[3] of influences and self-determinations; they have multiple layers of identity[4] they combine in a way that makes them unique. This counts for the individual as much as for the collective level. Culture is, thus, not a homogeneous entity,[5] but a form of debate, a set of actions, relevant at some time at some place, ever changing, and too rich and complex to be summarized by a single characteristic. To talk of American, Swiss, or German culture is, against this background, a loss in alternatives, in plurality, in difference. Not listening to the individuals' stories means not to pay respect to their creativity and engaged search for a sensible life.

b) Homogeneity v. plurality

Besides the question of how to approach each other – as enemy or as co-operators – a community also has to decide about the amount of variety it is willing to support. The more difference there is is not a handicap but an equal opportunity, the more freedom and justice are leading construction-

---

[2] Sen, Amartya (2006), p. 16
[3] Keupp, Heiner (1992), p. 100
[4] Beck-Gernsheim, Elisabeth (2004), p. 102
[5] In this sense see Sen, Amartya (2006), p. 112

principles. Using equal construction power and freedom as criteria, I distinguish *three levels of plurality*: Assimilation, core values absolutism, and cooperation.

aa) Assimilation

Assimilatory integration is based on exclusive and absolute truth. There is one true way of life, nothing else can be imagined. Alternatives are perceived as unduly critical or menacing of the majority's existence. To be different or to ask for difference means in an assimilatory "reality" to disagree, to think about and perhaps opt for alternatives. Such a relativization many a people can't bear. The idea that there are many truths and many ways to become happy indicates that the truth we have built up arduously over the years could be wrong. For assimilationists, life has to be simple and unambiguous, which is why exclusivity has to be upheld.

Simplicity and predictability can't be built, if we use Manichaean criteria: "Self" and "stranger" are irreconcilably different, equality is unthinkable, and the one's own identity is glorified whereas others' is vilified. The majority decrees the standard biography people have to comply with. Abnormality can't be tolerated, it has to be fought, excluded, or even eradicated. To easily recognize an enemy it has to be constructed by the use of a few simple criteria. It also has to be different in an essentialist way different. Their skin color, their language, their religion, their genetical pre-disposition to violence or fraud, their poverty, their ethnicity, or their laziness – are given and unchangeable character traits. To think of living together is, therefore, futile.

"Nationalism" is the prime example of an assimilatory integration. It was invented as a reaction to overwhelming philosophical, social, political, and economic changes that had begun in the middle of the 18th century. God was questioned; the monarchy as sole political organization-principle came under pressure; divine rights of the rulers couldn't be justified anymore; estate-based social structures were replaced; the natural order of rich and poor came to be the result of social processes; family-based economy was substituted by industrialized working-conditions; and social change was made a center point of the time concept.[6] A belief system that had structured life over centuries was abolished, which is why people were *looking for a new orientation*. "Nationalism" as celebration of the sovereign collective with an untainted past and a bright future was and still is the

---

[6] About these fundamental changes see Schulze, Hagen (1994), pp. 163 f.

answer to a need for stability. According to Guéhenno, nationalism is a defensive reflex, a reaction focused on ourselves against a world that seems to get out of control.[7] All different forms of "reality" construction like politics, art, science,[8] or philosophy contribute to the perfect national identity free of any self-doubts. The collective prevails over the individual, which is why serious sacrifices have to be made, culminating in the readiness to die for your nation. The primacy of the collective justifies coercion and violence outside and inside the nation state.[9]

Assimilatory integration leads to monoculture because plurality, difference, and novelty are eradicated. Even though the ruling majority wins important degrees of freedom because it is their construction-power that decides, they renounce, at the same time, to a wide range of possibilities. The more it becomes Manichaean, the more it restricts itself and turns into a narrow and conservative existence. This *absolutism of the collective self* is then mainly preoccupied with fighting the enemy it constructed. Lots of time, energy, money, and ideas are lost in this battle. Fear, anger, and hate dominate life. Trust in others and open-minded discovery of alternatives aren't available, which is why freedom is strongly reduced. That's why Glotz pleads for supranational cooperation instead of nationalism, for federalism instead of centralism, for individualization instead of a simple majority rule, for autonomy instead of assimilatory dictates.[10]

For many years and with great success the Swiss People's Party (SVP, right-wing populist party) has pursued assimilatory integration. Having reached almost 30 % in the elections of 2007 in the National Council, this demagogic party succeeded exclusively with xenophobic proposals. Very effectively using propaganda tools they always stage a play in two acts. First, they construct a problem that threatens the existence of the nation. Second, foreigners are made responsible. For example "pseudo-invalides" is one of their creations. According to the SVP, predominantly foreign workers feign being ill or injured to receive benefits from a duped state. This money is then missing for honest Swiss. Inquiries of the Federal Office of Social Security reported less than 1 % of fraud, and the percentage of fraudulent foreigners corresponds with their percentage of benefits-beneficiary.[11] To keep Switzerland clean from unwelcome subjects, the SVP launched a popular initiative to amend the Constitution, affording the right of the state to expel for-

---

[7] Guéhenno, Jean-Marie (1994), p. 24
[8] Kaschuba, Wolfgang (1993), p. 253
[9] Beck-Gernsheim, Elisabeth (2004), p. 197
[10] Glotz, Peter (1992), pp. 35 f.
[11] Neue Zürcher Zeitung of April 20, 2009, p. 13

eigners convicted of crimes ("Ausschaffungsinitative").[12] Whoever commits premeditated murder, rape, or social security fraud (of whatever amount) has to be expelled immediately without judicial review. On November 28, 2010, with a relatively high turnout, 53 % of the voters approved the constitutional reform.[13] Fearing globalization and change in general, and feeling insecure because of the crisis of the dogma of market integration, the voting majority hoped for Swiss purity. This "aggressive populism"[14] seeks for *more of the same forever.*

bb) Core value absolutism

Core value absolutism protects a restricted set of principles. All members have to adhere to the core values that are *undeniably given* and are usually defended by legal and state means. *Within specified limits differences are accepted.* Individuals and groups dispose of a wide array of possibilities, as long as they do not infringe the absolute limits imposed on the community's members. The German Grundgesetz (Constitution) explicitly rules that certain principles can't be questioned under any circumstances:

> **Article 79 GG**
>
> (3) Amendments to this Basic Law affecting the division of the Federation into Länder, their participation on principle in the legislative process, or the principles laid down in Articles 1 and 20 shall be inadmissible.
>
> **Article 1 GG**
>
> (1) Human dignity shall be inviolable. To respect and protect it shall be the duty of all state authority.
> (2) The German people therefore acknowledge inviolable and inalienable human rights as the basis of every community, of peace and of justice in the world.

---

[12] Swiss half-direct democracy knows the political right to submit an amendment to the vote of the people and the cantons if more than 100'000 people entitled to vote sign the initiative.
[13] Article 121 Section 3-6 BV
[14] EU Commission president José Manuel Barroso on French Radio Europe 1, November 29, 2010: "I see societies that have a great tradition of openness and democracy where a nationalist, chauvinist, xenophobic, sometimes even a very, very aggressive populism surge is swelling." "Populism is the manipulation of fears with irrational arguments, but it works sometimes."

(3) The following basic rights shall bind the legislature, the executive and the judiciary as directly applicable law.

Article 20 GG

(1) The Federal Republic of Germany is a democratic and social federal state.
(2) All state authority is derived from the people. It shall be exercised by the people through elections and other votes and through specific legislative, executive and judicial bodies.
(3) The legislature shall be bound by the constitutional order, the executive and the judiciary by law and justice.

Based on its National Socialist experience, this "eternity clause" is supposed to avoid anti-democratic and anti-constitutional developments. The constitution is expected to be a barrier against claims of parties and people who intend to install an authoritarian government irrespective of human rights and of the rule of law. Constitutional principles are, in my view, symbolic declarations, proposals (see p. 301 ff.). They are not unimportant and can be a crystallization point launching actions based on and focusing toward these norms. But their integrative effect only occurs if the interactors are able to develop a normative consensus and are ready to abide by these rules in their everyday life. A constitution is no firewall against violations of the enumerated principles if the legal staff isn't engaged and willing to fight against populist or demagogic developments.

In its "Rapport public 2004" the Conseil d'Etat[15] of France describes "la laïcité" as a diffuse concept, which generally speaking stands for the loss of influence of the state on religion. It rejects the subordination of politics under religion and recognizes, therefore, a pluralism of religious activities. Furthermore, a state neutrality toward churches is prescribed.[16] This separation of the political and religious realm can be traced back to the French Revolution and appears implicit in Article 10 of the Déclaration des droits de l'homme of August 26, 1789, and in most of the subsequent constitutions. Legally central is the law of 1905, which states in Article 1 freedom of conscience and in Article 2 separation of church and state. Because of the neutrality of the state, teachers in public schools, for example, play a particular role. Basically they are free to believe in whatever they want or

---

[15] Highest administrative court
[16] Conseil d'Etat (2004), p. 245, 272

not to believe at all. That's why, on the one hand, teachers can't be denied a job because of their faith. On the other hand, they are not allowed to wear religious signs in class because they represent the state and have to be and appear neutral.[17] In relation to individuals without state function the concept of "laïcité" wants to privatize religious aspects without excluding the appearance of religious signs in the public sphere.[18] Religious acts can take place in public, outside of churches, synagogues, or mosques as long as the public order is respected, whereas only exceptionally grave circumstances allow a restriction of these liberties.[19] On November 27, 1989, the Conseil d'Etat wrote in an opinion commissioned by the education minister, that public schools can't deny admission based on religious arguments, because the neutrality of state doesn't allow such discrimination. According to this, students are entitled to wear religious symbols in school or university. And schools are allowed to restrict religious activities of students if other students have to be protected (proselytization, propaganda, provocation), the functioning of the institution is seriously disturbed, the students lack respect toward teachers, or because of public disorder. A general interdiction however, so the Conseil d'Etat, can't be justified.[20] The request of the education minister was motivated by a conflict in the grammar school of Creil in the North of Paris. Its headmaster had interdicted Leila, Fatima, and Samira to wear their scarf in school. This conflict launched a religious and cultural controversy, and the Islamic scarf became the core object of an identity-"war." In 2004, the French parliament adopted "La loi sur les signes religieux dans les écoles publiques," which prohibited all religious signs in schools and colleges.[21] The legislator understood the scarf as a symbol of a patriarchal concept of family and of gender-relations, not in accordance with the fundamentals constituting French identity. For Altschull, the scarf stands for oppression and segregation and excludes women of all the emancipatory possibilities France offers. That's why it risks destroying republican morality.[22] For Leggewie, this prohibition leads to a retreat into the private sphere, where fundamentalists have easier access to recruit adherents.[23] Gaspard and Khosrokhavar, on their side, are convinced that the conflict is highly exaggerated, because the scarf is much more a symbol of

---

[17] Id., pp. 274 f.
[18] Id., p. 264
[19] Id., pp. 276 f.
[20] Id., pp. 338 f.
[21] Today Article L141-5-1 of the Code de l'éducation
[22] Altschull, Elizabeth (1995), pp. 57, 72 f., 121 ff.
[23] Leggewie, Claus (1993), p. 85

personal identity, of family membership, and/or of tradition than a political statement against the modern state or against civil rights in the sense of Hezbollah or FIS.[24] They distinguish three motives and meanings associated with the Islamic scarf:[25] First, so-called "traditional women" from the countryside who wore the scarf before arriving in France. Their mothers and grandmothers showed the example and it became part of their identity. Second, young teenagers or pre-teenagers, wanted to please their observant Muslim father. More or less newly immigrated, they try to reconcile both worlds and to find their own way and identity. If there are traditional parents, the scarf helps them leave the restricted family area and discover the other community. After a lapse of time they often renounce to the scarf out of their free decision, when, for example, entering college. In these cases, ideological pressure pushes them back into their family, into the traditional "reality."[26] A part of young teenagers experience intense control and pressure from their brothers. If state and society react repressively instead of supporting the girls and women when they ask for help, they will be traumatized a second time.[27] The third motive to wear a scarf is described by Gaspard and Khosrokhavar as the claimed or autonomous scarf, the scarf chosen because of personal conviction, sometimes supported by their parents, sometimes against their will.[28] These young women between the ages of sixteen to twenty-five develop their own identity out of "modern" and "traditional" elements. They are autonomous deciders wearing Islamic clothes.[29]

The French majority of parliament opted for an authoritarian republicanism. First, they interpreted the principles of the "republic" and the "laïcité" in a very restrictive, homogenizing way, against the recommendations of the Conseil d'Etat. Second, they supposed that there is a sort of natural, eternal French collective identity, as if the compromise between Catholic Church and the state wouldn't have taken decades to be established.[30] Taking women seriously who wear an Islamic scarf would mean to enter into discussions to see, if help is needed because of conflicts with parents, broth-

---

[24] Gaspard, Françoise/Khosrokhavar, Farhad (1995), pp. 54 ff. 59
[25] Id., pp. 34 ff.
[26] Id., p. 37
[27] Id., p. 38
[28] Id., p. 45
[29] Id., p. 47. Béji sees the scarf as a critic against certain modern developments, against to much of freedom, against the over-sexualization of all areas of life (Béji, Hélé [2011], p. 15).
[30] Conseil d'Etat (2004), pp. 249 ff.

ers, school, or classmates. Basically the scarf is only a clothing item that, in my opinion, doesn't hurt or injure other people. It is the everyday behavior of people, their concrete living situation that matters. To respect freedom means, in my view, defending the right to wear a scarf as well as the right to renounce to it. Forcing young women to renounce symbols they qualify as a part of their origins, or symbols important for their family, forces them to chose between their family and the ruling majority. Respecting these girls and women means to listen to their convictions, to pose questions if we don't understand their motives or their fears that they could be abused, and to talk on their behalf if necessary. There is a danger for freedom and equality if we make every difference an identity-conflict and if certain principles are declared absolute.

cc) Cooperation – masterpiece plurality

Difference is a chance. Cooperative integration proposes an *open debate about the common future.* There is no prerogative to be respected without need of justification, no absolute truth, no undeniable reality. Applying the basic values *relevant for now*, it is important to work together on equal terms. In this way, the richness of ideas, of different histories, and of hopes is respected and the dialogue that's held doesn't exclude on the basis of criteria that people can't influence. There is no use for dichotomous worldviews, no use for collective judgments doing everything to avoid a nuanced statement. There is no fixed minority, defined and constructed solely according to the needs of the majority. There is only *a common task to find solutions* that give all the participants a possibility to realize their goals in a respectful manner. Much more work has to be done than just decree others' behavior. We have to listen, propose, ask and discuss, criticize and reflect in order to secure what worked up to now and to change where people weren't integrated.

What seems to be a disadvantage – permanent work and frequent change – is, in my view a condition for a high quality of life. Thanks to respectful recognition people are able to trust each other, which is why stability and change are possible. Trusting each other helps us to confront new challenges brought forward by old and new members of the community (see p. 179 ff.). People who trust are able to be open minded, to be self critical because they know the others are not a danger but look for common grounds. We do not want others to fail because their failure is a loss for us, too. That's why cooperation helps us to risk new things, to be different, to make the function of the court jester possible, which develops wild speculations about the future. For "realities" based on the homo oeconomicus cooperation doesn't make any sense. According to the economic theory, human beings cooperate only because of selfish interests or because they are forced to. But why should people who are free to act by their own will not being able and even eager to act in a solidary and just way? The one who has made the experience of cooperation realizes its enormous potential and how much it goes beyond experiences one can make on her or his own. As stated by Bohnet and Frey, cooperation follows communication: "[...] simply talking to each other already changes individual behavior and enhances cooperation."[31] Getting to know somebody, overcoming anonymity increases drastically the generosity of people.[32] Against this background an integration mode based on mutual interest and not on fear, on curiosity instead on rejection, on plurality instead on homogeneous reductionism, will help bring people together instead of excluding the ones currently without enough power to defend their interests. There is a risk in difference because possibly we won't like it. But to fight difference increases the risks to lose what we currently like, because counterpower will quite probably be developed. Listening to the ones willing to be different will give them the possibility to listen to us and to work toward common goals. We, therefore, *have to take risks to minimize risks.*

Turkish Prime Minister Erdogan visiting Germany in February 2008 demanded Turkish speaking schools and universities to be build.[33] He pointed out that nobody can expect of Turkish people to assimilate because "assimilation is a crime against humanity." Accordingly, they should have the possibility of their own education system. On the other hand, he asked Turkish people to be cooperative, to learn German and play an active role in German society. The conservative right qualified these statements as an aggressive threat and defended their assimilatory integration concept, which is why a cooperative approach wasn't possible. For Wolfgang Bosbach, for example, party whip of the Union and member of CDU, Erdogan wasn't entitled to interfere in German domestic politics.[34] CSU chief Erwin Huber

---

[31] Bohnet, Iris/Frey, Bruno S. (1994), p. 459
[32] *Id.*, p. 460
[33] And again in February 2011, see: Spiegel-Online of February 27, 2011 (http://www.spiegel.de/politik/deutschland/0,1518,747991,00.html), retrieved on July 27, 2011
[34] Bosbach warnt Türkei vor Einmischung, in: Spiegel-Online of February 12, 2008 (http://www.spiegel.de/politik/deutschland/0,1518,534617,00.html), retrieved on July 27, 2011

qualified Erdogan's statement as anti-European.[35] For Chancellor Merkel, Erdogan defended the wrong concept of integration because, in her view, people have to be loyal to the German state alone.[36] The CSU group in the Bundestag was angry that Erdogan's speech was given in Turkish. They qualified this as an insult.[37] The conservatives refuse to cooperatively debate a possible future and they even forbid critical statements. To question the current state is qualified as gross and there is no level playing field on which the interactors can meet. Thus, the feeling of not being recognized and respected is increased.

c) Manichaeism and collectivism

Carl Schmitt, one of the leading National Socialist jurists, defended a Manichaean concept of politics: "The real political distinction is the distinction between friend and foe."[38] The foe is in a essentialist way different from us; he is the stranger with whom we have existential conflicts. They are existential because they can't be rationalized in the form of legislative procedures or decided by an independent third party. For Schmitt, it is the undeniable reality[39] of politics that war or revolution are the final and always possible consequences of politics.[40] The state incorporates, according to him, the jus ad bellum (the right of the sovereign state to wage war) and has, therefore, the right to determine and to fight the foe and to decide over the life of human beings. It is entitled to require blind obedience and can oblige the people to die and to kill[41] because the life of individuals can be sacrificed for the collective's sake.[42] Every limitation of the state's power is, according

---

[35] Erdogan bekräftigt Warnung vor "Assimilierung", on: Welt-Online of February 2, 2008 (http://www.welt.de/politik/article1663412/Erdogan_bekraeftigt_Warnung_vor_Assimilierung.html), retrieved on July 27, 2011

[36] Merkel: Bin auch die Bundeskanzlerin der Deutschtürken, on: Faz.Net of February 2, 2008 (http://www.faz.net/artikel/C30923/integrationsdebatte-merkel-bin-auch-die-bundeskanzlerin-der-deutschtuerken-30109579.html), retrieved on July 27, 2011

[37] Deutschland soll türkische Schulen einrichten, on: Neue Zürcher Zeitung of February 9, 2008 (http://www.nzz.ch/nachrichten/politik/international/deutschland_tuerkei_1.667889.html), retrieved on July 27, 2011

[38] Schmitt, Carl (1933), pp. 7 f.

[39] Id., pp. 9 f.

[40] Id., p. 13

[41] Id., p. 28

[42] Id., p. 51

to Schmitt, unjustifiable, which is why constitutional states are weak states that try to avoid every real conflict.[43] And a system of checks and balances is consequently subversive because it negates the essential character of the state, its omnipotence.[44] Political power doesn't have to be justified. It is entitled to use whatever it needs to win the battle.[45] Schmitt's nationalist collective is understood as *homogeneous entity, based on some evident and truthful criteria which justifies the supremacy of the one over anything else.*

This collectivist concept within a set of hostile entities is also used by Huntington. His construction of the world after the Cold War is not interested in differences, nuances, or complexity. The post-Cold War world is, according to Huntington, "a world of seven or eight major civilizations. Cultural commonalities and differences shape the interests, antagonisms, and associations of states. The most important countries in the world come overwhelmingly from different civilizations."[46] Cultures are, according to Huntington, defined by several criteria, the most important being religion.[47] He differentiates the following civilizations: Sinic (Chinese), Japanese, Hindu (India), Islamic (spread across Africa, Turkey, the Middle East, and Asia), Orthodox (Russia), Western (Europe, North America, Australia, New Zealand), Latin America, and (possibly) African.[48] It is, to Huntington, a "highly simplified [picture]. It omits many things, distorts some things, and obscures others. Yet if we are to think seriously about the world, and act effectively in it, some sort of simplified map of reality […] is necessary".[49] "Every model or map is an abstraction and will be more useful for some purposes than for others."[50] But what is indisputable for him, is the constant anthropological need for Manichaean judgements: The civilized "we" and the barbarian "others" are unavoidable.[51] Even more: "It is human to hate. For self-definition and motivation people need enemies: competitors in business, rivals in achievement, opponents in politics. They naturally distrust and see as threats those who are different and have the capability to harm them."[52]

---

[43] *Id.*, p. 25
[44] *Id.*, pp. 42 f.
[45] *Id.*, pp. 46 ff.
[46] Huntington, Samuel P. (1998), p. 29
[47] *Id.*, p. 42, 47
[48] *Id.*, pp. 45 ff.
[49] *Id.*, p. 29
[50] *Id.*, p. 30
[51] *Id.*, p. 32, 129
[52] *Id.*, p. 130

As Huntington mentions: Every model is useful for specific purposes. His "clash of civilizations" is ideal if a collective intends to construct its identity by hating others. In 2007, a group consisting of members of the Swiss People's Party (SVP), members of the Federal Democratic Union (conservative Christian right), and the "Egerkingen Committee" (local politicians fighting against concrete plans to build a minaret in their constituency) launched a popular initiative to amend the Swiss Constitution. The amendment text stated: "The construction of minarets is forbidden." Originally motivated by an actual minaret building project, the initiative fast became a spearhead against "Islam." One of the main arguments of its proponents was that "Minarets are symbols of the secular and metaphysical claim to power inherent to Islam." A threat had to be constructed to give the demagogues the opportunity to portray themselves as saviors. There hadn't been terrorist attacks in Switzerland; there weren't up to this point any conflicts between religious groups; most of the about 400'000 Muslims living in this country are as secular as the Christian majority, as only 5 % attend regularly a mosque; the first minaret built in Switzerland in 1963 in Zurich didn't cause any legal objection; in 2009 four minarets exist and no problems are known due to their existence. Because any planned construction has to pass building laws and has to be approved by the competent authority, there wasn't any legal need for this amendment. But there seemed to be a need for psychological stabilization, a need for the construction of a polarized collective identity that gave the majority the assurance being absolutely right. The initiator of the constitutional amendment identified Islam with Sharia law, forced marriages, "honor" killings, female genital mutilation, the burqa, and other forms of oppression of women. Paradoxically, this right-wing groups had up until now never fought for equal rights for men and women (on the contrary), suddenly they discovered the usefulness of this claim. Their proposal was approved by 57,5 % of the participating voters (at a participation rate of 53,4 %, which is quite high, as the average of the last twenty years has been 44 %). They justified this initiative by the need to protect the secular against religious claims. However, it is this their political fight that made religion a discussed principle of Swiss identity. Classic scapegoat strategy was applied: First, you create an enemy which you, second, describe as threatening, so that you can, third, fight this danger by all means. It is this defamatory construction that made some Muslims unite and react to defend the common interests they didn't have before. As a result, a schism was built up that helped the populist party mobilize their adherents.

"Islam" took over the role the east-west schism played during the Cold War: "Since the 1990s there yawned a gap there."[53] On the other hand, fundamentalists like Al Qaeda nurture fear by the casualties and injuries they orchestrate appropriately for the needs of modern media. This exceptional rage is then used by non-violent Christians and other fundamentalists to fight everything they don't like. In their search for simplicity scapegoat politics needs terrorists in a certain way.[54] As a result, a reductionist religion-based and stigmatizing Muslim-identity is constructed which excludes other perceptions.[55] Because this fundamentalist identity is the only one offered by the majority, Muslims have to possibilities: Hide their personal convictions and try to avoid every hint of their religious or cultural identity. Or they can adhere to the fundamentalist offer supported by the majority because they are socially, politically, or economically disadvantaged.[56] The currently dominating picture of "Islam" constructed by the majority is characterized by historical references or citations from the Koran and the tradition of the prophet. Anti-Islam fundamentalists do not accept the possibility that "Islam" could have changed over the centuries.[57] If Muslims are quoted, most of the time they are fundamentalists.[58] And to talk about Muslims doesn't mean to talk about individuals and their banal everyday life, but about "islamic Masses"[59] causing or being part of violent crises.[60] The very heterogeneous, courageous acts of the protesters in Egypt and Tunisia, in Libya and Syria, in Bahrain or in Jordan, will hopefully question this pejorative collectivization and open the door to a respectful interest in individuals. Sen criticizes Huntington's collectivization as over-simplifying because, for example, the Hindu civilization stands for a country within which live, after Indonesia and Pakistan, the world's largest number of Muslims (145 million). Huntington doesn't take them into consideration. The same accounts for the Sikhs, the Jains, Buddhists, Christian, Jews, Parsees,

---

[53] Czempiel, Ernst-Otto (2003), p. 120. See also Kandil, Fuad (2000), p. 138; Haug, Wolfang (2003), p. 16
[54] Scheerer, Sebastian (2002), p. 108, 136, 139
[55] Kandil, Fuad (2000), p. 129
[56] Id., p. 131
[57] Lueg, Andrea (1993), p. 21
[58] Id., p. 22. See also Bishara, Azmi (1993), p. 140. Heine states, that of the around 1,5 billion Muslims on the world, 1 to 2 % are expected to be fundamentalists (Heine, Peter [2010]).
[59] Lueg, Andrea (1993), p. 24
[60] Hippler, Jochen (1993), p. 143

agnostics, and atheists.[61] Simplifications, though, are not innocuous: In my opinion, they determine our perception of the other. Men and women are no longer individuals with a unique story. Their identity is widely determined by the collective we force them into and they have to represent. And what is even more, we have to hate them, as hate is, according to Huntington human, natural, and therefore inescapable.

The American founding fathers intended a pluralistic and cooperative religious setup. They didn't fear new religions. On the contrary, they hoped for a multitude of establishments, making sure that there was not one dominating. "They saw religion as a power necessary to the good order of society, giving the revolutionary political arrangements their validity. [...] Their problem was how to encourage the practice of religion without allowing it to oppress the people. [...] By not establishing a church, they would control the dangerous potential of a religion while encouraging the beneficial powers and moral impulses that arise from it. They would temper sectarian religions by balancing one church against another, believing thus that no single one would become dominant enough to oppress people's minds as they had done in Europe."[62] In American statements God is much more often mentioned than in Europe. This "God," however, is not a specific one, but stands, in my view, for an engagement in favor of the common good and the readiness to be responsible for one's own acts. It seems to me that religion per se is not a problem, but the use people make of ideas. Religious convictions that are made absolute are as much a threat to freedom and justice as political or economic convictions. What makes them dangerous is their claim for exclusivity and the Manichaean collectivization. Insofar is the respect we have for the individual's performance, for their everyday engagement for a good life, a safeguard against totalitarianism. Conflicts occur, in my perception, not because of religious, ethnical, or cultural differences, but because of the refusal to recognize and respect others. Manichaean collectivizations, hence, aren't a solution. They get their tempting effect from exclusion and denigration, which leads to intensified conflicts. Manichaeism in the form of science claims objectivity and is a powerful part of the cultural violence.

---

[61] Sen, Amartya (2006), pp. 46 ff.
[62] Meyer, Jeffrey F. (2001), pp. 53 f.

4. Reciprocity

"For human beings living […] means to be with people."[1] In the consensus-based constructivism this is the fundament of human existence. There is no survival without social contact, at least in the first years. And quality of life depends on interactions: *Being humane means to establish reciprocal relationships*. Reciprocity is a concretization of solidarity and stands for a sense of

- commonality, of a
- shared future, of
- trust, and of
- mutual responsibility.

A relationship is "reciprocal" if there is a form of *give and take*. It contains a mutual obligation to support each other when needed, to exchange some form of valuables to consolidate social bonds, or to equalize unjust distribution of wealth. A constant point of debate is the balancing of freedom and obligation, of independence and dependence, of autonomy and support.

Reciprocity generates meaning by incorporating people into a relationship defined by specific roles. One is entitled to expect something from others. The payback doesn't have to be of exactly the same value or the same sort and the timing of the refund does not have to be fixed. If the exchange takes place step-by-step, the integrative effect lies in the reproduction of expectations and institutions. So, for example, in a political compromise is made possible within a legislative procedure. If the support is given without instant return, the endeavor contains a certain risk. One has to trust the others that in the long run there will be community actions in favor of the current giver. If trust is confirmed, it introduces a long-term bond that stabilizes the community. Social security, which is built on an assessment system, is an example of this.

Reciprocity is *not a gift*, it is an *act in favor of the community*. It, therefore, profits others and myself at the same time. Writing about different native communities, Mauss points out the importance to return something, to answer the given.[2] At the same time, there is a duty to give, to take one's own responsibility to support decisions that bring a solution to actual conflicts.[3]

---

[1] Arendt, Hannah (1987), p. 15
[2] Mauss, Marcel (1990), pp. 25, 33
[3] Id., p. 36

The more the "give and take/expect" is related to people the interactors know personally, the higher the integrative effect of reciprocity. Formalized institutions mainly convince by their performances. As long as they deliver according to the expectancies established, the readiness to contribute to the reciprocal mechanism will endure and bind individuals to the institution.

a)   Morality first

The immigration of the Puritans on American soil is an immigration based on *strong religious beliefs and moral principles*. It is also an example for the powerful integrative effect reciprocity yields. The sixteenth century England of Catholic Mary I was an unpleasant place for Protestants, which is why a significant group left the country and went to Geneva, where they were influenced by the Calvin. Protestant Elizabeth I restored religious tolerance, what made the now Calvinistic Puritans go back to England, radicalized by the new ideas they had encountered abroad. The Puritans played an important role because many of them were educated men, working on the pulpits and in the courts. Increasingly, however, their anti-hierarchical convictions and their democratic claims led to conflicts with the authority. Denying royal supremacy over ecclesiastical affairs and propagating the set up of churches independent of the queen or bishops enabled them to be qualified as a "sect of Separatists."[4] The designation "Puritan" was originally an insult created by a Catholic mocking that the Protestants were looking for the "authentic Christianity"[5] and wished to get rid of every trace of Romanism. The Puritans called themselves "professors of the Gospel," "professors of sincerity," or "the godly."[6] Nevertheless, the great majority of the Puritans agreed to adapt to the actual power and to stay within the queen's church.

Scottish theologian Andrew Melville, giving a speech in the presence of James VI, King of Scots, demonstrated the revolutionary side of independent Puritans: "I tell you, sir, there are two kings and two kingdoms in Scotland. There is Christ Jesus the King, and his kingdom the Kirk, whose subject James VI is, and of whose kingdom not a king, nor a lord, nor a head, but a member. And they whom Christ hath called to watch over his kirk and govern his spiritual kingdom have sufficient power and authority so to do both together and severally."[7] When in 1603 James VI became

---

[4]   Fiske, John (2005), p. 66
[5]   Bunker, Nick (2010), p. 85
[6]   Id., p. 75
[7]   Quoted in Fiske, John (2005), p. 69

King of England and Ireland, now called James I., he enforced conformity against Catholics who didn't accept the idea that the Pope hadn't any prerogatives over the king, and against Puritans questioning his religious authority. Fleeing this forced assimilation, some of the Puritans escaped to the Dutch Republic, which was at the time a place of tolerance attracting dissenters from all of Europe: "All persons who came to Holland, and led decorous lives there, were protected in their opinions and customs."[8] From 1609 on they lived in Leyden and their number increased from 300 to over 1'000. They didn't assimilate with Dutch society and kept up their distinct collective identity by preserving their organization, talking English, and cherishing their traditions. "Leyden was a thriving city of forty thousand, but it was also a commercial center that required its inhabitants to work at a pace that must have come as a shock to farmers from Nottinghamshire and Yorkshire. […] As the years of ceaseless labor began to mount and their children began to lose touch with their English ancestry, the Pilgrims decided it was time to start over again."[9] Not to have to work raised their doubts, as they adhered to Protestant work ethics. They feared losing the possibility to worship God and to take the time to organize their life in a godly way. There was no English grammar school and religion was of no particular importance in the city. Industrial conditions were unhealthy and it seemed difficult to preserve a close family life. Furthermore, the place became politically instable because of increasing protests against inequality and intolerance.[10] Unwilling to give up their convictions and identity they started to look for a new place overseas.

In 1617, the Pilgrim society of Leyden sent a detachment to Northern America to lay the corner-stone of a Puritan state, which following the colonization movement, the British government had supported since the beginning of the century. A second detachment left Delft in 1620. It shipped on the Speedwell first to Southampton, where they met friends from London, and then shipping on the Mayflower. The Speedwell sprang a leak, which is why all of them had to go on the Mayflower to start the passage from Plymouth on September 6, 1620. Because of the bad weather they didn't land in the south where they hoped to find their community members, but rather on Cape Cod on November 9, 1620. Half of the 102 Mayflower passengers were Puritans, the other half were strangers to them. All of them agreed upon the necessity of cooperation to build up a successful settlement. After the experience of a secular government in Holland and based on the rec-

---

[8] *Id.*, p. 74
[9] Philbrick, Nathaniel (2006), p. 17
[10] Bunker, Nick (2010), pp. 219 ff.

ommendations Pastor John Robinson had given, the Puritans were ready to adopt a treaty based on political and not on religious terms only. Before disembarking the passengers agreed on the *Mayflower Compact*, a covenant that was based on *equality* and stipulated the *responsibility of everyone for each other*. The civil body politic should be democratically organized and should enact "just and equal laws," focused on "the general good of the colony." No religious creed or specific faith was needed to adhere to the covenant.[11] They chose John Carver as their governor and all the men had to sign the compact.

On Clark's Island, an area already cleared by the Natives, they decided to build up their settlement. It took them five months to enter into official contact with the Natives, who for the first time were confronted with Europeans. After the death of John Carver, William Bradford was elected as governor. Thanks to the help of the Native Massasoit, sachem ("leader") of the Pokanokets, half of the Pilgrims survived the first winter. "For the Pilgrims [...] the Indians [...] were not a despicable pack of barbarians [...]; these were human beings, much like themselves – 'very trust[worth]y, quick of apprehension, ripe witted, just', according to Edward Winslow."[12] The Pilgrims bought a grant of land from the Virginia Bay Company[13] in 1621 and called it "Plymouth," according to the place in England where they had set sail. The pre-existing family ties, shared religious beliefs, and a working political culture made possible the construction of a community based on disciplined cooperation. Families were the core element of the community's structure and morally a mixture of personal and economic freedom and of moral and religious obligations characterized their world.

The Wessagussett Colony, on the other hand, consisted of unattached men who had arrived in Plymouth in 1622 before going further to the north. Badly organized, not ready to cooperate with each other or with the Natives, they stole from the older colony and from the Natives, desecrated graves, and insulted their leaders.[14] This confrontational, power orientated, respectless, and basically selfish behavior[15] led to hostilities with the Natives, which also tarnished their relationship with the Plymouth Colony.

---

[11] *Id.*, pp. 285 f.
[12] Philbrick, Nathaniel (2006), p. 119
[13] Also called "Plymouth Company" or "Virginia Company of Plymouth". One of the two joint stock companies chartered by James I. in 1606 to establish settlements on the coast of North America. The other company was the "London Company" or "Virginia Company of London".
[14] Bunker, Nick (2010), p. 327
[15] Philbrick, Nathaniel (2006), pp. 149, 153

A military preemptive attack by the Pilgrims was supposed to secure an allegedly threatened colony. "Standish's raid had irreparably damaged the human ecology of the region."[16] And the more materialistic demands increased, the more the basic respect vanished; the more hunger for land grew, the more power politics replaced cooperation.[17]

In the 1620s, wealthy businessmen and university-educated scholars and ministers decided to leave England and to settle in America. In 1628, they obtained a charter, allowing the Massachusetts Bay Company to establish its own government for the colony, subject only to the king. After making two preliminary reconnaissance voyages they settled on Cape Ann in Salem harbor. Like the Pilgrims they were religious nonconformists, defending an uncorrupted concept of the church. But contrary to the separatist Pilgrims, the Puritans didn't want to break up with the Church of England. Furthermore, they were class-conscious and less equalitarian, defending a more authoritarian and elitist concept of political organization. But both groups had left their home country mainly because of religious and political reasons, unlike, for example, the colonists in the Chesapeake, which were only economically motivated. The Pilgrims and Puritans alike intended to establish a community based on specific values like the right to religious conviction, freedom, and democracy. Even though there were quite a few members who were interested in more economic freedom, looking for new business opportunities[18] or even owing their own land (something that was impossible in England for many of them), the concept of a moral economy prevailed. Their main goal was to create the foundations of God's kingdom on earth. But the Puritans were more dogmatic and more exclusionary than the Pilgrims: "[…] the Puritans of Massachusetts Bay developed a more rigorous set of requirements for church membership than had been used at Plymouth, where it had been assumed […] that only God ultimately knew whether a person was or was not a Saint."[19]

In 1630 John Winthrop led seventeen ships carrying 1'000 men, women, and children, animals, and the materials needed to build houses to the Massachusetts Bay Colony. During this "Great Migration," which lasted from

---

[16] Id., p. 155. See also p. 149 and 153. Miles Standish was the first Commander of the Plymouth Colony militia.
[17] Bunker, Nick (2010), p. 318, 322; Fiske, John (2005), p. 121; Philbrick, Nathaniel (2006), p. 203
[18] Newell, Margaret Ellen (1998), pp. 24 f.
[19] Philbrick, Nathaniel (2006), p. 174

1620 to 1643,[20] over 20'000 people emigrated to New England – at the time about 30 % of the English emigration to America. Even though the population increased quickly, the social structure of the Puritans was much more stable than in other colonies. The moral and social basis of the communities were quite homogeneous, as the needy and shiftless people were excluded on the ground of a pronounced working ethic.[21] Also existed a mere equation of men and women, what made family building and procreation much easier. Further, most of them were middle class members, contrary to the majority of poor settlers and the dependent and vulnerable serfs of the Chesapeake. Their social conditions and their moral and religious motivation[22] made integration much easier and more effective. Their common ideological background also helped build up a sensible collective identity, rooted far back in the past. Defending a pure concept of church, their congregations "asserted consistency with the primitive Christianity of the era before the corrupt Roman Popes."[23]

A good life meant a godly life, which was manifest in hard work and discipline, respect for moral principles, reading the Bible, and going against fatalism by actively shaping the world. Sufficiency instead of abundance and justice instead of inequality were the guidelines. They were aware, that *a big gap between rich and poor was a source of disintegration*. A just community had to recognize its members as equal and to assure *comparable opportunities*. Hence, all men were provided enough land to support their families. It was land they completely owned (freehold), which protected them from rising rents. Private property and freedom of contract were institutionalized within a highly integrated social network that asked for civic mindfulness. Absolute egality was not intended, they were not levelers.[24] *Social inequality was tolerated as long as it wasn't disruptive for the group's cohesion*. People had to do the work according to their social origin. And class distinctions were upheld for example by the use of dress codes.[25] Even though the Puritans had left England because of an authority they weren't willing to accept, they didn't oppose subordination. Hierarchical structures were seen as part

---

[20] The Great Migration ended because of the overthrow of King Charles and his execution in 1649. During the upheaval many settlers went back to England to support the revolution. And afterwards, England having become a Puritan state which started to be the center of the world, there was no need anymore to leave the country.
[21] Fiske, John (2005), pp. 141 f.
[22] Bremer, Francis J./Botelho, Lynn (2005), p. 9
[23] Hart, James S./Ross, Richard J. (2005), p. 265
[24] Morgan, Edmund S. (1966), p. 18
[25] Durst Johnson, Claudia (2002), p. 88

of the divine order. "The essence of the social order lay in the superiority of husband over wife, parents over children, and master over servants in the family, ministers and elders over congregation in the church, rulers over subjects in the state."[26] The leaders of the Massachusetts Bay Colony were quite wealthy people. So, for example, the merchants or the clergymen were "[…] the most highly educated people in the community, clergymen were the powers behind the legislators. From the beginning, their influence was tremendous."[27] Nevertheless, the absence of an aristocracy made the community quite equal,[28] and the moral restrictions on self-interested money making kept social inequality within a certain range. The importance of equality also becomes apparent in gender relations. Compared to many other women at this time, the status of Puritan wives in New England was relatively high.[29] The "husband's authority was strictly limited"[30] and had to be guided by love, by real affection, kindness, and respect.[31] Furthermore, the women's decisive responsibility for the inculcation of religious knowledge within the family made them play a prominent role in the community.[32] And economically they were engaged in a wide range of trades, later qualified as "male."[33] Human beings were recognized as universally equal, which is why the Puritans didn't trade with slaves. Contrary to the Quakers, however, they accepted slavery and the possession of slaves in Massachusetts. But they had to be treated in a Christian way and "shall have the liberties […] which the Law of God established in Israel."[34]

In Puritan and Pilgrim communities the idea of justice dominated all realms of life. Accordingly, the *economy was morally embedded and was no end in itself*. An autonomous and decent life for everybody wasn't achievable by the capitalistic principle of material greed, but by a commonwealth founded on reciprocity and freedom, responsibility and solidarity. They were "in the service of God, not Mammon,"[35] as "the essential principle was that economic dealings not take place at the expense of social justice."[36] It

---

[26] Morgan, Edmund S. (1966), p. 19
[27] Durst Johnson, Claudia (2002), p. 60
[28] Bremer, Francis J. (2005), p. 210
[29] Innes, Stephen (1995), pp. 31 f.
[30] Morgan, Edmund S. (1966), p. 45
[31] Id., pp. 47 f.
[32] Peterson, Mark A. (2005), p. 87
[33] Godbeer, Richard (2005), p. 297
[34] Resolution the Court of the colony passed in 1641.
[35] Innes, Stephen (1995), p. 43
[36] Id., p. 166

was a "commitment to the common good" secured by "checks on economic individualism."[37] In the foreground stood the integration of the community, the stability of the social arrangement. Individual greed, individual interests in making fast money had to step back. "Usury stood for a form of exchange that disregarded the moral dynamics of neighbor-to-neighbor relations and looked instead to rational laws of supply and demand."[38] A form of political economy took place because "the principles of prudence, productivity, and oversight that worked in the household context [were extended] to the state's administration of the entire community's resources."[39] Equity, amity, and order were central values that politics had to take care of.

Their cooperatively structured community was very successful. "Through their civic ecology, Protestant work ethic, and sense of communal purpose, seventeenth-century New Englanders created a stable, thriving, 'middling'-rank society. This was a society that offered the mass of its inhabitants level of prosperity, educational attainment, family stability, material culture, and life expectancy not duplicated elsewhere in British America."[40] As opposed to the Chesapeake, there weren't any fabulously wealthy people exceeding far the majority. "Equal opportunity" wasn't a lure used to calm the many who were exploited by the few, but a lived-by principle. Even servants and slaves got their chance, albeit relativized. At the end of the 18th century 80 percent of the families owned and worked their own land. "When we measure colonial societies by their ability to offer economic autonomy and decent comforts to *all* their households (including servants and slaves) [...] the New England colonies along with Pennsylvania demonstrably exceeded all others."[41]

The families were the core of the communities. Favorable climate, an integrative family and community structure, and a good diet enabled parents to raise six to seven children to maturity. Most of the servants working in New England came with the family and accounted for about five percent in 1700. At the same time, around two percent of the people were slaves (13 percent in Virginia, 78 in the West Indies). Being part of a community was a compelling element of a godly life, why singles were obliged to enter a family for example as a servant or as a boarder.[42] They preferred small social

---

[37] Newell, Margaret Ellen (1998), p. 7
[38] Valeri, Mark (2005), p. 151. See also p. 159. And p. 161: "Ministers preached with remarkable consistency against self-serving business practices."
[39] Newell, Margaret Ellen (1998), p. 8
[40] Innes, Stephen (1995), p. 6
[41] *Id.*, pp. 24 f., 7
[42] Morgan, Edmund S. (1966), p. 27

and economic entities, based on solidarity and mutual responsibility, which is why the building of towns was favored over the scattered settlements of isolated farms.

The high integration level the community intended to achieve necessitated a comprehensive education. Home education, public schools, and the local church were the most important institutions for this very spiritual community. To make sure that everybody would be able to read the Bible and to become an integrated part of this word-based culture, they promoted literacy. "The life of the Puritan was in one sense a continuous act of worship, pursued under an unremitting and lively sense of God's providential purposes and constantly refreshed by religious activity, personal, domestic and public."[43] "Knowing God through the Bible and serving God through action were the most important human activities."[44] That for they developed a culture of intellectuality, of reflection that prevailed over materialism. Book ownership was very important and the first press in America was established in Cambridge in 1640. In 1636 Harvard College was founded to educate an orthodox Puritan ministry. The parents were held responsible for their children's "ability to read & understand the principles of religion & the capitall lawes of this country."[45] In 1647, the General Court of Massachusetts decided, that in all towns of fifty or more families reading schools had to be established because it was "one chief project of that old deluder, Satan, to keep men from the knowledge of the Scriptures."[46] Towns including more than one hundred families were compelled to set up a grammar school. By the end of the 17th century a publicly founded school system was established. Grammar schools and the university, though, remained the prerogative of the sons of wealthy families.

To establish a church, a group of men was simply needed who were ready to be the "pillars of the church." These men were approved by their peers and when a sufficient number of members were convened, they constituted a congregation. Based on their democratic concept of religion and church and the maxim that "each man is his own priest," they incited a critical discourse of the culture and the ministers' work. On the other hand, the Puritans were quite authoritarian hierarchies, which they used to bring into line the individuals with deviant behavior. A tightly knit community with high moral uniformity was the goal. That's why, for example, priests and the

---

[43] Collinson, Patrick (1967), p. 356
[44] LaPlante, Eve (2004), p. 43
[45] Decision of the General Court of Massachusetts in 1642, quoted in: Hall, David D./Walsham, Alexandra (2005), p. 352.
[46] Old Deluder Satan Act of 1647

authorities were entitled to intervene in family matters that were judged unsuitable for a devout life. And the clergy had an enormous influence on elections, appointments, and legislation.[47] Moreover, every town had to sustain a church and all inhabitants had to attend midweek lectures and two hour Sunday services. In 1650, Massachusetts had eight times more priests per inhabitant than, for example, Virginia. But the integration-burden didn't solely rest on formal institutions. On the contrary, what we would call today a civil society played a the dominant role. Social obligations were taken very seriously and freedom was not an end in itself, but the result of a morally sound life. Churches, schools, the market, an important and active public sphere, and above all, the family built up a strong social fabric. God developed churches and states out of the family, the very first society, the foundation of all societies,[48] "a little commonwealth."[49]

According to the charter given by the king, the General Court comprised a governor, his deputy, and a council of eighteen assistants, to be elected annually by the company. John Winthrop was elected governor out of twelve members before the emigrants left England. Arriving in New England, the members of the company were the first and only freemen with the right to vote,[50] constituting the General Court, and having the power to make laws and to elect the governor. Contrary to the intention of the charter, which had supposed the government of the colony to remain in England, the Company called the first General Court in Massachusetts in 1630. At the beginning, there was no intention to build up an equalitarian democracy. This New England oligarchy[51] decided to raise a tax in 1631, but had to realize that the people weren't ready to pay without having a say. As the village of Whatertown refused to pay the tax that had been levied without consultation, the government allowed the election of two deputies of every township. From this point, on the General Court was no longer the executive council of a company, but the democratically elected government of a community. Increasingly, the government had to give in and to enlarge the participation of the people, which is why, in 1634, a second legislative body was created that represented the townships. However, the vote was only given to the few men admitted to the right church membership. To secure the political autonomy of the townships town meetings were organized. At this political level selectmen were most of the time chosen by the

---

[47] Durst Johnson, Claudia (2002), p. 26
[48] Morgan, Edmund S. (1966), pp. 133, 143, 185
[49] Innes, Stephen (1995), p. 13
[50] Durst Johnson, Claudia (2002), p. 35
[51] Id., p. 36

entire free male population, including all the settlers and not only the freemen. The settlement of Rhode Island, established by Roger Williams, and the one of Hartford, established by Reverend Hooker, enfranchised all men, independent of church membership.

The right to decide over taxation, to erect a court system with final powers of adjudication, and to legislate were the competencies the colonies had illegally taken over. This usurpation wasn't contested by the king who at the time was too busy with Asia and not interested in the Americas. To base the state institutions within the community, the colonists established a decentralized government structure with town meetings, selectmen, and country courts. Taking up an English tradition that existed in Elizabethan England, the alliance of local magistrates with godly ministers, both of them provided with considerable local autonomy,[52] was perceived as essential. Ministers, though, were barred from civil authority, because the godly and the profane had to be separated. The high moral expectations were vigorously enforced. People not ready to act in a solidary way, to behave decently, or to work earnestly were, for example, pressed by the Grand jury to live with an upright community member to be brought back to the right track. Defending principles of equity, of commutative justice, wealthy Robert Keayne was fined £200 by the Massachusetts General Court for having sold his wares at excessive rates. "For taking 50 and 100 percent profit on his business transactions, Robert Keayne became a pariah."[53] John Winthrop declared the idea "that a man might sell as dear as he can, and buy as cheap as he can" as a false principle. A man had not to sell above the "price that is usual in the time and place, and as another (who knows the worth of the commodity) would give for it."[54] Protecting their moral values of reciprocity and solidarity, "Keayne symbolized the fear that a headlong rush for prosperity would lead New Englanders to forget that they were their brothers' keepers."[55]

Freedom was not an individualized freedom *from* any obligation. Community prevailed over an individualistic approach,[56] which is why "freedom" was mainly understood as freedom *for* building up one's own community based on religious criteria. Insofar it was a freedom *against* the king and *for* the "city upon a hill." To be free meant to choose conscientiously a life abiding by the principles the scripture contained. "Although Puritans

---

[52] Bremer, Francis J. (2005), p. 196. The same accounts for many of the elements of government in New England copying familiar English forms (see p. 224).
[53] Innes, Stephen (1995), p. 161
[54] Jehlen, Myra/Warner, Michael (ed.) (1997), pp. 444 f.
[55] Boyer, Paul S./Clark, Clifford et al. (2010), p. 49
[56] Valeri, Mark (2005), p. 149

believed that a free consent was essential to a covenant, they also believed that freedom consisted in the opportunity to obey the will of God."[57] Making this goal absolute made them as effective as intolerant: Their moral high ground had a strongly unifying impact on the adherents but as much an exclusionary effect on the "heretics." It was this "radical coupling of devotional piety and state formation by expelling powerful dissenters"[58] that created a strong, unified, and by this durable community. But the price of disrespect had to be paid by others, by the excluded minorities and individuals. Not willing to stand otherness they fought difference by all means. Independent thinkers like the Quakers, for example, who put "private judgment" at the center of their "reality," were viewed as representatives of the Devil and as an attack upon the Puritan theocratic idea,[59] which is why they were persecuted. Laws banishing Quakers were introduced which punished shipmasters who brought Quakers to New England and gave the colonial governments the right to flog, imprison at hard labor, cut off an ear, or perforate the tongue of Quakers if they really came back after having been expelled. The Natives had to endure the same harsh treatment. The Puritans' religious absolutism couldn't accept the Quakers' difference and couldn't support their independence and autonomous way of life. Following an assimilatory integration concept, the Natives had to convert or to die.[60] Inside the community, the Puritans were progressive, equalitarian, and fundamentally democratic, and criticized by monarchists as "hotbed of republicanism." However, against those they had constructed as "others," they acted aggressively and in a Manichaean way. Understanding themselves as "the chosen people" they had a particularly close covenant with God and felt obliged to fight the continual attacks from Satan. Their liberty of conscience was much more a "liberty to believe orthodoxy,"[61] which is why dissent about the fundamentals of their believe had to be eradicated. According to the respect of others who are different, the Puritans paradoxically behaved like the government officials in Old England they had fled.[62] The cases of Roger Williams and Anne Hutchinson are examples of this absolutism. Williams was not only a precursor to the universal understanding of freedom of conscience and the separation of church and state, he also criticized the colonial attitude that betrayed the Natives and violated their

---

[57] Morgan, Edmund S. (1966), p. 26
[58] Peterson, Mark A. (2005), p. 85
[59] Fiske, John (2005), p. 182
[60] Taylor, Alan (2001), p. 197
[61] von Til, L. John (1972), p. 57; see also p. 69.
[62] *Id.*, p. 73

equal rights. After the General Court of Massachusetts had ordered his deportation to England, he fled south and founded, in 1636, the Providence Plantation. One year later, in 1637, Governor Winthrop wanted to make sure that the process against Anne Hutchinson would be successfully used as a symbolic confirmation of the community's nascent identity. Hutchinson symbolized two threats that Winthrop wanted to address: First, she had held religious meetings that attracted a great number of people. Being a celebrity, she had gained power, which was an unfitting importance for a woman. With this behavior, she questioned the humble role women were expected to play. Second, she doubted the Calvinistic concept of a "covenant of work," which meant that our performance on earth indicates who God has elected for salvation. Consequently, one had to live by the rules and laws of the church and state to be assured of being saved. In Hutchinson's theological opinion, however, only God's grace was decisive, a godly gift not to be influenced by such mundane work. She concluded that the needed a strong personal communion with the Holy Spirit could be developed by every individual, independent of the church. Her "covenant of grace" questioned, therefore, the moral basis of the community, which expected people to work hard relentlessly, and questioned the power of the church and its ministers, which was the moral authority of the time. For Winthrop, a strong and unambiguous reaction to her critical statements and the good reputation she had with a portion of the people was supposed to unify the colony.[63] He, therefore, changed the makeup of the Great and General Court of Massachusetts to make sure that nobody who was pro-Mistress Hutchinson would judge over the heretic. Nevertheless, the result of the trial wasn't evident because Hutchinson had quite some support in Boston and also from many merchants and businessmen who were criticizing the restrictive immigration policy that Governor Winthrop had imposed on dissenters. This is why the Governor chose Cambridge as the place of jurisdiction. The General Court of Massachusetts found her guilty of the crime of heresy and of sedition. Using her as "the community scapegoat,"[64] the trial was the perfect pretext to eliminate the political opposition for quite a time. In the aftermath, all supporters of Hutchinson were removed from power, disfranchised, and fined. And the ones who had signed a petition in favor of the defendant were disarmed. The court also decided to found a college in order to indoctrinate young male citizens in order to avoid the emergence of further dissenters.[65] John Harvard bequeathed half his estate

---

[63] LaPlante, Eve (2004), p. 7
[64] Id., p. 191
[65] Id., p. xxi, 133

and his library to the Congregationalist College. Anne Hutchinson was allowed to remain in Massachusetts for the winter, but had to respect the house arrest. In the meanwhile, her supporters were looking for a place for a new settlement, and Roger Williams recommended the area called Rhode Island. There, Hutchinson was active again, but she didn't establish a formal church. Massachusetts threatened to take over Rhode Island, which is why Anne Hutchinson went to the Dutch settlement of New Amsterdam.

Massachusetts Bay stood by their absolutist concept of religion for quite a time, whereas other colonies made important steps toward an equalitarian and universal understanding that respected different forms of belief: Providence in 1638; Maryland in 1649; New York, Bahamas, and Bermuda in 1650; Carolina in 1665; and Pennsylvania in 1682. Roger Williams managed after years of political battle to fuse four towns into a single colony called Providence. And, in 1663, he succeeded in uniting Providence with Rode Island. Both times his main motive was to protect the independence of these communities from the expansive power politics of Massachusetts. The Charter of the new colony stated that "no person within the said colony, at any time hereafter shall be any wise molested, punished, disquieted, or called in question, for any differences in opinion in matters of religion – so long as he keeps the peace." It's only by 1760 that Massachusetts was ready to give up its exclusionary and homogeneous community ideal. And the Revolution brought the breakthrough of universality.

Over the time the Puritans began to develop more materialistic interests, giving up the original idea that had motivated the Pilgrims: The community of Saints based on moral purity. "Instead of the afterlife, it was the material rewards of *this* life that increasingly became the focus of the Pilgrims' children and grand-children."[66]

b) Greed alone is not enough

The colonies set up in the Chesapeake by the Virginia Company of London were in the beginning solely motivated by material interests: *A purely economic endeavour*. There weren't any political or social intents that would have moderated the quest for fast money. Economic motives alone, however, aren't enough to inspire people to be responsible for the community, particularly when these interests are implemented within a competitive setup. It is a highly volatile engagement that is broken off as soon as the returns aren't as expected. From the moment the colonists decided to stay,

---

[66] Philbrick, Nathaniel (2006), p. 198

the construction of a collective identity with reciprocal duties developed. Unbound individuals had to convene to become a community and to establish a form of cooperation based on shared interests.

The first British settlement in Virginia looked for riches and served as a base to rob Spanish ships carrying gold. Queen Elizabeth I granted Sir Walter Raleigh a charter for the colonization – a right limited to ten years if by then no colony was erected. A first attempt launched in 1585 ended unsuccessfully. In 1587, John White led a second group of colonists to Roanoke in Virginia. The colony, though, couldn't be upheld because of a lack of supplies due to the Anglo-Spanish war and weather conditions. In 1606, James I of England chartered the Virginia Company he had set up to colonize America. Their main goal was "a search for minerals, particularly gold, silver, and copper, and for rivers that flowed into 'the East India Sea.'"[67] The king was the owner of the land and the company his tenant. Settlers were subtenants of the Virginia Company and had the same legal rights like those living in England. The company was organized as a joint-stock company, controlled by the Council of the Company. Its members, in turn, were elected by the General Court of the stockholders. It "was primarily a commercial enterprise, set up in the hope of bringing a profit to both adventurers, those who risked their money, and planters, who risked their persons."[68] In 1607, Jamestown was established, which was the first lasting settlement of the English in Northern America. A new charter changed the government-structure of the colony and entrusted the whole power into the hands of the governor alone, who was appointed for life and endowed with absolute authority. John Smith was appointed as third governor and first vested with this far reaching power; a power he used skillfully to make the government much more efficient. One of the many difficulties the settlers encountered were high mortality rates during the summers in Jamestown. Observing the Natives' behavior, Smith realized that semi-nomadism was the key to the problem: Too many people in the same location in summer amplified the dangers of infection, which is why the Natives scattered and met again in winter. Doing the same in 1609, almost all of the settlers survived.[69] After Smith left Jamestown due to illness, this knowledge got lost and the death rate increased again. It is only in 1624 that a fundamental change occurred, because the people dispersed to their tobacco plantations and the settlements moved inwards "away from the deadliest parts of the James and onto the hills, ridges, and drainage divides where fresh springs

---

[67] Abbot, William W. (1975), pp. 18 f.
[68] Morton, Richard L. (1960), p. 7
[69] Earle, Carville V. (1979), pp. 106 ff.

provided a safe water supply."⁷⁰ In 1618 the company's leader decided to democratize its government and to reinstall the rights the charter of 1606 had guaranteed. The General Assembly of Virginia was established, within which the Councilors, assisting the Governor, and the elected Burgesses, representing the plantations, convened, made laws, and gave advice. Any law could be vetoed by the Governor and needed the approval of the Company's Court.

Lacking experience, the first years were incredibly harsh. Many people starved to death, died of diseases, and the confrontational style Smith adopted toward the Natives led to intense warfare. One of the company's goals was to subdue the Natives and to force them to convert to Anglicanism. "[…] to be acceptable [the Natives had to] forsake their native culture."⁷¹ Among other things, the company therefore kidnapped the Natives' children. To justify direct violence against the Natives and "to get the country behind the war," a Native bogeyman had to be constructed by wrongfully contending that the Natives had killed John White's colony in Roanoke.⁷² Subsequent governors Gates and Dale went on with a "stern attitude toward" the Natives, reaching, however, in the mid-1610's a peaceful state by negotiation.⁷³ Thanks to this pacification, people could focus on their housing and the development of plantations. The prolific cultivation of tobacco made the investment in Virginia profitable. No gold had been found, but the tobacco industry, which expanded rapidly after 1616,⁷⁴ promised satisfying returns. The improved quality could be sold well in England. The more tobacco was successfully sold/exchanged, the more settlers came and the more land was needed. This very land was also one of the main inducements which motivated people to emigrate. In the first years of colonization, the settlers approached the Natives in a cooperative way, trading different products for their land. This reciprocal arrangement was born out of necessity, not of equal recognition and respect. Increasing economic activities intensified the need for land so much so that the colonizers weren't interested anymore in a fair relationship. Justifications were needed to exclude the Natives from their land. One argument was that the Natives had to obey the order of the indisputable masters: "If we finde the countrey populous, and desirous to expel us … that seeke but just and lawfull trafficke, then by reason that we are lords of navigation, and they are not so, we

---

[70] *Id.*, p. 122
[71] Vaughan, Alden T. (1978), p. 84
[72] Miller, Lee (2000), pp. 218, 222
[73] Hatch, Charles E. (1957), p. 12
[74] Morton, Richard L. (1960), p. 40

[can] [...] in the end bring them all in subjection and to civilitie."[75] As soon as the Natives began to protect their interests against European expansionism, as soon as they claimed recognition, the colonists' reaction was violent: "[...] Jamestown's early colonists made more use of the sword than the olive branch."[76] Another form of justification was a religious one. It was morally compulsory and for the Natives' own good to convert them to Christianity. Well-known preachers were engaged in marketing the oppression at home, so to convince the nation and privates to support the company.[77] According to preacher Gray, the Natives' land could be seized and no legal titles had to be respected: "[...] these Savages have no particular propertie in any part or parcel of that countrey, but only a general residence there, as wild beasts have in the forest ... so that if the whole land should be taken from them, there is not a man that can complaine of any particular wrong done unto him."[78] This expansionist logic led to intense warfare with many casualties on both sides. In the Massacre of 1622, for example, 350 settlers were killed, which in the aftermath led to up to six hundred deaths by famine and disease. In the long run this disrespectful and destructive behavior led to the decline of the Natives.

The Virginia Company finally failed. A failure caused by an important lack of experience, insufficient organization and management, dire infrastructure, conflicts between the different factions, permanent warfare with Natives, diseases (especially the plague),[79] and the economic interests of the king.[80] Launched as a merchants project, as a "production plant," "much of the Virginia social and institutional pattern derive[d] from the merchant-colonizers' efforts to make the colony a producer of crops for the English market and a consumer of goods the English had to sell."[81] Merchants as well as the king, aristocrats, and wealthy landholders were involved in this mercantile project to secure and enhance English trade and to support imperial aspirations. But the failure had made clear that *colonization couldn't be undertaken as mere investment project, run like a company*, and "owned by men in England and worked by servants sent out by English masters."[82]

---

[75] Written in 1585 by Richard Hakluyt, English geographer and writer, quoted in: Vaughan, Alden T. (1978), p. 58
[76] *Id.*, p. 62
[77] Manahan, Karen B. (2011)
[78] Quoted in Manahan, Karen B. (2011)
[79] Morton, Richard L. (1960), p. 86
[80] *Id.*, p. 95
[81] Abbot, William W. (1975), p. 8
[82] *Id.*, p. 22

Communities had to be built up, based on reciprocal structures with sufficient political autonomy to act and react according to local needs. Also, the focus had to be changed to a long-term engagement.[83] Even though the Governor and the Council were appointed by the king, they couldn't build up real autonomy because the General Assembly, which was established in 1619, established itself in the 1630s as "an integral, even indispensable, part of colonial government."[84] And the colonial offices were perceived as "public businesses" or "profitable employments," as a "share of government" used to protect the interests of the investors in England only.[85] Political participation wasn't built on representative principles, but rather on landholding.[86] And the purely competitive character of the endeavor made it impossible to generate a common ground, a shared project.

As no lasting community had been established, a workforce had to be imported, until the last quarter of the 17th century.[87] Indentured servants weren't seen as community members but simply as cheap workers: "[…] idle, lazie, simple people … such as have professed idlenesse, and will rather beg than work; who are perswaded […], they shall goe into a place where food shall drop into their mouthes: and being thus deluded, they take courage, and are transported. But not finding what was promised, their courage abates, & their minds being dejected, their work is according."[88] The majority of the people (mostly indentured servants[89] and slaves) were used for the benefit of others in a disrespectful environment that makes cooperation impossible. Because of economic reasons men were almost exclusively hired,[90] which is why few families came into being. Without this reciprocal social fabric, though, long term stability, trust, and, hence, success is highly improbable. It is only about a century after the first settlement that

---

[83] Innes, Stephen (1995), p. 78: "For Smith, the lust for present profit was what destroyed the Virginia Company. […]. Immediate rather than long-term returns on investments of time or money were sought and no sense of working for the greater collective good was recognized."
[84] Abbot, William W. (1975), p. 32
[85] Shammas, Carole (1979), p. 279
[86] Abbot, William W. (1975), p. 41
[87] Horn, James (1979), p. 51
[88] Bullock, William (1649), p. 14
[89] Walsh, Lorena S. (1979), p. 127
[90] Horn, James (1979), p. 62: "For every female servant who left London for Virginia in 1635, there were six males." Green Carr, Lois/Menard, Russell R. (1979), p. 209: "The proportion of women among immigrants doubled by the 1650s and continued to increase slowly thereafter, but men still outnumbered women by about two and a half to one among new arrivals at the end of the century. "

the investors decided to make the colony their home. At the end of the 17th century, immigrating English nobility, gentry, and wealthy merchants filled the shortage. And from the 18th century on an oligarchy of big, intermarrying families ruled the colony.[91] Now, a collective identity became important and they started to describe themselves as "Virginians." In "1705 Virginia acquired a history."[92]

Because of a quite equal social structure, high moral expectations, a shared community project and, hence, a widely supported meaning of life, the Massachusetts colonies were much more stable than the economic projects in the South. As a result of this elaborate elementary consensus the "New England settlements suffered far less violence and unrest and attained rather mature and stable governing institutions within a few years of their founding. Political leadership resided in a respected ruling elite that enjoyed a remarkable continuity of service and that transferred its power quite successfully to its sons and grandsons."[93] The *readiness to engage in favor of the community, of the common good* is the constitutive precondition of every working political institution. That's why reciprocity is vital for successful recognition and the establishment of trust. A res publica is needed, something the Pilgrims and Puritans had from the beginning, whereas the colonists of the Chesapeake had only their private material interests motivating them. What finally made the revolution and, hence, the United States possible, were the convictions and practices of the reciprocally organized Pilgrims and Puritans, it was their political idea[94] and ideal of a new world, of the "City upon a Hill."

---

[91] Morton, Richard L. (1960), p. 166, 168; Jordan, David W. (1979), p. 269
[92] Shammas, Carole (1979), p. 294. Robert Beverley wrote "The History and present State of Virginia".
[93] Jordan, David W. (1979), p. 243
[94] McKenna, George (2007), p. 7: "They managed to envisage an America long before there was a United States of America. America is a work of the imagination as much as it is a juridical entity, and it was their imagination that played the seminal role in creating it."

5. Trust

Trust is a social arrangement that *tremendously enhances the quality of life*. It *makes freedom and creativity possible and diminishes fear*. A positive future becomes thinkable and, thanks to trust, the potential of human beings can unfold comprehensively.

a) Functions of trust

Trust is *confidence about the future*. To trust means to know what comes, to be sure that a specific action will take place. We know that our neighbor will take care of our plants during our absence. We know that the emergency rooms of the hospital are running a reliable 24-hour operation. We know that refuse collectors will do their job after the next football game. The supplier we used to work with over the last years will, as always, deliver on time. And most human beings expect the sun to shine year in and year out. We trust all this to happen because of our experiences in the past, which were confirmed again and again. Or because the stories we heard had never been questioned to date. The more our expectations are met, the more we trust it will happen again. Trust is, therefore, nurtured by the past, applied in the presence, and used as "resource to cope with the future."[1] It takes quite some time to build up trust, a highly fragile resource, however, destructible in no time. One unfulfilled expectation may be enough to rise doubts about future interactions.

Trust is built up best if we take part in the interaction that yields specific expectations. Having met somebody face-to-face and seen her making decisions we think are convincingly justified, it becomes easy to be sure about her future actions. The less we encounter people personally, the more we have to rely on other people or on some certifying mechanisms to corroborate our impressions and expectations. Thus, there is a paradox that people have to deal with: Personal relationships are the best grounds to build up trust. As long as we are in contact with most of the people relevant to us, we do not need too much trust, because we can check ourselves how they behave and if they keep their promises. The more distanced and anonymous relationships are, the more our information about others is indirect, the more we have to rely on third parties who themselves get their information from somebody else. All participants have to do a good job of providing us with the information we need, and most of them can't be controlled by

---

[1] Sztompka, Piotr (1995), p. 255

ourselves.² So the chain of trust becomes longer and longer and our interdependence increases. Modern society has, therefore, more than a traditional one to rely on trust. Its size and its geographical range, the rarity of binding face-to-face contacts and the enhanced individualization, its functional differentiation and an augmented focus on material values make trust the inevitable glue holding together loosely organized actors. But contrary to many things in modern society, trust can't be bought or ordered.³ It is *the result of personal engagement and the readiness to recognize and respect others as part of a reciprocal arrangement.* Our scope of action being limited, we rely on others to solve our problems. An important part of the decisions relevant to our life are delegated to people acting on our behalf.⁴ It is therefore crucial to cultivate our relationships by cooperation.

aa)   Increase and reduction of complexity

People trusting each other have two big advantages: First, a trustful relationship is basically a complexity-reducing arrangement, making planning and deciding easier. Acting within a trustful environment narrows possible actions we have to take into account. The contingency of the human existence isn't abolished by trust because everything can change anytime. But the relationships built up over time make the occurrence of negatively surprising actions less probable. Second, the more people trust each other, the more it is possible to go beyond the everyday routine and to create difference. Trusting each other, the risky new ideas aren't perceived as a threat, but rather as a never-thought-of chance or the crazy fantasizing of well-known scientists. These trust-based creations increase complexity in a positive sense and hence enlarge the realm of freedom.⁵

The absence of trust augments complexity negatively because others are then a potential threat, the competitors or the enemy. Every interaction can lead to exclusion, to injury, or to death. Most of the people become risk-averse in such an environment and are preoccupied with observing and controlling others. Instead of engaging in a cooperative integration process, instead of listening to the proposals of the interactors and debating pros and cons, people engage in a paralyzing fight over the control of "reality."

---

[2]   Petermann, Franz (1996), p. 43, highlights the risk, that sharing information in a competitive setup can be.
[3]   Hartmann, Martin (2001), p. 34
[4]   Endress, Martin (2002), p. 29
[5]   Petermann, Franz (1996), p. 12; Offe, Claus (2001), p. 258

This fearful, power-orientated concept of interaction is highly costly because it absorbs people, ideas, time, and money.[6] Violence and oppression are used to achieve the main goals, leading to a poor quality of life for all and an inherent tendency to dissolution.[7] Trustful relationships, on the contrary, have a stabilizing effect, avoiding the build up of a counterpower by establishing a recognizing, respecting, and reciprocal social arrangement. The interactors do not have to check and control everything, which is why the community becomes able to focus its attention and energy on core challenges and increases therefore its efficiency.[8] Establishing trustworthy institutions is another step toward higher integration and efficiency (see pp. 295 ff.).

The success of the Hudson's Bay Company in the 18th century is mainly attributable to trustworthy employer-employee relationships. Trade companies didn't have the possibility to control their employees abroad. Boats and the cargos leaving and arriving could indeed be checked, but the time it took to react to irregularities was way too long. The company, therefore, had to rely on employees qualified as trustworthy and who were paid above average. The reciprocity structure that got established showed the employees how much they were respected and valued, which in turn yielded a lifelong bond. Board and lodging were free, the pension granted was generous, and the company took care of the family if an employee was seriously injured or died.[9] Trust is not at least the result of distributive justice,[10] which is why structural violence has a negative effect on this central integrative resource. Current long-distance economic activities like, for example, on Internet pose the same problem trade companies had centuries ago: How can I make sure that my investments and my payments are secure? Thanks to the cooperation of users the lack of personal contact can be overcome. Former users/clients qualify the services and post them on the web site. This feedback and our own experiences make it possible to estimate the amount of trust we reasonably may spend.[11] Organizations like credit card companies or consumer associations, symbols like the seals of quality, brands

---

[6] Gambetta, Diego (2001), p. 215
[7] Prime minister Lee Hsien Long of Singapore sees in trust-based stability an important advantage: "The people support the government and work with the government. That reservoir of trust is one of our most valuable and sustainable competitive advantages" (on Charlie Rose of April 15, 2010).
[8] Arrow, Kenneth J. (1974), p. 23
[9] Osterloh, Margit/Weibel, Antoinette (2006), pp. 214 f.
[10] Id., pp. 132 f.
[11] Brinkman, Ulrich/Seifert, Matthias (2001), p. 43

that stand for reputation, or specific professions that are supposed to be trustworthy like physicians, lawyers, or priests – all these standardized tools help to establish integrated and by this stable long-distance relationships. We accord them trust even when we never had these positive experiences ourselves – as long negative ones are absent.[12]

bb) Trust – doubts – distrust

Trust is destroyed within a glimpse. Being a human construction, it is an ever contingent performance. However long trust existed between interactors, it can be questioned at any time. One unexpected action that violates norms or is perceived as elementary can be enough to raise doubts or generate distrust. As long as we trust we do not think of being deceived, because to trust means to be sure about a specific future behavior. If there is *insecurity* about somebody's action to come, we *doubt* –a state between trust and distrust.

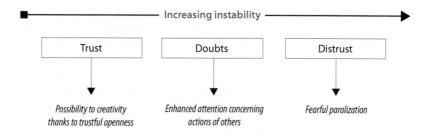

The insecurity raised by doubts doesn't make acting impossible. The one we doubt will be checked, we will look for more information and be quite attentive to her or his actions. If our doubts are overcome, trust will be established. If the doubts, however, are validated, distrust with all its negative effects, may result. Distrust paralyzes, makes us fear the dominant state, forces people to be vigilant all the time, and, hence, to increase the control and command of others. If command isn't possible, contact will be avoided because the risk to fail has become unbearable. Distrust develops a tendency to escape or to violence, which is why it is highly destructive.

Trust and cooperation are constitutively intertwined. Without cooperation trust won't occur. It follows the free and critical test and approval of the

---

[12] Endress, Martin (2002), p. 75

behavior of others. Even though dictatorships force people to act according to their rules, that doesn't mean that trust is developed. People will consent to overwhelming power for different reasons. If they are convinced that the dictatorship is the best solution to actual problems, then they trust. Or they may profit greatly from the political-economic structure established and, therefore, support or at least do not fight against the dictator. Or they simply adapt to a power that currently excludes any alternatives (see about the different forms of consensus p. 61 ff.). Besides the ones who directly support the dictator and are part of his entourage, the rest of the population doesn't trust him. They may make profits or adapt to his power, but they basically doubt or even distrust him, because one of the outstanding characteristics of this form of government is its arbitrariness.

Cooperation yields trust because we know that our interests are taken into account. Competition leads to doubts or even to distrust and using force to stabilize a society only yields *adaptation* – a deceptive calm based on doubts and distrust that ends sooner or later in fundamental opposition.

b) With trust to democracy

In the 19th century, the Spanish monarchy began to be seriously questioned by liberal democratic forces. Spanish society was torn between, on the one hand, liberal and social forces that intended to reshape the country in a more open and more equal way, and, on the other hand, the traditional oligarchic elite that tried to preserve their prerogatives. Because of these internal problems and the lack of a solidly established state, Spain lost its international influence: "The country ceased to be the great world-wide empire it had been during the entire Early Modern period from the sixteenth to the eighteenth centuries and was reduced to the condition of small European power."[13] Traditionalism, different nationalisms, liberal upper- and middle-class aspirations, and workers' claims for equal opportunities tried to make their impact on a society in fundamental transition. The Republican Movement, for example, came to power from 1873 to 1874, but was overthrown by a military coup supported by the king. During the subsequent Restoration, liberal constitutionalism was the form of government, which was characterized by "excessive fragmentation and personal rivalries," "heterogeneous and deeply divided [...] parties."[14] In 1921, a widely shared wish for

---

[13] Moradiellos, Enrique (2000), p. 110
[14] Arranz, Luis/Cabrera, Mercedes/Del Rey, Fernando (2000), p. 205

a strong and efficient government, along with the backing of King Alfonso XIII, helped establish the dictatorship of General Prima de Rivera. The dictator tried a form of cooperation with the labor movement, which refused the offer. In 1931, the dictatorship, which had had a negative effect on the democratization of the country, came to an end. "By delaying and repressing the political mobilization, it led to polarization and radicalization."[15] Finally, the people got back the right to vote and used it to elect Republican candidates in the local and municipal elections of 1931. This victory was also directed against the king's involvement in the dictatorship. Realizing that he no longer had the support of most of the people, the king left the country for Rome without abdicating. In the general election of June 1931, the coalition of Republicans and Socialists won a landslide victory.

aa) Justice and solidarity

The Second Spanish Republic was proclaimed and the Republican forces in the Constituent Cortes (parliament) drafted the new Constitution which was adopted on December 9, 1931. The Constitution of the Second Republic was democratic, based on the rule of law and the equality of people, and it was secular. It consented universal suffrage (women included), democratic elections of the head of state, the complete separation of church and state in government and in schools, the abolition of religious orders, constitutional freedoms including religious freedom, the elimination of nobility's prerogatives, legal procedures for the nationalization of public services, and it granted the right to autonomy for every Spanish region. The army would be democratized by establishing the prerogative of politics over military power, by reducing its costs (reduction of officers, regiments, and bureaucracy, and the closing of four of the six military academies[16]), and by restricting the army's task to the sole protection of Spain against external attacks. Military forces would no longer be a central pillar of Spanish identity, but rather a tool in the hands of democratically elected politicians. Even though General Franco strongly disapproved of all these developments, he had to acknowledge that for the moment the new power had to be accepted. Accordingly, the army didn't use its power to overturn the Repub-

---

[15] Tusell, Javier/Queipo de Llano, Genoveva (2000), p. 220

[16] Franco perceived the closing of the Academy of Saragossa as "motivated by jealousy of his impressive military record, and a personal spite" (Ashford Hodges, Gabrielle [2000], p. 66).

lic[17] and declared it would serve and defend the government. The measures concerning the Catholic Church fundamentally questioned this centuries old enormously powerful institution. The church would have to give up its legitimizing, educational, and cultural role, which had thoroughly determined Spanish society. In respect to the social structure of the society, the Second Republic opted for a new set of basic values, whereby justice and solidarity would be given a central place. The Republican politic aimed to reduce the economic and social inequality because "thousands of landless labourers in Andalusia, Extremadura, Castile, and Aragon lived in abject poverty, while the handful of families who owned vast areas of land in those regions enjoyed enormous social, economic, and political influence."[18] The government recognized the right to private property, but expected property to be used in a social way (the "social function of property"). Compensated expropriations were intended to distribute the land more equally and give the labourers economic opportunities and, thus, a certain autonomy.

The Second Republic was unmistakably on the way to revolutionize Spanish society. Long-lasting power arrangements were threatened, the prerogatives of the conservative upper class, the aristocracy, the Catholic Church, the Society of Jesus, the army, and the conservative rich had to be given up in favor of a more equal society, in favor of the urban working and middle classes. What had been true for centuries and had been taken for granted, couldn't be trusted anymore. According to right wing Spanish surrealist Giménez Caballero, the Republic "had destroyed the very substance of our being. The very soul of us as Spaniards and as men … The Catholic Spain had lost his God. The monarchist, his King. The aristocrat, his nobility. The soldier, his sword."[19] Strong reactions from the conservatives ensued and the Republicans failed to win over an unquestionable majority of people for their project.[20] As a result, a class conflict occurred which divided the country[21] and led to violent fighting. Churches and cloisters were burnt, peasant riots took place. In December 1931, la Guardia Civil shot a peasant after a peaceful demonstration at Castilblanco. Later they shot in a crowd of socialists, killing several of them. In 1932, a coup d'état was attempted, but didn't succeed.

---

[17] Ellwood, Shelagh (1994), p. 41
[18] *Id.*, p. 45
[19] Richards, Michael (1998), p. 3
[20] Martin, Claude (1995), p. 56
[21] *Id.*, p. 100

bb) Civil war

With the Left not united and the anarchists abstaining, the elections of 1933 were won by centre-right and far-right parties. Most of the initiated reforms were reversed by the new centre-right government. The electoral defeat, the abolishment of the reforms, and the systematic oppression against the Left in Germany, Austria, and France made clear that society projects based on justice and solidarity wouldn't be realized. Trying to build up counterpower, socialists and anarchists launched, in 1934, protests and the miners a general strike in Asturias. The government promoted General Francisco Franco to full general and summoned him to repress the popular movement. Government forces aided by right-wing armed movements systematically oppressed, persecuted, and even tortured protesters and strikers. About 3'000 miners were killed and over 35'000 people arrested. "Franco was hailed as a savior; the personification of the triumph of military strength over both liberal ineptitude and Marxist evil."[22] For the General, this was the way the world was organized. Throughout his life he was convinced that there was the ever truthful Right, on the one hand, and the malign Marxist forces on the other. Negotiations and compromises were unthinkable within his Manichaean "reality." The enemy had to be fought by any means. What at the beginning was a the fundamentalist concept, widespread in Europe, became totalitarian, especially after World War II. Totalitarianism was his deep conviction and he wasn't able to trust people who held different views to his very narrow concept of "normality".

Contrary to 1933, the Left (Socialists, Communists, and Republicans, now called the "Popular Front") united for the elections of 1936 and won a narrow victory, resulting, though, in a huge number of parliamentary seats (263 against 156). Fearing the Popular Front's democratic and equalitarian politic, high-ranking army officers (including Franco and other generals) met in Madrid to organize armed resistance. The Spanish Civil War began in July 1936 with an attempted revolt against the Republican government. General Mola led the Nationalist uprising supported by the bigger part of the Spanish army, conservatives, monarchists, and the Fascist Falange. After this failure, the Nationalists decided to organize more effectively and to center all the power in one man to avoid further frictions within the insurgents. In September 1936 the Junta de Defensa National appointed Franco Generalísimo (supreme chief) of the Nationalist Armed Forces and Chief of State. Cabanellas, president of the Junta, feared the unlimited power given to Franco because of the Genralísimo's personality: "You don't

---

[22] Ellwood, Shelagh (1994), p. 56

know what you've just done because you don't know him like I do since I had him under my command in the African army ... If, as you wish, you give him Spain, he is going to believe that it is his and he won't let anyone replace him either during the war or after until he is dead."[23] To celebrate the new Chief of State, a ceremonial investiture was organized in Salamanca on October 1, 1936. He moved into the Episcopal Palace and wanted to be called "Caudillo", paralleling the German "Führer" and the Italian "Duce." Building up cultural violence, massive propaganda, censorship,[24] and education programs constructed Franco as the savior of Spain. In 1937 Franco decreed the unification of the fascist Falange, the monarchist Carlists, and the right-wing parties into one party, the Moviemiento, often called the Falange. Until the death of Franco this was the only authorized party in Spain. All members of the armed services had to join the party and were obliged to use the fascist salute, a political ritual symbolizing his adulation.

The Civil War opposed working-class Republicans on the one hand and the nationalist movement, on the other. The nationalists were supported with transport planes, fighters, pilots, and machine guns by Nazi Germany, Fascist Italy, Portugal and by important American corporations like Texaco, GM, Ford, and Firestone. The working class in this internationalized conflict was backed by the Soviet Union (sending weapons, tanks, and ammunition, Generals and consultants), the Comintern, the International Brigades, and volunteers coming from different European countries, and from the US and Latin-America. Even though the Right got much more backing, "without the support of the Soviet Union, the Republic would have foundered during the early months of the war."[25] About 300'000 people died in a war that lasted three years and couldn't be overcome because of absolutist positions, of Manichaean perceptions of the enemy, of a total lack of shared values, the absence of trust, and the incapacity to imagine a shared future. The ones who over decades and centuries had all advantages on their side were not ready to give up power; whereas the others didn't see any room for compromise and wanted immediate results. Both sides committed horrific murders and used any means to reach their goal.

---

[23] Ashford Hodges, Gabrielle (2000), p. 105
[24] On July 20, 1949, Franco declared himself being the First Journalist of Spain.
[25] Ashford Hodges, Gabrielle (2000), p. 112

cc) Francoism

Legitimized by the defeat of the Republican forces in 1939, Franco "the providential saviour and guardian of the true Spain" established himself as head of state, entitled to legislate on his own without needing the assent of parliament or justice. The "Law of Political Responsibilities" of 1939 made possible persecutions of people who supported the Republic or fought against the National Movement. The law included a retroactive application back to October 1934. People, however, were judged for actions dating back to 1909. Many tens of thousands of working class members were executed and in total 500'000 people had to endure proceedings. Left-wing parties and trade unions were banned and the expropriations carried out during the Second Republic were reversed, without obliging the former proprietors to give back the compensation they got from the Republic. Concentration of wealth on behalf of the landed elites was the intended and realized goal. Nationalism became the leading construction principle thoroughly put through: At the expense of Catalan, Galician, and Basque, Castilian Spanish became the only accepted language for all official affairs, for speeches outside private matters, for teaching, the press, and literature. Catholic belief was declared the official religion of the state. Being Catholic qualified people, which is why, for example, civil servants had to be Catholics. Divorce and abortion or contraceptives were forbidden and women were subjugated to their husband's will. Bullfighting, as well as flamenco were promoted as national traditions. Imports were replaced as much as possible by national products. The dictator launched a cultural revolution, using propaganda and direct violence to re-educate the people who had to "accommodate their ideas, their vocabulary, and their expectations."[26] Nationalist uniqueness was realized by erecting "a cultural and economic barrier [...] around Spain and around Spaniards. The monopolization of public memory and the public voice"[27] is symptomatic of totalitarian systems, determining every element of the current "reality." Based on the idea of "autarky", everything in Spain had to be a part of Francoism, nobody and nothing could claim to be different. Private, economic, political, and cultural actions – all were subjected to the one and only way of thinking and behaving. A closed self-sufficient system focused on the leader. Instead of political cooperation,[28] violence became the standard form of integration,

---

[26] Cazorla Sánchez, Antonio (2010), p. 4
[27] Richards, Michael (1998), p. 4
[28] Id., p. 27: "[...] a persistent and explicit denial of reconciliation or integration."

justified by naturalistic arguments. The pure Spanish had to be protected against the sick proletarians, who one of Franco's press officers called "slave stock. They are good for nothing but slaves [...]. They're like animals [...] and you can't expect them not to be infected with the virus of Bolshevism."[29] They "explained class and ideology as a result of biological differences. According to them, 'red' Spaniards were not only socially inferior but also degenerate, resentful individuals. This biological degeneration was what made poor people embrace left-wing ideas."[30]

dd) The monarchical dictator

For over thirty years Franco made himself the symbolic link (see p. 387 ff.) of "conservative Spain's deep-seated desire for a leader who would restore and conserve the country's identity as a great world power."[31] At the same time he was aware of the symbolic and emotional power the monarchy and the king had had in Spain over centuries. To secure his position, he prevented the return of Alfonso XIII or of his son Juan de Borbón and prevented them playing an important role in the Civil War. The conflict between dictatorship and monarchy intensified after the Civil War when Juan de Borbón opposed since 1941 Franco's dictatorship, claiming the reintroduction of monarchy. In 1943, the king and others urged Franco to restore the monarchy before the end of World War II. The dictator answered with the sacking of people who held official positions and supported this plan. And anyway, nobody but him was able to fight communism and anarchy. He had to guarantee a united conservative Spain, a God-given mission and onerous duty. Therefore, the government had to be totalitarian: "Little will be saved of the liberal democratic system." As "the totalitarian regime has fully demonstrated its superiority ... it is the only one which is capable of saving a nation from ruin."[32] Franco made use of the monarchical symbolism to demonstrate his greatness and to legitimize his limitless power. He resided in the El Pardo Palace, wore the uniform of a Captain General (traditionally reserved for the king), sat on the throne near the high altar, walked beneath a canopy, used eighteenth-century coaches drawn by plumed horses, or minted coins and printed stamps with his portrait, adding the phrase "by the grace of God." Victory parades of medieval heroic

---

[29] *Id.*, p. 47
[30] Cazorla Sánchez, Antonio (2010), p. 22
[31] Ellwood, Shelagh (1994), p. 113
[32] Preston, Paul (1993), p. 464

figures were repeatedly re-enacted. He was convinced he was the leader of the Crusade, the ruler of a quasi-monarchical, sacred state.[33] The regime inserted itself in a century-long tradition and became a quasi natural part of the past, present, and future of Spain.

Besides the monarchical symbolism and tradition, Franco relied heavily on religious justifications. Ideologically, church and dictator shared the same convictions because for the Spanish Catholic Church Republicans were monsters.[34] In 1936, Cardinal Gomá had tried to convince the Vatican to support Franco, which it did carefully by appointing Gomá as the Vatican's confidential in Spain. German and Italian warplanes destroyed the small town of Guernica in 1937, supporting the Nationalist forces. Many Catholics were appalled because of the 1'500 people killed within three hours.[35] To reconcile the believers with Franco, many high ranking Spanish Church officials signed the letter "To the Bishops of the Whole World" published on July 1, 1937. This letter legitimized the military rebellion and defended the Nationalist State.[36] In 1939, Pope Pius XII congratulated the dictator for winning the Civil War: "'With immense joy,' the Pope gave his apostolic blessing to the victors, reserving special praise for 'the most noble and Christian sentiments' of the Chief of State."[37] Franco's regime got full recognition by the Vatican in 1953 and in 1954, Pope Pius XII granted the dictator the highest Vatican decoration, the Supreme Order of Christ.

About half of the population was attracted by Franco's mixture of absolute power, traditionalism, and religiosity. Rich landowners, Catholic peasantry, industrialists, parts of the petit-bourgeoisie and the lower middle class supported the ideology and politic of the dictator. "Spanish society was, therefore, not 'hi-jacked' by a handful of reactionary generals. The coup d'état against the Republic, and the regime which ultimately followed, were actively supported by a genuine social base."[38] Mainly motivated by the need to preserve their prerogatives and what they possessed, and fearing fundamental social change heading toward an uncertain future, the new "King" guaranteed at least the "present." Many a people feared another

---

[33] Richards, Michael (1998), p. 11
[34] Cazorla Sánchez, Antonio (2010), p. 28
[35] The number of killed and injured people is often debated (Martin, Claude [1995], p. 131). What isn't questioned, however, is the important negative effect the bombing of a city (among others) had on the international reputation of the regime.
[36] Preston, Paul (1993), p. 273
[37] Id., p. 323
[38] Richards, Michael (1998), p. 21

bloody conflict, which only he would be able to avoid. The other half of the population had to endure fierce, systematic, and limitless oppression, and was denied recognition and respect.

The Spanish dictatorship got its international blessing because of its irrefutable battle against Bolshevism. When, in 1947, a series of strikes broke out across Spain, the regime reacted instantly by sending in the army, Guardia Civil, and police. Employers had to fire the strikers, otherwise they were imprisoned. This reaction convinced London and Washington that Spain was an effective ally against nascent Communist-inspired revolutions. The intensification of the Cold War (the atomic bomb of the Soviet Union, the Chinese Revolution, McCarthyism in the USA, the North Korean invasion of South Korea) helped the dictator find more international support and legitimacy together with Salazar's Portugal. The Defense Pacts between the USA and Spain, signed in 1953, established economic and military help for Spain and the permission accorded to the USA, to construct and utilize air and naval bases on Spanish ground. Even though Franco had had to give up parts of his cherished sovereignty and his feigned neutrality, the recognition of the most powerful state was worth it.

The "Law of Succession" re-introduced monarchy in 1947, declaring Franco Head of State for life, and he gave himself the competence to designate his successor. Intense propaganda in favor of the law and the interdiction to say anything against it, yielded the predictable result of 14 million "yes" votes against 1 million "no" votes. To make sure that he would have an impact on Spain even after his death, he started very early to prepare his succession. Franco and Juan de Borbón agreed in 1948 to educate Juan Carlos (son of Juan de Borbón) in Spain under the dictator's guidance. "Juan Carlos in Spain would be a hostage to justify Franco's indefinite assumption of the role of regent and an instrument to control the political direction of any future monarchical restoration."[39] On November 9, 1948, Juan Carlos was dispatched to Spain – "a major public relations coup for Franco."[40] Afterward Juan de Borbón had to realize, that he had lost all influence on the education of his son. The future of monarchy was now totally in the hands of the dictator.

---

[39] Preston, Paul (1993), p. 578
[40] Ashford Hodges, Gabrielle (2000), p. 210

ee) The trusted leader

Totalitarian systems are very expensive because they spend money on highly unproductive things: 45 % of the budget of 1946 was used for the police, the Guardia Civil, and the army. The strikes, revolts, and demonstrations of an intensely suffering working class were severely suppressed by a widely stable government. Economically, the General supported the rich landowners by sustaining inefficiency and low productivity, paying guaranteed prices, and keeping down and even lowering rural wages to punish the Republic's supporter. Forty-six percent of working people were, in 1950, active in the agricultural sector, like in 1930.

During the 50s, the unity of the nationalist movement developed some fissures. Claims to reintroduce the monarchy, criticism on the length of Franco's reign, and his family's unfettered extravagance divided not only the members of his government. The new and, because of the criticism, overhauled cabinet included young politicians, technocrats and liberals, who wanted to push economic and political modernization. They hadn't experienced the Second Republic, the Civil War, or the following autarkic economic system and were open to the surrounding world. On their agenda were the liberalization of the widely regulated economy and the industrialization of the country. Increasingly, Franco's "nacional-Catolicismo", his traditionalist and reactionary interpretation of Catholicism, started to be questioned. During the Second Vatican Council, the position of the Catholic Church underwent important changes. Pope John XXIII's ideas were strongly opposed to dictatorships as he defended freedom of religion and the church's independence of politics. Portions of the Spanish priests changed their attitude toward the under class and toward workers. Two priests wrote in 1964: "I am not ashamed to say that, like most of my generation, I was wrong when I believed that Spanish workers were little more than a bunch of savages, full of vice and hatred, lazy people who wanted to live without having to work."[41] The important waves of strikes and protests from 1962-64, starting in Asturias and spreading further, then the student demonstrations, and agitations in the regions stand for a growing delegitimization and an increased courage of the people, to stand up against the system.[42] Adapting to the criticism and the upcoming consumer society, Franco moved his image from the winner of the Civil War to the "provider of material wealth and prosperity,"[43] and economic growth became the leitmotiv of the 1960s.[44]

---

[41] Cazorla Sánchez, Antonio (2010), p. 137
[42] Marín Arce, José María (2003), pp. 73 f.
[43] Ellwood, Shelagh (1994), p. 184, 190
[44] Id., p. 187

This growth, however, was very unevenly distributed and profited Franco's usual clientele. A laissez-faire liberal economy in the form of comprising low taxes, an inexpensive and widely unorganized workforce, because the unions had been crushed, and an increasingly important consumer market offered ideal conditions for the wealthy and for capital investment. Despite the economic reforms, the General didn't soften his totalitarian regime.

With Franco suffering from Parkinson's disease, the Caudillo designated, in 1969, Prince Juan Carlos as his successor. Juan Carlos was called King of Spain, not Princípe de Asturias, which would have been the correct title in continuation of the monarchy, because the dictator wanted to present the monarchy as his own heritage. By 1973, the dictator renounced his function as Prime Minister and remained only head of state and commander-in-chief. Two days after Franco's death on November 20, 1975, the Cortes Generales appointed Juan Carlos King of Spain. In his last speech, read after his death by the Prime Minister, Franco invoked the people of Spain to support his successor as they had supported him. The central question now was: Where would the new King lead the country to?

Intense hopes and fears were projected on Juan Carlos: On the one hand, all the dictator's victims hoped for liberation after decades of heavy suffering. On the other hand, the groups that had made big profits thanks to Franco's regime and had been in power over decades, feared losing their prerogatives and feared the vengeance of the oppressed. Insecurity about the future role of the king dominated because he almost never had taken a position in political conflicts over the years. At the age of 37 Juan Carlos was practically unknown and he had always been overshadowed by the dictator. Further, Franco had made clear that his successor would have to work within narrow limits and not be allowed to reintroduce liberal democracy.[45] Called "Juan Carlos the little" or "Juan Carlos the short," he had to demonstrate character in a basically hostile environment. If he wanted to *have a real impact on the future, he had to build up trust*. On the other hand, he had to trust the people in power not to betray him: "It is possible that people will hand me the crown on a velvet cushion. As well, the Guardia Civil could be sent to me with a warrant of arrest."[46] However, the enormous power the king had received didn't corrupt him. Against all temptations, he stood firm in his conviction to establish a democratic and just community. "I had inherited the immense power of Franco. During one year I could do and say what I wanted. I used this power first and foremost to tell the Spaniards

---

[45] Preston, Paul (2004), p. 214
[46] De Vilallonga, José Luis (1993), p. 79

that it's up to them, to say what they want."⁴⁷ His coronation took place on November 27, 1975, two days later than foreseen, to permit the attendance of as many foreign democratic Head of States as possible. General Pinochet, the only Head of State present at the funeral of Franco, wasn't invited. In his inaugural speech Juan Carlos talked about the future and the necessity of pluralism and change. But change wouldn't be easy because people often prefer to stick to the well-known bad state than to risk the unknown new. Until the mid-70s, "54 % of the people said that they preferred Spain's present system of government and did not want to risk change"⁴⁸ as they feared violence – something they had had to endure often enough. Life after the dictator's death was difficult not only for his admirers and supporters, but also for the opposition. Even though they finally had the possibility to live their convictions without risking being killed, they had gotten used to the existence of their enemy. Some said later: "We lived better *against* Franco."⁴⁹ The dictator had been a determining orientation point, forced on them and difficult to replace by a concrete political project. Even hated "reality" elements become routine and start to be so natural that a life without them has first to be created almost out of nothing.

Juan Carlos developed his new legitimacy step by step because trust and by this power are things one has to work on. According to Desazars de Montgailhard, the following measures helped to establish his credibility with a large portion of the Spanish people. He was able to neutralize the extreme right, establish a direct link with the Spanish people, integrate the opposition, communicate internationally about things he had to silence on the domestic front, and to put his allies on decisive positions.⁵⁰ Juan Carlos had to calm the army to avoid a coup d'état. That's why he kept Arias as Prime Minister, even though Arias had announced in February 1976 being willing to continue Francoism. On the other hand, the ETA in the Basque country hadn't renounced their claims of independence, which is what gave the army a welcomed justification for a hard-line course. The king asked Arias to resign in June and chose Suárez, a former leading member of the Movimiento. As a Francoist, he wouldn't be distrusted by the Right and was because of his readiness for reforms, was able to win the trust of the anti-Francoists. The same year, Juan Carlos and the Cortes amended the penal code to allow unions and political parties. Carlos didn't want to legal-

---

[47] *Id.*, p. 224
[48] Cazorla Sánchez, Antonio (2010), p. 198; see also p. 211
[49] Ashford Hodges, Gabrielle (2000), p. 258
[50] Desazars de Montgailhard, Sylvia (2003), p. 55

ize the Communist Party at this time, not to provoke too much.[51] Carrillo, secretary-general of the Communist Party, began to challenge the government and the new liberties by holding meetings. At the same time, he assured Suárez of his support for a peaceful transition. The Prime Minister on his part was sure that his reform politics would only be convincing, if the Communist Party would be legalized. In January 1977 a group of extreme rightists killed five people of the communist movement, which led to an impressive but peaceful demonstration of tens of thousands in Madrid. On April 9, 1977, the Communist Party, the evil of the former decades, was legalized. The secure the prerogative of politics over the army, several measures were taken. A Ministry of Defense was created and a civilian was appointed secretary of state. The number of army officers was reduced. Military education had to be changed because soldiers and officers had to learn their new role: Being at the service of democratically elected politicians and the people of Spain as a whole, acting according to the constitution, and refusing to obey orders that violate national and international law. Further, the military justice had to be reformed. To overcome the economy, which was in dire straits in 1977 (high inflation, high deficits, increasing unemployment, and a slowdown of productivity), the government proposed an integrative solution in the form of an all-parties consensus called the Moncloa Pacts of 1977. Cooperation between the former irreconcilable enemies took place for the first time ever. Thanks to this power-sharing a respectful form of politics got established and initial steps toward trust were taken.

To strengthen his son and to reinstall an hereditary monarchy instead of the dictator's one, Juan de Borbón abdicated in favor of his son on May 14, 1977. Symbolically, the king could connect this way to the glorious history of 16th century Spain. The Constitution of 1978 established in Article 1 a parliamentary monarchy, the rule of law, and federalist principles. It was an act of compromise and consensus, as the king and the monarchists had to accept the prerogative of democracy over monarchy, and the Socialists had to live with a monarch as Head of State. Spanish regions – especially Catalonia and the Basque country were granted a form of autonomy.

To make sure that the suffering endured in the past wouldn't sabotage the shared future, a "willful strategy of ignorance and oblivion"[52] was chosen. They didn't negate what had happened, but renounced revenge. This reconciliation process only works if it isn't imposed, but is accepted and espoused by as many as possible. To deconstruct the old and construct anew

---

[51] He was already as Prince convinced, that one day, the PCE would have to be legalized; De Vilallonga, José Luis (1993), p. 101.
[52] Daguzan, Jean-François (2003), p. 65; Rozenberg, Danielle (2003), p. 168

a community that integrates factions who were until now in war with each other is an incredible challenge becoming effective in everyday interactions. Every participant in this process has to compromise and be willing to change. And a form of cooperation has to be established that recognizes and respects, as well as supports, the members of the community to come. The workers, who were organized in unions were longing for a change, after all this time, using demonstrations and strikes as a form of pressure. In 1976 the strikes had increased ten-fold in relation to 1975. The unions launched a "wave of strikes throughout the country,"[53] which often led to violent clashes between protesters and security forces. The still very powerful establishment, and especially the military, who was accustomed to make use its power at its own means, had now to renounce their almightiness. And there were terrorist attacks from autonomist and the extreme right and left groups. This overall violence, which had been part of Spanish society for so long, burdened the identity-finding process. All these actors were using violence for political purposes: The Left justified it because of the persistent totalitarianism. The Right needed it to fight the communist and anarchist threat. And the autonomists saw no other path to their independence.[54] However, long-term integration is only possible on cooperative grounds, which prohibits the use of violence.

Three days after having been crowned, the king pardoned all political crimes committed before November 22, 1975. To the disappointment of the Left, only 235 out of a total of 4'000 political prisoners were released. An amnesty law of 1976 and one of 1977 exempted from criminal liability all political acts that had tried to re-establish public liberties and regional autonomy. At the same time, criminal acts committed by the state during the dictatorship were also amnestied. To make the last point acceptable to the Left, all political prisoners were freed, the communist party was legalized, and free elections were set up for June 1977. The amnesty law of 1977 rehabilitated operatives, teachers, and members of independent professions, giving them back their jobs and guaranteeing their pensions. Some symbols of Francoism were abolished, such as, for example, street names. But this symbolic purification took quite some time. It's only in 1995 that the coins minted with Franco's face were withdrawn from circulation. Besides this symbolic presence, the dictatorship was officially ended with the free elections of June 15, 1977: The UCD, Suárez's center party, won with 34,3% of the vote, the Socialists (PSOE) reached 28,5%. Alianza Popular, the Fran-

---

[53] Marin Arce, José Maria (2003), p. 76. About the compromises the unions had to make, see p. 73.
[54] Baby, Sophie (2003), pp. 93 ff.

coists, polled 8,4 %, in spite of their plentiful financing. And the PCE (Communists) realized 9,3 %. At a participation rate of 80 %, 90 % of the voters made a clear statement for change.[55]

Four times the transition was challenged by the army. Frightened of its loss of power, it fell back on violence to push through its interests. Francoists, Falangists, right-wing conservatives, and monarchists tried different coups d'état. The first was in 1978, operation Galaxia, which failed. The improvised attempt intended to oblige the King to appoint a new government of national salvation, which would launch a war against the ETA. The perpetrators were punished with short imprisonment, as the government feared of antagonizing the army. In 1981, the same people, supported now by high-ranking generals, tried a much bigger coup. On January 29, Suárez resigned under intense threats of a military intervention, which was revealed by the intelligence services and published in El Alcázar (an ultra-rightist newspaper). To avoid the parliamentary investiture of his successor Sotelo, a group of Civil Guards and Army officers took hostage the Chamber of Deputies on February 23. At the same time tanks from Valencia started toward Madrid. The decisive role the king played in this crucial moment for the young democracy has a lot to do with personality, symbolic power, and trust. Appearing on TV at 1.15 a.m., he declared that he would neither abdicate nor leave Spain – meaning that the rebels would either have to shoot him or acknowledge defeat.[56] "The crown, symbol of the permanence and unity of the Fatherland cannot tolerate any actions or attitudes by those who aim to interrupt by force the democratic process determined by the popularly ratified Constitution."[57] For a right-wing soldier a regicide was not an option. The king, with no power besides his personal integrity, his ritualized connection to the mighty past of monarchical Spain, his formal status as Commander-in-Chief of the Armed Forces, his personal contacts to different members of the army, many public appearances in favor of the army as an important institution, and the moral support of more and more people nationally and internationally was too powerful for armed soldiers, who were aware of their *lack of legitimacy*. This time, the traitors were punished severely with long prison sentences.

Institutions aren't stable tools, usable at the will of the rulers, but rather a form of social arrangement leading to an effective integration, if all its constituent parts are consented (see pp. 295 ff.). Juan Carlos's duty was to transform his power, created by the dictator, to a monarchical as much as a

---

[55] Preston, Paul (2004), p. 392
[56] De Vilallonga, José Luis (1993), p. 173.
[57] Preston, Paul (2004), pp. 481 f.

democratic institution, possibly outlasting himself. Establishing an institution happens step by step and depends at the beginning on the engagement and personality of the responsible actors. In Spain, the transition worked in the first place because of the king's personality and engagement and the readiness of Suárez, as a representative of the old system, to risk the change. With Felipe González (general secretary of the PSOE at this time): "[…] it wasn't the abstract institution monarchy that convinced the Spaniards, it was the king."[58] Besides his personal engagement and the symbolic importance of the monarchy, it was also his willingness to listen to people, to recognize all of them as valuable that played an essential role. Contrary to his grandfather Alfonso XIII, he entertained contacts to the opposition. He acted as the king not only of the Right, but of all Spaniards. Cooperating with everybody he bridged the divide that had been erected and seemed to be insurmountable. The dictator was succeeded "by a constitutional monarch and a generation of political leaders was born after the Civil War, who were intent upon breaking down the barriers Franco had erected between different groups of Spaniards and between Spain and the outside world. Unlike Franco, their guiding principle was not 'divide and rule,' but the search for consensus and the peaceful coexistence of all Spanish citizens."[59] And finally, the support of the majority of the people had to be won. According to the king, it was the Spanish people, patient and trustful enough, that made the change possible.[60] On February 27, 1981, as a reaction to the attempted coup d'état, three million people demonstrated across Spain supporting democracy and the king. This convincing manifestation in favor of democracy ended a declining trust in this form of government. Democracy had lost its approval, from 90% in 1977 to 40% in 1981. Slow progress, chaos, and mistakes that in an open society became visible, and uncertainties tarnished democracy's image. It may be easier to have a dictator: At least you know whom to hate and to blame. In a democracy, it is basically you who's responsible for the current problems. And democracy is not a solution, is not an end in itself. It is just a form of debate, recognizing the people's existence and right to be heard and to decide themselves. If this debate doesn't yield betterment as hoped for, authoritarian solutions become attractive again. However, the attempts of the army to end democratization called its importance to mind.

Parts of the army who were still not ready to accept their new serving role, attempted further overthrows of the government, in June 1981 and in

---

[58] De Vilallonga, José Luis (1993), p. 7
[59] Ellwood, Shelagh (1994), p. 227
[60] De Vilallonga, José Luis (1993), p. 94, 223

1982 (the quite ambitious operation Cervantes), but didn't succeed. Their failure was the final approbation democracy had needed to be firmly established. And the victory of the Socialist Party in 1982 demonstrated that Manichaean scapegoat politics had ended. For the first time in the history of Spain, a left-wing party governed the country without being threatened by the army, Guardia Civil, or police. The PSOE won 48 % of the votes and, hence, the absolute majority in parliament, staying in power for fourteen years.

6. Decision-making process

We often hear that "the market" has decided, that "the state" has to solve the problem, that "human nature" dictates, that "God" wants us to do something, that "the unconscious" rules, or that "the reality" has to be accepted. Suppose, however, we think individuals are important and suppose we are convinced that freedom, responsibility, and justice are defendable values. Then it is sensible to base our perception of the community and of institutions not on existing systemic entities and taking their influence independent of human beings (see p. 153 ff.), but on interacting individuals. Thus, nothing is pre-given, nothing has to be accepted as unchangeable. Everything follows out of the personal engagement of individuals who are ready to spend time, energy, passion, ideas, and, if necessary and where existing or available, money. What we call "the state" is, against this background, a *relationship between individuals* that has to be updated every day so it will be of lasting character. Neither governmental functions nor the constitution are immutable fixed points. They are temporary arrangements, the sense of which has to be established anew endlessly.

a) Monopoly of violence by consensus

Establishing a monopoly of violence is a challenge between trust and doubts. It means, on the one hand, giving up private armament in favor of a few people called "government." The citizens accept that these few people have the exclusive authority to dispose of police and armed forces. The intention is to control the use of weapons and to securitize the public and private sphere. There is, on the other hand, no guarantee that this monopoly will not be used against the citizens. People, therefore, need an impressive amount of trust in their government to consent to their self-disarmament, all the more in modern times where government's power has reached unseen levels. Never was there such a concentration of armaments in such a small number of hands. Medieval kings had to build up an army prior to every conflict, and they had to convince the aristocracy to provide themselves weapons, horses, soldiers, and money. There wasn't any deployable standing army at any time. And the aristocracy made the king pay with feudal tenures, political power and civil rights. What makes modern times "modern" is the almost limitless development of armaments, deployable more or less when the government pleases, and it is able to destroy many times the people who agreed to this concentration of power. The disarmament of individuals and the renouncement of self-justice makes, on the one hand, society more peaceful. On the other hand, there are critical mechanisms needed to ensure, that the commissioned power isn't misused. The rulers have also to demonstrate again and again their ability to apply their power responsibly.

A monopoly of violence doesn't lead per se to justice. It simply means that physical violence is institutionally concentrated. Justice is established if the monopoly is used in an equitable way. Like any social arrangement, the monopoly of violence, once established, stays fragile and may be hijacked by whom ever. Revolutions, civil wars, terrorist attacks, lynchings, or police violence show that this arrangement for peace can't be taken for granted. Without the everyday readiness to act peacefully and to look for integrative conflict resolutions that respect those involved, violence is a constant menace that impacts the quality of life.

An elementary consensus is needed to build up trustworthy institutions. Otherwise, the renouncement to violence won't take place and permanent fights between the different factions become a heavy burden. Disarmament is a necessary condition to recognize equal construction power, to respect individual freedom, and to secure an open space of negotiations – elements currently described as "democracy."

aa) Elementary consensus

Different Spanish and English expeditions arrived by ship on the Pacific coast of the American continent during the 16th and 17th century and claimed the land as theirs. However, it took more than hundred years till the Spanish started to settle in California because it was too far away and to expensive. For most Europeans the area wasn't attractive, which is why they had to be forced to move to the West Coast.[1] In the 18th century, Spanish government decided to expel the Jesuits because they treated Native Americans too benignly. The substituting Franciscan friars were assigned to proselytize the Natives, who as "gente sin razón" were lacking reason, could be treated as children,[2] and had to be rescued by conversion. This conversion didn't only concern religious matters, but also the way they were clothed, spoke, organized socially, and the way they were housed.

Spanish settlements were religiously and militarily motivated and, in 1776 established the Anza expedition the Presidio at the Golden Gate of San Francisco Bay. In 1810 Mexican-born Spaniards launched the Mexican

---

[1] Starr, Kevin (2005), p. 37
[2] *Id.*, p. 41

War of Independence against the Spanish colonial authority. Mexico became independent with the signing of the Treaty of Córdoba and California became part of the new state. According to its republican convictions adopted the Mexican congress adopted in 1833 the Revolutionary Secularization Act, which ended the Franciscan's control of the missions. Their vast land holdings were supposed to be distributed to Hispanicized Natives and new colonists. Governor of California José Figueroa applied the law but died too early, which is why "only a small percentage of mission Indians ever came into possession of the properties."[3] Most of the land was sold at whatever price and taken over by large cattle barons – the Californios – who became the dominant social and political force in Mexican California.[4] A rancho society developed that was based on the big landowners' families. The governor had assigned the army to take care of security matters and to guarantee the northern frontier. Mariano Guadalupe Vallejo (1835, Sonoma) and John Augustus Sutter (1839, Nueva Helvetia) were commissioned to build presidios and protect California against Russian or Native incursions. Far into the 19th century, California didn't develop a collective identity or integrative political institutions, and civil institutions were rare. It was much more an aggregate of rich families living on immense estates with Mexican and forced Native workers.

In 1835, President Andrew Jackson offered to purchase San Francisco Bay and Northern California, but Mexico declined. Jackson's proposal was part of the United States' imperial aspirations, justified later by the concept called "Manifest Destiny."[5] This ideology comprised "the right of [the European-American's] manifest destiny to overspread and to possess the whole of the continent which Providence has given us for the development of the great experiment of liberty and federative self government entrusted to us."[6] The expansionist logic "from sea to shining sea"[7] was motivated by power politics and economic interests and justified by religious and racist arguments. Senator Thomas Hart Benton, speaking in the Senate on May 28, 1846, qualified the direct access to the Pacific of great economic interest because it would open the door to India.[8] Furthermore, the Caucasian white race was, according to him, far above all other races, which is why it would be of great benefit not only to the western coast of America, but to

---

[3] *Id.*, p. 49
[4] Richards, Rand (2007), p. 36
[5] Remini, Robert V. (2010), p. 29
[6] John L. O'Sullivan, quoted in Remini, Robert V. (2010), p. 31
[7] Stone, Ilene/Grenz, Suzanna M. (2005), p. 23
[8] Congressional Globe, 29:1 (1846), pp. 915 f.

humanity in general.⁹ The "White race alone received the divine command, to subdue and replenish the earth! [...] The Red race has disappeared from the Atlantic coast: the tribes that resisted civilization, met extinction. [...] For my part, I cannot murmur at what seems to be the effect of divine law. [...] Civilization, or extinction, has been the fate of all people who have found themselves in the track of the advancing Whites, and civilization, always the preference of the Whites, has been pressed as an object, while extinction has followed as a consequence of its resistance."¹⁰ The Mexican-American War (1846-1848) was incited to fulfill the United States' imperial dreams. Under the pretext of outstanding payments and injuries done to its citizens, President Polk ordered General Zachary Taylor to move his troops into the disputed border area at the Rio Grande. He hoped to provoke a military reaction by Mexico.¹¹ "Polk [baited] Mexico into war over the Texas boundary question in order to get California."¹² By winning the war the United States would get the expansion to the Pacific, a goal "that was foremost in the minds of President Polk and his associates in their whole conduct of the war."¹³ Mexico wasn't interested enough to defend its Californian territory: "The problems of the Presidio mirrored those of California. It was remote, underdeveloped, and its status unclear in the eyes of Spanish or Mexican rulers, who never had a clear purpose or priority. The earlier grand vision of the Presidio as a bastion of empire, a guardian of the riches of the Pacific, faded into obscurity."¹⁴ After the United States had won the war it paid Mexico in the Treaty of Guadalupe Hidalgo $18.25 million for an area that today includes California, Nevada, Utah, New Mexico, and parts of some other states.

To become an integrated political community, California had to build up two forms of cooperation. First, cooperation was needed between the people living in the geographical area called "Alta California." Second, they had to convince the members of the United States to include them in their union. On the West Coast an elementary consensus had to be established which would also include the decision-making process. This comprised rules about the people who, under specific circumstances, would have the right to decide on a certain form. A civil society agreeing widely on the

---

[9] *Id.*, p. 917
[10] *Id.*, p. 918
[11] Remini, Robert V. (2010), pp. 31 f.
[12] Morison, Samuel Eliot/Commager, Henry Steele/Leuchtenburg, William E. (1983), p. 243
[13] Rives, George Lockhart (1913), pp. 657 f.
[14] Benton, Lisa M. (1998), p. 19

relevant basic values had, therefore, to designate and support what in the sociology of law is called the "Rechtsstab" ("legal staff" or "enforcement staff") – the people acting on behalf of and abiding by the law, such as governors, lawyers, judges, civil servants, policemen, and so on. The integration of California into the United States was a claim that challenged the collective identity of the Union. Slavery had encumbered the country for decades because it crystallized the unsolved conflict about the basic values. Time and again the Union risked splitting up as shaky compromises were established to disguise insurmountable differences. This elementary disagreement about human dignity, freedom, and justice could not be ignored. To use people as a tool for the fulfillment of economic interests regardless of the possible costs to them, or to respect them basically as equal human beings – these two worldviews had to clash. Several times politics has had to decide whether the interest of the majority in unity and international power was more important than the economic, social, and political practice of negating human dignity and life of many a people. Decades before, the pro- and anti-slavery states had arduously negotiated a balance of power, neutralizing effectively slavery as origin of discord. In 1819, Missouri wanted to be admitted into the Union as a slave state. Making sure that neither would have the majority, a complex mix of assets and drawbacks for the North as well as the South was agreed on. What is called the Missouri Compromise contained the following elements: Missouri became the twelfth slave state, slavery was forbidden north of the Mason-Dixon-Line (36° 30'), Maine was admitted as the twelfth free state, and slavery as an institution stayed untouched. The request of California in 1848 to become a member of the Union brought the innate division within U.S. identity to the fore because it would have changed the balance between the fifteen free and fifteen slave states in favor of the free ones. Once again, states that saw slavery as an integral part of their identity, as "peculiar institution," had to come to terms with states that found slavery abhorrent. This conflict divided states as well as communities, as, for example, in 1844/45, both the Methodists and the Baptists split over the question of slavery. Congress finally adopted the Compromise of 1850, which saved the union once again. California was recognized as a free state and the New Mexico and Utah territories were free to decide about the question. The slave trade was also abolished in the District of Columbia. The Fugitive Slave Act, on the other hand, gave slave-owners a powerful tool to catch their fleeing possession. Authorities in the free states were now obliged to return fugitives to their masters. Remini is right when he writes that the achievement of important goals needs compromises of the people involved,[15] because the compromise is a form of integration that respects freedom, equity and often solidarity. But he's wrong in qualifying the Compromise of 1850 as a success. According to him, it was an achievement because it gave the North ten years to develop its economic, technical, and infrastructural advance that finally made its victory in 1865 possible.[16] To uphold a union for the price of about 665'000 lives is only justifiable if the nation is more valued than the life of individuals. And even this toll didn't bring a stable integration, as the country stayed deeply divided over the status of African Americans. A country unified by force and not by basic value consensus quite probably will not last or it has to clash repeatedly.

bb) Govern the rush

Almost from the beginning US-California was confronted with an existential consensus problem. Building up state institutions had to take place within a short time. As long only a few people were interested in living on the West Coast, the army was able to rule and solve conflicts.[17] When, however, in January 1848 sparkling pebbles were found by James Marshall, a partner with Sutter in building a sawmill, everything changed. Many basic problems had to be solved to make sure that conflicts wouldn't reach a level that was no longer controllable. Sutter and Marshall had hoped to acquire the land where the gold was found. They negotiated an agreement with the Natives, but it wasn't accepted by the military governor of California, Colonel Richard B. Mason. The land had been conquered by the United States and was, therefore, its property. He decreed that the goldfields were freely available and the gold belonged to the one who found it, laid legal claim, and extracted it.[18] The first regional Gold Rush developed within months, bringing thousands of gold seekers to California. President Polk's confirmation in Congress on December 5, 1848 that "gold" had been found launched the international Gold Rush of 1849. At the end of 1848, 8'000 to 10'000 miners were at the digging. Within three years, the population rose to 255'000. This instant mass immigration couldn't be organized by the overwhelmed military administration, so it had to organize itself. In his Official Report on the Gold Mines, Colonel Mason described the profound

---

[15] Remini, Robert V. (2010), p. 1
[16] Id., p. 158
[17] Starr, Kevin (2005), p. 90
[18] Id., p. 82

effect the Gold Rush had on the social fabric of California:

> "The discovery of these vast deposits of gold has entirely changed the character of Upper California. Its people, before engaged in cultivating their small patches of ground, and guarding their herds of cattle and horses, have all gone to the mines, or are on their way thither. Labourers of every trade have left their work-benches, and tradesmen their shops. Sailors desert their ships as fast as they arrive on the coast; and several vessels have gone to sea with hardly enough hands to spread a sail. Two or three are now at anchor in San Francisco, with no crew on board. Many desertions, too, have taken place from the garrisons within the influence of these mines. [...] I really think some extraordinary mark of favour should be given to those soldiers who remain faithful to their flag throughout this tempting crisis. [...] if the government wish to prevent desertions here on the part of men, and to secure zeal on the part of officers, their pay must be increased very materially. [...] No capital is required to obtain this gold, as the labouring man wants nothing but his pick and shovel and tin pan, with which to dig and wash the gravel, and many frequently pick gold out of the crevices of rocks with their knives, in pieces of from one to six ounces."[19]

The military government was ill equipped to manage all the problems the gold rush boom originated. The army had taken over the government in 1848 and acted on *military law*, using the *alcalde system* established by the Mexicans. "Alcaldes" were mayors who presided over town councils (*ayuntamiento*), executed their decisions and were responsible for public order. Administering justice, they tried criminal and civil cases. If there wasn't an ayuntamiento the alcalde himself acted as legislator. As long as just a few people were living on ample land the need for administrative work was small: "In [...] Mexican times, there had not been a great demand for lots, so there was not much pressure to keep records in a businesslike way. The record of deeds to town lots was kept on a penciled map behind the bar in a popular saloon. When Americans first came, conditions did not change a great deal; as alcaldes, Bartlett and Bryant pretty much granted town lots to whom they wanted."[20] The more the political and economic interests in California rose, the more conflict-avoiding and conflict-solving mechanisms had to be institutionalized. "[...] at the end of 1848, while San Francisco awaited the flood of 49ers, the criminal justice establishment of the town consisted of a lone alcalde with ill-defined executive and judicial

---

[19] Mason, Richard B. (1848), pp. 61 f.
[20] Mullen, Kevin J. (1989), pp. 30 f.

powers and a single sheriff or constable to carry out his orders."[21] In the Spring of '48, the absence of effective state institutions wasn't too much of a problem because people were busy mining for gold so that there was no time for crime and hardly anybody left to commit them. It is only in the Summer 48, when the people came back to the city, that the inhabitants of San Francisco began to organize volunteer militia companies like the San Francisco Guard. In the mines, the miners organized themselves, because the whole mining region with only two alcaldes was underresourced. They convened summary courts, a "well-established frontier tradition. [...] Common sense was the rule of law and legal technicalities were dispensed with [...]. A guilty finding resulted in almost immediate punishment, most often banishment, whipping, or hanging, in the absence of any jails or anyone willing to watch prisoners."[22]

Brigadier General Riley was appointed governor in 1849 and organized the transition to an ordinary civil government. A legislative assembly had to be created, courts established, a government installed, and sensible legal rules had to be enacted for a fast growing community that lacked a collective identity and stood under the pressure of an ever changing population. The U.S. Congress was competent to establish a territorial government and to authorize the election of a convention to prepare the constitution of California, which would have to be approved by Congress itself. But it didn't act because of the political gridlock between the North and South over slavery. Therefore, the army decided to abuse of its power: Trying to bring order on the legal basis of the emerging community, in 1849 Riley called to elect a constitutional convention. The convention relied on the constitutions of New York and Iowa as guidelines. "Only white males were granted the franchise. [...] African Americans, Chinese, and Native Americans were denied the rights of citizenship and prohibited from testifying against Whites in court. [...] On the other hand [...] slavery was prohibited in California."[23] Not humanitarian, but economic motives led to this decision. It seemed clear for the majority that slave owners were planning to bring their slaves to California, freeing them there on the condition that they worked in the mines as indentured servants.[24] To attract women to an area almost exclusively populated by men, the convention adopted a provision that allowed married women to keep the property they had before the marriage.

---

[21] *Id.*, p. 45
[22] *Id.*, p. 44
[23] Starr, Kevin (2005), pp. 92 f.
[24] Bean, Walton Elbert (1978), p. 107; Lee Johnson, Susan (2001), p. 70

Governor Riley proclaimed general elections on November 13, 1849. Half of the electors went to the polls and the constitution was approved with 12'061 against 811. Peter Burnett was elected governor and Riley resigned, giving the way free for civil structures, even though the army went on playing an important role in the state.[25]

cc) Solidarity, responsibility, reciprocity

Communities exist over time if they develop a collective identity and if their members are willing to engage in the long run. People have to make the community to their "home" and must take over a supportive and responsible role by building up reciprocal structures. One has to be ready to spend time or money for a common cause – an investment that doesn't pay back instantly but secures relationships and services that make life valuable and one day perhaps will support ourselves.

The Hounds riot of '49 made it clear to many people that cooperation was needed if they wanted to live peacefully and pursue their interests effectively.[26] California as a widely unstructured and barely integrated El Dorado was an attractive environment for organized crime. The Hounds were a gang of bullies who had come into being in late 1848. Its members were mainly from the New York Volunteers who were "recruited in New York by Jonathan D. Stevenson, a Tammany Hall leader, to aid in the conquest of California."[27] They later called themselves the "San Francisco Society of Regulators," whose services were mainly used by leading businessmen to, for example, "return runaway sailors to their ships,"[28] to control the voting of people, or to carry out the orders of the alcalde.[29] These hoodlums grew fast and reached up to hundred members, becoming increasingly a public nuisance. Through threats of physical violence they extorted money from shopkeepers, didn't pay for meals in restaurants, and liked to frighten people in the city.[30] Highly xenophobic they were decided to oust foreigners from American soil. Chileans, especially, were their targets because they perceived them as the main competitors of Americans in the rush for gold. In the middle of July 1849, they attacked the encampments of the Chileans on Telegraph Hill in San Francisco, stole gold and silver, and destroyed

---

[25] Starr, Kevin (2005), p. 219
[26] Richards, Rand (2009), p. 102
[27] Ellison, William Henry (1950), p. 206
[28] Richards, Rand (2009), p. 98
[29] Browning, Peter (ed.) (1995), p. 338; Richards, Rand (2009), p. 103
[30] Richards, Rand (2009), p. 99

everything else. Thirty-eight Chileans were assaulted or intimidated and one Chilean and one American died. Outraged citizens summoned alcalde Leavenworth to act on behalf of security and to arrest the gangsters. He "claimed that he could do nothing without an armed constabulary."[31] Hence, a group of about 230 citizens took the law into their own hands and captured 19 members of the Hounds, including their leader Sam Roberts. A trial was organized, including a jury, prosecutors, and counsels for the defendant. And the judgments were pronounced within a week, banishing the perpetrators from California. This rather light punishment seems to be attributable to the influential parties that had engaged the Hounds for their own needs and were against a monopoly of violence in the hands of the alcalde.[32]

To avoid this sort of conflicts difficult to control, the new alcalde John White Geary decided to establish a professional police department, permanently visible and representing law and order, which, hopefully, would have a preventive effect. A police chief was appointed and his assistant, three sergeants and 30 patrolmen were hired. However, there was not enough money to pay the police force seriously. They were paid less than half of the salaries of skilled laborers. Many cities at this time burned down time and again because they consisted of wooden houses. Besides accidents, arson was very often the cause. Arson fires were set, for example, to conceal another crime, to intimidate competitors, to get rid of stocks unsolvable or only to too low a price,[33] as a mean of revenge, or because of the fascinating feeling of power. This common disaster was, on the one hand, fatalistically accepted. On the other hand, people weren't ready to pay for services like police and fire protection or the construction of jails. The laissez-faire philosophy,[34] the unusual idea to pay for something that people up until then perceived as a voluntary service, and the absence of a notion of responsibility for the bigger collective, led to this destructive inactivity. Furthermore, the institutions needed for this fast growing society were a form of administration that many of the group-experienced immigrants didn't know. Conflicts in traditional, agrarian cultures and in the world of westward pioneers were avoided and solved on a personal and small-group level. There were no third-party conflict-resolution delegations. "Culprits were haled before an

---

[31] Monaghan, Jay (1973), p. 168
[32] Richards, Rand (2009), p. 104
[33] Senkewicz, Robert M. (1985), p. 73: "[…] fires performed a useful commercial function. When the market was glutted, fires were one way of seeing inventories reduced."
[34] Mullen, Kevin J. (1989), p. 85

improvised bar of justice. The entire group or jury would hear the evidence, weigh it, and pronounce judgment. A sentence would be carried out immediately and then the miners would return to their usual routine. This system had a number of desirable features: Justice was rendered by one's peers; sentences were carried out immediately and were generally appropriate to the offense; and since there were no regular officials or facilities available, the convicted offender was punished and usually banished. [...] these ad hoc groups which donned judicial robes and acted in the name of justice whipped, hanged, banished, or tarred and feathered."[35] San Francisco, however, needed institutional arrangements that were of unusual scale, weren't rooted in the culture of most of its inhabitants, and had to be developed against a background of the upcoming and forced industrialization and the generalization of the market principle. Individualization started to take place, family businesses became less and less important, and time started to be dictated by the rhythm of employers and their machines. An anonymity resulted that had an impact on the capacity of small communities to keep up mutual support and to integrate people. In Gold Rush California the social fabric was even more put under pressure because:

- Young men overwhelmingly predominated.

- People came from different geographical areas and spoke many different languages.

- Most of the people only wanted to make money as fast as possible and weren't interested in becoming a member of a lasting community. The sooner they would leave and head home the better. "San Francisco residents did not yet think of themselves as 'San Franciscans'; they were still New Yorkers or Bostonians temporarily away from home."[36]

- The miners didn't stay very long at the same place, running from gold strike to gold strike.

- The commercial establishment was not willing to pay higher taxes.[37]

- The high rate of poor and frustrated miners who hadn't been able to fulfill their high hopes. As long as not too many had arrived and the gold was easy to find, abundance made conflicts few. However, the more it became clear that just a few would get rich and the source of

---

[35] Beck, Warren A./Williams, David A. (1972), pp. 172 f.
[36] Richards, Rand (2009), p. 107
[37] Mullen, Kevin J. (1989), p. 118

hope would perish, confrontations increased in numbers and intensity."

Even though the "overlanders" had shared, during their trips to the West, a sense of community and mutual support,[38] it wasn't grounds enough to support new rules and institutions. Furthermore, the never seen before fast growth of the population made it quite difficult to generate a community's sense sufficiently that would be important to rein in the greed that had motivated most of the people heading West. As a result, corruption and fraud committed by the officials and the upper class were widespread, and social unrest, petty, and serious crimes committed by members of the underclass increased in the 1850s.

In the beginning, heading west meant heading into "a no man's land." Space seemed to be inexhaustible and the regulation concerning the acquisition and delimitation of land was quite lax. Also the Native Americans were a negligible quantity. Even though the alcalde-system was effective and fulfilled its task most of the time, land titles, for example, were difficult to determine exactly. The deeds often defined property boundaries in vague terms.[39] The more the value of the land increased, the more it was important to find conflict resolution mechanisms that were consented to by the majority of concerned individuals. Under Mexican law, the main intention "was to avoid reserving indefinitely to single individuals the rights to vast expanses of vaguely identified property."[40] This open range principle came under pressure as soon as the land became limited financial investments were put at risk, and the principle of common ground was "privatized." "With the first arrival of white men in the West, the federal government allowed private livestock to graze in its rangelands without restraint or compensation. As public land gradually became private in the hands of homesteaders, railroads, and others, the same open range practices transferred to private lands as well. [...] By law, if a landowner wished to exclude others' livestock from his land, he needed to erect a legal fence to do so. Without a fence, he had no complaint against their incursions. As western populations grew and competition for land uses multiplied, so too did breaches, violations, and assaults on these simple range practices. Legal agitation to limit the open range crystallized in the U.S. Supreme Court case of Lazarus v. Phelps, decided in 1894."[41]

---

[38] Eifler, Mark A. (2002), p. 87
[39] *Id.*, p. 120
[40] Kens, Paul (2000), p. 346
[41] Andes, Roy H. (2000), p. 338

A lasting community can't be built on greed alone. It is barely possible to trust somebody who is exclusively motivated by material interests. To establish effective institutions that are capable of solving conflicts in a just and, therefore, integrative way, long-term engagement is needed. Short-term oriented fortune-seekers and upper class investors – all of them resembling the selfish individualists of the free-market ideology – were not willing to take responsibility for the community. An increase in social inequality combined with an unmitigated fight over limited resources intensified conflicts and disengagement at a time that needed more cooperation, given the volatility of the social fabric. What finally changed the West from an unregulated market into a community's home, was the decision of individuals to stay. As soon as a long-term relationship is intended, as soon as people don't want simply avoid each other, the concept of a selfish competitive war of all against all doesn't work anymore. Integration is needed and arrangements have to be found that make recognition, respect, reciprocity, and, therefore, trust possible. From the moment on that Sacramento and San Francisco became more than just walkways serving the simplest needs of people staying in the mines during the summer and in the city in wintertime, institutions were needed that could be responsible for everyday conflict-resolutions. Moving to another place was no longer an option, and the interests in other people became political, which meant that: The quality of life depended primarily on the relationships one could build up, and only secondary or tertiary on money. "Orientation" and "sense" occur in a human's life because of interactions with others. Being member of a community provides the experience of something bigger than the isolated individual. Families played an evermore important role because the people began arriving as families, individuals were "adopted" as members of families, or men created families with women now coming increasingly to California. Besides the intimacy of families there were working associations or communities of people with same language or origin.

"Sacramento's founders sought only to make a quick profit. They saw the people passing through Sacramento's streets not as potential settlers, but as temporary, transitory customers."[42] Enrichment was the order of the day, not integration, not quality of life for all, but quantity of wealth for the few. On this materialistic basis democracy or the rule of law are handicapping restrictions because they are typically orientated toward long-term integration and protection of minorities and individuals. Being "just" means to

---

[42] Eifler, Mark A. (2002), p. 55

take the time[43] to listen to people and to be ready to change not only the political organization, but also the social arrangement and the distribution of wealth, so that everybody has the possibility to construct interactively the "reality" one hopes for.

dd) The common good

In my opinion, capitalistic logic of limitless accumulation does not fit with a long-term communal existence. Mechanisms of self-restraint and equalization are needed to secure mutual obligation, and reciprocity. Vigilantism in San Francisco illustrates two things: First, violence is not related to a social strata. It is a tool people use to fulfill their interests, independent of their economic, social, or political status. Second, state institutions do not work if they are founded on a deeply divided and disinterested society. Mainly wealthy entrepreneurs were politically active in the California of the mid-eighteenth century because they had long-term investments in mind. The majority of the people were passionately occupied with finding gold and were too greedy to be interested in public affairs or in building a government. As a result, politics became a "private" club for the upper class – a club focused on "the business interests of the city's largest businessmen"[44] and accessible solely to members. Leading merchants of San Francisco used their membership of the ayuntamiento or the office of the justice of peace to sell town lots of the city at cheap prices and bought them as privateers, especially when they were located in promising development areas.[45] They assigned to themselves exclusive access to the city's waterfront, the economically most interesting part of the nascent city. Furthermore, they monopolized access to political institutions.

"Sacramento City's first government came from essentially self-appointed officials."[46] Vacant places in the council didn't lead to elections, the elite co-opted new members at their own discretion. Accordingly, they drafted laws that pleased themselves and built up an important degree of organization that helped them simulate democracy. And yet, even under such manipulative circumstances political power is disputed and has to face resistance. The upper class had usurped all politically relevant positions, but had

---

[43] Insofar are "expediency and justice often antithetical" (Beck, Warren A./Williams, David A. [1972], p. 173).
[44] Eifler, Mark A. (2002), p. 70
[45] Mullen, Kevin J. (1989), p. 96
[46] Eifler, Mark A. (2002), p. 68

to note that their power wasn't consented to. The politicians had decided that the waterfront had to be cleared. The people, however, claimed the waterfront to be common ground and went on using it at their own will. That there was an important gap and a lack of trust between the council and the people became evident when nearly 60 % of the electorate rejected the draft of a city constitution. To increase their influence, the wealthy needed to broaden their support. Hence, the council, which until now was dominated by the "city's great speculators," opened itself for enterprising residents.[47] These two groups then worked against new immigrants. At this time land titles were the main source of wealth, which is why many of the conflicts were about land rights and often ended in violent confrontations. Conflicts frequently occurred because of new immigrants, the transient miners who had to live somewhere during the winter months when gold digging wasn't possible. For the rich and the already settled, these miners were squatting on private property. The settlers, however, were convinced to stay on public ground because the newly conquered frontier land, "the vacant land in Sacramento City [was] open for all, free of charge."[48] The Settlers' Association demonstrated and attacked land speculators and members of the Common Council to make them pay attention to their living problems. The latter, on the other hand, humiliated the new immigrants and sometimes evicted them by force.[49] Trying to regulate the conflict, the transitional Senate and Assembly of the State of California passed in April 22, 1850, the act "Concerning forcible and unlawful Detainers." This act favored plaintiffs bringing charges against squatters because they didn't have to prove their entitlement. On this legal ground the Common Council of Sacramento issued an ordinance forbidding the erection of tents, shanties, or houses on any vacant lot belonging to a private person. By suing one of the settlers, the establishment tried to enforce the new rules. But the defendant appealed and, supported by the Settlers' Association, they were ready to take all necessary legal steps. Even though the legal system was, in their opinion, corrupt, they were encouraged by the support claims of settlers had received in 1849 and 1850 by the state legislature, the state supreme court, and the federal district court.[50] Not sure about the outcome of the lawsuit and judging the

---

[47] Id., p. 98
[48] Id., p. 136
[49] Id., pp. 123, 145
[50] Pisani, Donald J. (1994), p. 292: The first legislature (1849-50) awarded "preemption rights to those 'now occupied and settled upon' up to 160 acres of public land. The boundaries had to be clearly marked, the parcel had to be continuously occupied, and claimants had to spend at least $100 on improvements. The legislature did not

legal path as too slow, the speculators mobilized the "Law and Order Association" and formed and drilled militia companies, which destroyed several housings of squatters. The upper class was willing to use all means because their whole system was based on the future development of the city and on inflated land prices: A fragile system that would work as long as people believed in never ending prosperous development.[51] Camping wild settlers put at risk the willingness of people to invest in this carefully built up market. For the Settlers' Association, the city government was extra-legal as "it had violated basic precepts of unwritten laws, and consequently, its edicts were null and void."[52] However, the legal hopes of the settlers ended quite fast. Having lost in the City Recorder's Court, they appealed to the County Court, where Judge E. J. Willis ruled against them. He stated in his ruling, that because of the uncertain status of California within the Union an appeal to a higher court probably wasn't possible. As Judge Willis himself was a speculator, it was evident to the Settler's Association, that he had unjustly defended the interests of his friends.[53] This lack of legal opportunities "left the squatters but to powder and ball."[54] Their leader, Charles Robinson, issued the following manifest: "The people in this community called settlers, and others who are friends of justice and humanity [...] have determined to disregard all decisions of our courts in land cases, and all summonses or executions by the sheriff, constable, or other officer of the present county or city touching this matter. They will regard the said officers as private citizens."[55] On August 14, 1850, the armed squatters assembled and walked down to the contested area and intended to liberate imprisoned members of their association. Mayor and Sheriff mobilized their troops and the Squatter Riots began when city officials and settlers opened fire on each other. Four people died.

Since the American Revolution it had become much more difficult to justify inequality and the absence of reciprocity. The Revolution philosophically and legally promised equal opportunities to everybody. Gold seekers had taken this promise seriously and were convinced that, in the newly acquired part of the country, there shouldn't be any private prerogatives that would restrict the access for others who wanted to build up an exis-

---

require the land to be surveyed or fenced, but leaving it for longer than three months constituted abandonment and the forfeiture of all rights."
[51] One is tempted to think of 2007 ...
[52] Pisani, Donald J. (1994), p. 281
[53] Hurtado, Albert L. (2006), p. 283
[54] Royce, Josiah (1898), p. 339
[55] Id., p. 335

tence. "[…] the American newcomers were, in a goodly proportion of the cases, men from the regions of our Middle West, where land ownership had very generally been determined either directly by settlement, or through conformity to easily comprehensible general laws. […] the settlers in California were ill-prepared to be patient with the Californian laws, and with mysterious sources of land ownership. To add to the confusion of men's ideas, the lands of the gold region were, in general, actually free to all. […] They were […] public lands of the United States."[56] "[…] the right to squat on vacant land had come to seem to them traditional and inalienable."[57] "The uncertainties of land ownership irritated and frustrated the American settlers most of all. They had come to the new territory assuming that its acres would be as open to homesteading as other territorial lands west of the Mississippi, but they soon found that the best land was already claimed by earlier Mexican or American settlers and that the American government was prepared to recognize these prior claims."[58] The old conflict between land-aristocracy and the poor was repeated here, not justifiable anymore in a world oriented toward the democratic ideal of equal opportunities. Hence, the resentment of many a people against the capitalistic development toward important, even enormous private fortunes and the increasing privatization of what before was common ground and assets. "Many political thinkers of the second quarter of the nineteenth century regarded the monopolization of money, natural resources, goods, and services as a perversion of law and government by self-serving elites. It was not the natural or inevitable by-product of a nascent market economy."[59] For John Morse, writing in 1851, social instability is the result of the philosophy "to make the most money in the shortest possible time, out of the least capital, and with perfect indifference to the consequences so far as the State was concerned; and also without any very fastidious notions of honor or propriety."[60]

In the aftermath of the riots, people realized that an elementary consensus was needed, that they had to develop an integrative community project if a peaceful life in Sacramento was intended. It had become apparent that the confrontational mode was too costly. The outbreak of a cholera epidemic further motivated them to overcome the schism that had limited the city's potential. Also, the Gold Rush had ended in 1850. Easily accessible gold was gone, which is why many of the miners who hadn't the money

---

[56] *Id.*, p. 300
[57] *Id.*, p. 307
[58] Valentine, Alan (1956), pp. 17 f.
[59] Pisani, Donald J. (1994), p. 284
[60] Cited in Eifler, Mark A. (2002), p. 197

to seek for gold in a industrialized way, had to look for alternatives. They became shopkeepers, merchants, or craftsmen and, in this way, paid the debts they had accumulated for travel and their stay in California. The efforts of the land speculators "to use Sacramento as a speculative enterprise eventually gave way to a more welcoming attitude toward newcomers. Land and settlement in Sacramento needed to be opened, not restricted to the profiteering motives of a relative few."[61] Speculators as well as Squatters had generally lost their authority, which is why the middle-class became the leading force.

ee) Upper class violence

It is justice that leads to an effective monopoly of violence. The ones in power who do not recognize and respect "their subjects", who obviously favor one fringe of the community won't last. Upper class vigilantism in San Francisco is another example of power abuse based on selfish class interests. They wanted to take the shortcut to wealth, getting rid of everyone and everything hindering them. Samuel Brannan was the typical homo oeconomicus: Selfish, greedy, and focused on immediate success. He was born in Maine in 1819, son of an Irish immigrant, and became member of the Church of Jesus Christ of Latter-day Saints (Mormons) in 1842. When in 1844, their leader Joseph Smith got killed, they decided to flee from the persecution they had had to endure in the East and Midwest. In 1846, Brannan was commissioned by the church to lead a contingent of 224 members around Cape Horn to California. The community hoped to create a Mormon state in the northern territories of Mexico, in a free land beyond the jurisdiction of the United States. Brannan set up a covenant that guaranteed him a nice return on his investment.[62] In July 1846 they arrived in Yerba Buena (San Francisco), tripling the population of the mission. Not out to make money but to create a new home, the social and economic structure of the community was sound and played an important role in the future development of California: "The Mormons brought to California, at a critical point in its development, social solidarity and much-needed manual skills as sawyers, carpenters, millwrights, farmers, and irrigationists."[63] In 1847, the overland expedition under their leader Brigham Young joined them. Young, though, favored the isolation of the Rocky Mountains to Cali-

---

[61] Avella, Steven M. (2003), p. 38
[62] Eifler, Mark A. (2002), pp. 41 ff.
[63] Starr, Kevin (2005), p. 77

fornia, because he feared being dominated soon by the Gentiles (the non-believers). That's why the majority of the church went to the area of today's Utah and founded Salt Lake City. Brannan had to chose between religious conviction or business and, staying in San Francisco, opted for the latter. He established the California Star, the first newspaper and became one of the wealthiest men in California, thanks to land speculation and the building of stores selling goods to the miners in San Francisco, as well as in Sacramento, the city he founded with Sutter Jr. "From the start, the Star was an organ of protest against what its publisher considered the tyranny of the military government."[64] Not interested in the common good, power-broker Brannan used his media influence to discredit people he didn't like or who dared oppose him. Because of his lack in community interests, the Mormons disfellowshiped Brannan in 1951 "due to his personal sins, general apostasy, and leadership of vigilante movements in Sacramento and San Francisco."[65]

On February 19, 1851, merchant C.J. Jansen was beaten and robbed in his shop. Samuel Brannan, an experienced demagogue, seized the opportunity and effectively incited a popular outcry. "The press seized upon the case to trumpet a litany of all that was wrong with the justice system."[66] The Star, the Herald, the Alta California, and the Courier launched a campaign – "inflammatory urgings"[67] – calling for severe reactions: "Something must be done to strike terror into the hearts of the miscreants."[68] Looking for perpetrators to satisfy the stirred up anger, two Australian men were seized. Still recovering Jansen had to be roused to consciousness and hesitantly "recognized" his assailants after having seen them "for barely a minute by the dim light of a single candle burning in a large room."[69] By chance the Washington Guard (a militia unit) was able to save the two allegedly culpable from being lynched. Nevertheless, Brannan tried everything to hang the suspects, but the following extralegal "people's court" came to a hung jury of nine to three result, which is why the accused were turned over to the regular authorities. The district court convicted both men to several years of imprisonment. Latter it was found that they were innocent.

The outcry instigated on the occasion of the attack on Jansen wasn't due to an extraordinary high crime rate, but to the social status of the victim. The establishment felt threatened and wanted to send a clear message to

---

[64] Mullen, Kevin J. (1989), p. 19
[65] Eifler, Mark A. (2002), p. 47
[66] Mullen, Kevin J. (1989), p. 123
[67] Stewart, George R. (1964), p. 16
[68] Id., p. 8
[69] Id., p. 11

uphold and strengthen the social distinctions: He was "a solid citizen ... and other solid citizens immediately began to think 'I might have been the victim.'"[70] With this hunt for scapegoats[71] they claimed their leading role in the emerging society and hoped to divert the attention from economic problems. They chose a group of immigrants, the Australians, who were arriving in important numbers in California, and declared them a great threat to the settled community. Using the construction-power of the press, they built up cultural violence against a group of people, so that, "by 1851, 'Australian' was virtually synonymous with 'criminal.'"[72] When, on May 4, 1851, in San Francisco the fifth and greatest fire occurred, Brannan called for a meeting of citizens ready to fight criminality, and the Committee of Vigilance of 1851 was born. "Without any doubt, the 1851 vigilance committee was a businessmen's club,"[73] a "mercantile cooperation."[74] About one hundred San Franciscans were members of the Committee, when John Jenkins got caught after having stolen a small safe in a merchant's store. He was immediately tried and hanged. In the aftermath, more and more "influential men" became Committee members: Merchants, bankers, real estate operators, and shipmasters. Common workmen were accepted, but couldn't take a seat in the Executive Committee, which was the central power. The hundred-man vigilante police force was active on land and on the water. Till September 1851, the committee made about 90 arrests, hanged four, whipped one man, sentenced 28 to deportation, handed 15 over to the authorities for trial and released 41. The effect of the vigilante movement on criminality is contested because the decrease in criminal acts after its installment can also be attributed to the seasonal fluctuation of large numbers of people going back to the mines in summer. But this large and powerful mobilization of people had most probably a short-term influence on behavior which is now clearly and fast sanctioned. "[…] jail escapes declined after the rise of the committee. With a determined group outside the walls waiting for any excuse to hang them without observing the niceties of the law, the inmates no doubt made the observation that they were safer in jail."[75] Volunteer activities by the committee ended soon because institutionalization wasn't intended and their members had more rewarding business to

---

[70] Id., p. 7
[71] Senkewicz, Robert M. (1985), p. 82: "[…] merchants were groping toward a scapegoat."
[72] Id., p. 79. See also p. 75.
[73] Id., p. 86
[74] Id., p. 72
[75] Mullen, Kevin J. (1989), p. 175

do. In the long run, however, this business corporation didn't have an influence on crime rates. In 1852 crime was back on the level of the Gold Rush period, without, though, leading to the re-mobilization of the Committee. Their political and economic goals had been achieved thanks to the criminalization and prosecution of selected victims.

The vigilantes were much more than a law and order movement to protect the community. As a group of upper class members they tried to gain hegemony in the developing society of California. It's not the common good, universal democracy, or justice they were fighting for. But for their material interests,[76] for their social and economic privilege not to be infringed by competitors of the same social status or the lower classes. Racial criteria also played an important part in this collective identity-construction, as "vigilance committees were more concerned with punishing wrongs done to Anglo Americans than wrongs done by them, especially wrongs done by them to non-Anglo Americans."[77] The wealthy were ready to use every means possible to make sure the would remain in a good position. The class-character of vigilantism becomes evident when we have a look at the case of Robert Waterman, captain of the clipper ship Challenge. The shipping company, N.L. & G. Griswold, promised him a bonus of $10'000 if he managed to sail in record time from New York to San Francisco. To achieve this exploit, he and his first mate Douglas abused their power, wounded crew members, and Douglas killed at least one sailor. Back in San Francisco after 108 days on sea, boatmen, sailors, and dock workers spread news about the evens that had taken place on the boat, which is why many a people wanted to hang both men. However, because the two had vigorously fought, injured, and put to death for the interests of the entrepreneurs, the vigilantes protected the perpetrators. "It was the merchant/shipmaster establishment that prevailed again – the establishment that founded San Francisco, that framed its first laws, that abandoned the law and imposed summary rule when its interests seemed in danger, and […] that mobilized to support the agents of the law again when it suited the welfare of its own adherents."[78] No complaint was filed against Waterman, and an inquiry exonerated him,[79] while Douglas was convicted of murder, but as it seems not executed. In this capitalistic world, more than sixty years were needed to

---

[76] According to Mullen, "trade […] preceded the flag" (Mullen, Kevin J. [1989], p. 240). "From the first they opposed governmental controls of any type, and damned the public weal."

[77] Lee Johnson, Susan (2001), p. 321

[78] Mullen, Kevin J. (1989), p. 219

[79] New York City WPA Writer's Project (2004), p. 150

establish regulations that were in favor of the workers on the ships (Seamen's Act of 1915), protecting their interests, and trying to avoid working conditions on what were frequently referred to as "hellships."

The executive committee of the Vigilantes of 1856 was again a Businessman's Revolution, although this time it was directed against elected politicians they wanted to replace with some of their own. Following the successful procedure, they first constructed the threat of overwhelming criminality. Second, a concrete crime had to be exploited to demonstrate strength and effectiveness. On May 14, 1856, county supervisor James Casey shot publisher James King. King had written in his pugnacious journal a devastating personal attack against Casey, criticizing his corrupt practices. Led by William Coleman, around 2'500 well-drilled vigilantes armed with rifles and bayonets, seized the opportunity and captured Casey and Charles Gora, who had allegedly killed William Richardson, U.S. Marshal for the Northern District. Governor Neely Johnson and William Sherman, major-general of the California militia, tried to convince Coleman to respect the regular procedure and guaranteed the execution of Casey, would he be convicted. The vigilantes, however, refused, because they were eager to make use of this opportunity of symbolic politic. A cannon was brought to the building where Casey and Gora were imprisoned and the regular forces were coerced to hand over the accused. In the vigilantes' headquarters the executive committee judged them guilty and hanged them on May 22, 1856. Having gained attention and political drive, the vigilantes attempted to remove the current city and county officers, but they had to conceal their intentions so as not to lose the support of the public: "The members of the executive committee feared that if their political purposes became known, they would lose the considerable backing they expected to maintain so long as they themselves remained publicly 'non-partisan.'"[80] A sort of civil war ensued between the regular forces and the vigilantes. Governor Neely Johnson declared on June 2, 1856, the state of insurrection in the city of San Francisco and ordered Sherman to deploy his troops. Lacking money, the major-general couldn't mobilize enough militia members and weapons and resigned.[81] The vigilantes were also short of resources. Even though they had a government, a police, a court and an intelligence system, and even though they seized the government of the city and declared Governor J. Neely Johnson as deposed, they too had problems to keep up their effectivity, as the thousands of men had to be paid, facilities maintained, and

---

[80] Senkewicz, Robert M. (1985), p. 183
[81] Beck, Warren A./Williams, David A. (1972), p. 176

the motivation was difficult to upheld over time. Long-lasting effects need organizational skills, personal knowledge, financial resources, and the consensus of the people to provide these funds.

The leader of the vigilantes moved the fight from the military to the political field, forming the People's Party. In the city elections of November 1856, the party won most of the offices and stayed in power for the next 10 years. "Its primary objective was drastic tax reduction."[82] The Party still pretended being disinterested, just serving the public.[83] But the people they fought against always were Democrats.[84]

One of the favorite narratives of the upper class is the anarchic underclass mob that has to be reined in by a sensible and reflective elite. Stability and prosperity, so the story goes, are guaranteed by the rational, educated wealthy people, who make sure that the society works. For Valentine, for example, the vigilantes were the protectors of San Francisco against the "law of the jungle, working its way painfully back to law and order. [...] The citizens of San Francisco in the 1850s were fighting not only an invasion of criminals from without, but an inner social corruption born of their own earlier indifference to their social responsibilities."[85] "[...] one must give them credit for a unique nobility of motive and restraint."[86] In my view, though, selfishness, illegality, or violence are not linked to class, but to the basic values and forms of action people think are important. Not the common good, but personal wealth motivated Samuel Brannan, "who did more than anyone else to instigate vigilantism in San Francisco" and built up "the first great California fortune in money that he had diverted from church property and tithes to his personal use and profit."[87] Using violence to achieve economic goals seemed to be a character trait of the time, used independent of social or economic background. "Some of these practitioners [Sutter's agents and business associates], like Sam Brannan, ... wore the mask of Puritanism and of patriotism to wage war upon the small-fry bandits and were themselves wholesale robbers and despoilers of the law."[88] Sacramento and Sutterville fiercely competed for the role of the most important city in the area, which is what led Brannan and the Sacramento merchants to destroy McDougal's

---

[82] Bean, Walton E. (1978), p. 130
[83] Senkewicz, Robert M. (1985), p. 190
[84] Beck, Warren A./Williams, David A. (1972), p. 178
[85] Valentine, Alan (1956), p. VIII
[86] Id., p. IX
[87] Bean, Walton E. (1978), p. 120
[88] Zollinger, James P. (1939), p. 307

stock of goods, the leading merchant of Sutterville. Thus, what took place in California was much more a free-for-all battle than the building up of a community. The more social inequality increased, the more the fight took place along class distinctions. Capitalism in the sense of enhanced material greed had no civilizing effect on people,[89] on the contrary. The Spanish, the Mexicans, and then the Americans brought lawlessness into the West, where, before, anarchy had had an integrative effect over millennia. *It is not the savages who were civilized. It is the savage civilized who brought chaos into a fairly organized world that knew and defended the common good.*

ff) A culture of non-violence

The so-called "Wild West" is the result of a fast growing number of homines economici meeting by chance, without any concept of a shared future. This highly violent culture was not inevitable, it was not a natural part of community-developments to be seen elsewhere. Canada for instance, where immigrants developed at the same time economic and political structures, didn't now these exactions.[90] Besides vigilantism, lynching was a widely practiced form of violence, also used to secure the prerogatives of one group over another. This time, though, the Whites united against the Natives, African Americans, Chinese or Latinos. These groups "constituted the majority of cases of lynchings and extrajudicial executions in California."[91] Anglo-Americans or Europeans were also hanged. But Blacks, Latinos, Asians, or Natives were lynched in a disproportionally high number.[92] Lynchings, however, shouldn't be "mischaracterized as an inevitable consequence of Western expansion."[93] It was a tool to protect the wealthy against claims of the underclass by using scapegoat politics. Killing the outsiders helped to attenuate the anger of the white underclass, highlighting the common ground unifying the Whites, their race. Newmark stressed the use of lynching for the "better classes:" "While upon the subject of lynching, I wish to observe that I have witnessed many such distressing affairs in Los Angeles; and that, though the penalty of hanging was sometimes too severe for the crime (and I have always deplored, as much as any of us ever did, the administration of mob-justice) yet the safety of the better classes in

---

[89] Pisani, Donald J. (1994), p. 307, 305
[90] Stewart, George R. (1964), p. 14
[91] Gonzales-Day, Ken (2006), p. 14
[92] *Id.*, pp. 26 f.
[93] *Id.*, p. 39

those troublous times often demanded quick and determined action, and stern necessity knew no law."[94] Lynching helped integrate the Whites because they all became part of the killing and were, therefore, jointly responsible. It also gave the perpetrators and the supportive public the comforting feeling of controlling the fast changing world. The mass mobilization was intended to justify the violence: "News reports of executions tended to point out that many women and children had attended, presumably because their presence contributed both to the sense of public spectacle and to the social legitimacy of the event."[95] Public displays of violence further pursued the goal of behavior control. "[...] most public lynchings resembled modern theatrical entertainment. The style of new, sensational journalism at the turn of the century exploited the violence by paying lurid attention to the pain and suffering of both the violated white woman and the lynching victim."[96] This show of power intended to intimidate excluded minorities, to demonstrate that nothing was certain for them, that the rulers could hit however, whenever, and wherever they wanted. To know that at any moment one's life was at risk, disciplined the potential victims,[97] made them renounce their claim for justice.

A non-violent culture develops forms of communication and conflict resolution that provide for the majority of its members recognition, respect, and reciprocity. To renounce direct violence is part of the deal. *One gives up power to get power.* Instead of using direct violence, equal opportunities to take part in the construction process have to be established. It is within a cooperative arrangement of "reality"-builders that people will be willing to support the community project. Justification by arguments becomes the core element of communication in a culture of debates instead of violent oppression. If the conflicting parties aren't able to solve the problem themselves, third-party intervention has to take place. This may take the form of mediation, arbitration, or of a state court. The court's decision has to be abided by, and self-justice excluded. Formalized conflict resolutions based on law are established by the people themselves or the parliament they have elected. Administration and courts apply the rules adopted by the majority and decide over the conflicts assigned to them. To make this effective, the members of the community have to agree on the basic values, have to be educated to understand and accept the conflict mechanisms, and have

---

[94] Newmark, Harris (1916), p. 141
[95] Wood, Amy Louise (2009), p. 33
[96] *Id.*, p. 10
[97] *Id.*, p. 2. In the South, "execution days were mass spectacles that made very evident the stat's and the church's authority" (p. 27).

to have the experience that, within this arrangement, their needs and their dignity are respected.

A monopoly of violence is, therefore, much more than just a political decision. Economic interests aren't enough either. *To renounce violence and to entrust with its use to a few, becomes possible with people ready to commit themselves for the common good.* It is the women coming to California who made this engagement possible.[98] It is thanks to them that a community built on responsibility developed and the homo oeconomicus could be overcome. Churches, synagogues, and schools are the symbols of the moral ground originating reciprocity, mutual obligation and restraint. *Effective state power follows cultural integration*: "[…] the ordering processes that occurred on cultural ground in post-gold rush San Francisco were every bit as far-reaching, profound, and integral to nation-making as the military and political conquest of the late 1840s."[99] It took the European Americans decades to establish a common interest and identity (see p. 146 ff.), and, thus, to establish consented state institutions. Not a comprehensively just society was constructed, as big minority groups were excluded, killed in wars, aggressed, and sexually abused (see pp. 371 ff.).[100] But just enough to make the majority feel at home.

b) Interactive construction of the state – consented state power

States do not have to be. There is no anthropological inevitability to states. States are constructed to attain specific goals, to fulfill particular interests. Whatever communities define as "state," it is just a form of organization, helpful or dangerous, effective or useless and exceedingly costly. There are some who criticize the state for being responsible for everything negative. Others, in turn, are convinced that the state is the savior of all our problems. From the point of view of an interactive construction of institutions, "the state" is nothing more than the product of people and is dependent on them and their engagement.

---

[98] Starr, Kevin (2005), p. 88, 109
[99] Berglund, Barbara (2007), p. 15
[100] Lee Johnson, Susan (2001), pp. 234, 239, 298 f.

aa)   Anarchy – valuable alternative

> "I am convinced that those societies (as the Indians) which live without government, enjoy in their general mass an infinitely greater degree of happiness than those who live under the European governments. Among the former, public opinion is in the place of law, and restrains morals as powerfully as laws ever did anywhere. Among the latter, under pretense of governing, they have divided their nations into two classes, wolves and sheep. I do not exaggerate ... Experience declares that man is the only animal which devours his own kind; for I can apply no milder term to the governments of Europe, and to the general prey of the rich on the poor."[101]

The area called "California" had been home to Native Americans for thousands of years. Many different tribes, belonging to more than twenty linguistic families (including around 135 languages), had lived here. It is estimated that in the end of the 18th century about 300'000 dwelled in Alta California. Natives didn't build up a centralized power in the form of what is called a "state." Nevertheless, they lived for millennia in a democratic way with a pronounced reciprocal structure. Large-scale political organizations oriented around a central power weren't known. Contrary to the expectations of Hobbes, these communities lived over tens of thousands of years without decimating each other. For most of the existence of human beings there wasn't any Leviathan controlling anti-social individuals. Hunter-gatherers lived in anarchy: There was no leader, no institutionalized domination, no segmentation.[102] "Conflicts […] are solved in self-regulated processes, most of the time by reaching consensus."[103] The amount and the form of warfare depended on the communities' culture. But, in general, the conflicts were not destructive like the ones Europeans had invented. Armed conflicts were regulated and were limited in their impact on people. There were no professional armies and there was no interest in overthrowing or eradicating the other conflict party. "The natives waged short raids intended to kill a few warriors, take some captives, and humiliate a rival, then beat a hasty retreat homeward to celebrate. […] To conquer a land, Europeans fought for years and even decades, with the massacre of entire villages and cities a standard technique meant to intimidate others into surrender. The English mode of total war introduced by the colonists shocked the Indians of Virginia as

---

[101] Jefferson, Thomas (1903 [1787]), p. ME 6:58
[102] Luig, Ute (1990), p. 83
[103] Wesel, Uwe (1985), p. 29

pointless and wasteful."[104] If chiefs were provided with some prerogatives, reciprocity rules obliged them to use their power and wealth to strengthen the integration of the community. They had to develop a network "that gathered and redistributed tribute."[105] Moreover, they couldn't rely on their authority to push through a decision.[106] Giving orientation and convincing the community to take a specific decision was possible only, if the chief listened, recognized, and respected the statements of the others and if he was an outstanding personality. This reciprocal structure is, for example, to be found with the Siuai of Bougainville Island. Their chief is called "Big Man" and becomes "big" because he is more than others "ambitious, industrious, skilled at many tasks, and good, meaning generous, cooperative, genial, and decent. A Big Man's authority is largely the natural result of his being able to run a successful enterprise."[107] Integration happens by motivating people to work for the chief, guaranteeing that their part of the surplus will be distributed on the occasion of one of the big feasts. By this redistribution of the accumulated wealth, a generalized and balanced reciprocity[108] takes place. The more people the Big Man can win over to work on his team, the bigger and more stable the network he is able to develop. He keeps loyal adherents as long as he keeps up his reputation as "big provider." The central element of his power is the amount of commodities and comestibles he gives away.[109] According to Kohl, societies of several hundred thousands members are known having existed in this acephalous way, without any institution that could use physical force on its members. What motivated the individuals to stay together was the common project, the economic rule to share what has been produced, and the principle to avoid too big a social inequality.[110] Aware that wholesome integration is only possible if people are recognized economically, the hunter-gatherers guaranteed "[…] direct access of all members to the primal resources like water, land, and food."[111] The Natives' understanding of property is fundamentally an inclusive communal concept, not an individual and exclusive one.

Native people differentiate from the modern world also by their relative modesty. Human life is perceived as part of nature, adapting to the

---

[104] Taylor, Alan (2001), p. 127
[105] *Id.*, p. 126
[106] Kohl, Karl-Heinz (2000), p. 54
[107] Moore, Alexander (1998), p. 265
[108] *Id.*, pp. 263 f.
[109] Harris, Marvin (1978), pp. 104 f.
[110] Kohl, Karl-Heinz (2000), p. 57
[111] Luig, Ute (1990), p. 84

environment and not intending to dominate and change it. Nature is understood as a well ordained set of existences, that lived in harmony and were made for each other.[112] Over the millennia they had developed a lifestyle adapted to their environment, living "by a complex and seasonally shifting mix of hunting and gathering that made the most of their abundant environment."[113] Unfortunately their pre-ecological cooperation with nature, their autonomous subsistence strategies decayed because of forced colonization by Europeans. As a result, "the newcomers distressed the California environment."[114] Natives seemed to have a much higher quality of life than the so called "civilized" Europeans. Dutch columnist Nicolaes von Wassenaer (1571-1630) wrote after his first encounter with Native Americans: "It is somewhat strange that among these most barbarous people, there are few or non cross-eyed, blind, crippled, lame, hunch-backed or limping men; all are well-fashioned people, strong, and sound of body, well fed, without blemish."[115] Others were astonished to note that "there are among them no simpletons, lunatics or madmen as among us."[116]

For Henry D. Thoreau, freedom had two meanings: Absence of authoritarian centralized state power and freedom from material greed. Dominant materialism as an ideology that makes the human being unfree and unhappy is not having the time to enjoy relationships free of an instrumentalist focus, as in "he has no time to be any thing but a machine."[117] "Most of the luxuries, and many of the so called comforts of life, are not only not indispensable, but positive hindrances to the elevation of mankind."[118] Besides these economic and social restrictions he refuted political constraints: "[…] government is best which governs not at all."[119] He didn't advocate rulelessness, but questioned authoritarian power-arrangements. "Anarchy," therefore, doesn't stand for chaos nor for a battleground on which everyone fights everyone else, but for a self-regulated community, within which individual autonomy, mutual obligation, and reciprocity play the central integrative role.[120] Thoreau points out autonomy when he writes that "the mass of men serve the State thus, not as men mainly, but as machines, with their bod-

---

[112] Debo, Angie (1970), p. 3
[113] Taylor, Alan (2001), p. 455
[114] *Id.*, p. 462
[115] Quoted in Eisen, George (1977), p. 192
[116] Burrows, Edwin G./Wallace, Mike (1999), p. 11
[117] Thoreau, Henry D. (2008), p. 7
[118] *Id.*, p. 13
[119] *Id.*, p. 227
[120] Degen, Hans-Jürgen (1987), p. 25; Wesel, Uwe (1985), pp. 86 f.

ies. [...] In most cases there is not free exercise whatever of the judgment or of the moral sense."[121] "I think that we should be men first, and subjects afterward. [...] The only obligation which I have a right to assume, is to do at any time what I think right."[122] Anarchy is a strong statement in favor of freedom, not in the liberal sense, but combined with social obligations and responsibility – a *socially embedded freedom*. Interestingly, modern society is much more fascinated with "freedom" than native people were. This was possibly because freedom was less in danger than today since there wasn't any central state power, unduly wealthy people, or big companies trying to influence society and politics according to their interests. Did we possibly loose freedom by building up institutions that are supposed to secure freedom? The more institutions with an increasing amount of power are built up, the more the idea of freedom as a corrective becomes important.

bb) Institutions – interactions in reproduction phase, routine

To take responsible freedom seriously means to attribute "reality" to interacting individuals. That also holds true for institutions, which, against the backdrop of consensus-based constructivism, aren't objects by themselves or entities that individuals have to cope with. The term "institution" stands for

- *relationships*, for social arrangements which
- have been *reproduced over time*, are supposed to
- *perpetuate* a
- *particular performance* for the community, and are
- *secured by a set of norms and sanctions*.

A community convinced about the positive effects of a social arrangement tries to reproduce it, tries to make sure that its performance is available in the future. What has been built up with engagement in negotiations and has incurred construction costs but has yielded valued outcomes, shall be preserved for the future. Institutions like family, school, state, church, police, army, parties, or the media consist of a set of *expected generalized behavior* called *roles*, which are standardized[123] to guarantee long-term validity independent of particular individuals. "Roles" unfold their intended effects

---

[121] Thoreau, Henry D. (2008), p. 229
[122] *Id.*, p. 228
[123] Berger, Peter L./Luckmann, Thomas (1980), pp. 78 f.; Parsons, Talcott (1986), p. 188

only under distinct circumstances. The role of the judge isn't played in the swimming pool and, to be successful in trials, the court procedures have to be precisely respected. If elected, a former actor becomes president of the United States and has to play a totally different role with much more power and constraints than in Hollywood (even though both "realities" have some similarities). To make sure that their stabilizing effects can occur and be preserved, relatively strict procedures and a set of rules and sanctions are established.

Routinized reproduction eases the burden of thinking through all the details of a decision and makes decisions more effective and stabilizes our existence.[124] As standardizations they enhance predictability. The more often institutional behavior is reproduced, the less it is questioned, the more people take institutions for granted,[125] and the more these relationships achieve the status of natural law.[126] Routinized actions have a tendency to acquire objectivity[127] and, over the years or even generations, they get reified, seeming to be chiseled in stone and perceived as objects, independent of individual actions. At this stage, routine becomes a risk for freedom and responsibility because the institutions are increasingly withdrawn from critical questions. According to Nietzsche there is, however, a danger to presume that categories which are useful for some are also true, of a higher quality, justified by their sole existence.[128] The original construction process, as well as its permanent reproduction, are blinded out and become visible again only when dissent occurs, when the institution's validity is questioned. Not to discuss the content of judicial or administrative decisions or the decisions of companies because they followed the rules, reduces individuals to followers and opens the door to atrocities. That is the way totalitarianism is established. Not to think about the content, the values we are creating, but only trying to function smoothly, supports unreflected power-politics. Our own responsibility for everyday's "reality" construction is denied.[129]

---

[124] Sennett points out, that routine has as much a positive effect on individuals, as it can have a corrosive impact on the character: "Routine can demean, but it can also protect; routine can decompose labor, but it can also compose a life" (Sennett, Richard [1998], p. 43).

[125] Jepperson, Ronald L. (1991), p. 147, 149; Wittgenstein, Ludwig (1992), pp. 46 f.

[126] Meyer, John W./Rowan, Brian (1991), p. 42

[127] Laing, Ronald D. (1969), p. 69; Simmel, Georg (1992), pp. 556 f., 858; Sofsky, Wolfgang/Paris, Rainer (1994), p. 12; Peters, Bernhard (1993), pp. 317, 346

[128] Nietzsche, Friedrich (1996), pp. 350 f.

[129] Benasayag, Miguel/Sztulwark, Diego (2000), p. 25

The state as an institution originates in the actions of individuals and may break down any time because of a lack of support. The same can be said about the monopoly of violence or the *separation* of state and society. According to the constitutive contribution every individual makes to the existence of state and society, the liberal schism between a bad state and a good society doesn't make sense. This concept is based on a fundamentally free society, on the one hand, and the liberty-threatening state on the other, with both understood as ontological entities.[130] In my opinion, this schism stems from the conflict between monarchy and the upcoming bourgeoisie that is eager to get at least a part of the power. The state was qualified as the enemy because it excluded people based on immutable hereditary principles, it excluded the steadily becoming richer class of traders and industrialists. It is, therefore, a political concept that serves specific interests and not an unquestionable given. The concept of civil society, identified as a free, democratic meeting of individuals, applies the same ontological differences. Civil society is then understood as neither state nor economy, as a somehow pure and perfect form of human community, not affected by greed or power.[131] But then, where do greed and power come from? Who invented them? And why are there some pure and some bad existences? Is it possible to change the bad people responsible for the economy and politics or are they lost forever? The separation of state and society or the separation of civil society and the state and economy portrays the state and economy as impenetrable entities threatening the born free individual. Most of the time, though, at least for the homo interactivus, the ones who are important in the economy or in society have their say in state affairs – and vice versa. Everyone also contributes with her or his quotidian support to the existence of the current state and economy. Not to resist means to build up and keep alive what for now exists. To postulate the objective separation of these different spheres helps the ones who are active in all of them hide their influence and negate responsibility. Or it gives the possibility to blame *the* state or *the* economy for everything that doesn't work. Another threat for responsibility and freedom is to be found in the *identification of state and society*. Fascism, soviet and other communism, anti-communism, or the war against terrorism – in all these cases the collective preponderates

---

[130] See for example Köbl, Wolfgang (2006); Mayer-Tasch, Peter Cornelius (1991), p. 92, 105, 216; Tschannen, Pierre (1995), p. 303; Pernthaler, Peter (1996), pp. 69 ff.; Böckenförde, Ernst-Wolfgang (1992), p. 209-243.

[131] Habermas, Jürgen (1992a), p. 445; Habermas, Jürgen (1990), p. 46; Honneth, Axel (1994), pp. 83 f.; Matjan, Gregor (1998), p. 292

over the individual, which is reduced to a servant. The individual has to be sacrificed for the bigger interest, if necessary.

In my view, there is no ontological difference between the state, economy, and (civil) society. We should debate the repartition of power,[132] exclusion/inclusion-mechanisms, and the question of how much construction power every individual gets. Where and how do we construct minorities, what are their rights and possibilities to protect their "realities" against the majority, and do minorities have any chance to win over the majority for their interests? These questions have to be discussed not only according to the state, but also according to the economy, the society, to the cultural production of identity, and in the realm of religion.[133] Giddens points out, that the separation of state and civil society is the most important accomplishment of liberal democracy.[134] It seems to me, however, that the most important criteria should be the interactive individuals who are responsible for the "reality" they construct. Against this background of a comprehensively political community,[135] it is much easier to discuss integration processes and in-/exclusion-mechanisms and the dreadful effects of denied recognition.

cc) State actors – commissioned and lent power

> "The President so fully represents his party, which secures political power by its promises to the people, and the whole government is so identified in the minds of the people with his personality that they are inclined to make him responsible for all the sins of omission and of commission of society at large. [...] The President cannot make clouds to rain and cannot make the corn to grow, he cannot make business good; although when these things occur, political parties do claim some credit for the good things that have happened in this way."[136]

Building up state power and the states monopoly of violence needs time, a lot of conviction, and the readiness of people to accept the loss of a part of their personal power. The drafting of legal rules is done quite easily. To un-

---

[132] Lietzmann, Hans (1994), p. 101
[133] According to Seiler, Hansjörg (1994), pp. 216 f., the power repartition of all societal systems has critically to be checked.
[134] Giddens, Anthony (1997), p. 164
[135] Castoriadis, Cornelius (1990), p. 87, speaks of a "truly political society".
[136] Taft, William Howard (1916), p. 52. Taft was pleased about this lack of (federal) power, defending the states' autonomy and their knowledge about local problems.

derpin and accompany critically these rules by an ethical and moral structure has to be established that can't be decreed. Cultural integration work is needed that takes time. People have to be convinced of the advantages that the restriction they are enduring yields. If the arrangement is well done, the community members will gain something out of this cooperation. If badly organized, giving up power in favor of a small group of people can mean loss of life.

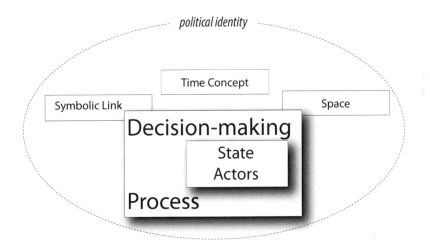

"The State" is only one, and not the decisive part, of a rich, always risky and creative integration process. Many decisions have to be taken and many people convinced before a group of individuals can be designated as "state actors" with defined competencies. To call somebody "president" doesn't make her or him a representative of the community. The power of the President will be accepted if this institution is part of a story that makes sense and is based on a shared set of values. Also, a community structure is needed that recognizes people in their everyday existence, culturally as well as economically. Further, the members have the possibility of influencing and, if necessary, recalling the president. *"State power" is delegated power, is commissioned power.* State power is also lent power, such as the power of the "senator," "policewoman," or "judge" that has to be used in the interests of the principals. Power is powerful as long as the elementary consensus isn't violated. The roles the state actors fulfill are a part of the decision-making process. Besides them, there are journalists, party members, lobbyists, priests, artists, CEO's, and many others who are influencing, creatively en-

riching, or blocking the decisions relevant for the community. State actors, though, are commissioned to solve problems in a basically determined way. They have to act according to the broad guidelines established in the constitution or the law. Nevertheless, there is a considerable leeway for making decisions and many of them will find their critics. But as long as the criticism doesn't impinge on the function itself, the state actor can go on deciding. If she doesn't listen to the opposition, she will, in the long run, be confronted with increasing counterpower and loose her ability to influence the "reality" construction.

Sometimes state actors are able to lead because the majority is willing to follow. Often, though, they have to react to the proposals of others and see if they can manage to reconcile the task they were commissioned for with the opposition raised. In consensus-based constructivism, it is always individuals who stand for and exercise state power. All the buildings, memorials, constitutions, museums, exhibitions, or parades symbolize and objectify the power generated by the elementary consensus and are attempts to make the power last. If serious doubts or distrust develops, the carefully built up arrangement crashes. The break of the Wall in 1989 and the revolutions in South Africa, Egypt, or Tunisia illustrate how much state power is provisionary and can break up at any moment.

The following factors play a decisive role in the establishment of institutions that have the power to integrate a community effectively, meaning that they are able to solve problems in a way that convinces most of the people over time:

- Guaranteeing recognition and respect within the political discourse (to be heard/to be different).

- Avoiding to big power imbalance.

- Securing the community's most important values.

- Acting predictably, being trustworthy, applying clear rules and simultaneously being responsive to individuals' need and differences.

- Taking care of the ideological and symbolic orientation of the community.

- Procuring support where needed.

c) Integration by law

The law doesn't like instability; it likes to *stabilize what is stable*. Revolutionary changes are per se anti-legal because you can't rule them. You do not control a revolution, you do not know the outcome of a revolution. Law gets into the game when an established consensus has to be reproduced and secured. That's why law can't guide a fundamental new construction or the construction of a community out of nothing. It is *during* the *new construction phase* that the interactors agree on certain legal rules. However, the law unfolds its integrative effects when the community is set up. In the *reproduction phase, law becomes an effective tool* to guide the actors and to secure important achievements (about the construction phases see pp. 64 ff.). The law, therefore, is conservative, it *preserves what is dear to the rulers*, be it a dictator or the democratic majority. Against a constructivist backdrop there is no innate content of law.

Rulers use law to enforce their worldview, which is why it is *directed against a minority*. For the ruling majority law stabilizes the present and tries to guarantee the future, whereas for the minority it is an authoritarian obstacle,[137] a source of restricted freedom, sufferance, and/or exclusion. In order to be controlled the minority has to be small, otherwise the legal staff[138] commissioned to apply the rules will be overwhelmed. The rulers may be the democratic majority, the economic oligarchy, or the dictatorial individual – all of them depend on the readiness of people to fulfill the legal expectations by themselves, to comply with the law out of personal conviction, satisfaction, convenience, or fear. Everything else is an overload the legal and the enforcement staff can't cope with. Legal rules are rarely directed against the majority. Civil rights law, for example, is a protection of the minority against the majority. This protection, however, becomes effective only if the majority is considerate enough to respect the minority's freedom. The ones in power have, first, to establish a norm and, second, to restrain themselves from violating the norms, and, third, to defend the norms against offenders.

---

[137] About the authoritarian side of law, see for example Coing, Helmut (1993), p. 218.
[138] Max Weber defines law as the rules protected by a set of people declared responsible (Weber, Max [1980], pp. 17 f.). There is a according to him a legal system as soon people are commissioned to apply the rules using means of coercion (Weber, Max [1960], p. 59, "Zwangsapparat").

aa) Stabilizing the stabilized

Law stabilizes communities if it

- helps to solve conflicts,
- supplies rules to structure interactions,
- symbolizes the community's most important "reality" elements, and
- supports managed adaptations of the governing rules.

All these functions only take place if the community has already developed an elementary consensus that is concretized in legal rules. Legal rules, therefore, become the symbol of the basic values and the forms of action the interactors agree upon. These rules do not belong to a higher order, or to a higher form of justification, like Ryffel seems to speak of as "over-positive destination."[139] He is convinced that law has to structure "the plastic human existence,"[140] representing an order that "has to become reality by all means."[141] Contrary to his ontological difference of law and politics, law is, in my constructivist point of view, *part of politics,* with no superior origin. *The law is, therefore, not defined by its content, but by its function,* the task the community decides to assign the legal staff. There is no innate sense of justice or freedom that defines law because *it simply reflects the interests of the current rulers.* "Opposition to slavery came from the public, not from judicial, executive, or legislative actions. Individual Americans, untutored in the fine points of constitutional law, viewed slavery as repugnant to fundamental political and legal principles [...]. The essential antislavery documents were private writings and speeches, not court decisions or legislative statutes."[142] Legal staff is commissioned to solve conflicts, to decide, who's right and who has to pay. They have to control the building of nuclear plants or private houses, to check if companies pay their taxes, if banks abstain from insider dealings, if parents bring their children to school. They have to prosecute people who infringed penal law and judge them. Legal staff organizes elections, amendments of the constitution, makes sure that the procedure is respected.

The more different forms of conflict resolution exist, the better the integrative effect because a varied approach to dissent may help find a way out. Parliament brings together the different factions to debate over the future in

---

[139] Ryffel, Hans (1978), pp. 518 f.
[140] Ryffel, Hans (1969), p. 161
[141] *Id.*, p. 169
[142] Fisher, Louis/Harriger, Katy J. (2011), pp. 764 f.

generalized terms. With the help of expert-commissions, of lobby-groups, of the media, and other information-generating actors, the elected representatives or senators try to reach a solution. Dependent on the political system, parliament as one form of conflict resolution has, for example, to count with the president's veto (USA), the sanction by the Supreme Court (BRD, F), or an intervention by the voters (CH). Courts and the administration try to find a solution for individual cases, have perhaps another understanding of freedom or justice, questioning and reopening by this the debate over the principles the law-makers fixed.

Legal actors aren't machines applying unambiguously determined norms. They are free individuals confronted with different problems. No conflict is identical with another, every conflict party brings in their own story. The legal staff has to find a compromise between the general-abstract norm representing the standardized expectations of the majority and the specific interests of the concerned subjects: A challenging creative process that shouldn't uncoil schematically. To generate a just solution, the interests of the community as well as the ones of the individual have to be taken into account. Both expectations have to be recognized and respected, even though, according to the principle of legality and democratic legitimization, the rulers' claim basically prevails. Thus, while legal actors are mainly reproducing accepted interpretations, they are also proposing new constructions. They can anticipate future conflicts and try to avoid them; they can develop unexpected alternatives the law-maker, for example, didn't think of. This wide scope of interpretation can be used as long as there is no serious opposition criticizing what has become law.

The effect of routinization and reification also affects the actions of the legal staff. Unchallenged reproduction strengthens the belief in the rightness of the rules, and over time, legal institutions become independent of the individual. It is at this stage that law is most effective: Reproduction runs smoothly and the legal guidelines fulfill their integrative function. As long as reproduction prevails and law is, therefore, used exclusively against individuals or powerless minorities, legal expectations are trustworthy during the integration mode of stabilization (see p. 64 ff.). As soon as criticism becomes intense and the rightness of legal activities are doubted or even distrusted, its integrative effect quickly decreases. Thus, *the law stabilizes a community during good weather periods, when a community is widely stabilized*, but becomes useless as soon as the specific institution is distrusted or the elementary consensus gets lost.

bb) Law-proposal

"Law" is man-made, it is action, it is somebody pretending that this action is "law". In consensus-based constructivism, law is a "reality" proposal that has to be consented to by a considerable majority. Otherwise, it doesn't have any effect, it is empty words. Attempts to eternalize legal rules serve to strengthen the validity of their claim and to exclude critics. Different forms of justification are then used to move responsibility toward extra-human instances. Referring to the eternal principles of nature, when the validity of natural law is claimed, referring to God, when divine right is invoked, referring to a century-old tradition, when common law is the basis of our decision – in all these cases, law-making is no longer a human decision. To make law means then: To recognize the objective truth of law,[143] to recognize what nature,[144] God, or the everlasting historical wisdom have decided in our stead. There is no room left for debates, and the ones able to recognize the truth become the priests everybody else has to follow. A similar concept is the sanctification of legal texts, so that there is just the one and only understanding of the scripture (see p. 400).

In my opinion the content of law is a proposal of, for example, a member of the legal staff. And it is the interaction of the legal staff and all the other participants of the decision-making process that decides what happens with this proposal and if it becomes the law. The same accounts for the idea of the state, for its role within society. People build their notion of the state and the law based on the currently relevant set of basic values and the concept of humankind.[145]

---

[143] See, for example, Höffe, Otfried (1990a), pp. 98, 115 f., 124; Höffe, Otfried (1990b), pp. 255 f.; Starck, Christian (1990), pp. 54 ff.

[144] Zippelius, Reinhold (1994), p. 105. For example, he describes as "natural" and, therefore, decisive the maternal instinct, the readiness to respect the possession of others, permanent pair bonding, and the respect of existing couples and of older group members (pp. 182 f.). Furthermore, if the natural sciences prove that we are not free, the lawmaker, according to Zippelius, will have to accept this verdict (p. 152). Contrary to his natural concept of values and law, the following authors see these social phenomena as the result of a construction process: Mead, Margaret (1992), p. 219, Janssen-Jurreit, Marielouise (1978), pp. 565 f.; Thurer, Shari (1995); Badinter, Elisabeth (1992); Farrell, Michèle (1990), pp. 112 f.; Wesel, Uwe (1985), p. 132; Olbricht, Ingrid (1993), pp. 259 f.

[145] With regard to the social contract states Kersting: "Describe the determining influence of nature and I tell you which is the state you are looking for" (Kersting, Wolfgang [1994], p. 327). And for Hofman, the definition of the original position decides on all other elements of the theory of contract (Hofmann, Hasso [1996], p. 16).

After the landslide victory of Franklin D. Roosevelt over Herbert Hoover in 1932 and the even more important defeat of the Republicans in the midterm elections of 1934, it became clear that the president had all the power on his side to realize his political intentions. Up to this point, freedom of contract and the protection of private property against the claims of workers was one of the core elements of the dominant worldview and, therefore, of the American legal order. Besides the intermezzo of the progressive era, during which a more just democracy was achieved, free-market ideology had prevailed in politics and in many Supreme Court cases. The state Roosevelt inherited had, compared to today, a few tasks. At the time of Calvin Coolidge (president from 1923–1929), for example, most of the employees of the federal government worked in the Post Office. Roosevelt had first to develop the tools that seemed necessary to him to react to the Great Depression.[146] Even though he could rely on developments that had taken place during the Progressive era, he had to improvise and find a non-ideological way out of this unprecedented crisis. Among other things, he gave up the highly venerated concept of fiscal orthodoxy.[147] "Until 1937 he experimented to solve a gaping incongruence between his goals and the limited powers and resources of the office. The consequence was a brilliant improvisation of policy experimentation, public appeals, prime ministerial leadership, and bargaining."[148]

Roosevelt and his party intended to fundamentally change the set of basic values relevant for American society. Justice in the sense of equal opportunities and construction power, solidarity, and responsibility became principles changing the concept of freedom, which up to this point was understood in a negative sense (see p. 136). First, people had to survive, and, second, they had to have the resources to use the freedom they formally were guaranteed. Consequently, they were the first to defend rigorously the interests not only of the owners of major companies, but also of the men and women in the street.[149] "'He was the only president who understood that my boss is a son-of-a-bitch,' said one workman. Millions of others thought the same." Already as governor of New York, he had been "the first [...] in the United States to establish state aid for unemployment relief," understanding it as "social duty."[150] Yet this champion of the poor, the greatest vote-winner in US history, had been raised in lonely splendor, the only child of

---

[146] Badger, Anthony J. (2008), pp. 7 f.
[147] *Id.*, pp. 49 f.
[148] Arnold, Peri E. (2009), p. 207
[149] Rauchway, Eric (2008), p. 87
[150] Renshaw, Patrick (2004), pp. 65 f.

one of the nation's oldest, proudest and richest families."[151] His thorough engagement in favor of the common good and of justice didn't only make him friends, but aroused "unprecedented upper-class hostility."[152] For the wealthy, he had betrayed his social origins and had chosen the wrong side of an intensifying class conflict.

Making use of the political support that had come from the voters, Roosevelt and the democratically dominated congress enacted an unprecedented number of laws during the first 100 days. The Republicans' last hope against this governmental engagement in favor of solidarity and justice was judicial activism, based on a conservative interpretation of the constitution. From 1873 on, the Supreme Court had undeniably favored economic interests over the protection and support of people, which is why the liberty of contract had "reached its apogee."[153] The "four horsemen," as the four conservative judges were called (Butler, McReynolds, Sutherland, van Devanter), were strongly opposed to the politics of Roosevelt, which were often seconded by Justice Owen Roberts. The hopes of the Republicans would be heard. The decision Railroad Retirement Board v. Alton R. Co., 295 U.S. 330 (1935) was the first of a series of Supreme Court decisions that invalidated New Deal legislation. Adhering to laissez-faire liberalism, the court declared every intrusion in the freedom of contract as unconstitutional. The Railroad Retirement Act gave older workers the possibility of retiring from the hard work, giving their jobs to young workers desperately in need. Railroad companies were required to pay 4 percent of their payrolls to a pension pool, to which the employees had to contribute 2 percent of their wage. Roberts wrote the opinion of the majority, exclusively defending the interests of the private companies, neither recognizing nor respecting the needs of the workers.[154] His opinion reflects the conservative judges' elitist concept of the relationship between employer and employee. For Roberts, it went without saying that the employee owes "loyalty or gratitude to the employer."[155] There was no right of workers for a pension fund. If railroad companies did or would establish such support, it was only because of their "largess," their "gratuity," or their "bounty."[156] For Roberts, social ends weren't important enough to prevail over the conduct of business.[157]

---

[151] Id., p. 3
[152] Jenkins, Roy (2003), p. 1
[153] Labbé, Ronald M./Lurie, Jonathan (2005), p. 11
[154] Leuchtenburg, William E. (1995), pp. 35 f.
[155] Railroad Retirement Board v. Alton R. Co., 295 U.S. 330 (1935), p. 372
[156] Id., pp. 377, 349, 351
[157] Id., p. 371

If workers lost their jobs, it was because of their unfaithful behavior or because they had decided to look for something else.[158] Visibly, the structural violence that was part of the Great Depression and its victims didn't bother this defender of the homo oeconomicus. Joblessness was one's own fault and responsibility and neither solidarity nor reciprocity could be expected. The right to hire and fire freely was one of the most important elements of the market society, which had to be protected by the Supreme Court against workers' claims.

Nevertheless, the democratic support for Roosevelt's politics was beyond doubt. Measures like social security, unemployment benefits, and the right of workers to organize and bargain collectively found the support of the people. In 1936, Roosevelt got reelected with another landslide victory: 61 % of the working and middle class voted for him, and he won all states except Maine and Vermont. Despite this overwhelming democratic verdict, the Supreme Court went on nullifying the laws congress had enacted. The involved institutions tried to solve the conflict according to the respective institutional rules and the convictions of the main actors. They all referred to the constitution and claimed to know, what this law-proposal was supposed to mean. For chief justice Charles E. Hughes, the division of competencies was evident: "We are under a Constitution, but the Constitution is what the judges say it is, and the judiciary is the safeguard of our liberty and of our property under the Constitution."[159] The president, however, pointed out: "We want a Supreme Court that will do justice under the Constitution, not over it. In our courts, we want a government of laws and not of men."[160]

The "law" is the result of a wide array of actors, contributing in different ways to protect what they currently think is important. Defending his politics that the people had legitimized several times, Roosevelt first thought of amending the constitution. "If, however, the Constitution is construed technically, if it is held that one hundred and fifty years have no bearing on the case, and that the present generation is powerless to meet social and economic problems that were not within the knowledge of the founding fathers, and therefore not made the subject of their specific consideration, then the President will have no other alternative than to got to the country with a Constitutional amendment that will lift the Dead Hand, giving the people of today the right to deal with today's vital issues."[161] But the

---

[158] *Id.*, p. 349
[159] Hughes, Charles Evans (1908), p. 139
[160] Quoted in Bennett, William John (2007), p. 132 (Franklin D. Roosevelt, Radio Broadcast, Fireside Chat of March 9, 1937).
[161] Roosevelt, quoted in Leuchtenburg, William E. (1995), p. 94

amendment process would take very long and its result was more than uncertain. Also, it wouldn't automatically restrain the Supreme Court, which could still decide according to its conservative view. Roosevelt, therefore, developed his Court-packing scheme of 1937. The conservative majority of the court had clearly demonstrated its determination not to give in to the pressure of the president or the people. And its life tenure made it quite probable it wouldn't see any change in the near or distant future. Roosevelt decided to draft a bill that would increase the number of justices. By appointing only justices in favor of the New Deal, the majority situation would tip in favor of the solidary politic. This legislative threat and the discontent of the people made Justice Roberts change his mind, which is why he voted along with the liberals in West Coast Hotel Co. v. Parrish, 300 U.S. 379 (1937). From then on, he gave up the idea of judicial supremacy and accepted the prerogative of the congress.[162] "[…] the Justices had sensed political danger, if not from Court packing then by some other means to curb their power, and simply decided that 'a switch in time saves nine.'"[163] This conflict had demonstrated the power and importance of the worldviews of individual justices and the power one justice had to decide in favor or against millions of people, who had clearly made their statement for a changed interpretation of the constitution. The Supreme Court, however, didn't give up power, but focused afterwards on the protection of the civil rights. Roosevelt's engagement in favor of the community in general had a positive impact on the society as a whole: "Public works programs led to the building of a vast infrastructure, including valley resource development and regional economic diversification; highways and air transport facilities; electric power generation and transmission, especially for rural, underdeveloped areas; water supply and sewers, as well as flood control; national park facilities; and urban housing."[164]

The aforementioned conflict has been called the "constitutional revolution of 1937." According to the basic values that were changed, to the relativization of property and the freedom of contract, a revolution took place. It is an example of constructive politics (see p. 322 f.), intense negotiations about the core elements of the society. The almost absolute dominance of the free-market principle and of liberalism was ended and justice and solidarity were made defining new elements. The adjustments between the institutions, between the Government, Supreme Court, and Congress, though, weren't, in my view, a revolution. They were adaptations within an

---

[162] *Id.*, p. 219
[163] Lawson, Alan (2006), p. 177
[164] Rosen, Elliot A. (2005), p. 151

institutional arrangement that otherwise was kept up (reproductive politics; see p. 322). The Supreme Court had to give in to the democratic principle, but preserved its important role.

The constitution isn't the truth, it isn't an objective guide indicating unambiguously what the people have to do, regardless of the place, the time, or the conflict. It is a guideline proposed by some people who thought it would be an effective recommendation for times of conflict. What the actors do with this suggestion when they have to find a way out of their dissent depends on their basic values, the concrete circumstances, and the readiness to cooperate now and in the future. The framers of the Constitution didn't anticipate a civil war nor the problems that such a conflict would generate.[165] In war, the American Constitution wasn't able to play its stabilizing role anymore. There was no consensus about central elements of the collective identity, which is why reproduction stopped and deconstruction began. The North and the South had taken different paths philosophically, politically, socially, and economically. The gap that had already existed at the foundation of the United States had widened and become irreconcilable. "The Union that they [had] created was built on sand. [...] and [...] as time passed the difference was becoming more, not less, pronounced."[166] "The outbreak of the Civil War had highlighted the fault lines in America's national fabric."[167] This schism was routed in three fundamental differences. First, the South wanted to preserve its very successful agrarian society, which was based on cotton, whereas the North focused on heavy industrialization. "[...] one of the striking features of the Southern economy was its inability to urbanize or industrialize on a significant scale."[168] Second, this was for the North a problem economically because they were heading toward an economy based on free market, on the free movement of capital and people. Free workers were needed in the North, but were "imprisoned" in the South, owned by rich planters. The third issue concerned slavery, which had become a core element of Southern identity. The South defended its hierarchical authoritarian social structure and its autonomy to organize life according to its wishes. The conflict crystallized around slavery,[169] because it collided with the basic values mainly relevant in the North, a *universally* understood justice and freedom. Furthermore, slavery affected the reputation of the United States in the world. It was shameful

---

[165] Urofsky, Melvin (2000), p. 2142
[166] Grant, Susan-Mary (2010), pp. 300 f.
[167] *Id.*, p. 309
[168] Ashworth, John (2010), p. 170
[169] Vile, John R. (1997), p. 179

being the last of the Western countries allowing slavery.[170] Dred Scott v. Sandford, 60 U.S. 393 (1857) highlighted the differences over basic values that divided the country. Dred Scott had been slave in Virginia and then Missouri. From 1833 to 1843, he had lived as a slave with his owners in the free state of Illinois, as well as in the Louisiana Territory. According to the Missouri Compromise of 1820 (see p. 270), slavery was forbidden in the Louisiana Territory. Brought back to Missouri, Scott first tried to purchase his freedom, but his owner denied him. Then he sued for freedom, arguing that he had lived twice on free soil. Defending the interests of the slave owners and the slave states, the Supreme Court declared, first, that Scott was a slave and not a citizen, so he couldn't sue in a Federal court. Second, being resident of Missouri there was no possibility to invoke the laws of Illinois. Third, the Missouri Compromise, an act of Congress in force for over thirty years, was, according to the judges unconstitutional because it violated the right of property guaranteed by the Fifth Amendment to the Constitution. With one decision the Justices[171] overruled an act of Congress that had brought the explosive slavery issue to a halt for one generation. The democratically elected Representatives and Senators had debated for months to find a compromise that would keep the union together. The right to property prevailed over popular sovereignty and a universal understanding of freedom and human dignity.

Even though Lincoln had accepted slavery as an institution in the states where it already had existed, not one of these voted in his favor in 1860. Not surprisingly, because he hadn't been put on the ballot papers of most of the Southern states, Lincoln was ready to compromise and would even had accepted an amendment protecting slavery in the slave states.[172] But he insisted that no new ones would be admitted. When, in 1861, six Southern states seceded, opting for deconstruction, they quit an arrangement that had been fragile from 1776 on. Favoring the union, the states agreed in the Declaration of Independence, as well as in the Constitution on arrangements combining concepts of humankind and worldviews that were incompatible. Slavery, voting qualifications, and the women's rights were set aside in the Declaration.[173] And the Constitution approved slavery in different provisions, which "gave the South a strong claim to 'special treatment' for its pe-

---

[170] Keegan, John (2009), p. 19
[171] According to Keegan, the justices were in their majority pro-Southern, because of a long series of Southern presidents appointing suitable people (Keegan, John [2009], p. 30).
[172] Smith, Adam I. P. (2007), p. 61
[173] Ellis, Joseph J. (2007), p. 51

culiar institution."¹⁷⁴ This "general proslavery tenor of the Constitution [...] helped create a race-based jurisprudence that led to discrimination against nonwhites."¹⁷⁵ To protect their way of life and their economic basis, the seceding states mostly referred to "the right of a State to govern itself; and the right of a people to abolish a Government when it becomes destructive of the ends for which it was instituted."¹⁷⁶. And for the state of Mississippi, slavery was an indispensable element of the State's identity and resources: "Our position is thoroughly identified with the institution of slavery – the greatest material interest of the world. Its labor supplies the product which constitutes by far the largest and most important portions of commerce of the earth. These products are peculiar to the climate verging on the tropical regions, and by an imperious law of nature, none but the black race can bear exposure to the tropical sun. [...] a blow at slavery is a blow at commerce and civilization. That blow has been long aimed at the institution, and was at the point of reaching its consummation. There was no choice left us but submission to the mandates of abolition, or a dissolution of the Union, whose principles had been subverted to work out our ruin."¹⁷⁷ The Mississippi declaration held that slavery had been under pressure from the North from the beginning, already in the Ordinance of 1787. And California's entrance into the Union as a free state in 1850 was perceived as a "first sign of defeat,"¹⁷⁸ as a turning point in favor of the power of the North. And "Lincoln's resounding victory" demonstrated for the Cotton South "that the Union had devolved into two irrevocably hostile sections."¹⁷⁹ This election threatened slavery in the short and for sure in the long term.¹⁸⁰ For the seceding states, living together with the North was no longer possible. The Constitution had been a shaky compromise, not solving the problem, just bringing the conflict to a provisional halt. The differences about the basic values made serious integration and cooperation inconceivable, which is why sooner or later a clash would be inevitable. Northern states were no longer ready to support the compromise and the changes they wanted to

---

[174] Finkelman, Paul (2010), p. 5: Article 1, Section 2, Clause 3; Article 1, Section 9, Clauses 1 and 4; Article 4, Section 2, Clause 3, Article 5.
[175] *Id.*, p. 8
[176] Declaration of the Immediate Causes Which Induce and Justify the Secession of South Carolina from the Federal Union, from December 24, 1860.
[177] A Declaration of the Immediate Causes which Induce and Justify the Secession of the State of Mississippi from the Federal Union, from January 1861.
[178] Schoen, Brian (2009), p. 197
[179] *Id.*, p. 246
[180] Wilentz, Sean (2009), p. 27

make were perceived by the South as betrayal. As a result, distrust occurred, making co-existence out of question (see pp. 248 f.). Quickly the Confederate States of America was established, with its own government, constitution, army, currency, flag, and Post Office. Accepting the division and going on with two confederations on American soil would have been a possibility. Given the elementary consensus in the South about the basic values and the economic and social organization, two autonomous and viable political entities would have existed side by side. Sure, a confederation of slave states was a blatant violation of freedom and justice. But the war only brought to an end the legal institution, not the direct, structural, and cultural violence Blacks had to suffer. In his State of the Union Address on December 3, 1860, President James Buchanan highlighted the importance of an elementary consensus to make the union possible:

> "[…] it may be safely asserted that the power to make war against a State is at variance with the whole spirit and intent of the Constitution. Suppose such a war should result in the conquest of a State; how are we to govern it afterwards? Shall we hold it as a province and govern it by despotic power? In the nature of things, we could not by physical force control the will of the people and compel them to elect Senators and Representatives to Congress and to perform all the other duties depending upon their own volition and required from the free citizens of a free State as a constituent member of the Confederacy. […] The fact is that our Union rests upon public opinion, and can never be cemented by the blood of its citizens shed in civil war. If it can not live in the affections of the people, it must one day perish."

War, thus, wasn't inescapable, but nationalist interests prevailed: The union had to be preserved by all means. "Lincoln was convinced of the supreme value of the Union for its own sake."[181] "I hold, that in contemplation of universal law, and of the Constitution, the Union of these States is perpetual. Perpetuity is implied, if not expressed, in the fundamental law of all national governments. It is safe to assert that no government proper, ever had a provision in its organic law for its own termination."[182] The war had to be fought, not because of the aberration of slavery, but because of the preservation of the great nation.[183] Southern states, on the other hand, were willing to risk a war, out of ideological reasons, to protect their identity,

---

[181] Smith, Adam I. P. (2007), p. 64
[182] Abraham Lincoln in his inaugural address of March 4, 1861
[183] According to Carwardine, Lincoln justified with the time the Civil War as a war against slavery because of public opinion purposes (Carwardine, Richard [2010], p. 128). Even though himself convinced, that slavery violated equality and freedom.

but as much because they were "greedily looking for ways to protect their near monopoly in raw cotton and expand their commercial and industrial capacity."[184] The forced unification finally cost 665'000 human lives, left thousands of veterans suffering from physical disablement and/or mental illnesses[185] – a heavy toll that didn't solve the basic problems. Even more important, the military and political humiliation put a heavy burden on future cooperation. Also, the South had lost its political and economic primacy within the Union. "[...] the South emerged from the Civil War as a backward economic region, characterized by low wages, low productivity, underdevelopment and a chronic shortage of productive capital."[186] In hindsight, the story is told in a way that lessens the divisions yielded by the military conflict, making co-existence easier and sensible. Today, the war is seen as an important part in the process of unification, a "struggle which completed the Revolution."[187] There is a "glow of pride, at the sacrifice a previous generation was ready to make in the cause of ideals held central to its life [...], the bravery and patriotism."[188] After the Civil War though, it took the American community more than ten years to develop a new legal consensus, that led to a fragile stability. Three elements were at stake and had to be re-discussed and re-defined in the amended Constitution: The

- distribution of power between federal government and the states, the
- respective competencies of the different branches of the federal government, and the
- set of relevant basic values, like the universality of freedom and justice.

The legal consensus didn't solve the integration problem because it was, first, a forced consensus, and, second, it didn't alter the dissent according to the basic values. The amended Constitution remained, therefore, a *proposal* for about a century before the new set of basic values was comprehensively consented to and became a supported part of the elementary consensus.

One of the results of the Civil War was an intensified gap between the Southern and Northern identities. Thanks to the conflict, the Northern industrial bourgeoisie was massively strengthened and made a lot of profit from government contracts. In organizing the war effort, the government

---

[184] Schoen, Brian (2009), p. 269
[185] Brundage, Fitzhugh W. (2009), pp. 127 f.
[186] Ashworth, John (2010), p. 173
[187] Keegan, John (2009), p. 356
[188] *Id.*, p. 356

had established a national paper currency and banking system and developed the infrastructure. "In their unprecedented expansion of federal power and their effort to impose organization upon a decentralized economy and fragmented polity, these measures reflected what might be called the birth of the modern American state. On the eve of the Civil War, the federal government was 'in a state of impotence', its conception of its duties little changed since the days of Washington and Jefferson. Most functions of government were handled at the state and local level. [...] But the exigencies of war created [...] a 'new government', with a greatly expanded income, bureaucracy, and set of responsibilities."[189] The South, on the other hand, had lost the war and saw its collective identity threatened with extinction. Recognition and respect became the main problem: Would they be treated equally and, most important, was there room for a different lifestyle in this forced union?

For Southerner President Andrew Johnson the renouncement of slavery would have been enough to justify the integration of the Southern states on equal terms. Republican dominated Congress, on the other hand, wanted to make sure that the price the North had had to pay would have more effect than just some readjustments. The 13th Amendment which was introduced in 1865 abolished slavery and made federal interventions in the states possible. It was an important step toward a centralized federal government, restricting not only the autonomy of the states, but also of institutions or individuals, disallowing both to have slaves or authorize servitude.[190] Reconstruction wasn't a "re-construction" in respect to the construction phases described here. It was a "new construction" redefining central elements of the collective identity. According to the Supreme Court (of 1980), the 13th, 14th, and 15th Amendments "were specifically designed as an expansion of federal power and an intrusion on state sovereignty."[191] An intense political and legal fight between the President and Congress ensued, including a series of vetoes and even an almost successful impeachment of Johnson, demonstrating that constitutions are what the people decide them to be.

President Johnson was a vehement defender of Southern interests and a central actor in the battle over the law during Reconstruction. Congressional elections in 1866, though, brought a landslide victory for the Republicans, which now could override Johnson's vetoes. This victory was in no small part due to the absence of the Confederacy, which the winners until that time hadn't readmitted as equal members in the union. Despite this

---

[189] Foner, Eric (2002), p. 23
[190] Hyman, Harold M. (2000), p. 2691
[191] City of Rome v. United States 446 U.S. 156

important defeat and the clear statement of the voters, Johnson didn't stop defending the interests of the South. "The events of 1867, with continuing tensions between President and legislature, led to a political impasse unforeseen by the Framers – a chief executive who, repudiated at the polls, refused to accept that judgment and who did his best, not to execute duly passed laws of Congress, but to thwart their implementation."[192] In 1867 Congress amended the Judiciary Act of 1789, authorizing the Supreme Court to protect the habeas corpus right of *all* state prisoners, including the freed slaves (Habeas Corpus Act of 1867). Fearing that the court could use this right to declare the Reconstruction laws unconstitutional, Congress amended the Judiciary Act in March 1868, restricting the power of the justices. In July 1868, the 14th Amendment established universal freedom, which fundamentally changed the basic values relevant for the new community. It further tackled the Black Codes. By abolishing the three-fifths clause that had originally been in the Constitution (Article 1, Section 2), the former slaves counted now as much as Whites. Thanks to this equal recognition of human beings, previous slave states gained power in Congress and in the electoral college. Consequently, it was important for the Republicans to have loyal governments in the South; otherwise, the losers of the war would increase their power thanks to the war.

Despite the consensus of the majority, the new legal basis incorporating a universal understanding of freedom and justice didn't change the society in the South. All the power the Republicans had in Washington didn't mean control of the social, economic, and political situation in the South, where the congressional law-proposals weren't taken seriously. Exclusion, inequality, degrading treatment of Blacks went on, no longer based on the concept of slavery, but of a segregated community, an apartheid of the early days. "[…] following the war, Southern Whites expected the freedmen to behave much the same way they had under the antebellum slave codes."[193] The legal basis for this oppression were, first, the Black Codes, later, the Jim Crow laws. Because it was no longer possible to own the workers, employers organized the labor market in a way that the built up structural violence would force the Blacks to work under the same conditions as before.[194] Legally freed from slavery, their economic options were limited; only plantation labor was left. And state power was used to "enforce labor agreements and plantation discipline, punish those who refused to contract, and prevent

---

[192] Urofsky, Melvin (2000), pp. 2143 f.
[193] Wade, Wyn Craig (1987), p. 19. During the war, the slave-owners were appalled and embittered that so many of their properties fled the plantations (p. 12).
[194] Finkelman, Paul (2010), p. 36

Whites from competing among themselves for black workers."[195] According to the Black Code of Mississippi of 1865, euphemistically titled "The Civil Rights of Freedmen in Mississippi," intermarriage between black and white was forbidden (Sec. 3) and Blacks were obliged to have a lawful home or employment (Sec. 5). Sec. 7 gave the state, as well as private citizens the right to arrest and bring back to their employers "every deserting employee." In many states, the movement of Blacks was controlled "by systems of passes;" residence had to be proven, congregations of groups of Blacks were forbidden, Blacks weren't allowed to reside in certain areas,[196] and they were excluded from public office or voting. In reaction and to make sure that the intended universal understanding of freedom and justice would prevail, Congress enacted the 14th Amendment in 1868 and the Civil Rights Act in 1875. Aware that law is only a proposal that has to be accepted by the people in their everyday life, Joseph Hawley (Republican congressman from Connecticut) stated: "There is a social, and educational, and moral reconstruction of the South needed that will never come from any legislative halls, State or national; it must be the growth of time, of education, and of Christianity. We cannot perfect that reconstruction through statutes, if we had all the powers of the State Legislature and of Congress combined. We cannot put justice, liberty, and equality into the hearts of a people by the statutes alone."[197] I wasn't helpful that the Supreme Court didn't support the acts of Congress to enforce the 13th Amendment. Using a restrictive interpretation, the Court held in Civil Rights Cases, 109 U.S. 3 (1883) that the Civil Rights Act was unconstitutional, because the Amendment didn't ban discriminatory behavior. And in Hodges v. United States, 203 U.S. 1 (1906), the Supreme Court denied Congress the right to legislate against racial discrimination, because neither the 13th nor the 14th Amendment entitled the federal government to do so, which is why the 10th Amendment had to be respected.[198] It took almost another sixty years to finally get rid of the legal racist discriminations by enacting the Civil Rights Act of 1964, which, this

---

[195] Foner, Eric (2002), p. 199

[196] Wiecek, William M. (2000), p. 189

[197] Congressional Record, 43rd Cong., 2nd Sess., 1853 (February 26, 1875)

[198] Hodges v. United States, 203 U.S. 1 (1906), pp. 1 f.: "The result of the Amendments to the Constitution adopted after the Civil War was to abolish slavery, and to make the emancipated slaves citizens, and not wards of the nation, over whom Congress retained jurisdiction. This decision of the people is binding upon the courts, and they cannot attempt to determine whether it was the wiser course." The same formalistic interpretation used in favor of a racist understanding of political exclusion is to be found in United States v. Resse (1876) or United States v. Cruikshank (1876).

time, was upheld by the Supreme Court on the basis of Article 1, Section 8, Clause 3 (Commerce Clause). The moral, philosophical, social, and cultural fabric had changed, and so, too, the Constitution. An important player within the decision-making process was the courageous and relentless Civil Rights Movement. Not a legally foreseen actor, not part of the legal staff, but decisive to bring to an end the new-construction launched hundred years ago.

Even though slavery was widely concentrated on the South, racism was a construction principle applied in the whole country. "The determination to keep the United States a white man's country, they would say, has been the central theme of American, not just Southern, history. Racism has been America's tragic flaw. Questions of color and race have been at the center of some of the most important events in American experience."[199] "By linking 'whiteness' so closely to the prerogatives and rights of citizenship and political participation, the Jacksonian construction of racial modernity defined not merely the South but the entire American nation-state as a 'white man's country.' Thus racial modernity shaped a powerful national self-definition."[200] One could fight slavery and still being convinced that there were different races with varying aptitudes. Lincoln himself was persuaded that the Blacks were "the white's inferior and irredeemably so."[201] "[…] his opposition to slavery had never included advocacy of racial equality."[202] In his race for Senator in Illinois, Lincoln stated:

> "I am not, nor ever have been, in favor of bringing about in any way the social and political equality of the white and black races, that I am not nor ever have been in favor of making voters or jurors of negroes, nor of qualifying them to hold office, nor to intermarry with white people; and I will say in addition to this that there is a physical difference between the white and black races which I believe will forever forbid the two races living together on terms of social and political equality. And in as much as they cannot so live, while they do remain together there must be the position of superior and inferior, and I as much as any other man am in favor of having the superior position assigned to the white race."[203]

Consequently he defended the position that colonization, the emigration of freed Blacks to Africa or Latin America, was "the best solution to the

---

[199] Fields, Barbara J. (1982), p. 143
[200] Ford, Lacy K. (1999), p. 737
[201] Keegan, John (2009), p. 31
[202] Fehrenbacher, Don E. (1987), p. 97
[203] Debate at Charleston in 1958

American race problem."²⁰⁴ To refer to the mindset of the time to explain Lincoln's racism isn't convincing because since the 17th century, abolitionist movements existed on American soil, demonstrating that a universally equal construction of human beings was at least thinkable. In the North, there was no consensus about the political rights of Blacks, about enfranchisement. White voters in the lower North, for example, rejected several times the unrestricted enfranchisement of Blacks. And the Republicans, unwilling to risk the cohesion of the party, decided at their national convention in 1868, that "each northern state could decide black suffrage without federal interference, but southern states must accept black voting as a matter of national policy."²⁰⁵ In this way, the Republicans secured the votes of Blacks they needed to succeed in the South. For the same reason, the governing party pushed for an amendment of the Constitution: Democratic idealism alone did not motivate the enactment of the 15th Amendment, but also the Republican's "objective of ensuring party hegemony."²⁰⁶

Violence is an important integration tool of racist societies because this blatant inequality can't be upheld without the use of direct, structural, and cultural violence. Under pressure from the North, as well as critically judged by the international community, the violence in the South increased, clinging to the identity, the "home," they had learned to be the natural order. It was a truth built up over generations, justified and shored up socially, economically, culturally, politically, and legally; it was a truth developed by a network of actions, all of them oriented toward eternal white supremacy. "Violence [...] had been endemic in large parts of the South since 1865. But the advent of Radical Reconstruction stimulated its further expansion. By 1870, the Ku Klux Klan and kindred organizations like the Knights of the White Camelia and the White Brotherhood had become deeply entrenched in nearly every Southern state."²⁰⁷ White supremacists intimidated Blacks whenever they trespassed the formal and informal barriers they had erected. Blacks were economically blackmailed to cast the right vote, whipped, injured, or killed. Victims of this violence sweeping through the South were also white office holders who were implementing the new Northern politics or white supporters of universal equality. Every sign of the new order imposed from the outside was fought. Unwilling to change and to cooperate and *lacking alternatives*, the were determined to understand the world in a

---

[204] Donald, David Herbert (1995), p. 221. See also Fehrenbacher, Don E. (1987), pp. 110 f.
[205] Gillette, William (2000), p. 1039
[206] *Id.*, p. 1040
[207] Foner, Eric (2002), p. 425

Manichaean way, and *were condemned to resort to violence.*

The Ku Klux Klan was a counter-revolutionary terrorist organization.[208] It had existed before, but gained its strength and set about to use terrorist methods as soon as the Blacks began to have rights imposed by the federal government. "[…] after Democratic persuasion and economic pressure had failed to sway Negro voters, terrorism represented the only remaining way of seizing political control."[209] The Klan was supported by many Whites actively and passively, and those who disagreed feared limitless repercussions.[210] Its members were sympathetic to the Democratic party and stemmed from all social strata. "Professional men – doctors, lawyers, and university professors – were also Klansmen. Such members, however, preferred to operate behind the scenes in supportive roles."[211] Officials like sheriffs or judges, on the one hand, or former Confederate officers, on the other hand, were also part of this secretive, demonstrative organization. On the victims' side, the vast majority of the Blacks were Republican voters. And, more importantly, the more they were political, the more they risked to be assaulted. "The purposes were clearly to destroy the basis of Negro political effectiveness by driving out its leaders, white and black."[212] Besides political targets, the Ku Klux Klan also attacked the institutions necessary to build up a group identity, such as churches or schools.[213] The violence Blacks had to suffer was even worse than under slavery, because the owner's protection for his property had been lost. Gradually, state power, the monopoly of violence, got totally lost in the South. "By 1871, the Klan had rendered Southern Republicans, law officers, and military commanders equally helpless."[214] Following the logic of vigilantes, there was no respect for state officials: "We can inform you that we are the law itself and that an order from these Headquarters is supreme above all others."[215] The Klan was more a set of loosely organized groups than a strongly centralized, hierarchical organization[216] and perceived itself as "self-appointed police organization" responsible to enforce the right law,[217] against the Northern occupation of their territory and its arrogant claim to prescribe the South how to live.

---

[208] Trelease, Allen W. (1971), p. xi
[209] *Id.*, p. xlvii
[210] Wade, Wyn Craig (1987), p. 49
[211] *Id.*, p. 57; See also Foner, Eric (2002), pp. 432 f.
[212] Chalmers, David M. (1987), p. 14
[213] Foner, Eric (2002), p. 428
[214] Wade, Wyn Craig (1987), p. 79
[215] Newton, Michael (2010), p. 31
[216] Chalmers, David M. (1987), p. 2
[217] *Id.*, p. 9

The Ku Klux Klan Act of 1871 (and the Force Act of 1870) contained several provisions intended to protect the victims of the Klan. It was highly disputed because it gave the federal government the right to intervene militarily on the local level, and to punish individuals interfering with federal forces. But the power to penalize crimes, to the critics, was a power of the states.[218] The Grant administration used its federal power in South Carolina, arrested or made flee about eight hundred Klansmen and judged many of them. As a result, the Klan was effectively dissolved in South Carolina, with similar effect on other states. Lacking the means, the courts were overwhelmed with all the cases they had to try, which is why most of them had to be dropped. This temporary end of the Klan, though, didn't end the violence against Blacks. They were further hindered to vote and apartheid was maintained until the 1960s. The Civil Rights Act of 1875 never was enforced in the South. "The North may have won the war, but the South had now won the peace. It was a peace in which Southern Blacks found themselves noncitizens, unable to vote, consigned to inadequate housing and menial employment, and their children to inferior schools. This was the peace that marked the end of both the Ku-Klux and Reconstruction."[219] And the Klan came back into action in 1915.

What finally helped to overcome the profound schism that from the beginning of the union had been a heavy burden, was a story that relativized the past and promised a prolific future: It was a "story of national progress and triumph."[220]

cc) Interactive law-construction

The highly venerated Constitution and the reverenced Founding Fathers are, in my view, important symbolic links (see pp. 394 ff.), that helped integration as much as hindered it. On the one hand, it anchors a collective identity in the heroic past, giving the present a meaning and assuring a hopeful future. On the other hand, it is permanently used to justify present politics by delegating the construction responsibility to the infallible founders. According to Kammen, the Constitution occupies a very important role in America and has over time "been swathed in pride,"[221] become a sacred object to be worshipped. Furthermore, it is a very rigid document because Article 5 doesn't foresee a procedure in favor of change. The barriers are

---

[218] In United States v. Harris, 106 U.S. 629 (1883)
[219] Wade, Wyn Craig (1987), p. 111
[220] Silber, Nina (2009), p. 107
[221] Kammen, Michael (1986), p. 3

much too high to accompany and react to social, philosophical, economic, or political changes. It seems the founders opted for preservation, not for a structure that would make innovation easy. According to Madison, "frequent appeals would in great measure deprive the government of that veneration, which time bestows on every thing, and without which perhaps the wisest and freest governments would not possess the requisite stability."[222] He also distrusted public passions[223] and was convinced that the Constitution of 1787 had found the "equilibrium of government."[224] Out of over 11'000 amendments proposed in Congress, only 27 finally succeeded gaining the approval of three-fourths of the states.[225] It took 203 years to the ratification of the 27th Amendment, which intends to regulate the compensation of members of Congress. Proposed by James Madison to the House of Representatives on June 8, 1789, only six states ratified it up to 1791. In 1873, Ohio approved, in 1978 Wyoming approved, and in 1992 Alabama approved as the 38th state, so Congress could confirm the amendment's ratification on May 20, 1992.

This constitutional rigidity may be a problem for people who have to solve a conflict, who, on the one hand, try to respect the rule of law but have, on the other hand, problems reconciling the old constitution with a current conflict they have to solve. In my opinion, the debate over what is constitutional takes place in many different areas and often with changing participants. Sometimes it is the point of view of Congress, or sometimes it is the view of the president that prevails. Another time it may be the Supreme Court who brings a conflict to a temporary end or a state that tries to initiate or block new constitutional understandings. More often than the procedural understanding of law lets expect, it is an informal political protest or an unsatisfied part of the people that has the greatest impact on constitutional interpretation. The Constitution is in my point of view more than just the relatively short text adopted in 1787. Because to be "constitutional" is to be qualified as *the expectations people perceive as elementary, the norms they understand as core elements of their collective identity, the forms of action people are ready to engage or even fight for*. According to the construction phases described earlier (see p. 64 ff.), there are three forms

---

[222] Hamilton, Alexander/Madison, James/Jay, John (2003 [1787-1788]), p. 307, The Federalist No. 49: Madison
[223] Id., p. 310, The Federalist No. 49: Madison: "The passions therefore not the reason, of the public, would sit in judgment. [...] it is the reason of the public alone that ought to control and regulate the government."
[224] Id., p. 308, The Federalist No. 49: Madison
[225] Vile, John R (1997), pp. 115 f.

of constitutional work: Constructive, reproductive, and deconstructive politics. During *constructive politics*, (new construction), negotiations about the future core elements of the collective identity take place that involve a wide variety of actors. These negotiations often do not respect procedures, are of a highly dynamic character, tend to revolutionize the ways people acted before, or to create relationships nobody until now thought of. "Tradition" or the "prevailing opinion" doesn't determine the debate, a debate the result of which is totally unknown. Constructive politics isn't controllable and can't be regulated in a way that guarantees certain values because these values themselves could be questioned. It is an open debate, a search for a future that will be shared by an until now unknown number of people. *Reproductive politics* (reproduction) occurs within a quite narrow realm of possibilities; is regulated and can be measured against a tradition of expectations reproduced/confirmed over time. It is in this case that the "rule of law" finds its application: Governmental actions are controlled by comparing them to the consensus acquired over the course of foregoing conflicts. Dissent during reproductive politics concerns details and doesn't affect the basic values the community is built on. *Deconstructive politics,* on the contrary, intends to break up an arrangement. The elementary consensus is no longer given because people do not see enough common ground to go on with their political project. Perhaps they separate or engage in constructive politics, in a new construction based on different principles with another people. In deconstructive politics, as well as in constructive politics, to have alternatives and to be able to think creatively new, is decisive.

Constructive Politics	Reproductive Politics	Deconstructive Politics
Negotiations *about the future core elements of the collective identity.*	**Regulated debate** *about adaptations of the current identity.*	**Break up** *Consensus can't be uphold anymore, reproduction fails.*

All three configurations can occur at any time. There is no constitutional guarantee of avoiding deconstruction or new construction. Even though law is used for reproduction, it is because of the contingency of human actions that we only see in times of conflict whether law is accepted and can be used as an integrative tool, or if it is an ineffective proposal. Bogdanor states about the constitutional conventions of British law:

"The question of which conventions are relevant during a constitutional crisis is not primarily a theoretical issue capable of abstract resolution through a process of reasoning. It is fundamentally political, and at bottom an issue of political power. [...] Constitutional crises, then, cannot be resolved through a statement of principles; nor, by the very nature of the constitution, could there be a 'hidden code' with the power of determining how such crises are to be resolved. It is not that the constitution consists of 'instantly invented precedents,' but rather that, when the precedents conflict, as they invariably will, there can be no authoritative guidance as to which are relevant in advance of a particular crisis. There is, inevitably, a conflict of principles, and how that conflict is to be resolved cannot be determined until the crisis actually arises. [...] A codified constitution [...] does little to resolve the problem [...]; a codified constitution cannot provide a right answer to a constitutional conflict any more than Britain's uncodified constitution can. [...] Perhaps, indeed, constitutional crises are the process through which the 'living constitution,' as opposed to the codified constitution, adapts to changing political conditions. A constitutional crisis may be the means of bringing the constitutional rules up to date."[226]

We, therefore, may conclude that, because of the interactive structure of law, the constitution is concretized and changed on the one hand using the regular procedure. On the other hand, there are many other open ways with varying participants to define what the constitution is supposed to be.

The negotiations between the Federalists and the Anti-Federalists from 1789 to 1791 are an example of constructive politics. It was about core elements of the future identity, about the power of the federal government and the protection of individual freedom against a too powerful state. The first ten amendments, the Bill of Rights, were the price the Federalists were willing to pay for the union. Another example are the three Reconstruction amendments (13th to 15th) after the Civil War. They were essential for the development of universal equality and of the modern state. This process, however, lasted about hundred years and led to a comprehensive democratization of the society, a fundamentally different "reality" than the one of slavery and racism that existed before. The Progressive movement is at the origin of further democratization (17th and 19th Amendment) and the beginning of the welfare state (16th Amendment). In 1924, a Child Labor Amendment was proposed, intended to regulate, limit, and prohibit the labor of persons under eighteen years of age, but it was ratified only by 28 states. Beside these "revolutionary" amendments as part of constructive

---

[226] Bogdanor, Vernon (1995), pp. 180 f.

politics, there were amendments concerning procedural changes (such as, for example, the 22th, the 25th, or the 27th Amendment) without having an effect on the collective identity. These reproductive politics adjusted some aspects of an otherwise uncontested "reality." In the 1990's, the religious right unsuccessfully proposed different amendments like the authorization of school prayers, the end of school busing for racially mixed schools, and the interdiction of abortion.

Besides the formal changes of the Constitution, there are constitutional changes that do not alter the text. The New Deal legislation mainly concerned equality of opportunities, solidarity with the less fortunate, and social equalization and had a fundamental impact on society without amending the Constitution. Many different actors were involved: The President, the people electing the President and Congress, Parliament, the parties, and the Supreme Court. The result of this intense negotiation about political power wasn't foreseen by the Founders. On the other hand, the Constitution expects certain actions but doesn't get them. Article 1, Section 8, Clause 11 of the U.S. Constitution states that Congress has the power to declare war. The Korean or the Vietnam War, the Gulf or the Libyan War didn't get the parliamentary declaration the Founders had thought of. "[…] Congress did authorize the war in Vietnam – at least its public aspects, at least as the law of authorization stood at the time. But it did so backhandedly, generally without anything resembling serious consideration of the consequences of its actions, and where possible so ambiguously that when things went wrong it could continue to claim mere bystander status. Who, us? This isn't *our* war. […] What is at stake […] is the judgment that no single individual should be able to take the nation into war and thereby risk the lives of all of us."[227]

There are basically two positions on the question of who is entitled to interpret the Constitution and how far they are allowed to go.[228] A prudent one is favored by scholars who argue that moderate adaptations can be made by the Supreme Court, a more reflective institution than the populist political process.[229] Greater changes, though, have to comply with the procedure of Article 5.[230] On the other hand, there is a position defending popular sovereignty and criticizing idolatrous reverences to the existing text. Vile, for example, is convinced that the courts have a duty not to stick too thoroughly to the text of the Constitution. Through interpreta-

---

[227] Ely, John Hart (1993), p. 47
[228] Sullivan, Kathleen M. (2000), p. 76
[229] Murphy, Walter F. (1995), p. 189
[230] Dow, David R. (1995), p. 118

tion the courts have to open a path for reforms, otherwise conflicts would reach too high an intensity: "Even if the courts had the courage to oppose the raging tides of opinion in such contingencies [...] there is little reason to believe they would be successful in doing anything other than sparking revolution."[231] And Amar defends "a majoritarian and populist mechanism akin to a national referendum, even though that mechanism is not explicitly specified in Article 5."[232] The "We the people", the "deliberative popular sovereignty," has to prevail and is according to Amar, the core element of the Constitution. Never mind which form is used to change the Constitution, the procedure of Article 5 or the way of new interpretation, in his opinion, popular sovereignty is the criterion to be respected.[233] Ackerman, too, defends an interactive understanding of law, calling it dialectical.[234] He perceives the fight between Roosevelt and the Supreme Court as positive and important:

> "My reinterpretation of the law of the middle republic[235] challenges this view. The Old Court's defense of its comprehensive synthesis helped, not hurt, the democratic process through which the People gave new marching orders to their government in the 1930s. By dramatizing the fundamental constitutional principles raised by the New Deal, the Old Court contributed to a more focused, and democratic, transformation of constitutional identity than might otherwise have occurred. By holding up a mirror to the American people that re-presented the fundamental principles of the middle republic, the Old Court made it easier, not harder, for the citizenry of the 1930s to clarify what they found wanting in the traditional structure – and finally give constitutional legitimacy to a new vision of activist national government that did not have deep popular roots in our previous constitutional experience."[236]

For Ackerman, the law proposed and established by Roosevelt and the Democratic Congress is a form of "higher lawmaking"[237] (in my words: constructive politics, new construction), not normal politics[238] (reconstructive politics, reconstruction). And it is up to the people to decide, whether

---

[231] Vile, John R. (1995), p. 199
[232] Amar, Akhil Reed (1995), p. 89
[233] *Id.*, p. 77
[234] Ackerman, Bruce (1993), p. 161
[235] The time of Reconstruction, E.D.
[236] Ackerman, Bruce (1993), p. 104
[237] *Id.*, pp. 266 ff.
[238] *Id.*, pp. 230 ff.

they want to accept the new proposal and, thus, "transform our fundamental principles" or stick to the preservationist understanding the Court has to offer.[239] To make sure that extra-legal changes do not take place easily, that the higher lawmaking finds really the support of the people, Ackerman requests a years-long period of mobilized deliberation.[240] The conservative attitude the Court often demonstrates is a necessary safeguard against populist rush. On the other hand, this conservatism had the effect of oppressing people over decades, people who didn't find support or weren't able to develop power enough to change the current living constitution. The Supreme Court didn't seize the opportunity to act in favor of justice and solidarity. Ackerman's understanding seems to me too procedural, not enough focused on the power relationships involved in the conflict. If both conflict parties have the same possibility to influence popular approval, conservatives and progressives would meet on a level playing field. But if the construction power is distributed unevenly, it is not a fair deliberation that takes place. In my view, every legal actor has to take her or his responsibility to avoid or at least to minimize direct, structural, or cultural violence. *Referring to the supremacy of law can't justify every form of oppression.*

Because of the considerable interpretative scope and the changing concepts of humankind and of community, expectations toward the Constitution and toward law in general are permanently altered. Interactively speaking, there is no inherent limit to constructive politics. It depends on the conflict parties, if the new understanding of law is acceptable or goes beyond currently imaginable change. One, therefore, has to take the risk and try the *fundamentally new* to find out if change is possible and which is the most promising path to be taken. Quite often, intended fundamental changes do not respect the constitutional procedure because these formal restrictions are perceived way too obstructive to bring about the looked for improvement. It probably was a mistake of the Founding Fathers to claim so high an approval. Even though it was helpful to protect the autonomy of the states and to make sure that an important majority approves the changes, this federalist and democratic safeguard may motivate people who seek for change to use broad interpretative liberties or to blatantly disrespect the rules.

The establishment of the American Constitution was quite a creative process.[241] Article 13 of the Articles of Confederation stated the perpetual existence of the union and required the confirmation of every state to change

---

[239] *Id.*, p. 162, 303

[240] *Id.*, p. 285

[241] See the detailed description with Ackerman, Bruce (1998), pp. 34 ff.

the compact. Article 7 of the Constitution of 1787, however, asked only for the approval of nine states. Furthermore, the Constitutional Convention was not duly assembled, as Rhode Island was absent (refusing to participate) and the delegations of New York and Delaware were not legitimated to decide on behalf of their states. And, finally, the ratification processes performed in the states were at least doubtful. The enactment of Amendments 13th and 14th reveals similar procedural largess. Southern states weren't represented in the Congress which debated on the amendments.[242] They were forced to ratify Amendment 13; otherwise their exclusion from Congress would go on. President Andrew Johnson even threatened with "indefinite military rule if ratification failed."[243] The First Reconstruction Act of 1867 abolished civil governments in the South (except the one in Tennessee) and subjected the states to the Union Army – a measure to last, as long as the 14th Amendment wasn't ratified.[244] It is by simple power politics that these constitutional changes occurred, even though they didn't change society (see p. 315 ff.).

An interactive concept of law is characterized by different goals and is not easily combined, but interconnected to each other:

- Having a constitution that *prevents power-abuse* by the majority, as well as by an elitist minority, is to be welcomed from the point of view of individual freedom and the freedom of minority groups.

- Constitutions, however, *have to be interpreted*. They do not force upon the people and the legal staff a specific and exclusive form of action. Furthermore, to accept one and only one norm-application is dangerous for freedom and justice, because individual case justice isn't possible anymore. Governments and justices treating everybody the same won't meet the needs of unique individuals.

- Whatever is recognized as a normative foundation of the community, its integrative effect depends on the *readiness to support and the engagement of people to defend* these relationships. A concept of law that is firmly established is problematic because it is withdrawn from the actions of interacting individuals. Against the background of consensus-based constructivism, there is always contingency, there is always the possibility to act differently. As long as people demand

---

[242] *Id.*, p. 134, 174
[243] Hyman, Harold M. (2000), p. 2691; Ackerman, Bruce (1998), p. 230
[244] Morison, Samuel Eliot/Commager, Henry Steele/Leuchtenburg, William E. (1983), p. 338

each other to stick to the rules, the rules will have their integrative effect. As soon as reproduction ends, however, and new construction launched, the rules' character as a proposal becomes visible again. A new consensus has to be established.

What is needed is, first, a *multitude of forms of conflict resolutions* that are never absolute, never exclusive, holding the possibility to criticize in different ways and on different grounds the decisions of each other. Second, all members of the community have to have *equal access to these forums to be heard*. Exclusionary politics incites revolutionary claims unwilling to cooperate and trying to overthrow violently the excluders. Third, the legal staff has to be attentive and legal institutions have to be permeable to *hear the criticism and protests*. And fourth, a *readiness to deliberate freely* is needed, not restricted by absolute, unquestionable truths.

Legal interpretation is, according to Ackerman, restricted by the tradition built up over centuries, which established rules and expectations. In his view, the professional narrative and the built-in arguments shape the legal staff more than it supposes.[245] To trust the integrative force of tradition seems, from an constructive point of view, dangerous. According to Rüthers, it is mainly the Judiciary that changed the republican German law into the "National Socialist law-perversion."[246] Legislative changes were not responsible for the totalitarian genocide that followed, but judge-made law.[247] In his view, it is possible to re-evaluate a whole legal system only by interpretation,[248] a position that Ackerman also defends: "Like all languages, [the language of the Constitution] may be used to accomplish great evils as well as great goods."[249] Tradition is, therefore, not a value per se; it has an impact on the actions of people only if claimed and respected by the members of the community. Ackerman's understanding of the constitution seems to me ambivalent, demonstrating that the law or constitutions are a *self-service store*. On the one hand, he states that the Founding Fathers helped to establish "the most powerful slave-ocracy of the nineteenth century," to slaughter Natives, and to protect the upper class against workers.[250] "The Founders established an oligarchy. While they spoke for the People,

---

[245] Ackerman, Bruce (1993), p. 39
[246] Rüthers, Bernd (1989), p. 14
[247] *Id.*, p. 100
[248] *Id.*, p. 181. See also Rüthers, Bernd (1995), pp. 163, 193.
[249] Ackerman, Bruce (1993), p. 322
[250] *Id.*, p. 314

they only tried to win the mobilized consent of white men."[251] On the other hand, he is convinced, that it is the same Constitution which is at the origin of the women's and the civil rights movement, using "the country's higher law-making heritage" to fulfill their goals.[252] In my opinion, there is nothing unavoidable, compulsory built in a text drafted by human beings. It can be used as a symbolic link, as a representation of the core values of the community for any purpose whatsoever, which is why its integrative effect lasts as long as people refer to it. If there is a need for an eternally relevant Constitution with one unique interpretation, it will be constructed. The Constitution is, then, an order, not to be discussed, that represents the pensée unique, the exclusive way of thinking. Or we understand the Constitution as an orientation point, a basis for discussions, easily changeable to avoid concealed circumvention. Those who intend to preserve a specific constitutional understanding have to justify their conservatism as much as those who aim for a change have to advance their arguments. As long as the conservative and the progressive position are willing to listen, to ask, and to take responsibility for their proposals, stability *and* change can be realized in an integrative way.

According to Woods and Gutzman the American Constitution is dead. "It died a long time ago. [...] The crisis we face today is the culmination of decades of offenses against the Constitution by Democrats and Republicans, justices, presidents, and congresses alike, all of whom have essentially rejected the idea that the Constitution possesses a fixed meaning limiting the power of the U.S. government. That idea was not a minor aspect of the Constitution; it was the very purpose of the Constitution."[253] But which is the "fixed meaning" that has undeniably to be respected? Tamanah, too, criticizes the moral relativism and "the multiplication of groups aggressively pursuing their own agendas, convinced in the rightness of their claims."[254] He complains about a collapse of the higher law and the deterioration of the common good. In his view, first, basic principles of the constitution have to be respected. Second, the law has to represent the common good, public welfare.[255] "Lost in this transformation was the time-honored understanding that there are certain things the government and legal officials absolutely cannot do with and through law."[256] However, if we want to fix

---

[251] *Id.*, p. 315
[252] *Id.*, p. 316
[253] Woods, Thomas E./Gutzman, Kevin R.C. (2008), pp. 1 f.
[254] Tamanaha, Brian Z. (2006), p. 4
[255] *Id.*, p. 215
[256] *Id.*, p. 218

certain rules and to make sure that the powerful respect them, too, we have to do more than invoke a man-made text and hope for clear answers like an oracle. It is the everyday critical observation of the legal staff and the state actors that helps to push through what people think is important. To trust a text to do this work has in my opinion a lot to do with animistic convictions – a belief not shared by the constructivist concept defended here. Using the different conflict resolving mechanisms, we should try to convince others and to gain consensus.

British constitutional law is not easy to describe, as there is no single defined text containing the most important rules about the rights and duties of state actors. Accordingly, there is no formal criterion to determine which rules are constitutional.[257] British "constitutional law" circumscribes two elements: The law of the constitution (rules, written or unwritten, in form of statutes, tradition, custom, or case law) which is enforceable by the courts, and the conventions of the constitution (conventions, understandings, practices), that are not enforceable, even though they regulate the conduct of the Crown or Ministers and the relationship of the Government with Parliament. An important part of the rules determining the way political power is to be used,[258] therefore, can't be judged by courts,[259] but has to be claimed by politicians, parties, and people. This "jumble of diffuse statutes and court rulings, supplemented by extra-legal conventions and practices"[260] is validated by its long-lasting existence. Instead of placing the trust in a document that fixes the core elements of the community, it is the confidence in an immemorial practice that stabilizes relevant expectations, the reference to *tradition*. This "traditional Constitution"[261] has proved to be "one of the most successful political structures ever devised by the wit of man."[262] What King George III described as "the most perfect of human formations", what hasn't been made but has grown over centuries, what wasn't the fruit of abstract theory but "of that instinct which [...] has enabled Englishmen, and especially uncivilized Englishmen, to build up sound and lasting institutions"[263] – all this can't be wrong, and has to endure. Analogous

---

[257] Barendt, Eric (1998), p. 28
[258] Hailsham, Lord (1992), p. 12: "[...] in some fundamental respects, we are governed by conventional practices and not by law in its strict sense."
[259] Birch, Anthony H. (1998), p. 21: "[...] the limited influence of the courts of law." See also Barendt, Eric (1998), p. 45.
[260] Barendt, Eric (1998), p. 33
[261] Hailsham, Lord (1992), p. 13
[262] *Id.*, p. 1
[263] Dicey, Albert Venn (1982 [1915, 8th ed.]), p. CXXVI

to the Americans, the British are also lucky to have found the best solution ever built up. And both argumentations use history to justify the present, even though the British have more years to brag about. The Americans have their Founding Fathers, the British, however, can't exactly fix the origins. "[…] no precise date could be named as the day of [the Constitution's] birth; no definite body of persons could claim to be its creators, no one could point to the document which contained its clauses."[264] The reference to the past, to an extended time frame to defend a current solution seems to me problematic. Over centuries Blacks were oppressed, women the subordinates of their husbands, people forbidden to vote, or children forced to work: Is it therefore a just arrangement to be upheld? What the British concept demonstrates, though, is that stable integration doesn't depend on the form of law, but on the way it is established and adapted to the needs of the people. A *cooperative approach to the drafting, as well as to the enforcement of law, stabilizes the community*. According to Bagehot, the British constitution changed slowly over the centuries, "because a quick [development] would have destroyed the executive and killed the State, and because the most numerous classes, who changed very little, were not prepared for any catastrophic change in our institutions."[265] Whatever the justification, be it that the creators of the legal fundaments were exceptional or that the legal rules were in force since time immemorial, what counts is the story told. The story has to be sufficiently convincing to make people support the community's fundament. And it has to be a story within which the individuals can play a respected role. "Every constitution must gain authority, and then use authority; it must first win the loyalty and confidence of mankind, and then employ that homage in the work of government."[266] An interactive understanding of politics and law invites all participants to work on their comprehension of the Constitution and the consequences to be taken. That counts even more in a legal system that makes constitutional amendments an exceptional event. Paradoxically, a very rigid Constitution leads to more creative interpretation than a flexible one that can simply be adapted to current interests. Within a flexible arrangement a living constitution reflects the understanding of the good life of the people who are living, adapting continuously to their ever changing needs. The fundamental text, then, isn't this shining symbol anymore, reaching back in time, pointing the way into the future. It becomes a more technical document, that helps to solve problems during reproduction, stands for the current or former elementary

---

[264] *Id.*, p. CXXVI
[265] Bagehot, Walter (1966 [1867, 1915]), p. 255
[266] *Id.*, p. 61

consensus during constructive politics or deconstruction, but is less suitable to become the crystallization point of the integration process.

From the point of view of civil rights, there is, interactively speaking, unfortunately no safeguard making sure that they are respected. Whatever the legal rule that's established, it is still the majority that has to be willing to protect the minority. Lacking this will, no legal text will restrain the unwilling from persecuting the minorities they constructed when establishing their own collective identity. Violations of civil rights can take place in different relationships. So, for example, in the relationship of the individual to the state, or between individuals in private matters, at the working place, or in the church. If there is not a comprehensive readiness to accuse and prosecute these violations and to support the victims, these rights do not exist. The same accounts for human rights, where, on the one hand, an international consensus has to be established. On the other hand, their enforcement is often difficult because of the dearly defended state sovereignty and because of a lack of solidarity and resources.

d) Law and identity

France and Switzerland have a fundamentally different approach to conflicts and know by this a fundamentally different decision-making process. Whereas Switzerland does everything to avoid conflicts and to control debates by referring to legal structures, the French politic is much more chaotic, spontaneous, unruly, and dynamic.

aa) France – a revolutionary monarchy, an elitist democracy

Since Louis XIV, France oscillates between two extremes: absolutism and revolution. After the absolutist monarchy of the Sun King came the revolution, which intended a sort of a constitutional monarchy (1789–1792), which was followed by the First Republic (1792–1799), which, in turn, developed into the totalitarian empire of Napoleon Bonaparte (until 1814). The restored constitutional monarchy lasted 34 years and was replaced in 1848 by the Second Republic, which, in turn, was succeeded after three years by the relatively mild dictatorship of Napoleon III. What is described as the "Third Republic" (1871–1940) was a succession of governments which weren't bothered too much by the very short constitution. Arbitrary interpretation led to a permanent change of the legal foundations, so that law of 1871 didn't have many things in common with the law of 1940. This parliamentary democracy is replaced by the factual dictatorship of Maréchal

Pétain from 1940–1944. The fourth republic, from 1946 on, serves mainly to hinder president de Gaulle to become to powerful.

The *alternating revolutionary and authoritarian politics* is motivated, on the one hand, by the fear that revolutions generate, and, on the other hand, by the need for justice and freedom. Even though the French revolution is highly venerated because of its liberating effect, it is also something people fear because of its unpredictability and destabilizing consequences.[267] Favoring stability over change (see p. 92 ff.), people for a long time didn't want to overthrow monarchy, an order perceived as natural. Compromises in favor of the third estate would have sufficed to save the king.[268] But the greed and the arrogance of the aristocracy finally beheaded the monarchy. After the revolution the need for stability was satisfied by dictatorship and monarchy, which, in turn, came under revolutionary threat. French history and identity contains, thus, "monarchy/empire/dictatorship" as element for stability and order, "revolution" as an element for freedom and justice.[269] The Fifth Republic mixes authoritarian elements with democracy in the constitution, or authoritarian elements with revolution if we look at the political culture in general. The constitution itself doesn't give the people much power besides the elections of the parliament and the president. It incorporates an elitist understanding of leadership and reflects the absolutist tradition. The extensive protest-culture, on the other hand, stands for the revolutionary tradition. And the combination of both in the Fifth Republic can be seen as integration of this century-old conflict.

Another element characterizing the French political culture is its elitism, which follows the authoritarian logic. French elitism is rooted in two formidable rulers: The Sun King and Napoleon Bonaparte. The kingdom of Louis XIV was the most impressive in Europe in the 17th century. He created the modern state. Napoleon Bonaparte, in turn, established the modern administration and a very effective police state. Both needed well-educated and informed people to implement their political visions. The king, therefore, developed an idea that Cardinal Richelieu had had: The collective identity of the nation should emanate from one man, using all political, economic, and cultural tools available. To make sure that the French kingdom would be the unsurpassed and most glorious one on earth, the most talented artists would have to work for the king (see pp. 388 ff.). On the other hand, the national integration needed a unification in thinking and

---

[267] Furet, François/Richet, Denis (1963), p. 450
[268] *Id.*, pp. 23, 74, 101, 120; Bluche, François (2000), p. 13; Richard, Guy (1979), p. 101
[269] According to Nicolet the empire appeared for the French as syntheses of the old monarchy and the young republic (Nicolet, Claude [1992], p. 170).

speaking. Richelieu "wanted to acquire control of the state over all cultural activities, both for the aggrandizement of France as a centre of literary activity and eventually also of learning, but also for the ability it would give the state to manipulate the personal and social values of France."[270] The Académie française was a political project[271] created in 1635 to unify and standardize language and to use culture for the celebration of the political power.[272] Culture became political and the French "exception culturelle"[273] was born. The revolution abolished the Académie française because of its absolutist character. Aware of the power rooted in cultural production as well as in education, Napoleon I. restored the academy and established in 1804, the first empire – a dictatorial regime much more absolutist than the one Louis XIV had built.[274] For the first time in European history the modern administrative state with its focus on bureaucratic effectiveness and its tendency to total control and standardization got established. Everything is regulated, everything is legislated.[275] Such a strongly extended administration needed well-trained personnel, no longer recruited because of its membership of a particular rank, but because of its proficiency. In the mid-nineteenth century, the "École libre de science politiques" (Sciences Po) was founded, a school supposed to form an elite capable to prohibit or rein in popular uprising. In reaction to the dishonor of the German "Blitzkrieg" and mobilizing against communism, the "École Nationale de l'Administration (ENA)" was founded 1945 and was expected to strengthen the state. Today, one has to graduate from ENA or Sciences Po to get access to administrative or governmental power. Rare is the important politician let alone member of the administration who wasn't or isn't a former member of one of these "grandes écoles." "Without administration, politics wouldn't exist. [...] The French administration is more than anywhere else the motor of politics."[276]

Against this backdrop, it isn't surprising that the Constitution of 1958 is based on "monarchical" principles: A strong hierarchical orientation toward the president, a centralist representative democracy, and the relative powerlessness of the parliament, which can't dismiss the most powerful ac-

---

[270] Levi, Anthony (2001), p. 164
[271] Thuau, Etienne (2000), p. 219
[272] Solnon, Jean-François (1987), p. 267
[273] Rigaud, Jacques (1995), p. 32
[274] Richard, Guy (1979), p. 186
[275] Castelot, André (2001), p. 368
[276] Tenzer/Delacroix (1992), p. 88. About Sciences Po and ENA see Garrigou, Alain (2001), Bourdieu, Pierre (1989), Gaillard, Jean-Michel (1995).

tor, the president. Weak federal elements were introduced in 1982. Direct democracy is limited to the right to elect parliament and the president every five years. There are four forms of referendums:

- Referendum concerning constitutional amendments (Article 89 Section 2 Constitution)
- Referendum concerning draft bills of a certain importance (Article 11 Section 1 Constitution)
- Popular initiative concerning the amendment of ordinary bills (Article 11 Section 3 Constitution)
- Territorial referendum (Article 53 Section 3 Constitution)

These referendums, however, aren't tools people can use to control the rulers. They are much more measures the president uses at his own discretion. During the Fourth Republic, de Gaulle had made negative experiences with a fragmented parliament. To make sure that the president wouldn't be blocked by the legislative, he intended to introduce the direct election of the head of state. The prescribed procedure of Article 89 Section 2 and 3 Constitution needed the approval of parliament, which, however, wasn't interested in losing power. Quite sure about his popular support, he chose to appeal directly to the people, based on Article 11 Section 1 Constitution. He succeeded in 1962, but was widely criticized for having used the wrong legal basis. What was qualified as a breach of the constitution is today accepted as legal.

The power of the French president is of a monarchical character. He is entitled to dissolve parliament and decides over the appointment of the prime minister and the ministers if he is in control of the majority party. France can therefore be qualified as a "demonarchy:"[277] A quite authoritarian system with a selective access of "We the people" to power. It is only in times of the "Cohabitation" that there is a form of checks and balances limiting the immense power of the president. "Cohabitation" means that the two main political forces have to cooperate because the president's party doesn't have the majority in parliament. The executive responsibility is then shared between Prime Minister and President and the Parliament has its own will. In ordinary times, though, the President uses the Prime Ministers and ministers according to the actual political needs. They serve as scapegoats, are replaced as soon as problems occur, to give the impression that the people have been heard.

---

[277] See Georgel, Jacques (1990), who talks about the "démonarchie".

Beside the voting rights, France is, legally speaking, a presidential system following the autocratic tradition of the country. That accounts also for the popular initiative introduced in 2008 in Article 11 Section 3 Constitution. What is supposed to enhance the power of the people, is a steeplechase in the hands of the state institutions. Called a "popular initiative" it is much more a parliamentary initiative of at least one fifths of the members of parliament (184), supported by one tenth of the voters (approximately 4,5 mio.). The initiative is monitored twice by the Conseil constitutionnel (French supreme court). First the supreme court has to check whether the bill deals with the organization of the public authorities or with reforms relating to the economic, social or environmental policy of the Nation (Article 11 Section 1 Constitution). If this precondition is respected, the support of one tenth of the voters has to be organized. Afterwards, the Conseil constitutionnel checks if the initiative itself is constitutional. A referendum only takes place if the Parliament doesn't decide about the initiative within a period defined by the law. There are no grounds to suppose that this new right will ever be used, as the preconditions are way too high and the whole procedure much too time-consuming.

Article 5 Section 1 Constitution stipulates that the President has to be the guarantor of the Constitution, the one who ensures as an umpire the proper functioning of the public authorities and the continuity of the State. In my view, though, the President is the republican king, using state power largely at his own discretion. A major precondition, therefore, is that he has to control the majority party. Consequently, it can be said, that the constitution is not an authoritative text that imposes itself against the will of the powerful. This impression is confirmed by an important element of French politics that isn't mentioned in the Constitution: street protests. "The street" is the revolutionary element of French political culture, which puts into perspective the almighty President. An effective counterpower developed in places and on the streets, forcing the formal institutions to listen and to react. This symbolic power gains its importance because of the venerated tradition of the revolution.

In 1986, Prime Minister Jacques Chirac decided to reform higher education in France. His education minister, René Monory, and delegated minister, Alain Devaquet, submitted, in June 1986, a draft bill that was accepted by the Conseil des ministres. In autumn 1986, the parliament discussed and approved the bill; the current distribution of institutional power guaranteed the President to push through his political goals. However, on November 17, 1986, the students at the University of Villetaneuse (Paris) launched a strike against the so-called law Devaquet. This protest continued by colleges and reached on the 27th the provinces. Supported by the unions, the movement becomes quite impressive. As usual in this sort of conflict, the formal institution, in this case, education minister Monory, attacked the unions and their right to protest and he declared being the only one responsible for national education.[278] The union "Fédération de l'éducation nationale" (FEN) answered on November 23, with a demonstration of about 200'000 teachers and students. Faced with this massive protest, Chirac understood that he had to compromise, that he had to launch indirect negotiations. On November 30, he proposed to submit to Parliament a new draft bill within two weeks. But this offer didn't ease the situation. Devaquet declared, that Tuesday, December 4, the day of the next demonstration, will be the crucial moment.[279] During these "negotiations" between formal and informal politics, both sides do not try to convince with arguments but mainly with symbolic power. The bigger and longer the demonstrations, the more the formal institutions have to react and give in. These conflicts sometimes lead to serious negotiations of the content of a law, but most of the time they are about the withdrawal of an existing law or a proposal. The demonstration of December 4th, in Paris mobilized between 200'000 (information of the police), 500'000 (Le Monde), or up to 1'000'000 (organizers) students. A delegation met at 7 p.m. with the education minister without finding a compromise. Just after 8 p.m. riots occurred resulting in casualties. Protests against the actions of the police during the demonstration of December 4th were countered by the police with excessive force, leading to the death of the student Malik Oussekine. This was literally the death blow for the draft bill. Against such a powerful symbol, institutionalized politics had to give in: On December 6, Devaquet resigned and on December 8, Chirac retrieved the draft bill. Even though they are not part of the legal framework, even though are legally inexistent, the street revolutionaries prevailed and shaped in an important way the political "reality."

Following his (neo)-liberal politics, Prime Minister Alain Juppé, declared on September 4, 1995, to would modify the social security and the retirement arrangements of the civil servants. According to Juppé, civil servants are privileged, which is why a reduction of their entitlements would help his austerity plan. Surprisingly, on October 10, the civil servants organized a country-wide general strike, comprised of 55 % of the staff in general and about 60 % of the educational system. In the view of this massive resistance, Juppé agreed to discuss the retirement pay, but was not willing to

---

[278] "Le vrai patron de l'éducation nationale, c'est moi, pas les syndicats", in: Le Monde November 24, 1986
[279] Année Politique 1986, p. 367

negotiate the basic principles of his wage policy. The new proposal did not satisfy the unions, which is why they started new strikes from November 17-24, paralyzing the entire public traffic in France from the 24th on. While pretending to be willing to negotiate, Juppé and President Chirac made the Conseil des ministres adopt the draft on November 28. The unions again mobilized, from December 5th on, a large number of people (one million on December 7 and 12, respectively). From the moment the government was seriously ready for further compromises, the protests faded. Even though the users of public traffic had to organize themselves privately to get to work, the entire "revolution" was perceived much more as a public festival than as an annoyance. The majority supported the strikers, motivated not in the least by the arrogant reactions of Juppé and the contradiction between his politics and the promises the President had made during the election campaign. Juppé, like most of the elite, was too convinced that politics is made by decrees, not by negotiation. This lack of recognition launched a reaction from the people outside the elitist area of politics, important enough to force the rulers to listen and to adapt.

Protests of the police and of the gendarmerie[280] are very rare. First, it is not part of their culture; they are fundamentally responsible for law and order and because of this always on the other side of the protesters. Second, they have to observe the strike ban, which is why protesting for them is illegal. Because of its rarity, law and order protests are already effective when a small group of people is mobilized. Police or gendarmerie in the streets has an important symbolic impact that a government is ready to recognize quickly. In November 2001, first 4'000, then around 8'000 police officers demonstrated in Paris for better working conditions and less restrictions based on rule of law. Secretary of the Interior Vaillant opens negotiations, which did not lead to a consensus. The police answered with a protest of 20'000 officers. At the end of the month, a compromise could be reached, that would cost approximately € 380 million. That same year, the gendarmerie struck and demonstrated for the first time in its five hundred years history. In the beginning they used forms of protest notable for their originality. In this way, they intended to conceal the breach of law they were committing. First, they asked 250 of their women to demonstrate in Grenoble with uniform caps and whistles, making the demands of their husbands. Not allowed to express themselves in public, they set up their own web site, containing a discussion forum and serving as a wailing wall. Secretary of Defense Richard proposed a package of measures worth € 380 millions.

---

[280] Army troops responsible for homeland security.

Not satisfied, 300 soldiers went in uniform and by office car to the doctors offices, because the proposals of the defense minister had made them sick. Only now the demonstration became public, in the classic form, beginning with 2'000 and ending with 12'000 marchers. Finally, an agreement was reached that satisfied the gendarmerie and ended the protests. Besides the uniqueness of their demonstration, the upcoming election campaign made the government ready to compromise. Even more, because the campaign focused on criminality and homeland security, these sort of pictures had to be avoided. Regardless of the illegally of their acts, no charges were pressed against them. French street revolution is not understood as an aggression against the state, it is not intended to overthrow the state. But it is an effective and strong claim for negotiations, for recognition and respect, for being heard.

There is no guarantee that protesters will have an impact. Even big mobilizations over quite a time can be in vain. The year 1966 is marked by an intense strike movement, costing 2'245'000 working days, but yielding almost no result.[281] A unified appearance, a long-lasting large mobilization, and the support of the people are most important. Contrary to the well organized and permanently mobilized small group of institutionalized politicians, the revolutionaries have to constitute their power from scratch again and again. They have to rally an impressive number of people who have to be willing to bear private and/or professional inconveniencies.

To avoid these intense and costly conflicts, a law on the "modernization of social dialogue"[282] was adopted in 2007. It obliges the government to negotiate with the social partners all draft bills about work, professional education, or employment. Up to today, the law got applied quite arbitrarily, probably because until now it didn't suit the political culture.

bb) Switzerland – mitigating conflicts, concordance democracy

The political culture of France likes conflicts, it likes the display of power, strong claims, intense fights over right and wrong, of the elite against the people, and of the "king" against the man and woman in the street. Decisions have to be made quickly and changes may come from one day to the next. Law is, therefore, often understood to be at the disposal of the elite. Switzerland, on the other hand, organizes everything in a way that hides conflicts, makes them small and manageable, tries to avoid systematic ex-

---

[281] Année Politique 1966, S. 213
[282] Loi du 31 janvier 2007 de modernisation du dialogue social

clusion, too radical positions, and makes sure that changes take their time. This concordance democracy is based on the following constitutional arrangements:

- Popular initiative for total or partial revision of the Constitution (Article 138 and 139 Constitution). 100'000 people can claim an amendment of the Constitution. The new provision comes into effect, as soon as the majority of the voters and the cantons (states) have approved.
- Mandatary referendum for amendments of the Constitution or the introduction of important federal decrees (Article 140 Constitution)
- Optional referendum for ordinary legislation (Article 141 Constitution). 50'000 people can require a vote over a law that has been passed by the parliament. The majority of the voters decides whether the bill becomes effective.
- There is no government-opposition-system. All important parties build a coalition-government (so called "Zauberformel", not defined by law), which can't be deselected during a four years' term. Its seven members have to represent as well as possible the different geographical areas and the linguistic regions (Article 175 Section 4 Constitution).

It is the widely respected political culture and the constitutional arrangements that make Swiss politics stable, predictable, and sometimes boring. To avoid an optional referendum, bills are drafted in a way that possible opposition is avoided in the run-up to a parliamentary debate. During an extensive consultation process, the administration invokes all organizations, unions, cantons, lobby-groups, associations, or individuals who could be concerned by a draft bill to take a stand on the proposed changes. Their criticism is either introduced into the bill or the project ends because of strong opposition. It's not worth fighting for a draft that will after its parliamentary approval be denied by the majority of the voters or not applied by the cantons or responsible organizations. Popular initiative and optional referendum provide the possibility to launch and change the law. There is, so the common sense, no protest needed. Protests are nothing more than an annoying and noisy disturbance of a well-greased law-making machine which provides everything necessary to make yourself heard. Stick to the rules and avoid too much visibility. Revolutionary movements do not fit the conflict-controlling culture that has been densely woven and effective for many decades.

This focus on procedures is motivated by the lack of a unifying language or culture. Four national languages are spoken and recognized in Switzerland: German (63.7%), French (20.4%), Italian (6.4%), and Romansh (0.5%) (Article 4 Constitution). And the different parts of Switzerland are culturally oriented to themselves and much more to the outside, the surrounding cultures (Germany, France, and Italy) than to the other linguistic parts of the country. Nevertheless, what holds this community together is not the intense conflict oriented debate or a conflict about fundamentals, or the celebration of a unique and exclusive culture like in France or in other culturally more homogeneous states. It is the political procedure, the widely used political rights, which make the people experience the collective identity. Four times a year there are votes, and every four years elections. It is during these debates and decisions that the other parts of the country matter most. This *political* (and not cultural) *integration* also becomes visible in the federal structure of Switzerland. This small nation (only 41'285 km^2) affords itself the luxury of 26 cantons (Article 1 Constitution) with considerable autonomy and state power, and about 2'500 communes. Compared to other countries, this is an incredibly intense state structure with two advantages: First, it connects the people directly with political institutions, strengthening the collective identity. Second, federalist logic asks for cooperation between the different levels (Article 44 et seq. Constitution), making sure, that the major actors are heard and fundamental opposition is avoided. And Article 50 Constitution guarantees the communal autonomy in accordance with cantonal law and demands the federation to consider the consequences its activities have for the communes.

Law-making in Switzerland takes years, whereas the French government can pass a law within months or even weeks. The French government, on the other hand, doesn't know, if the law adopted by the parliament will be accepted and implemented. And during the parliamentary debate or when the draft is announced, street protest can occur any time, which contains considerable political risks that nobody can control. Changes to the French retirement system were done very fast in September/October 2010, leading to big demonstrations of one to two million people. President Sarkozy had to give in on certain aspects of the law, but, nevertheless, he did succeed on the major question of the retirement age. During this intense conflict nobody knew who would win. In this case, the President was successful because the majority of the people was convinced of the necessity of reform. Winning this fight strengthened his position. There is, though, always the risk that the loser has to pay with his political career. In Switzerland, however, the retirement age will probably also be raised. But it will take years. In 2003, Federal Councillor Couchepin declared that 67 should be the age of retirement for everybody. A lot of criticism was heard, but in the following years many people became accustomed to this idea. A bill will be drafted, pass the consultation process and the parliamentary debate, and pass a possible referendum. When the bill is finally enacted, people will have had lots of possibilities to influence the law and enough time enough to adapt their life to the new "reality," why protests won't occur and implementation will take place smoothly.

This permanent process of generalized law-making unites people in debates. There is, on the other hand, a risk that demagogues with more money than others can set the discussion's agenda and influence the outcome.[283] Especially the right wing SVP has, thanks to sponsors like Christoph Blocher or Walter Frey, the possibility to be permanently in campaign. Another problem is the very restrictive naturalization practice that leads to a population of 20 % of foreigners, who do not have the right to vote. As a member of the community, the participation possibilities are quite high. Being excluded from this main integrative discourse is even more humiliating, because the membership is essentially experienced during votes or elections. A further problem is that the countless possibilities to influence the law-making process are mainly used by right and right-wing politicians and lobby groups, which are numbered by Kriesi at about 1'200 people.[284] So it is, on the one hand, a fairly cooperative and respectful political culture, that avoids effectively intense clashes. On the other hand it is a closed, quite xenophobic, and elitist system, sold to the people as highly democratic.

---

[283] Linder, Wolf (1994), pp. 113 f.; Gruner, Erich/Hertig, Hans Peter (1983), pp. 133 ff.; Longchamp, Claude (1991), pp. 311 ff.
[284] Kriesi, Hanspeter (1980), pp. 263, 577 f.

7. People – Space

People define who they are, who they want to be, and who doesn't belong to them (see also p. 89 f. and p. 107 ff.). Against the background of constructivism defended in this book, there isn't any natural criteria that imposes itself when it comes to the construction of "we the people." Depending on our basic values, the "people" can, for example, be understood in a universal or in an essentialist sense. A *universal concept of human beings* can be based on equal freedom: Every man and every woman is free economically, socially, and politically. Furthermore, every individual is unique, different, and has to be treated as if all were equal, respecting his or her individuality. Collectivism in the sense that group-criteria dominate individuality, has to be avoided. An individual may be part of a group, of a family, country, nation, religious, cultural, or professional group, but group membership shouldn't prevail over the uniqueness of the individual character. Being part of a group is a part of one's identity, but doesn't determine her or him. Human contingency makes individuals organize the chosen memberships in a distinct way, changing its meaning, enriching it, and creating new appearances. This arrangement is a more *fragile, floating set of memberships and soloist performances* than an entrenched structure. If we want to take equal freedom seriously, identity is the *individual understanding about oneself and the relationships to others*.

Essentialist concepts of people, on the other hand, fix specific attributes as given, as natural. Traits of individuals, as well as of communities, are declared as characteristic and unchangeable and are absolutized and immunized against quests for change or criticism. Protecting what is their own, essentialist constructions tend to be exclusionary and oppressive. Other forms of living are judged much more a threat than a valuable alternative. Fearing what is different, others have to be outside of one's own "reality" and are made scapegoats for all the problems occurring in the perfect world. Negating the human and equal quality of others helps to stabilize the essentialist existence; e.g., "Niggers" that can be enslaved, "immigrants" or "refugees" deported regardless of their dire straits.

Space is another construction form used to build up collective identities (see also p. 391 ff.). It is more than just the physical arrangement of objects. "Space" is action, it is the relationships people create between people and between people and things. As geographical anchor point it helps to create a lasting link for many a people. In the history of humankind personal relationships prevailed over geographical attachments. It is mainly with the nation state that geographical space and political borders gain the importance we ascribe to them today. To have land of one's own can be helpful to unite people and to protect them and their culture against demands or threats from other communities. People calling themselves "Palestinians," for example, are longing for a state of their own with secure borders recognized by their neighbors and making an autonomous existence possible. Natural frontiers like mountains or the sea do not impose themselves as identity-criterion. Borders are social constructions having an identity-building effect as long as the community refers to them and the neighbors take sovereignty seriously. In 1884, people living in Africa weren't consulted if the borders drawn by fifteen states[1] were sensible, if the identities forced onto them had an integrative effect on them and their life-style. At the request of Portugal, German Chancellor Bismarck called a conference to find a solution that would satisfy the economic claims of the powerful states of the time. Their major interest was the exploitation of Africa's minerals. Even though 80 % of the continent was organized by African communities, the historical structures weren't taken into account. Looking today at a map of the borders of Africa demonstrates the arbitrary almightiness the colonial states applied to what they understood to be "their world." This lack of recognition and respect, this compelled unification led to conflicts still happening today. "The African politico-geographical map is, thus, a permanent liability that resulted from three months of ignorant and greedy acquisitiveness during a period when Europe's search for minerals and markets had become insatiable."[2]

Space is an area people have to embrace and occupy by using it. It can be the public space, belonging to nobody and everybody, freely usable, as it was the case during most of the time of mankind. Or it takes the form of a private space, so that the king, the aristocracy, and/or the wealthy bourgeoisie become owners and the rest have to stay away from the now private grounds. Parks can be built for the exclusive pleasure of the king, hunting, for example, his game in his forest. Or parks are conceived as the places where the subjects can meet their king, reminding them of their rank within society and the greatness of the ruler. In 1662, Charles II opened St. James's Park to the public, following the model of Louis XIV and of his architect, Le Nôtre. His subjects got familiar with this use and began to understand it as a right. "George II's Queen Caroline later inquired of Sir Robert Walpole what it would cost to shut the royal parks to the public: 'Only three Crowns,' was the reply."[3] *It is in public space that the notion of the*

---

[1] Austria-Hungary, Belgium, Denmark, Germany, Spain, France, Great Britain, Italy, Netherlands, Norway, Portugal, Russia, Sweden, Turkey, and United States of America.
[2] de Blij, H.J./Muller, Peter O. (2008), p. 305
[3] Porter, Roy (2000), p. 130

community becomes palpable, where the multitude of memberships is visible, different social strata interact more or less willfully, and where in- and exclusion mechanisms take place. For homeless people, the public space becomes "home." Regulations to "remove homeless people lead to a specific, and highly constricted sort of public sphere. [...] it speaks of a highly sanitized city and a fully deracinated politics – a politics that elevates the importance of aesthetics over the needs of some people simply to survive."[4] On the other hand, the public space is a political place, where, for example, French unions and student organizations challenge their government's policies, where democracy in its direct or revolutionary form comes into being. Consumption temples are publicly used private grounds, highly regulated and excluding political manifestations in favor of undisturbed consumption.[5] Increasing economization and privatization of public space makes the available "democratic space" shrink. As a result, political engagement is increasingly replaced by the homo oeconomicus, who is only satisfied if her or his material possessions increase. Shopping malls and one's own four walls become the center of the individual's life, which is why mobilizations for common interests become difficult to realize. To integrate a community, visiting shopping malls, bars, or concerts will not suffice.

Public space is needed to build up a counterpower that's characterized by the number of participants. This space is the result of interactive debates or, if competition rules, of a power struggle. When workers made use of non-private space to claim just working conditions, the rulers didn't judge this as free speech and rally which are protected by the Constitution, but as violence because "all concerted struggle against employers was understood to be violent."[6]

a)   Racist market

The history of South Africa can be constructed as a highly effective economic integration of cheap workers, while at the same time totally excluding them from the social and political realm. The majority of the population got debased, had to suffer a degrading and humiliating treatment to make the white upper class wealthy and to give the white middle class and the white poor the satisfaction of not being the worst off. The lowest place on the social ladder was foreseen for the Blacks, "with unskilled jobs, infertile

---

[4]   Mitchell, Don (2003), p. 9; see also pp. 134 ff.
[5]   Schroer, Markus (2006), p. 233
[6]   Mitchell, Don (2003), p. 55

land, broken families and, above all, the all-pervading poverty and inhuman living conditions."[7]

aa) Human material

Before the Dutch East India Company came to the South of Africa in 1652, the Khoikhoi ('men of men'), Nama, San, Tshu-Khwe, and others had been living there as hunter-gatherers for at least 10'000 years. Around 300 AD Bantu-speaking people like the Xhosa and Zulu moved from West to South Africa. The size of the communities ranged from a few hundred to about 50'000. They were democratically organized with a chief and bound into a network of reciprocity. The typical capitalist class-structure based on social inequality and the absence of a solidary corrective didn't exist.[8] It was imported and forced upon them by Europeans. Conflicts were divisive but not destructive because their basic values were not perceived as absolute. Accordingly, conflicts took on a bigger scale in the form of rebellions, not of war in the sense of bloody destruction.[9] "[…] there is no evidence of large-scale warfare before the early nineteenth century."[10] Power politics based on an all-or-nothing logic was a European importation, too.

The Dutch East India Company used the Cape only as a supply base for its travels to Asia. In the beginning, the exchange of goods with the local Africans didn't pose any problems because it was a relationship based on respect and equity. When the Dutch began to change the terms of trade at the expense of the Khoi, the latter were opposed and the Dutch fought some war to drive them of and establish farms run by European settlers. Losing a series of battles against the East India Company at the end of the 17th century, the Khoi "lost their cattle and were reduced to tributary status. From then on, some Khoikhoi began to work alongside imported slaves as laborers on the settler farms, a clear sign of their loss of economic independence."[11] Fast-growing numbers of settlers (who called themselves Afrikaner and were called by others "Boer," Dutch for "farmers") with an increasing hunger for grazing lands led to conflicts with Africans who were not ready to give up the land that had been their base of life and home for thousands of years.

---

[7] Kaur, Abnash (1995), p. i
[8] Guy, Jeff (1987), p. 29
[9] Id., p. 26
[10] Study Commission on U.S. Policy toward Southern Africa (1981), p. 26
[11] Worden, Nigel (2007), p. 11

Like the Dutch, the new world power, Great Britain, was in the beginning not interested in settling on a big scale in Southern Africa. They took the Cape in 1795 to keep control of the sea route to Asia. In 1799, a rebellion started of Khoi and San which lasted four years and convinced the British to cooperate with the Xhosa. Realizing that the British position on the Cape wasn't secured and the settlers were under serious threat, Great Britain decided to engage more seriously. Not ready to fight costly wars against the Natives who had much more to lose than just economic opportunities, the British ordered Dutch settlers not to expand into the lands of Africans. Nevertheless, over 10'000 Boers went north (the so-called "Great Trek" of 1830 to 1840) mainly because of their dire and unequal economic situation. They "were not members of the new capitalizing wool gentry and many of them still rented land from the state."[12] They established new settlements in the form of three independent states, which the British countered by invading one of them and founding the British colony of Natal in 1843. Most Boers fled to the other two states and developed there quite isolated communities there. Many armed conflicts between British, Boers, and for example the Xhosa or the Zulus led over the decades to thousands of deaths on both sides.

Having abolished the slave trade in 1807 and in 1833 slavery throughout the Empire,[13] British and Dutch settlers had to find another way to force people working for them as cheaply as possible. A racially based construction of land use and borders seemed to be the most effective answer. The first segregated areas called *"Native Reserves"* were built for four reasons: First, the Whites intended to establish large-scale commercial plantations, reserving the best land for themselves and excluding others based on the criterion of race. Second, Africans would be used as a cheap workforce. The exclusion and confinement of Africans helped, third, to control the potentially disruptive Natives who were ready to defend their interests and to fight for recognition and justice. And fourth, assigning scattered African refugees to reserves helped to uphold the racial and social difference and to protect white areas from squatting Natives. Creating an artificial scarcity of land and depriving Africans of their means of agricultural production,[14] the Natives had to look elsewhere to make a living, so they took the badly paid jobs Whites offered. To increase the pressure, the Natal "hut tax" was introduced in 1850, imposing seven shillings a year on Africans. As a result, Africans had to sell their cattle to pay the tax or to sell their workforce to

---

[12] *Id.*, p. 14
[13] The emancipation of the slaves in the Cape Colony took place from 1834-38.
[14] Kaur, Abnash (1995), p. 6

white farmers.

Till the 1860s, the economy in the South of Africa was predominantly agricultural. The discovery of diamonds in 1867 changed fundamentally British engagement. From this point on they intended to overthrow the whole region, brake African resistance, control mineral deposits, and build up the mining industry plus the therefore needed infrastructure. Finding gold in 1886 further emphasized the desire to invest in Southern Africa. The demand for a cheap workforce increased because the mines were rich but difficult to exploit. Their deposits lay very deep and between vast quantities of rock. Though many Africans migrated to the mines in search of work, the need of white employers increased. Had there been free negotiations between workers and potential employers, a considerable increase of wages would have resulted. The British had, therefore, to construct the market adapted to their interests. Using the same mechanisms as before, this "British market" was made by the use of structural violence (see p. 77 ff.). That meant avoiding equal construction power for Blacks and worsening their living conditions in a way that forced them to accept any job and to work for almost nothing. To control the influx of migrants and the reservoir of workers, the British conquered all the rest of the land the Native tribes lived on, set up a labor recruiting system throughout the area, housed black unskilled laborers in dormitories without their families, and increased taxes. "In the new industrial cities, African workers were subjected to a bewildering array of discriminatory laws and practices, all enforced in order to keep workers cheap and pliable."[15] Based on the Glen Grey Act of 1894, the rulers raised another labor tax. Besides the interest in low salaries[16] they intended to re-educate the Natives to get a standardized European style workforce better suitable to the needs of the white economy. Presenting the act in parliament, Prime Minister Cecil Rhodes highlighted the danger of class conflicts because they had occurred in Great Britain or in the U.S. That's why he felt "rather glad that the labor question [in South Africa] is connected with the native question."[17] In this way, unjustified claims for higher wages or redistribution could be excluded easily. According to Rhodes government by the people had to be avoided. "[…] if the Whites maintain their position as the supreme race, the day may come when we shall be thankful that we have the natives with us in their proper position."[18] He noted that the number of Natives was increasing very fast because "the old diminutions by war and

---

[15] Clark, Nancy L./Worger, William H. (2004), p. 14
[16] Rhodes, Cecil (1900), p. 375
[17] Id., p. 371
[18] Id., p. 372

pestilence do not occur" and "our good government prevents them from fighting."[19] But what had to be done with this increasing number of Natives? In his opinion, they were not the same as the British or the Boers because they lacked civilization and were "still children."[20] The labor tax was needed to "give some gentle stimulus [...] to make them go on working. [...] These young natives live in the native areas and locations with their fathers and mothers, and never do one stroke of work. But if a labor tax of 10s. were imposed, they would have to work. [...] We want to get hold of these young men and make them go out to work and the only way to do this is to compel them to pay a certain labor tax."[21] "[...] the gentle stimulant of the labor tax [will] remove them from a life of sloth and laziness; you will thus teach them the dignity of labor, and make them contribute to the prosperity of the state, and give some return for our wise and good government."[22] During the mining revolution large companies were built that were powerful enough to control black workers by applying registration passes, fixed contract terms, and closed compounds. This comprehensive control of the life of black workers contrasted with the ones of the Whites who lived in boarding houses.[23] To prevent the Natives from negotiating with different employers, they were recruited and contracts were signed directly in the rural areas. Cecil Rhodes wasn't only Prime Minister, he was also and foremost a businessman, mining magnate, co-founder of De Beers Mining Company, and, at this time chief of the magnates.[24] It is, therefore, not surprising that economic interests dominated everything, and that notions of the common good, justice, or solidarity were of no importance. Natives weren't recognized as human beings. Stripped of their dignity, they were used simply as working tools.

bb) Making others to unite

Most of the profits made in the mines fell into British hands and were reinvested in America or Europe. Inequality didn't only affect the Natives, but also many Whites. Increasingly, a class-struggle within the Whites developed, as white farmers were confronted with British merchants and local

---

[19] *Id.*, p. 373
[20] *Id.*, p. 380
[21] *Id.*, p. 381
[22] *Id.*, p. 390
[23] Worden, Nigel (2007), p. 43
[24] Wilson, Francis (1972), p. 2

financial institutions with imperial banks. Giliomee talks of a "farmer-merchant, rural-urban, Afrikaner-English division" which engendered Afrikaner Nationalism, "made people express sentiments of ethnic solidarity or 'Africaanderism.'"[25] Being excluded from power and wealth made them unite under an ethnical criterion: "Not-British," "Not-Upperclass," "Not-Rulers," on the one side and of course: "Not-Slave," "Not-Black," "Not-Underclass" on the other. It was an economic structure that excluded a majority from the riches of the country, the unjust repartition of wealth and income, and the lack of cooperation and reciprocity that led to the South African War between the Boers and the British in 1899 to 1902, a war primarily about the control of mineral resources. Too interested in gold, the British moved an immense amount of troops to the Cape and Natal and even armed 30'000 Africans to outnumber the Boers and, finally, winning the war. Still, the British had understood that a certain form of cooperation was needed to stabilize the situation, which is why they took care not to subdue the Boers. Also, their agricultural production was needed for the urban areas. "Economic and political stability required incorporation of Afrikaner politicians into the central organs of government. [...] white unity was thus upheld at the expense of black political and land rights."[26] The Whites united, therefore, against the Blacks to secure white supremacy and avoid conflicts with the ones who had not much in common besides the color or their skin. Thanks to these exclusion mechanisms, the excluders confirmed and strengthened their identity. The problems of social inequality between Whites could be lessened by the hatred on the constructed minority. The white underclass, happy to avoid being in the lowest status, became, therefore, part of the oppression of others, but also of themselves, because they supported indirectly the class society that fixes their chances of success, too.

Alfred Milner, governor of the South African colonies wanted to attract as many English-speakers as possible to outnumber the other language groups and build up a British society. However, the wages paid by the South African mining industry were too low to attract British workers, which is why the shortage of workforce prevailed. Based on an agreement with Portugal, thousands of Blacks from Mozambique were forced to migrate to the gold mines. A more effective solution was the importation of 60'000 Chinese indentured laborers in 1904, who were ready to work for even less than the Africans. On the other hand, the Chinese became competitors of white workers as soon as their contracts were fulfilled, which is why the Afrikaners and the British wanted to get rid of them as fast as possible.

---

[25] Giliomee, Hermann (1987), p. 63, 58
[26] Worden, Nigel (2007), p. 36

However, still in need of a workforce, the pressure on Blacks had to be increased. The Vagrancy Act of 1909 declared vagrancy illegal. The only way the law accepted to proof that one wasn't vagrant was to be in possession of a written contract with a white employer. "African farmers had responded to these pressures by increasing their agricultural production and successfully participating in the commercial sale of their crops in competition with white farmers."[27] To break this economic resistance, the Natives Land Act of 1913 used the same technique that had been already effective in the previous century and allocated 7.3 per cent of the land of the Union to 4/6 of the population. The land for Africans was far removed from white-owned farms and the key areas of commercial agriculture. It couldn't be bought by white people and Blacks were forbidden to buy any land outside these reserves. The Native Reserves weren't only used to control Africans and to make sure, that the reservoir of workforce was secured. "They could also be used as a dumping ground for the waste discarded by the urban and mining industries."[28] Taking control over all the living space, the Urban Areas Act was adopted in 1923, which gave the municipalities the right to enforce residential segregation and force Africans to carry permits in the cities. In this way, the cities became white, and Blacks had to live in rural areas, except if they were needed by white townspeople.

cc) Resistance

In the late 19th century, the Blacks began to develop counter-power. While at first they were cooperative, the futility of their engagement led to radicalization. Many organizations like the South African Native Congress (later the South African Native National Congress and, in 1923, renamed African National Congress [ANC]), the Native Vigilance Association, the African Political Organization, or the Natal Indian Congress were established to defend the rights of the oppressed and to mobilize resistance in the form of demonstrations, protests, or even armed rebellion.[29] Besides the black movement, the white rulers were also confronted with white criticism. The extreme inequality between upper class Whites and white workers and the detrimental effects of industrialization made socialist or communist thinking for the underclass quite attractive. Thanks to this, they were able to develop a consciousness of their own rights and to perceive inequality as a social construct. Because of the industrialization, people were now widely

---

[27] Clark, Nancy L./Worger, William H. (2004), p. 22
[28] Kaur, Abnash (1995), p. 13
[29] Clark, Nancy L./Worger, William H. (2004), pp. 18 f.

dependent on their employers, which made them much more vulnerable. The South African Labour Party, formed in 1908, had to be taken into account as a powerful representation of the interests of white workers. To break their momentum and to avoid class conflicts within the Whites, the rulers decided early on to block the economic advancement of Blacks. The Mines and Works Act of 1911 (also called Color Bar Act) barred Blacks the access to skilled jobs.

In 1919, the Industrial and Commercial Workers' Union (IUC) was created. In 1920 it organized the first large African strike of over 70'000 men in 21 mines. Even though the strike was ended by a police and military force that killed 11 workers, the employers began to fear a workers' revolution in South Africa. The Whites followed, highlighting in their turn that social and economic inequality is an important integration problem. Nevertheless, because of economic reasons, the Chamber of Mines began to dilute the color bar and announced in December 1921 the firing of two thousand highly paid Whites in semiskilled occupations and to replace them with Blacks. They justified this step by the falling gold price which threatened smaller mines with foreclosure. White coal miners were confronted with cuts in wages and with cheap black competition on a skilled level. On January 1, 1922, the white Mine Workers' Union launched a strike that affected the whole Rand mining region and lasted for almost three months (Rand Revolt). Within ten days 22'000 miners joined in. After violent clashes between strikers and the police, the state, defending the interests of the mine owners, declared martial law and attacked the miners with military force, using seven thousand troops, tanks, artillery, and even air support. About 200 people died in this class warfare. On March 18, the strike was ended. The Martial Law Inquiry Commission concluded, that the conflict was the result of a communist influence interested in abolishing the color bar that had led to this conflict. Several leaders of the strike were hanged.

The subsequent elections, however, led to a government change, as Prime Minister Jan Smuts' South African Party was sanctioned for their abuse of state power. They lost the majority to the Nationalist Party (formed in 1914) and the Labour Party. The new government entrenched the color bar to make sure that the Whites wouldn't fight against each other again. Enhancing the racist focus they hoped to strengthen their collective identity by creating a shared menace. Again, one of the main preoccupations of the government was to avoid a development to be seen in many other countries: The solidarity between the workers against the rulers. The race-experience "militated very strongly against the development of a common working-class identity."[30] The race card, however, was relativized by a pronounced ethnicizing which drove a wedge between Whites. The Nationalist Party's identity politic became increasingly important. Afrikaans language was pushed, Afrikaans culture was supported and promoted, and a unique historical identity developed. The Broederbond, established in 1918, and the Federation of Afrikaner Cultural Organizations of 1929 engaged in events to cherish Afrikaner music and art. The history of the Boers had to make them unique and proud, which is why the Great Trek of the 1830s and 1840s became the core element of the new identity: Victims of the British, this courageous people left the oppressor and built up their own republics. Identity work was easy by excluding Africans because the Boers could use the previously constructed collectivization of the "black Bantus". To distance themselves from the British, however, was quite difficult because they shared the same basic values concretized in capitalism and anti-communism.

dd) Apartheid

In the 1930s, the rulers of South Africa were mainly motivated by economic interests. Racist segregation was used whenever necessary. At the beginning of the 1930s, the Depression and droughts made the government establish a support system to uphold the prices of white farmers in dire economic situation. Relief-schemes and job-creation programmes for Whites were introduced and black workers were fired and replaced by Whites. Because of economic reasons total segregation couldn't be upheld. The new industrial sector in the cities required an increasing nimber of workers to satisfy the need for goods the war had rapidly engendered. Furthermore, many white men were at war, which is why Blacks were even hired for skilled jobs, and women got a chance to work outside the home. Defending the interests of the companies, the United Party approved therefore eased the access of Blacks to work and white space. By the end of the war, Africans constituted more than half of the industrial workforce. And many black servants worked in white households in the cities.

In 1948, the National Party came into power. They were aware that the end of World War II had brought important changes to the basic values on the international level. After the experiences with the National Socialists, racism was despised and human rights became very popular. And the strengthened de-colonization movement highlighted the importance of a

---

[30] Alexander, Peter (1999), p. 40

now universally understood equal freedom. Analogous to the development in the USA a hundred years earlier, the South African felt their collective identity threatened by these external changes. Unwilling to adapt, and determined to keep their power, the small minority of ruling Whites decided to continue the economic violence and to intensify the political control. A safeguard was needed, because the racist social, political, and economic structure would no longer be supported internationally, and the lack of legitimization made violent upheavals more than probable, even understandable. Therefore, the rulers intensified the totalitarian system and built up a tightly woven net of oppressive measures that were enforced regardless of the consequences: Total "apartheid" (Afrikaans word for "apartness" or "separateness") was established and *the principle of segregation became a central element of this essentialist understanding of identity*. The racist structure went further than economic interests would have gone. Racism and segregation became a comprehensive construction mode, affecting every part of the individual's and the collective's life. Tough racist behavior became the ticket for respect within the white "reality:" "No European politician, provincial councillor, or town or city councillor will get elected to power in South Africa if he does not show that his stand against African advancement is stronger than those who compete with him."[31]

"Apartheid was a new term for an old idea."[32] The National Party didn't have to invent a new concept, it carried on the reserve-politic "almost as old as the European occupation of South Africa."[33] It relied on a mode of society many rulers before had used. Nevertheless, the "sheer brutality of its implementation and its ultimately overarching impact on the country,"[34] its comprehensive, totalitarian application using the power of modern states made it uniquely radical and brutal. Apartheid meant "permanent denial of human rights, permanent baasskaap,[35] a master race, and inferiority for anything non-white."[36] Because of the worldwide delegitimization of racism, the National Party had to work on the justification of apartheid. For the rulers, racism was no longer a mere anthropological fact but became a "divine mission, the service entrusted by God to the Afrikaner nation (*volk*) acting on behalf of the white race. As the vanguard of white supremacy, the Afrikaner *volk* simultaneously fulfilled its 'natural' role as 'trustee' (*voog*)

---

[31] Mokgatle, Naboth (1971), p. 247
[32] Mandela, Nelson (1995), p. 111
[33] Rogers, Barbara (1976), p. 5
[34] Clark, Nancy L./Worger, William H. (2004), p. 35
[35] Afrikaans for "the white is always the boss."
[36] Mokgatle, Naboth (1971), p. 271

of the African peoples, by undertaking to protect their distinct ethnic and cultural identities."[37] Using one of the standard arguments of dictatorships, apartheid was needed to protect the oppressed: "The policy of apartheid is a concept historically derived from the experience of the established white population of the country and in harmony with such Christian principles as justice and equity. It is a policy which sets itself the task of preserving and safeguarding the identity of the indigenous peoples as separate racial groups with opportunities to develop into self-governing national units; of fostering the inculcation of national consciousness."[38]

The National Party consolidated the Native Reserves and amplified segregation and migration-control, fearing the economic power Blacks had developed over the last decades.[39] The Prohibition of the Mixed Marriages Act of 1949 and the Immorality Amendment Act of 1950[40] wanted to make sure that the races would not mix. Only races held pure could justify the dichotomic worldview. Like the Nürnberger Rassengesetze"[41] during the National Socialist dictatorship, marriage between the races and extra-marital sexual intercourse were forbidden. Space had to be organized the same way, which is why the Group Areas Act was adopted at the same time. Residential and ownership areas were designated and had to be cleaned from the wrong race, which led to massive dislocations[42] and the far reaching uprooting of communities. The Population Registration Act classified and registered everybody according to their racial characteristics. Political rights, educational and economic opportunities, and social status were attributed based on this classification. Because there were obviously more forms of appearance than only White and Black (who were also called "Native" and "Bantu"), a third group, the Coloureds, had to be created. This third category contained Chinese and Indians, but also the descendents of the intermingled European-Malay-Khoi-Slave population of the 17th century and of the emancipated slaves (Griqua and Cape Malay). The Indians had been indentured servants brought to Natal by the British. They had been expected to leave Africa for India after having completed their contracts.

---

[37] Posel, Deborah (1987), pp. 125 f.
[38] The National Party cited in Kaur, Abnash (1995), pp. 11 f.
[39] Kaur, Abnash (1995), p. 14
[40] An extension of the Immorality Act of 1927.
[41] They included the "Gesetz zum Schutze des deutschen Blutes und der deutschen Ehre", to be translated as the "Law for the protection of German Blood and German honor."
[42] Over thirty years about 3,5 million Africans were moved out of white areas, to "erase black spots" as the government described it.

To counter de-colonization claims, the Boers developed Bantustan politics in the 1950s. Conceding the principle of autonomous development, the Blacks were given land for their disposal. Prime Minister Hendrik Verwoerd pointed out, in 1962, that the Bantustans were to be a form of independence and cooperation that would be attractive enough to prove the humanity of South African politics: "I believe that these people [the Africans] should be given their own States as they desire [...] I have confidence in the mass of our Bantu, with the exception of a small group of agitators. I believe that they will see what is taking place in the rest of Africa, and this will strengthen the bonds between us, rather than lead to their joining up with foreign countries, which will result in conflict and chaos [...] We are trying to establish well-disposed little black neighboring States and to safeguard them from such dangers by being prepared to render all kinds of services to them."[43] Verwoerd's concept of humankind and especially of the Blacks becoming visible in this quotation is striking: One has to perceive millions of people as inferior, dumb, child- or animal-like existences when he believes, that oppression and exploitation will find their appraised consensus. The Bantustans, however, weren't intended to achieve real autonomy or equal cooperation between political communities. It was a lure for international critics and strengthened the exclusionary and oppressive space organization based on apartheid-logic. The Bantu-Self-government Bill of 1959 established eight national territorial units, based, according to the government, on the main tribal groups. As stated in the standard South African history books, the Bantustans were "the areas of South Africa where the Bantu had always lived and which belonged to them."[44] These identities, though, weren't traditional ones, but the ethnical classifications that had resulted from the conquests of the 1870s and 1880s. The over 1'500 years' history of the Natives was much more pluralistic than the nationalistic thinking that Europeans could imagine. Population movements and social interactions had led to a variety of communities and sub-communities.[45]

Aware that direct and structural violence alone wouldn't restrain the Africans from fighting back, the Bantu Education Act of 1953 intended to keep them lower educated and away from revolutionary ideas. "By blindly producing pupils trained on a European model, the vain hope was created among Natives that they could occupy posts within the European community despite the country's policy of 'apartheid.' This is what is meant by the

---

[43] House of Assembly Debates (Hansard) of January 23, 1962, quoted in Rogers, Barbara (1976), p. 8.
[44] So a standard South African history book, quoted in Rogers, Barbara (1976), p. 5
[45] Clark, Nancy L./Worger, William H. (2004), pp. 12 f.

creation of unhealthy 'White collar ideals' and the causation of widespread frustration among the so-called educated Natives ... The school must equip [the Bantu pupil] to meet the demands which the economic life of South Africa will impose upon him."[46] For the economy the production of further low-skilled workers, was helpful.

In 1970, the "Bantus" were given the citizenship of their Bantustan[47] and, in 1974 the governments of the Bantustans received far-reaching formal power to control any organization with African members. They could restrict them or individuals to a specific area or prohibit publications or speeches in order to monitor opposition effectively. But at no point could the chiefs use their own discretion, as they needed the approval of the Minister of Bantu Administration and Development.[48] The appointment of the chiefs, as well as any legislative act in the Natives' areas, could be vetoed by the South African Government. And the administration kept control over the schools, colleges, and universities and determined the budget of the Banustans. So, despite the rhetoric of independence and self-government, the Bantustans remained what the Native Reserves always were: "[...] the reservoir of cheap labor for the white economy." And they were "the dumping grounds for Africans who [...] were no longer needed in 'white' South Africa,"[49] like unemployed, old and infirm people or unmarried mothers.[50] According to Roberts, the per capita income in the Bantustans was one of the lowest in whole Africa.[51] Beside Lebowa and Bophuthatswana, the Reserves didn't have any significant mineral resources and their soil was rugged, depleted, and eroded because of over population, as half of the population of South Africa had to live on 14 per cent of the land. Were mineral resources found removed government the area from the reserve or sold the prospecting rights to companies. "An estimated 30'000 to 50'000 African children died every year from the effect of hunger" and the "infant mortality rate for the Africans living in the Bantustans (282 per 1000) was 23 times higher than the rate for the white South Africans (12 per 1000)."[52] Black agriculture could, in the beginning, compete with that of the Whites,

---

[46] Statement made by H.F. Verwoerd, Minister of Native Affairs in 1954 in the senate of South African parliament, quoted in: Clark, Nancy L./Worger, William H. (2004), p. 51. About Bantu Education see Rose, Brian W. (1965), pp. 208 ff.
[47] Bantu Bantustans Citizenship Act of 1970
[48] Rogers, Barbara (1976), p. 23; see also p. 41.
[49] Kaur, Abnash (1995), p. 19
[50] Rogers, Barbara (1976), p. 35
[51] Id., p. 29
[52] Kaur, Abnash (1995), pp. 59 f.

but it was systematically excluded from access to cheap credit, from irrigation support, or from the distribution and the marketing infrastructure.[53] The same logic is to be found in regard to industrialization, as four-fifths of South Africa's industrial output was produced in the four metropolitan centers.[54] Financially, the Bantustans depended heavily on the goodwill of South Africa, which "never aimed at developing the Bantustans."[55] Only public services like education, health, and social security were paid for.

The only thing white Europeans had looked for over the centuries was a cheap workforce. "It must be understood very fundamentally that the Bantu who are working in the industries in South Africa on the basis of our policy [...] are not there on an integrationary basis [...] to become equal workers, equal entrepreneurs, equal partners."[56] With material greed as primal motive, the system could be upheld for such a long time because so many powerful, wealthy people made massive profits with it, including the white upper class minority of South Africa, as well as international investors and companies. Whatever the consequences for the Africans, the profits, which averaged annually nearly 25 per cent at the beginning of the 1980s, and the unrivaled cheap workforce, led many companies to invest in this officially racist country. Social inequality was extremely high: The white minority lived on average a better life than in most industrialized countries, whereas the real value of African mine wages was inferior in 1971 to 1911 and amounted to 18 per cent of the wages of their white co-workers.[57] "Despite the enormous development of the gold mines during the first eighty years of their existence, the real wages of black miners did not increase at all; indeed, over the period of 1889 to 1969, they seem actually to have fallen. Meanwhile real earnings of Whites increased by at least two-thirds."[58] However, apartheid did achieve one of its main goals perfectly well: Very low wages and, thanks to this, extremely high productivity and gains for rulers and investors.[59] Economic inequality was the result of political decisions upheld over decades. It is the repartition of power and the set of values underlying the "reality" construction that defines justice and the quality of life, not impersonal market forces that nobody is responsible for.

---

[53] *Id.*, p. 62
[54] *Id.*, p. 70
[55] *Id.*, p. 94
[56] Mr. Botha, House of Assembly Debates [Hansard] of February 6, 1967, quoted in Rogers, Barbara (1976), p. 10.
[57] Clark, Nancy L./Worger, William H. (2004), p. 63
[58] Wilson, Francis (1972), p. 141
[59] *Id.*, p. 16

ee) Revolution

Although there had been many negotiations, protests, boycotts, defiances, or strikes over the decades, it is after the Sharpville Massacre of 1960 that the Africans' fight against apartheid radicalized and became violent. In the aftermath, ANC[60] and PAC[61] were banned and important leaders jailed. To free themselves from the forced Bantu-identity and to counter the cultural violence, the Africans had to build up their own identity. The Black Consciousness Movement was an important step in this direction. As a part of this movement Stephen Biko organized the SASO,[62] which was supposed to promote self-reliance and to develop a powerful and independent self-perception. In 1973 a series of about 160 strikes mobilized over 60'000 industrial workers. And in December 1974, the "Black Renaissance Convention" took place, in which delegates from all black communities in the country and Coloureds as well as Indians convened. They claimed a truly democratic South Africa based on the principle of "one man, one vote" and an equitable distribution of wealth. The independence of Angola and Mozambique in 1975 motivated them to take more risks. The government's decision that mathematics, social studies, history, and geographic had to be taught in Afrikaans, mobilized students. Bantu Education, which had tried to bring up docile Africans, visibly hadn't had the intended effect. On June 16, 1976, hundreds of high-school students marched toward the Orlando Stadium in Soweto to protest against the government's plans. The police instantly charged the students, which led to several deaths. The next day the schools were closed and the military put on alert. Fights went on and over the following months, many hundreds of people were killed. Soweto became a strong symbol for black consciousness and the arbitrary abuse of power of the white rulers. On September 12, 1977, Steve Biko died in custody of the security police. Since 1963, he was the forty-fourth black dying while in the hands of the police under suspicious circumstances. The consciousness of Africans, however, had fundamentally changed. Based on the idea "don't mourn – mobilize," the Blacks launched one attack after the other against the apartheid system: School boycotts, strikes, marches, demonstrations, burning of symbols of white oppression, or even sabotage attacks against official buildings and government-owned corporations were perpetrated by guerrilla soldiers of the ANC and the PAC operating from neighboring countries. All these forms of resistance made apartheid a topic on the inter-

---

[60] African National Congress
[61] Pan Africanist Congress
[62] South African Students Organization

national agenda, successfully engendering calls for disinvestment. "Western governments and businesses were reassessing South African stability."[63] And the employers began to fear the politicization of the workforce, which is why they urged the government to legalize black and mixed unions that they would be able to negotiate with.[64] It was, in my opinion not a sense of humanity and justice that motivated the rulers to change, but economic problems, the end of the material success-story for Whites over more than two hundred years. But the hopes of the employers to have an unresisting workforce weren't fulfilled, as the black trade unions like NUM (National Union of Mineworkers) or COSATU (Congress of South African Trade Unions) became increasingly important in the economy as well as in the political protests. From 1986 to 1990, more labor days were lost due to work stoppages than during the previous 75 years. And the membership in COSATU rose from 1985 to 1994 from 450'000 to more than 1.3 million.[65]

From 1979 on, the last government upholding its colonial structure used two strategies to try to come to grips with the increased criticism from within and without. First, they empowered the police and army, giving them carte blanche for controlling disorder in the country by using a "Total Strategy." Second, a constitutional reform was proposed that included enfranchisement of the Coloureds and Indians (Article 52 Constitution of 1983) and separate parliaments for every group created by the apartheid-system except for the Africans, who would be represented by the homeland governments. "This new vision of apartheid was intended to present an image of rights and freedom for all, within group-identified institutions that in reality had little power and remained firmly under the control of the white South African parliament."[66] However, the basic power arrangement wasn't altered. The white House of Assembly with 178 members could outvote the House of Representatives of the Coloureds with 85 members and the House of Delegates of the Indians with 45 (Article 37 § 1, 41-43 Constitution of 1983). And, whatever was decided in the different houses, the State President as part of the legislative power (Article 30 Constitution of 1983) remained the most powerful institution, having many possibilities to alter decisions or to dissolve parliament (Article 32, 33, and 39 § 2, lit. a Constitution of 1983).

---

[63] Study Commission on U.S. Policy toward Southern Africa (1981), p. 187
[64] What was done by the Industrial Conciliation Amendment Act of 1979 and the Labour Relations Amendment Act of 1981.
[65] Murray, Martin J. (1994), pp. 142 f.
[66] Clark, Nancy L./Worger, William H. (2004), p. 82

White voters approved the new constitution with two-thirds vote in 1983. This different form of apartheid, however, didn't bring political integration. On the contrary; mobilized by another injustice, it helped to unite the opposition. The United Democratic Front was created, bringing together a multitude of different organizations and colors. After all this time of oppression, the Africans began to use their sheer numbers to construct the power that would challenge the Whites' racist prerogative. The civil society of the oppressed and the popular movement that contained organizations active in many different fields like labor, women's right, civic rights, health, education, housing, legal advice, church, or media had developed over the years organizational structures, knowledge, and support networks that could be used now.[67] This civic movement had its origins in the late seventies in the form of 'self-help' grassroot organizations at the township level.[68] They were social movements which had fought, on the one hand, for resolving day-to-day problems in the townships. On the other hand, they had played an important part in the development of an African consciousness by attributing concrete problems to the apartheid system. It took the ANC quite some time to view itself as a popular movement. From the beginning and into the 1960s, it was an elitist and conservative organization led by middle-class Blacks. Revolution never was intended. Their main goal was the abolishment of racism and the building up of a classic liberal-democratic society based on the principle of equal chances.[69] "ANC leadership was detached from any popular base [...] and it failed to mobilize and coordinate widespread unified protest, as much because of its limited financial and administrative resources and heightened state repression as because of the conscious alienation of its leaders from popular or working-class interests."[70] In 1963-64 Mandela disputed in court that "the ANC and the Communist Party were one and the same. [...] The ANC has never at any period of its history advocated a revolutionary change in the economic structure of the country, nor has it [...] ever condemned capitalist society."[71] Building up a black identity, building up a Black Consciousness took place in the 1960s and it wasn't an easy process, as black inferiority had, after all these years, become a decisive element of self-perception. But "only after the banning of Black Consciousness organizations in 1977 did [the] leaders [of the ANC] advocate a more radical socialist programme."[72]

---

[67] Marais, Hein (1998), pp. 200 f.
[68] Murray, Martin J. (1994), p. 168
[69] Alexander, Neville (2001), pp. 56 ff.
[70] Worden, Nigel (2007), pp. 113 f.
[71] Mandela, Nelson (1995), p. 366
[72] Worden, Nigel (2007), p. 129

In April 1985, the ANC launched the campaign: "Make apartheid unworkable! Make the country ungovernable!" The strategy was to drive state authority out of the townships. Police stations and other government buildings of the black local government representing apartheid were attacked, homes of black policemen and town councillors assaulted, and collaborators killed. The state repression had been built up "to destroy opposition, and [...] was accompanied by the extensive use of the army [...] mass detention and torture of suspects."[73] Notwithstanding the reckless state power, the protesters managed to push the police and army out of the townships and to claim their possession of the spaces and places.[74] Botha proposed releasing Mandela if he renounced to violence – an offer Mandela rejected: "What freedom am I being offered while the organization of the people remains banned? What freedom am I being offered when I may be arrested on a pass offense? [...] Only free men can negotiate. Prisoners cannot enter into contracts."[75] "South Africa was embroiled in a civil war"[76] the government could no longer control. For the first time in history, the protesters had managed to build up equal counterpower. The mobilization of large parts of the oppressed, the majority unarmed, effectively challenged professional police and army units and finally succeeded to push "the townships, ghettos, and squatter settlements beyond the frontiers of governability and rendering 'the system' unworkable."[77]

The ferocious state repression accompanied by "militarization of the state," "draconian security legislation," and almost freely acting security forces[78] impinged seriously on the international reputation of South Africa. Foreign bankers and investors became increasingly concerned for their investments, which is why they began to pull out their money. After the US Congress decided in October 1986 – against President Reagan's veto (!) – on mandatory economic sanctions, a 50 % decline in American investments resulted. In 1987, the following reasons made even the white rulers conclude that serious negotiations had to take place: The economic disaster; the gridlock between government and protesters because of a resistance that had destroyed the "total strategy;" international sanctions in the field of economy, sports, culture, and politics. Business leaders became highly critical of the government and even went to visit the ANC in Lusaka.

---

[73] Parker, Peter/Mokhesi-Parker, Joyce (1998), p. 28
[74] Bozzoli, Belinda (2004), p. 73
[75] Mandela, Nelson (1995), p. 523
[76] Clark, Nancy L./Worger, William H. (2004), p. 96
[77] Murray, Martin J. (1994), p. 79
[78] Id., pp. 75 ff.

Following the urgent request of members of his cabinet P.W. Botha stepped down in August 1989 and National Party leader de Klerk became State President. On February 2, 1990, de Klerk rescinded the banning orders on the ANC, PAC, SACP, and 31 other organizations. Then on February 11, Mandela was released from prison. The main apartheid laws were repealed. "In a single stroke that went far beyond what virtually all his critics has expected [de Klerk wanted] to break the political impasse that had developed after months of semi-secret discussions with the ANC by removing the remaining stumbling blocks to nascent negotiations over a proposed new constitution."[79] This courageous step that nobody had expected highlights the importance of individual acts in the construction of "reality." It also demonstrates the importance of trust needed in such an existential situation as is the transition from systematic oppression to democracy. There is no guarantee for the future. Only the reliability of the participants, only their trustworthiness makes it possible to take the huge steps necessary to overcome the walls of hatred built up over centuries. That holds true for the beginning of negotiations and even more for the decisive steps afterwards on the way to a new power-arrangement that risks to fundamentally change everything. After over two hundred years of racist politics, after almost forty years of heightened state terrorism surrounded by a world within which the civil rights and, especially, equality and freedom had become leading values, the protagonists had to find a way out of this highly polarized and absolutized Manichaean system. This revolution needed an enormous amount of courage and trust on both sides: The non-Whites risked being trapped and killed by the police or the army, which happened countless times before. The Whites knew that fair elections would lead to the victory of the non-Whites and, thus, possibly to the long-awaited (violent) revenge. The challenge was enormous because there was a new community to be built up and there was nothing in common beside an incredibly long history of disrespect, exclusion, abuse, injury, and killing. Besides the wish to live in the space called "South Africa," everything had to be developed.

During the very difficult negotiation process between the ANC and NP, which lasted from 1990 to 1994, both sides upheld the violence, which is why 14'000 people were killed. To assure the support of the Whites, de Klerk decided to hold a national referendum on the ongoing of the negotiations and the end of apartheid. Having lost three by-elections the NP wanted to mute the right-wing critics against reform-politics. Sixty-nine per cent of the voters approved the course de Klerk had chosen two years ago. The ANC, on its side, had to come around with the Inkatha Freedom

---

[79] *Id.*, p. 7

Party of Buthelezi, which opposed the ANC and was financially supported by the government and backed by military training. Many ANC members also disapproved of the negotiations as long as people were killed in the townships. Others, in turn, intended total revolution and refused reforms that wouldn't change the fundamentals of the society. Against the appeal of Mandela, violent protests occurred again and again.

The negotiations led to a political settlement in 1993 (Interim Constitution) which outlined the principles that would be part of the Constitution of 1996:

- Truly universal suffrage,

- separation of powers,

- elections every five years, and

- a Bill of Rights containing individual and collective rights.

To secure the approval of all the participants, the majority rule would come into force only in 1999. Until then they agreed that the Government of National Unity would take over power. Even though it was quite clear that the ANC would win the majority in free elections, it agreed on many compromises in the Interim Constitution, such as the acceptance of racist members in local governments (30% of local council seats were reserved for existing local authorities and a disproportionate representation for Whites was guaranteed) and the continuity of anti-democratic traditional leadership as a concession to Inkatha. The Truth and Reconciliation Commission (TRC, see p. 415 ff.) was decided, on the one hand, to investigate what had happened during the years of oppression. But, on the other hand, it was supposed to help to avoid resistance within the security forces by amnestying those ready to disclose their crimes. For the National Party neoliberal principles were sensible because they helped to secure the economic advantages built up over the decades and centuries. Thus, the very liberal settlement of 1993 included two elements that favored the interests of the capital. First, they protected property rights, a protection that made redistributive politics less probable. Second, the institutional independence of the Reserve Bank was guaranteed, which in the past had been attuned and subservient to the needs of capital.[80] It can be said that this impressive case of constructive politics was made possible because the ANC was willing to accept a capitalist future without questioning the actual distribution of wealth.[81]

---

[80] Marais, Hein (1998), p. 92
[81] Alexander, Neville (2001), p. 68

The first universally free elections in the history of South Africa took place from April 26 to 29, 1994. Every party that would get at least 20 seats in the National Assembly (5 %) was entitled to one or more Cabinet portfolios in the Government of National Unity (Article 88 Section 2 Constitution of 1993). The new government would have the task of drafting a new constitution. To protect minorities, it was convened that the new constitution needed the approval of at least 66 % of parliament's members to become law. First, though, the elections had to be carried out. On the side of the Africans (Inkatha for example) as much as on the side of the Whites (like right-wing racists Constand Viljoen and Eugene Terreblanche) there were minorities intending to sabotage the transition. Two days before the election white separatists had launched a *blitzkrieg* against the daunting democracy. But the car-bomb that killed nine and injured ninety-two and the dozen other bombs on April 26, didn't deter the 22.7 million voters (75 % of which were newly enfranchised). In spite of the menaced and executed violence, the elections took place in a serene and disciplined manner. Ninety-one percent of registered voters cast their ballots. The ANC won 62.6 % of the vote, the National Party 20.4 %, making de Klerk deputy president beside Thabo Mbeki of the ANC. From an integrative point of view, the result was ideal because the parties were obliged to cooperate on drafting the new constitution. The ANC didn't win the qualified majority needed to amend the constitution by itself, and the minority parties were sure to take a seat in the government. On May 9, 1994, the National Assembly unanimously elected Mandela President of South Africa. The integrative role of Nelson Mandela can't be overstated.[82] He incorporated the "principles of reconciliation, tolerance, moderation, consistency and trust"[83] and made acceptable the peaceful change for the discriminated majority. Besides a symbol of trust, he also became a symbol for the new collective identity. The Government of National Unity passed the new constitution in December 1996. Its preamble makes clear that the basic values have been revolutionized: "Heal the divisions of the past and establish a society based on democratic values, social justice and fundamental human rights." And Article 9 § 3 forbids discrimination: "The state may not unfairly discriminate directly or indirectly against anyone on one or more grounds, including race, gender, sex, pregnancy, marital status, ethnic or social origin, color, sexual orientation, age, disability, religion, conscience, belief, culture, language and birth."

---

[82] *Id.*, p. 63
[83] Marais, Hein (1998), p. 257

The political schism had widely been overcome. Against the background of the history of South Africa, this result has to be qualified as "revolutionary", as an astonishing new construction. Nevertheless, many blatant economic and social injustices prevailed. Even though the focus is most often on democratic participation and the rule of law (recognition and respect), *effective integration needs a solidarity structure, fundamental support (reciprocity) that overcomes historical or current inequalities.* Everybody had now the right to elect their candidates, civil rights were guaranteed, and the arbitrary abuse of state power ended. This formal part of justice is, to be certain, an incredible and very important achievement, but substantial justice wasn't realized, because the new government pursued years of fiscal restraint to consolidate public finances. Only a limited amount of money could be spent to compensate victims of past discriminations. And too little had been done to redistribute the wealth to give every member of society the opportunity to live decently. After years of apartheid, South Africa was heavily in debt, – the price paid for racism.[84] It had taken almost two decades for the state to recognize that political reform was a necessary precondition of any attempt at economic recovery. "Without this, the continuing spiral of ever-worsening poverty, disaffection and repression was inevitable."[85] The focus on primary product exports and inward industrialization based on a "violently regimented labor supply"[86] led to high costs of oppression and to an impoverished majority of the population. As a result domestic demand was limited. The sinking gold price (in 1990 minerals accounted for about half of the exports, gold for 31 per cent), the steady decline of manufacturing in the 1980s, as well as the decline of commercial agriculture because of neoliberal reductions of state subsidies and regulations,[87] low investment rates as there was a tendency of the private sector to direct its funds abroad, and international economic and financial sanctions – all these developments had a very negative effect on the economy in general and on the financial situation of the state. Furthermore, the agricultural economy, which for many people had secured at least a basic income, had been destroyed decades earlier.

In 1990, the ANC declared nationalization as one of the major economic means it intended to use after having taken over power. But in 1994, Nelson Mandela stated in reaction to national and international criticism from business organizations, banks, Western governments, or foreign lend-

---

[84] Worden, Nigel (2007), p. 145
[85] *Id.*, pp. 151 f.
[86] Marais, Hein (1998), p. 100
[87] Murray, Martin J. (1994), pp. 28 ff.

ing institutions: "In our economic policies ... there is not a single reference to things like nationalization, and this is not accidental. There is not a single slogan that will connect us with any Marxist ideology."[88] This change in mindset was motivated by four aspects: First, the former apartheid state lacked of the means to seriously fight poverty and to make possible economic and social redistribution.[89] Apartheid politics had been extremely costly without generating anything valuable, and the government had privatized many of the state enterprises, which was once 57 % of the country's fixed assets. On the one hand, these sales took place to make money and honor the debts. On the other hand, the rulers wanted to avoid too many assets falling into black hands after a government change. Mandela's second reason for the change in attitude toward nationalization was to include the people with economic power and to motivate international support for the new South Africa. Third, the revolution of 1989 in Eastern Europe and before in the Soviet Union had had a delegitimizing effect on centralized economic planning.[90] "Unable to project an all-embracing programme for socioeconomic restructuring independent of the existing worldwide capitalist consensus, the ANC leadership was forced to fall into line, complying with the rules and protocols of market-driven orthodoxy."[91] The intention was to improve the economy of South Africa, which suffered a crisis of frightening proportions by increasing productivity, educating the labor force, restoring business confidence, and attracting foreign investment. After that, social inequality could be confronted. Fourth, Mandela was decided to renounce the politics perceived as "extreme," because for a fundamental change he needed people to trust the new power and to be willing to cooperate: "From the moment the results were in and it was apparent that the ANC was to form the government, I saw my mission as one of preaching reconciliation, of binding the wounds of the country, of engendering trust and confidence. I knew that many people, particularly the minorities, Whites, Coloureds, and Indians, would be feeling anxious about the future, and I wanted them to feel secure."[92] According to Bond, a "transition from a popular-nationalist anti-apartheid project to official neoliberalism [had taken place] – by which is meant adherence to free market economic principles, bolstered by the narrowest practical definition of democracy (not the radical participa-

---

[88] Quoted in Marais, Hein (1998), p. 122
[89] Gumede, William M. (2007), p. 101
[90] Murray, Martin J. (1994), p. 22
[91] Id., p. 23
[92] Mandela, Nelson (1995), pp. 619 f.

tory project many ANC cadre had expected)."[93] In general it can be said, that the ANC throughout its history has favored the political over the economic, what "allowed for the possibility of a settlement based on significant restructuring of the political sphere, and broad continuity in the economic sphere."[94]

There were, however, several progressive policy directives, such as affirmative action in the civil service, water delivery projects, sliding tariff scales for water, universal access to telecommunication, actions to secure basic nutritional needs, free primary health care and the construction of health care facilities, guaranteed human rights and workers rights, and a strengthening of the civil society.[95] Many of the provisions foreseen in the Reconstruction and Development Programme (RDP) adopted by the ANC during the election campaign in 1994 weren't realized, but would have had an important impact for the lower classes and the poor, such as, for example, the land reform (redistribution of agricultural land[96]), employment creation through public works, housing and municipal services, enhanced social welfare, or restructuring of the financial sector's commanding heights.[97] But the interim multi-party government had inherited more than $20 billion in foreign debt from the apartheid state. Should that be repaid? The loan from the IMF of over $850 million, purportedly for drought relief, had to be used for servicing the foreign debt. Moreover, the IMF requested a decrease in wages across the board, as black workers were in their opinion overpaid.[98] The ANC was convinced that these measures would have to be financed by neoliberal economic policies like contained government spending, lowered taxes, and trade liberalization, which is why "a tightly controlled macroeconomic balance took precedence over redistribution."[99] Already in the ANC government's initial term the RDP-programme was abandoned[100] and the

---

[93] Bond, Patrick (2000), p. 1
[94] Marais, Hein (1998), p. 85
[95] Bond, Patrick (2000), pp. 113 f.
[96] Murray, Martin J. (1994), p. 69: "[…] South Africa has been a net exporter of foodstuffs while millions of impoverished, landless black families are undernourished and virtually starving. The enormous disparity of land ownership […] was an emotion-laden issue, riddled with layers of competing interests."
[97] Bond, Patrick (2000), p. 117
[98] *Id.*, pp. 178 f.
[99] Marais, Hein (1998), p. 177, 182; p. 189: "[…] a perspective that predicated reconstruction and development on liberalization, free markets, and the cultivation of business and investor confidence."
[100] Bond, Patrick (2000), p. 91

RDP Office was shut down in 1996. The Growth, Employment and Redistribution Policy (GEAR) was launched in 1997 and stood for free market capitalism and the privatization of state-owned enterprises and tax-reductions. "By 1996 [...] the ANC government's economic policy had acquired an overt class character, and was unabashedly geared to service the respective prerogatives of national and international capital and the aspirations of the emerging black bourgeoisie."[101] Black Economic Empowerment (BEE) – economic programs aimed to reduce inequality – helped not the poor, but a small black elite to become rich fast.[102] Former black radicals became part of the class of capitalists, supporting a conservative economy.[103] "The black and the white middle class [...] built up an open alliance against the impoverished workers."[104] For some of the formerly excluded Blacks the color bar was abolished. For the big majority though, the class barrier endured.

Not surprisingly, therefore, "levels of poverty and income inequality actually rose in the late 1990s."[105] Fifty percent of the Africans were (and are) unemployed (20% Coloureds, 12,5% Asians and 4% Whites) and poverty has still a racial bias because 95% are black, 4% are coloured and 1% white people are concerned.[106] Over half of the people do not have any education and 14% of men and 16% of women are illiterates. Fifty percent of the population live below the poverty line.[107] Against this background, it is not surprising that these massive levels of unemployment and inequality have fueled crime throughout the country.[108] From 1998 to 2000 31'918 homicides by force of arms were registered, compared to for example 384 cases in Germany, a country with twice the population.[109] The experience of fundamental and comprehensive exclusion widely explains (without justifying!) the high degree of violence against women in South Africa: The country is at the top of rape statistics worldwide,[110] on the one hand, because of a macho-culture and the belief that sex with a virgin heals AIDS. On the other hand, because of a need for recognition and to overcome the

---

[101] Marais, Hein (1998), p. 147
[102] Ellmer, Jutta (2008), p. 70
[103] Alexander, Neville (2001), p. 72
[104] *Id.*, p. 81
[105] Worden, Nigel (2007), p. 162
[106] Bond, Patrick (2000), p. 19
[107] Ellmer, Jutta (20008), p. 65
[108] Clark, Nancy L./Worger, William H. (2004), p. 116; Worden, Nigel (2007), p. 164; Murray, Martin J. (1994), p. 214
[109] Ellmer, Jutta (2008), p. 82
[110] *Id.*, p. 41

feeling of powerlessness. As a result of this high level of insecurity, a majority of the people wishes the re-introduction of the death penalty, which was abolished in 1995. And many do not really bother about the police violence which in some respects has gotten even worse than during apartheid: Almost two people per day died because of police actions since 1998.[111] Insecurity perceived as existential instability leads people to accept high degrees of incivility, of counter-violence, of exclusion. And the lack of trust resorts to an increased amount of aggression. The late 1990s witnessed many forms of protest like land invasions, building occupations, rent and bond boycotts, urban rioting, strikes, and demonstrations.[112]

South Africa is another example for the neoliberal's and liberal's market disinterest in justice. Much more, it works according to the principle that he who has plenty of goods shall have more. Democracy understood solely in formal terms doesn't lead by itself to equal chances and to decent living conditions, especially when the repartition of income and wealth is so blatantly unequal. According to Alexander, we shouldn't be misled by the form of representative democracy, even though this form of government is very important for the organization of the exploited and oppressed.[113] "The principles of conciliation and concession [had] replaced conflict and triumph"[114] – an incredible step toward a recognizing and respectful integration path, necessary to end the merciless fight based on absolutist categories. However, accepting capitalism as fate and the dissociation from class-concepts and social-economic transformation played finally much more the game of the rich than the poor.[115] This class-bias is also reflected in the Constitutions of 1993 and 1996: A consensus was reached about civil rights as a protection against state action, "whereas those concerning socioeconomic and welfare rights [in the interim Constitution of 1993] are weak and muted."[116] The same can be said about the Constitution of 1996, which guarantees, for example, property in § 25 in a classical liberal form. § 26 and 27 contain positive rights like housing, health care, food, water and social security. But these positive rights are only guaranteed in the form of "reasonable legislative and other measures, within [the states'] available resources." Historically the classical liberal rights were claimed by the bourgeoisie interested in political and economic freedom to pursue their own

---

[111] NZZ of April 27, 2011, p. 7
[112] Bond, Patrick (2000), p. 84
[113] Alexander, Neville (2001), p. 11
[114] Marais, Hein (1998), p. 94
[115] Id., p. 96
[116] Wilson, Richard A. (2001), p. 6

interests. As upper-class rights, they weren't concretizations of solidarity or of equity in the sense of equal chances and reciprocity, because the bourgeoisie didn't need this sort of social arrangement. Being able to decide over one's own life, however, is only possible if the necessary resources are available. Otherwise, the promise of freedom becomes a mockery. Formal democratization[117] can yield the impression that democracy and civil rights are powerless show-events only played to calm people by giving them the luring but deceiving impression of having power. In the end, the elite became multi-colored, opposing an impoverished majority which was still predominantly black: South Africa, thus, moved from a dominantly racist society toward a class society.

b) Imposed and chosen ghettos

Rulers confine others to circumscribed areas for different reasons: Sometimes it's because they want to exclude and reduce competitors, because they want to reserve the valuable space for themselves, because they want to control what they have constructed as "minority," and/or because they want to protect and hide their unjustified wealth behind gates. In the case of South Africa, the organization of the space and the construction of "We" and "the others" fulfilled all these criteria. Similar mechanisms are to be found in the construction of ghettos. These prisons are based on structural violence if they are used to exclude and control others. Or they are a self-inflicted loss of freedom in gated communities.

aa) Chinatown

Tourists visiting San Francisco in the 19th century were fascinated and attracted by Chinatown. Guided tours were organized to satisfy the curiosity of the white upper and middle class who were eager to discover an exotic, dangerous, and miserable world they didn't have to live in. Fearing the creatures they would possibly meet, the wealthy and the petit bourgeois took their protection with them. "Police guides [...] were known for deploying quite brutal, invasive, and generally disrespectful tactics that included kicking doors open, forcing their way into private living quarters, waking people from sleep, and shining bright lights into people's faces."[118] This behavior reflects the contempt with which white people treated the Chinese. From

---

[117] Alexander, Neville (2001), pp. 131 f.
[118] Berglund, Barbara (2007), p. 106

the middle of the 19th century on, the Chinese were ranked on the lowest class-level in San Francisco's society and constructed as unassimilable, inclined toward vice, risky for public health, and a threat to free white labor.[119] People visiting Chinatown were eager to identify the conditions seen there as typical for Chinese: Overcrowded, unsanitary, malodorous, dark and seemingly impenetrable. "That the crowding and lack of public sanitation […] were in large measure products of the poverty of its residents coupled with the denial of basic municipal services was of little interest."[120] This collective judgment, this collectivism of thousands of people on ethnic or cultural grounds was used to construct and contour the American identity as clean, virtuous, and civilized. It is the majority who needed the minority to define itself, excluding and oppressing at the same time the unlucky fellows who were at the wrong time at the wrong place.

At the beginning of Chinese immigration in California, the Chinese weren't perceived as a threat, their eateries were even praised for their cheap and tasty food and an important support structure for the men working all day long. The more the Chinese were seen as competitors in the run for gold, the more the digging for gold became difficult and the yields decreased, the more many Anglo-Americans began to look for scapegoats. In this way, the exclusion of competitors from the race for wealth[121] became easier. And it would help to forge an identity of white Americans and, thus, to reduce conflicts within this developing community: "[…] the shared anti-Chinese sentiment that crossed class and ethnic lines helped give shape to San Francisco's circle of whiteness, uniting Whites across lines that in other contexts often served to divide them."[122] In 1850, the California State Legislature passed a Foreign Miners Tax bill, a structural violence directed against Mexican and South American diggers. By forcing foreign miners to pay a prohibitively high price for a digging license, they hoped to keep competitors away. Because in 1851 the number of Chinese immigrants increased from 4'000 to 25'000, the California Legislature enacted the second Foreign Miners Tax bill in 1852, requiring the Chinese to pay a monthly fee of three dollars. The Chinese's average earning being of about six dollars a month, the tax was clearly intended to have a deterrent effect. Nevertheless, the tax paid by hard working immigrants accounted during the next twenty years for about a third of the state budget.[123] This aggressive politics

---

[119] *Id.*, p. 96
[120] *Id.*, p. 113
[121] Senkewicz, Robert M. (1985), p. 66
[122] Berglund, Barbara (2007), p. 10
[123] Leung, Peter C.Y. (2001), pp. 34 f.

against non-Whites or non-European-Americans was supported by all state institutions which were dominated by a group of people who understood themselves as privileged rulers. In People v. Naglee, the California State Supreme Court validated the Tax bill.[124] Ordinary legal procedures were not effective enough to control undesired people, so the ruling majority used direct violence and forced their Chinese competitors out of the mines, intimidated them at home, "kicking down doors, smashing furniture, beating up the men, and abusing the women."[125] To make sure that these exactions of Whites would go unpunished, Blacks, Mulattos, and Indians were forbidden from giving evidence in court against Whites (Act of April 16th, 1850, regulating Criminal Proceedings). In 1854, when a Chinese miner, Ling Sing, was murdered in Nevada County, three Chinese men had witnessed George W. Hall as the perpetrator. Using its interpretative power creatively, the Supreme Court of the State of California held in People v. Hall, 1854, that the term "Indian" mentioned in the Criminal Proceedings Act stood for all people of the Mongoloid race, and "black" for all non-Whites, which is why Chinese witnesses couldn't give testimony.

> "We are of the opinion that the words 'white', 'Negro', 'mulatto', 'Indian', and 'black person', wherever they occur in our Constitution and laws, must be taken in their generic sense, and that, even admitting the Indian of this continent is not of the Mongolian type, that the words 'black person', in the 14th section, must be taken as contradistinguished from white, and necessary excludes all races other than the Caucasian. [...] The same rule which would admit them to testify, would admit them to all the equal rights of citizenship, and we might soon see them at the polls, in the jury box, upon the bench, and in our legislative halls. This is not a speculation which exists in the excited and overheated imagination of the patriot and statesman, but it is an actual and present danger. [...] a race of people whom nature has marked as inferior, and who are incapable of progress or intellectual development beyond a certain point, as their history has shown; differing in language, opinions, color, and physical conformation; between whom and ourselves nature has placed an impassable difference, is now presented, and for them is claims, not only the right to swear away the life of a citizen, but the further privilege of participating with us in administering the affairs of our Government."[126]

---

[124] Heizer, Robert F./Almquist, Alan J. (1971), p. 121
[125] Leung, Peter C.Y. (2001), p. 37
[126] People v. Hall 4 Cal. 399 (California Supreme Court 1854)

Hall, who had been convicted for murder ,was freed, what indirectly incited riots of Whites against Chinese. Federal legislation (Chinese Exclusion Act of 1882) increased the pressure, suspending Chinese immigration for ten years and denying them the right of naturalization. The ones already living in the States had to obtain a certification to re-enter, if they left the country.

As a result of this overt racist exclusion and violence, the Chinese of San Francisco, for example, "withdrew into an enclave – Chinatown – where they were among friends and were relatively safe from the predations of white ruffians."[127] People who wouldn't have lived together and not under such dire circumstances in their country of origin, were forced to group as a community,[128] to build up mutual support-structures and, thus, to develop a collective identity.

bb) Brooklyn and Harlem

During the 19th and the 20th centuries Brooklyn and Harlem became the ghettos for African-Americans, who had been discriminated above all in the areas of work, living, and education. This deleterious structural violence had a disintegrative effect on individuals and communities. Exclusionary politics was used to protect the ones who perceived themselves as "white Europeans" against working-place competition, to reserve living areas for the white middle and upper class, and to make valuable investments possible. Blacks were just allowed to do the work nobody else wanted to do. And within these jobs it was important for the Whites to prevent African Americans from acquiring knowledge that would qualify them for skilled jobs. This job-control was achieved through the exclusion of African Americans from skilled jobs,[129] by barring their access to unions (which intensified during the Second World War),[130] by threatening industrialists with strikes, and by taking away the jobs of African Americans when the Europeans needed them such as during the Great Depression. According to Wilders, "African Americans' future was determined when white laborers reacted to the industrial collapse by snatching jobs that were once unacceptable and by hoarding government-funded employment and training programs. New

---

[127] Richards, Rand (2007), p. 110
[128] Schwartz, Stephen (1998), pp. 84 f.
[129] In their dissenting opinion to Ricci et al. v. Destefano, 557 U. S. 1 ff. (2009), justices Ginsburg, Stevens, Souter, and Breyer describe the racially based discrimination in the public domain, especially in the firefighting profession and in the police. The majority of the Court didn't take into account the historical or social context of the recruitment practice and relied exclusively on a formalistic understanding.
[130] Wilder, Craig Steven (2000), p. 157; as well pp. 226-233

Deal funds flowed into the borough to relieve unemployment, but black workers received no immediate benefits since that money inflated building trades and defense industries that excluded people of color."[131] Over the decades, Brooklyn was increasingly built as the home of African Americans, paying high rents for miserable housing. The number of houses continually decreased, the population grew, and there weren't any alternatives available for Blacks, which is why they had to pay what reckless landlords demanded.

Until 1915, nearly 50 % of the tenements were constructed in Brooklyn. This cheap housing wasn't built anymore because the investors saw higher profits concentrating on middle-income residences. Poor people, and especially the Blacks, therefore, had to endure an critical shortage of affordable accommodations at the beginning of the Great Depression. This problem intensified because of an increasing black population and the destruction of tenements and dilapidated houses. Whites progressively moved to South Brooklyn and investors followed. This exclusionary racist market built by European realtors was justified "as a purely economic or market imperative," as "a financial business proposition" that had nothing to do with white prejudice.[132] Once again the market-metaphor was used to hide the responsibility of individuals for a politic that took place nation-wide. The National Association of Real Estate Boards (NAREB) in 1924 established a national code, Article 34, which held: "A Realtor should never be instrumental in introducing into a neighborhood a character of property or occupancy, members of any race or nationality, or any individuals whose presence will clearly be detrimental to property values in that neighborhood."[133] The Brooklyn Real Estate Board adopted this code in 1927. Racial homogeneity was perceived as "a natural characteristic of residential neighborhoods."[134] In its textbook "Fundamentals of Real Estate" the NAREB wrote in 1946: "The tendency of certain racial and cultural groups to stick together, making it almost impossible to assimilate them in the normal social organism, is too well known to need much comment."[135] The book further pointed out how much the races are incompatible: "The prospective buyer might be a bootlegger who could cause considerable annoyance to his neighbors, a madam who had a number of Call Girls on her string, a gangster who wants a screen for his activities by living in a better neighborhood, a colored

---

[131] *Id.*, p. 160; see also p. 137. For the racial practice during the Second World War, see pp. 167 ff.
[132] Freund, David M. P. (2007), p. 15
[133] Wilder, Craig Steven (2000), p. 182
[134] Gotham, Kevin Fox (2002), p. 35
[135] *Id.*, p. 35

man of means who was giving his children a college education and thought they were entitled to live among Whites ..."¹³⁶ Real estate agents, political leaders, and the neighborhoods themselves were those responsible for the ghettos, for the racial space established. Local improvement associations organized covenant-writing campaigns (agreements included in deeds restricting the resale of property) and actions to build up a sense of communal solidarity. Owners were put under pressure or even intimidated to motivate them not to sell to Blacks. "Ultimately, however, violence served as a last resort that underscored the general determination to confine the growing black population."¹³⁷ The private practice of restrictive covenants was challenged before the Supreme Court, which in Shelley v. Kraemer, 334 U.S. 1 (1948) ruled against the black family. "Yet even while acknowledging the unfairness of restrictive covenants, the Court's decision provided justification, legitimization, and guidance for resisting racial desegregation. Although it prevented states from enforcing restrictive covenants on their own, the decision did not make it illegal for property owners to adhere to them voluntarily."¹³⁸

In Brooklyn these segregationist developments were amplified by the politics of the HOLC (Home Owners' Loan Corporation). Created in 1933 as a New Deal emergency measure, it was charged to intervene in the mortgage market to prevent wide scale foreclosures and bank failures. This neutral tool in principal turned in the hands of its main actors into a corporation that helped the developers, lenders, and financial institutions to protect their investments.¹³⁹ Not interested in North Brooklyn, the money went to the South where the people with more money lived and would live. It can be said that "North Brooklyn's decay was written into government policy."¹⁴⁰ The newly built white areas should be kept clean to make sure that it's inhabitants agreed to pay for their new middle- and upper-class home. An early form of gated communities arose. Because of the discriminatory lending practices and the targeted investment activity "[…] Central Brooklyn was [in 1945] the primary locale of nonwhite residency in the borough. And, in 1953, when President Truman left office, a vast black ghetto stretched across Brooklyn and was becoming the largest concentration of its kind."¹⁴¹ On the one hand, Whites were ready and able to pay more for

---

[136] Hirsch, Arnold R. (1993), p. 75
[137] Id., p. 75
[138] Lipsitz, George (2006), p. 26
[139] Wilder, Craig Steven (2000), p. 187
[140] Id., p. 193
[141] Id., p. 177

a racially clean living space. African Americans, on the other hand, had to live with considerable decay in the quality of housing and an increase in rents. Excluded from any alternatives, they had to accept whatever was imposed on them. "Rents increased as much as ten dollars per month when black tenants replaced white occupants."[142] Making profits anyway were the realtors and their financiers, the banks and insurance companies, who took advantage of the upward mobility of the ones and the downward mobility of the others.

Osofsky describes the same developments in Harlem. And, again, it is not an impersonal market which is at the origin of this structural violence, but individual speculators responsible for exclusion and injustice. At the end of the 1870s and 1880s, when the newly built railroad came to Harlem, this area was supposed to be a fancy upper- and upper-middle-class residential suburb.[143] Enhanced by the new subway built in the 1890s, a second wave of speculation was set off: "Speculators who intended to make astronomic profits when the subway was completed bought the marshes, garbage dumps and lots left unimproved or undeveloped in the 1870s and 1880s."[144] This speculation led to an anomalous increase in land prices and in the cost of houses. This real estate bubble burst in 1904-05 because too many houses had been built and the rents were too high for the general population.[145] Now, the realtors profited from the African Americans' the lack of choice. Black people had never been allowed to choose the place where to live,[146] they had to take what was allocated to them. As the immigration of African Americans had increased and the previous living quarters had been destroyed,[147] the pressure toward the reserved black areas aggravated and changed a formerly promising area into a slum. "The most important factor which led to the rapid deterioration of Harlem housing was the high cost of living in the community. Rents, traditionally high in Harlem, reached astounding proportions in the 1920s – they skyrocketed in response to the unprecedented demand created by heavy Negro migration and settlement within a restricted geographical area. 'Crowded in a black ghetto,' a sociologist wrote, 'the Negro tenant is forced to pay exorbitant rentals because he cannot escape.' [...] the typical white working-class family in New York City in the late twenties paid $6.67 per room, per month, while Harlem

---

[142] *Id.*, p. 180
[143] Osofsky, Gilbert (1971), p. 71, 77
[144] *Id.*, p. 87
[145] *Id.*, p. 90
[146] *Id.*, p. 127
[147] *Id.*, p. 93

Negroes were charged $9.50. [...] High rents and poor salaries necessarily led to congested and unsanitary conditions."[148]

The structural violence exerted by the construction of a racist space segregation was reinforced by educational means – by cultural violence. Reproducing social and economic barriers, the schools in Brooklyn, for example, lacked public resources. They were therefore of incomparably worse quality than the one for Whites. Main factors were, for example, the older facilities, fewer veteran teachers, limited class time because of overcrowding, the disrepair of the physical plant, or the program shortages.[149] This was all the more a problem because the severe discrimination in the field of work could only be fought if the education was at least at the same level as the one of the privileged. African Americans had to outperform white people if they wanted to have a chance at all to reach the same status. In the words of civil-rights activist, Reverend Milton A. Galamison, pastor in Brooklyn: "Negroes don't need segregated or integrated schools in themselves. What Negroes do need is an equal education and it happens that this is impossible in a segregated school."[150]

In the 1960s, riots broke out in many cities of the United States. These protests were "intimately related to the attempts of Blacks to move out of the grip of the neocolonial characteristic of the ghetto, to remove the control of modern-day white carpet-baggers over their lives. [...] politically disruptive acts [are, E.D.] one of the ultimate weapons of any people whose political aspirations remain significantly unfulfilled and other alternatives have been tried."[151]

cc) Gated communities out of high inequality and distrust

The ghettos of the rich, the "gated communities," are contrary to the ghettos of the poor and the powerless not a form of structural violence, but *a self-induced isolation to protect and hide what can't be justified*. The more a society splits up in different groups of unequal status and power, the more the ones with power try to protect themselves against political protest and the unworthy life of the under class. Poverty was one of the main negative consequences industrialization generated in the late 19th century. Many people had lost their economic autonomy and had, therefore, serious prob-

---

[148] *Id.*, pp. 135 f.
[149] Wilder, Craig Steven (2000), p. 224
[150] Quoted in Wilder, p. 220
[151] Feagin, Joe R./Hahn, Harlan (1973), p. 54

lems making the ends meet. Not to be confronted with this social misery, the better off tried to distance themselves from the poor: "Traditionally urban slums had lain outside of the boundaries that most respectable citizens recognized as the true city. As long as a cordon sanitaire had sealed the world of hovels from theirs, they did not have to concern themselves about the very poor. Officials, reflecting this attitude, had made little effort to police these outcast districts, only to contain them. [...] Trouble in the tenements potentially touched everyone, and knowing nothing about the slum except that it frightened them, respectable citizens demanded aggressive protection."[152] This spatial segregation based on excessive wealth-difference highlights distrust and a fundamental lack of responsibility, justice, solidarity, and freedom. Instead of sharing their abundant wealth they anyway wont be able to spent during their lifetime, the small upper class prefers to renounce freedom and lock themselves up. Sharing this experience with a vanishingly small group of people, everything is done to avoid contact with others.

The number of people willfully living apart from the others is increasing. "The Villages," "Florida's Friendliest Hometown," is a standardized paradise for retirees that's inhabited by about 80'000 people who are predominantly Republican. Sharon Morse, the residence's CEO's wife, declared on the radio station of the hometown: "Our community grew in the past year by 23%, though there is decline around us. Luckily, we live under a safety dome."[153] All the aspects of life that do not have to do with sun, fun, and happiness are excluded. That means, for example, that people who need care have to leave the compound. The minimum age is 50 and one is expected to move before dying, as there is no cemetery and dying is not entertaining. Unsurprisingly, this phenomenon has increased over the last decades, when neoliberalism motivated people to be individualistic, selfish, and irresponsible, conveniently forgetting that they originated in and thanks to a community made up of many different people. It is also a reaction to a *deterioration of public space*, which showed an increase in crime and social ills – a decline due to a lessened engagement of the community and the state.

Giving up the idea of a common good poses a serious disintegration problem. A community that doesn't take care of what belongs to everybody gets fragmented and disintegrates into private lots that lack a comprehensive common project. From 36'000 Common interest communities (CICs) in 1980 to 286'000 in 2007, about 20% of Americans live today in these

---

[152] Wiebe, Robert H. (1967), pp. 38 f.
[153] Neue Zürcher Zeitung of December 4, 2010, p. 11

artificial communities.[154] The "common" in these companies' name doesn't represent mutual support and the readiness to accept all the people a community brings together. It is more about a greatly simplified and homogenized community convening because of specific and exclusive interests. Also, this type of residence is more an investment and business for the real estate company and others than a living organism. Every member of the Villages, for example, has to pay a one-time fee of $20'000 for the building of guardhouses, golf courses, or small parks. But the company spent only $8 million out of the $60 million for actual construction.[155]

In many countries a process of gentrification is noted and perceived as a challenge for the integration of the community.[156] Not the least because of the tax competition between the cantons (Switzerland[157]) or states, areas to attract wealthy people are built. As a result, house and apartment prices substantially increase, so that the middle- and underclass can no longer afford them. "The gated communities phenomenon has enormous policy consequences. It allows some citizens to secede from public contact, excluding others from sharing in their economic and social privilege."[158] And this wealth isn't something they owe only to themselves. It is the result of the cooperation of many a people who contributed their moral and political support, their workforce, their knowledge, or their money. Other parts of the country that are left with those who have little or nothing, have to take over public tasks but lack tax resources.[159] The state in general has been neoliberally handicapped because the good taxpayers have moved away, and solidarity has become an outdated concept.

Motives of class and elitist distinction, of pleasure and entertainment, and/or of security create CICs. They are based on the idea that the "reality" has to be a totally controlled form of living. Every moment and into every detail of life has to be predictable and the unexpected excluded. This totalitarian approach to others loses creativity and, hence, freedom of alternatives. "Unlike conventional communities, which are made up of a hodgepodge of privately owned homes and businesses and publicly owned and

---

[154] Franzese, Paula A./Siegel, Steven (2007), p. 1116
[155] The New York Times of July 10, 2009, p. A15
[156] Blakely, Edward J./Snyder, Mary Gail (1999), p. VIII
[157] About the situation in Switzerland see Mäder, Ueli/Aratnam, Ganga Jey/Schilliger, Sarah (2010), pp. 313 ff. Describing the self-exclusion of the better off, pp. 322 ff. For France see: Résidences fermées : la recherche de l'entre-soi, in: Le Monde of December 26, 2010, p. 7.
[158] Blakely, Edward J./Snyder, Mary Gail (1999), p. 3
[159] Huissoud, Thérèse et. al. (2003), pp. 195 f.

maintained resources and amenities, CICs are totally commodified living spaces. Public spaces and public property do not exist. And unlike in traditional communities, which allow for the free flow of people, goods, and services, access in CICs is tightly circumscribed and a principal reason why people choose to live there."[160] Membership fees and the price of the houses make sure that only people from the same social stratum have access. Homogeneity and security are the most important values, which makes life a product to be consumed without any risk. It is a consumption life-style where freedom is no longer important. "The phenomenal growth of CICs in the past quarter of a century speaks volumes to the change in thinking that has brought commercial values to the fore and shunted civic values to the periphery of human life."[161] However, individualization, material greed, and selfishness do *not* produce "home," an identity one can be proud of, an identity that is part of a story, that has a past, is lived in the present, and points toward a shared future. According to Blakely and Snyder, CICs are governed by legal contract, not by social contact.[162] This sort of community is bought and not built up cooperatively; it is industrialized and, therefore, lacks human imperfection. "They are wholesale fabrications, designed by specification and plopped down onto a cleared space without historical referencing."[163] Freedom is considerably reduced. The CICs offer only limited possibilities to shape the house of our dreams. An uncountable number of prescriptions have to be fulfilled to live up to the standard-existence. The basic logic is "a 'command and control' rule regime that attempts to regulate all manner of land use and behavior."[164] Thus, there is only one way of living, narrowly described in the declaration of "covenants, conditions and restrictions" (CC&Rs). For example, forbid a residential association in California the installation of a basketball hoop over the garage door. In Boca Raton a 30-pound limit for pets is prescribed. Another CIC forbids more than one dog per unit. In Santa Ana, the condominium association cautioned a 51-year old woman against "kissing a friend good night in her driveway."[165] As these CC&Rs require a qualified majority to be amended, these regulations most often last over time. "Because the developer retains ownership of unsold lots and enjoys enhanced voting rights, he or she has effective control over all association decisions until well into the development of the

---

[160] Rifkin, Jeremy (2000), p. 116
[161] *Id.*, p. 123
[162] Blakely, Edward J./Snyder, Mary Gail (1999), p. 20
[163] Rifkin, Jeremy (2000), p. 132
[164] Franzese, Paula A./Siegel, Steven (2007), pp. 1110 f.
[165] Quoted in Kennedy, David J. (1995), pp. 762 f.

community."[166] Furthermore, the access of people is restricted and there is no public space where people may assemble, protest, criticize, claim, and speak freely, as "every square foot of living space is part of a commercial arrangement."[167] It is this privatization of space that functionally should be public or, at least, usable in a free common way, that poses problems for the use of civil rights. The freedom of speech, of movement, of meetings, or the protection against racial discrimination of members and nonmembers are restricted. The members, one could say, renounced these freedoms, using their freedom of contract. On the contrary nonmembers, and society in general, are confronted with the loss of public property, a reduction of places where exchange, debates, and the building up of a shared experience is possible. "Residential associations cause harm to nonmembers by developing exclusive communities, by gating formerly public streets and neighborhoods, and by increasing the fiscal burdens of cities and states. These semiprivate governments, or quasi-governmental actors, have to take their responsibility for the community in a wider sense."[168] From the point of view of power control and democratic legitimization, the quasi-governmental power of residential associations is problematic because they do not assume the corresponding liabilities that state governments have to deal with.[169] And most of the time the infrastructure of these exclusionary private worlds were paid for by the state, by the public in general.[170] Thus, the excluded had to pay for their exclusion.

Democracy originates on public space, a space, many people had to fought for, a space free from private domination or aristocratic prerogatives. Revolutions highlight how important it is to have a meeting ground where people get to know each other, where things can be discussed, where rulers can be criticized, and alternatives developed. Furthermore, this meeting ground is an important source for trust. The public is a social space[171] where we can see and experience others, which helps us to understand, to compromise, and to reduce fear. Public space has to be freely accessible, without any limits of wealth, power, status, origins, religion, or race. The CICs are an anti-political area because they're mainly ruled by private investment interests and exclude people on the grounds of wealth and (at least indirectly) race. A common cause beyond the (segre)gated communities becomes im-

---

[166] Rifkin, Jeremy (2000), p. 119
[167] Id., p. 119
[168] Kennedy, David J. (1995), p. 763
[169] Id., p. 768
[170] Id., p. 774
[171] Habermas, Jürgen (1992a), p. 436

possible. Democracy, however, means to be willing and able to confront others and to reach a compromise, not to exclude them.

dd) Virtual "reality" – the other space

"Virtual" spaces are not less real than "physical" spaces. In consensus-based constructivism, there is no meter point, no Archimedean position from which we can undeniably state the objectivity and truth of a living form. Referring to Oldenberg, Turkle describes "real" and "unreal" forms of encounter. Face-to-face meeting-points like bistros or cafés are understood as "real,"[172] whereas the virtual "reality" is based on a culture of simulation.[173] If face-to-face relations are the relevant criterion, then most of the actions taking place in modern society are "virtual", because, according to Giddens, "the advent of modernity increasingly tears space away from place by fostering relations between 'absent' others, locationally distant from any given situation of face-to-face interaction."[174] I agree with Debray that the need of people for face-to-face contact will stay important.[175] But, it is, in my opinion, a need supported or suffocated by social, economic, and political circumstances. The more the others are presented as our enemies we have to fight and the more life is constructed as a permanent competition between isolated individuals, the more people will try to avoid direct contact and the less they will be able to trust in human beings. It is, therefore, this generalized distrust forwarded against the background of an enhanced materialistic worldview that makes a technical, controllable "reality" attractive. In the simulated "reality" the control of the "reality" elements is quite high, everything is staged and predictable. Direct social contacts are minimized and people retract behind their own four walls.[176] Furthermore, virtual "reality" offers many forms of entertainment, of distractions, so that one doesn't have to think anymore about the sense of life or what to do next. It can also be a "reality" with a low level of complexity, restricted to some few elements, controllable, and therefore free of ambiguity.

Physical criterion does not help, in my view, to differentiate the "reality" of realism from the virtual "reality". Turkle seems to have similar doubts: "[…] where does real life end and a game begin? Is the real self always

---

[172] Turkle, Sherry (1995), pp. 233 f.
[173] *Id.*, p. 235
[174] Giddens, Anthony (1990), p. 18
[175] Debray, Régis (2007), pp. 86 f.
[176] Turkle, Sherry (1995), p. 235

the naturally occurring one? Is the real self always the one in the physical world? As more and more real business gets done in cyberspace, could the real self be the one who functions best in that realm?"[177] But still does she fear an escape into imaginary refuges instead of solving personal and social problems.[178] And she is convinced that there is an insurmountable reality, as "the real fights back."[179] According to my constructivist conviction, the problem is not one of reality vs. virtuality, but of *responsibility vs. irresponsibility*. Are we ready to take responsibility for the world we live in? Are we ready to feel responsible for ourself and for the people who share our "reality," and who are confronted with our actions? Furthermore, we do not have to discuss the ontological quality of the "reality" we live in, but, rather, its structure. How is construction-power distributed? Who can influence "reality" and, therefore, be a recognized part in the construction process? Moreover, we do have to make sure that we control the information about ourselves, that we master the identity built up based on our appearances in the world. To be free means to be able to qualify information, to reflect on the "reality" proposals of others, to make knowledge out of information.[180] What, in my opinion, makes the difference is the amount of rules, expectations, embeddedness, and social structuration applied to the communication. On the one hand, there is established behavior, a network within which the actors have to give account. On the other hand, there are fast changing relationships that are terminable at any time.

The new digital space is not per se beneficial. It is a form of communication used in many a different ways. From an integrative point of view, it is important that its potential for a critical public discourse can be used freely by responsible individuals in a recognizing and respectful manner. Equal access has to be possible and the discourse should be public. On the other hand, privacy claims of the participants have to be respected, in order to avoid, for example, cyber-mobbing or unfounded defamations. From a democratic standpoint, the opportunity to have a critical and responsible debate about the state power, about the common future and the rights and duties of each other, is to be welcomed. The danger that conventional mass media becomes the monopole of investors or that the economic pressure

---

[177] *Id.*, p. 241
[178] *Id.*, p. 244
[179] *Id.*, p. 267
[180] Strauss, Botho (1999), p. 101: "Information exists without a self. Knowledge doesn't." Against the background of consensus-based constructivism is a self also needed to construct information. But knowledge is the reconstruction of perceived actions based on our relevant principles.

leads to an uncritical reproduction of standardized information, can be lessened by the Internet. It can make decentralized and informal interaction possible[181] – the fundament of democracies. Thanks to the low-threshold access (at least for developed countries) information can be shared about dire working conditions or working-opportunities, imprisonment of people, living situations, housing, or environment. That sort of "sub-institutionalized basis communication"[182] is elementary to sensitize people to problems, to allow free statements about everything, and to develop a sense of common concern. The social network makes possible communication-intensities formerly known in face-to-face relationships. What is called the "Arab Spring" demonstrates the opportunities these networks can unfold. The same can be said about protests against a G7, 8, or 20-meeting, demonstrations of solidarity for the victims of WTO-politics, or the bombarding of MNU's with standardized protest letters. On the other hand, the state reactions in Egypt or Syria, Iran or China are examples of abuses of the new communication form by authoritarian rulers. The more power somebody has, the more one's action are influencing the life of others, and the more he or she has to act in public and to be accessible for criticism. There is, for example, a private digital network used by "wholesale financial markets, a corporate intranet, and corporate networks that bring together lenders and borrowers in a private domain rather than in the public domain of stock markets."[183] The neoliberal deregulation-dogma led to "a shift in authority from the public to the private when it comes to governing the global economy."[184] Sassen describes this transformation as "a privatizing of capacities for making norms, capacities we have associated with the state in our recent history. This brings with it strengthened possibilities of norm-making in the interests of the few rather than the majority."[185]

Provided everybody gets access to the digital space and knows how to use it, a comprehensive and free democratic would technically be possible. This communication, however, should be reflective and thoughtful. There is, constructively speaking, no objective criterion to measure thoughtfulness. But current forms often are characterized by quantity and not by quality, by instant reaction and not by creative reflection. As well in established commercial as in informal communications there is a strong tendency to "much ado about nothing," to hypes that everybody feels obliged to consume and

---

[181] Geser, Hans (1996), Chapter 2.1.
[182] *Id.*, Chapter 2.2.
[183] Sassen, Saskia (2006), p. 336
[184] *Id.*, p. 246
[185] *Id.*, p. 247

to sustain. The consumption of fast changing information piecemeal dominates. That is more of a problem when the actors do not have to justify their statements, when nobody claims an explanation, and when it is easy to quit the communication because there is no obligation (neither moral nor legal) to stay, to respect, or even to take care of others. The challenge, therefore, is to embed the communication socially, to establish long-term communication forms besides the fast-food consumption. More listening and thinking and less talking. Consumerism as an integration principle renounces the innumerable opportunities that enable human beings.

Another problem is to develop power within the digital space that represents the common good and lasts over time. Private companies use these technical possibilities very effectively, but only for their own interests and largely without democratic oversight. On the other hand, it is difficult for the civil society to build up counter power that lasts longer than a one-time mobilization. Interestingly, most social movements aren't initiated by spontaneous assemblages, but by targeted actions of pre-existing associations or "social entrepreneurs."[186] A lasting structure based on the civil society, national state actors, and international organizations has to be developed so that the liberty of the new space can be used responsibly and in a solidary way. This dominant discourse has no inherent prerogative and has to justify itself to the innumerable forums developing critical positions.

---

[186] Geser, Hans (1996), Chapter 2.1.; see also Rucht, Dieter (1994), p. 340

8. Symbolic link – Time concept

Mohammed Bouazizi set himself on fire and became the symbol for the Tunisian revolution, a symbol for the past oppression, for the present courage to fight the dictatorship, and the hope for a brighter future. Rosa Parks played an important role in the Civil Rights Movement by sitting on the wrong bus seat. Mandela symbolized resistance against apartheid by being imprisoned and he symbolized with de Klerk reconciliation. Contrary to what we were told over the last thirty years, it is not material greed that matters most, it is the *meaning of life*. Contingency makes us fear a lack of meaning, of perspective, of past and future. Material greed can be our meaning of life. But it is the least satisfying and sustainable, because it doesn't transcend the individual's existence. Material resources are necessary and helpful, but can't compare with human interactions, human hopes, human love, human cooperation, or human creativity. Collective projects transport individuals beyond the present, giving them the possibility to step out of the day-to-day routine and to be a part of the big story. Contingency makes human beings receptive to symbolic meaning, which gives sense to their existence and that indicates a path to take, decisions to make, and institutions to believe in.

a)   Symbolic link

Edifices, streets, or houses can incorporate meaning, they can be used as symbols turned to stone, representing ideas, concepts of the community, worldviews. The same can be said of texts, books, tunes, songs, flags, or food. A community's origin may be connected to a mountain, a river, or a field. An innumerable number of possibilities can be used to indicate the existence of the collective or of relationships people identify with. These symbols stand for a story told by the people. A story that explains and justifies the existence and the power of specific institutions. The stories told have to be convincing. And they are convincing the bigger the challenges the community had to overcome and the more the main characters were ready to sacrifice themselves for the common good. If the community is supposed to last forever, the story of the brave people who made this possible has to be heroic, unsurpassed, unique.

Symbols stand for ideas, for a specific "reality." They are reductions of complex interactions and help to focus on some core elements that people can engage in.¹ Symbols further evoke commonality, reminding the community's members of their affiliation and tasks to support the reproduction of the shared "reality."

aa) Versailles – unrivalled greatness

For the French, some of the important symbols carrying their collective identity are, for example, "Marianne," the allegory of liberty and reason to be found in every town hall, court, and on stamps. Another one is the Marseillaise, the national anthem, or the flag the Tricolor, or the Phrygian cap, the symbol for the fight for liberty. These are the symbols associated with the revolution. But absolutist Louis XIV and the Napoleonic dictatorship are as much venerated, not their authoritarian or totalitarian excesses, but their cultural, political, administrative, military, and legal output.

At the age of four Louis XIV became king. Being minor, he wasn't allowed to govern. His father Louis XIII had, therefore, appointed his mother, Anne of Austria, to be head of the Council. In 1643, she nominated Mazarin as Prime Minister. Cardinal Mazarin pursued the politics of his predecessor, Richelieu, who had strengthened the power of the king at the expense of the parliament and the nobility. This "modernization" of state power toward a centralized monopoly of force reduced the influence of the army based nobility (noblesse d'épée), which gradually got replaced by the nobility of the robe (noblesse de robe). Hence, military abilities were no longer the key to state power, but rather knowledge acquired at the university. Mainly responsible for governmental activities in the field of finances and jurisdiction, the nobility of the robe gained considerably in importance. Already displeased by this intellectualization and bureaucratization of power, the former leading social classes risked to losing another privilege when Mazarin, in 1648, attempted to tax the hereditary members of the "Parlement de Paris." Up tho this point they hadn't had to pay taxes or just to a little amount. Fighting their slow but steady disempowerment, parliamentarians refused to comply and didn't enact the draft law. French parliament at this time, however, wasn't a legislative organ. Even though it was a powerful institution, it was mainly responsible for jurisdiction. Contrary to the British, the French never developed to the same degree the negotiated cooperation between court and parliament that led to a quite autonomous legislature. Reacting to the parliament's obstinacy, the minister arrested some of its im-

---

[1] About the relevance of symbols in the political realm see Loewenstein, Karl (1961), pp. 289 ff.

portant members to demonstrate his power. The rich, the rentiers, aristocrats, officers, and the little trade bourgeoisie – all of them protested in the streets of Paris against a state that wanted to increase its power and needed, therefore, more and more money from its people. Barricades were erected and angry protesters broke into the Palais Royal to see the king. The queen liberated the prisoners and made some concessions, flew with her son out of Paris and sent 4'000 mercenaries to besiege the capital, whereupon the parliamentarians surrendered and laid down their arms.

For Louis XIV the experience of this so-called "Fronde Parlementaires" and the following "Fronde des Princes," – the experience of a hostile Paris, a hostile nobility and middle class – was an determining shock. He realized that his position wasn't secure, that his power depended on the consensus of the powerful elite or the great number of the people. It became clear for the future king that he couldn't trust and rely on the aristocracy. Accordingly, he decided to avoid his opponents as much as possible and to make the powerful dependent on him. Living mainly in Vincennes and St. Germain, he projected Versailles as the future center of his kingdom.[2] Building Versailles, Louis XIV pursued two goals: First, this chateau would glorify and symbolize the magnificence of the king and, by this, of France. Second, he intended to move the court of the king from Paris to Versailles. In this way, he hoped to be able to counter the claims to power of the nobility on his own battleground.[3] All the means at his disposal were used to reach this goal: The best artists in the field of architecture (Le Vau, Le Nôtre, Le Brun, Hardouin-Mansart), sculpture (Bernini), music (Lully), theatre (Molière), painting, dance, and the best scientists and writers (Racine) would create masterpieces, make new discoveries, and invent things without precedent. Royal patronage became one of the most important sources for cultural development.[4] In order to control the creative production in France, the "république des lettres," Louis XIV and Colbert made use of the Académie française created by Richelieu in 1635, paying gratifications to artists who convincingly praised the king. With great personal engagement the king oversaw the construction of the new symbolic incarnation of France, the new "roi-soleil." A combination of power and esprit, of politics and art would be brought to its apogee.

Versailles became, thanks to its architectural and cultural greatness, and thanks to its never before seen festivities, the ballets, the operas, and

---

[2] Beaussant, Philippe (2000), p. 133, 94; Meyer, Daniel/Saule, Béatrix (1999), p. 4
[3] Newton, William R. (2000), p. 16
[4] Petitfils, Jean-Christian (2002), pp. 278 ff.

the parades, the symbolic attraction point of Europe.[5] From his god-father Mazarin, Louis XIV had learned that festivities can be used as an effective political weapon.[6] And he attained his goal. Many other nations copied the style of Versailles without ever equaling it. To be a part of this unique celebration of power, the court of the king moved to Versailles. Even though the living conditions in the chateau were, compared to their palaces in Paris, miserable (very small rooms, cold in winter), the nobility wanted to be in the proximity of the king[7] to make sure that his greatness would shine on them. And despite of the grand size of Versailles the number of rooms was limited, allowing Louis XIV to use it as an effective tool of favoritism to control the aristocrats. He personally allocated the rooms according to the political and economic advantages he intended to gain.[8]

Modern politics also became visible in Louis XIV's notion of public relations. The king perceived and used the chateau as well as the gardens as public space. His own role was a public role that he performed day in and day out.[9] "Versailles was public, more open than today, accessible without any tickets nor guided tour, less guarded […] than a […] presidential residence at the present time."[10] To access the state apartments one just had to be dressed correctly and to be neither monk nor beggar. Certain ceremonies like the king having lunch or dinner or going to bed, or the queen giving birth were public, but reserved for the nobility. He kept a certain privacy, as the chateau of Marly and the Trianon were only accessible to people invited by the king.[11] But, otherwise, the roi-soleil "justified" the incredible amount of money the people had had to pay for the construction of this politico-cultural space by sharing it with the public. It is in Versailles as a living and public space that Louis XIV confined the nobility and aggrandized common people as a proud part of the unrivalled nation.

In consensus-based constructivism, institutions originate in the engagement of individuals and depend on them. "[…] the absolute monarchy […] only worked at the time of Louis XIV"[12] because it was constructed by him and based on his character. His successor Louis XV had problems fulfilling the public role the "great king" had created. Unable to live up to the expec-

---

[5] Verlet, Pierre (1998), p. 130
[6] Petitfils, Jean-Christian (2002), p. 285
[7] Solnon, Jean-François (1987), pp. 327 f.; Verlet, Pierre (1998), p. 349
[8] Newton, William R. (2000), p. 78
[9] Verlet, Pierre (1998), p. 160
[10] Id., p. 354
[11] Solnon, Jean-François (1987), p. 331
[12] Bluche, François (2000), p. 201

tations Louix XIV had installed in the minds of his subjects, he preferred his privacy,[13] tried to avoid Versailles, and lived most of the time in the chateau of Vincennes and in the Tuileries. When he used Versailles for representative tasks, he stuck to the dispositions the great king had decreed years ago.[14] Louis XVI amplified the tendency toward privacy as he "wasn't something other than a bourgeois" and "all representative tasks bored him."[15] His major passion was hunting, an activity he could pursue endlessly,[16] but didn't have any symbolic impact. Absolutism was "absolute" as long as the deal offered by the king was attractive enough to rein in the powerful and to attract the majority of the people. Its rationale was to be a symbol for the greatness and power that exceeded the individuals and the society, as well as the neighboring countries. Without this transcendental effect, the monarchy had to adapt, democratize, or to go.

bb) Cities – militarily effective, symbolically great

Paris at the end of the 18th century and the beginning of the 19th century was an over-crowded, filthy city confined within the medieval borders, and dominated by poor people because the rich increasingly lived outside the old walls. The upper class barricaded within their luxurious hotels and the poor clustered in the blocks. Social unrest and political protests played an increasing role and the public space was more and more used not solely for the admiration of the king, but for the gathering of people developing their "public opinion" and pointing out their discontent. Too many people were moving to the city, putting enormous pressure on the infrastructure, which couldn't support the needs. The cholera epidemics of 1832 and of 1849 blatantly demonstrated the unsanitary state of the city. In 1841, the government decided to make Paris the center of the national railway-system, which is why the people coming by train needed means of transport to reach the center. Motivated by sanitary, security, aesthetic, and symbolic interests Claude-Philibert de Rambuteau, prefect of the Seine-Département, began to rebuild certain areas in the center of Paris during the 1840s. After the revolution of 1830 and even more after the one of 1848, strategic reflections began to dominate: The long and straight Boulevards were built to ease the move of the troops fighting the mob[17] and to optimize commercial

---

[13] Id., pp. 135 ff., 198 f., 37
[14] Verlet, Pierre (1998), p. 318
[15] Id., p. 512; Lever, Evelyne (1985), p. 414
[16] Lever, Evelyne (1985), p. 409
[17] Jordan, David (1996), pp. 126, 129

traffic.¹⁸ Besides this military motive, there was also a symbolic one. Louis Napoléon (president of the Second Republic and emperor from 1852-1870) wanted to use the capital to symbolize and legitimize his importance. He, therefore, intended to liberate the city from the poor and their slums and to enlarge shining monuments like the Louvre and finish the Hotel de Ville. Furthermore, this construction program should create jobs. Not to be restricted by the law, the Expropriation Act was amended in 1850. From 1853 on, Georges Eugène Haussmann was appointed prefect and was ordered to recreate the city according to the intentions of the emperor. Haussmann developed a network of large Boulevards and big places, on which important monuments were displayed. He further forced onto the city symmetric strength and uniformity. According to the idea of modernity, efficiency, simplicity and usability for ceremonies were dominating. Military aspects faded into the background. For the first time a city got rebuilt on the basis of a major idea and on such a scale.¹⁹ On the one hand, many lovely and time-honored districts had to give way to the new city. Lots of identity-space got lost, lots of history got replaced by a fascinating because grandiose staging. On the other hand, the salubrious conditions necessitated an architectural answer. That the answer was almost exclusively in favor of the bourgeoisie²⁰ demonstrates the self-service attitude of the upper class: The state as a tool not in favor of the common interest, but to please the already rich, make them richer, and secure their wealth.

This comprehensive approach, this urban construction on such an enormous scale makes a fascinating experience possible: Being part of a large space structured by one central idea. Greatness was also the intention of Hitler and Speer. The planned capital of "Germania" should combine fear with fascination and surpass Paris and Vienna.²¹ National Socialist constructions were intended to frighten the enemies and amaze foreign politicians, on the one hand, and thrill and entrap people on the other hand: "The enemies will guess it, but especially our followers have to know that to strengthen our authority our buildings unfold."²² It should function as an anchor for identity-formation and be a long-lasting heritage.²³ Aware of the symbolic power of willfully structured space, the transformation of the cities was one of Hitler's priorities. The same counts for the construction of

---

[18] Köstler, Andreas (1996), p. 133, 143
[19] Jordan, David (1996), p. 193
[20] *Id.*, p. 266
[21] Ellenbogen, Michael (2006), p. 35
[22] Hitler, quoted in: Nerdinger, Winfried (2004), p. 77
[23] Ellenbogen, Michael (2006), p. 7, 26

a dense network of highways. Basically this architecture wasn't new, it was a part of the classical architecture since the beginning of the twentieth century. Gigantism in the sense of a total reconstruction[24] was not an invention of the National Socialists, but much more a sign of modernity. Enormous constructions are to be found attractive in Manhattan[25] and fascinate in its historical appearances like Versailles, triumphal arches, Escorial, or the Capitol in Washington. What makes the plans of Hitler and Speer threatening is their immensity, their exclusive focus on quantity.[26] Everything existing had to be overshadowed. However, not focused on cultural creativity or on architectural originality, the limitless aspiration to subject the world was their motivation. This architecture symbolized the totalitarian dominance of the collective over the individual, the loss of freedom in favor of membership, and the destruction of everything and everyone trying to stop them. The "Great Hall of the People" would have had a size embracing seventeen times the volume of St. Peter's Church in Rome. And the vault of the planned triumphal arch would have contained forty-nine times the volume of the existing Parisian arch.[27] Sheer size would have to demonstrate the unsurpassable power of the regime. Based on the "natural" rights of the racially predominant Aryans and combined with their aggressive expansionist notion of space, it was a totalitarian claim to power[28] that negated every right of the individual or of the different other. Furthermore, the modern conviction of bureaucratic administration carried the National Socialist "reality" to the extreme, exterminating everything that didn't fit their understanding of clean and efficient space structuration.[29] Their architecture was "part of a hierarchically organized space-concept."[30] Mass parades, mass gatherings, and mass symbols represented the collective. Monuments everywhere stood for the party and the state, and highways connected these symbols. Following Kracauer,[31] this concept can be called "the principle of the mass:" Total size, total uniformity, total order, total symmetry, and a to-

---

[24] Speer intended for example to tear down appartements for about 150'000 to 200'000 people in the area of the planned axes in Berlin/Germania. A destruction of Berlin about identical with the one the city had to suffer in the end of World War II. The planing, however, took place during peace (Flierl, Bruno [1998], p. 47).
[25] Ellenbogen, Michael (2006), pp. 22 ff.
[26] Nerdinger, Winfried (2004), p. 77
[27] Ellenbogen, Michael (2006), pp. 37, 39
[28] Münk, Dieter (1993), p. 73
[29] Id., pp. 80 f.
[30] Id., p. 148
[31] Id., p. 123

tal collective. Combined with the total control of the cultural creation, there was no way to escape the National Socialist space. The public space wasn't constructed to liberate individuals for a critical debate about the common future, but to mobilize people and subjugate them to the absolute power of the Führer. The individual melts into this body called "Volksgemeinschaft:" "Du bist nichts, Dein Volk ist alles." ("You are nothing. Your people is all."). And all this was ordered by and oriented toward the Führer.

Luckily, the constructors of the New-Paris ran out of money, which is why some old areas are still left (such as Montmartre, Marais, Quartier Latin). All the symbols of different times are emanating statements about the "reality" relevant than and reconstructed by the people of today. That engenders a discourse between medieval and modern-authoritarian; social housing, private villas, and rental housing; or modern-capitalist points of view. It is a debate of values over, for example, a neoliberal or a community-oriented understanding of space. It is a discourse that takes place with every new construction, as, for instance, with the Grande Arche de la Défense. Its construction can be understood as a conflict between democracy and capitalism. Originally thought as an internationally networked and publicly accessible communication centre, the project was stopped by the conservative government of Jacques Chirac, which wanted a commercial use of the building. In the end a compromise resulted thanks to the engagement of state secretary Robert Lion.[32]

The public space people live in should also be a place for the unplanned, different, unique, and abnormal. Otherwise, public space becomes the symbol and the restricting structure of sterility and compulsory uniformity, which destroys plurality and freedom. Interestingly, Speer himself stated that the realization of Germania would have been not just crazy, but also boring.[33]

cc) Washington – hoard of the scriptures

Washington D.C. is on the one hand the place where the Federal politic is enacted and, for a part, executed. On the other hand, Washington is a museum, a symbolic focal-point harboring an immense amount of references to the past and to the collective identity of the nation. For the community, important elements are petrified and made eternal in order to highlight their importance against the fast flow of present changes.

---

[32] Seidl, Ernst (1996), pp. 311 ff.
[33] Ellenbogen, Michael (2006), p. 31

The American nation needed a capital to demonstrate its equality with other states. Paradoxically, the nascent democracy had to use, at least for a part the recognized symbolism that monarchies had used over the time because an alternative "democratic" architectural style wasn't known and wouldn't have been valued. Accordingly, French architect L'Enfant was commissioned to draft the future seat of government. Even though the plans contained the typical French elements developed for monarchical greatness in Versailles and Paris,[34] the arrangement of the buildings hosting the three branches of government demonstrated its democratic character. The Congress House, the Capitol (referring to the Roman model), was located in the center, representing the people as the power with the highest legitimacy. For its most important buildings Jefferson recommended "the adoption of some one of the models of antiquity which have had the approbation of thousands of years."[35] In combination with the Mall, thought to be the prime avenue, the people's prominent role becomes evident. Implementing the idea of checks and balances, L'Enfant positioned the Supreme Court and the President's seat surrounding the Capitol. Compared to the power we attribute to the President today, the President's House[36] is strangely insignificant in relation to the Capitol. That reflects the basic constitutional arrangement that L'Enfant had in mind when he planned the elevated Capitol, in the centre of the city, with many radiating streets emanating from it including long vistas.[37] The President's House was linked to the people's representation by the Pennsylvania Avenue, pointing out its role as the people's agent.

Contrary to many of the American cities dominates in Washington the symbolic aspect over the functionalist or economic one: Symbolism transcends short-term logic and pure materialistic goals. A story of lasting greatness is told by using grand vistas and impressive diagonals, breaking through the simple and rigid grid of streets, and establishing important green spaces to highlight the symbols of government and bringing to a halt everyday's rush. In its modern use, Washington is supposed to offer the opportunity to develop an enduring relationship between the past and the visitors of the monuments and memorials. In this way, a collective identity

---

[34] Meyer, Jeffrey F. (2001), p. 8, 15
[35] *Id.*, p. 27
[36] Till 1812 the home of the president was called President's House. During the War of 1812 British troops set fire to the house which had to be reconstructed. It is only then that it got painted white and became the popular name of "White House", officialized in 1901.
[37] Meyer, Jeffrey F. (2001), p. 116

is built up and reproduced by the parents who educate their children and the teachers who inculcate their students with what the young generation has to know to become supportive members of the society. Visitors and the media taking photos or filming reproduce the stories told by the monuments. And politicians use this stage for inaugural speeches, on the Fourth of July, or during election campaigns.

Establishing a permanent capital wasn't an easy thing to do. It took time and many negotiations until a consensus about its location could be found. The Continental Congress moved, over the time, from Philadelphia to Baltimore, Lancaster, York, Princeton, Annapolis, Trenton, and New York. To make sure, that no precedent was set in favor of a city or state, some members of Congress thought of a continually moving capital or of dual capitals. Many cities wanted to fulfill this privileged role. To this point, symbolic integration was mainly and effectively incorporated by President Washington; however, a lasting and institutionalized solution was needed. The Constitution provided, in Article 1 Section 8 the authority of Congress to establish the Seat of Government. To be a totally independent federal government and not to favor any state, the city would have to be built in a federal district exempt from any state control.[38]

On September 8, 1789, Congress voted for a permanent capital on the east bank of the Susquehanna. But Madison and Jefferson wanted to bring the capital to the Potomac, in order to enhance the political and economic power of Virginia and Maryland. The so-called Compromise of 1790 would be the result of a deal between Hamilton, Secretary of the Treasury, and Madison, and their respective supporters. Hamilton wanted the Federal government to assume the debts accumulated during the Revolutionary War to restore the credit of the American nation (Assumption Bill). He had to demonstrate that the United States was willing and had the means to honor its debts. Having built up trust, new money could be raised and invested in national development. The South wasn't pleased because, on the one hand, they would have to accept new federal taxes, and on the other hand, Virginia, for example, had already paid back half of its debts. Furthermore, the plans of the Secretary of the Treasury would strengthen the federal government, which was difficult to justify after a war for independence against a centralized monarchical government. Slavery was another important conflict, which had been brought up by two petitions of the Quakers, which asked the federal government to end slave trade, as well as a petition

---

[38] Madison: The Federalist No. 43, in: Hamilton, Alexander/Madison, James/Jay, John (2003 [1787-1788]), p. 262. Passing the Organic Act in 1801, Congress created the District of Columbia.

from the Pennsylvania Abolition Society, which called for the abolition of slavery. The country split over this question, Congress declared not to have the authority to emancipate slaves or to interfere into the autonomy of the states. Even though Hamilton was a staunch opponent of slavery, he was ready to accept this injustice if his Assumption Bill would pass. Knowing most of the votes of the Northern members were in favor of his plan, he was in the strong position to deal the Bill of the site of the new capital, the third fundamental dissent in the young nation. On the other hand, Madison had enough votes to block the Bill indefinitely. On July 16, 1790, the Congress approved the Residence Act, making the Potomac the site of the capital. Shortly after the Assumption Bill was adopted. The capital wasn't instantly moved to the South because for the next ten years Philadelphia would play this role, a concession made to win over the Pennsylvanians. To make sure that the capital would be finished in time, Congress commissioned President Washington to build the city and gave him complete executive authority. Free to choose the concrete site he opted for an area where the Patowmack Navigation Company had previously bought vast tracts of land.[39] That he was president of the company likely helped him make this decision. In 1791, the city was called "Washington," honoring the man who had represented the nation until then.

The construction of Washington D.C. became not the intended heroic demonstration of the power of the new nation, but much more an exhibition of "its impotence […] by its inability to lay even a few streets or erect a pair of buildings for its own government."[40] However, it is thanks to the engagement of George Washington that the capital finally could be realized,[41] even though President John Adams had to move into an unfinished Presidents House on November 1, 1800. "Not a single room was finished, closet doors were missing, and a three-hole 'necessary' had barely been finished in time for [Abigail Adams'] arrival. The main stairs had not even been installed, and no fewer than thirteen fires had to be kept burning just to make the damp house habitable."[42]

Over the time Washington gained two opposite statuses. On the one hand, it was the site of everyday's federal politics with its seldom heroic debates and negotiations, its power game, its lobbying, its party politics, its humane mediocrity, its a-moral affairs. It was a symbol for hope for the ones dependent on federal protection and support, and a symbol for hatred

---

[39] Bordewich, Fergus M. (2008), pp. 61 ff.
[40] Id., p. 95
[41] Id., p. 241
[42] Id., p. 250

for the others, who characterized the modern federal state as a threat to individual liberty. On the other hand, it became the venerated symbol of the American collective identity, of an heroic past, an untainted battle for everlasting values and institutions, a time and people transcending place for public worship. "[…] for millions of […] Americans and foreign visitors, to travel to Washington is to seek some kind of communion with the secular civic religion that is embodied in its templelike buildings and the democratic institutions they enshrine."[43] As guardian of the three most important American ideological symbols, the Declaration of Independence, the Constitution, and the Bill of Rights, Washington is an actively staged and visited "pilgrimage center."[44] The ideological performance of these three documents had to be built up. After their enactment and during the following decades, what at present is called "The Nation's Vital Documents" hasn't been regarded with much reverence.[45] In the 20th century they became part of an ideological battle against totalitarianism. Fighting fascist and communist enemies in the 1940s and 1950s, the charters of freedom were understood as the symbol and assertion of American values. Pearl Harbor made evident that these identity creating documents had to be protected, which is why they were sent to the Bullion Depository at Fort Knox and, in 1952, to the National Archives, which was built in 1934 and has now become a shrine,[46] "the unequivocal temple of the American State."[47] Analogous to the itinerant king, who had to travel throughout the country to stage his existence to a people who otherwise, lacking modern media, would never have had the opportunity to get a glimpse of its ruler, the Freedom Trains of 1947–1949 and 1975–1976 wanted to make sure that the fundamental texts which were at the origin of the nation could be seen and venerated by everybody.

The Declaration of Independence fulfilled and fulfills its function as ideological symbol in an exemplary way. The legally decisive step toward self-government was taken by the Second Continental Congress. On July 2, 1776, it approved the resolution of independence.[48] Even though New York abstained, freedom from Great Britain had been declared and had united the colonies just in time, as the British landed their troops on Staten Island

---

[43] *Id.*, p. 4
[44] Meyer, Jeffrey F. (2001), p. 10
[45] Maier, Pauline (1997), p. XI
[46] *Id.*, p. XV
[47] Meyer, Jeffrey F. (2001), p. 81
[48] Hogeland, William (2010), p. 173

the next day. The Continental Congress was convinced that this key political moment needed symbolization and justification to mobilize people against the actual world power. "If the delegates expected thousands of Americans to put their lives at risk voluntarily, they knew they had to draft a manifesto that would lay out the reasons why."[49] They also hoped to gain support from France or other foreign powers against Great Britain, if they could give good reasons for their decision against the monarchy. "The task assigned to Jefferson was to act as advocate of his country's cause before the bar of world opinion."[50] Why should the monarchy, the form of government that had prevailed over centuries and had become a natural state of politic, be overthrown? Congress discussed and amended Jefferson's draft on July 3rd and 4th and adopted the text on the 4th. The text was printed and made known by publication or public reading in the states. On July 19, New York approved the text, which now was written on parchment and given an official title: "The Unanimous Declaration of the Thirteen United States" and signed by the members of Congress during the following months. Having fulfilled its primal symbolic function, the document was largely forgotten.[51] It's only years later that the political text would become revered "as a sacred text"[52] and achieve a transcendent status. "The modern reputation of the Declaration of Independence was born in the bitter partisan politics of the 1790s and reached a recognizably mature form, complete with quasi-religious attributes, thirty years later. [...] after the execution of Louis XVI and the onset of the Terror, the Federalists shed any enthusiasm they once felt for the French Revolution; and the assertions of equality and unalienable rights in the second paragraph of the Declaration of Independence [...] still seemed too 'French' for the Federalists' comfort. [...] It was, then, the Republicans [...] who began to celebrate the Declaration of Independence as a 'deathless instrument' written by 'the immortal Jefferson.'"[53]

The longer a symbol is unquestioned in use, the more its integrative effect is taken for granted, and the more it gets a somewhat canonical, iconic status.[54] The content of the Constitution or the Declaration isn't then defining anymore, it's pure existence suffices to mobilize passion and interest and to recall the common heritage and the shared reasons to live. The Re-

---

[49] Parkinson, Robert (2008), p. 12
[50] Boyd, Julian (1999), p. 20
[51] Hogeland, William (2010), p. 178
[52] Parkinson, Robert (2008), p. 11
[53] Maier, Pauline (1997), p. 170
[54] Meyer, Jeffrey F. (2001), p. 89, 91

publicans of the 112th Congress tried to connect to this eternal integrative validity to make their politics unquestioned. Reacting to the landslide success of the Tea Party movement, they intend to establish rules making sure that their Constitution of the United States would be respected, supported and defended.[55] In their Pledge to America on September 2010, the House Republicans stated that every bill would be required to cite its specific constitutional authority. The standing Rules of the House would be amended, so that each bill or joint resolution introduced in the House had to contain "a statement appropriately citing the specific powers granted to Congress in the Constitution as a basis for enacting the law proposed by the bill or joint resolution."[56] However, the unique interpretation of the Constitution that the Republicans look for won't be found this way. To mention a specific constitutional basis in order to justify a new law doesn't bring to an end the interpretative leeway every rule embodies. On January 6, 2011, the Republicans tried to make profit of the aura the iconic text retains, which is why they let read the Constitution aloud in the House of Representatives. This event illustrated best the willful use of what is pretended to be an unequivocal guide and source. Republicans used their interpretative freedom and opted not to read the whole constitutional text, but a sanitized version. Making sure that their symbolic act would demonstrate the greatness of the Constitution, they blinded out the less glorious parts of American history. They didn't want to hear about a country that had counted a Black as three-fifths of a white person, that had allowed slavery, denied women the right to vote, or banned liquor. For Representative Jesse L. Jackson Jr., a Democrat from Illinois, this procedure "was whitewashing history and ignoring the blood, sweat and tears paid to achieve the amendments."[57] Making the constitution a scripture, a holy text, unquestionable and superhuman, is a form of self-incapacitation or a tool to exclude other ways of thinking, is an absolutist approach to conflicts that have to be solved on the basis of the only truth. For this "non-instrumental view of law, [...] the process of lawmaking is not a matter of creation but one of discovery; [...] law is not the product of human will; [...] law has a kind of autonomy and internal integrity; [...] law is, in some sense, objectively determined."[58] To work with the concept of the universal truth means to exclude the possibility of change. Based on this "originalism" everything new has to be wrong, and people

---

[55] Republican John A. Boehner quoted in Washington Post of December 30, 2010, "Two new rules will give Constitution a starring role in GOP-controlled House."
[56] Bill Text, 111th Congress (2009-2010), H.RES.1754.IH
[57] The New York Times of January 7, 2011, A15
[58] Tamanaha, Brian Z. (2006), p. 11

have to lose the chance to try out solutions for problems they didn't have until now. Other views, other interpretations of the Constitution risk being qualified as unpatriotic, treacherous.[59]

According to consensus-based constructivism, symbols develop their effect not because of an inner truth or their connection to objectivity or to a godly existence. Symbols integrate people and bring people together when they represent a story the interactors like to hear, a story they want to be a part of and to live up to. A little part of this story is incorporated in "The Nation's Vital Documents," which stand for the adventure told in books or in the Smithsonian museums, such as the National Portrait Gallery, the National Museum of American Art, the Air and Space Museum, the American history Museum, or the American Indian Museum. All of them and many more tell a story of the artistic, scientific, political, and military heroines and heroes that people want to be relevant. Using these symbols to exclude others is missing the intense cooperation of thousands and millions of people engaged for their community.

dd) Northern Ireland – to whom belong the streets?

The Irish-British conflict in Northern Ireland was on the one hand a conflict over governmental power, justice, and freedom. On the other hand, it was an intense fight over the collective identity of the involved parties. Besides violent battles, terrorist attacks, torture, imprisonment, or hunger strikes, the conflict had an important symbolic aspect: The use of the public space and the living areas was highly contested. Within an imperialistic context, the Catholic minority tried to gain political freedom, recognition, and respect. And the Protestant majority, as "representative" of the rule of Great Britain, could rely on the British Army and the Royal Ulster Constabulary to enforce its supremacy. In addition, the Protestants occupied the streets and places by telling the story of their victory over the Catholics, beginning in the seventeenth century. They wielded their power effectively not in the least by using symbols of identity.

When in 1922, the Irish Free State was established, the six North-eastern counties had, according to the Anglo-Irish Treaty the right to opt out and to decide whether or not to stay a part of the United Kingdom. The Parliament of Northern Ireland decided on December 7, 1922, to opt for Great Britain by addressing to the King the legally required request. From this point on, the Protestants saw themselves even more than before as a

---

[59] Epps, Garrett (2011)

small minority on a Catholic-Irish island. Demonstrating their supremacy in the North and reassuring their own identity, the Protestants celebrated themselves and their successful history using different rituals. At the core of this identity-reproduction stood the reference to the Battle of the Boyne, during which Protestant King William III (Prince of Orange) won over the Catholic troops of King James on July 12, 1690. The leading group in this reproduction process is the Orange Order which commemorates William of Orange. It was founded at the end of the 18th century and is meant to defend the interests of the Protestants in Ireland. Early on, the Protestants didn't feel comfortable with their role as colonizers and oppressors and needed to affirm their right to rule over the Catholic majority. Even though the Acts of Union of 1801 established the United Kingdom of Britain and Ireland and left the Catholics of Ireland at the bottom of the social hierarchy,[60] the Protestants were not confident about their own position. Every time Great Britain gave in to claims of the Catholics, the Protestants reacted with symbolic demonstrations to mark and reaffirm their dominating position. During Catholic Emancipation, which took place at the end of the 18th and the beginning of the 19th century and removed restrictions the Catholics had had to endure, the Protestants paraded intensely to build up connections between themselves and their living areas and to demarcate their identity. The Orange Order lost importance up to the end of the 19th century, but got reactivated when the Irish request for autonomy was heard by Prime Minister Gladstone in 1886, and who introduced the Home Rule Bill. Parliament didn't enact the Bill, not in 1886 nor in 1893, but the Orangemen, nevertheless, paraded again to demonstrate their presence. And the ascent of Gaelic movements asserting their difference intensified the Orangemen's feeling of insecurity. The creation of the Republic of Ireland in 1922 posed a fundamental threat to the Protestants' position on the isle, which is why the Orangemen amplified their use of symbolic tools to secure their control over the geographical space. The following symbolic forms of actions are used to this day:

- Marches throughout the year but especially on the Twelfth of July: Thousands of Orangemen take to the streets, parading among others pictures of William III. These marches are accompanied by music bands playing tunes recalling past glories. Flags and banners symbolizing the British heritage are carried with.
- Before the marches start, bunting is hung between the houses.

---

[60] Rolston, Bill (1998), p. i

- Wooden, metal or floral arches are installed in the centres of towns and villages.
- Bonfires are lit and by this occasion flags of the Republic of Ireland or effigies of the Pope burnt.

As lasting symbols,
- kerbstones are painted in red, white, and blue,
- lampposts are color-coded,
- graffitis sprayed to mark an area, and
- murals painted on house walls, telling identity relevant stories.

Mural paintings are to be found worldwide and fulfill different functions. In Tanzania's oral tradition they relate popular tales and play an important role in the construction of the collective identity. In Egypt they are part of the religious art, whereas, for example, in Nicaragua the murals have been used by the FSLN in the 1980s to mobilize and convince people to fight against American imperialism. In San Francisco the murals illustrate actual problems like racism, drugs, unemployment or political solidarity.[61] In the Irish context, murals were applied to comfort the identity of Protestants, to indicate as well as to delimit the areas Catholics were allowed to live in,[62] and to point out who rules.

From the 19th century till the 1960s, the unionist domination of the symbolic "reality" construction and of the geographical space wasn't really challenged. The Protestants in power adopted all possible means to control political institutions and the use of the public sphere. Through laws,[63] gerrymandering (electoral districts are bounded in a way that the chances of a specific group to win the majority is assured), and police force, they secured their power because they were a "Protestant Parliament and a Protestant

---

[61] Rolston, Bill (1998), p. viii
[62] Guildhall Press (2008), p. 12; Jarman, Neil (1998), p. 83
[63] For example the Special Powers Act of 1922 or its replacement regarding the governance and control of Northern Irish parades of 1951: the Public Order Act. "Customarily held processions" were exempt from authorization, what privileged the parades of the Orange Order. Another example is the Flags and Emblems Act of 1954, which gave the RUC the right to remove any flag or emblem from public or private property likely to cause a breach of peace. Exempt was the Union Flag. About the unequal application of the Special Powers Act of 1922 see: Dohonue, Laura K. (1998).

State."[64] But, in the 1960s the Republican (catholic) movement began seriously to question the Protestants' symbolic construction power. From January to April 1969 clashes between the Royal Ulster Constabulary (RUC, police forces of the Northern Ireland Government) and Republicans took place. One cause was the Republicans' support for the Civil Rights Movement, which had taken high risks challenging the inequalities in Northern Ireland. These fights led to the death of Samuel Devenny, who died after a heart attack probably caused by a severe police beating. The Unionists, on the other hand, tried to counter the mounting resistance threatening their supremacy.[65] The closer the annual parade of the (Protestant) Apprentice Boys on August 12 approached, the more the tensions rose. This demonstration of power took place across the residential area of the Republicans: "Parades through Catholic areas [...] looked [...] like invasions,"[66] and were intended to humiliate the enemy. Catholics, however, couldn't pay back in kind: "[...] loyalist parades were allowed to pass through Catholic areas but attempts by nationalists to parade or erect visual displays were often highly restricted or banned outright. Even the temporary erection of the Irish tricolour was seen as a challenge and an affront."[67] In 1969, though, this provocation could no longer be suffered. The Catholics had requested to renounce to the traditional parading routes. Their demand was refused and the Derry Citizens Defence Association (DCDA) evacuated women and children to safer parts of the city and started to build barricades to prevent the parade from entering into what they perceived as their home. Using the enemy's techniques, the slogan "You are now entering Free Derry" was painted on the gable wall of the house at the corner of Lecky Road and Fahan Street. "[...] people began to [...] redefine the symbolic identity and status of the estates. [...] Behind the barricades the power of the state was restricted and the agents of the state were excluded."[68] Different riots between the residents of the Bogside area and the RUC followed and calm was only restored after the British government ordered the deployment of British troops.

After a vain year-long protest of Republican inmates to be recognized the status of political prisoners, they opted, in 1981, for hunger strikes – one of the most powerful forms of symbolic protest. Ten of them died. In

---

[64] Statement of James Craig, first Prime Minister of Northern Ireland from 1921–1940, in Parliament on April 24, 1934.
[65] Bryan, Dominic (2000), p. 85
[66] Id., p. 96
[67] Jarman, Neil (1998), p. 84
[68] Id., p. 85

the aftermath, the use of murals by the Unionists increased dramatically. Many intense battles ensued: The Battle of Drumcree in Portadown in 1985 and 1986 (following the Anglo-Irish Agreement of 1985, giving the Irish government an advisory role in Northern Ireland's government);[69] and after the cease-fires of 1994, when intense fights over the right and the ways of parading occurred in Belfast (Lower Ormeau Road), Derry (Bogside), and Portadown (Garvaghy Road). In 1985-86 and 1995-96. loyalists asserted their identity they perceived threatened. And in 1995, Sinn Fein and the IRA "transferred the theatre of conflict with Unionists to the local level [...] by mobilizing the residents of Catholic areas [...] to resist Orange marches."[70] The Protestants, on the other hand, had to realize that the British Government had secretly negotiated with Sinn Féin and suddenly "everyone appeared to be courting Gerry Adams, President of Sinn Féin."[71]

Against the background of consensus-based constructivism, there is no symbolic resource that has inevitably to be used. That accounts as much for religion as for ethnicity, race, or tradition. Even if the history of this conflict can be traced back to the 17th century, that doesn't mean that we are confronted with an inevitable social clash: "Ireland is all too readily regarded as a society trapped in the past: the contemporary conflict has been likened to medieval religious wars, or alternatively described as an unresolvable conflict between two mutually hostile tribes."[72] "While an ethnic or national identity is often seen as an essential and unchangeable feature of one's being, it is in practice a much more fluid and unpredictable formation."[73] During the 17th century, Protestants and Catholics worked together for an independent, or at least an autonomous, Irish state. Religion played a role but it wasn't as unchangeable and categorical as it became later. The "formations of the distinct Ulster-British Protestant and Irish Catholic ethnicities in Northern Ireland were largely a product of the 19th century; but they are nonetheless real for all that as people live according to this scheme."[74] Religious community constructions are effectively rallying people when they're understood in an absolutist way. As a dichotomous construction they enhance the conflict intensity and presume inescapability. And the physical fixation of symbols gives the relationship an historical or even an eternal character. But history is, like everything else, a story we would like to be

---

[69] Kaufmann, Eric P. (2007), p. 122; Bryan, Dominic (2000), p. 158
[70] Id., p. 149
[71] Bryan, Dominic (2000), p. 169
[72] Jarman, Neil (1997), p. 2
[73] Id., p. 6
[74] Id., p. 6

told of ourselves and of our descent. So the victory of William of Orange of 1690 only started to play an important role in the later 19th century, as a unionist political consciousness was needed. The same accounts for the parades that had to be politically established as an accepted form of symbolic identity construction. Parades were, first, a privilege of the ancien régime, of the great and the good. In this way they demonstrated their power, their military force and their control of the public space: "They represent their reign […] in front of the people" by celebrating their status based on "regalia (insignia, weapons), habitus (clothes, haircuts), gesture (greeting and behavior form)."[75] Lacking mass media to stage government, the physical appearance in the public space was a condition sine qua non for demonstrating the existence and, thus, the relevance of monarchical power. In the 1770s, the rural gentry of Northern Ireland discovered the use of parades as an effective tool for mobilization and unification, and employed them to amplify their claims against London. From 1795 to 1868, parading was largely seen as a dangerous, often seditious, behavior to be controlled by state authority, which is why they were restricted.[76] Even though Orangeism was politically supporting the government, the elite in power wasn't quite sure about the characterization of this loud and overtly visible manifestation: "[…] Orangeism was […] a popular culture that developed in shebeens and pubs, the site of much political resistance in early modern Europe. It developed out of more direct lower-class sectarian confrontations that put at risk the economic and political stability of the country."[77] More and more, local landlords, magistrates, and the elite in Dublin supported the movement. Unable to eradicate parading, the government had to give in and accept this popular form of political communication: In 1872, parades were legalized. The parading commemoration of the Williamite campaign became, from then on, a core element of Protestant identity. The reassuring importance of symbolic action in a political fight becomes evident when we look at the number of marches that took place in the 1990s: There were around 2'500 parades held by loyalist organizations (Orangemen, Royal Black Preceptory and others) every year[78] and around 300 nationalist ones. Symbolic action can be used as cultural violence to exclude others and force an identity on them. It is, on the other hand, an effective possibility to bring people together, to tell a uniting story.

---

[75] Habermas, Jürgen (1990), p. 61
[76] Jarman, Neil (1997), pp. 27 f. Bryan, Dominic (2000), p. 9
[77] Bryan, Dominic (2000), pp. 35 f.
[78] Id., p. 26

Finally, the Good Friday Agreement of 1998 brought this intense conflict to an end. A just sharing of the power helped to overcome this century-old conflict. Even though the Protestants first had to renounce to power, they gained power thanks to the cooperative approach they chose. All the energy, time, and resources invested in a destructive conflict are freed for common projects. And instead of the stalemate due to a Manichaean understanding of others, an open future becomes possible. Creativity is needed[79] to overcome "realities" which seemed to be engraved in stone and to avoid the emptiness the absence of the former foe can yield. Symbolically, the world changes when hateful and violent imagery gets replaced by murals reflecting the new cooperation, a process called "re-imaging communities."[80] However, new murals have appeared, which are as aggressive as before and accompanied by violent attacks and murder. For sure, there is much less violence than before. But these clashes show that there are still individuals who are not integrated enough to become a part of the new community, and that the former symbolism is appropriated by people not feeling recognized.

b) Time concept – past, present, future

Developing a narrative is an integrative process. Constructing a community's tale is not a question of truth or of scientific recognition, but of building "home." The main question is: Who gets integrated and how? The "time" we live in is more than just a sequence of events. It is a specific, interactively constructed experience that gains its sense out of the contributions of the participants. Thus, "history" and supposed "future" are the result of the need of people who aspire to a satisfying picture of themselves. This social arrangement helps to solve present problems and to motivate actions to come. *"History" is what we need now to have been.* Time – the story of the past, present, and future – is a permanent discourse about a community's place in history and about the role of individuals. If life, freedom, justice,

---

[79] Kenney, Mary Catherine (1998), pp. 155 f., 166
[80] Belfast City Council (retrieved July 12, 2011, from http://www.belfastcity.gov.uk/re-image/): "The Re-Imaging Communities Project (established by the Shared Communities Consortium) aims to transform communities by improving their environment and reflect the positive changes in Belfast. Sectarian murals, emblems, flags and graffiti will be replaced by positive images which reflect the community's culture, as well as highlight and promote the social regeneration taking place in communities today."

solidarity, and responsibility are of importance, we should avoid story-telling of the sort of absolutist hopes for salvation or nationalistic-heroic tales of the one and only chosen people who are entitled to kill whoever gets in their way.

To tell the story of a community is not an innocuous act. It constructs "reality" and builds up expectations for the future. There is a tendency to reproduction because of a need for stability. Still, to make the past become a reliable element of our collective identity, steady reproduction is needed through, for example, commemorations, statues, museums, and such. Once a narrative is established it has a propensity to endure and to be taken for granted. Many tales are proposed that suit the basic values of their defenders. Sometimes the ideas and concepts of historians converge, only to diverge again. Scientific "reality" proposals are helpful to nurture and enrich a discussion about the shared identity. But they can't bring these discussions to an end by claiming to have found *the* narrative to be followed. It is, therefore, constructively speaking, not a fight over "hard facts"[81] that can't be denied, but a creative exploration of possibilities, hopefully rich, surprising, and different, to provide a choice.

Every community develops its own understanding of the past, present, and future. The majority has what can be called a *dominant narrative*, whereas the minorities have to fight for and develop their own understanding of their origins and the time to come. Depending on the amount of recognition and respect the majority manifests toward the minority, I differentiate a *won* or an *independent narrative*. When a minority has to defend its own narrative against the imposed story of the majority, they have to fight for their identity. The majority's claims for supremacy make it difficult to uphold what is dear to the relatively powerless. With imagination and cleverness, they uphold their origins. Hiding the signs of their membership, the symbols of the collective, the texts and sources justifying and explaining their existence, they counter the majority's cultural violence. This hard-won narrative has to be told and retold again and again to make it a stable element of identity. The same accounts for the independent narrative, which can be developed freely if the dominant narrative allows different collective identities within its sphere of influence.

An important part of every community is the narrative over its origins. What brought this community into existence? What were the decisions to be made, the adventures lived, the obstacles overcome, so that this unique relationship could be developed? As much as the concept of the past does

---

[81] Mattioli, Aram (2010), p. 147

our understanding of the future characterize the collective's identity. What are the goals that people hope to achieve? How bright or dismal is the future? How confident are we to forge the impending "reality?" What will we look like in the future? To talk about the present means to talk in the present about the past or the future. In my opinion, we can't seize the present because the present is the moment of action, the moment we are doing something. When we talk about what we are doing, we talk in the present about what we just did or what we should do. *We are what we were and what we will be.*

The consumer society has a very limited time frame within which it acts and lives. The nearest future, the immediate consumption is the raison d'être. What we were and what we will be is of no importance because the permanent change is an end in itself and short-termism dominates the way to think and to decide. The need for a sense of life is answered with speeded up modifications of the goods offered for consumption. Having what is new, being part of the next trend is central and determines our notion of time and responsibility. Whatever the effects of our short-term satisfaction culture are in the long run, and whatever was needed in the distant or near past to produce the cheap consumer goods is, at least for a neoliberal, of no interest. Individuals just have to focus on their own greed, because the market will harmonize the interests involved; it will take care of the children who have to work, of the environment destroyed by low-cost production, of the people dying because of overwork or of harsh working conditions.

aa) The past we need ...

Iraq 2010: The American invasion of Iraq in 2003 didn't happen. Saddam Hussein never existed. At least that's the story told in Iraq's school curriculum. The education ministry avoids topics that could question the more than fragile and still developing elementary consensus. What for some was an invasion, is for others Operation Freedom.[82] History isn't innocent. *The story we tell about our past is the result of politics we want to realize in our future.* There is, according to consensus-based constructivism, no objective history to be recognized. Communities tell *the stories they think best suit their current needs.*

There existed a so-called European "Meistererzählung", a dominant narrative orientating the collective identity in time. Part of this narrative

---

[82] In Rewriting Its History, Iraq Treads Cautiously, in: The New York Times of June 30, 2010, p. A4

was the consensus to exclude from the democratic discourse people who defend National Socialist, Fascist, racist, and/or totalitarian ideas, such as, for example, Le Pen, Schönhuber, or the successors of Mussolini. At least they shouldn't have access to government. Part of this "Meistererzählung" was the Italian narrative, called the "Resistenza." Since World War II this story of the proud resistance against Fascism has been told. Contrary to the Germans, in this story the Italians were ready to risk life and liberty fighting Mussolini. "From the beginning the [resistenza-myth] blinded out Fascism as a socially widely supported societal experiment."[83] Describing themselves as the good Italian ("bravo italiano") and the others as the "bad German" ("cattivo tedesco")[84] helped to integrate the Italian nation that had lost the war and had, in its majority, supported Mussolini. The "Resistenza"-narrative was a compromise between the ones who had fought the totalitarian government and its adherents or the collaborators. It helped to overcome a deep schism and to make a common future possible. Everybody got the chance to be part of the new community if he or she was ready to accept the victory of the resistance over the Fascist forces.

Berlusconi, however, is fascinated by Mussolini, by Fascism, and by authoritarian governments. During the several years of his tenure, he quite successfully took one step after another to establish a society based on two elements. On the one hand, an authoritarian government that could do whatever pleases the small elite ruling the country, not controlled by the justice, the parliament, or the media. The media, on the other hand, are owned or controlled by the government and used to entertain the majority in a way that makes them forget the political duties they have in a democracy. Berlusconi, therefore, needs strong police and military forces, wants to abolish unions, to control the justice, and to limit the freedom of the press. This authoritarian political program is based on a leader who isn't restricted by the rule of law, and corresponds, not surprisingly with the program of the lodge "Propaganda Due (P2)," which was a secret lodge that had tremendous influence on the Italian government from 1945 to 1981. It defended a strong anti-Communism, intended to "destroy the independence of the judiciary" and pursued the "strategy to take over key elements of the media."[85] A proud member of the lodge, Berlusconi supported its ideas and used his membership mainly for networking and to build up his economic and media empire. Still, caught in this dichotomous logic of good and evil, he perceive's and presents himself as the leader preventing Italy from com-

---

[83] Mattioli, Aram (2010), p. 27
[84] Bidussa, David (1994), pp. 62 f.
[85] Ginsborg, Paul (2005), p. 32

munism, the evil incarnate. This friend-foe-scheme described and defended by Carl Schmitt (see p. 221) perceives chaos and civil war everywhere,[86] which is why drastic measures have to be taken to protect a menaced core of basic values. The dominant worldview is one of "warfare," which is why "politics" as a democratic debate over the common future on a level playing field is excluded.[87] Mussolini's world was based on the same principles: "War was the natural, fatal, and not reversible result of the Fascist concept of the right of the stronger."[88] Similar in its logic and justification, criticism of "il Cavaliere" Berlusconi is viewed as treason. State institutions like the Justice or the President, which try to control the Prime Minister's abuses of state power, are treated by il Cavaliere as Communists who are responsible for the weakening of powerful Italy.[89]

Berlusconi's problem was that the Resistenza-narrative made authoritarian governments illegitimate. He, therefore, had to rewrite history to whitewash Fascism. Propagating the new narrative shouldn't be too big of a problem for a Prime Minister controlling a dominant part of the media and having been elected three times (1994, 2001, 2008). However, Italy knew the biggest resistance movement in Europe. Unfortunately for Berlusconi, its majority was consisted of Communists. This Left pride and moral performance always was a thorn in the side of the revisionist Right. The main target of their rehabilitation of Mussolini is to disqualify the first anti-Fascist Republic as infested by "Marxist culture."[90] And the responsibilities of the Fascists and the Resistenza during World War II shall be equalized. According to authoritarian and right-extremist movements, "Mussolini's was a mild dictatorship" basically a good thing. It is only its collaboration with the Nazis that had to be judged as a mistake.[91] This good-natured Fascism (Fascismo bonario)[92] (Berlusconi: "Mussolini didn't kill anybody. He only sent people into exile on holiday"[93]), shall be understood as a positive community experience. To avoid supporting and reproducing the Resistenza-

---

[86] See Frankenberg, Günter (2003), p. 23
[87] Buber, Martin (1992), p. 254
[88] Camilleri, Andrea (2010), p. 18
[89] Galluzzo, Marco: Berlusconi: il leader pd è un cattocomunista, in: Corriere della Sera of March 13, 2009 (http://www.corriere.it/politica/09_marzo_13/berlusconi_cattocumunista_Galluzzo_a684c0c4-0f97-11de-948b-00144f02aabc.shtml), retrieved on July 27, 2011
[90] Mattioli, Aram (2010), pp. 20 f., 59
[91] *Id.*, pp. 54 f.
[92] *Id.*, p. 57
[93] La Repubblica of Mai 27, 2010 (http://www.repubblica.it/politica/2010/05/27/news/berlusconi_mussolini-4385926/), retrieved on July 27, 2011

narrative which is a moral and political success story of the Left, Berlusconi, since his entry into politics never participated at the commemoration of April 25, the "day of liberation" (liberazione) from Fascism. This "red celebration" provided the Left with a heroic place in history, whereas the Right in its majority chose the wrong side. That's why Berlusconi always insisted that the real danger was and still is Communism, and that the Republican Constitution of 1948 has a "Soviet character."[94] After their success in the elections of 2001 the new majority tried to transform the "day of liberation" into a "celebration of freedom," but it finally didn't take place. In 2004, however, the right-wing Italian parliament introduced the Foibe celebration, which commemorates the Italians killed by the Yugoslavian guerillas and who were forced to migrate from 1943 to 1947.[95] The fall of the Berlin Wall on November 9, 1989 is also celebrated as victory over communism. The proposal to equate Mussolini's soldiers, militia, and collaborators with the resistenza, however, went too far because it led to a storm of protest in 2003. Nevertheless, legitimizing the "Duce" became an important part of the politics of Berlusconi et al. – something they did very effectively, as an "apology of Fascism and 'Duce'-admiration arrived in the middle of society."[96] Fascist ideas and convictions aren't solely represented by right extremists anymore, but by "ordinary" people and the so called "elite" (professors of history, journalists, or writers). These ideas also began to be a part of everyday life, as, for example, the best selling iPhone app in Italy in January 2010 was "iMussolini," a collection of speeches of and documents about the Duce.[97] Other blockbusters are calendars with Mussolini slogans and wine labelled with the portrait of the Italian leader.[98] About 100'000 people visit the family vault of the Mussolinis in San Cassiano every year. Besides the historical and symbolic normalization of Fascism, Berlusconi has also made the access of right-wing and former Fascists to the government possible.[99]

Il Cavaliere doesn't like democracy and the rule of law because of their negative effects on government: They restrict power in favor of the people, something an absolutist leader can't accept. In May 2010, he complained: "Let me quote Benito Mussolini, whose journals I have recently been reading, […] 'All I can do is tell my horse to go left or go right. That's my power.'

---

[94] Mattioli, Aram (2010), p. 56
[95] See about the history of this commemoration and its political use Sluga, Glenda (1999).
[96] Mattioli, Aram (2010), p. 11
[97] Martin: Mussolinis iPhone-Erfolg erregt Italien, on: Welt.de of January 29, 2010
[98] Italien: Das Geschäft mit Mussolini boomt, in: Die Presse.com of January 4, 2010
[99] Mattioli, Aram (2010), p. 17

[…] I've never felt like I had power. When I was a businessman with thousands of employees, then I felt like I had power."[100] "In a real democracy you have to be at the service of everybody, and everybody is entitled to criticize or even insult me."[101] That Berlusconi identifies companies with a democratic constitutional state highlights his understanding of freedom, equality, and responsibility. Democracy and the rule of law are supposed to serve the people, which is why the state monopoly of violence is subjected to strict rules and the rulers have to justify what they do. In my opinion, it is not the state that has to be made company-like, but the companies that have to be democratized and held accountable for their use of power and its effects within the company and in society. By quoting Mussolini, he demonstrated his conviction, that il Duce was a statesman like many others, that he himself is like the Duce, and that, unfortunately, political power isn't structured anymore in a way that suits great leaders like him.

The intended and partly-achieved new construction of Italian history is problematic because it facilitates exclusion and oppression. The Führer-principle and collectivism are legitimized and the construction of bogeymen is simplified. That authoritarian politics are part of the government's repertoire and has penetrated society becomes apparent in the groundless attacks against leftist teenagers, against homeless, and against migrants.[102] The Roma and Sinti, especially, were and are the currently favored victims of rowdies and of rightist politics. A mob beat Roma and Sinti and set fires to their camp in May 2008 in Napoli. The arson was repeated three times to make sure that the inhabitants wouldn't come back. It wasn't the first time that camps of Roma and Sinti were set on fire: In 2007 arson attacks were acted out in Catania, Milano, and in the capital. And it seems quite probable that the fire in Livorno, which cost the lives of four Roma and Sinti children, had been set willfully.[103] Collectively judged as criminals, different regions proclaimed, in Mai 2008, a "state of emergency of nomads," followed by the national government in July, declaring a "state of emergency of security." This decree of the council of ministers gave the administrative authorities the right to observe the Roma and Sinti, to record their identity and deport illegal inhabitants. Fingerprints were taken, photos made, and private data collected. In August, 3'000 soldiers were deployed to control internment camps and to protect public places and the infrastructure. This

---

[100] The New York Times of May 28, 2010, p. A6
[101] La Repubblica of Mai 27, 2010 (http://www.repubblica.it/politica/2010/05/27/news/berlusconi_mussolini-4385926/), retrieved on July 27, 2011
[102] Camilleri, Andrea (2010), p. 19
[103] Vivaldi, Elisabetta (2009)

scapegoat politic was used to demonstrate governmental power and activism. A serious principled reaction of the opposition was missing.

bb) End the past, begin the future – forgiveness

Wars, genocide, fundamental political defeats, or crushed hopes lead to a schism between groups of people, making cooperation highly improbable. If there shall be a common future, the friend-foe scheme has to be given up in favor of a modest form of co-existence,[104] of cooperation. The hatred used to fight each other has to become part of a story that basically recognizes the others existence on an equal basis, has to respect their difference, and has to point out the common task for the future. Our basic values, the normative grounds of our identity[105] have to be rethought and an elementary consensus needs to be built up that makes delimitations possible without excluding people (see p. 89 ff.). To be able to cooperate, former enemies have to forgive committed cruelties. That doesn't mean that violations of important values have to be forgotten. They should be memorized, displayed in museums, documentaries, and in the stories told in school. It is important not to forget because "the struggle of humanity against power is the struggle of memory against forgetting."[106] Memory, however, is not longer used as a weapon to exclude or kill others, but as a critical sort of philosopher's stone, a touchstone, that helps to highlight our current state of mind, our prerogatives, and what we should try to avoid in the future.

On October 31, 2007, the Spanish parliament passed without the votes of the conservatives the "ley de memoria histórica" (law of remembrance). By this the actual majority wanted to recognize the rights of the victims of the Civil War and the dictatorship and to make possible the reconstruction of individual and familial histories. Symbols of Francoism had to be removed from state buildings and places, mass graves were opened so that people can get information about the fate of their family members and friends.[107] This politic tries to strengthen democracy and the constitutional state by criticizing authoritarianism and by bringing to the fore the victims it caused. Not an innocuous decision as it questions, at least indirectly, the

---

[104] Sloterdijk, Peter (2008), p. 10, writes about "the emancipation from heroism and tragicism".
[105] Id., p. 23
[106] Kundera, Milan (2001), p. 10: "Der Kampf des Menschen gegen die Macht ist der Kampf des Gedächtnisses gegen das Vergessen."
[107] Schlee, Beatrice (2009), pp. 206 f.

compromise found in 1977 in the form of the Amnesty Law (see p. 262). Part of the ensuing debate was the trial against Judge Baltasar Garzón, who had launched the first investigation into the crimes during the dictatorship of General Franco. Contrary to Berlusconi's use of history for his own sake and at the expense of the widely powerless minorities, the debate in Spain was about the collective identity of a community still deeply divided about the past.

The South African political revolution was made possible by a cooperative work on the burdensome past of the country. The Constitution of 1993 stated in Chapter 16 (National Unity and Reconciliation) the principle that reconciliation is needed if the unity of the nation should be upheld:

> This Constitution provides a historic bridge between the past of a deeply divided society characterized by strife, conflict, untold suffering and injustice, and a future founded on the recognition of human rights, democracy and peaceful co-existence and development opportunities for all South Africans, irrespective of color, race, class, belief or sex.
>
> The pursuit of national unity, the well being of all South African citizens and peace require reconciliation between the people of South Africa and the reconstruction of society.
>
> The adoption of this Constitution lays the secure foundation for the people of South Africa to transcend the divisions and strife of the past, which generated gross violations of human rights, the transgression of humanitarian principles in violent conflicts and a legacy of hatred, fear, guilt and revenge.
>
> These can now be addressed on the basis that there is a need for understanding but not for vengeance, a need for reparation but not for retaliation, a need for ubuntu[108] but not for victimization.

Without a notion of commonality and of mutual dependence, cooperation doesn't take place. Against the background of South African history, a reconciliation was less than probable. Centuries of oppression, of killings, of discrimination, of exclusion had to be overcome. The Truth and Reconciliation Commission (TRC) was constituted by three commissions. The first was responsible for human rights violations between 1960 and 1994; the second had to decide over reparations, rehabilitations, and to make sure that the dignity of the victims would be restored; the third had to check requests for amnesty. Individual crimes and guilt of direct violence, would be worked on. The structural and cultural violence, which were effective and destructive as the direct one, weren't dealt with. Apartheid's systemic

---

[108] "I am what I am because of who we all are."

basis, the social inequality inherent in the capitalistic economy that produced existential exclusion, and the educational, philosophical, and cultural imposition of a collectivist identity – all this wouldn't be taken into consideration. That was the compromise the ANC and the NP had been able to reach and the way the past should be approached. The victims had to pay an incomparably higher price than the perpetrators to make a shared future possible. "Reconciliation was the Trojan Horse used to smuggle an unpleasant aspect of the past (that is, impunity) into the present political order, to transform political compromises into transcendental moral principles. [...] It creates a moral imperative which portrays retributive justice as blood-lust and 'wild justice' and as an affront to democratization and the new constitutional order."[109]

Only gross human rights violations would be heard.[110] "The Truth and Reconciliation Commission [...] was *the* archetypal transitional statutory body created to promote a 'culture of human rights' in South Africa."[111] According to Act 34, 1995, the TRC had "to provide for the investigation and the establishment of as complete a picture as possible of the nature, causes and extent of gross violations of human rights committed during the period from 1 March 1960 to the cut-off date."[112] The focus of the TRC was "the violation of human rights through the killing, abduction, torture or severe ill-treatment of any person."[113] Because the commission didn't have funds to pay compensation, it made recommendations in its final report to the government. About 22'000 victims should receive $ 3'000 per year of a six-year period. The government, however, paid $ 3'900 once and nothing more. "We have been betrayed. The previous government gave the killers golden handshakes and the present government gave them amnesty. [But] the victims have been left empty handed," spoke Duma Khumalo, a former human rights activist.[114]

This extreme discrepancy motivated former victims to file class actions against foreign companies that had supported apartheid and had made profits thanks to the unjust racist system, such as Deutsche Bank, Commerzbank, Barclays Bank, Chase Manhattan, UBS, Credit Suisse, Daimler Chrysler, Ford, General Motors, Fujitsu, IBM, Rheinmetall, Implatts, BP, Exxon Mobil, Holcim, Novartis and many others. According to Ed Fagan,

---

[109] Wilson, Richard A. (2001), p. 97
[110] Alexander, Neville (2001), p. 144
[111] Wilson, Richard A. (2001), p. 13
[112] Act No. 34 of 1995: Promotion of National Unity and Reconciliation Act
[113] Act No. 34 of 1995, ix a)
[114] Wilson, Richard A. (2001), pp. 22 f.

the plaintiffs want "the financial institutions and industry groups that provided the funding and support for the apartheid system [to] be held accountable and liable for the profits earned because of their support of apartheid and for the related damages caused by or attributable to this support."[115] The plaintiffs, furthermore, criticize the companies' direct role in apartheid violence[116] and stress their participation in gross human rights violations.

As mentioned earlier, the consensus that brought apartheid to an end didn't include a fundamental rethinking of the social and economic basis of South Africa. There was no generalized will to address the origins of injustice or to develop a comprehensive form of solidarity and responsibility. Focusing on compromise and individual guilt "[…] a deeper analysis of the apartheid system – also according to all its economic implications – wasn't possible."[117] The TRC's historical report paid much attention to the petty murderers and torturers of the system, thus relieving the economic, political, and cultural elites of their responsibility.[118] Paradoxically, the concept of individual rights becomes an obstacle to rebuild a society on just grounds, because its community-based roots and the wide array of pre-conditions necessary to live these rights aren't developed and secured. Only direct violence is discussed, structural and cultural violence are blinded out. The first and very important step was done. But if there has to be a lasting integrative answer to apartheid, it has also to be found in a fundamental change in the economic disparities, and the enormous inequality in education and housing, not only in the realm of politics. "[…] unless a radical redistribution of material resources is realized within the lifetime of the present generation, all the glib rhetoric of social transformation, national democratic revolution, and African renaissance will come to mock their authors and exponents."[119]

cc) Change

Change can be a demonstration of freedom, of the possibility to act differently than before, to chose new targets, to build new "realities." Or, change happens, regardless of what we do in favor or against it. We have to adapt

---

[115] New Statesman of August 12, 2002 (http://www.newstatesman.com/200208120012), retrieved on July 27, 2011
[116] The New York Sun of November 12, 2007 (http://www.nysun.com/foreign/apartheid-suit-puts-corporations-on-notice/66266/), retrieved on July 27, 2011
[117] Alexander, Neville (2001), p. 151
[118] Id., pp. 157 f.
[119] Id., p. 166

to processes we can't influence. In the first case, individuals are responsible for keeping up with what is and for inducing new possibilities. In the second case, the laws of economy or of the civilization process determine our future and it is up to the forces within society to make what is necessary. A third group of people is convinced that the current state of affairs is the best ever and that nothing better is to come, which is why preservation for them is the modus operandi. For this conservative approach, the present is the future and critics are denigrators of what great generations of ancestors have painfully built up. A fourth approach will even renounce human influence on change and perceive the future as created by godly power or the evolution, given and unstoppable. A pronounced need for stability as described (see p. 92 ff.) will make people go for this fatalistic acceptance of whatever comes. I will title these different approaches

- progressive-interactive,
- progressive-systemic,
- conservative, and
- fatalistic.

These represent four different sets and understandings of basic values as well as four different time concepts. In my view, change as much as preservation, should be possible; i.e., stable change (see p. 106 f.). Revolutions show that change needs to be possible to react cooperatively to claims of community members who are not satisfied with the current state. Stubborn resistance to claims of people who try to improve their situation, to overcome structural and cultural violence, most likely will lead to violence. And justice and solidarity are only possible if people are able to find compromises to their problems, what means to change. On the other hand, being forced to change relentlessly without having a say, excludes freedom and responsibility and puts a lot of psychological, social and economic stress on people. Change has integrative effects if it is done cooperatively. That means that everybody is welcomed to the debate and is able to profit from the chosen alterations. So-called "losers of modernization" or the "losers of globalization" highlight the failure of a society to develop a common project for the future.

Besides the quantity and importance of change, there is also the question about the "reality" elements that need to be changed. Not every modification has the same impact on the interactors. Consumer societies made change their dogma: Everything new is great, everything that lasts suffers the opprobrium of the old. Hip, young, and always looking for the hottest deal – these are the keys to a fulfilled life, whereas tradition, loyalty, or fairness are outmoded. This shallow prima facie change doesn't have an important impact on individuals and the social fabric. It is a form of change supposed to divert the attention from politics and from injustice, from a critical engagement in favor of a better world. However, an a-political consumption monade is created, losing the capacity to take its fate into its own hands. Serious changes, changes that affect political and civil rights as are currently being discussed in Tunisia or Egypt, are a serious matter. Even more challenging is the attempt to establish comprehensive justice. Equal repartition of wealth needs those who have to renounce and to share with the have-nots. They have to give up a part of their power in order to gain stability, reliability, and solidarity and to get the chance to live up to their responsibility.

Change may provoke a feeling of insecurity, but it seems to be inevitable if we accept the right of others to be and become different. That's why we have to develop forms of *inclusive change, based on mutual respect and cooperative conflict resolution*. Stable change can take different forms. The authoritarian one as seen in China or Singapore can be as or more effective than a democratic model, if this form of government is widely consented to. The consensus can be uphold as long as the promises of a better future are kept. The combination of fast development and satisfying returns for the individual makes this model attractive and the price of a lack of freedom acceptable. Democrats, on the other hand, sometimes doubt the efficiency of their government. Time-consuming procedures may bring the debate to a halt, which can be frustrating. However, the advantage of democratically organized change is that more alternatives are produced and a higher level of criticism is established, which helps to avoid mistakes and increase freedom.

dd) Responsible for the future, solidary with the next generations

Fudai, the Japanese coastal town, survived without damage the tsunami of March 11, 2011. Thanks to their Mayor who had built against all odds a 16 meter-high protection wall, which broke the enormous impact of the 20m waves. Fifty years before, many inhabitants weren't read to pay for a construction that nobody would ever need. And the landowners who were forced to sell their land were deeply dissatisfied. Mayor Kotaku Wamura, though, was convinced of the danger to the town, because of many historical indications about past tsunami experiences. Two massive earthquakes in 1896 and in 1933 had triggered tsunamis that killed 439 peoples. But most of the inhabitants had forgotten these events. Remembering disastrous tsunamis in medieval times, many path markers and inscriptions on monuments urged the following generations not to build too near to the coast and to settle on elevations.[120] This *eternalized solidarity turned to stone* wasn't read and heard, except by the Mayor, who started the construction in 1967, which saved the lives of 3'000 people in 2011.

Being interested in the fate of future generations and listening to former ones is cooperation over time that enlarges our field of experiences. Especially for a society that is preoccupied with itself and focuses on the present, long-lasting perspectives into the past as much as into the future can enhance its construction power and give a sense to the individual's and the collective's life. Ecological conflicts are difficult to construct in a consumer society because the time concept of consumption is the unrestricted present. The biosphere, on the other hand, is characterized by limits and a long-term orientation.[121] Our present actions have long-term effects, that may not concern us. But taking into consideration the ones suffering or profiting from our constructions gives us the opportunity to last beyond our limited existence, gives a certain sustainability to what we are doing. In this way, the continual running after "change" can be replaced by an enduring establishment of relationships, within which the present of future generations plays a role.

---

[120] "Riesenmauer rettete japanisches Dorf vor Tsunami," in: Der Spiegel of May 13, 2011 (http://www.spiegel.de/wissenschaft/technik/0,1518,762341,00.html), retrieved on July 27, 2011

[121] Bourg, Dominique/Whiteside, Kerry (2010), p. 10

9. Elementary consensus

a) Approval of the core elements

Acting is proposing "realities" to others, who must consent to make the proposal become effective. A community consists of thousands of proposals from many different individuals concerning a wide array of topics. To become a community, the variety of actions has to be related to each other, they have to be orientated toward shared goals and based on common ground. Only if people decide to be part of a sensible story will their collective identity come into being.

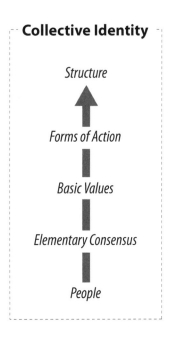

To consent to a collective identity doesn't mean to approve the myriad of actions that are taking place day in and day out. Individuals have to endorse a big enough part of the actions, to align with the majority or at least the most important forms of behavior. As long as we think of human beings as unique and creatively different, there will always be conflicts, dissent, dissimilarities. That, however, isn't a problem if the discord doesn't affect elements most of the people think are central and have for now to be supported. Total conformity, homogeneity, thus, isn't needed. People have to approve the values that characterize the relationships. The arrangement of rights and duties they incorporate should be reproduced in everyday interactions, regardless of their number, type, or the power arrangement they stand for. The values characterizing the community are *general* expectations of other's actions. There is, thus, quite a leeway for personal interpretations, for concretizations.

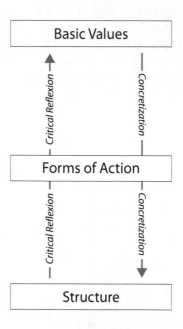

The same accounts for the forms of action the community opts for. They are, on the one hand, concretizations of the basic values, and, so, are more restrictive. Uniqueness, though isn't excluded because they do not determine in detail and in every single case how to act. The structure that ensues is again one of different possibilities, more concrete, widely conditioning the possibilities the individuals have and the role they are expected to play. It is important to point out, that the process of concretization doesn't take place linearly at all. It is much more a back and forth of proposals and approval/application on the different levels of concretization. Sometimes the meaning of the involved elements is changed, new expectations are added that have to be debated. Other times reproduction runs smoothly and an almost boring routine takes place. To make sure that the community can be upheld, it is important to foresee a change mechanism. It provides an opportunity to adapt to new interests of the members without risking disintegration. And it helps people to accept compromises, as they know, that current affairs don't have to last for ever and can be changed if necessary.

The decision-making process is one of the elements to be consented to; it is of great importance, even though it's not decisive for integration. The organization of the decision-making process decides about the repartition and the use of physical power, the possibility to control it, and the way people are involved in making mandatory resolutions relevant for the community. State actors are effective under the following circumstances:

- In a *competitive setup* they will effectively defend the interests of the ruling minority (dictators, oligarchs, priests and so on), as long as the different sets of violence can be used without meeting too severe an opposition;
- in a *mainly cooperative setup* the majority commits state actors to control a minority of people; and
- in a *comprehensively cooperative setup* state actors focus on organizational duties and moderate debates over conflicts, without having the power to subdue people who defend different ideas.

As long as there is no generalized elementary consensus, the structural as well as the cultural violence will increase. Social injustice will be upheld by the use of direct violence which, in turn, will motivate counter-violence or even revolution. Avoiding this sort of destructive development means to build up a decision-making process based on justice and solidarity. *Choosing cooperation as the main interaction form avoids or at least minimizes any form of violence and has the most comprehensive impact on integration.*

On December 20, 2001, the United Nations Security Council decided by Resolution 1386 to engage in war with Afghanistan. The first operations of the International Security Assistance Force (ISAF) were targeted at stabilizing the region of Kabul, allowing the establishment of the Afghan Transitional Administration. The Talibans were ousted quite fast. But they weren't weakened enough, which is why they regrouped in Pakistan. Washington opted for a troop-lite approach[1] and was, from 2003 on mainly involved in Iraq. In 2004, a new constitution was adopted and a president was democratically elected. Parliamentary elections followed in 2005. In 2006, the Taliban launched a large-scale insurgency in the south of the country. Like all the great powers before in the history of the Afghanistan – Alexander the Great, the British, the Russians, or the Soviet Union – the USA and its allies had to recognize that Afghanistan can't be ruled from the top, against its people. Without an elementary consensus reached with an important majority of the people, stability won't be achievable. This consensus is to

---

[1] Mills, Greg/Richards, David (2010)

be developed by cooperation, by the integration on equal grounds of the traditional social structures that play a major role in the construction of the collective identity. That the ISAF is often perceived as a foreign occupation power leads to active or hidden opposition and withdraws the necessary support. Contrary to the top-down strategy of the ISAF, the Taliban in the 1990s had developed a bottom-up policy, trying to win over the tribal leaders, militia commanders, and soldiers. "It was a strategy accomplished on a very personal level: Taliban leaders who spoke the local dialect traveled to the Pashtun villages and district centers. [...] while they focused on securing urban areas, they successfully cut deals with local commanders [...] in rural areas."[2] Where this cooperation couldn't be established, violence "convinced" the reluctant ones. Lacking this cooperative support, the ISAF has problems implementing their military and political goals. "[...] the local population is the most important group; it is for their hearts and minds that the war is being fought in the first place. The support of the population is the sine qua non of victory in counter insurgency warfare."[3] You can't bomb people to democracy. They have to be attracted by a serious offer that recognizes and respects their wishes. Against the background of all the integrative problems that prevail in Afghanistan, it is not a simple task. For example, there is a high degree of insecurity that gives the Taliban a justification for taking control back: They made the area safer. They also used the absence of state power to threaten people and to impose their will. At the same time, people experienced the official Afghan government as widely inexistent and when existing, as corrupt and unreliable. "In some areas there is now a parallel Taliban state, and locals are increasingly turning to Taliban-run courts, which are seen as more effective and fair than the corrupt official system,"[4] even though they apply the not much appreciated sharia. Developing respectful relationships would mean to enhance the representation of the traditional tribal structures, and to hand over administrative power on the district and local level. "To create a lasting peace that includes the country's main ethnic and sectarian groups – as well as elements of the insurgency – Afghanistan will require a more inclusive, flexible, and decentralized political arrangement."[5] Intended centralization has to be given up and a serious devolution has to take place. There possibly will be some local solutions that do not please the convictions of one or the other. But to cooperate and compromise means also to respect differences that may hurt to a certain degree. Ongoing cooperation will then

---

[2] Jones, Seth G. (2010), pp. 59 f.
[3] Id., p. 153
[4] Rubin, Barnett R. (2007)
[5] Biddle, Stephen/Christia, Fotini/Thier, Alexander J. (2010)

likely lead to an adaptation, a mutual learning and, consequently, a higher integration. "Near-ideal internal political and developmental outcomes in Afghanistan"[6] shouldn't be the only possible goal, as this limits alternatives and forces on others the exclusive living-mode.

Instead of a total war, a political solution is needed, because *a lasting elementary consensus can't be forced onto people*. Both conflict parties seem to view the current situation as a stalemate that can't be solved by military means.[7] To make integration work, a political ending of the conflict has to be found as well as a convincing economic strategy.[8] That not only means a fundamental change of mind for the absolutist Taliban, but also for the American approach, which following Bush's neocons logic, wasn't interested in nation-building processes.[9] "[…] the first thought of the Bush administration after the Afghan war ended was how to declare victory, get out, and move on to Iraq. The administration wanted no responsibility for reconstructing the now-occupied nation of Afghanistan and was unwilling to learn about the people or the country."[10] Since Obama, though, foreign policy is no longer a one-sided event, but intended as a cooperation between equally treated nations. Negotiations over the end of war and the participation of the different forces is only possible, if a minimal form of trust can be built up. Without confidence, that the other side is seriously interested in integrative compromising, sufficient steps won't be possible. Economic integration will be difficult because of the immense inequality (the third-most unequal society in the world after Angola and Equatorial Guinea[11]), the massive joblessness, and the poverty, which is why many young people lack prospects and, therefore, are willing to fight. The twenty years of continuous war has also comprehensively destroyed the country.[12] That the Pakistani Inter-Services Intelligence has supported the Taliban since the early 1990s doesn't help either. The serious cooperation of Pakistan, ending its role as a safe heaven for the Taliban, would make a significant contribution. If there is no chance to find an accord over the basic values, cooperation isn't possible. Under these circumstances, the partitioning of the area and the establishment of two communities that are able to agree on the central elements would probably be the most integrative solution.[13]

---

[6] Chipman, John (2010)
[7] Brahimi, Lakhdar/Pickering, Thomas R. (2011), pp. 17 f.
[8] *Id.*, pp. 22 f., 36 ff.
[9] Rashid, Ahmed (2009), pp. 172 f.
[10] *Id.*, p. XLIX
[11] Mills, Greg/Richards, David (2010)
[12] Rashid, Ahmed (2009), p. 171
[13] Favoring partition, see: Blackwill, Robert D. (2010)

b) Integration is more than democracy or politics

Is democracy the end of history as described by Fukuyama? Is democracy a natural political state, an organization principle toward which every human community develops inevitably? Is there "a fundamental process at work that dictates a common evolutionary pattern for all human societies – in short, something like a Universal History of mankind in the direction of liberal democracy?"[14] According to Fukuyama, "the success of democracy in a wide variety of places and among many different peoples would suggest that the principles of liberty and equality on which they are based are not accidents or the results of ethnocentric prejudice, but are, in fact, discoveries about the nature of man as man."[15] As the revolutions in South Africa, Poland, the Czech Republic, or in the former GDR all led to democracy, one can see the thesis confirmed, that liberal democracy is the culmination of political ideas. However, the concept of democracy, on the one hand, found many different concretizations. On the other hand, there are ecological, economic, and social inequality challenges that need to be solved. And democracy by itself doesn't answer to this. *Political participation alone doesn't integrate people sufficiently.* There are many economic and social conditions to be fulfilled to ensure that an *equal* debate can take place. Does everybody have the resources to engage politically and what are their chances to be heard? And decisive, in my view, is the ability of the debaters to establish and defend a notion of the common good. Democracy is too often hijacked by economic interests that aren't interested in the common good at all. "Jefferson [...] feared commercial avarice; he argued that merchants loved nobody and that commerce bred manipulation and a cold heart."[16] And John Adams "feared the corrupting influence of commerce."[17]

Democracy is by no means exclusively benevolent. It is an organization principle that is able to be used for any purpose. Basically it means that the people rule. But who are "the people"? Rarely has it stood for all the people living in the community. What about the effect on the minorities that every majority decision produces? And who are these minorities? Are they delimitated or excluded (see p. 89 ff.)? Nationalism and the construction of the demos as "ethnos" are examples of *democratic abuse of power*. Horrific killings, torture, persecution, massive imprisonment, forced emigration and other violations of life, freedom, and justice were decided by democ-

---

[14] Fukuyama, Francis (1992), p. 48
[15] *Id.*, p. 51
[16] Hill, John E. (2007), p. 36
[17] *Id.*, p. 31

racies. "Murderous cleansing is [...] the dark side of democracy."[18] "Ethnic hostility rises where ethnicity trumps class as the main form of social stratification, in the process capturing and channeling classlike sentiments toward ethnonationalism. Cleansing was rare in the past because most big historic societies were class-divided."[19] To exclude or even eliminate others constructed as ethnicities can take place by direct, structural, or cultural violence. The Natives' fate in North America is an example of ethnic cleansing within or by a democracy.[20] Kosovo-Albanians were cleansed by Milosevic's majority. In Croatia the Krajina was cleansed of the Serbs in 1995. Today in Kosovo, only a few Serbs have stayed. After 1991, the Russian democracy intervened massively militarily against independence claims of Chechnya. And in Northern Ireland, the British democracy over centuries oppressed the Catholics.

To make integration universally equal and to respect the people's differences, democracy has to limit itself. As a counterpower to democracy, to the rule of the people, there is the constitutional state and the rule of law needed. They protect human rights and control democratically elected state power. However, the constitutional state itself depends on the people; it is built up and kept alive by the people it is supposed to rein in. To protect freedom is, therefore, a paradoxical task: It is "we the people" which rules and sets itself free from authoritarian governments. At the same time it is "we the people" which controls itself to make sure that freedom can be kept up and, foremost, that freedom is guaranteed equally. This paradox seems to me unavoidable, because there is nobody else to do the job. If there was, we would lose the freedom we looked for. The rulers, therefore, have to be willing not to use the power they basically have. Without this limitation, democracy may become an authoritarian or even totalitarian regime. Besides power-control, comprehensive integration needs an elaborated solidarity structure. Without solidarity, individual existences will often be miserable, materially speaking. Furthermore, the potential of interacting people won't be realized. That's why social security in a wide sense is needed: Financial as well as moral support, a concept of the community as a shared chance and task, and the willingness to take over responsibility for the acts committed by individuals, collectives, or companies. Gross injustice or inequality will burden the relationships and lead to disintegrative conflicts. Even more, when political participation is made possible. Against this background injustice appears even more as a lack of recognition and respect, affecting the

---

[18] Mann, Michael (2005), p. 2
[19] *Id.*, p. 5
[20] See Mann, Michael (2005), pp. 83 ff.

willingness to cooperate and to trust. Democracy, therefore, is not good enough. This governmental structure has to be embedded in a net of interdependent and mutually supportive relationships to become the home of people.

c) Greatness thanks to cooperation

Gordon Wood reproduces the sacrosanct origins of the national American narrative, pointing out that "we can never again replicate the extraordinary generation of the founders."[21] The great and noble act that these courageous men accomplished is, according to Woods, unimaginable today, because democracy levelled out the capacities of people: "One of the prices we had to pay for democracy was a decline in the intellectual quality of American political life and an eventual separation between ideas and power."[22] Wood sees the strength of the founding fathers lying in their elitist understanding of themselves, as "they were not democrats [...]. They were never embarrassed by talk of elitism, and they never hid their sense of superiority to ordinary folk. But neither were they contemptuous of common people; in fact they always believed that the people in general were the source of their authority. [...] they were the beneficiaries of a semiaristocratic political system, and their extraordinary leadership was due in large measure to processes that we today would consider undemocratic and detestable. [...] a self-created aristocracy largely based on merit and talent."[23] And, finally, it is thanks to this elitism that the revolutionary characters defended a concept of "absolute values and timeless truth."[24] Relativizing the depicted greatness of the founders, Wood emphasizes that "the revolutionary leaders were certainly not demigods or superhuman individuals; they were very much the product of specific circumstances and a specific moment in time."[25]

Different points in Wood's argumentation seem problematic to me. First, referring to the advantages of elitism, on the one hand, and pointing out, on the other hand, that this elite was convinced being dependent on the people's support, appears contradictory. If the people had to be ready to follow the propositions of the founders, it is not an elitocracy we are talking about, but a democracy. Without women and men ready to sacrifice their

---

[21] Wood, Gordon S. (2006), p. 28
[22] *Id.*, p. 10
[23] *Id.*, p. 11
[24] *Id.*, p. 8
[25] *Id.*, p. 11

lives, the revolution wouldn't have happened. The founders had to do the conventional work of politicians who have to convince others to change the world. The values written down in an adroit and tactically intelligent way, were ideas widely accepted by many people when the revolution started. A large number of them had left Europe to live differently. And during the following 150 years, they had enjoyed the liberty a British king, who was largely disinterested in America, had made possible. It is, therefore, not a hierarchical-authoritarian concept of elitist power, but the interactive cooperation that shaped the New World, because it "turned out that [the founders] did not control their society and culture as much as they thought they did."[26] What in my opinion makes the fundamental difference between today and the time of the founding fathers is *another set of basic values*. In the revolutionary times community was of great importance (solidarity) and responsibility was an indispensable part of liberty. Our neoliberal "reality" of the last thirty years, on the contrary, has been characterized by an absolutist, individualistic, greed-based understanding of freedom. When we compare the notion of "disinterest" of today with the one at the time of the revolution, the difference between these "realities" becomes evident. "Disinterest" today means being focused solely on one's own advantages, only looking out for the individualized self. Pure egoism negates politics as passion and goal. There is no political project, no engagement for a form of community, but only the short-term and short-range goal to increase one's own material wealth. For the founders, however, life was much more than just shopping. "Disinterestedness was the most common term the founders used as a synonym for the classical conception of virtue or self-sacrifice; it better conveyed the threats from interests that virtue seemed increasingly to face in the rapidly commercializing eighteenth century."[27] Where the founders were convinced that politics and, hence, community and solidarity had to prevail over economy and greed, the neoliberal worldview turned these principles upside down and made the individual monad walking through a social desert to be the only touchstone.

Wood's negative characterization of the post-revolutionary time can be perceived differently using the construction phases described at the beginning of this book (p. 64 ff.). During new construction or deconstruction heroes are much more likely to come to the fore than during times of reproduction, when a certain routine develops that's based on an established elementary consensus. In reproduction, extremes are avoided, stability is

---

[26] *Id.*, p. 26
[27] *Id.*, p. 16

cherished, and a more risk-averse behavior takes place. Wood criticizes the decline of the intellectual quality, a judgment I share because the selfish greed-ideology that has become the dominant mentality and alternatives are disqualified as unrealistic, naive, and grounded in social-Romantism. But it's not intellectuality that made the founders great, it is their willingness to risk their wealth, their reputation, their social status, or even their life for an idea of humanity, for a community to come that was based on much more than materialistic greed. Washington "never seemed to have very much to say. He was almost certainly not what we today would call an intellectual. [He] was a man of few words and no great thoughts. [...] he was a man of affairs."[28] "He was trying to live up to the age's image of a classical disinterested patriot who devotes his life to his country. [...] Many of his actions after 1783 can be understood only in terms of this deep concern for his reputation as a virtuous leader."[29] That's why Aaron Burr would be the ideal of today, though not a role model back then because he "spent so much time and energy so blatantly scheming for his own personal and political advantage. And no one of the other great revolutionary statesmen was so immune to the ideology and the values of the Revolution as Burr was."[30]

It's on the basis of republican values that this amazing change was made possible. Central to a republican notion is the common good, the res publica, combined with equality and liberty. That is more than just the coincidental "common wealth" that results luckily out of the actions of selfish atomistic individuals[31] acting on the market place. To achieve this common good, this social cohesion,[32] people have to a certain degree to sacrifice their individual interests.[33] "A strong moral-ethical-religious base with a focus

---

[28] *Id.*, pp. 34 f.

[29] *Id.*, pp. 42 f.

[30] *Id.*, p. 234

[31] Taylor, Charles (1995), p. 188

[32] Wood, Gordon S. (2005), p. 90

[33] Wood, Gordon S. (1993), p. 53: "The sacrifice of individual interests to the greater good of the whole formed the essence of republicanism and comprehended for Americans the idealistic goal of their Revolution." And on p. 55: "To make the people's welfare - the public good – the exclusive end of government. [...] No phrase except 'liberty' was invoked more often by the Revolutionaries than 'the public good'." P. 69: "For most Americans in 1776 vicious behavior by an individual could have only disastrous results for the community. A man racked by the selfish passions of greed, envy, and hate lost his conception of order; 'his sense of a connection with the general system – his benevolence – his desire and freedom of doing good, ceased.'"

on economic justice for all was central to the thought of Adam Smith, John Adams, and many of the founders of the new American republic [...]. [...] the United States was a society based on the interplay of individual drive, energy, creativity, *and* mutual support within values-based communities. [...] they assumed that liberty would be within a community context."[34]

This republican readiness to fight for the common good didn't end after the revolution and is to be found up to today. Many heroes are still willing to engage on behalf of others for justice, freedom, and solidarity. The labor movement, the suffragettes and feminism, the Civil Rights Movement, or the generation of '68. Nelson Mandela, Václav Havel, or Lech Wałęsa, and quite some others risked their life, their freedom, their families, their wealth for solidarity, for the common good. They decided like the Founding Fathers to fight injustice and authoritarian or totalitarian governments. They, like the Founding Fathers, needed the support of many people to realize their hopes. And, like the Founding Fathers, they used ideas others had developed before and adapted these to their specific context and later became a symbolic link for the construction of the collective identity. Compared to the American Revolution, these fundamental changes occurred without any war – insofar an enormous progress.

People are fascinated by *the stunning performances that are possible when it comes to passionate cooperation*. It is this commonality that "the nation's vital documents" stand for. It is, therefore, not a problem of the structure of government, but of basic values that have to change if we want to realize the limitless potential that cooperating individuals bring to the fore.

d) Cooperation instead of confrontation

Business leaders or market apologists who are eager to make as much money as fast as possible like to focus on the state as the centre of power. For workers or consumers who every day experience their modest possibilities to influence their situation in the work- or in the so-called marketplace the companies seem most powerful. They appear to have as much or even more influence on their lives as the state. Many more are confronted in their daily routine with economic than with state power. The decisions of their employers can have an immediate existential impact on their life, like those of the state. And in a democracy the decisions of the state actors more often take the form of support than of restriction. Contrary to most of the economic leaders, state actors can be replaced with the vote and can be

---

[34] Hill, John E. (2007), pp. 9 f.

controlled by the representatives we elect. The neoliberal focus on the state intends to hide the power the non-state actors have and are allowed to apply. This juxtaposition of state and society/individuals and the individualistic concept of freedom, however, hinder justice and solidarity, because they hinder fundamental changes to the power arrangement. The state is neither the source of all evil, the enemy, nor is it the solution to everything, the redemption. It is a common task, the fruit of the quality of the relationship that characterizes the community at its basis. That's why relationships have to become the focus of attention, *relationships and their integrative quality*. Besides the central power, there are many other areas where integration takes place, and an uncountable number of actors are involved in the integration process, such as neighborly help, civil society's engagement, familial support, nonprofit charities and foundations, or work in unions or associations, to name just a few.

If we take equal construction power seriously, and if we intend to abolish violence in all its appearances, we have to enlarge the integration focus. Force should not be the first tool to resort to, it is the ultima ratio for integration, solely to be used in exceptional cases. To rely mainly on military and police resources demonstrates the considerable weakness or even absence of an elementary consensus. *All relationships have to be democratized.* Power, wherever it is found, has to suffice the criteria of justice and responsibility. Are the people currently in power doing an integrative job? Do they recognize and respect the interests of the ones who follow their instructions or orders? This also means *democratization of economic relationships* by, for example, pushing cooperatives or the power of stakeholders instead of the shareholders alone.

Neoliberalism led people to renounce the incredible potential that justice and solidarity offer. The most salient effect that neoliberalism has had on people is to make them believe, that there is no alternative to the atomistic greed. An intellectual revolution is needed that brings back the importance of the common good. Furthermore, social injustice has to be countered by serious redistribution in the form of, for example, a minimum guaranteed income. A common project has to be developed, one that is courageous, creative, willing to plan and engage for the long term. There is, though, a risk that those who are well-off, who most often rule societies, aren't interested in a serious engagement for the common good. What Galbraith described as "culture of contentment," is the ruling of satisfied people, doing everything to preserve or increase what they have; they are not interested in the community as a whole,[35] which could hinder every serious attempt for change.

Two conflicts will, in my view pose serious integration problems in the future:

- Social and economic inequality and
- Cultural racism.

Integration is only complete if all aspects of life are taken into account. Political rights are one part of the set of recognition practices important for integration. However, "elections are generally not an endpoint, but only one of many necessary steps to build local legitimacy."[36] Letting people talk and vote is not too high a risk for the rulers, as long as they control the economy and have an important, even decisive impact on the construction of public opinion. But to redistribute wealth effectively seems to be of another order. In too many countries it is social and economic inequality combined with the disinterest of a client state that legitimizes fundamentalist movements, which, in turn, perform supportive functions: Building schools, organizing affordable food and health care, they justify their existence for people who in their majority otherwise wouldn't be attracted by such absolutist community concepts. The small class of profiteers of the client states prepares the bedrock of disintegrative and potentially violent extremists who are not ready to compromise. The second integration challenge is, in my view, collectivist exclusionary politics. "Traditional" biological racism is in most countries either forbidden or morally reprimanded. Nevertheless, the ones interested in effective exclusion refer now to cultural, ethnical, or religious

---

[35] Galbraith, John Kenneth (1992), p. 6: "[…] the fortunate and the favored […] do not contemplate and respond to their own longer-run well-being. Rather, they respond, and powerfully, to immediate comfort and contentment." "[…] the controlling contentment and resulting belief is not that of many, not just of the few. It operates under the compelling cover of democracy, albeit a democracy not of all citizens but of those who, in defense of their social and economic advantage, actually go to the polls. The result is government that is accommodated not to reality or common need but to the beliefs of the contended, who are now the majority of those who vote" (p. 10). "In past times, the economically and socially fortunate were […] a small minority – characteristically a dominant and ruling handful. They are now a majority, though, as has already been observed, a majority not of all citizens but of those who actually vote" (p. 15). "[…] self-regard is […] the dominant, indeed the controlling, mood of the contended majority" (p. 17).

[36] Krasner, Stephen D./Pascual, Carlos (2005), p. 160

attributes to justify their views of inequality. Qualified as unchangeable criteria, they have to be taken into account. The new bogeymen "Islam" or "Muslims" is the most recent example.

Social change toward a just society is possible as soon as the involved actors are willing to cooperate. Competing with each other, people will only be ready to take minimal risks. Furthermore, too much energy and time will be invested in beating the others instead of developing valuable alternatives. Against a cooperative background, though, *integrative revolutions* can take place. Most people are looking for a decent, stable life with an enriching and positively challenging exchange with each other. There is no need for a war of all against all, which profits only a few in society. Developing trustful cooperation is the most heroic and humane task human beings can undertake. Unrealistic and naive for neoliberals, who never thought in alternatives. Liberating and elevating to the creatively new for the ones courageous enough to leave behind what limited our possibilities during the last generation. It is time, for something fundamentally different. Why not returning to a modus vivendi that has been successful for the major part of human history: Cooperation.

Acknowledgments

Like all human activities, this book came into existence thanks to the contribution of innumerable people. Those who are specifically germane to this book are listed in the references. Many of their writings were enriching and challenging and made new ways of thinking for me possible. Others made me angry, motivating me to develop arguments against their worldview and their concept of humankind.

I am indebted to my editor, Otto Kammerlander of Springer Publishers, for his readiness to support this unusual project and his very positive attitude. I am also very grateful for the technical and layout services that Eva-Maria Oberhauser provided.

Further, my sincere thanks go to Charlotte Mills Seligman for her very professional, efficient, and needed text editing!

The readers of this book are to be thanked for their interest and their willingness to share, at least for a time, my thoughts.

References

Abbot, William W. (1975) The colonial Origins of the United States – 1607-1763. John Wiley & Sons, New York – London

Abosch, Heinz (1993) Das Ende der grossen Visionen. Junius, Hamburg

Ackelsberg, Martha A./Addelson, Kathryn P. (1990) Anarchistische Alternativen zur Konkurrenz, in: Miner, Valerie/Longino, Helen E. (ed) Konkurrenz – Ein Tabu unter Frauen, pp. 156-167. Frauenoffensive Verlag, München

Ackerman, Bruce (1993) We the People – Foundations. Harvard University Press, Cambridge

Ackerman, Bruce (1998) We the People – Transformations. Harvard University Press, Cambridge

Adam, Heribert (1994) Fremdenfeindlichkeit, Einwanderungspolitik und Multikulturalismus in Kanada und Deutschland, in: Leviathan 1/1994, pp. 60-77

Albert, Hans (1978) Traktat über rationale Praxis. Mohr Verlag, Tübingen

Alexander, Neville (2001) Südafrika. C.H. Beck Verlag, München

Alexander, Peter (1999) Coal, Control and Class Experience in South Africa's Rand Revolt of 1922, in: Comparative Studies of South Asia, Africa and the Middle East, 1/1999, pp. 31-45

Alexy, Robert (1995) Recht, Vernunft, Diskurs. Suhrkamp Verlag, Frankfurt am Main

Altschull, Elizabeth (1995) Le voile contre l'école. Éditions du Seuil, Paris

Aly, Götz (1995) Endlösung. Fischer Verlag, Frankfurt am Main

Amann, Anton (1991) Soziologie. Böhlau, Wien – Köln – Weimar

Amar, Akhil Reed (1995) Popular Sovereignty and Constitutional Amendment, in: Levinson, Sanford (ed) Responding to Imperfection, pp. 89-115. Princeton University Press, New Jersey

Amar, Akhil Reed (2000) Amendment Process, in: Levy, Leonard W./Karst, Kenneth L.: Encyclopedia of the American Constitution, Volume 1, 2. ed, p. 77. Macmillan Publishers, New York

Amendt, Gerhard/Schwarz, Michael (1990) Das Leben unerwünschter Kinder. Universität Bremen, Bremen

American Labor Studies Center (2010) (http://labor-studies.org/by-education-level/elementary/labor-quotes/), retrieved on May 15, 2011

Andes, Roy H. (2000) Lazarus v. Phelps and the Closing of the open Range, in: Bakken, Gordon Morris (ed) Law in den western United States, pp. 338-342. University of Oklahoma Press, Norman

Anhut, Reimund/Heitmeyer, Wilhelm (2000) Desintegration, Konflikt und Ethnisierung, in: Heitmeyer, Wilhelm/Anhut, Reimund: Bedrohte Stadtgesellschaft, pp. 17-75. Juventa Verlag, Weinheim – München

Arendt, Hannah (1987) Vita activa. Piper Verlag, München

Arendt, Hannah (1993) Was ist Politik? Piper Verlag, München

Armey, Dick (2010) Give us Liberty. Harper Collins Publishers, New York

Armitage, David (2007) The Declaration of Independence. Harvard University Press, Cambridge

Arnold, Peri E. (2009) Remaking the Presidency. University Press of Kansas, Lawrence

Arranz, Luis/Cabrera, Mercedes/Del Rey, Fernando (2000) The assault on liberalism, 1914-1923, in: Alvarez Junco, José/Shubert, Adrian (ed) Spanish History since 1808, pp. 191-206. Hodder Education, London

Arrow, Kenneth J. (1974) The Limits of Organization. Norton & Company, New York

Ashford Hodges, Gabrielle (2000) Franco. Weidenfeld & Nicolson, London

Ashworth, John (2010) Capitalism and the Civil War, in: Grant, Susan-Mary/Holden Reid, Brian: The American Civil War, pp. 169-182. Pearson Education, Harlow

Aust, Anthony (2010) Handbook of International Law. Cambridge University Press, Cambdrige

Avella, Steven M. (2003) Sacramento. Arcadia Publishing, Dover

Babka von Gostomski, Christian (2003) Gewalt als Reaktion auf Anerkennungsdefizite?, in: Kölner Zeitschrift für Soziologie und Sozialpsychologie 2/2003, pp. 253-277

Baby, Sophie (2003) Violence et transition en Espagne, in: Dulphy, Anne & Léonard, Yves (ed) De la dictature à la démocratie – voies ibériques, pp. 85-103. P.I.E.-Peter Lang, Bruxelles

Badger, Anthony J. (2008) FDR: The first hundred Days. Hill and Wang, New York

Badinter, Elisabeth (1992) Die Mutterliebe. Piper Verlag, München

Baecker, Dirk (2006) Wirtschaftssoziologie. Transcript Verlag, Bielefeld

Bagehot, Walter (1966 [1867, 1915]) The English Constitution. Cornell University Press, Itaca

Bandmann, Günter (1998) Mittelalterliche Architektur als Bedeutungsträger. Gebr. Mann Studio Reihe, Berlin

Barber, Benjamin R. (2010) America's Knowledge Deficit, on: The Nation of November 10, 2010

Barendt, Eric (1998) An Introduction to Constitutional Law. Oxford University Press, Oxford

Barth, Boris (2006) Genozid. Verlag C. H. Beck, München

Bauby, Jean-Dominique (1998) The Diving Bell and the Butterfly – A Memoir of Life in Death. Vintage, New York

Bauman, Zygmunt (1989) Modernity and the Holocaust. Polity Press, New York

Bauman, Zygmunt (1994) Dialektik der Ordnung. Europaeische Verlagsanstalt, Hamburg

Bauman, Zygmunt (1995) Ansichten der Postmoderne. Argument Verlag, Hamburg

Baykan, Aisegul (1999) Women Uprooted, in: Apitz, Ursula (ed): Migration und Traditionsbildung, pp. 157-164. Westdeutscher Verlag, Opladen – Wiesbaden

Bean, Walton E. (1978) California. McGraw-Hill, New York

Beaussant, Philippe (2000) Le Roi-Soleil se lève aussi. Editions Gallimard, Paris

Beck-Gernsheim, Elisabeth (2004) Wir und die Anderen. Suhrkamp Verlag, Frankfurt am Main

Beck, Ulrich (1993) Die Erfindung des Politischen. Suhrkamp Verlag, Frankfurt am Main

Beck, Warren A./Williams, David A. (1972) California. Doubleday & Company, New York

Becker, Gary S. (1993) Ökonomische Erklärung menschlichen Verhaltens. Mohr Verlag, Tübingen

Becker, Jurek (1976) Jakob der Lügner. Suhrkamp Verlag, Frankfurt am Main

Beemyn, Brett Genny (2006) The Americas, in: Aldrich, Robert (ed) Gay Life and Culture in a world History, pp. 145-165. Universe Publishing, New York

Beinhocker, Eric D. (2006) The Origin of Wealth. Harvard Business School Press, Boston

Béji, Hélé (2011) Le voile est une dissidence au sein du féminisme, in: Le Monde of February 26, 2011, p. 15

Benasayag, Miguel/Sztulwark, Diego (2000) Du contre-pouvoir. Éditions la découverte, Paris

Benhabib, Seyla (1989) Der verallgemeinerte und der konkrete Andere. Ansätze zu einer feministischen Moraltheorie, in: List, Elisabeth/Studer, Herlinde (ed) Denkverhältnisse. Feminismus und Kritik, pp. 454-487. Suhrkamp Verlag, Frankfurt am Main

Bennett, William John (2007) America – The last best Hope, Volume 2, Nashville

Benton, Lisa M. (1998) The Presidio. Northeastern University Press, Boston

Bercus, Costel (2005) Die Situation der Roma in Rumänien, in: Matter, Max (ed) Die Situation der Roma und Sinti nach der EU-Osterweiterung, pp. 29-45. V&R unipress, Göttingen

Berger, Peter L./Luckmann, Thomas (1980) Die gesellschaftliche Konstruktion der Wirklichkeit. Fischer Taschenbuch Verlag, Frankfurt am Main

Berghahn, Sabine (1998) Der Geist des Absoluten in Karlsruhe und die Chancen der Demokratie in der Abtreibungsfrage II, in: Leviathan 3/98, pp. 400-422

Berglund, Barbara (2007) Making San Francisco American. University Press of Kansas, Lawrence

Bertho, Alain (1999) Contre l'État, la politique. La Dispute, Paris

Betzler, Monika (1998) Objektivität als epistemische Norm feministischer Erkenntnistheorie, in: Deutsche Zeitschrift für Philosophie 5/1998, pp. 783-797

Biddle, Stephen/Christia, Fotini/Thier, Alexander J. (2010) Defiing Success in Afghanistan, on: Foreign Affairs July/August 2010 (http://www.foreignaffairs.com/articles/66450/stephen-biddle-fotini-christia-and-j-alexander-thier/defining-success-in-afghanistan?page=show), retrieved on July 26, 2011

Bidussa, David (1994) Il mito del bravo italiano. il Saggiatore, Milano

Birch, Anthony H. (1998) The British System of Government. Routledge Publishers, London – New York

Bishara, Azmi (1993) Religion und Politik im Nahen und Mittleren Osten, in: Hippler, Jochen/Lueg, Andrea (ed) Feindbild Islam, pp. 92-141. Konkret Verlag, Hamburg

Blackburn, Robin (1998) The Making of New World Slavery. Verso Publishers, London – New York

Blackwill, Robert D. (2010) A de facto partition for Afghanistan, on: Politico of July 7, 2010 (http://www.politico.com/news/stories/0710/39432.html), retrieved on July 26, 2011

Blakely, Edward J./Snyder, Mary Gail (1999) Fortress America. Brookings Institution, Washington

Bloche, Gregg M. (2005) Managing Conflict at the End of Life, in: New England Journal of Medicine of June 9, 2005, pp. 2371-2373

Bluche, François (2000) Louis XV. Librairie Académique Perrin, Paris

Böckenförde, Ernst-Wolfgang (1992) Recht, Staat, Freiheit. Suhrkamp Verlag, Frankfurt am Main

Bogdanor, Vernon (1995) The Monarchy and the Constitution. Clarendon Press, Oxford

Bohley, Bärbel (1992) An den Widerständen in diesem Lande bin ich ICH geworden, in: Glaessner, Gert-Joachim (ed) Eine deutsche Revolution. Peter Lang Verlag, Frankfurt am Main

Bohnet, Iris/Frey, Bruno S. (1994) Kooperation, Kommunikation und Kommunitarismus, in: Kölner Zeitschrift für Soziologie und Sozialpsychologie 3/1994, pp. 453-463

Bok, Derek (2010) The Politics of Happiness. Princeton University Press, Princeton

Bond, Patrick (2000) Elite Transition. Pluto Press, London

Bordewich, Fergus M. (2008) Washington – The Making of the American Capital. Harper Collins Publishers, New York

Bosc, Serge (2008) Sociologie des classes moyennes. Éditions de la Découverte, Paris

Botschaft betreffend das Übereinkommen über die Verhütung und Bestrafung des Völkermordes sowie die entsprechende Revision des Strafrechts vom 31. März 1999 (1999), in: Bundesblatt 1999, pp. 5327-5362, Bern

Bourdieu, Pierre (1989) La Noblesse d'État. Les Éditions de Minuit, Paris

Bourg, Dominique/Whiteside, Kerry (2010) Vers une démocratie écologique. Éditions du Seuil, Paris

Boyd, Julian (1999) The Declaration of Independence. University Press of New England, Hanover – London

Boyd, Nan Alamilla (2003) Wide open Town. University of California Press, Berkeley

Boyer, Paul S./Clark, Clifford et al. (2010) The enduring vision. Wadsworth, Boston

Boyer, Paul/Nissenbaum, Stephen (1974) Salem Possessed. Harvard University Press, Cambridge

Bozzoli, Belinda (2004) Theatres of Struggle and the End of Apartheid. Edinburg University Press, Edinburgh

Brahimi, Lakhdar/Pickering, Thomas R. (2011) Afghanistan – Neogitating Peace, The Report of the Century Foundation, International Task Force on Afghanistan. Century Foundation, New York

Brandt, Lewis Wolfgang (1982) Gedanken zum Angreifen, in: Hilke, Reinhard/Kempf, Wilhelm (ed) Aggression, pp. 164-185. Verlag Hans Huber, Bern – Göttingen – Toronto

Braudel, Fernand (1997) Die Dynamik des Kapitalismus. Klett – Cotta Verlag, Stuttgart

Bréchon, Pierre/Laurent, Anne/Perrineau, Pascal (2000) Introduction, in: Bréchon, Pierre et al. (ed) Les cultures politiques des français, pp. 11-16. Presses de Science Politiques, Paris

Bremer, Francis J. (2005) The County of Massachusetts, in: Bremer, Francis J./Botelho, Lynn A. (ed) The World of John Winthrop, pp. 187-236, Boston

Bremer, Francis J./Botelho, Lynn (2005) Introduction, in: Bremer, Francis J./Botelho, Lynn A. (ed) The World of John Winthrop, pp. 1-21, Boston

Breuer, Tilman (1996) Gestaltung von Landschaft durch Politik, in: Hipp, Hermann/Seidl, Ernst (ed) Architektur als politische Kultur: philosophia practica, pp. 53-66. Reimer Verlag, Berlin

Brinkman, Ulrich/Seifert, Matthias (2001) Face to Interface, in: Zeitschrift für Soziologie 1/2001, pp. 22-46

Bronfen, Elisabeth/Marius, Benjamin/Steffen, Therese (ed) (1997) Hybride Kulturen. Stauffenburg Verlag, Tübingen

Browning, Christopher R. (1993) Ganz normale Männer. Rowohlt Verlag, Reinbek bei Hamburg

Browning, Peter (ed) (1995) To the golden Shore. Great West Books, Lafayette

Brundage, Anthony (2002) The English Poor Laws, 1700-1930. Palgrave, Hampshire

Brundage, Fitzhugh W. (2009) Redeeming a failed Revolution, in: Cooper, William J./McCardell, John M.: In the Cause of Liberty, pp. 126-135. Louisiana State University Press, Baton Rouge

Bryan, Dominic (1998) Ireland's very own Jurassic Park, in: Buckley, Anthony D. (ed) Symbols in Northern Ireland, pp. 23-42. The Queen's University of Belfast, Belfast

Bryan, Dominic (2000) Orange Parades. Pluto Press, London

Buber, Martin (1992) Das dialogische Prinzip. Lambert Schneider, Gerlingen

Büchler, Andrea/Cottier, Michelle (2002) Transsexualität und Recht, in: FamPra.ch 1/2002, pp. 20-47

Bullock, William (1649) Virginia impartially examined. Hen: Whaley, London

Bunker, Nick (2010) Making Haste from Babylon. Alfred A. Knopf, New York

Burgherr, Simone/Chambr, Siegfried/Iranbomy, Shahram (1993) Jugend und Gewalt. rex, Luzern – Stuttgart

Burns, Ric/Sanders, James/Ades, Lisa (2008) New York. Routledge Publishers, New York

Burrows, Edwin G./Wallace, Mike (1999) Gotham. Oxford University Press, Oxford – New York

Camilleri, Andrea (2010) Was ist ein Italiener? Verlag Klaus Wagenbach, Berlin

Cannon, Lou (1991) President Reagan. Simon & Schuster, New York

Cappai, Gabriele (2000) Kulturrelativismus, in: Zeitschrift für Soziologie 4/2000, pp. 253-274

Carwardine, Richard (2010) Abraham Lincoln, the Presidency, and the Mobilization of Union Sentiment, in: Grant, Susan-Mary/Holden Reid, Brian: The American Civil War, pp. 124-150. Pearson Education, Harlow

Cassel, Elaine (2005) The Terri Schiavo Case, in: FindLaw's Writ of June 23, 2005 (http://writ.news.findlaw.com/cassel/20050324.html), retrieved on July 26, 2011

Castelot, André (2001) Napoléon. Librairie Académique Perrin, Paris

Castoriadis, Cornelius (1990) Das Gebot der Revolution, in: Rödel, Ulrich (ed) Autonome Gesellschaft und libertäre Demokratie, pp. 54-88. Suhrkamp Verlag, Frankfurt am Main

Castoriadis, Cornelius (1997) Gesellschaft als imaginäre Institution. Suhrkamp Verlag, Frankfurt am Main

Cazorla Sánchez, Antonio (2010) Fear and Progress. John Wiley & Sons, Chichester

Chalmers, David M. (1987) Hooded Americanism. Duke University Press, Durham

Chandler, Alfred D. (1977) The visible Hand. Harvard University Press, Cambridge

Chipman, John (2010) A Strategy for Afghanistan, in: International Herald Tribune of September 10, 2010

Chrétien, Jean-Pierre (2000) L'Afrique des grands Lacs – deux mille ans d'histoire. Aubier, Paris

Civai, Mauro/Toti, Enrico (1997) Siena. Der gotische Traum. Edizioni Alsaba, Siena

Clark, Nancy L./Worger, William H. (2004) South Africa. Pearson Education Limited, Harlow

Coelho, Paulo (2001) Handbuch des Kriegers des Lichts. Diogenes Verlag, Zürich

Coing, Helmut (1993) Grundzüge der Rechtsphilosophie. De Gruyter Verlag, Berlin – New York

Collinson, Patrick (1967) The Elizabethan Puritan Movement. University of California Press, Berkeley

Conseil d'Etat (2004) Rapport public 2004: jurisprudence et avis de 2003. Un siècle the laïcité. La Documentation française, Paris

Cornelissen, Christoph (2003) Was heisst Erinnerungskultur?, in: Geschichte in Wissenschaft und Unterricht 10/2003, pp. 548-563

Czempiel, Ernst-Otto (2003) Weltpolitik im Umbruch. Beck Verlag, München

Daguzan, Jean-François (2003) La révolution incroyable?, in: Dulphy, Anne & Léonard, Yves (ed) De la dictature à la démocratie – voies ibériques, pp. 61-69. P.I.E.-Peter Lang, Bruxelles

Dahrendorf, Ralf (1979) Lebenschancen. Suhrkamp Verlag, Frankfurt am Main

Dahrendorf, Ralf (1999) Ein neuer Dritter Weg? Mohr Siebeck, Tübingen

Dahrendorf, Ralf (2006) Homo Sociologicus. VS Verlag für Sozialwissenschaften, Wiesbaden

Därmann, Iris (2002) Fremderfahrung und Repräsentation, in: Därmann, Iris/Jamme, Christoph (ed) Fremderfahrung und Repräsentation. Velbrück Wissenschaft, Weilerswist

de Blij, H.J./Muller, Peter O. (2008) Geography – Realms, Regions, and Concepts. Wiley & Sons, Inc., Hoboken

de Saint Martin, Monique (2003) Der Adel. UVK Verlagsgesellschaft, Konstanz

de Vilallonga, José Luis (1993) Juan Carlos. Bertelsmann Verlag, München

de Waal, Frans (1989) Behavioral contrasts between Bonobo and Chimpanzee, in: Heltne, Paul G./Marquardt, Linda A. (ed) Understanding Chimpanzees, pp. 154-175. Harvard University Press, Cambridge

de Waal, Frans (1991) Wilde Diplomaten. Hanser Verlag, München de Waal, Frans/Lanting, Frans (1997) Bonobo. University of California Press, Berkeley – Los Angeles – London

Debo, Angie (1970) A History of the Indians of the United States. University of Oklahoma Press, Norman

Debray, Régis (2007) L'obscénité démocratique. Flammarion, Paris

Debray, Régis (2009) Le Moment Fraternité. Editions Gallimard, Paris

Degen, Hans-Jürgen (1987) Vorwort, in: Degen, Hans-Jürgen (ed) "Tu was du willst, pp. 13-25. Schwarzer Nachtschatten, Berlin

Desazars de Montgailhard, Sylvia (2003) Les élites espagnoles et la transition démocratique, in: Dulphy, Anne & Léonard, Yves (ed) De la dictature à la démocratie – voies ibériques, pp. 45-60. P.I.E.-Peter Lang, Bruxelles

Dicey, Albert Venn (1982 [1915, 8th ed.]) Introduction to the Study of the Law of the Constitution. Liberty Classics, Indiana

Dickinson, Alice (1974) The Salem witchcraft Delusion, 1692. Franklin Watts, New York

Dieth, Eric (2000) Politisiertes Recht oder verrechtlichte Politik? Schulthess Juristische Medien, Zürich

Dietz, Alexander (2005) Der homo oeconomicus. Gütersloher Verlag, Gütersloh

Döbert, Rainer (1996) § 218 vor dem Bundesverfassungsgericht. Verfahrenstheoretische Überlegungen zur sozialen Integration, in: van den Daele, Wolfgang/Neidhardt, Friedhelm (ed) Kommunikation und Entscheidung, pp. 327-367. Edition Sigma, Berlin

Dohonue, Laura K. (1998) Regulating Northern Ireland: The Special Powers Acts, 1922-1972, in: The Historical Journal 4/1998, pp. 1089-1120

Donald, David Herbert (1995) Lincoln. Simon & Schuster, New York

Donne, John (1839) The Works of John Donne, vol. III., ed. by Henry Alford. John W. Parker, London

Dostojewski, Fjodor M. (1966) Der Grossinquisitor. Insel Verlag, Frankfurt am Main

Douglas, Mary (1991) Wie Institutionen denken. Suhrkamp Verlag, Frankfurt am Main

Dow, David R. (1995) The plain Meaning of Article V, in: Levinson, Sanford (ed) Responding to Imperfection, pp. 117-144. Princeton University Press, New Jersey

Dreier, Ralf (1991) Recht – Staat – Vernunft. Suhrkamp Verlag, Frankfurt am Main

Dundes, Alan/Falassi, Alessandro (1994) La Terra in Piazza. Nuova immagine editrice, Siena

Dupront, Alphonse (1978) La religion populaire dans l'histoire de l'Europe occidental, in: Revue d'histoire de l'Église de France 173/1978, pp. 185-202

Durkheim, Emile (1990) Der Selbstmord. Suhrkamp Verlag, Frankfurt am Main

Durst Johnson, Claudia (2002) Daily Life in colonial New England. Greenwood Press, Westport

Earle, Carville V. (1979) Environment, Disease, and Mortality, in: Tate, Thad W./Ammerman, David L.: The Chesapeake in the Seventeenth Century, pp. 96-125. University of North Carolina Press, Chapel Hill

Egli, Andina (1998) Die Bekämpfung des Landfahrertums. Zürich

Eifler, Mark A. (2002) Gold Rush Capitalists. University of New Mexico Press, Albuquerque

Eisen, George (1977) Voyageurs, Black-Robes, Saints, and Indians, in: Ethnohistory 3/1977, pp. 191-205

Eisenberg, Götz/Gronemeyer, Reimer (1993) Jugend und Gewalt. Rowohlt Taschenbuch Verlag, Reinbek bei Hamburg

Elkins, Stanley M. (1959) Slavery. University of Chicago Press, Chicago

Ellenbogen, Michael (2006) Gigantische Visionen. Ares Verlag, Graz

Ellis, Joseph J. (2007) American Creation. Random House, New York

Ellison, William Henry (1950) A self-governing Dominion. University of California Press, Berkeley

Ellmer, Jutta (2008) Kontroversen. Novum Verlag, Neckenmarkt

Ellwood, Shelagh (1994) Franco. Longman, London

Ely, John Hart (1993) War and Responsibility. Princeton University Press, Princeton

Emerson, Ralph Waldo (1971) Journals and miscellaneous notebooks of Ralph Waldo Emerson, Volume IX: 1843-1847. Harvard University Press, Cambridge

Emerson, Ralph Waldo (1993) Essays – First and second Series. Gramercy Books, New York

Emirbayer, Mustafa (1997) Manifesto for a Relational Sociology, in: The American Journal of Sociology 2/1997, pp. 281-317

Endress, Martin (2002) Vertrauen. Transcript Verlag, Bielefeld

Engel, Uwe/Hurrelmann, Klaus (1993) Was Jugendliche wagen. Juventa Verlag, Weinheim – München

Epps, Garrett (2011) Stealing the Constitution, on: The Nation of January 20, 2011 (http://www.thenation.com/article/157904/stealing-constitution), retrieved on July 26,2011

Erikson, Erik H. (1999) Kindheit und Gesellschaft. Klett – Cotta Verlag, Stuttgart

Eser, Albin (1994) Schwangerschaftsabbruch – Auf dem verfassungsgerichtlichen Prüfstand. Nomos Verlag, Baden – Baden

Faderman, Lillian/Timmons, Stuart (2006) Gay L.A.. Basic Books, Berkeley

Farber, Daniel A./Sherry, Suzanna (2002) Seeking Certainty. University of Chicago Press, Chicago

Farr, James (1986) "So vile and miserable an Estate – The Problem of Slavery in Locke's political Thought, in: Political Theory 2/1986, pp. 263-289

Farrell, Michèle (1990) Mutterschaft nach Mass, in: Miner, Valerie/Longino, Helen E. (ed) Konkurrenz – Ein Tabu unter Frauen. Frauenoffensive Verlag, München

Farrow, Anne/Lang, Joel/Frank, Jenifer (2006) Complicity. Ballantine Books, New York

Fasching, Gerhard (1996) Verlorene Wirklichkeiten. Springer Verlag, Wien – New York

Feagin, Joe R./Hahn, Harlan (1973) Ghetto Revolts. MacMillan, New York

Fehrenbacher, Don E. (1987) Lincoln in Text and Context. Standford University Press, Stanford

Feyerabend, Paul K. (1999) Knowledge, Science and Relativism. Cambridge University Press, Cambridge

Fields, Barbara J. (1982) Ideology and Race in American History, in: Morgan Kousser, J./McPherson, M.: Region, Race, and Reconstruction, pp. 143-177. Oxford University Press, Oxford

Finkelman, Paul (2010) Race and the Constitution. American Historical Association, Washington

Finkelstein, Norman H. (2007) American Jewish History. Jewish Publication Society, Philadelphia

Finzsch, Norbert/Horton, James O./Horton Lois E. (1999) Von Benin nach Baltimore. Hamburger Edition, Hamburg

Fisher, Louis/Harriger, Katy J. (2011) American Constitutional Law. Carolina Academic Press, Durham

Fiske, John (2005) The Beginnings of New England. Adamant Media Corporation, Boston – New York

Flanagan, Robert J. (2005) Has Management strangled U.S. Unions?, in: Journal of Labor Research 1/2005, pp. 33-63

Flierl, Bruno (1998) Gebaute DDR – Über Stadtplaner, Architekten und die Macht. Verlag für Bauwesen, Berlin

Fogel, Robert William/Engerman, Stanley L. (1974) Time on the Cross. Norton & Company, New York

Foner, Eric (2002) Reconstruction. Perennial Classics, New York

Ford, Lacy K. (1999) Making the "White Man's Country white: Race, Slavery, and State-Building in the Jacksonian South, in: Journal of the Early Republic 4/1999, pp. 713-737

Forrester, Viviane (1997) Der Terror der Ökonomie. Zsolnay Verlag, München

Forster, Kurt W. (1996) Baugedanken und Gedankengebäude, in: Hipp, Hermann/Seidl, Ernst (ed) Architektur als politische Kultur: philosophia practica, pp. 253-271. Reimer Verlag, Berlin

Forte, Dieter (1995) Der Junge mit den blutigen Schuhen. Fischer Verlag, Frankfurt am Main

Forte, Dieter (1998) In der Erinnerung. Fischer Verlag, Frankfurt am Main

Foucault, Michel (1976) Mikrophysik der Macht. Merve Verlag, Köln

Foucault, Michel (1978) Dispositive der Macht. Merve Verlag, Köln

France, Anatole (1894) Le Lys Rouge. Paris

Francia, Peter L. (2006) The Future of organized Labor in American Politics. Columbia University Press, New York

Frank, Robert H. (2007) Falling behind. University of California Press, Berkeley

Frankenberg, Günter (1994) Solidarität in einer "Gesellschaft der Individuen?, in: Frankenberg, Günter (ed) Auf der Suche nach der gerechten Gesellschaft, pp. 210-223. Fischer Taschenbuch Verlag, Frankfurt am Main

Frankenberg, Günter (2003) Autorität und Integration. Suhrkamp Verlag, Frankfurt am Main

Franzese, Paula A./Siegel, Steven (2007) Trust and Community: The Common Interest Community as Metaphor and Paradox, in: Missouri Law Review 4/2007, pp. 1111-1157

Fraser, Nancy/Gordon, Linda (1994) Civil Citizenship against social Citizenship?, in: van Steenbergen, Bart: The condition of citizenship, pp. 90-107. Sage, London

Frehsee, Detlev (1991) Zur Abweichung der Angepassten, in: Kriminologisches Journal 1/1991, pp. 25-45

French, Marilyn (1992) Der Krieg gegen die Frauen. Albrecht Knaus Verlag, München

Freund, David M. P. (2007) Colored Property. University of Chicago Press, Chicago

Friedman, Milton (1970) The Social Responsibility of Business is to Increase its Profits, in: The New York Times Magazine, September 13, 1970, pp. 232 ff.

Friedman, Milton (2002) Capitalism and Freedom. University of Chicago Press, Chicago – London

Frisch, Max (1965) Vorwort, in: Seiler, Alexander J.: Siamo italiani – die Italiener, pp. 7-10. EVZ-Verlag, Zürich

Fromm, Erich (2001) The Fear of Freedom. Routledge Publishers, London – New York

Fuchs, Peter (1992) Die Erreichbarkeit der Gesellschaft. Suhrkamp Verlag, Frankfurt am Main

Fukuyama, Francis (1992) The End of History and the last Man. Free Press, New York

Furet, François/Richet, Denis (1963) La Révolution française. Hachette Littératures, Paris

Gadamer, Hans-Georg (1990) Hermeneutik 1: Wahrheit und Methode. Mohr Verlag, Tübingen

Gaillard, Jean-Michel (1995) L'E.N.A, Miroir de l'Etat. Editions Complexe, Brüssel

Galbraith, John Kenneth (1992) The Culture of Contentment. Sinclair-Stevenson, London

Galbraith, John Kenneth (1994) A short History of financial Euphoria. Penguin Books, New York

Galbraith, John Kenneth (2005) Die Ökonomie des unschuldigen Betrugs. Siedler Verlag, München

Galle, Sara/Meier, Thomas (2009) Von Menschen und Akten. Chronos Verlag, Zürich

Galtung, Johan (1969) Violence, Peace, and Peace Research, in: Journal of Peace Research, 1/1969, pp. 167-191

Galtung, Johan (1978) Peace and Social Structure. Christian Ejlers, Kopenhagen

Galtung, Johan (1990) Cultural Violence, in: Journal of Peace Research, 3/1990, pp. 291-305

Galtung, Johan (1994) Menschenrechte – anders gesehen. Suhrkamp Verlag, Frankfurt am Main

Gambetta, Diego (2001) Können wir dem Vertrauen vertrauen?, in: Hartmann, Martin/Offe, Claus (ed) Vertrauen, pp. 204-237. Campus Verlag, Frankfurt am Main

Ganssmann, Heiner (2003) Marktplatonismus, in: Zeitschrift für Soziologie 6/2003, pp. 478-480

Garfinkle, Norton (2005) Nurturing economic Growth and the Values of American Democracy, in: Garfinkle, Norton/Yankelovich, Daniel (ed) Uniting America. Yale University Press, New Haven

Garrigou, Alain (2001) Les élites contre la République. Éditions la Découverte, Paris

Garry, Patrick M. (2008) An entrenched Legacy. Pennsylvania State University Press, Pensylvania

Gaspard, Françoise/Khosrokhavar, Farhad (1995) Le foulard et la République. Éditions la Découverte, Paris

Gauchet, Marcel (1996) Die totalitäre Erfahrung und das Denken des Politischen, in: Rödel, Ulrich (ed) Autonome Gesellschaft und libertäre Demokratie, Frankfurt am Main

Geiger, Thomas (1987 [1947]) Vorstudien zu einer Soziologie des Rechts. Duncker & Humblot Verlag, Berlin

George, Henry (1911) Progress and Poverty. J.M. Dent & Sons, London – New York

Georgel, Jacques (1990) La cinquième république: und démonarchie. Librairie générale de droit et de jurisprudence, Paris

Geser, Hans (1996) Auf dem Weg zur Cyberdemocracy. Auswirkungen der Computernetze auf die öffentliche politische Kommunikation, in: Sociology in Switzerland: Towards Cybersociety and Vireal Social Relations (http://socio.ch/intcom/t_hgeser00.htm), retrieved on July 26, 2011

Giddens, Anthony (1984) The Constitution of Society. Polity Press, Oxford

Giddens, Anthony (1990) The Consequences of Modernity. Stanford University Press, Stanford

Giddens, Anthony (1997) Jenseits von Links und Rechts. Suhrkamp Verlag, Frankfurt am Main

Gildemeister, Regine/Wetterer, Angelika (1992) Wie Geschlechter gemacht werden, in: Knapp, Gudrun-Axeli/Wetterer, Angelika (ed-): Traditionen Brüche. Kore Verlag, Freiburg im Breisgau

Giliomee, Hermann (1987) Western Cape Farmers and the Beginnings of Afrikaner Nationalism, 1870-1915, in: Journal of Southern African Studies, 1/1987, pp. 38-63

Gillette, William (2000) Fifteenth Amendment, Section 5, in: Levy, Leonard W./Karst, Kenneth L.: Encyclopedia of the American Constitution, Volume 3. Macmillan Publishers, New York

Ginsborg, Paul (2005) Silvio Berlusconi. Verso, London

Glaessner, Gert-Joachim (1992) Der schwierige Weg zur Demokratie. Westdeutscher Verlag, Opladen

Glotz, Peter (1992) Der Irrweg des Nationalstaats. Deutsche Verlags-Anstalt, Stuttgart

Godbeer, Richard (2005) Performing Patriarchy, in: Bremer, Francis J./Botelho, Lynn A. (ed) The World of John Winthrop, pp. 290-333, Boston

Goffman, Erving (1982) Das Individuum im öffentlichen Austausch. Suhrkamp Verlag, Frankfurt am Main

Gonzales-Day, Ken (2006) Lynching in the West 1850-1935. Duke University Press, Durham – London

Goss, David K. (2008) The Salem Witch Trials. Greenwod Press, Westport

Gotham, Kevin Fox (2002) Race, real estate, and uneven development. State University of New York Press, Albany

Gourevitch, Philip (1999) We wish to inform you that tomorrow we will be killed with our families. Picador, London

Graf, Martin/Lamprecht, Markus (1991) Der Beitrag des Bildungssystems zur Konstruktion von szialer Ungleichheit, in: Bornschier, Volker (ed) Das Ende der sozialen Schichtung?, pp. 73-96. Seismo Verlag, Zürich

Graham, Carol (2009) Happiness around the world. Oxford University Press, Oxford

Grant, Susan-Mary (2010) From Union to Nation? The Civil War and the Development of American Nationalism, in: Grant, Susan-Mary/Holden Reid, Brian: The American Civil War, pp. 295-316. Pearson Education, Harlow

Grass, Günter (2000) Ohne Stimme. Steidl Verlag, Göttingen

Grasso, Piero (2010) Trauer, Tränen und Tod, in: Das Magazin vom 31.7.2010

Green Carr, Lois/Menard, Russell R. (1979) Immigration and Opportunity, in: Tate, Thad W./Ammerman, David L.: The Chesapeake in the Seventeenth Century, pp. 206-242. University of North Carolina Press, Chapel Hill

Green, E.H.H. (2002) Ideologies of Conservatism. Oxford University Press, Oxford

Greene, Lorenzo Johnston (1942) The Negro in Colonial New England, 1620-1776. Columbia University Press, New York

Greven, Michael Th. (1999) Die politische Gesellschaft. Leske & Budrich Verlag, Opladen

Gruner, Erich/Hertig, Hans Peter (1983) Der Stimmbürger und die «neue» Politik. Haupt Verlag, Bern – Stuttgart

Gschwend, Lukas (2002) Gschwend, Lukas: Hilfswerk für die Kinder der Landstrasse der Pro Juventute – Ein Fall von Völkermord in der Schweiz?, in: Donatsch, Andreas u.a. (ed) Festschrift für Stefan Trechsel zum 65. Geburtstag, Zürich 2002, pp. 373-392. Schulthess Juristische Medien, Zürich

Guéhenno, Jean-Marie (1994) Das Ende der Demokratie. Artemis & Winkler Verlag, München – Zürich

Guildhall Press (2008) Murals of Derry. Guildhall Press, Derry

Gumede, William M. (2007) Thabo Mbeki and the Battler for the Soul of the ANC. Zebra Press, Cape Town

Günter, Roland (1996) Die politische Ikonographie des Ruhrgebietes in der Epoche der Industrialisierung, in: Hipp, Hermann/Seidl, Ernst (ed) Architektur als politische Kultur: philosophia practica, pp. 213-224. Reimer Verlag, Berlin

Guy, Jeff (1987) Analysing pre-capitalist Societies in Southern Africa, in: Journal of Southern African Studies, 1/1987, pp. 18-37

Habermas, Jürgen (1990) Strukturwandel der Öffentlichkeit. Suhrkamp Verlag, Frankfurt am Main

Habermas, Jürgen (1992) Faktizität und Geltung. Suhrkamp Verlag, Frankfurt am Main

Habermas, Jürgen (1996) Die Einbeziehung des Anderen. Suhrkamp Verlag, Frankfurt am Main

Hacker, Jacob S./Pierson, Paul (2010) Winner-Take-All Politics. Simon & Schuster, New York

Hagemann-White, Carol (1984) Sozialisation: Weiblich – männlich? Leske & Budrich Verlag, Opladen

Hahn, Alois (1994) Die soziale Konstruktion des Fremden, in: Sprondel, Walter M. (ed) Die Objektivität der Ordnungen und ihre kommunikative Konstruktion. Suhrkamp Verlag, pp. 140-163, Frankfurt am Main

Hailsham, Lord (1992) On the Constitution. Harper Collins Publishers, Glasgow

Hall, David D./Walsham, Alexandra (2005) "Justification by Print alone?, in: Bremer, Francis J./Botelho, Lynn A. (ed) The World of John Winthrop, pp. 334-385, Boston

Hamilton, Alexander/Madison, James/Jay, John (2003 [1787-1788]) The Federalist Papers. Bentam Classic, New York

Hamm, Thomas D. (2003) The Quakers in America. Columbia University Press, New York

Harris, Marvin (1978) Kannibalen und Könige. Umschau Verlag, Frankfurt am Main

Hart, James S./Ross, Richard J. (2005) The ancient Constitution in the Old World and the New, in: Bremer, Francis J./Botelho, Lynn A. (ed) The World of John Winthrop, pp. 237-289, Boston

Hartmann, Martin (2001) Einleitung, in: Hartmann, Martin/Offe, Claus (ed) Vertrauen, pp. 7-37. Campus Verlag, Frankfurt am Main

Hassauer, Friederike (1990) Weiblichkeit – der blinde Fleck der Menschenrechte?, in: Gerhard, Ute/Jansen, Mechthild u.a. (ed) Differenz und Gleichheit, pp. 320-337. Ulrike Helmer Verlag, Frankfurt am Main

Hatch, Charles E. (1957) The First Seventeen Years, Virginia 1607 1624. University Press of Virginia, Williamsburg

Haug, Wolfang (2003) Ein Verbrechen gegen die Menschlichkeit, in: Haug, Wolfang (ed) Angriff auf die Freiheit?, pp. 7-31. Trotzdem Verlagsgenossenschaft, Grafenau

Hayek, Friedrich A. (1949) Individualism and Economic Order. Routledge & Kegan Paul, London

Headey, Bruce/Muffels, Ruud/Wagner, Gert G. (2010) Long-running German panel survey shows that personal and economic choices, not just genes, matter for happiness, in: PNAS October 4, 2010; PNAS 2010 : 1008612107v1-201008612

Heckhausen, Heinz (1987) Intentionsgeleitetes Handeln und seine Fehler, in: Heckhausen, Heinz/Gollwitzer, Peter M./Weinert, Franz E. (ed) Jenseits des Rubikon: Der Wille in den Humanwissenschaften, pp. 143-175. Springer Verlag, Berlin – Heidelberg – New York

Hedges, Chris (2009) Empire of Illusion. Nation Books, New York

Heidegger, Martin (1979) Unterwegs zur Sprache. Neske Verlag, Pfullingen

Heilbroner, Robert (1994) Kapitalismus im 21. Jahrhundert. Hanser Verlag, München – Wien

Heine, Peter (2010) "Man sollte die Gefahr nicht übertreiben, in: Der Spiegel Online of January 3, 2010 (http://www.spiegel.de/politik/deutschland/0,1518,669852,00.html), retrieved on July 26, 2011

Heitmeyer, Wilhelm (1997) Gibt es eine Radikalisierung des Integrationsroblems?, in: Heitmeyer, Wilhelm (ed) Was hält die Gesellschaft zusammen? Suhrkamp Verlag, Frankfurt am Main

Heitmeyer, Wilhelm/Anhut, Reimund (2000) Einleitung, in: Heitmeyer, Wilhelm/Anhut, Reimund: Bedrohte Stadtgesellschaft, pp. 9-14. Juventa Verlag, Weinheim – München

Heizer, Robert F./Almquist, Alan J. (1971) The other Californians. University of California Press, Berkeley

Hellinger, Marlis (1990) Kontrastive feministische Linguistik. Hueber Verlag, Ismaning

Hening, William Waller (1819) The Statutes at Large, Being the Collection of all the Laws of Virginia from the Third Session of the Legislature in the Year 1619, 13 vols. W. Gray Printers, Richmond

Higham, John (1984) Send these to me. Johns Hopkins University Press, Baltimore

Hilberg, Raul (1999) Die Vernichtung der europäischen Juden. Fischer Taschenbuch Verlag, Frankfurt am Main

Hill, John E. (2007) Democracy, Equality, and Justice. Lexington Books, Plymouth

Hill, Lisa (2001) The hidden theology of Adam Smith, in: European Journal of the History of Economic Thought 1/2001, pp. 1-29

Hindle, Steve (2001) Exhortation and entitlement, in: Braddick, Michael J./Walter, John (ed) Negotiating Power in Early Modern Society, pp. 102-122. Cambridge University Press, Cambridge

Hipp, Hermann (1996) Aristotelische Politik und frühneuzeitliche Bauaufgaben, in: Hipp, Hermann/Seidl, Ernst (ed) Architektur als politische Kultur: philosophia practica, pp. 93-114. Reimer Verlag, Berlin

Hippler, Jochen (1993) Islam und westliche Aussenpolitik, in: Hippler, Jochen/Lueg, Andrea (ed) Feindbild Islam, pp. 142-184. Konkret Verlag, Hamburg

Hirsch, Arnold R. (1993) With or Without Jim Crow – Black Residential Segregation in the United States, in: Hirsch, Arnold R./Mohl, Raymond A. (ed) Urban policy in twentieth-century America, pp. 65-99. Rutgers University Press, New Brunswick

Hirsch, Joachim (1998) Vom Sicherheitsstaat zum nationalen Wettbewerbsstaat. ID Verlag, Berlin

Hirschman, Albert O. (1994) Wieviel Gemeinsinn braucht die liberale Gesellschaft, in: Leviathan 2/1994, pp. 293-304

Höffe, Otfried (1990a) Kategorische Rechtsprinzipien. Suhrkamp Verlag, Frankfurt am Main

Höffe, Otfried (1990b) Transzendentale Interessen: Zur Anthropologie der Menschenrechte, in: Gauch, Peter (ed) Das Menschenbild im Recht. Universitätsverlag Freiburg, Freiburg

Hofmann, Hasso (1996) Neuere Entwicklungen in der Rechtsphilosophie. De Gruyter Verlag, Berlin – New York

Hogeland, William (2010) Declaration. Simon & Schuster, New York

Hondrich, Karl Otto (1992) Lehrmeister Krieg. Rowohlt Taschenbuch Verlag, Reinbek bei Hamburg

Hondrich, Karl Otto/Koch-Arzberger, Claudia (1992) Solidarität in der modernen Gesellschaft. Fischer Taschenbuch Verlag, Frankfurt am Main

Honegger, Claudia (1991) Die Ordnung der Geschlechter. Campus Verlag, Frankfurt am Main – New York

Honegger, Claudia/Neckel, Sighard/Magning, Chantal (2010) Strukturierte Verantwortungslosigkeit. Suhrkamp Taschenbuchverlag, Berlin

Honneth, Axel (1992) Kampf um Anerkennung. Suhrkamp Verlag, Frankfurt am Main

Honneth, Axel (1994) Desintegration. Fischer Taschenbuch Verlag, Frankfurt am Main

Honneth, Axel (1994) Die soziale Dynamik von Missachtung, in: Leviathan 1/1994, pp. 78-93

Honneth, Axel (ed) (1993) Kommunitarismus. Campus Verlag, Frankfurt am Main – New York

Horn, James (1979) Servant Emigration to the Chesapeake in the Seventeenth Century, in: Tate, Thad W./Ammerman, David L.: The Chesapeake in the Seventeenth Century, pp. 51-95. University of North Carolina Press, Chapel Hill

Hughes, Charles Evans (1908) Addresses and Papers – 1906-1908. The Knickerbocker Press, New York

Huissoud, Thérèse et. al. (2003) Strukturen und Tendenzen der Differenzierung in den städtischen Räumen der Schweiz, in: Wicker, Hans-Rudolf/Fibbi, Rosita/Haug, Werner (ed) Migration und die Schweiz, pp. 183-206. Seismo Verlag, Zürich

Human Rights Watch (2004) France – L'interdiction du port du foulard viole la liberté de religion, New York

Huntington, Samuel P. (1998) The Clash of Civilizations and the Remaking of World Order. Simon & Schuster, London

Hurtado, Albert L. (2006) John Sutter. University of Oklahoma Press, Norman

Hyman, Harold M. (2000) Thirteenth Amendment – Framing, in: Levy, Leonard W./Karst, Kenneth L.: Encyclopedia of the American Constitution, Volume 6, 2. edition, p. 2691. Macmillan Publishers, New York

ILO (2009) The cost of coercion. Geneva

Imhof, Kurt/Romano, Gaetano (1996) Die Diskontinuität der Moderne. Theorie des sozialen Wandels. Campus Verlag, Frankfurt am Main – New York

Innes, Stephen (1995) Creating the Commonwealth. W.W. Norton Company, New York – London

Jacobs, Harriet (pseudonym "Linda Brent") (1861) Incidents in the Life of a slave Girl. Boston

Jäger, Herbert (1989) Makrokriminalität. Suhrkamp Verlag, Frankfurt am Main

Jak i, Bo idar (2005) Lebensbedingungen von Roma Binnenvertriebenen in Serbien und Montenegro, in: Matter, Max (ed) Die Situation der Roma und Sinti nach der EU-Osterweiterung, pp. 47-67. V&R unipress, Göttingen

Jamme, Christoph (2002) Gibt es eine Wissenschaft des Fremden?, in: Därmann, Iris/Jamme, Christoph (ed) Fremderfahrung und Repräsentation. Velbrück Wissenschaft, Weilerswist

Janssen-Jurreit, Marielouise (1978) Sexismus. Carl Hanser Verlag, München – Wien

Jarman, Neil (1997) Material Conflicts. Berg, Oxford

Jarman, Neil (1998) Painting Landscapes, in: Buckley, Anthony D. (ed) Symbols in Northern Ireland, pp. 81-98. The Queen's University of Belfast, Belfast

Jefferson, Thomas (1853) Notes on the State of Virginia. J. W. Randolph, Richmond

Jefferson, Thomas (1903 [1787]) The Writings of Thomas Jefferson. Memorial Edition. Letter to Edward Carrington. Lipscomb and Bergh, Washington

Jehlen, Myra/Warner, Michael (ed) (1997) The English literatures of America, 1500-1800. Routledge, New York

Jenkins, Roy (2003) Franklin Delano Roosevelt. Times Books, New York

Jepperson, Ronald L. (1991) Institutions, Institutional Effects, and Institutionalism, in: Powell, Walter W./DiMaggio, Paul J. (ed) The new institutionalism in organizational analysis, pp. 143-163. University of Chicago Press, Chicago

Joas, Hans (1992) Die Kreativität des Handelns. Suhrkamp Verlag, Frankfurt am Main

Joffrin, Laurent (2001) Le gouvernement invisible. Arléa, Paris

Jones, Seth G. (2010) In the Graveyard of Empires. W. W. Norton & Company, New York

Jordan, David W. (1979) Political Stability and the Emergence of a Native Elite in Maryland, in: Tate, Thad W./Ammerman, David L.: The Chesapeake in the Seventeenth Century, pp. 243-273. University of North Carolina Press, Chapel Hill

Jordan, David (1996) Die Neuerschaffung von Paris. Fischer Verlag, Frankfurt am Main

Jullien, François (2010) Le Pont des singes. Éditions Galilée, Paris

Kammen, Michael (1986) A Machine that would go of itself. Alfred A. Knopf, New York

Kandil, Fuad (2000) Zwischen kultureller Stigmatisierung und ideologischer Ausgrenzung, in: Robertson-Wensauer, Caroline Y. (ed) Multikulturalität – Interkulturalität?, pp. 119-141. Nomos Verlagsgesellschaft, Baden – Baden

Kantorowicz, Ernst H. (1994) Die zwei Körper des Königs. Princeton University Press, Princeton

Kaplan, Sidney (1976) The "Domestic Insurrections of the Declaration of Independence, in: The Journal of Negro History 3/1976, pp. 243-255

Kaschuba, Wolfgang (1993) Nationalismus und Ethnozentrismus. Zur kulturellen Ausgrenzung ethnischer Gruppen in (deutscher) Geschichte und Gegenwart, in: Jeismann, Michael/Ritter, Henning (ed) Grenzfälle, pp. 239-273. Reclam Verlag, Leibzig

Kaufmann, Eric P. (2007) The Orange Order. Oxford University Press, Oxford

Kaur, Abnash (1995) South Africa and Bantustans. Kalinga Publications, Delhi

Keegan, John (2009) The American Civil War. Alfred A. Knopf, New York

Kennedy, David J. (1995) Residential Associations as State Actors – Regulating the Impact of Gated Communities on Nonmembers, in: The Yale Law Journal 3/1995, pp. 761-793

Kennedy, Gavin (2009) Adam Smith and the Invisible Hand: From Metaphor to Myth, in: Econ Journal Watch 2/2009, pp. 239-263

Kenney, Mary Catherine (1998) The Phoenix and the Lark, in: Buckley, Anthony D. (ed) Symbols in Northern Ireland, pp. 153-169. The Queen's University of Belfast, Belfast

Kens, Paul (2000) Disputed Ownership in Sacramento, in: Bakken, Gordon Morris (ed) Law in den western United States, pp. 343-346. University of Oklahoma Press, Norman

Kersting, Wolfgang (1994) Die politische Philosophie des Gesellschaftsvertrags. Wissenschaftliche Buchgesellschaft, Darmstadt

Keupp, Heiner (1992) Identitätsverlust oder neue Identitätsentwürfe?, in: Zoll, Rainer (ed) Ein neues kulturelles Modell. Zum soziokulturellen Wandel in Gesellschaften Westeuropas und Nordamerikas, pp. 100-117. Westdeutscher Verlag, Opladen

Kirchgässner, Gebhard (1991) Homo oeconomicus. Mohr Verlag, Tübingen

Kirsch, Jan-Holger (1999) Identität durch Normalität, in: Leviathan 3/1999, pp. 309-354

Kissack, Terence (2008) Free Comrades. AK Press, Edinburgh

Kissling, Hans (2008) Reichtum ohne Leistung. Rüegger Verlag, Zürich – Chur

Kleger, Heinz (1993) Der neue Ungehorsam. Campus Verlag, Frankfurt am Main – New York

Klocke, Andreas (2000) Methoden der Armutsmessung, in: Zeitschrift für Soziologie 4/2000, pp. 313-329

Köbl, Wolfgang (2006) Zivilgesellschaft und staatliches Gewaltmonopol, in: Mittelweg 36, 1/2006, pp. 61-84

Kohl, Karl-Heinz (2000) Ethnologie – die Wissenschaft vom kulturell Fremden. Beck Verlag, München

Kohn, Alfie (1986) No Contest. Houghton Mifflin, Boston

Kolchin, Peter (2003) American Slavery. Hill and Wang, New York

Köstler, Andreas (1996) Gloire und simplicité französischer Platzanlagen, in: Hipp, Hermann/Seidl, Ernst (eds.): Architektur als politische Kultur: philosophia practica, pp. 131-147. Reimer Verlag, Berlin

Krasner, Stephen D./Pascual, Carlos (2005) Adressing State Failure, in: Foreign Affairs 4/2005, pp. 153-163

Kriesi, Hanspeter (1980) Entscheidungsstrukturen und Entscheidungsprozesse in der Schweizer Politik. Campus Verlag, Frankfurt am Main – New York

Kronauer, Martin (2002) Exklusion. Campus Verlag, Frankfurt am Main

Krugman, Paul (1996) Pop Internationalism. MIT Press, Cambdrige

Krugman, Paul (1999) Der Mythos vom globalen Wirtschaftskrieg. Campus Verlag, Frankfurt am Main – New York

Krugman, Paul (2009) The Conscience of a Liberal. Norton & Company, New York – London

Krugman, Paul (2011) Wisconsin Power Play, in: The New York Times of February 21, 2011 (http://www.nytimes.com/2011/02/21/opinion/21krugman.html), retrieved on July 26, 2011

Kundera, Milan (2001) Das Buch vom Lachen und Vergessen. Deutscher Taschenbuch Verlag, München

Labbé, Ronald M./Lurie, Jonathan (2005) The Slaughterhouse Cases. University Press of Kansas, Lawrence

Laing, Ronald D. (1969) Phänomenologie der Erfahrung. Suhrkamp Verlag, Frankfurt am Main

Lamont, Michèle (1992) Money, Morals, and Manners. University of Chicago Press, Chicago

Langford, Paul (2001) The Eighteenth Century, in: Morgan, Kenneth O. (ed) The Oxford History of Britain, pp. 399-469. Oxford University Press, Oxford

Lapeyronnie, Didier (2008) Ghetto urbain. Éditions Robert Laffont, Paris

LaPlante, Eve (2004) American Jezebel. Harper Collins Publishers, New York

LaPlante, Eve (2007) Salem Witch Judge. Harper Collins, New York

Lawson, Alan (2006) A Commonwealth of Hope. Johns Hopkins University Press, Baltimore

Lazarus, Edward (2005) Why Congress's Intervention Predictably Didn't Help the Schindlers, in: FindLaw's Writ of March 31, 2005 (http://writ.news.findlaw.com/lazarus/20050331.html), retrieved on July 26, 2011

Lee Johnson, Susan (2001) Roaring Camp. W. W. Norton & Company, New York

Leggewie, Claus (1993) multi kulti. Rotbuch Verlag, Berlin

Legislative Reference Bureau (2011) January 2011 Special Session, LRB-1383/2

Leidgeb, Ellen/Horn, Nicole – Roma-Union Ffm. (ed) (1994) Opre Roma! Erhebt Euch! AG SPAK-Bücher, München

Leimgruber, Walter/Meier, Thomas/Sablonier, Roger (1998) Das Hilfswerk für die Kinder der Landstrasse. Schweizerisches Bundesarchiv, Bern

Lemke, Christiane (1991) Die Ursachen des Umbruchs 1989. Westdeutscher Verlag, Opladen

Lerner, Gerda (1991) Die Entstehung des Patriarchats. Campus Verlag, Frankfurt am Main – New York

Leuchtenburg, William E. (1995) The Supreme Court Reborn. Oxford University Press, New York

Leung, Peter C.Y. (2001) A Glimpse of Chinese Gold Miners in California, in: Sacramento Chinese Culture Foundation: 150 Years of the Chinese Presence in California, pp. 26-40. Sun Printing, Sacramento

Lever, Evelyne (1985) Louis XVI. Librairie Arthème Fayard, Paris

Levi, Anthony (2001) Cardinal Richelieu. Carroll & Graf Publishers, New York

Levi, Primo (1998) Ist das ein Mensch? Deutscher Taschenbuch Verlag, München

Lewy, Guenter (2001) "Rückkehr nicht erwünscht." Propyläen Verlag, München

Licata, Salvatore (1981) The homosexual Rights Movement in the United States, in: Licata, Salvatore/Petersen, Robert (ed) Historical Perspectives on Homosexuality, pp. 161-189. The Haworth Press, New York

Liessmann, Konrad Paul (2006) Theorie der Unbildung. Paul Zsolnay Verlag, Wien

Lietzmann, Hans (1994) Staatswissenschaftliche Abendröte, in: Gebhardt, Jürgen/Schmalz-Bruns, Rainer (ed) Demokratie, Verfassung und Nation, pp. 72-101. Nomos Verlagsgesellschaft, Baden – Baden

Lindberg, Leon N./Scheingold, Stuart A. (1970) Europe's would-be polity – Patterns of change in the European community. Prentice-Hall, Englewood Cliffs

Linder, Wolf (1994) Swiss Democracy. St. Martin's Press, New York

Lindner-Braun, Christa (1990) Soziologie des Selbstmords. Westdeutscher Verlag, Opladen

Linke, Angelika (2007) Wer ist "arm"?, in: Renz, Ursula/Bleisch, Barbara (ed) Zu wenig, pp. 19-41. Seismo Verlag, Zürich

Lippold, Michael W. (2000) Schwangerschaftsabbruch in der Bundesrepublik Deutschland. Evangelische Verlangsanstalt, Leipzig

Lipsitz, George (2006) Investment in Whiteness. Temple University Press, Philadelphia

Lipsmeier, Gero (1999) Die Bestimmung des notwendigen Lebensstandards, in: Zeitschrift für Soziologie 4/1999, pp. 281-300

Locke, John (1824) Two Treatises of Government. London

Loewenstein, Karl (1961) Beiträge zur Staatssoziologie. Mohr Verlag, Tübingen

Longchamp, Claude (1991) Herausgeforderte demokratische Öffentlichkeit, in: Direkte Demokratie, Schweizerisches Jahrbuch für politische Wissenschaften 31/1991, pp. 303-326

Longino, Helen E. (1990) Die Ideologie der Konkurrenz, in: Miner, Valerie/Longino, Helen E. (ed) Konkurrenz – Ein Tabu unter Frauen, pp. 183-195. Frauenoffensive Verlag, München

Lorber, Judith/Farrell, Susan A. (1991) Principles of Gender Construction, in: Lorber, Judith/Farrell, Susan A. (ed) The Social Construction of Gender, pp. 7-11. Sage Publications, Newbury Park

Löw, Martina (2001) Raumsoziologie. Suhrkamp Verlag, Frankfurt am Main

Lueg, Andrea (1993) Das Feindbild Islam in der westlichen Öffentlichkeit, in: Hippler, Jochen/Lueg, Andrea (ed) Feindbild Islam, pp. 14-43. Konkret Verlag, Hamburg

Luhmann, Niklas (1988) Erkenntnis als Konstruktion. Benteli Verlag, Bern

Luhmann, Niklas (1989) Legitimation durch Verfahren. Suhrkamp Verlag, Frankfurt am Main

Luhmann, Niklas (1991) Soziale Systeme. Suhrkamp Verlag, Frankfurt am Main

Luhmann, Niklas (1993) Das Recht der Gesellschaft. Suhrkamp Verlag, Frankfurt am Main

Luhmann, Niklas (1997) Die Gesellschaft der Gesellschaft. Suhrkamp Verlag, Frankfurt am Main

Luhmann, Niklas (1999) Grundrechte als Institution, 4. ed. Duncker & Humblot Verlag, Berlin

Luhmann, Niklas (2000) Die Politik der Gesellschaft. Suhrkamp Verlag, Frankfurt am Main

Luig, Ute (1990) Sind egalitäre Gesellschaften auch geschlechtsegalitär?, in: Lenz, Ilse/Luig, Ute (ed) Frauenmacht ohne Herrschaft. Orlanda Frauenverlag, Berlin

Lukes, Steven (1977) Essays in social Theory. Macmillan, London

Mäder, Ueli/Aratnam, Ganga Jey/Schilliger, Sarah (2010) Wie Reiche denken und lenken. Rotpunktverlag, Zürich

Maier, Pauline (1997) American Scripture. Vintage Books, New York

Malanczuk, Peter (1997) Akehurst's modern Introduction to International Law. Routledge, London

Malinowski, Bronislaw (1922) Argonauts of the Western Pacific. Routledge & Kegan Paul, London

Manahan, Karen B. (2011) Robert Gray's "A good Speed to Virginia – accessed on February 24, 2011 (http://digital.lib.lehigh.edu/trial/justification/jamestown/essay/4/), retrieved on July 26, 2011

Mandela, Nelson (1995) Long Walk to Freedom. Hachette Book Group, New York

Mandelbaum, Maurice (1959) Societal Facts, in: Gardiner, Patrick: Theories of History, pp. 476-488. Free Press, Glencoe

Mankiw, Gregory/Taylor, Mark (2008) Grundzüge der Volkswirtschaftslehre. Stuttgart

Mann, Michael (2005) The dark Side of Democracy. Cambridge University Press, Cambdrige

Marais, Hein (1998) South Africa – Limits to Change. University of Cape Town Press, Cape Town

Marín Arce, José María (2003) La mobilisation politique et sociale pendant le post-franquisem et la transition démocratique, in: Dulphy, Anne & Léonard, Yves (ed) De la dictature à la démocratie – voies ibériques, pp. 71-83. P.I.E.-Peter Lang, Bruxelles

Markl, Hubert (1982) Naturwissenschaftliche und kulturwissenschaftliche Perspektiven der Aggresionsforschung, in: Hilke, Reinhard/Kempf, Wilhelm (ed) Aggression, pp. 21-43. Verlag Hans Huber, Bern – Göttingen – Toronto

Martin, Claude (1995) Franco. Leopold Stocker Verlag, Graz – Stuttgart

Mason, Richard B. (1848) Report of Col. R.B. Mason, Military Governor of California, in: House documents, otherwise published as Executive documents, 30th congress, 2d session, Volume 1, Document 1, pp. 56-64. A. O. P. Nicholson, Washington

Matjan, Gregor (1998) Auseinandersetzung mit der Vielfalt. Campus Verlag, Frankfurt am Main – New York

Matter, Max (2005) Zur Lage der Roma im östlichen Europa, in: Matter, Max (ed) Die Situation der Roma und Sinti nach der EU-Osterweiterung, pp. 11-28. V&R unipress, Göttingen

Mattioli, Aram (2010) "Viva Mussolini. Verlag Neue Zürcher Zeitung, Zürich

Maturana, Humberto R. (1994) Was ist Erkennen? Piper Verlag, München

Mauss, Marcel (1990) Die Gabe. Suhrkamp Taschenbuchverlag, Frankfurt am Main

Mayer-Tasch, Peter Cornelius (1991) Politische Theorie des Verfassungsstaates. Deutscher Taschenbuch Verlag, München

Mayntz, Renate (1997) Soziale Dynamik und politische Steuerung. Campus Verlag, Frankfurt am Main – New York

McKenna, George (2007) The Puritan Origins of American Patriotism. Yale University, New Haven & London

McQuade, Aidan (2008) Foreword, in: Skinner, Benjamin E.: A Crime so Monstrous, pp. 7-11. Mainstream Publishing, Edinburgh – London

Mead, George Herbert (1993) Geist, Identität und Gesellschaft. Suhrkamp Verlag, Frankfurt am Main

Mead, Margaret (1992) Mann und Weib. Ullstein Verlag, Frankfurt am Main

Meckseper, Cord (1996) Oben und Unten in der Architektur, in: Hipp, Hermann/Seidl, Ernst (ed) Architektur als politische Kultur: philosophia practica, pp. 37-52. Reimer Verlag, Berlin

Meier, Christian (2004) Wo liegt Europa?, in: Leggewie, Claus (ed) Die Türkei und Europa, pp. 32-38. Suhrkamp Verlag, Frankfurt am Main

Merlin, Pierre (1998) Les banlieues des villes françaises. La documentation française, Paris

Meyer, Daniel/Saule, Béatrix (1999) Versailles. Éditions Art Lys, Versailles

Meyer, Jeffrey F. (2001) Myths in Stone. University of California Press, Berkeley

Meyer, John W./Rowan, Brian (1991) Institutionalized Organizations, in: Powell, Walter W./DiMaggio, Paul J. (ed) The new institutionalism in organizational analysis, pp. 41-62. University of Chicago Press, Chicago

Meyer, Thomas (1994) Die Transformation des Politischen. Suhrkamp Verlag, Frankfurt am Main

Meyer, Thomas (1997) Identitäts-Wahn. Aufbau Taschenbuchverlag, Berlin

Meyersohn, Harald (2011) Wisconsin is only part of the GOP war against unions, in: The Washington Post of February 23, 2011 (http://www.washingtonpost.com/wp-dyn/content/article/2011/02/22/AR2011022207093.html), retrieved July 26,2011

Michalowski, Raymond (1988) Radikale Kriminologie in den USA – Die Evolution marxistischer Analysen von Staat, Recht und Kriminalität, in: Janssen, Helmut/Kaulitzky, Reiner/Michalowski, Raymond (ed) Radikale Kriminologie. AJZ Druck und Verlag, Bielefeld

Mike Leigh (2008) Happy-go-lucky (Movie). Great Britain

Miller, Lee (2000) Roanoke – solving the mistery of the lost colony. Arcade Publishing, New York

Mills, Greg/Richards, David (2010) The Binds that tie us, in: Foreign Affairs of November 24/2010 (http://www.foreignaffairs.com/articles/67015/greg-mills-and-david-richards/the-binds-that-tie-us), retrieved on July 26, 2011

Minowitz, Peter (2004) Adam Smith's invisible Hands, in:, in: Econ Journal Watch 3/2004, pp. 381-412

Mitchell, Don (2003) The Right to the City. Guilford Press, New York

Mitterer, Josef (1992) Das Jenseits der Philosophie. Passagen Verlag, Wien

Modelmog, Ilse (1989) Die zwei Ordnungen. Westdeutscher Verlag, Opladen

Mokgatle, Naboth (1971) The Autobiography of an unknown South African. University of California Press, Berkeley

Monaghan, Jay (1973) Chile, Peru, and the California gold rush of 1849. University of California Press, Berkeley

Monti, Martin M. et al. (2010) Willful Modulation of Brain Activity in Disorders of Consciousness, in: New England Journal of Medicine of February 3, 2010

Moore, Alexander (1998) Cultural Anthropology. Collegiate Press, San Diego

Moore, Barrington (1982) Ungerechtigkeit. Die sozialen Ursachen von Unterordnung und Widerstand. Suhrkamp Verlag, Frankfurt am Main

Moradiellos, Enrique (2000). Spain in the world, in: Junco, José Alvarez/Shubert, Adrian (ed) Spanish History since 1808, pp. 110-120. Hodder Education, London

Morgan, Edmund S. (1966) The puritan Family. Harper & Row, New York

Morgan, Kenneth (2007) Slavery and the British Empire. Oxford University Press, Oxford

Morgenson, Gretchen/Story, Louise (2011) In financial Crisis, no Prosecutions of top Figures, in: The New York Times of April 14, 2011, p. A1

Morin, Edgar (2008) Pour une Politique de Civilisation. Arléa, Paris

Morison, Samuel Eliot/Commager, Henry Steele/Leuchtenburg, William E. (1983) A concise History of the American Republic. Oxford University Press, New York – Oxford

Morris, Thomas D. (1996) Southern Slavery and the Law, 1619-1860. University of North Carolina Press, Chappel Hill – London

Morton, Richard L. (1960) Colonial Virginia. University of North Carolina Press, Chapel Hill

Mouffe, Chantal (1998) Für eine anti-essentialistische Konzeption feministischer Politik, in: Deutsche Zeitschrift für Philosophie 5/98, pp. 841-848

Mullen, Kevin J. (1989) Let Justice be done. University of Nevada Press, Reno – Las Vegas

Müller, Jörg Paul (1999) Der politische Mensch – menschliche Politik. Helbing & Lichtenhahn Verlag, Basel – Genf

Münch, Richard (1976) Legitimität und politische Macht. Westdeutscher Verlag, Opladen

Münch, Richard (1994) Politik und Nichtpolitik. Politische Steuerung als schöpferischer Prozess, in: Kölner Zeitschrift für Soziologie und Sozialpsychologie 3/1994, pp. 381-405

Münk, Dieter (1993) Die Organisation des Raumes im Nationalsozialismus. Pahl-Rugenstein, Bonn

Murphy, Walter F. (1995) Merlin's Memory, in: Levinson, Sanford (ed) Responding to Imperfection, pp. 163-190. Princeton University Press, New Jersey

Murray, Martin J. (1994) Revolution Deferred. Verso, London

Myrdal, Gunnar (1996) An American Dilemma. Transaction Publishers, New Brunswick

Nairn, Tom (1997) Faces of Nationalism. Verso Publishers, London

Nassehi, Armin (2004) ICH-Identität paradox, in: Nollmann, Gerd/Strasser, Hermann (ed) Das individualisierte Ich in der modernen Gesellschaft, pp. 29-44. Campus Verlag, Frankfurt am Main

National Geographic Society (1993) Menschenaffen. Reise- und Verkehrsverlag, Berlin

Neckel, Sighard (1992) Das lokale Staatsorgan. Kommunale Herrschaft im Staatssozialismus der DDR, in: Zeitschrift für Soziologie 4/92, pp. 252-268

Neckel, Sighard (1999) Blanker Neid, blinde Wut?, in: Leviathan 2/1999, pp. 145-165

Neckel, Sighard (2003) Kamp um Zugehörigkeit, in: Leviathan 2/2003, pp. 159-167

Nerdinger, Winfried (2004) Architektur – Macht – Erinnerung. Prestel Verlag, München – Berlin – London – New York

New York City WPA Writer's Project (2004) A maritime History of New York. Going Coastal, New York

Newell, Margaret Ellen (1998) From Dependency to Independency. Cornell University Press, Ithaca – London

Newman, Alizabeth (1992) For richer, for poorer, till death do us part: India's response to dowry deaths, in: ILSA Journal of International Law XV/1992, pp. 109 ff.

Newmark, Harris (1916) Sixty Years in Southern California. The Knickerbocker Press, New York

Newton, Michael (2010) The Ku Klux Klan in Mississippi. McFarland & Company, Jefferson

Newton, William R. (2000) L'espace du roi. Librairie Arthème Fayard, Paris

Nichols, John (2011) Wisconsin's political Crisis is a good Deal more serious than its fiscal Crisis, in: The Nation of February 21, 2011 (http://www.thenation.com/blog/158776/wisconsins-political-crisis-good-deal-more-serious-its-fiscal-crisis), retrieved on July 26, 2011

Nicolet, Claude (1992) La République en France. Éditions du Seuil, Paris

Nietzsche, Friedrich (1996) Der Wille zur Macht. Kröner Verlag, Stuttgart

Nollert, Michael (2005) Waging the War of Ideas, in: Imhof, Kurt/Eberle, Thomas (ed) Triumph und Elend des Neoliberalismus, pp. 39-58. Seismo Verlag, Zürich

Norris, Clive/Armstrong, Gary (1999) The Maximum Surveillance Society. Berg, Oxford

Norton, Mary Beth (2002) In the Devil's Snare. Alfred A. Knopf, New York

Nozick, Robert (1974) Anarchy, State, and Utopia. Basic Books, New York

Nozick, Robert (1981) Philosophical Explanations. Harvard University Press, Cambridge

O'Neill, Onora (1993) Wie wissen wir, wann Chancen gleich sind?, in: Rössler, Beate (ed) Quotierung und Gerechtigkeit, pp. 144-157. Campus Verlag, Frankfurt am Main – New York

Offe, Claus (2001) Wie können wir unseren Mitbürgern vertrauen?, in: Hartmann, Martin/Offe, Claus (ed) Vertrauen, pp. 241-294. Campus Verlag, Frankfurt am Main

Ong, Walter J. (1982) Oralität und Literalität. Opladen

Onuf, Peter S. (2008) Introduction, in: Dupont, Christian Y./Onuf, Peter S. (ed) Declaring Independence, pp. IX-XII. University of Virginia Library, Charlottesville

Osgood, Herbert L. (1907) The American Colonies in the seventeenth Century. The Macmillan Company, New York

Osofsky, Gilbert (1971) Harlem – The Making of a Ghetto. Harper & Row, New York

Osterloh, Margit/Weibel, Antoinette (2006) Investition Vertrauen. Betriebswirtschaftlicher Verlag, Wiesbaden

Pamuk, Orhan (2005) Schnee. Hanser Verlag, München

Parekh, Bhikhu (1998) Integrating Minorities, in: Blackstone, Tessa/Parekh, Bhikhu/Sanders, Peter (ed) Race Relations in Britain, pp. 1-21. Routledge, New York

Parker, Peter/Mokhesi-Parker, Joyce (1998) In the shadow of Sharpeville. New York University Press, New York

Parkinson, Robert (2008) Twenty-seven reasons for Independence, in: Dupont, Christian Y./Onuf, Peter S. (ed) Declaring Independence, pp. 11-18. University of Virginia Library, Charlottesville

Parsons, Talcott (1986) Aktor, Situation und normative Muster. Suhrkamp Verlag, Frankfurt am Main

Pascal, Blaise (1977) Pensées; ed of Michel Le Guern. Éditions Gallimard, Paris

Pascal, Blaise (1995) Pensées – A new translation by Honor Levi. Oxford University Press, Oxford

Paugam, Serge (1998) Poverty and Social Exclusion, in: Rhodes, Martin/Mény, Yves (ed) The Future of European Welfare, pp. 41-62. MacMillan Press, London

Pernthaler, Peter (1996) Allgemeine Staatslehre und Verfassungslehre. Springer Verlag, Wien – New York

Persad, Govind/Wertheimer, Alan/Emanuel, Ezekiel J. (2009) Principles for allocation of scarce medical interventions, in: Lancet 2009, 373, pp. 423-431

Petermann, Franz (1996) Psychologie des Vertrauens. Hogrefe Verlag, Göttingen

Peters, Bernhard (1993) Die Integration moderner Gesellschaften. Suhrkamp Verlag, Frankfurt am Main

Peters, Helge (1989) Devianz und soziale Kontrolle. Juventa Verlag, Weinheim – München

Peterson, Mark A. (2005) The Practice of Piety in Puritan New England, in: Bremer, Francis J./Botelho, Lynn A. (ed) The World of John Winthrop, pp. 75-110, Boston

Petitfils, Jean-Christian (2002) Louis XIV. Librairie Perrin, Paris

Philbrick, Nathaniel (2006) Mayflower. Penguin Books, New York

Phillipson, Michael (1974) Die Paradoxie der sozialen Kontrolle und die Normalität des Verbrechens, in: Lüderssen, Klaus/Sack, Fritz (ed) Seminar: Abweichendes Verhalten 1. Die selektiven Normen der Gesellschaft, pp. 126-145. Suhrkamp Verlag, Frankfurt am Main

Pisani, Donald J. (1994) Squatter Law in California, 1850-1858, in: The Western Historical Quarterly 3/1994, pp. 277-310

Plumelle-Uribe, Rosa Amelia (2001) La Férocité Blanche. Éditions Albin Michel, Paris

Popper, Karl R. (1979) Objective Knowledge. Oxford University Press, New York

Popper, Karl R. (1994a) Alles Leben ist Problemlösen. Piper Verlag, München

Popper, Karl R. (1994b) Auf der Suche nach einer besseren Welt. Piper Verlag, München

Popper, Karl R./Eccles, John C. (1996) Das Ich und sein Gehirn. Piper Verlag, München

Porter, Roy (2000) London – a Social History. Penguin Books, London

Posel, Deborah (1987) The Meaning of Apartheid before 1948, in: Journal of Southern African Studies, 1/1987, pp. 123-139

Postman, Neil (1999) Die zweite Aufklärung. Berlin Verlag, Berlin

Potter, Wendell (2009a) The health care Industry vs. health Reform, on: prwatch.org, June 24, 2009 (http://www.prwatch.org/node/8422), retrieved on July 26, 2011

Potter, Wendell (2009b) "Bill Moyers Journal" of July 10, 2009, Transcript (http://www.pbs.org/moyers/journal/07102009/profile.html), retrieved on July 26, 2011

Potter, Wendell (2009c) Testimony before the U. Senate Committee on Commerce, Science and Transportation of June 24, 2009 (http://voices.washingtonpost.com/ezra-klein/Potter%20Commerce%20Committee%20written%20testimony%20-%2020090624-%20FINAL.pdf), retrieved on July 26, 2011

Preston, Paul (1993) Franco. Harper Collins Publishers, London

Preston, Paul (2004) Juan Carlos. Harper Collins Publishers, London

Pusch, Luise F. (1984) Das Deutsche als Männersprache. Suhrkamp Verlag, Frankfurt am Main

Quill, Timothy E. (2005) Terri Schiavo – A Tragedy Compounded, in: New England Journal of Medicine of April 21, 2005, pp. 1630-1633

Radbruch, Gustav (2006 [1945]) Five Minutes of Legal Philosophy (1945), in: Oxford Journal of Legal Studies, Vol. 26, No. 1 (2006), pp. 13–15

Rammstedt, Otthein (ed) (2003) Georg Simmels Philosophie des Geldes. Suhrkamp Taschenbuchverlag, Frankfurt am Main

Rashid, Ahmed (2009) Descent into Chaos. Penguin Books, London

Ratcliffe, Donald (2010) The State of the Union, 1776-1860, in: Grant, Susan-Mary/Holden Reid, Brian: The American Civil War, pp. 3-35. Pearson Education, Harlow

Rauchway, Eric (2008) The Great Depression & the New Deal. Oxford University Press, New York

Rauer, Valentin (2004) Ausländerghettos und die neue multiethnische Mittelklasse, in: Eder, Klaus/Rauer, Valentin/Schmidtke, Oliver (ed) Die Einhegung des Anderen, pp. 99-130. VS Verlag für Sozialwissenschaften, Wiesbaden

Rawls, John (1993) Gerechtigkeit als Fairness – politisch und nicht metaphysisch, in: Honneth, Axel (ed) Kommunitarismus, pp. 36-67. Campus Verlag, Frankfurt am Main – New York

Reagan, Ronald (1981) Inaugural Address of January 20, 1981

Reagan, Ronald (1982) Speech about the Caribbean at the Organization of American States, 1. Januar 1982

Reich, Kersten (1998) Die Ordnung der Blicke. Perspektiven des interaktionistischen Konstruktivismus, Band 2. Luchterhand Verlag, Neuwied

Reichel, Peter (1996) Berlin nach 1945 – eine Erinnerungslandschaft zwischen Gedächtnis-Verlust und Gedächtnis-Inszenierung, in: Hipp, Hermann/Seidl, Ernst (ed) Architektur als politische Kultur: philosophia practica, pp. 273-296. Reimer Verlag, Berlin

Remini, Robert V. (2010) At the Edge of the Precipice. Basic Books, New York

Renan, Ernest (1875) La Réforme intellectuelle et morale. Michel Lévy Frères, Paris

Renshaw, Patrick (2004) Franklin D. Roosevelt. Pearson Education, Harlow

Renz, Ursula/Bleisch, Barbara (ed) (2007) Zu wenig. Seismo Verlag, Zürich

Rhodes, Cecil (1900) His political Life and Speeches. Chapman and Hall, London

Richard, Guy (1979) Les Institutions politiques de la France. Flammarion, Paris

Richards, Michael (1998) A Time of Silence. Cambridge University Press, Cambridge

Richards, Rand (2007) Historic San Francisco. Heritage House Publishers, San Francisco

Richards, Rand (2009) Mud, Blood, and Gold. Heritage House Publishers, San Francisco

Riesebrodt, Martin (1988) Fundamentalismus und Modernisierung. Zur Soziologie protestantisch-fundamentalistischer Bewegungen in den USA im 20. Jahrhundert, in: Kodalle, Klaus-M. (ed) Gott und Politik in USA, pp. 112-125. Athenäum Verlag, Frankfurt am Main

Rifkin, Jeremy (2000) The Age of Access. Penguin Putnam, New York

Rigaud, Jacques (1995) L'Exception culturelle. Éditions Grasset & Fasquelle, Paris

Rischin, Moses (1977) The promised City. Harvard University Press, Harvard

Rives, George Lockhart (1913) The United States and Mexico – 1821-1848. Charles Scribner's Sons, New York

Roach, Marilynne K. (2004) The Salem Witch Trials. Taylor Trade Publishing, Lanham

Rockefeller, Steven C. (1992) Kommentar, in: Taylor, Charles: Multikulturalismus und die Politik der Anerkennung, pp. 96-108. Fischer Verlag, Frankfurt am Main

Rödel, Ulrich/Frankenberg, Günter/Dubiel, Helmut (1989) Die demokratische Frage. Suhrkamp Verlag, Frankfurt am Main

Roeck, Bernd (1996) Die Ohnmacht des Dogen und die Macht der Kunst, in: Hipp, Hermann/Seidl, Ernst (ed) Architektur als politische Kultur: philosophia practica, pp. 79-92. Reimer Verlag, Berlin

Rogers, Barbara (1976) Divide & Rule. International Defence & Aid Fund, London

Roloff, Juliane (1997) Schwangerschaftsabbruch in West- und Ostdeutschland. Bundesinstitut für Bevölkerungsforschung, Wiesbaden

Rolston, Bill (1998) Drawing Support 2. BTP Publications, Conway Mill

Romani, Rose (1989) Ein Mahnmal für alle Opfer, in: Die Zeit vom 28.4.1989, Nr. 18 (http://www.zeit.de/1989/18/ein-mahnmal-fuer-alle-opfer), retrieved on July 26, 2011

Rorty, Richard (1989) Kontingenz, Ironie und Solidarität. Suhrkamp Verlag, Frankfurt am Main

Rorty, Richard (1994) Hoffnung statt Erkenntnis. Passagen Verlag, Wien

Rosa, Hartmut (2006) Wettbewerb als Interaktionsmodus, in: Leviathan 1/2006, pp. 82-104

Rosanvallon, Pierre (1998) Le peuple introuvable. Editions Gallimard, Paris

Rose, Brian W. (1965) Bantu Education as a Facet of South African Policy, in: Comparative Education Review 2/1965, pp. 208-212

Rose, Michael E. (1988) The disappearing pauper, in: Sigsworth, Eric (ed) In search of Victorian Values, pp. 57-72. Manchester University Press, Manchester

Rosen, Elliot A. (2005) Roosevelt, the Great Depression, and the Economics of Recovery. University of Virginia Press, Charlottesville

Rosenthal, Bernard (ed) (2009) Records of the Salem Witch-Hunt. Cambridge University Press, Cambridge

Rössler, Beate (ed) (1993) Quotierung und Gerechtigkeit. Campus Verlag, Frankfurt am Main – New York

Royce, Josiah (1898) Studies of Good and Evil. Appleton and Company, New York

Rozenberg, Danielle (2003) Mémoire et oubli dans la construction démocratique espagnole, in: Dulphy, Anne & Léonard, Yves (ed) De la dictature à la démocratie – voies ibériques, pp. 167-184. P.I.E.-Peter Lang, Bruxelles

Rubin, Barnett R. (2007) Saving Afghanistan, in: Foreign Affairs of January/February 2007 (http://www.foreignaffairs.com/articles/62270/barnett-r-rubin/saving-afghanistan), retrieved on July 26, 2011

Rucht, Dieter (1994) Öffentlichkeit als Mobilisierungsfaktor für soziale Bewegungen, in: Neidhardt, Friedhelm (ed) Öffentlichkeit, öffentliche Meinung, soziale Bewegungen, pp. 337-358. Westdeutscher Verlag, Opladen

Rufer, Marc (1988) IrrSinn Psychiatrie. Zytglogge Verlag, Bern

Rüssmann, Kirsten et. al (2010) Soziale Desintegration und Bindungsstil als Determinanten von Fremdenfeindlichkeit, in: Zeitschrift für Soziologie 4/2010, pp. 281-301

Rüthers, Bernd (1989) Entartetes Recht. Beck Verlag, München

Rüthers, Bernd (1995) Die Wende-Experten. Beck Verlag, München

Ryffel, Hans (1969) Grundprobleme der Rechts- und Staatsphilosophie. Luchterhand Verlag, Neuwied bei Berlin

Ryffel, Hans (1978) Recht und Ethik heute, in: Kaulbach, Friedrich/Krawietz, Werner (ed) Recht und Gesellschaft, pp. 507-525. Duncker & Humblot Verlag, Berlin

Sackmann, Rosemarie (2004) Zuwanderung und Integration. VS Verlag für Sozialwissenschaften, Wiesbaden

Sala-Molins, Louis (2005) Le Code Noir. Quadrige, Paris

Samuelson, Paul A./Nordhaus, William D. (2001) Economics, Boston

Sandel, Michael (1984) The Procedural Republic and the Unencumbered Self, in: Political Theory 12/1984, pp. 81-96

Sartre, Jean-Paul (1943) L'être et le néant. Éditions Gallimard, Paris

Sartre, Jean-Paul (1996) L'existentialisme est un humanisme. Editions Gallimard, Paris

Sassen, Saskia (2006) Territory – Authority – Rights. Princeton University Press, Princeton – Oxford

Sax, Leonard (2002) How Common Is Intersex?, in: The Journal of Sex Research, 3/2002, pp. 174-178

Scheer, Léo (1994) La Démocratie virtuelle. Flammarion, Paris

Scheerer, Sebastian (2002) Die Zukunft des Terrorismus. Zu Klampen Verlag, Lüneburg

Schlee, Beatrice (2009) Endstation Vergangenheit?, in: Schmidt, Siegmar u.a. (ed) Amnesie, Amnestie oder Aufarbeitung?, pp. 203-228. VS Verlag für Sozialwissenschaften, Wiesbaden

Schmitt, Carl (1933) Der Begriff des Politischen. Hanseatische Verlagsanstalt, Hamburg

Schmölzer, Hilde (1990) Die verlorene Geschichte der Frau. Edition Tau, Mattersburg – Bad Sauerbrunn

Schneider, Wolf (1989) Wörter machen Leute. Piper Verlag, München

Schnepf, Robert (2007) "Armut ohne Bedürftigkeit ist ein Gut"|, in: Renz, Ursula/Bleisch, Barbara (ed) Zu wenig, pp. 110-135. Seismo Verlag, Zürich

Schoelcher, Victor (1998 [1842]) Des colonies françaises, abolition immédiate de l'esclavage. Paris

Schoen, Brian (2009) The fragile Fabric of Union. Johns Hopkins University Press, Baltimore

Schopenhauer, Arthur (1987) Die Welt als Wille und Vorstellung, Volume 1. Cotta-Insel Verlag, Frankfurt am Main

Schroer, Markus (2000) Gewalt ohne Gesicht, in: Leviathan 4/2000, pp. 434-451

Schroer, Markus (2001) Die im Dunkeln sieht man doch, in: Mittelweg 35 5/2001, pp. 33-46

Schroer, Markus (2006) Räume, Orte, Grenzen. Suhrkamp Taschenbuchverlag, Frankfurt am Main

Schülein, Johann August (1990) Die Geburt der Eltern. Westdeutscher Verlag, Opladen

Schultz, Hans-Dietrich (2004) Die Türkei: (k)ein Teil des geographischen Europas?, in: Leggewie, Claus (ed) Die Türkei und Europa, pp. 39-53. Suhrkamp Verlag, Frankfurt am Main

Schulze, Hagen (1994) Staat und Nation in der europäischen Geschichte. Beck Verlag, München

Schulze, Hans K. (1998) Grundstrukturen der Verfassung im Mittelalter, Band 1. Kohlhammer, Stuttgart – Berlin – Köln

Schulze, Hans K. (2000) Grundstrukturen der Verfassung im Mittelalter, Band 2. Kohlhammer, Stuttgart – Berlin – Köln

Schwarberg, Günther (1997) Der SS-Arzt und die Kinder vom Bullenhuser Damm. Steidl Verlag, Göttingen

Schwinn, Thomas (1997) Die Entstehung neuer Ordnungen im antiken Griechenland, in: Kölner Zeitschrift für Soziologie und Sozialpsychologie 3/1997, pp. 391-409

Seidl, Ernst (1996) Monument im Dienst der Demokratie?, in: Hipp, Hermann/Seidl, Ernst (ed) Architektur als politische Kultur: philosophia practica, pp. 311-326. Reimer Verlag, Berlin

Seiler, Hansjörg (1994) Gewaltenteilung. Staempfli Verlag, Bern

Seligman, Martin E.P. (1999) Erlernte Hilflosigkeit. Beltz Verlag, Weinheim – Basel

Sen, Amartya (1999) Development as Freedom. Oxford University Press, Oxford

Sen, Amartya (2006) Identity & Violence. Penguin Books, London

Senkewicz, Robert M. (1985) Vigilantes in gold rush San Francisco. Standford University Press, Stanford

Sennett, Richard (1998) The Corrosion of Character. W. W. Norton & Company, New York

Sennett, Richard (2003) Respect. Norton & Company, New York

Sennett, Richard (2006) The Culture of the New Capitalism. Yale University Press, New Haven – London

Shammas, Carole (1979) English-Born and Creole Elites in turn-ofthe-century Virginia, in: Tate, Thad W./Ammerman, David L.: The Chesapeake in the Seventeenth Century, pp. 274-296. University of North Carolina Press, Chapel Hill

Shaw, Malcolm N. (2003) International Law. Cambridge University Press, Cambdrige

Shorto, Russell (2007) New York. Rowohlt Taschenbuch Verlag, Reinbek bei Hamburg

Shyaka, Anastase (2005) The Rwandan Conflict – Origin, Development, Exit Strategies, NURC 2005 (http://www.grandslacs.net/doc/3833.pdf), retrieved on July 26, 2011

Silber, Nina (2009) Emancipation without Slavery, in: Cooper, William J./McCardell, John M.: In the Cause of Liberty, pp. 105-125. Louisiana State University Press, Baton Rouge

Simmel, Georg (1992) Soziologie. Suhrkamp Verlag, Frankfurt am Main

Simon-Muscheid, Katharina (2002) Missbrauchte Gaben, in: Gilomen, Hans-Jörg/Guex, Sébastien/Studer, Brigitte (ed) Von der Barmherzigkeit zur Sozialversicherung, pp. 153-165. Chronos Verlag, Zürich

Skinner, Benjamin E. (2008) A Crime so Monstrous. Mainstream Publishing, Edinburgh – London

Sloane, Hans (1706) A Voyage to the Islands, Vol. I, London

Sloterdijk, Peter (2008) Theorie der Nachkriegszeiten. Suhrkamp Taschenbuchverlag, Frankfurt am Main

Sluga, Glenda (1999) Italian National Memory, National Identity and Fascism, in: Bosworth, R.J.B./Dogliani, Patrizia (ed) Italian Fascism – History, Memory, and Representation, pp. 178-194. Palgrave, Houndmills

Smith, Adam (1980 [1795]) The Principles which lead and direct philosophical Enquiries; illustrated by the History of ancient Physics, in: Essays on philosophical Subjects, pp. 106-117, Oxford

Smith, Adam (1994 [1776]) The Wealth of Nations. Random House – Modern Library Edition, New York

Smith, Adam (2006 [1759]). The Theory of Moral Sentiments, Mineaola: Dover Publications

Smith, Adam I. P. (2007) The American Civil War. Palgrave Macmillan, Houndmills

Sofsky, Wolfgang (1993) Die Ordnung des Terrors: Das Konzentrationslager. Fischer Verlag, Frankfurt am Main

Sofsky, Wolfgang/Paris, Rainer (1994) Figurationen sozialer Macht. Suhrkamp Verlag, Frankfurt am Main

Solnon, Jean-François (1987) La Cour de France. Librairie Arthème Fayard, Paris

Soros, George (2008) The new Paradigm for financial Markets. Public Affairs, New York

Spescha, Marc (1988) Rechtsbruch und sozialer Wandel. Duncker & Humblot Verlag, Berlin

Spescha, Marc (2002) Zukunft Ausländer. Haupt Verlag, Bern

Starck, Christian (1990) Zur Notwendigkeit einer Wertbegründung des Rechts, in: Dreier, Ralf (ed) Rechtspositivismus und Wertbezug des Rechts. Franz Steiner Verlag, Stuttgart

Starr, Kevin (2005) California. Random House, New York

Steiner, Udo (1995) Das zweite Grundsatzurteil zum Schwangerschaftsabbruch, in: Piazolo, Michael (ed) Das Bundesverfassungsgericht, pp. 107-124. Hase & Koehler Verlag, Mainz – München

Stevenson, Adlai (1952) Speech to the American Legion convention in New York City on August 27, 1952

Stewart, George R. (1964) Committee of Vigilance. Houghton Mifflin, Boston

Stiglitz, Joseph (2002) Die Schatten der Globalisierung. Siedler Verlag, Berlin

Stöger, Roman (1997) Der neoliberale Staat. Deutscher Universitäts Verlag, Wiesbaden

Stone, Ilene/Grenz, Suzanna M. (2005) Jessie Benton Frémont. University of Missouri Press, Columbia

Strange, Susan (1998) Mad Money. University of Michigan Press, Manchester

Strauss, Botho (1999) Der Aufstand gegen die sekundäre Welt. Carl Hanser Verlag, München – Wien

Study Commission on U.S. Policy toward Southern Africa (1981) South Africa: Time running out. University of California Press, Berkeley

Sullivan, Kathleen M. (2000) Amending Process – Update, in: Levy, Leonard W./Karst, Kenneth L.: Encyclopedia of the American Constitution, Volume 1, 2. edition. Macmillan Publishers, New York

Süskind, Patrick (1985) Das Parfum. Diogenes Verlag, Zürich

Sztompka, Piotr (1995) Vertrauen – Die fehlende Ressource in der postkommunistischen Gesellschaft, in: Nedelmann, Birgitta (ed) Politische Institutionen im Wandel, pp. 254-276. Westdeutscher Verlag, Opladen

Taft, William Howard (1916) Our chief Magistrate and his Powers. Columbia University Press, New York

Takahashi, Lois M. (1998) Homelessness, AIDS, and Stigmatization. Oxford University Press, New York

Taleb, Nassim Nicholas (2008) The Black Swan. Penguin Books, New York

Tamanaha, Brian Z. (2006) Law as a Means to an End. Cambridge University Press, Cambridge

Tanner, Jakob (2007) Der Kampf gegen die Armut, in: Renz, Ursula/Bleisch, Barbara (ed) Zu wenig, pp. 80-109. Seismo Verlag, Zürich

Tatz, Colin (2003) With Intent to destroy. Verso Publishers, London

Taylor, Alan (2001) American Colonies. Penguin Books, New York

Taylor, Charles (1988) Negative Freiheit? Suhrkamp Verlag, Frankfurt am Main

Taylor, Charles (1992) Multiculturalism and "The Politics of Recognition. Princeton University Press, Princeton

Taylor, Charles (1995) Philosophical arguments. Harvard University Press, Cambdrige

Tenzer, Nicolas/Delacroix, Rodolphe (1992) Les élites et la fin de la démocratie française. Presses Universitaires de France, Paris

Terray, Emmanuel (2004) Interview, in: Europäisches BürgerInnenforum CEDRI (ed) Bittere Ernte, pp. 121-126. Verlag Europäisches Bürgerforum, Basel

Teubner, Gunther (1989) Recht als autopoietisches System. Suhrkamp Verlag, Frankfurt am Main

Thatcher, Margaret (1987) Interview for Woman's Own, 23.9.1987 (http://www.margaretthatcher.org/document/106689), retrieved on July 26, 2011

Thoreau, Henry D. (2008) Walden, Civil Disobedience and Other Writings. W. W. Norton & Company, New York

Thuau, Etienne (2000) Raison d'État et pensée politique à l'époque de Richelieu. Éditions Albin Michel, Paris

Thurer, Shari (1995) Mythos Mutterschaft. Droemer Knauer Verlag, München

Todorov, Tzvetan (1996) Abenteuer des Zusammenlebens. Versuch einer allgemeinen Anthropologie. Verlag Klaus Wagenbach, Berlin

Tönnies, Ferdinand (1991) Gemeinschaft und Gesellschaft. Wissenschaftliche Buchgesellschaft, Darmstadt

Traoré, Aminata (2002) Le viol de l'Imaginaire. Librairie Arthème Fayard et Actes Sud, Paris

Trelease, Allen W. (1971) White Terror. Louisiana State University Press, Baton Rouge – London

Trömel-Plötz, Senta (1992) Vatersprache – Mutterland. Frauenoffensive, München

Trömel-Plötz, Senta (ed) (1984) Gewalt durch Sprache. Fischer Verlag, Frankfurt am Main

Tschannen, Pierre (1995) Stimmrecht und politische Verständigung. Helbing & Lichtenhahn Verlag, Basel – Frankfurt am Main

Turkle, Sherry (1995) Life on the Screen. Simon & Schuster, New York

Tusell, Javier/Queipo de Llano, Genoveva (2000) The dictatorship of Primo de Rivera, in: Alvarez Junco, José/Shubert, Adrian (ed) Spanish History since 1808, pp. 207-220. Hodder Education, London

Twenge, Jean M./Foster, Joshua D. (2010) Birth Cohort Increases in Narcissistic Personality Traits Among American College Students, 1982–2009, in: Social Psychological and Personality Science 1/2010, pp. 99-106

Urofsky, Melvin (2000) Reconstruction, in: Levy, Leonard W./Karst, Kenneth L.: Encyclopedia of the American Constitution, Volume 5, 2. ed. Macmillan Publishers, New York

Vacarie, Isabelle/Allouache, Anissa/Ginon, Anne-Sophie/Ferkane, Ylias/Leroy, Sonia (2008) Crise de l'État-providence ou crise de la régulation économique?, in: Droit Social 11/2008, pp. 1103-1114

Vairan, Hal R./Buchegger, Reiner (2007) Grundzüge der Mikroökonomik. München

Valentine, Alan (1956) Vigilante Justice. Reynal & Company, New York

Valeri, Mark (2005) Puritans in the Marketplace, in: Bremer, Francis J./Botelho, Lynn A. (ed) The World of John Winthrop, pp. 147-186. University of Virginia Press, Boston

van Wolferen, Karel (1989) Vom Mythos der Unbesiegbaren. Droemersche Verlagsanstalt, München

Vaughan, Alden T. (1978) "Expulsion of the Savages" – English Policy and the Virginia Massacre of 1622, in: The William and Mary Quarterly 35, 1/1978, pp. 57-84

Verlet, Pierre (1998) Le Château de Versailles. Librairie Arthème Fayard, Paris

Vester, Michael (1997) Kapitalistische Modernisierung und gesellschaftliche (Des-)Integration, in: Heitmeyer, Wilhelm (ed) Was hält die Gesellschaft zusammen?, pp. 149-203. Suhrkamp Verlag, Frankfurt am Main

Vilas, Carlos (1996) Neoliberals Social Policy – Managing Poverty (Somehow), in: NACLA Report on the Americas of June 19, 1996, pp. 16-25

Vile, John R. (1995) The Case against implicite Limits, in: Levinson, Sanford (ed) Responding to Imperfection, pp. 191-213. Princeton University Press, New Jersey

Vile, John R. (1997) A Companion to the United States Constitution and its Amendments. Praeger Publishers, Westport

Vivaldi, Elisabetta (2009) Der Wind der Intoleranz, in: pogrom – bedrohte Völker 254 (3/2009)

von Beyme, Klaus (1996) Politische Ikonologie der Architektur, in: Hipp, Hermann/Seidl, Ernst (ed) Architektur als politische Kultur: philosophia practica, pp. 19-34. Reimer Verlag, Berlin

von Beyme, Klaus (1998) Kulturpolitik und nationale Identität. Westdeutscher Verlag, Opladen – Wiesbaden

von Cube, Felix (2001) Fordern statt verwöhnen – die Erkenntnisse der Verhaltensbiologie in der Erziehung. Piper Verlag, München

von Til, L. John (1972) Liberty of Conscience. Presbyterian and Reformed publishing Company, Nutley

Wade, Wyn Craig (1987) The fiery Cross. Oxford University Press, New York – Oxford

Wagner, Gerhard (1996) Differenzierung als absoluter Begriff? Zur Revision einer soziologischen Kategorie, in: Zeitschrift für Soziologie 2/1996

Waldenfels, Bernhard (1998) Der Stachel des Fremden. Suhrkamp Verlag, Frankfurt am Main

Waldenfels, Bernhard (1999) Topographie des Fremden. Suhrkamp Verlag, Frankfurt am Main

Walsh, Lorena S. (1979) "Till Death us do part", in: Tate, Thad W./Ammerman, David L.: The Chesapeake in the Seventeenth Century, pp. 126-152. University of North Carolina Press, Chapel Hill

Warnke, Martin (1984) Einführung, in: Politische Architektur in Europa vom Mittelalter bis heute – Repräsentation und Gemeinschaft, pp. 7-18. DuMont, Köln

Warnke, Martin (1996) Bau und Gegenbau, in: Hipp, Hermann/Seidl, Ernst (ed) Architektur als politische Kultur: philosophia practica, pp. 11-18. Reimer Verlag, Berlin

Warren, Elizabeth/Warren Tyagi, Amelia (2003) The Two-Income Trap. Perseus Books, New York

Watkins, John W. N. (1959) Historical Explanation in the Social Sciences, in: Gardiner, Patrick: Theories of History, pp. 503-514. Free Press, Glencoe

Weber, Max (1960) Rechtssoziologie. Hermann Luchterhand Verlag, Neuwied

Weber, Max (1973) Soziologie – Universalgeschichtliche Analysen – Politik. Kroener Verlag, Stuttgart

Weber, Max (1980) Wirtschaft und Gesellschaft. Mohr Verlag, Tübingen

Weisman, Richard (1984) Witchcraft, Magic, and Religion in 17th-Century Massachusetts. University of Massachusetts Press, Amherst

Weiss, Johannes (1993) Vernunft und Vernichtung. Zur Philosophie und Soziologie der Moderne. Westdeutscher Verlag, Opladen

Werlen, Benno (1997) Gesellschaft, Handlung und Raum. Franz Steiner Verlag, Stuttgart

Wesel, Uwe (1985) Frühformen des Rechts in vorstaatlichen Gesellschaften. Suhrkamp Verlag, Frankfurt am Main

Wiebe, Robert H. (1967) The Search for Order – 1877-1920. Hill and Wang, New York

Wiecek, William M. (2000) Black Codes, in: Levy, Leonard W./Karst, Kenneth L.: Encyclopedia of the American Constitution, Volume 1. Macmillan Publishers, New York

Wierlacher, Alois (1993) Kulturwissenschaftliche Xenologie, in: Wierlacher, Alois (ed) Kulturthema Fremdheit. iudicum Verlag, München

Wiese, Harald (1994) Ökonomie des Lügens und Betrügens, in: Kölner Zeitschrift für Soziologie und Sozialpsychologie 1/1994, pp. 65-79

Wieviorka, Michel (2001) Nationalismus, Populismus, Ethnizität, in: Mittelweg 36, 5/2001, pp. 75-90

Wilde, Oscar (2005) De Profundis, in: The Complete Works of Oscar Wilde, Volume 2, pp. 157-193. Oxford University Press, Oxford

Wilder, Craig Steven (2000) A Covenant with Color. Columbia University Press, New York

Wilentz, Sean (2009) Why did Southerners Secede?, in: Cooper, William J./McCardell, John M.: In the Cause of Liberty, pp. 25-39. Louisiana State University Press, Baton Rouge

Williams, Mary Floyd (1921) History of the San Francisco Committee of Vigilance of 1851. University of California Press, Berkeley

Willke, Helmut (1992) Ironie des Staates. Suhrkamp Verlag, Frankfurt am Main

Wilson, Francis (1972) Labour in the South African Gold Mines 1911-1969. Cambridge University Press, Cambdrige

Wilson, Lory Lee (1997) The Salem Witch Trials. Lerner Publications Company, Minneapolis

Wilson, Richard A. (2001) The Politics of Truth and Reconciliation in South Africa. Cambridge University Press, Cambridge

Wittgenstein, Ludwig (1992) Über Gewissheit. Suhrkamp Verlag, Frankfurt am Main

Wittgenstein, Ludwig (1995) Werkausgabe. Band 1: 1. Tractatus logico-philosophicus; 2. Tagebücher 1914-1916; 3. Philosophische Untersuchungen. Suhrkamp Verlag, Frankfurt am Main

Woll, Artur (2000) Allgemeine Wirtschaftslehre. München

Wolton, Dominique (1998) La Ville, l'Espace public et la Politique, in: Charzat, Michel: Le Paris cotoyen, pp. 167-195. Editions Stock, Paris

Wood, Amy Louise (2009) Lynching and Spectacle. University of North Carolina Press, Chapel Hill

Wood, Gordon S. (1993) The Creation of the American Republic. Norton & Company, New York – London

Wood, Gordon S. (2005) The American Revolution. Phoenix, London

Wood, Gordon S. (2006) Revolutionary Characters. Penguin Books, New York

Woods, Thomas E./Gutzman, Kevin R.C. (2008) Who killed the Constitution? Three Rivers Press, New York

Worden, Nigel (2007) The Making of modern South Africa. Blackwell Publishers, Oxford

Wright, Les (1999) San Francisco, in: Higgs, David (ed) Queer Sites – Gay urban histories since 1600, pp. 164-189. Routledge, London – New York

Yergin, Daniel/Stanislaw, Joseph (1998) The Commanding Heights. Simon & Schuster, New York

Zedler, Johann Heinrich (1732-1754) Grosses vollständiges Universal-Lexikon. Halle – Leipzig

Zernike, Kate (2010) Boiling mad. Times Books, New York

Zhou, Min/Bankston, Carl L. III (1998) Growing Up American. Russell Sage Foundation, New York

Zingerle, Arnold (1993) Fremdheit und Verfremdung, in: Wierlacher, Alois (ed) Kulturthema Fremdheit. iudicum Verlag, München

Zinn, Howard (1999) A people's History of the United States. New York

Zippelius, Reinhold (1994) Recht und Gerechtigkeit in der offenen Gesellschaft. Duncker & Humblot Verlag, Berlin

Zola, Émile (1979) Thérèse Raquin. Editions Gallimard, Paris

Zollinger, James P. (1939) Sutter – The Man and his Empire. New York

Index

A

Abnormality 71–73, 149, 157, 213. *See also* Deviant behavior
Aborigines 104
Absolutism 76, 214–215, 237, 332, 391. *See also* Economic absolutism
Académie française 389
Africa 344
Alternatives, need for 9, 25, 43, 59, 62, 74, 86, 141–149, 318, 322
Altruism 17–18, 86
Anarchy 292–296
Apartheid 353–359
Archimedian point 13
Architecture. *See* Symbolic link
Assimilation 213–215
Authoritarian government 221, 410–414
Autonomy 8–9, 24, 58, 71, 76, 86, 112, 118, 124, 130, 155, 157, 196, 209, 214, 236, 243, 261, 294, 402
Autopoietic systems 154–155

B

Basic values 3, 21, 124–179, 270–271, 305, 414, 421, 429. *See also* Values
 - freedom. *See* Freedom
 - justice. *See* Justice
 - life. *See* Life
 - responsibility. *See* Responsibility
 - solidarity. *See* Solidarity

Black Codes 201, 315–316
Bonobos 8
Border 344
Brooklyn 374–378
Bureaucratization 103, 104, 156–159, 314, 334, 388, 393

C

Capitalism 182, 188–189, 289
 - inequality 282, 346
 - violence 78
Carlos, Juan 259–265
Change 417–419
 - inclusive change 419
 - stable change 106–107, 219, 418–419, 422
 - value per se 40, 84
Checks and balances 171–172, 222, 335, 395
Chesapeake 230
 - immigration 65–66
Chimpanzees 8
Chinatown 371–374
Chosen people 79, 97, 237, 408
Circular argument 22–24
Civil disobedience 76, 144, 209
Civilization 93, 102, 134–135, 158, 222–223, 269, 311, 349, 418
Civil rights 266, 301, 308, 316, 320, 329, 332, 370, 382
Civil Rights Movement 387
Civil society 297–298, 361–362, 368, 386
Civil war, U.S. 271, 309–314

Classic liberalism 28, 39, 121, 361, 370
Class society 350, 371
Client state 433
Cold War 222, 224, 257
Collective identity 3–5, 107–110, 173–174, 176–177, 195–200, 274, 321, 333, 343, 372, 421. *See also* Delimitation
- dominant narrative 408
- independent narrative 408
- won narrative 408
Collectivism 211, 221–225, 343, 372
Common good 35, 175, 244, 279–283, 345, 349, 379, 426, 430–431, 432
Common space. *See* Public space
Common wealth 31, 32, 33. *See also* Common good
Communitarianism 121
Community 48–52
- concept of community 27–54
Competition 81–84
- negative effects 83–84, 173–179, 209, 249, 289, 383
Concept of humankind 2, 4, 5, 22, 27–54, 182, 304, 343, 356
Conflict resolution 302
Consciousness 58
Consensus 21, 57–63
- constitutive consensus 57–58
- institutional consensus 60
- legitimation consensus 61–63
- overview 63
- routine consensus 58–59
- value consensus 57–58
Consensus-based constructivism 20–26, 45, 51, 53, 56, 71, 108, 126, 212, 295, 300, 304, 327, 390, 401, 409

Constitution 216, 266, 310, 321
- interpretation 321–332, 400–401
- symbolic link 70, 309–311, 320, 329
Constitutional conventions 322
Constitutional state 59, 91, 171–172, 180, 222, 413–414, 427
Construction opportunities 165
- equality of 23, 119
Construction phases 64–76
- deconstruction 66–70, 117
- new construction 64–65, 117, 301
- overview 64
- reproduction 65–66, 117, 301, 429
Construction power 91, 106, 124, 136, 156, 171, 175, 204, 207, 298, 305, 326, 348, 404, 420, 432
Construction responsibility 52, 320
Constructive politics 322, 325, 364
Constructivism 2, 7–26. *See also* Social construction of "reality"
Consumer society 61, 119, 124, 189, 205, 345, 381, 409, 418, 420
Contingency 24, 30, 45, 66, 92–94, 136–137, 202, 246, 322, 387
Cooperation 85–87, 92, 180
- advantages 1, 86–87, 173–179, 219–220
- definition 85
- preconditions 85–86, 89–90
Counterpower 72, 80, 83, 91–92, 101, 126, 140, 145, 166, 179, 195, 220, 247, 252, 300, 319, 336, 423, 427
Counter-violence. *See* Counterpower
Court jester 25, 219
Creativity 3, 25, 54, 83, 149, 179, 212, 245, 380, 387, 393, 407, 431

Criticality 72
Criticism 19, 43, 59, 64, 66–70, 73, 86, 107, 142, 209, 300, 303, 328, 343, 419
- as chance for improvement 19, 74
- as existential threat 73
Cultural violence 3, 15, 77–79, 140–141, 147, 189, 198, 203, 253, 356, 378, 406, 408, 415–417, 423
Culture 9, 43, 49, 79, 83, 101, 212, 222

D

Decision-making process 82, 109, 266–342, 423
Declaration of Independence 70, 113, 137–138, 194, 310, 398–400
Deconstruction. *See* Construction phases
Deconstructive politics 322
De Gouges, Olympe 139
Delegitimization 69, 258, 354
Delimitation 89–90, 135, 277, 414
Democracy 104, 170–171, 264–265, 278, 279, 344–345, 382, 384, 426–428
- definition 8–9
- formal 171–172, 366, 370–371
- problems 8
Destabilization. *See* Integration modes
Deviant behavior 38, 66, 71–76, 116–117, 147, 234
Dichotomous "reality" 47, 148, 219, 405, 410
Dictatorship 24, 61–62, 67, 122, 142, 249–250, 255–257, 332–333
Difference. *See* Alternatives, need for
Direct violence 3, 77–79, 104, 140, 189, 198, 203, 279, 289–291, 356, 373, 415–417, 423

Discourse 24, 171
Disintegration. *See* Integration modes
Dissent
- function 76
- fundamental dissent 62, 67
- specific dissent 62, 66
- validity test 73
Distraction 41, 383
Distrust 167, 174, 222, 248, 300, 303, 312, 379, 383
Doubts 214, 248–249, 266, 300

E

Economic absolutism 1, 55, 84, 165, 168, 180–202, 188
Economic power 170–171, 431–434
Efficiency 33, 50–51, 58, 82, 111, 156–159, 171, 180, 247, 392–393, 419
Elementary consensus 267–271, 282, 299, 301, 302, 409, 414, 421–434
Elitism 19, 333, 428–429
Equal construction power 91, 119, 124, 163–172, 202–204, 267, 432
Equality 174, 192–193, 202, 229, 232, 250, 316–318, 323, 399, 426, 430
Equal opportunities 1, 76, 119, 163–164, 171, 177, 249, 281–282, 290, 305
Essentialism 42, 213, 221, 343, 354
Ethnic cleansing. *See* Genocide
Ethnicity, social construction 42, 88, 135, 212, 213, 405, 426
Ethnonationalism 427
Exclusion 15, 16, 75–76, 82, 83, 89–91, 98–106, 155, 177, 225, 315
- exclusion mechanism 88, 98, 141, 298, 350

F

Fight for recognition. *See* Recognition
Financial market crisis 37, 125, 150–151
Founding Fathers 225, 307, 320, 326, 328, 331, 428–432
France 332–339
- collective identity 388–391

Freedom 136–149, 294. *See also* Neo-liberalism – freedom
- economic freedom 32, 40, 55
- freedom of contract 231, 305, 306, 308, 382
- individualistic freedom 30, 112, 121, 432
- interactive freedom 112, 137–141, 159, 178–179, 427–428, 431
- liberal 140
- negative freedom 29, 83, 112, 136, 140
- political freedom 32
- positive freedom 136, 236
- responsible 295
- responsible freedom 136, 236, 295
- social construction 137. *See also* Freedom – interactive freedom
- universal freedom 309–310, 313, 315, 354

Free-market principle 39, 150, 278, 305, 308, 367, 369
French Declaration of the Rights of Men and of the Citizen 137–139
Friend-foe-scheme 411
Functional differentiation 153, 246
Fundamentalism 39, 91, 224, 252, 433
Future 219, 226, 245, 289, 301, 320, 407, 409, 420

G

Gated communities 376, 378–383
Gendercide 206–207
Genocide 103–104, 134–135, 328, 414, 427
Gentrification 380
Globalization 90, 99, 215, 418
Gold rush 271–291
Government 266, 267–271. *See also* State actors; *See also* Decision-making process
Great Depression 70, 165, 177, 305, 307, 374
Greed. *See* Materialism

H

Happiness 119–121, 179
Harlem 374–378
Harmonization. *See* Integration modes
Heterogeneity 74. *See also* Pluralism
Heterosexuality 143–149
History 331, 405
- social construction 407, 409

Holocaust 62, 101, 103, 134, 157–158
Home 58, 64, 66, 81, 93, 108, 274, 345, 381, 404, 407
Homogeneity 73, 212–221
Homo interactivus 28, 41–54, 58, 92, 161, 172
Homo oeconomicus 27, 29–31, 39, 136, 283, 291, 307. *See also* Neo homo oeconomicus
Homosexuality 143–149
Homo sociologicus 27, 50
Hope 20, 111–112, 116, 120, 126, 132–133, 409
Human dignity 80, 91, 98, 109, 111, 126, 159–163, 175, 207, 211

Human nature 2, 8, 41, 82, 93, 108, 126, 133, 266
Human rights 117, 133, 171, 206, 216, 332, 427. *See also* Civil rights
Hunter-gatherers 41, 84, 293, 346

I

Identity. *See* Collective identity; *See* Individual identity
- essentialist concept 343

Identity construction
- by exclusion 98–106, 350

Immigration 56, 57, 98, 189, 204, 227, 238, 271, 372, 377
Indentured servant 184, 197, 243, 273, 350, 355
Indeterminism 20, 106, 136–137
Individual identity 42–45, 173–174, 343–344
- interactive construction 42–45
- uniqueness 42, 44, 94, 160, 179, 211–212, 225, 327, 421

Individualization 1, 10, 13, 15, 28, 82–83, 115, 121, 125, 178, 179, 276
Industrialization 10, 13, 213, 276, 351, 378
Inequality 32–33, 78, 83, 91, 98, 106, 120, 163–172, 175, 176, 212, 228, 231–232, 251, 278, 281, 289, 293, 318, 378, 425–428. *See also* Equal construction power; *See also* Justice
- social construction 167–169, 358

Infinite regress 20, 23–24
Insecurity 92, 120, 248, 370, 402, 419, 424
Institution 60, 65, 263, 266–267, 295–298

Integration
- authoritarian integration 80–81
- definition 3–4, 27, 55–57, 70
- equal construction power 91
- integration quality 3, 9, 13, 76–91
- integration work 87–88
- market integration. *See* Market – integration by the market
- model 3

Integration modes 64
- basic integration 64
- criticism 66–70
- destabilization 67–71, 97
- disintegration 67, 117
- harmonization 66, 117
- stabilization 65, 117

Integration quality. *See* Integration
Interaction 24
Interdependence 20, 24, 35, 45, 51, 58, 70, 85, 199, 212
Internet 385–387
Interpretation. *See* Law – interpretation
Invisible hand 31, 33, 35, 52
Islam 117, 224, 434
Italy 410–414

J

Jasmin Revolution 67–69
Justice 159–172, 192. *See also* Equal construction power
- formal justice 164, 203, 366
- substantial justice 171, 366

K

King 60, 95, 138–139, 257, 259–265, 266, 332–333, 344, 388–391, 401–402
- itinerant king 398
Ku Klux Klan 318–321

L

Laïcité 117, 216–219
Law
- interactive construction 320–332
- interpretation 71, 184, 190, 303, 321, 400–401
- rule of law. *See* Rule of law
- stabilizing function 65, 302–303

Legality 303, 326
- social construction 72

Legal staff 216, 270, 301, 302–303
Liberalism. *See* Classic liberalism; Neoliberalism
Liberal state 117
Life 126–135
- absolute value 126–131
- social construction 126–132
- value of life 127–128

Lynching 267, 289–290

M

Majority rule 171, 214, 364
Manichaean worldview 40, 47, 98, 213–215, 221–225, 252, 407
Market
- integration by the market 31–38, 52–54, 124, 151, 156, 165–170, 178
- market equilibrium 33–38, 39, 53, 70
- religious belief in the market force 1, 33, 35, 38–39

Market absolutism. *See* Economic absolutism
Material greed. *see* Materialism
Materialism 10, 40–41, 83, 163, 179, 181, 188–189, 278, 294, 383, 387
- criticism 41

Meaning of life 84, 93, 106, 112, 133, 174–179, 177, 202, 208, 212, 226, 244, 278, 387
Media
- social construction of "reality" 171

Middle class 166–168, 283
Minority
- protection 332
- social construction 75–76, 332

Mirroring-effect 174–179
Missouri Compromise 270, 310
Modernity 84, 156–159, 383, 392–393
Modernity-loser 84, 418
Modern society 111, 115, 153–156, 266
Modern state 157–158, 334, 388
Monarchy 113, 124, 193, 213, 332, 399
Monoculture 214
Monopoly of violence 266–291, 297, 298, 319, 413
Multi-community community 143, 152–153
Multicultural society. *See* Multi-community community

N

Narcissism 178
Narrative. *See* Collective identity
Nationalism 213–221, 254, 343, 426
National Socialism 62, 157–158, 180, 392–394
Nation state 343. *See also* Nationalism
Natives 138, 145, 180, 183, 188, 195, 226, 237, 240–241, 267–268, 292–294, 347
- basic values 114, 293
- political organization 292–294
- reciprocity 346

Naturalistic fallacy 127
Negative freedom. *See* Freedom – negative
Neo homo oeconomicus 28, 28–41, 53, 58, 156. *See also* Homo oeconomicus
- community concept 48
Neoliberalism 1–2, 28–41, 35, 90, 121, 150–151, 379, 429–431, 432
- anti-social individualism 175, 178
- basic values 3, 40–41, 112
- community concept 48
- concept of humankind 6, 16, 28–41
- freedom 140, 429
- injustice 53, 370
Neutrality 79, 116–119
New construction. *See* Construction phases
New Deal 169, 305–309, 324, 325
Nihilism 111
Norm
- interpretation 71
- social construction 71–73
Normality 71, 156–159
Northern Ireland 401–407

O

Objectivity 7–9, 22, 79, 225, 296, 383, 401
Other 46–47
- cooperative construction 25–26
Outer-consciousness 59

P

Pensée unique 20, 329–332
People 343–386
Permanent losers 42, 91, 106, 176–177

Personality. *See* individual identity – uniqueness
Pilgrims 228–230
Pluralism 74, 115–119, 141–149, 211, 212–221, 216, 260
Political system 155–156
Poverty 9–26, 120, 167, 175, 213, 346, 366, 367, 369, 372, 378, 425
- definition 14–17
- social construction 13–16
Power 136
- economic power 170–171
- state power 170–171
Predictability 30, 38, 92, 136
Preferences 29
Present 26, 59, 78, 114, 175, 301, 320, 331, 387, 409, 418
Privatization 184, 277, 282, 367, 369, 382, 385
Property 114, 277, 280, 293, 305, 308, 364, 375, 381
Public space 344, 379, 382–383, 390, 391, 394, 406
Puritans 65, 94–98, 227–239

Q

Quakers 232, 237
Queen 60, 390

R

Race, social construction 88, 405
Racism 88, 98, 103–123, 192–193, 197, 212, 317–320, 353–356, 375
- cultural racism 222–225, 433–434
- economic motives 345–371
Rationality 28–30, 104, 111, 158–159
- as power tool 79
Realism 2, 17–20, 24, 383

"Reality" 20
- multitude of "realities" 9–16, 24
- social construction 7–26, 14

"Reality" proposal 20–23, 27, 44, 45, 57

Rechtsstab 270

Reciprocity 9–12, 17, 176–178, 226–244, 274–279, 292–293, 346
- definition 226

Recognition 180–210, 293
- constitutive recognition 45–46, 202
- denial of recognition 208–210
- fight for recognition 15, 68, 80, 91, 171–172, 191, 378
- recognition of potential 202
- universal recognition 202–205

Reconstruction, U.S. 201, 314–316

Reconstructive politics 325

Reification 108, 296, 303

Religion 42, 84, 100, 212, 213, 216–219, 222, 223–225, 405

Reproduction. *See* Construction phases

Reproductive politics 322

Republicanism 217–218, 237, 328, 336, 430

Responsibility 10, 15–16, 20–23, 45, 150–159, 291, 295, 297, 305, 326. *See also* construction responsibility
- delegation of 33, 39, 93, 150–151, 275, 278, 296, 320
- individual 363

Res publica 202–203, 244, 430

Revolution 11, 67, 69, 79, 101, 113, 139, 175, 216, 281, 300, 301, 308, 328, 333, 340, 382, 418, 423

Role 49, 116, 295, 299

Roma and Sinti 99–106, 413

Routine 58–59, 65, 71, 87, 260, 296

Rule of law 216, 273, 278, 321, 321–322, 427

Rwanda 134–135

S

Sans-papiers 57

Scapegoat politic 74, 92, 94–106, 135, 157, 198, 210, 223, 238, 241, 285, 289–290, 343, 372
- islam 47, 117

Schiavo, Terry 128–131

Science 27, 31, 225
- a power tool 79
- role of 25–26

Secular state 117, 216–219

Selfishness 1, 3, 6, 29–31, 32, 40, 86, 179, 220, 278, 283, 288, 381, 430–431

Serfdom 181

Slavery 180–202, 203–205, 270–271, 309–312, 397

Social change. *See* Change

Social construction of "reality" 7–26, 14

Socialism 112, 123, 163
- authoritarian 122

Social question 10. *See also* Poverty

Society 49–52

Solidarity 30, 55, 62, 91, 109, 121, 133, 172–179, 226, 250, 427

South Africa 345–371, 415–417

Space 343–386, 391–394, 401–407. *See also* Public space

Spain 249–265
- civil war 252–253
- General Franco 252
- Second Republic 250–252

Stability 65, 92–107, 244, 247
- need for stability 92–94, 136, 214, 223, 260, 333, 408, 418–420

Standardization 19, 30–31, 59, 156–159, 213, 296, 379
- and simplification 27
State 297, 432
- definition 266
- integration 299
- interactive construction 4, 52, 60, 291–300
- medieval state 266
- modern state 157–158, 334, 388
- monopoly of violence 266–291
- stabilizing function 65
State actors 175, 298–301, 330, 423, 431
State and society 297–298
State power 170–171, 175, 291, 298. See also Monopoly of power
- consented state power 291–300
Stigmatization 73, 88
Structural violence 3, 15, 77–79, 104, 105, 140, 155, 189, 198, 203, 206, 348, 356, 371, 374–375, 415–417, 423
Structure 42, 51, 64, 65, 78, 175
- structural change 175
Subconsciousness 59
Suicide 103, 133, 209–210
Support. See Solidarity
Sustainability 420
Switzerland 339–342
Symbolic link 387–407
Symbolic politic 287
System theory 115, 153–156

T

Taken for granted 58–59, 66, 108, 135, 408
Tea Party 69–70, 171, 400
Time concept 407–420
- social construction 407
Tolerance 146, 148, 211, 227, 228, 365

Totalitarianism 2, 180, 225, 252, 262, 296, 354, 393–394, 398
Tradition 59, 328, 330, 405
Trickle down effect 3, 165, 169
Trust 87, 219, 245–265, 266, 278, 363, 367, 370, 382, 389
- functions of trust 245–249
Truth 7–9, 13, 18, 20, 113, 130, 304, 328, 400
Truth and Reconciliation Commission 364–365, 415–417
Tunisia 67–69

U

Uniqueness. See Individual identity
Universalism 79, 117, 138–139, 192–194, 202–205, 203, 211, 239, 343, 427
Universality. see Universalism

V

Values 111–123. See also Basic values
- absolute 132
- definition 111–112
- social construction 113–115
Versailles 388–391
Victims 105
Vigilantism 279, 281, 283–289, 319
Violence 77–80, 318–320. See also Direct violence; Structural violence; Cultural violence
- culture of non-violence 289–291
- definition 77–80
- social construction 77, 134–135, 289–291, 345
- upper class violence 283–289
Virtual reality 383–386

W

War of all against all 2, 83, 90, 93,
    278, 292, 294, 434
Washington 394–398
Welfare state 13, 37, 91, 123, 323, 368
Wild West 289
Winner-takes-it-all 1
Witches of Salem 94–98
Working immigrants 204–206
Worldview 2, 4, 8, 11, 24, 27, 109,
    111, 301, 305

About the author

Dr. iur. et lic. phil. Eric Dieth

Mr. Eric Dieth is lecturer at the University of Applied Sciences HTW in Chur as well as at the Private University in the Principality of Liechtenstein. Convinced that an interdisciplinary construction of "reality" helps to overcome "normality," he studied law and sociology and has done research in Paris, London, New York, San Francisco, and Boston. Combining a variety of ways of thinking, he hopes to develop persuasive alternatives to the "realities" that are today declared as givens and used to justify the power of the few. A just and solidary freedom may become possible if we are ready to take responsibility for the world we live in.